THE GENESIS CREATION ACCOUNT

and Its Reverberations
in the NEW TESTAMENT

"Creation in the Bible" Series
Ekkehardt Mueller, General Editor
Deputy Director, Biblical Research Institute

The Genesis Creation Account and
Its Reverberations in the Old Testament
Gerald A. Klingbeil, Volume Editor
Research Professor of Old Testament
and Ancient Near Eastern Studies, Andrews University

The Genesis Creation Account and
Its Reverberations in the New Testament
Thomas R. Shepherd, Volume Editor
Professor of New Testament, Andrews University

The following entities collaborated in the preparation of this volume:

Biblical Research Institute

A doctrinal and theological resource center that serves the General
Conference of Seventh-day Adventists through research, publication, and
presentations. adventistbiblicalresearch.org

Geoscience Research Institute

Assists the Church through the scientific study of the natural world in the
area of origins and other related matters. Findings are made available
through publications and presentations. grisda.org

Faith and Science Council

A body of the General Conference of Seventh-day Adventists created to
study the interrelationships of science and Scripture with particular
attention to creation. It provides for the two Institutes above to interact
and collaborate on projects. fscsda.org

THE GENESIS CREATION ACCOUNT

and Its Reverberations in the NEW TESTAMENT

EDITED BY THOMAS R. SHEPHERD

Andrews University Press
Berrien Springs, Michigan

Andrews University Press
Sutherland House
8360 W. Campus Circle Dr.
Berrien Springs, MI 49104–1700
Telephone: 269–471–6134
Fax: 269–471–6224
Email: aupo@andrews.edu
Website: http://universitypress.andrews.edu

ISBN 978–1–940980–29–4 (paperback)

Printed in the United States of America
26 25 24 23 22   1 2 3 4 5

Library of Congress Cataloging-in-Publication Data

Names: Shepherd, Thomas R., 1951- editor.
Title: The Genesis creation account and its reverberations in the New
    Testament / edited by Thomas R. Shepherd.
Description: Berrien Springs, Michigan : Andrews University Press, [2021] |
    Series: "Creation in the Bible" series | Includes bibliographical
    references and indexes.
Identifiers: LCCN 2020055051 | ISBN 9781940980294 (paperback)
Subjects: LCSH: Bible. New Testament--Relation to Genesis. | Bible.
    Genesis--Relation to the New Testament. | Bible. New
    Testament--Criticism, interpretation, etc. | Creation--History of
    doctrines. | Creation--Biblical teaching.
Classification: LCC BS2387 .G46 2021 | DDC 225.6/6--dc23
LC record available at https://lccn.loc.gov/2020055051

CONTENTS

BACKGROUND AND BIBLICAL THEOLOGY STUDIES

BIBLICAL STUDIES

CONCLUSION

ABBREVIATIONS

1 Apol.	Justin Martyr, *The First Apology*
1–3 Bar.	*1–3 Baruch*
1–3 En.	*1–3 Enoch*
1 Esd.	1 Esdras
2 Fort.	Dio Chrysostom, *Fortune 2*
1–4 Macc.	*1–4 Maccabees*
A	Codex Alexandrinus
AB	Anchor Bible
ABD	*Anchor Bible Dictionary*. Edited by David N. Freedman. 6 vols. New York: Doubleday, 1992
Abr.	Philo, *De Abrahamo*
ABR	*Australian Biblical Review*
ABRL	Anchor Bible Reference Library
ACNT	Augsburg Commentaries on the New Testament
Add. Esth.	Additions to Esther
Aet.	Philo, *De aeternitate mundi*
Ag. Ap.	Josephus, *Against Apion*
Agr.	Philo, *De agricultura*
ALGHJ	*Arbeiten zur Literatur und Geschichte des helle-nistichen Judentums*
Am.	Ovid, *Amores*
Amat.	Plutarch, *Amatorius*
Ant.	Josephus, *Antiquities of the Jews*
Ant. rom.	Dionysius of Halicarnassus, *Antiquitates romanae*
AnthLyrGreac	*Anthologia Lyrica Graeca*. Edited by Ernst Diehl. Leipzig: Teubner, 1954
Apoc. Ab.	*Apocalypse of Abraham*
Apoc. Adam	*Apocalypse of Adam*
Apoc. El.	*Apocalypse of Elijah*
Apoc. Mos.	*Apocalypse of Moses*
Apoc. Sedr.	*Apocalypse of Sedrach*
Apos. Con.	*Apostolic Constitutions and Canons*
ArBib	The Aramaic Bible
Aristob. Frag. 1–5	Aristobulus Fragment 1–5
ASNU	Acta seminarii neotestamentici upsaliensis
AsTJ	*Asbury Theological Journal*
ATSDS	Adventist Theological Society Dissertation Series

AUSDDS	Andrews University Seminary Doctoral Dissertation Series
AUSS	*Andrews University Seminary Studies*
Autol.	*Ad Autolycum*
b. Ned.	Babylonian Talmud, *Nedarim*
b. Pesah.	Babylonian Talmud, *Pesahim*
b. Sanh.	Babylonian Talmud, *Sanhedrin*
BA	*Biblical Archaeologist*
Bar.	Baruch, *Apocrypha*; 2–4 Baruch, *Pseudepigrapha*
BBET	Beiträge zur biblischen Exegese und Theologie
BBR	*Bulletin for Biblical Research*
BDAG	Danker, F. W., W. Bauer, W. F. Arndt, and F. W. Gingrich. *Greek-English Lexicon of the New Testament and Other Early Christian Literature.* 3rd ed. Chicago: University of Chicago Press, 2000
BDF	Blass, F., A. Debrunner, and R. W. Funk. *A Greek Grammar of the New Testament and Other Early Christian Literature.* Chicago: University of Chicago Press, 1961
BECNT	Baker Exegetical Commentary on the New Testament
Ben.	*De beneficiis*
BETL	*Bibliotheca Ephemeridum Theologicarum Lovaniensium*
Bib.	*Bibliotheca*
BM	British Museum
BNTC	Black's New Testament Commentaries
BSac	*Bibliotheca Sacra*
BTB	*Biblical Theology Bulletin*
Carm.	*Carmina*
CBQ	*Catholic Biblical Quarterly*
CBQMS	Catholic Biblical Quarterly Monograph Series
CC	Continental Commentaries
Cels.	*Contra Celsum*
Cher.	*De cherubim*
Christ.	*Contra Christianos*
Comm Jo.	*Commentarii in evangelium Joannis*
ConBNT	Coniectanea biblica: New Testament Series
ConcC	Concordia Commentary

Conf.	*De confusione linguarum*
ConJ	*Concordia Journal*
Contempl.	*De vita contemplativa*
Controv.	Seneca the Elder, *Controversies*
Crat.	*Cratylus*
CRINT	Compendia Rerum Iudaicarum ad Novum Testamentum
CSB	Christian Standard Bible
CTJ	*Calvin Theological Journal*
CTQ	*Concordia Theological Quarterly*
CTR	*Criswell Theological Review*
Curc.	*Curculio*
DARCOM	Daniel and Revelation Committee Series
DCLS	Deuterocanonical and Cognate Literature Studies
Det.	Philo, *Quod deterius potiori insidari soleat*
DOTP	*Dictionary of the Old Testament: Pentateuch.* Edited by T. Desmond Alexander and David W. Baker. Downers Grove, Ill.: InterVarsity Press, 2003
DSD	*Dead Sea Discoveries*
DtrH	Deuteronomistic History
EBib	Etudes bibliques
Ebr.	*De ebrietate*
EDNT	*Exegetical Dictionary of the New Testament.* Edited by H. Balz, G. Schneider. ET. Grand Rapids, Mich.: 1990–1993
EKKNT	Evangelisch-katholischer Kommentar zum Neuen Testament
Enn.	*Enneades*
Ep.	*Epistulae morales*
Ep. Arist.	*Epistle of Aristeas*
Ep. Jov.	*Epistula ad Jovianum* Letter to Jovian, Athanasius
ESV	English Standard Version
ET	English Translation
Eth. Nic.	*Nicomachean Ethics*
EUS	European University Studies
EvQ	*Evangelical Quarterly*
Exc. Ps.	*Excerpta in Psalmos*
Fab.	*Fabulae*

FGrH	F. Jacoby, *Fragmente der griechischen Historiker* (1923–)
Fin.	*De finibus*
Frag.	Fragment
Fug.	Philo, *De fuga et invention*
Gen. Rab.	*Genesis Rabbah*
Gk. Apoc. Ezra	*Greek Apocalypse of Ezra*
GNT	Grundrisse zum Neuen Testament
HÄB	Hildesheimer ägyptologische Beiträg
Haer.	*Adversus Haereses*
Hel. Syn. Pr.	*Hellenistic Synagogal Prayers*
Her.	*Quis rerum divinarum heres sit*
Hist.	*Historiae*
Hist. eccl.	*Historia ecclesiastica*
Hist. Rech.	*History of the Rechabites*
Hist. rom.	*Historiae romanae*
HCSB	Holman Christian Standard Bible
HSDAT	*Handbook of SDA Theology*
HTA	Historisch Theologische Auslegung
HTR	*Harvard Theological Review*
HvTSt	*Hervormde teologiese studies*
ICC	International Critical Commentary
Il.	*Iliad*
Inst.	*Divinarum Institutionum*
Int	*Interpretation*
Inv.	*De inventione rhetorica*
Is. Os.	*Isis and Osiris*
j. San.	Jerusalem Talmud, *Sanhedrin*
JAAR	*Journal of the American Academy of Religion*
JAOS	*Journal of the American Oriental Society*
JATS	*Journal of the Adventist Theological Society*
JBL	*Journal of Biblical Literature*
JBQ	*Jewish Bible Quarterly*
Jdt.	Judith
JETS	*Journal of the Evangelical Theological Society*
JHS	*Journal of Hellenic Studies*
Jos. Asen.	*Joseph and Aseneth*
JPS	Jewish Publication Society
JRE	*Journal of Religious Ethics*

JSJSup	Journal for the Study of the Judaism Supplements
JSNT	*Journal for the Study of the New Testament*
JSNTSup	Journal for the Study of the New Testament: Supplement Series
JSOT	*Journal for the Study of the Old Testament*
JSOTSup	Journal for the Study of the Old Testament: Supplement Series
Jub.	Book of Jubilees
KEK	Kritisch-exegetischer Kommentar über das Neue Testament (Meyer-Kommentar)
LAB	*Liber antiquitatum biblicarum*
LAE	*Life of Adam and Eve*
L&N	*Greek-English Lexicon of the New Testament: Based on Semantic Domains.* Edited by J. P. Louw and E. A. Nida. 2nd ed. New York, 1989
LCL	Loeb Classical Library
Lect.	Rufus Musonius, *Lectures*
Leg.	Philo, *Legum allegoriae*
Leg.	Plato, *Leges,* Laws
Legat.	*Legatio ad Gaium*
Let. Aris.	*Letter of Aristeas*
LNTS	The Library of New Testament Studies
LQ	*Lutheran Quarterly*
LSJ	Liddell, H. G., R. Scott, H. S. Jones, *A Greek-English Lexicon.* 9th ed. With revised supplement. Oxford: Clarendon, 1996
LXX	Septuagint
m. 'Arak.	Mishnah, *Arakin*
m. Git.	Mishnah, *Gittin*
m. Ketub.	Mishnah, *Ketubbot*
m. Šabb.	Mishnah, *Shabbat*
m. Sanh.	Mishnah, *Sanhedrin*
Marc.	*Ad Marcellam*
Mart. Isa.	*Martyrdom and Ascension of Isaiah*
Mem.	*Memorabilia*
Metam.	*Metamophoses*
Midr. Ps.	Midrash on the Psalms
Migr.	*De migratione Abrahami*

MNTC	Moffatt New Testament Commentary
Mor.	Plutarch, *Moralia*
Mos.	Philo, *De vita Mosis*
MSJ	*The Master's Seminary Journal*
ms. P	Manuscript P of 2 Enoch
MT	Masoretic Text
Mund.	*De mundo*
Mut.	*De mutatione nominum*
NAC	New American Commentary
NAS	New American Standard Bible
NASB	New American Standard Bible
Nat.	*Nature of Things*
Nat. d.	*De Natura Deorum*
NAWG	Nachrichten der Akademie der Wissenschaften in Göttingen
NCBC	New Century Bible Commentary
NCCS	New Covenant Commentary Series
NEB	New English Bible
NET	New English Translation
NIBC	New International Biblical Commentary
NIBCNT	New International Biblical Commentary on the New Testament
NICNT	New International Commentary on the New Testament
NICOT	New International Commentary on the Old Testament
NIDB	*New International Dictionary of the Bible.* Edited by J. D. Douglas and M. C. Tenney. Grand Rapids, Mich.: 1987
NIDNTT	*New International Dictionary of New Testament Theology.* Edited by C. Brown. 4 vols. Grand Rapids, Mich.: 1975–1978
NIDOTTE	*New International Dictionary of Old Testament Theology and Exegesis.* Edited by W. A. VanGemeren. 5 vols. Grand Rapids, Mich.: 1997
NIGTC	New International Greek Testament Commentary
NIV	New International Version
NIVAC	New International Version Application Commentary

NJB	New Jerusalem Bible
NKJV	New King James Version
NLT	New Living Translation
NovT	*Novum Testamentum*
NovTSup	Supplements to Novum Testamentum
NRSV	New Revised Standard Version
NTG	New Testament Guides
NTL	New Testament Library
NTS	*New Testament Studies*
Od.	*Odyssey*
Odes Sol.	*Odes of Solomon*
ONTC	Osborne New Testament Commentaries
Op.	*Opera et Dies*
Opif.	Philo, *De Opificio Mundi*
Or.	*De oratione*
Or. Bas.	*Oratio in laudem Basilii*
ÖTK	Ökumenischer Taschenbuch-Kommentar
Pan.	*Panarion*
Part. an.	*Parts of Animals*
Phaed.	*Phaedo*
Phaen.	*Phaenomena*
Phil.	*Orationes philippicae*
Phys.	*Physica*
Plant.	*De plantatione*
PNTC	Pelican New Testament Commentaries
Pol.	*Politicus*
Post.	*De posteritate Caini*
Pr. Azar.	Prayer of Azariah
Praem.	*De praemiis et poenis*
Praep. ev.	*Praeparatio evangelica*
Pr. Jos.	*Prayer of Joseph*
Pr. Man.	*Prayer of Manasseh*
PRSt	*Perspectives in Religious Studies*
Ps.-Phoc.	Pseudo-Phocylides
Pss. Sol.	*Psalms of Solomon*
PW	Pauly, A. F. *Paulys Realencyclopädie der classischen Altertumswissenschaft.* New edition G. Wissowa and W. Kroll. 50 vols. In 84 parts. Munich, 1980

QG	*Quaestiones et solutiones in Genesin*
Quaest. graec.	*Quaestiones Graecae*
Quaest. rom.	*Quaestiones romanae et graecae*
RBL	*Review of Biblical Literature*
Rep.	*The Republic of Cicero*
RevQ	*Revue de Qumran*
Rhet.	*Rhetorica*
RHPR	*Revue d'histoire et de philosophie religieuses*
RSV	Revised Standard Version
RTL	*Revue théologique de Louvain*
Sat.	*Satirae*
SBL	Society of Biblical Literature
SBLDS	Society of Biblical Literature Dissertation Series
SBT	Studies in Biblical Theology
SCL	Sather Classical Lectures
SDABC	*Seventh-day Adventist Bible Commentary*
Sel. Exod.	*Selecta in Exodum*
Sent.	*Sentences of Pseudo-Phocylides*
Sept.	*Septem contra Thebas*
SHBC	Smyth & Helwys Bible Commentary
Sib. Or.	*Sibylline Oracles*
Sir.	Sirach
SJT	*Scottish Journal of Theology*
SNTSMS	Society for New Testament Studies Monograph Series
Somn.	*De somniis*
SP	Sacra Pagina
Spec.	*De specialibus legibus*
SUNT	Studien zur Umwelt des Neuen Testaments
Superst.	*De superstitione*
Symp.	*Symposium*
T. Ab.	*Testament of Abraham*
T. Adam	*Testament of Adam*
T. Ash.	*Testament of Asher*
T. Benj.	*Testament of Benjamin*
T. Dan	*Testament of Dan*
T. Isaac	*Testament of Isaac*
T. Iss.	*Testament of Issachar*
T. Jos.	*Testament of Joseph*

T. Levi	*Testament of Levi*
T. Mos.	*Testament of Moses*
T. Naph.	*Testament of Naphtali*
t. San.	Tosefta, *Sanhedrin*
T. Sol.	*Testament of Solomon*
TDNT	*Theological Dictionary of the New Testament.* Edited by G. Kittel and G. Friedrich. Translated by G. W. Bromiley. 10 vols. Grand Rapids, Mich.: 1964–1976
TDOT	*Theological Dictionary of the Old Testament.* Edited by G. J. Botterweck and H. Ringgren. Translated by J. T. Willis, G. W. Bromiley, and D. E. Green. 15 vols. Grand Rapids, Mich.: Eerdmans, 1974–2006
Tg. Ps.-J.	*Targum Pseudo-Jonathan*
Tg. Yer. II	*Targum Yerušalmi II*
Them	*Themelios*
Theog.	*Theogony*
THOTC	The Two Horizons Old Testament Commentary
Tim.	*Timaeus*
TJ	*Trinity Journal*
TLOT	*Theological Lexicon of the Old Testament.* Edited by Ernst Jenni, with assistance from Claus Westermann. Translated by M. E. Biddle. 3 vols. Peabody, Mass.: Hendrickson, 1997
TNTC	Tyndale New Testament Commentaries
Tob.	Tobit
Top.	*Topica*
TOTC	Tyndale Old Testament Commentaries
TQ	*Theologische Quartalschrift*
TR	*Theological Review*
TWOT	*Theological Workbook of the Old Testament.* Edited by R. L. Harris. G. L. Archer Jr., and Bruce K. Waltke. 2 vols. Chicago: Moody Press, 1980
TynBul	*Tyndale Bulletin*
Virt.	*De virtutibus*
Vit. Phil.	Diogenes Laertius, *Vitae Philosophorum* Lives of Eminent Philosophers

WBC	Word Biblical Commentary
Wis.	Wisdom of Solomon
WMANT	Wissenschaftliche Monographien zum Alten und Neuen Testament
WTJ	*Westminster Theological Journal*
WUNT	Wissenschaftliche Untersuchungen zum Neuen Testament
ZAW	*Zeitschrift für die alttestamentliche Wissenschaft*
ZECNT	Zondervan Exegetical Commentary on the New Testament
ZNW	*Zeitschrift für die neutestamentliche Wissenschaft und die Kunde der älteren Kirche*

Thomas R. Shepherd,
PhD, DrPH

Andrews University
Berrien Springs, Michigan, USA

INTRODUCTION

The two great theological themes of creation and redemption run throughout Scripture like two golden threads in a magnificent tapestry. This book is about the former theme as it appears in the New Testament. In 2015 the companion volume to the current work —*The Genesis Creation Account and Its Reverberations in the Old Testament*—was published by Andrews University Press. The current volume now joins its Old Testament companion as an expression of just how beautiful, far-reaching, and complex is the theme of creation in the New Testament.

In the following pages, fifteen authors present studies in three sections: backgrounds and New Testament theology, studies in New Testament books, and a conclusion to the two volume set. In the first section, six studies present creation in background data and New Testament theology. Ekkehardt Mueller begins the section with an overview of creation in the New Testament. He provides a helpful list of references to Genesis 1–2 in the New Testament and to the following stories in Genesis 3–11. He goes on to illustrate how Jesus in the Gospels and major New Testament writers refer to creation again and again.

Cedric Vine's chapter situates the New Testament affirmation of divine creation within the wider context of the Greco-Roman world.

Vine begins with a review of the widely held Stoic view of creation in the first-century world. He goes on to provide examples of Greco-Roman creation accounts to provide background for comparison with New Testament accounts. Of interest, he documents Greco-Roman explanations of fossil bone discoveries. He further gives examples of Greco-Roman authors who challenged the predominant paradigm concerning creation in Greco-Roman culture.

What Vine provides in background from Greco-Roman sources, Jan Sigvartsen provides from Jewish sources of the Second Temple period. Sigvartsen documents how Second Temple writers from various sects explained the Genesis creation accounts and how they filled out or described what they saw as missing or needing elucidation in the text. They grappled with some of the same questions that readers wrestle with today—whether the creation accounts are literal or allegorical, what was created in the first week, was it created *ex nihilo*, are the stories scientific, theological, philosophical, ethical, religious, symbolic, or some combination of these? Sigvartsen details what Second Temple writers saw as preexisting creation and compares this to the New Testament witness. In an appendix he provides a wide-ranging and useful list of references to creation and creation theology in Second Temple literature.

Michael Hasel's chapter deals with the theological implications of accepting a nonliteral view of creation. He delineates the shift to this view following the Enlightenment and its consequent effect on exegesis. Hasel sets forth the implications for a plethora of topics—authority, inspiration, the unity of Scripture, theology, moral accountability, anthropology, the Sabbath, marriage and the family, sin, death, the plan of redemption, and eschatology.

Kayle de Waal's chapter to follow studies the biblical concepts of creation, new creation, and resurrection, and how they interact and intersect with each other theologically and intertextually. De Waal argues that New Testament authors refer to promises found in the latter part of Isaiah and, to a lesser extent, Jeremiah and Ezekiel. These promises, in part, shape the New Testament belief in resurrection.

Laszlo Gallusz rounds out the background and theological studies with his chapter, which argues that creation is of fundamental significance for New Testament eschatology. Without creation, the very category of eschatology loses it basis. Gallusz illustrates how eschatology is weaved throughout the warp and woof of New Testament writing. He notes that the resurrection of Jesus Christ is the initiation of the new creation, the turning point of salvation history. His resurrection leads to the creation of the new community, who live as the people of God. The transformation these people experience is called a new creation by Paul and this terminology parallels language linked to creation themes that other New Testament writers use. Gallusz finds all this language rooted in the Creation-Fall narrative of Genesis 1–3. He argues for a protology-eschatology schema. Creation and eschatology are intrinsically interconnected in New Testament theology.

The second section of the volume is a series of studies on creation as described in the writings of the New Testament authors. Clinton Wahlen notes that the first two words of Matthew, *biblos geneseōs*, allude to Genesis, perhaps even to the entire book. Wahlen goes on to illustrate the other allusions or references to creation—the use of *ginomai*, "heaven and earth," in the disputes over the Sabbath (12:1–14) and about divorce (19:3–9) and Jesus's power over creation in various miracles.

Thomas Shepherd follows a similar pattern in his discussion of creation in Mark. The clearest references to creation are parallel to those in Matthew about the Sabbath (2:23–28) and concerning divorce (10:1–12). Shepherd also notes a reference in 13:18–20 in the eschatological discourse and possible allusions in 1:1, 12–13, and 4:35–41. He concludes that creation theology and the historicity of the creation accounts in Genesis 1–2 are crucial to the truth and effectiveness of the second Gospel.

Kim Papaioannou surveys creation references in the large Luke-Acts corpus. Papaioannou insists that the evidence from Luke and Acts clearly supports a literal six-day creation. He presents his argumentation in three steps. First, he surveys Luke's view of the historical reliability of the creation story (Genesis 1–2). Second, he investigates allusions and echoes of the creation account. Third, he investigates four passages that make unambiguous reference to the creation event (Luke 3:23–38, the genealogy of Jesus; Acts 4:24, reference to God as creator of heaven and earth; Acts 14:8–18, Paul's sermon in Lystra; and Acts 17:22–31, Paul's speech on the Areopagus). Papaioannou concludes that Luke consistently assumes the historicity of the creation account. Further, he sees Luke's creation theology focusing attention on God's rulership and lordship.

Creation forms a sense of international care for all nations and care for the earth and its creatures. Papaioannou notes other themes as well, ranging from wholistic anthropology, the nature of evil rooted in the Fall, and the Sabbath.

Jon Paulien covers the Johannine literature. He notes there are few scholarly discussions of the topic of creation in this corpus. Those scholars that do discuss it see the Johannine purpose as talking of creation with spiritual intent rather than focusing on how or when the world was made. Paulien goes on to identify key passages dealing with creation. He places this discussion in context by a review of "new creation" in the Old Testament and Hellenistic Judaism. After studying these, Paulien concludes that John sees a spiritual new creation in the ministry of Jesus, modeled on Jesus's role in the original creation. He further concludes that John's argument in the prologue (1:1–18) only makes sense if the original creation account in Genesis describes a literal creation. The new creation theology John promotes only has meaning if the original creation described in Genesis is also real.

Richard Sabuin provides an overview of creation in the Pauline corpus in his chapter. He provides two useful charts that highlight both clear references to creation and allusions to it. Sabuin illustrates how much of Paul's theology has linkage to the Genesis creation account. The theological themes include God as creator, the entrance of sin, the restoration of God's image in humanity, salvation, ecclesiology, and several other issues. Sabuin also notes references in Paul's writings to events linked to specific days of the creation account. In his conclusion Sabuin argues that many details in Paul's writing point toward the apostle accepting the Genesis account as historical.

Wilson Paroschi presents a study on creation in Romans 1 and 2. He notes that creation plays an important role in Paul's argument in chapters 1–2, 5, and 8. Paroschi also notes other references that link to the Genesis creation account. However, his study focuses attention on Romans 1 and 2. He argues that creation plays a crucial role in the argument of these two chapters as Paul presents the sinfulness of humanity arising from their rejection of the clear revelation of God's creative power in nature. Paroschi outlines the implications for human behavior as described particularly in Romans 1 and concludes that Paul's appeal to creation would be irrelevant if the Genesis account were not normative, reliable and true.

Dominic Bornand describes Paul's usage of the Genesis creation account in the Corinthian correspondence. According to Bornand, the apostle accepts the historicity of the Genesis account and, from the way Paul argues, he takes for granted that his readers do as well. Paul does not rely on extracanonical materials to explain or describe creation. He only utilizes the Genesis account. Paul presents God as the sole creator and the only one worthy of worship. The apostle utilizes creation theology in giving practical instructions on idolatry, community behavior, and sexual behavior. In teaching about the resurrection, Paul makes reference to the created order and gives evidence of his acceptance of God as the creator of all the biodiversity on our planet.

Felix Cortez presents an extended discussion of creation in the book of Hebrews. He notes that other than the Apocalypse, Hebrews has the most references to the Genesis creation account in the New Testament. Cortez maintains that Hebrews teaches at least seven things about creation. God is the creator of the entire universe. God the Father and God the Son are cocreators. The Son of God not only created the world but also has acted through all time. God created the world by His word. To recognize God as the creator requires faith, something unpopular throughout human history. Belief that God created the universe is paradigmatic of true faith. Belief in God as creator is central to faith.

Thomas Shepherd presents creation as found in the General Epistles. He notes that the book of James has numerous linkages to both Genesis 1 and 2. James has reference to events or God's creative work from the first, fourth, fifth, and sixth days of creation. Further, James draws two great anthropological truths from the creation account—wholistic anthropology and humans made in the likeness of God. Shepherd sees the broad and consistent parallels to Genesis 1 and 2 as strong evidence that James accepted the historicity of these accounts.

Shepherd notes as well the very extensive usage of creation concepts in 1 and 2 Peter. In 1 Peter the apostle's reference to creation has three central foci. First, it is tied to salvation. God's plan of redemption was settled before the world began. Second, creation becomes the reference point for reordering human power structures.

Humanity is creature, not the creator. Third, creation is the guardian of trust in God during suffering. If God were not the "faithful creator," and humanity were seen, instead, as the result of a long line of evolutionary development, there would be no solace for those in turmoil, they would simply be a small cog in a large evolutionary machine.

In 2 Peter the apostle is fighting false teaching and brings up the subject of creation in response to the false teachers' objection that all things continue as they were from the beginning of creation. Peter deconstructs their argument and illustrates the immanence of God in the affairs of humanity. Eschatology is tied to protology. The God who created the world will be the one who destroys it by judgment fire. Jude only makes reference to Enoch, the seventh person from Adam, but this illustrates belief in the historicity of the Genesis account.

Ekkehardt Mueller concludes the second section of the volume with his study of creation in the book of Revelation. Mueller notes that Revelation has many allusions to creation with strong emphasis on the Genesis 1–2 account. Jesus's activity in changing lives in the present is also referenced using creation language. However, the major emphasis of the Apocalypse is on the eschatological new creation described using terminology from Genesis 1–2. Mueller argues that creation as a motif makes a major contribution to understanding the nature of God. God as Creator is foundational to His nature. The Creator seeks a relationship with His creation; His creative power and His redemptive power are inseparable. Creation language in Revelation is also linked to anthropology. It is tied to ethics, describing how humans should treat one another. We are called to worship the Creator and to act justly, obeying His will, living holy lives.

The final section of the book has the article by Kwabena Donkor that provides a conclusion for the two-volume series. He presents a theological perspective on creation in the entire Bible. He covers four key themes in this article—that the biblical view of creation is that it encompasses all of reality, that creation was from nothing (*ex nihilo*), that all reality came into existence through God's power, and that creation is willed by God—it is purposeful.

Donkor argues that the biblical view of creation is much broader than simply the question of origination—whether God created the world and the universe or it arose through evolutionary processes apart from God. Using the four themes listed above, Donkor comes to the conclusion that what God created is both dependent on Him and has God-given freedom. Creation serves as the doctrinal basis of all Christian thought. Protology is linked to eschatology and judgment, arising out of the charge to worship the Creator.

In conclusion, we note that the theme and reality of creation are affirmed throughout the New Testament, indeed, throughout the entire Bible. The biblical view of creation cannot be reduced to a simple statement that "God made the world, but how He did it is not important." Instead, what we see through the studies in this volume and those in the first volume on creation in the Old Testament is that the doctrine and reality of creation by God touches many themes and doctrines. Analyzing these carefully illustrates that the biblical writers considered creation a key doctrine and that it took place literally as the Genesis 1–2 account presents it. Otherwise key teachings of Scripture on anthropology, eschatology, soteriology, and ethics are undermined or rendered ineffectual or inconsistent. Accepted as the key foundational doctrine of Scripture, fiat creation sets the stage for all that follows and becomes the glorious beginning to which we return in the end.

BACKGROUND
AND BIBLICAL
THEOLOGY
STUDIES

Ekkehardt Mueller, DMin, ThD

Biblical Research Institute
Silver Spring, Maryland, USA

CREATION IN THE NEW TESTAMENT

INTRODUCTION

Scripture deals with humanity's most important questions: Who are we? Where do we come from? Where will we be going? Why are we here? Although the New Testament preaches the good news about salvation and points to a wonderful future for those who choose to follow Christ, it also addresses the issue of creation.

This study will take a look at New Testament references to creation, discuss the contribution of Jesus and His disciples to the theology of creation, and draw some conclusions for our present situation.[1] This chapter serves as an introduction to a series of studies in this volume that delve into books and passages dealing with creation explicitly or implicitly, as well as studies that discuss the theology of creation in the New Testament. The goal of this chapter is to give an overview in preparation for the deeper studies that follow—to provide a map or outline of what will follow. As such, this study illustrates the way creation is viewed and discussed by New Testament authors—surprisingly much more than is commonly recognized.

---

1. This chapter first appeared in an earlier form as an article in *JATS* 15, no. 1 (2004): 47–62. Used by permission.

NEW TESTAMENT REFERENCES TO CREATION

The New Testament refers to creation quite frequently. There are only a few New Testament books that do not contain a quotation or direct allusion to the Genesis 1 and 2 creation account. Typically, these are the shorter letters of the New Testament.[2] All the larger New Testament books—the Gospels, Acts, Romans, the Corinthian letters, Hebrews, and Revelation—as well as a number of the smaller epistles contain quotations or allusions to creation. The strongest emphasis on creation is found in the letters to the Romans and to the Hebrews, as well as in the book of Revelation.

In some cases, creation and the Fall are connected. At other times, the Fall is referred to alone. Yet, the creation context cannot be denied. This is because Genesis 1–2 and Genesis 3 are very closely linked. References to Cain's murder, the mention of several names listed in the genealogy of Genesis 5, and events found in Genesis 4–11 occur in the New Testament. The following list does not claim to be comprehensive but points to a number of important creation references in the New Testament. It also contains references to Genesis 3–11, found in various New Testament passages as seen below.

NT Book	References to Genesis 1–2 and to Creation in General	References to Genesis 3–11
Matthew	3:35; 19:4, 5; 25:34	4:1–11; 10:16; 23:35; 24:37–39
Mark	2:27; 10:6, 7–8; 13:19; 16:15	
Luke	3:38; 11:50	3:36–38; 17:26–27
John	1:1–3; 17:24	
Acts	4:24; 10:12; 11:6; 14:15; 17:24, 26	
Romans	1:20, 23, 25–27; 4:17; 5:12, 14; 8:19–22, 39; 11:36	5:17–19
1 Corinthians	6:16; 8:6; 11:8–9; 15:45	15:22
2 Corinthians	4:6; 5:17	11:3
Galatians	–	
Ephesians	1:4; 3:9; 5:31	
Philippians	–	

---

2. They are Galatians, Philippians, 1 Thessalonians, 2 Thessalonians, 2 Timothy, Titus, Philemon, and the Johannine letters.

NT Book	References to Genesis 1–2 and to Creation in General	References to Genesis 3–11
Colossians	1:15, 16, 23	
1 Thessalonians	–	
2 Thessalonians	–	
1 Timothy	2:13; 4:4	2:12, 14
2 Timothy	–	
Titus	–	
Philemon		
Hebrews	1:2, 10; 4:4, 10, 13; 6:7–8; 9:26; 11:3; 12:27	11:4, 5, 7; 12:24
James	1:18; 3:9	
1 Peter	1:20; 4:19	3:20
2 Peter	3:4, 5	2:5; 3:6
1 John	–	3:12
2 John	–	
3 John	–	
Jude	1:14	1:11, 14
Revelation	2:7; 3:14; 4:11; 5:13; 8–9; 10:6; 13:8; 14:7; 16; 17:8; 20:1, 3, 11; 21–22	12:9, 17; 20:2

QUOTATIONS FROM GENESIS 1–2

Genesis 1 and 2 are not the only creation texts in the Old Testament. Other important passages on creation are found in Job 38–42; Psalms 8, 19, and 104; Isaiah 40:26–28, 65–66; Jeremiah 10:11–13; 27:5; 32:17; 51:15–16; Amos 4:13, 5:8–9; 9:5–6; etc.[3] However, they refer back to Genesis 1 and 2. Therefore, Old Testament quotations in the New Testament dealing with creation are essentially taken from Genesis 1 and 2. In addition to numerous allusions, there are eight such quotations included in the list above: two each in the Gospels of Matthew and Mark and four in the Pauline writings.[4] The quotations used in the Gospels are all part of

---

3. Cf. William Shea, "Creation," in *HSDAT*, ed. Raoul Dederen (Hagerstown, Md.: Review and Herald, 2000), 419–36.

4. Gen. 1:27 is quoted in Matt. 19:4 and Mark 10:6; Gen. 2:2 is used in Heb. 4:4; Gen. 2:7 is found in 1 Cor. 15:45; and Gen. 2:24 is quoted in Matt. 19:5, Mark 10:7, 1 Cor. 6:16, and Eph. 5:31.

Jesus's response to the Pharisees when questioned on the problem of divorce.

The texts or parts thereof, which are quoted in the New Testament, are Genesis 1:27, "God created man in His own image, in the image of God He created him; male and female He created them";[5] Genesis 2:2, "By the seventh day God completed His work which He had done, and He rested on the seventh day from all His work which He had done"; Genesis 2:7, "Then the LORD God formed man of dust from the ground, and breathed into his nostrils the breath of life; and man became a living being"; and Genesis 2:24, "For this reason a man shall leave his father and his mother, and be joined to his wife; and they shall become one flesh."

Interestingly enough, these quotations refer to the creation of humankind and to the two divine institutions established for them at creation—the Sabbath and marriage.

THE WORD FAMILY *KTISIS, KTISMA, KTIZŌ*

Among the New Testament texts dealing with creation, we find many that use formulas such as "from the foundation of the world." In addition, the word family *ktisis, ktisma, ktizō* is used frequently. The noun *ktisis* ("creation, what is created, creature") is used nineteen times in the New Testament,[6] the noun *ktisma* ("what is created, creature") four times,[7] and the verb *ktizō* ("to create, to make") fifteen times.[8] In other words, this word family is used thirty-eight times in the New Testament and stresses the importance of the concept of creation in the New Testament.

The noun *ktisma* refers to "creatures" and "everything created." The word describes what God created in the beginning (1 Tim. 4:4). God's creatures also include humans and animals throughout the past, present, and future (James 1:18; Rev. 8:9).[9] Furthermore, creation surpasses our world and is not limited to this earth or solar

---

5. Unless otherwise indicated, Scripture quotations in this chapter are from the New American Standard Bible®, Copyright © 1960, 1971, 1977, 1995 by The Lockman Foundation. All rights reserved.

6. Mark 10:6; 13:19; 16:15; Rom. 1:20, 25; 8:19, 20, 21, 22, 39; 2 Cor. 5:17; Gal. 6:15; Col. 1:15, 23; Heb. 4:13; 9:11; 1 Pet. 2:13; 2 Pet. 3:4; Rev. 3:14.

7. 1 Tim. 4:4; James 1:8; Rev. 5:13; 8:9.

8. Matt. 19:4; Mark 13:19; Rom. 1:25; 1 Cor. 11:9; Eph. 2:10, 15; 3:9; 4:24; Col. 1:16; 3:10; 1 Tim. 4:3; Rev. 4:11; 10:6.

9. Although God does not create today in the way He did in Gen. 1–2, humans are still and will remain God's creatures.

system. There are created beings in heaven who were created by God (Rev. 5:13). Consequently, the New Testament teaches that God created not only the earth, its atmosphere, and life on this earth but also extraterrestrial life forms that are not part of the creation we encounter and to which we belong.

The term *ktisis* ("creation") is used once to refer to "every human institution [may also be translated "creation"]" (1 Pet. 2:13).[10] Usually, however, it describes God's work and initiative.[11] The addition of the adjective "human" indicates that the normal understanding of the term—namely, as God's action and its results—is abandoned in this case. But this does not affect any of the other usages of the term in the New Testament. *Ktisis* is found in the phrase "the beginning of creation" (Mark 10:6; 13:19; 2 Pet. 3:4), which takes us back to Genesis 1 and 2. Creation here is God's creative act at the beginning of this world's and humankind's history. In Romans 8, not only do the children of God wait for the future, the "whole creation groans" and wants to be "set free from its slavery to corruption" (Rom. 8:18–22). While in this passage "creation" probably refers to all created beings and is not limited to humankind, the term in Mark 16:15 and Colossians 1:23—when the gospel is preached to "all creation"—only describes humanity throughout the centuries of the Christian era.[12] In Romans 8:39 also, the context seems to suggest that the created beings include extraterrestrial beings—that is, beings who are not part of our creation. God has also established the heavenly sanctuary that is "not of this creation" (Heb. 9:11). "The firstborn of all creation" (Col. 1:15) and "the beginning [beginner] of the creation of God" (Rev. 3:14) is Jesus. Yet in Christ, people, although being creatures of God, can become "new creature[s]" (2 Cor. 5:17; cf. Gal. 6:15). In this case, a spiritual meaning is added to the literal and physical understanding. Both correspond. Because Jesus is the Creator, He can bring about a new creation—that is, people who are reconciled with God through Him and who proclaim the message of reconciliation.

The verb *ktizō* describes God's creative activity when He brought about creation, including humanity (Mark 13:19; cf. Matt. 19:4; 1 Cor.

---

10. For further discussion of this usage in 1 Pet. 2:13, see Thomas R. Shepherd, "Creation in the General Epistles," 373, in this volume.

11. Eighteen out of the nineteen times when *ktisis* is used in the New Testament, it describes God's creation.

12. Mark 16:15 may not have been original to the Gospel of Mark, but the parallel usage of "all creation" in Colossians 1:23 still affirms the usage of the terminology to refer to humanity.

11:9; Rev. 10:6). He is the Creator who has created all things (Rom. 1:25; Eph. 3:9; Col. 1:16; Rev. 4:11). Again there is a spiritual dimension because "we are . . . created in Christ Jesus for good works" (Eph. 2:10). Jesus has also broken down the barrier between Israel and the Gentiles. Since then, those who believe in Him are one church. He has made (*ktizō*) "the two into one new man" (Eph. 2:15). Christians are called to "put on the new self," which "has been created in righteousness and holiness of the truth" (Eph. 4:24; cf. Col. 3:10). Thus, in addition to its original meaning, the term "to create" has an ecclesiological dimension. It refers not only to the creation of this earth and life upon it but also to the creation of Christ's church, consisting of individuals who together form one body. This "spiritual creation" forms a smaller segment of the whole picture and cannot be used to reinterpret physical creation as known from Genesis 1 and 2 and other texts.

SUMMARY

The New Testament contains numerous references to creation. Among them are eight direct quotations from Genesis 1 and 2. The specific creation language of the word family *ktiz-* describes God's activity in all cases but one. Other vocabulary needs to be studied.[13] The New Testament texts assume over and over that the creation account is to be understood literally. God created the heavens, the earth, and various plants and beings. The concept of creation is not limited to the creation described in Genesis 1 and 2. It encompasses much more, although in a different sense. Jesus has created His church. People have become, and even today are becoming, new creations in Jesus Christ. But this ongoing creative activity of God does not question the specific creation of heavens, earth, and life upon it at a specific point of time in the past. Rather, because God was able to do the first creation, He is able to do the other as well.

JESUS CHRIST AND CREATION

The issue of creation is closely linked to the issue of Scripture as the Word of God. This is also the crux in the current debate. If we were not Christians, it probably would be much easier to choose, according to one's individual preference, either creation or evolution, or another

---

13. E.g., *poieō* ("to make") is also used to describe the creation process. In this case, the context must determine whether or not it refers to creation.

approach such as theistic evolution or progressive evolution. But we have Scripture, which plays an important role in the life of our faith community as well as in our private lives. Therefore, we must ask: Does Scripture have the final say in the creation/evolution debate, even if in some cases it seems to contradict data or theories produced by science, or does it not constitute a final authority? Should Scripture be reinterpreted in order to fit these scientific models of origins, or should it not?

JESUS AND SCRIPTURE

As we now turn to Jesus and His understanding of the creation issue, we will briefly summarize His position on the Old Testament, the Scripture of His time, as a starting point for the discussion of His view of creation. We know Jesus through what the Gospels and other parts of Scripture tell us about Him. This information can either be taken at face value or be questioned. But even a critical approach—one claiming that many New Testament texts ascribed to Jesus are not authentic, but are productions of the early church—would probably result in a similar outcome.

Some scholars suggest that Jesus favored traditionalism and was not ready to challenge wrong ideas. But the Jesus of the Gospels was clearly willing to address delicate and controversial issues. Wenham states, "He [Jesus] is prepared to face the cross for defying current misconceptions. Surely he would have been prepared to explain clearly the mingling of divine truth and human error in the Bible, if he had known such to exist."[14]

So, what did Jesus think and teach about Scripture?

1. Jesus believed in the inspiration of the human authors of the Bible of His time (Old Testament). All of Scripture is the Word of God, through which God has spoken. Jesus considered the prophets to be reliable mediators of God's Word[15] (Matt. 15:4; 22:31–32; Mark 12:36).

---

14. John Wenham, *Christ and the Bible*, 3rd ed. (Grand Rapids, Mich.: Baker, 1994), 27.

15. Cf. E. Earle Ellis, *The Old Testament in Early Christianity: Canon and Interpretation in the Light of Modern Research* (Grand Rapids, Mich.: Baker, 1991), 126: "Jesus' use of the Old Testament rests on his conviction that these writings were the revelation of God through faithful prophets." Peter van Bemmelen, "The Authority of Scripture" (unpublished manuscript), 12, writes, "The Gospel narratives give evidence that Jesus not only had an unparalleled knowledge and understanding of the Scriptures, but that He accepted all of Scripture as the authoritative Word of God. Following the resurrection He gently chided two of His

2. He accepted the historical reliability of Scripture, including important events of Israel's and humankind's history.[16] Scripture is interpreted both literally and typologically (Matt. 12:42; John 10:34–36).
3. Divine interventions in human history—for instance, in the form of miracles—were no problem for Jesus (Matt. 12:39–41).
4. He used Scripture as authority and as a weapon against temptations (Matt. 4:4, 7, 10).
5. God's will and His work can be recognized through Scripture. Biblical doctrines are derived from Scripture, which is the standard by which all behavior and all Christian doctrines must be checked (Matt. 9:13; 19:4–6; 22:31–32).
6. Jesus believed that Scripture contains genuine prophecy that has been or will be fulfilled. Jesus regarded many of those predictions as being fulfilled in Himself and in His ministry (Matt. 11:10; 24:15; Luke 18:31).
7. Jesus was persuaded that Scripture was directed not only to the original hearers and readers but also to His generation, centuries later (Matt. 13:14; 15:3–8; 19:18–19).
8. Jesus expects His followers to know, believe, and obey God's Word (Matt. 22:29; Luke 8:21; 11:28). When He interpreted Scripture, His disciples' hearts burned and a change occurred in their lives (Luke 24:25–27, 32–35).

JESUS AND CREATION

The words of Jesus as recorded in the four canonical gospels contain ten references to creation.[17] Matthew, Luke, and John have added explanations that contain additional creation statements. But this is not our concern here.

Jesus did not point back only to Genesis 1 and 2. In His speeches we also find persons and events from Genesis 3–11: Abel (Matt. 23:35), Noah (Matt. 24:37–39; Luke 17:26–27), and the Flood (Matt. 24:39).

---

disciples for their slowness of heart to believe in 'all that the prophets have spoken' (Luke 24:25)."

16. For instance, He referred to Abraham (Matt. 8:11), Lot and his wife (Luke 17:28–29, 32), Isaac (Luke 13:28); Moses (Matt. 19:8), David (Matt. 22:43, 45), Isaiah (Matt. 13:14), Jonah (Matt. 12:39–41), and Daniel (Matt. 24:15) and regarded them as historical persons.

17. Matt. 19:4, 5; 25:34; Mark 2:27; 10:6, 7–8; 13:19; 16:15; Luke 11:50, and John 17:24.

When reading these short passages we get the clear impression that according to Jesus, Noah and Abel were not mythological figures but real human beings, that Genesis 3–11 is a historical narrative that should not be understood symbolically, and that a global flood actually happened (Gen. 6–8).[18] We should expect that Jesus would use the same approach of biblical interpretation when it comes to the creation account, and this is precisely what we find in the Gospels. Jesus's statements about creation can be grouped as follows: (1) passing references to creation, (2) direct references to creation, and (3) the use of quotations from Genesis 1 and 2.

Passing References to Creation

In a number of passages Jesus makes a passing reference to the Genesis 1–2 creation account. These revolve around phraseology dealing with the foundation of the world.

The Foundation of the World:

Then the King will say to those on His right, "Come, you who are blessed of My Father, inherit the kingdom prepared for you from the foundation of the world." (Matt. 25:34)

So that the blood of all the prophets, shed since the foundation of the world, may be charged against this generation. (Luke 11:50)

Father, I desire that they also, whom You have given Me, be with Me where I am, so that they may see My glory which You have given Me, for You loved Me before the foundation of the world. (John 17:24)

The related phrases used by Jesus—"from the foundation [*katabolē*] of the world" (Matt. 25:34; Luke 11:50) and "before the foundation [*katabolē*] of the world" (John 17:24)—also occur in other places in the New Testament.[19] The word *katabolē* can be translated as "foundation," "beginning," and, to some extent, "creation." The phrase "from the foundation of the world" focuses on events that have taken place since creation. The phrase "before the foundation of the world" describes events prior to the creation of the world.

---

18. The comparison between the Flood and Christ's worldwide second coming as well as the statement that the unbelievers were destroyed seem to indicate that the flood was a global event (Matt. 24:39).

19. "From the beginning of the world" is found six times in the New Testament (Matt. 13:35; 25:34; Luke 11:50; Heb. 4:3; 9:26; Rev. 17:8) and "before the beginning of the world" four times (John 17:24; Eph. 1:4; 1 Pet. 1:20; Rev. 13:8).

Ten texts in the NT use "foundation of the world" terminology to identify the starting point for this world's history. . . . Thus the NT writers
knew Creation week as a finite point in time that divided the time and
events before it from those that took place after it. As Bible writers
referred to Creation, it was not vague or nebulous, but historically
specific.[20]

The phrases do not allow us to talk only about the creation of
humanity, thereby separating it from the rest of creation; rather, the
phrases "from/before the foundation of the world" "refer to the
beginning of the whole creation as described in Genesis 1."[21]

Preaching the Gospel to All Creation:

He said to them, "Go into all the world and preach the gospel to all
creation [every creature]." (Mark 16:15)

The proclamation of the gospel is directed to all human beings.
The parallel text in Matthew 28:19 talks about "all nations." The
book of Acts shows how that commission was carried out. "Creation"
or "creature" is used in a restricted sense, referring to humans only.
By calling people "creatures" or "creation," Jesus may be reminding
His audience that all human beings are created by God, have an
intrinsic value, and are God's property. As such, they deserve to hear
the gospel and be saved.

Direct References to Creation

The following are passages in which Jesus makes direct reference
to the Genesis creation accounts. These references are more specific
than the previous and engage events tied to the creation account or
reference God's creative activity itself.

The Sabbath Made for Man:

Jesus said to them, "The Sabbath was made for man, and not man for
the Sabbath. So the Son of Man is Lord even of the Sabbath." (Mark
2:27–28)

---

20. Shea, "Creation," 437.

21. Terry Mortenson, "Jesus, Evangelical Scholars and the Age of the Earth" (presentation, annual meeting of the Evangelical Theological Society, Atlanta, November 19, 2003), 5.
He also states, "In the absence of any contextual clues before or after *apo kataboles kosmou*
in Matthew 13:35; Matthew 25:34; Revelation 13:8; and Revelation 17:8, which might
restrict the meaning of the phrase to 'foundation or beginning of the human race,' we must
assume that the phrase in these verses also is referring to the very beginning of creation. . . .
In John 17:24 Jesus clearly meant by this phrase the beginning of all creation, for the Father
surely loved the Son eternally before the creation (not merely before the creation of man)."

This text refers back to the fourth commandment in Exodus 20:8–11, where the Sabbath is linked to creation. However, creation is also visible in Mark 2 itself. According to Jesus, the Sabbath is a creation by God, as is humanity. The purpose of the Sabbath is to be a blessing to humankind. It is one of the great gifts of paradise still available to us. This text also assumes that humanity is created by God—not created for the sake of the Sabbath, but created nevertheless.

> Just as the Sabbath and the original creation were linked in the OT, so also these two elements are connected in the NT. . . . Human beings were made on the sixth day, the Sabbath on the seventh. Humans were already in existence when the Sabbath was made; therefore, the day evidently was made for their use and benefit. Surprisingly, however, Adam was not made lord of the Sabbath. The "Son of man," Jesus Christ, holds that title.[22]

The shift from verse 27 to verse 28 is abrupt: "So [Therefore] the Son of Man is Lord even of the Sabbath." The term "so [therefore]" seems to make sense if the one who created humankind and the Sabbath is the Son of Man. If this conclusion is correct, Mark 2 is a remarkable text in which Jesus Himself maintains a hidden claim of being the creator of humankind and of the Sabbath. The New Testament stresses again and again that Jesus is Creator, but it seems that this claim is not found in Jesus's own statements directly.

Since the Beginning of the Creation God Created:

> For those days will be a time of tribulation such as has not occurred since the beginning of the creation which God created until now, and never will. (Mark 13:19)

This text is part of the Synoptic Apocalypse. It is a strong statement, connecting the verb "to create" with the noun "creation." Although it is obvious that God is the Creator, it is stressed anyway. The phrase "from the beginning of the creation" is shortened in a number of other statements by Jesus and His followers but still refers to creation.[23] A similar phrase is "in the beginning."[24] This beginning

---

22. Shea, "Creation," 438. Francis D. Nichol, ed., *SDABC*, 7 vols. (Washington, D.C.: Review and Herald, 1978), 5:588, notes, "God did not create man because He had a Sabbath and needed someone to keep it. Rather, an All wise Creator knew that man, the creature of His hand, needed opportunity for moral and spiritual growth, for character development. He needed time in which his own interests and pursuits should be subordinated to a study of the character and will of God as revealed in nature, and later, in revelation."

23. E.g., Matt. 19:4, 8; 1 John 1:1; 2:13–14.

24. See John 1:1–2 (*en archē*) and Hebrews 1:10 (*kat' archas*).

is not just the beginning of humanity but is inclusive of the entire creation process. Terry Mortenson concludes,

> Hebrews 1:10 says that "in the beginning" God laid the "foundation of the world," and Hebrews 4:3 says God's creation works were finished from the foundation of the world. That unequivocally means that the seventh day (when God finished creating, Gen 2:1–3) was at the foundation. So, the foundation does not refer to simply the first moment or first day of creation . . . neither "from the beginning of creation" nor "from the foundation of the earth" (nor any related phrase) is referring to the beginning of the human race. Rather they refer to the beginning of the whole creation as described in Genesis 1.[25]

The Use of Quotations from Genesis 1 and 2

> And He answered and said, "Have you not read that He who created them from the beginning MADE THEM MALE AND FEMALE, and said, 'FOR THIS REASON A MAN SHALL LEAVE HIS FATHER AND MOTHER AND BE JOINED TO HIS WIFE, AND THE TWO SHALL BECOME ONE FLESH'? So they are no longer two, but one flesh. What therefore God has joined together, let no man separate." (Matt. 19:4–6)

> But from the beginning of creation, God MADE THEM MALE AND FEMALE. FOR THIS REASON A MAN SHALL LEAVE HIS FATHER AND MOTHER, AND THE TWO SHALL BECOME ONE FLESH; so they are no longer two, but one flesh. What therefore God has joined together, let no man separate. (Mark 10:6–9)

Matthew 19:1–12 and Mark 10:1–12 are parallel texts dealing with the problem of divorce, which the Pharisees use to confront Jesus. Jesus is opposed to divorce, but while Matthew mentions an exception clause, such a provision is not made in Mark. But in both cases Jesus supports His position by pointing back to creation and showing God's intention when He instituted marriage.

Whereas Mark 2 deals with creation and Sabbath, Mark 10 and Matthew 19 deal with creation and marriage, the other institution left to us from paradise. These texts are the clearest reference to the Genesis creation account found in Jesus's teachings. He quotes Genesis 1:27 and 2:24.

---

25. Mortenson, "Age of the Earth," 5.

By using these texts and applying them to marriage, Jesus declares that they are foundational to Christians. Creation took place in the beginning. God created. He created the first couple, Adam and Eve. The distinction of genders was set by God. By quoting from Genesis 1 and 2, Jesus affirms the creation account and the mode of creation as described there. He understands Genesis 1 and 2 literally and takes the two chapters at face value. Two human beings, male and female, were directly created by God and subsequently became one flesh in marriage, which He instituted. Unity is emphasized, but a unity consisting of one husband and one wife. In the Hebrew text, the term "two" is missing. It is found in the LXX. By stressing that only two beings and beings of the opposite sex become one, Jesus rejects polygamy[26] as well as homosexuality. Obviously, for Jesus the creation account was not only descriptive but prescriptive, and it determines ethical and moral behavior. Francis Moloney suggests that the phrase "from the beginning of creation" "reflect both the beginning of creation and time, and the book of Genesis."[27]

SUMMARY

The New Testament stresses that Jesus accepted the Bible of His times as the Word of God, which is authoritative and can be trusted. Israel's history, traced back to the creation account, is reliable. All Old Testament characters were real people who lived in time and space. A real creation and a real flood happened. Jesus does not utter any doubts about Scripture; instead He stresses that "Scripture cannot be broken" (John 10:35). He would rely on Scripture even in the most challenging times of His life.

Jesus holds that creation took place. God created. Creation happened at a definite time. There was a beginning: creation week, which includes all of God's creative activities described in Genesis 1 and 2 and the establishment of the Sabbath. Because Jesus mentions major biblical characters, starting by name with Abel, indirectly referencing Adam and Eve, and touching all periods of Israel's history, a short chronology is in view. The beginning of humanity is not separated from God's other creative acts in the creation week.

26. Cf. Rudolf Schnackenburg, *The Gospel of Matthew* (Grand Rapids, Mich.: Eerdmans, 2002), 183–184.

27. Francis J. Moloney, *The Gospel of Mark: A Commentary* (Peabody, Mass.: Hendrickson, 2002), 194.

Humans were created before the Sabbath. They are worthy to attain salvation and must be able to hear the gospel. In Mark 2 the Sabbath is a twenty-four-hour day—a day as we experience it now. This Sabbath reference points back to the creation Sabbath. Obviously, according to Jesus the creation days were literal calendar days. A literal and close reading of Genesis 1 and 2 seems to be the proper approach to Scripture.

JESUS CHRIST AS THE CREATOR

The New Testament affirms repeatedly that Jesus is God, that He exists forever, and that He was incarnated as a human being "when the fullness of the time came" (Gal. 4:4). As such, He lived among us, died a shameful and painful death in our place, was raised from the dead, and was taken to heaven. He now serves as our High Priest and will come back as King of kings in order to take home His people. But in addition to all these functions, Jesus is described as the Creator and Sustainer of the entire creation.

This is a unique contribution to the theology of creation by the New Testament. Although the Old Testament points to Christ as the Creator in a somewhat hidden way,[28] it is the New Testament that clearly spells out that Jesus is the Creator. Although a number of texts emphasize that God has created all things,[29] crucial passages stress that Jesus is the Creator. Although Jesus provides some hints that He is the Creator and does this by His proclamation and His deeds—for instance, the stilling of the storm—it is left to His disciples to plainly tell us who Jesus is: the Creator, God.

> All things came into being through Him [the *Logos*, who is God], and apart from Him nothing came into being that has come into being. (John 1:3)

> He is the image of the invisible God, the firstborn of all creation. For by Him all things were created, both in the heavens and on earth, visible and invisible, whether thrones or dominions or rulers or authorities—all things have been created through Him and for Him. (Col. 1:15–16)

---

28. E.g., the plural in Genesis 1:26 and possibly wisdom in Proverbs 8. Birth language in Proverbs 8 should be understood as installment to an office. See Richard Davidson, "Proverbs 8 and the Place of Christ in the Trinity," *JATS* 17/1 (2006): 48–50.

29. E.g., Acts 4:24; 14:15; 17:24, 26; Rom. 1:25; 1 Pet. 4:19.

In these last days [God] has spoken to us in His Son, whom He appoint-
ed heir of all things, through whom also He made the world. . . . And,
"You, Lord [referring to Jesus], IN THE BEGINNING LAID THE FOUNDA-
TION OF THE EARTH, AND THE HEAVENS ARE THE WORKS OF YOUR HANDS.
(Heb. 1:2, 10)[30]

All of these passages and their contexts show that Jesus is God.[31]
Since He is God, He is also Creator; or vice versa: since He is Creator,
"He is the image of the invisible God." These texts exclude Jesus from
the realm of created beings. In fact, all things and all beings have
been created through Him. The cosmic perspective, which includes
more than the creation we encounter, is spelled out most clearly in
Colossians 1. In encountering Jesus, we encounter the Creator.

John 1:1–3 portrays Jesus as the Word, God, the Creator, and Life.
Creation is expressed in several ways: (1) This Word existed "in the
beginning," a reminder of Genesis 1:1. (2) The Old Testament background of the statement about the Word of God is at least partially
found in Psalm 33:6: "By the word of the LORD the heavens were
made, and by the breath of His mouth all their host." Three verses
later we read, "For He spoke, and it was done; He commanded, and it
stood fast" (Ps. 33:9). Jesus is this creative Word of God. (3) John
tells us explicitly that all things came into existence through Him.

Hebrews 1:10 applies a quotation from Psalm 102:25 to Jesus,
although the Old Testament context talks about Yahweh as the Creator. The phrase "in the beginning" takes us back to Genesis 1:1.

Colossians 1:15–20 is an extensive christological hymn with an
interesting structure. The first part stressing Jesus as Creator (vv.
15–16) corresponds with the last part (vv. 18b–20), in which Jesus is
the Reconciler who has "made peace through the blood of His cross"
(see chiasm below). The very same person who created all things is
able to reconcile all things through His blood shed on the cross.

Therefore, to claim Jesus as Savior but question Him as Creator
does not make sense. To claim that He has saved us through His
once-and-for-all death on the cross, a short event in history, and yet
maintain that He created us through an evolutionary process over
millions of years is inconsistent.

---

30. See also Rev. 3:14. "Beginning" (archē) must be understood in the active sense of
"originator." In Revelation 21:6 the same term is applied to God the Father. He is "the beginning and the end." In Revelation 22:13 Jesus is "the beginning and the end." Archē is also
found in Colossians 1:18, referring to Christ.

31. See John 1:1–3; Col. 2:9; Heb. 1:5–12.

Furthermore, Jesus's creative power is seen in the fact that His followers are spiritually re-created. Ephesians 2:10 talks about being "created in Christ Jesus for good works" and 2 Corinthians 5:17 about being a new creation or new creature in Christ. As discussed, Ephesians 2:15 points to Christ creating one church, one new person, out of two groups—Jews and Gentiles. None of these creative processes that depend on Christ's sacrifice on the cross require an evolutionary process taking billions of years.

A **He is** { the image of the invisible God
the **firstborn** of all creation.
For by Him all things were created …
all things have been created *through Him* and for Him.

    B He is before all things,

        C   and in Him all things hold together.

    B' He is also head of the body, the church;

A' **He is** { and He is the beginning,
the firstborn from the dead …
For it was His Father's good pleasure for all the fullness to dwell
in Him, *and through Him* to reconcile *all things* to Himself. . .

On the other hand, if the biblical testimony is trustworthy—if Jesus is the Creator—then He must know what creation is all about, and His words carry a weight that surpasses all human knowledge. If it is true that Jesus is the Creator, then He should know by which process He accomplished creation. To claim that it happened as described in Genesis, which is the picture presented in the Gospels, while actually having used an evolutionary process would be deceptive to say the least. Why should we trust Him in regard to our salvation, if we have to question the veracity of His statements on creation?

Since Jesus is the Creator, we cannot talk about the topic of creation and the problems related to faith and science without focusing on Him. As crucial as Genesis 1–11 is for the current debate, Jesus cannot be excluded from this discussion. Whatever we decide on protology, it has a direct impact on soteriology.

NEW TESTAMENT WRITERS AND CREATION

New Testament authors have much more to say about creation. We will summarize some of their statements.

PAUL AND SOME ADDITIONAL STATEMENTS ON CREATION

Paul's proclamation of the "living God, WHO MADE THE HEAVEN AND THE EARTH AND THE SEA AND ALL THAT IS IN THEM" (Acts 14:15) is probably a reference to the Sabbath commandment (Exod. 20:11). This God has "made from one man every nation" (Acts 17:26). In Romans 5 he mentions Adam by name and discusses the consequences of his sin but also the gift of salvation in Jesus Christ. "In Adam all die" but "in Christ all will be made alive" (1 Cor. 15:22). Creation groans and suffers, longing to be set free "from its slavery to corruption," while Christians eagerly wait for the final salvation (Rom. 8:18–23). Paul knows that Eve was deceived (2 Cor. 11:3), and that Adam was formed first and then Eve (1 Tim. 2:13). The catalog of vices in Romans 1 is presented in the context of creation.[32]

Twice Paul quotes Genesis 2:24, "For this reason a man shall leave his father and his mother, and be joined to his wife; and they shall become one flesh": once when he warns against sexual immorality (1 Cor. 6:16), and another time when he dwells on the relationship between husband and wife, which becomes a symbol for the relationship between Christ and His church (Eph. 5:31). In the context of his discussion of the first resurrection, Paul quotes part of Genesis 2:7, slightly expanded: "The first man, Adam, became a living soul" (1 Cor. 15:45).

In Hebrews 4:4, when the issue of rest is discussed, Genesis 2:2 is quoted: "AND GOD RESTED ON THE SEVENTH DAY FROM ALL HIS WORKS." The author knows Abel (Heb. 11:4; 12:24), Enoch (Heb. 11:5), and Noah (Heb. 11:7). In Hebrews 11:3 he states, "By faith we understand that the worlds were prepared by the word of God, so that what is seen was not made out of things which are visible."

Paul bases his theology on a literal reading of the creation account and the story of the subsequent fall. When he uses typology, he

---

32. While Romans 1:20 is set in the context of creation and mentions creation explicitly, the list of animals, the mention of humans, and the concept of "likeness"/"image" suggest that Romans 1:23 echoes Genesis 1:24–26. Romans 1:25 points out that the Gentiles worshiped created things instead of the Creator. Furthermore, Romans 1:26–27 seems to echo Genesis 1:27 by concentrating on the same terms—"male" (*arsēn*) and "female" (*thēlus*)—instead of using the terms "man" and "woman." Peter Stuhlmacher, *Paul's Letter to the Romans: A Commentary* (Louisville, Ky.: Westminster John Knox, 1994), 37, states, "With every indication of his loathing, the apostle now pictures how the Gentiles profane themselves (in a sinful reversal of Gen 1:27ff.) in lesbian love and sodomy. . . . What the Gentiles do is contrary to creation and characteristic of their fallen state of guilt."

compares historical persons with other historical persons. He follows Christ's approach to interpreting Genesis 1–11.

JOHN AND SOME ADDITIONAL STATEMENTS ON CREATION

Like Paul, John is strong in pointing out that Jesus is the Creator. In the book of Revelation, allusions to creation abound. All things are created by God (Rev. 4:11). God "CREATED HEAVEN AND THE THINGS IN IT, AND THE EARTH AND THE THINGS IN IT, AND THE SEA AND THE THINGS IN IT" (Rev. 10:6). Humankind is called to "worship Him who made the heaven and the earth and sea and springs of waters" (Rev. 14:7). Both texts not only point to creation but may refer to the Sabbath of the fourth commandment as its memorial (Exod. 20:11). The tree of life (Rev. 2:7; 22:2, 19), the springs of the water of life (Rev. 21:6), and even the serpent (Rev. 12:9, 17; 20:2) remind us of the original paradise (Gen. 2:9–10; 3:1, 3, 14, 22, 24). The seven trumpets and seven bowls seem to be an undoing and a reversal of creation, whereas the description of Revelation 21–22 points to the new Jerusalem and the new heavens and earth—a new creation.

Again the same understanding of creation employed by Jesus and Paul is used here by John. If at the end of the millennium God is able to create a new heaven and a new earth without time spans of millions or billions of years but brings them about right after the millennium, why should He not have used similar techniques right in the beginning? We may not be able to understand precisely how He did that, and there may be conflicting data that do not yet fit this biblical picture, but the New Testament obviously confirms a literal reading of the creation account, a creation week of calendar days, and a short chronology.

CONCLUSION

What are some of the implications for us? We are neither afraid of science nor opposed to it. We could hardly do without it. We appreciate both knowledge that can be gained through science and knowledge that comes through God's Word. That does not mean that we buy into all presuppositions, theories, and philosophical or scientific models on the market.

Thomas C. Oden suggests, "Classical Christian doctrines of creation do not necessarily deny an evolution, or the possibility of a natural evolutionary development of nature and history. . . . One can posit a gradual evolutionary process that is not a denial of creation."[33] It seems that Jesus has not left us this choice.

Another author discusses antinomies in science and theology: "Antinomies are resorted to when one single model of reality does not do justice to all the data" and apparently contradictory statements or laws are both believed to be true. He mentions the nature of light, Christ being totally God and totally human, the doctrine of the Trinity, and others, suggesting "that we now stand before two great antinomies: special creation and theistic evolution. Both models can legitimately appeal to supporting sets of data, both scriptural and scientific. . . . Both models have serious problems. . . . As a procedural strategy we must embrace both models."[34] This scholar may have overlooked that, for instance, in the case of the doctrine of the Trinity, the Bible itself furnishes two sets of data. However, this is not true when it comes to the issue of creation. Jesus does not propose a literal reading of Genesis 1 and 2 and at the same time a symbolic reading. Secondly, although antinomies are found in Scripture that does not mean that all biblical doctrines can be presented as antinomies. In some cases it is an "either-or," not a "both-and." This author would probably reject a position claiming that we are both justified by grace and saved by works, and so would we. At the end, one must allow Scripture to speak for itself. If it presents antinomies, fine. If not, then we do not construct them.

Peter van Bemmelen reminds us that

> Scripture not only focuses on Christ as Redeemer, but also as Creator, Lord of creation and of the whole history of the world since creation. Therefore, no area of knowledge is excluded from the authority of Christ and His Word, the Scriptures. Some claim that since the Bible is not a textbook of science or history, it should not be used as authoritative in these areas of knowledge. While this claim is true in a technical sense, it becomes a frontal attack on the authority of the Bible if the truthfulness of its clear record of the creation and its historical narratives is rejected or reinterpreted along lines of scientific theories or historical research. Neither Jesus nor any of the inspired prophets and

---

33. Thomas C. Oden, *The Living God*, Systematic Theology 1 (Peabody, Mass.: Prince Press, 1998), 265.

34. Robert M. Johnston, "The Necessity and Utility of Antinomies" (unpublished manuscript, 2004), 1–2.

apostles ever questioned the historical truth of the Genesis record or of any other part of the Scriptures. Rather, they affirmed the truthfulness and divine authority of them all.[35]

The authors of the New Testament, disciples of Jesus Christ, followed the footsteps of their Master. They followed His method of interpreting Scripture. By accepting the name "Christian," we acknowledge that we too intend to follow Christ in His understanding and interpretation of Scripture. The New Testament testimony to creation is not only informative; it is normative for today's followers of Christ. And the message of creation is part of God's last message to this world: "Fear God, and give Him glory, because the hour of His judgment has come; worship Him who made the heaven and the earth and sea and springs of waters" (Rev. 14:7).

---

35. Van Bemmelen, "The Authority of Scripture," 12–13.

Cedric E. W. Vine, PhD

Andrews University
Berrien Springs, Michigan, USA

GRECO-ROMAN CREATION ACCOUNTS AND THE NEW TESTAMENT

INTRODUCTION

This study situates the New Testament's affirmation of divine creation within its wider Greco-Roman setting. By "creation," we refer to the creation of the world, the natural environment, and humanity. Our sources will be of a literary nature.[1] The numerous religious and philosophical movements of the Greco-Roman world and their vast number of attendant texts preclude a general comparison with the New Testament and require us to be highly selective in choosing sources. The Greco-Roman world was broadly Stoic by the New Testament era.[2] Stoicism has been described as a "grown-up" version of paganism.[3] Earlier Stoics such as Zeno, Cleanthes, and Chrysippus tended toward a form of pantheism in which a material god, called the "active principle," dwells within the matter of the

---

1. Our reliance on texts demands a word of methodological caution in that religious texts may not have functioned in the same manner in early Christianity as in other ancient religions. For Larry W. Hurtado, *Destroyer of the Gods: Early Christian Distinctiveness in the Roman World* (Waco, Tex.: Baylor University Press, 2016), 105–41, early Christianity was an unusually "bookish" religion. In contrast, many pagans were skeptical of books; see Robert Parker, *On Greek Religion* (Ithaca, N.Y.: Cornell University Press, 2011), 16–20.

2. A. A. Long and D. N. Sedley, *The Hellenistic Philosophers: Translations of the Principal Sources with Philosophical Commentary* (Cambridge: Cambridge University Press, 1987), 2ff.

3. N. T. Wright, *Paul and the Faithfulness of God* (Minneapolis, Minn.: Fortress, 2013), 217.

universe, called the "passive principle."[4] By the New Testament era, however, Stoicism distinguished between matter and the logical principle (the *logos*) that organized it.[5] Stoics originally drew on the ideas of Heraclitus for their view of the origins of the world.[6] They believed that the world was constituted from a divine "designing fire" in its various forms.[7] Fire turned to air, air to water, water to earth, and earth back to fire. This process, guided by "God, Intelligence, Fate, and Zeus," resulted in the universe.[8] Early Stoics believed that the universe would end as it began—in a great fiery conflagration. The universe is currently in a period of stability. At the great conflagration, the whole cycle of creation and history would be repeated.[9] The New Testament era, while heavily influenced by Stoicism, cannot be reduced to Stoicism. For this reason, we will broaden our sphere of investigation to include a selection of competing alternatives. A number of scholars have produced excellent overviews of creationism in Greco-Roman thought.[10] It is not our purpose to replicate their work. Neither is it our purpose to define in detail the New Testament's position on creation. Other authors in this volume undertake this task. Rather, our approach is one of narrative—to retell a selection of Greco-Roman creation accounts typically unfamiliar to a pastoral or educated Christian readership, thereby enabling the reader to compare and contrast these sources with the biblical account of creation.

The choice of case studies in this chapter is guided by both a desire to communicate the nature of the world in which New Testament authors operated and the need to speak to current discussions on creation and naturalistic evolution. As such, we will start by considering

---

4. Diogenes Laertius, *Vitae Philosophorum* (hereafter *Vit. Phil.*) 7.134–35.

5. Craig S. Keener, *Romans: A New Covenant Commentary* (Eugene, Ore.: Cascade, 2009), 33.

6. Long and Sedley, *Hellenistic Philosophers*, 277–78.

7. Diogenes Laertius, *Vit. Phil.* 7.136ff.

8. Ibid., 7.135. This study adopts the practice of capitalizing those words that were understood as a personification of a god from the ancient writer's perspective.

9. Long and Sedley, *Hellenistic Philosophers*, 308–13.

10. David Sedley, *Creationism and Its Critics in Antiquity* (Berkeley, Calif.: University of California Press, 2007). Cf. W. K. C. Guthrie, *In the Beginning: Some Greek Views on the Origins of Life and the Early State of Man* (Ithaca, N.Y.: Cornell University Press, 1957), 31–45; Arnold Ehrhardt, *The Beginning: A Study in the Greek Philosophical Approach to the Concept of Creation from Anaximander to St John* (Manchester: Manchester University Press, 1968); Keith A. Burton, "The Faith Factor: New Testament Cosmology in its Historical Context," *JATS* 15, no. 1 (2004): 34–46; and Mary-Jane Rubenstein, *Worlds without End: The Many Lives of the Multiverse* (New York: Columbia University Press, 2014), 40–69.

Apollodorus's *Library*, an excellent example from the time of the New Testament of a retelling of Homer's and Hesiod's creation myths. These myths included the Gigantomachy, the battle between the giants and the gods. At a popular level, many in the Greco-Roman world still accepted them as authoritative accounts of creation. The earlier rejection of the Gigantomachy by natural philosophers resulted, however, in a profusion of competing creation accounts. We will consider a number of such alternatives to illustrate what happens when belief in a dominant creation account is rejected. Particular attention will be paid to Empedocles's early version of natural selection, Plato's benevolent craftsman god, and Aristophanes's comedic account in which he seeks to justify a particular view of gender quite at variance with that held by early Christians. Finally, in Xenophon's *Memorabilia* (hereafter *Mem.*), Socrates presents an argument from design that, through the Stoics, would become highly influential in the first century AD. These arguments find their counterpart in today's intelligent design movement. As most people in the ancient world believed in some form of creation, we will not cover its ancient critics.[11]

THE FOUNDING MYTH: APOLLODORUS' *LIBRARY*

One of the most significant ancient Greek accounts of origins is Hesiod's *Theogony* (hereafter *Theog.*). In it he deals with the origin and genealogies of the gods, the ascension of Zeus to the position of king, and the various struggles between the Titans and the Olympians. This "succession myth" has its parallels in earlier Akkadian and Hittite texts.[12] It is estimated that Hesiod wrote *Theogony* around 700 BC.[13] Many of the events Hesiod describes find their parallel in Homer's epics of the *Iliad* and *Odyssey* (hereafter *Il.* and *Od.*). The question of which of the two authors predates the other has been a matter of dispute since at least the fifth century BC.[14] Both authors predate the New Testament by a minimum of seven to eight hundred years. Despite this significant time gap and five hundred years of

---

11. Sedley, *Creationism*, 133–66.

12. Martin Lichfield West, "Hesiod," in *The Oxford Classical Dictionary*, ed. Simon Hornblower, Anthony Spawforth, and Esther Eidinow, 4th ed. (Oxford: Oxford University Press, 2012), 678.

13. Sedley, *Creationism*, 2.

14. See Xenophanes in Aulus Gellius, *Noctes Atticae* 2.11.2; Herodotus, *The Histories* 2.53; Ephorus, *Fragmente der griechischen Historiker* (*FGrH*) 70 F 101. Most in the ancient world accepted Homer's priority.

skeptical readings on the part of philosophers, such myths were taken at a popular level as a literal account of actual events. Evidence of the enduring appeal of these ancient myths is found in Apollodorus's *Library*, a work possibly contemporary to the New Testament.[15] In this work, comprised of five books, he faithfully retells the events earlier described by Hesiod and Homer. It is impossible to tell how many still believed these myths. Ritual kept them alive in the popular imagination. They were used for instruction "on an astonishing variety of subjects, from religion to military science or even boatbuilding."[16] As such, they had, notes W. K. C. Guthrie, a disproportionate influence on later writers.[17] Guthrie also makes the intriguing suggestion that during the Roman Empire these myths were promoted in order to attract tourists to Greece, as Greece was "already living on her past as a playground for tourists from all parts of the Roman Empire."[18] It seems little has changed.

First, a few words regarding Apollodorus's use of sources: Apollodorus treats his source material as authoritative accounts of real events. He is certainly aware of variant traditions. He describes, for example, Hera as giving birth to Hephaestus, whom she conceived without intercourse with the other sex. He then notes that according to Homer, Hephaestus was sired by Zeus (Apollodorus, *Bib.* 1.3.5). Apollodorus is not bound by a "canonical" account and feels free to pick and choose between his sources. This illustrates Robert Parker's observation that Greek religion was a religion without a revealed text.[19] This is not to say that Greek religion was devoid of texts. In fact, it abounded with texts. They simply did not carry the same status attributed to the Hebrew Scriptures by Jews and to the New Testament by early followers of Jesus. Nevertheless, Apollodorus remains faithful to his sources and provides no commentary or assessment of the events he recounts. He provides us with a simple

---

15. Many difficulties remain in dating Apollodorus's work. A *terminus a quo* may be determined from his quote of the chronicler Castor, a contemporary of Cicero and the author of a history which covered events up until the year 61 BC (Apollodorus, *Bibliotecha* [hereafter *Bib.*] 2.1.3). It thus follows that the *Library* cannot have been composed earlier than the middle of the first century BC. A *terminus ante quem* may be determined from an allusion to the *Library* in a collection of proverbs composed by Greek sophist Zenobius during the time of Hadrian (AD 76–138).

16. Guthrie, *In the Beginning*, 80.

17. Ibid.

18. Ibid., 29.

19. Parker, *On Greek Religion*, 1–39. On Greek religion, cf. Walter Burkert, *Greek Religion: Archaic and Classical* (Oxford: Blackwell, 1985), 216–75.

narrative in which he makes no claims to exclusive authority, presenting his account as though it were a description of actual events. There is no air of cynicism. There is no attempt to defend his account. This is somewhat surprising in that it is clear from sources predating Apollodorus that many Greek philosophers either rejected such accounts or read them in a nonliteral manner.[20] In contrast, Apollodorus feels no need to defend his account against such attitudes. In this sense, the manner in which the myths are presented in the *Library* reflects more the popular literal interpretations of the masses rather than the cynicism of the "scientific" and philosophic elites.

EARTH, SKY, AND THEIR CHILDREN

Let us turn to the account itself. In contrast to Genesis's emphasis on the creation of the heavens and earth and humanity, the *Library* focuses on the genealogy of the gods. The creation of humanity is just one of their many acts. David Sedley concludes, "By this symbolism it is already clear in outline that man is not a first-level component of the divine cosmic structure, but somehow a secondary product."[21] A brief description of the opening chapters, focusing on an era of earth-shaking battles known as the Gigantomachy, serve to highlight this characteristic. In contrast to Hesiod, for whom Chaos is the first immortal god to exist (Hesiod, *Theog.* 115), the existence of the earth and sky is presumed right from the start (Apollodorus, *Bib.* 1.1.1).[22] Personality is attributed to Sky (*Ouranos*) and Earth (*Gē*), who together beget three groups: the "hundred-handed" creatures with a hundred hands and fifty heads (Briareus, Gyes, Cottus), the Cyclopes (Arges, Steropes, Brontes), and giant deities called the Titans (Ocean, Coeus, Hyperion, Crius, Iapetus, and the youngest of all, Cronus) and their sisters, called Titanides (Tethys, Rhea, Themis, Mmemosyne, Phoebe, Dione, and Thia, *Bib.* 1.1.2).[23] The first intimation that anything is wrong is signaled early

---

20. For cynical responses, cf. Homer, *Il.* 15.187; Plato, *Gorgias* 523a.

21. Sedley, *Creationism*, 4. This observation is made with respect to Hesiod's *Theogony*.

22. Hesiod states that before Earth came into being there was Chaos (*Theog.* 116–17). While still with us, Chaos has been transformed through subsequent generations, particularly through the birth of Love. Later cosmologists debated how the *kosmos* ("order") came to be established out of chaos. See Sedley, *Creationism*, 2–4.

23. Hesiod, *Theog.* 132–54. There are some strong similarities between what is described here and the Egyptian cosmologies, which focus primarily on the creation of the pantheon originating from Shu and Tefnut; see Gerhard F. Hasel and Michael G. Hasel, "The Unique Cosmology of Genesis 1 against Ancient Near Eastern and Egyptian Parallels," in *The Genesis Creation Account and Its Reverberations in the Old Testament*, ed. Gerald A. Klingbeil (Berrien Springs, Mich.: Andrews University Press), 9–30.

on when we are told that Sky bound and cast the Cyclopes into Tarta-rus, "a gloomy place in Hades as far distant from earth as earth is dis-tant from the sky" (*Bib.* 1.1.2; cf. 2 Pet. 2:4).[24] This grieved Earth, who persuaded the Titans to attack their father, Sky (Apollodorus, *Bib.* 1.1.4). Cronus leads the Titans in rebellion and succeeds in disfiguring Sky by cutting off his genitals and throwing them into the sea. The Furies are born from the resultant drops of blood.[25] Having dethroned their father, the Titans release the Cyclopes and transfer sovereignty to Cronus (*Bib.* 1.1.4). This signals a key motif: the transfer of sovereignty through war and violence. This is a succession myth in which sover-eignty is fought over amongst an elite group of beings in a manner reflective of the behavior of the Greek ruling class. Cronus then binds and shuts up the Cyclopes in Tartarus and weds his sister Rhea. Earth and Sky then inform him that he would be dethroned by his own son. To prevent this, he swallows his offspring at their birth (*Bib.* 1.1.5). These include Hestia, Demeter, Hera, Pluto, and Poseidon.[26] Subse-quently, the pregnant Rhea, in anger at Cronus's earlier actions, retreats to Crete where she gives birth to Zeus in a cave.[27] She then deceives Cronus by giving him a stone wrapped in swaddling clothes to swallow as though it were the newborn child (*Bib.* 1.1.7).[28] The child, Zeus, survives and grows to manhood.

MAKING SENSE OF LARGE FOSSIL BONES

At this point a brief word is in order in defense of those ancient Greek authors who created myths relating to heroes, giants, and hybrid creatures such as griffins (bodies like lions, beaks like eagles), centaurs (half man, half horse), the chimaera (an amalgam of goat, snake, and lion), and the minotaur (half man, half bull). Such crea-tures may not simply have been the result of overwrought ancient imaginations. Adrienne Mayor argues at length for a link between heroes, giants, and mythological creatures and the ancients' knowl-edge of paleontological discoveries. She convincingly demonstrates that many of the heroes and strange creatures found in Greek myths

---

24. Hesiod, *Theog.* 617–23.

25. Ibid., 156–90.

26. Ibid., 453–67.

27. Ibid., 468–80

28. Ibid., 485–91; Pausanias, *Description of Greece* (hereafter *Descr.*) 8.36.3; 9.2.7; 9.41.6; 10.24.6. According to Pausanias, the stone remained at Delphi until the second cen-tury AD and was used for libations (10.24.6).

reflect attempts on the part of the ancients to make sense of collections of large fossilized bones found throughout the then-known world. The abundance of fossils on the island of Samos, including those of many mammoths, was interpreted as the remains of the battle between the god Dionysus's war elephants and the giant Amazons.[29] The griffin, widespread in Greco-Roman literature and art, reflects the griffin-like *Protoceratops* and *Psittacosaurus,* of which there are countless fossil skeletons in certain regions of central Asia. These regions had strong trade links with Greece and were mined by the Scythians for gold.[30]

Throughout ancient Greece, regular discoveries of collections of fossil remains were sensational events that attracted large crowds and provided physical evidence for belief in the Gigantomachy, in which fifteen-foot heroes had fought Titans and giants. In the sixth and fifth centuries BC, there was a bone rush in which cities frantically sought the remains of local heroes such as Theseus (legendary king of Athens), Pelops (hero worshiped at Olympia), Orestes (son of Agamemnon and Clytemnestra), and Ajax (king of Salamis).[31] The burial sites of these heroes, all men of great stature, correspond again and again to areas of Greece rich in fossils. Temples became de facto paleontological museums stashed with large collections of "holy" bone relics of heroes and giants. These were later plundered by Roman imperial rulers such as Augustus and Tiberius for public display in Rome and for their own private museums.[32]

It became a matter of competing civic pride to claim the bones of some ancient hero: "Anatolian Lydia, Spanish Cadiz, Thebes, and Olympia each claimed to have the body of Geryon, and his huge oxen were said to have been dispersed around mainland Greece (Arcadia, Attica, Epirus), in Italy, in Asian Minor, and on the shores of the Black Sea."[33] Knowledge of such finds was widespread and served to reinforce at a popular level the belief in the Gigantomachy. It also fed into a perception that nature was in decline, that there was once a period in which huge heroes, Titans, and giants stalked the land, a period now overtaken by one in which men and beasts of far inferior

---

29. Adrienne Mayor, *The First Fossil Hunters: Paleontology in Greek and Roman Times* (Princeton, N.J.: Princeton University Press, 2000), 55. Cf. Plutarch, *Quaestiones Graecae* 56.

30. Mayor, *Fossil Hunters*, 22–53.

31. Ibid., 110–42.

32. Ibid., 142–48.

33. Ibid., 197.

stature predominated. At a popular level, these paleontological finds validated the Gigantomachy for the ancients, and the Gigantomachy gave meaning to the finds.

Second Temple Jewish authors were not isolated from these developments.[34] Judith 16:6 refers to "the sons of the Titans" and "tall giants." Wisdom 14:6 alludes to a period "in the beginning," when arrogant giants (*gigantōn*) perished as a result of the Flood. Fossil finds in Judea led Josephus to comment, in relation to the conquest of Canaan, "There were still left there [near Hebron] some of the race of giants [*gigantōn*], who had such large bodies, and countenances entirely different from other men, that they were shocking to look at and terrible to hear. Their bones are still shown to this very day and are unlike those of any other men" (Josephus, *Antiquities of the Jews* [hereafter *Ant.*] 5.125).

In Greek mythology, the "beast of Joppa" was a giant monster who attacked the maiden Andromeda. She was chained to a rock at Joppa, enduring the monster's attacks, until it was killed by Perseus. The skeleton of the monster was so famous that it was a central feature of Marcus Aemilius Scaurus's extravagant victory celebrations in 58 BC.[35] According to Josephus, the stone promontory of Joppa's harbor consisted of Andromeda's chains, which, he suggests, "attest to the antiquity of that fable" (*The Jewish War* 3.9.3). Such examples amply illustrate a pervasive awareness that large creatures once existed and that their significance was often understood in sections of Second Temple Judaism through a synthesis of Greek myth and biblical imagery.

THE GENEALOGY CONTINUES

We return to Apollodorus. After Zeus achieves maturity, he is helped by his cousin, Metis, daughter of Ocean, to drug Cronus. As a result of the drug, Cronus disgorges first the stone and then the siblings of Zeus. With their help, Zeus wages a ten-year war against Cronus and the other Titans. Earth prophesies that if Zeus were to be

---

34. The LXX uses *ho gigas* forty-one times to translate the Hebrew *nĕpîlîm* ("giants, monsters," e.g., Gen. 6:4, LXX), *hēmmâ haggibbôrîm' ăšer mē'ôlām 'anšê haššem* ("men of renown," e.g., Gen. 6:4, LXX), and *rĕpā'îm* (e.g., Gen. 14:5, LXX), defined as "ancient inhabitants of Canaan and legendary race of giants" (David. J. A. Clines, *ed., Dictionary of Classical Hebrew* [Sheffield: Sheffield Phoenix Press, 2010], 7:536). On Jewish awareness of pagan creation ideas, see Ehrhardt, *The Beginning*, 168–71.

35. Mayor, *Fossil Hunters*, 138.

aided by the Cyclopes, he would achieve victory (Appolodorus, *Bib.* 1.2.1). Zeus fulfills the prophecy when he manages to release the Cyclopes from Tartarus. The Cyclopes provide Zeus with thunder, lightning, and a thunderbolt, and give Pluto a helmet and Poseidon a trident.[36] With these weapons the gods overcome the Titans and shut them up in Tartarus under the guard of the Hundred-Handers.[37] The gods then cast lots and give sovereignty of the sky to Zeus, dominion of the sea to Poseidon, and dominion of Hades to Pluto (*Bib.* 1.2.1).[38] The account continues with a long list of the sons and daughters of the Titans and the gods. Offspring of the Titans include, among others, the Dawn, Sun and Moon (*Bib.* 1.2.2), Victory, Dominion, Emulation, and Violence (*Bib.* 1.2.4).[39] Grandchildren quickly arrive on the scene. Dawn and Astraeus give birth to winds and stars (*Bib.* 1.2.4).[40]

Apollodorus continues these genealogies with an account of Zeus's children. He describes Zeus as wedding another consort, Hera, with whom he produces Hebe, Ilithyia, and Ares (*Bib.* 1.3.1).[41] He then notes that Zeus joined himself with, or had intercourse with, many women, both mortals and immortals. The introduction without explanation of the distinction between mortal and immortal indicates that, as argued by Robert Parker, there was essentially no difference between humanity and the Greek gods, bar the gods' immortality and ability to procreate at will.[42] The gods can, somewhat surprisingly, themselves die. One of Zeus's daughters, Calliope, gives birth to a son Linus, whom Hercules slays (*Bib.* 1.3.2).[43] Apollo accidentally kills Hyacinth, whom he loves, by the casting of a quoit, a flattened ring of iron used in a throwing game (*Bib.* 1.3.4).[44] The gods may also seek to make mortals immortal. Demeter, for example, seeks to make Demophon, the newborn child of Metanira and Celeus, immortal by casting the child on a fire to strip off its mortal flesh (*Bib.* 1.5.1).[45] Her attempt fails.

---

36. Hesiod, *Theog.* 501–06.

37. Ibid., 617–34, 717–20; Horace, *Carmina* 3.4.42–48.

38. Homer, *Il.* 15.187.

39. Hesiod, *Theog.* 371–415.

40. Ibid., 378–82.

41. So too Homer, *Il.* 5.889–98 (Ares); 11.270 (Ilithyia); *Od.* 11.603–4 (Hebe); Hesiod, *Theog.* 921–23.

42. Parker, *On Greek Religion*, 64–102.

43. For Apollo as father, see Hyginus, *Fabulae* 161.

44. Cf. Pausanias, *Descr.* 3.19.4-5.

45. See Frazer's "Putting Children on the Fire," in Apollodorus, *The Library, Volume II: Book 3.10-end Epitome,* trans. James G. Frazer, LCL 122 (Cambridge, Mass.: Harvard University

THE CREATION OF HYBRID CREATURES

Toward the end of the first book we encounter two additional creation accounts. The first is of a strange hybrid between man and beast that results from Earth having intercourse with Tartarus out of anger that the gods had overcome the giants (Apollodorus, *Bib.* 1.6.3). Paleontological discoveries of unknown creatures could have seemed to affirm the existence of such hybrids. The result of this union is the hybrid Typhon, a being that surpassed all others in strength and size. "As far as the thighs he was of human shape and of such prodigious bulk that he out-topped all the mountains, and his head often brushed the stars. One of his hands reached out to the west and the other to the east, and from them projected a hundred dragons' heads" (*Bib.* 1.6.3).[46]

Mayor suggests that the identification of Typhon's thighs as being of human shape reflects the fact that many dinosaur femurs are similar in shape to the human femur.[47] Typhon attacks Heaven, prompting the gods to flee in animal form to Egypt. Zeus resists, however, and enters into combat with Typhon. Typhon hurls rocks at Zeus, who responds with thunderbolts. Typhon overpowers Zeus and cuts the sinews of his hands and feet. He then deposits Zeus in the Corycian cave on the slopes of Mount Parnassus. Unknown to Typhon, Hermes and Aegipan steal the sinews and restore them to Zeus. Renewed in strength, Zeus recommences his struggle with Typhon, pursuing him with thunderbolts until eventually he subdues him by casting Mount Etna upon him, thereby ending the era of the giants and masters. The blasts of fire from Etna provide ongoing testimony to the thunderbolts used by Zeus in this climactic struggle.[48] Enough on this subject, notes Apollodorus, and so we move on to the second creation account—that of humanity.

FINALLY, THE CREATION OF HUMANITY

Apollodorus's account of the creation of humanity is a condensed version of what we find in Hesiod's *Theogony*. The fact that it occurs

---

Press), 311–317. Frazer argues that babies were passed over the fire rather than burnt in the fire.

46. Cf. Hesiod, *Theog.* 821.

47. Mayor, *Fossil Hunters*, 197.

48. Other traditions have Typhon's corpse buried in Syria, Cilicia, and Phrygia. See Mayor, *Fossil Hunters*, 197.

so late in the narrative indicates that humanity is neither the center nor the climax of creation. The world has not been created for humanity. It was the playground, or rather the battleground, of the gods long before man arrived on the scene. Fossil evidence provided more than adequate evidence that humanity, from the start, was a degenerate creature in comparison to earlier heroes. The actual creation of humanity occurs when Prometheus, son of the Titans Iapetus and Asia (cf. Apollodorus, *Bib.* 1.2.3), molds men out of water and earth (*ex hydatos kai gēs anthrōpous plasas, Bib.* 1.7.1). It is unclear from Apollodorus's account as to whether the act of making man is of itself an act of hostility on the part of the Titans toward Zeus, the king of the Olympians. What is clear is that Zeus reacts with anger to Prometheus for smuggling fire, hidden in a stalk of fennel, to men. He orders Hephaestus to nail Prometheus to Mount Caucasus, a Scythian mountain. Apollodorus retells how "on it Prometheus was nailed and kept bound for many years. Every day an eagle swooped on him and devoured the lobes of his liver, which grew by night. That was the penalty that Prometheus paid for the theft of fire until Hercules afterwards released him, as we shall show in dealing with Hercules" (*Bib.* 1.7.1; cf. 2.5.11).

As the account continues, it becomes clear that the distinction between immortal gods and mortal humanity is repeatedly blurred.[49] Prometheus has a son, Deucalion, the Greek Noah, who reigns in the regions about Phthia, a city in ancient Thessaly, and who marries Pyrrha, the daughter of Epimetheus and Pandora, the first woman fashioned by the gods (*Bib.* 1.7.2).[50] Only at this point in the account does it become apparent that Prometheus's creation of humanity was of man alone, and not of woman. The first woman was created separately by other gods. Apollodorus does not explain by whom, how, or why the first woman was created. It may well be that he assumes his readers are aware of Hesiod's earlier account in which the god Hephaestus, at the behest of Zeus, created the first woman, Pandora, out of a mixture of earth and water in the image of immortal goddesses.[51] Zeus's motive for having women created was to punish men for colluding with Prometheus in the theft of fire.[52] As part of

---

49. This is true for many of the ancient myths, including Atrahasis.
50. Cf. Hesiod, *Theog.* 571–612.
51. Hesiod, *Opera et Dies* 60.
52. Ibid., 55.

the creation process, Zeus orders Hermes to put in the first woman a "shameless mind and a deceitful nature" (Hesiod, *Opera et Dies* [hereafter *Op.*] 68–69). Hermes obeys and places within her "lies and crafty words and a deceitful nature at the will of loud thundering Zeus" (*Op.* 78–79). Woman is given to man as an act of divine revenge. In contrast to Hesiod's account, Apollodorus skips over these details and continues apace with a Greek equivalent of Noah's Flood.

THE FLOOD ACCOUNT

The flood account proceeds with Zeus's decision to destroy the men of the Bronze age with a flood (Apollodorus, *Bib.* 1.7.2). His motives are not stated. In response, Prometheus warns his son, Deucalion, of the impending catastrophe and instructs him to build a chest and to store provisions in it. Deucalion then rides out the flood in the chest with his wife Pyrrha. Zeus pours heavy rain from heaven and floods the greater part of Greece so that all are destroyed, except a few who fled to high mountains.[53] Apollodorus notes that it was at this time that the mountains in Thessaly parted and that "all the world outside the Isthmus and Peloponnese was overwhelmed" (*Bib.* 1.7.2). Xenophon refers to examples of "bivalve shells (Mesozoic-Tertiary mollusks) on mountains, impressions of fish and seaweed in quarries on Sicily, myriad sea creatures embedded in rock on Malta, and oodles of small fish (probably Oligocene-Miocene *Prolebias* species) in slabs of rock on the island of Paros."[54] Such evidence convinced many ancients that the seas had at one point covered existing lands.

After nine days and nights in the chest, Deucalion drifts to Parnassus and, once the rain has ceased, lands and sacrifices to "Zeus, the god of escape" (*Dii phyxiō, Bib.* 1.7.2). It is unclear as to whether this is the same Zeus who sent the flood. The Zeus who sent the flood then sends Hermes to Deucalion with an offer to fulfill any of his wishes. Deucalion requests that he create new men to replace those drowned by the flood. At Zeus's bidding, Deucalion takes up stones and throws them over his head. The stones become men. Pyrrha copies Deucalion, with her stones becoming women.[55] Apollodorus then notes

---

53. For Aristotle, the flood was local to Greece. By the time we get to Ovid, it affects the whole earth. See Guthrie, *In the Beginning*, 26.

54. Mayor, *Fossil Hunters*, 210–11.

55. Guthrie highlights numerous creation accounts in which men originate from the earth. The Thebans, for example, were known as Spartoi, "the sown men." They resulted from Cadmus's action of killing a snake and sowing its "teeth" in the ground, the teeth producing

that it is for this reason that people were metaphorically called people (*laos*)—from *laas*, "a stone" (*apo tou laas ho lithos*, *Bib.* 1.7.2). In parallel Greco-Roman accounts, novel and strange creatures emerge after the flood.[56] We are then told of the descendants of Deucalion and Pyrrha. Their first son was Hellen, after whom he named the Greeks.[57] Hellen had Dorus, Xuthus, and Aeolus by a nymph Orseis (*Bib.* 1.7.3). Hellen divided the country amongst his sons. Dorus, after whom the Dorians were named, settled the southern region of the Peloponnese and Crete. Xuthus received the northern region of the Peloponnese and became the father of Achaeus and Ion, from whom the Achaeans and Ionians are named. Aeolus reigned over the region around Thessaly and named the inhabitants Aeolians. What follows is an extended genealogy of Hellen's family, focusing on those who founded or ruled important Greek cities and regions.

COMPARISON WITH THE NEW TESTAMENT

A number of observations may be made about the nature of this creation account. First, it represents just one of many ancient Greek creation myths, albeit the one that came to dominate all others. Guthrie warns that we should avoid imposing a nonexistent unity or consistency on Greek myths.[58] Greece was divided into a number of small and competitive tribal states that each claimed to be the oldest inhabitants of Greece. As such, each one put forth their own myth centered on their own ancestral hero, each claiming to be the first true sons and daughters of the earth. In this sense, creation myths were inextricably linked to political propaganda promoting particular local identities and aspirations. What they held in common, according to Guthrie, was belief that the earth, sometimes with a little help from the gods, could spontaneously generate life.[59] In the myth of Pandora, however, we have a move to a more universal position in that she is presented as "the ancestress of the whole Greek world."[60]

---

this unusual crop. The Athenians boasted that they were *autochthones* ("aboriginal, native") to the land, whereas all other Greeks were immigrants. See Guthrie, *In the Beginning*, 21–22.

56. Ovid, *Metamorphoses* (hereafter *Metam.*) 1.140–43.

57. In the Greek language, the term for the Greek people is *hellēn*.

58. Guthrie, *In the Beginning*, 24–27. Cf. Jan N. Bremmer, "Pandora or the Creation of a Greek Eve," in *The Creation of Man and Woman: Interpretations of the Biblical Narratives in Jewish and Christian Traditions*, ed. Gerard P. Luttikhuizen (Leiden: Brill, 2000), 19–33.

59. Guthrie, *In the Beginning*, 41. Guthrie also raises the problem discussed by the ancients as to how to define the difference between living and dead (ibid., 46).

60. Bremmer, "Pandora," 33.

This tension between tribal and universal origins is also found in Second Temple Jewish literature.[61] Some sources portray Adam, for example, as the first Jew rather than the father of all humanity. The book of Jubilees, a retelling of Genesis 1–3, portrays Adam as the first patriarch of Israel.[62] The Sabbath is a gift to the "seed of Jacob" and the "children of Israel" rather than to all humanity (Jub. 2:20, 26). We find an explicit affirmation that the Creator "did not sanctify any people or nations to keep the Sabbath with the sole exception of Israel. He granted to them alone that they might eat and drink and keep the Sabbath upon the earth" (Jub. 2:31). The author of Jubilees projects later Israelite laws back onto Adam and portrays him as a Jewish priest (e.g., Jub. 3:10–13). In contrast, other Jewish sources depict Adam in more universalistic terms. Philo talks of Adam as "the first citizen of the world" (*De Opificio Mundi* [hereafter *Opif.*] 142). Josephus portrays God as a universal Father and Lord and Adam and Eve as the father and mother of all humanity (*Ant.* 1.20, 36, 67).[63] This reflects the more universalistic biblical account in which, Jan Bremmer suggests, Eve transcended Pandora in that she is presented as the "mother of all living" (Gen. 3:20).[64] It is this later approach that we find in the New Testament, affirming the Old Testament story. Paul portrays all of humanity as being both created by God and dying "in Adam" (1 Cor. 15:22; cf. Rom. 5:14).[65] Adam is not just the father of Jews, but of all humanity.

Second, Apollodorus's account is predicated upon a monist worldview in which the gods are nature and nature, in all its gory horror, is the gods. The first dualist philosophers emerged in the early to mid-fifth century BC (e.g., Anaxagoras), moving away from

---

61. John R. Levison, *Portraits of Adam in Early Judaism* (Sheffield: JSOT Press, 1988). Cf. Michael E. Stone, *A History of the Literature of Adam and Eve* (Atlanta: Scholars, 1992); Gary Anderson, Michael E. Stone, and Johannes Tromp, eds., *Literature on Adam and Eve* (Leiden: Brill, 2000); Michael D. Eldridge, *Dying Adam with His Multiethnic Family: Understanding the Greek Life of Adam and Eve* (Leiden: Brill, 2001); and Bob Becking and Susanne Hennecke, eds., *Out of Paradise: Eve and Adam and Their Interpreters* (Sheffield: Sheffield Phoenix Press, 2011).

62. Levison, *Portraits of Adam*, 89–97.

63. Ibid., 99–111. For other more universalist examples, see Jacques T. A. G. M. van Ruiten, "The Creation of Man and Woman in Early Jewish Literature," in Luttikhuizen, *Creation of Man and Woman*, 34–62.

64. Bremmer, "Pandora," 33.

65. Unless otherwise indicated, Scripture quotations in this chapter are from the New Revised Standard Version Bible, copyright © 1989 the Division of Christian Education of the National Council of the Churches of Christ in the United States of America. Used by permission. All rights reserved.

Parmenides's monistic pantheism in which nature is, as Thales famously remarked, "full of the gods," to a dualism of mind and matter.[66] This enabled later philosophers such as Plato to posit the presence in the world of a superior governing power separate from creation. Such a presence is conspicuously absent in Apollodorus's *Library*. The New Testament similarly assumes, as with the Old Testament, a worldview in which God and creation are separate entities (e.g., John 1:1–5; Col. 1:15–17). The important consequence of this is that it allows for the distinction between a good God and a fallen creation.

Third, throughout Apollodorus's account we find that the gods act like mortals and mortals act like gods. The essential likeness of the gods—who mix, procreate, and fight together—and humanity affirms the present "fallen" state of the world as having existed from the beginning. In contrast to the biblical narrative, with its description of a pre-Fall state of harmony followed by the Fall, Apollodorus's account presumes that conflict, struggle, murder, jealousy, infidelity, and death are a natural part of the cosmos ushered in by that first union of Sky and Earth. The current moral state of the world is affirmed as normal and in harmony with its origins. In such a cosmogony there is no sense of paradise lost. By the classical period of Greek thought, many accepted the view that man's earlier condition was "brutish" or "animal–like."[67] If anything needs restoring, it is the physical prowess of a lost era. Large fossilized bones told them that there was once a period when man and beast were altogether stronger and bigger. This emphasis on the physical contrasts with the assumption of all New Testament authors that there is something not just physically wrong with the world but morally wrong (e.g., Rom. 3:9–18). In the ministry, death, and resurrection of Jesus a new creation process has begun in which moral transformation accompanies physical restoration.[68] Later Greek creation accounts diverged from these earlier, rather bleak portrayals of origins to

---

66. Thales's remark is found in Aristotle, *De Anima* 411.a8-9. Cf. Sedley, *Creationism*, 6. Parmenides, the great predecessor of Anaxagoras, was the ultimate monist.

67. Guthrie, *In the Beginning*, 95.

68. Cf. "on the first day of the week" in John 20:1 and God "raised us up" with Christ in Ephesians 2:6. See Paul S. Minear, *Christians and the New Creation: Genesis Motifs in the New Testament* (Louisville, Ky.: Westminster John Knox, 1994); and Maarten J. J. Menken and Steve Moyise, eds., *Genesis in the New Testament* (London: Bloomsbury T&T Clark, 2012).

reflect a position more akin to that of Scripture.[69] It is to these more divergent accounts, usually assuming a worldview in which God is separate from matter, that we now turn.

OVERTURNING AND REPLACING THE DOMINANT CREATION MYTH: THREE EXAMPLES

Not everyone approached ancient Greek creation myths with the same deference of Apollodorus. Many philosophers had earlier rejected such myths. They posited in their place a number of models that sought to explain the regularity in the world's structure.[70] A significant weakness of these models is that, while they sought to explain patterns and regularities in the natural world, they failed to account for the creation of humanity. Philosophers struggled to combine into one narrative the creation of the world and the creation of humanity. The result was that they merged, in what seems to later readers a very ad hoc manner, observation-based ideas with allusions to earlier myths.[71] Three creation accounts attributed to Empedocles, Plato, and Aristophanes nicely illustrate these developments.

REJECTING MYTH: EMPEDOCLES AND NATURAL SELECTION

Natural philosophers sought to replace earlier creation accounts with versions reflecting their own observations of the natural world. A good example of this is the fifth-century BC Sicilian philosopher Empedocles, who deplored literal readings of the Gigantomachy.[72] He argued against Parmenides's belief in a static world in which nothing could move or change by positing a cyclical battle between Love and Strife.[73] When Love dominates, the world moves toward a

---

69. By the time we come to the New Testament era, many creation accounts have been stripped of their mythological elements and read almost like the biblical account. See, for example, Heraclitus's first-century AD allegorical reading of Homer's creation account in his *Homeric allegories*, referenced in Ehrhardt, *The Beginning*, 164–66. An account quite similar to Scripture is found in Ovid's *Metamorphoses* 1.1–151ff. In this account humanity starts off good and then, in a sense, "falls."

70. Sedley, *Creationism*, 5.

71. Cf. Plato, *Legacy* 680b (cf. Aristotle, *Nicomachean Ethics* 1180a28; *Politics* 1252b23); 681e (quoting Homer, *Il.* 216–18).

72. Mayor, *Fossil Hunters*, 215.

73. Heraclitus (a different Heraclitus from that of note 67), an older contemporary of Empedocles, had earlier argued that the world is in a continual state of flux (Heraclitus, *D65–66*, in *Early Greek Philosophy, Volume III: Early Ionian Thinkers, Part 2*, edited and translated by André Laks and Glenn W. Most, LCL 526 [Cambridge, Mass.: Harvard University Press, 2016], 168–71). His theory of flux is frequently taken as a precondition for later

homogeneous whole. When Strife dominates, the world breaks down or separates into its four constituent elements of fire, air, earth, and water.[74] Both Love and Strife have their own creative periods.[75] According to Empedocles, we are currently in a movement toward cosmic dissolution as Strife increasingly dominates. For this reason, heterosexual love should be ruled out as it represents resistance to Strife. Rather, we should cooperate with Strife until we experience impersonal immortality as we are dissolved into our constituting elements.[76] Ethical purity, the keeping of food laws, and abstaining from sex all help one progress through ten to twenty lifetimes of cosmic creation and destruction to a state shared by the long-lived gods. In context, Empedocles was just one of many Greek philosophers who held to a cyclical view of history in which the best we can hope for is to enjoy intermittent golden ages.[77]

Within this cyclical process, Empedocles holds in tension a combination of divine creation and natural selection.[78] His creation account is as follows:[79] The gods, who are not necessarily immortal, first created a large selection of very simple creatures, which we now know as individual body parts.[80] Each "creature" had one special function. They were independent of each other, floating around, seeking either to join with others (when influenced by Love) or to disassociate from each other (when influenced by Strife). Examples of these simple creatures include eyes without eyebrows, "naked arms" separate

---

theories of evolution. For a defence of Heraclitus as author of the key respective passage, see Heraclitus, *Fragments: A Text and Translation with a Commentary by T.M. Robinson* (Toronto: University of Toronto Press, 1987), 141–42.

74. Diogenes Laertius, *Vit. Phil.* 8.76; Empedocles in Brad Inwood, *The Poem of Empedocles: A Text and Translation within an Introduction* (Toronto: University of Toronto Press, 1992), 88–89.

75. Sedley, *Creationism*, 33–52.

76. Inwood, *The Poem of Empedocles*, 61–65.

77. Guthrie, *In the Beginning*, 63–79.

78. For ideas related to natural evolution in Egyptian religions, see Ángel M. Rodríguez, "Biblical Creationism and Ancient Near Eastern Evolutionary Ideas," in Klingbeil, *Genesis Creation Account*, 293–328. Anaximander argued that living creatures originated from moisture. It has been suggested that this represents the first theory of evolution. The paucity of surviving sources precludes this conclusion. It is, for Guthrie, Aristotle who "burdened science for centuries with the dogma of the fixity of species"; see Guthrie, *In the Beginning*, 31–34, 62.

79. Empedocles's account of creation is far more complex than presented here. For a discussion, see Guthrie, *In the Beginning*, 42–45; and Sedley, *Creationism*, 31–74.

80. Gods and demons, like the soul, are long-lived and survive a number of the cosmic dissolutions, but they are not necessarily immortal. Cf. Inwood, *The Poem of Empedocles*, 53–54.

from shoulders, "whirling feet," and an "undistinguishable hand."[81] These simple creatures were each designed for a single purpose. Empedocles thus recognizes that purpose and design are inherent to creation. How these simple creatures combine, however, has less to do with design and more to do with chance. They randomly combined to produce "super-organisms," rather like giant ant colonies, or species as we know them today—humans, cows, horses, etc. The result of this process was a mixture of complex creatures more or less suited to their environments. Those that were suited survived. Those that were unsuited, such as human-faced cows and other mythological beasts, died out. The ongoing survival of humanity testifies to its suitability to its environment. By holding together divine design of simple creatures, their random combination to form today's "complex" creatures, and their varying suitability to their natural environment, Empedocles provides a narrative that, while going considerably beyond earlier creation myths of Homer and Hesiod, explains many elements within those myths. In particular, he maintains a role for the divine in creation while also explaining why many of Homer's strange mythological beasts are no longer present with us today. Though they once existed, they were unsuited for their environments and so died out.[82] This creation account was subsequently critiqued by Plato, who argued that a perfect god would have created complex creatures from the beginning (*Timaeus* [hereafter *Tim.*] 30c), and Aristotle, who disputed how separate body parts could have come together randomly in the first place (*Physics in Early Greek Philosophy* [hereafter *Phys.*] 2.8).[83] For Aristotle, not only the parts but also the manner of their combination reveal intention and design. Despite these criticisms, contemporary scholarship is quick to herald Empedocles's vision as a precursor to Darwinian natural selection.[84]

---

81. Empedocles is referred to in Simplicius's commentary on Aristotle's *Physics* in *Early Greek Philosophy, Volume V: Western Greek Thinkers, Part 2*, edited and translated by André Laks and Glenn W. Most, LCL 528 (Cambridge, Mass.: Harvard University Press, 2016), 497–503. For comment, cf. Inwood, *The Poem of Empedocles*, 94–95, 225–27.

82. Mayor, *Fossil Hunters*, 215–16.

83. Ibid., 217–18.

84. C. Leon Harris, *Evolution, Genesis and Revelations, with Readings from Empedocles to Wilson* (Albany, N.Y.: State University of New York Press, 1981), 32; and H. James Birx, *Interpreting Evolution: Darwin & Teilhard de Chardin* (Buffalo, N.Y.: Prometheus Books, 1991), 42. Contrast Sedley, *Creationism*, 61–62.

RELATIVIZING MYTH: PLATO'S GOOD CRAFTSMAN GOD

Plato's *Timaeus* is another creation account quite dissimilar to those of the Greek poets.[85] Sedley describes it as "the most influential of all Plato's works, and probably the most seminal philosophical or scientific text to emerge from the whole of antiquity."[86] Its influence on early Christianity was profound.[87] In a quite daring move, Plato relativizes earlier myths of origin by suggesting that they are actually descriptions of events that occurred a long time after the original creation of the universe. This allows him to create a myth that functions as a backdrop to existing myths—a story behind the story.

The *Timaeus* presents an extended dialogue between Socrates and a number of interlocutors, chief among them being Critias and Timaeus. Critias reports early in the dialogue on a conversation between Solon the Athenian lawgiver and an Egyptian priest that occurred when Solon visited Egypt, where Athena the god of Athens originated. The priest informs Solon that the Greek account of the flood of Deucalion is not a description of a unique one-time event (Plato, *Tim.* 23b). Greece, so the priest asserts, was regularly flooded during the eight thousand years between the creation of the universe and Deucalion's flood. In most instances the survivors died without writing down their accounts. Thus, claims the priest, the flood and genealogical accounts so valued by Solon (and here we may infer an allusion to Homer and Hesiod, and later Apollodorus), are "little better than children's tales" (*Tim.* 23b). They are not describing a unique event, but rather just one of many such floods. Their uniqueness as accounts lies not in the events they describe, but in the fact that the events were actually written down.

In relativizing the flood to being just one of many such floods, the priest also relativizes the associated Gigantomachy. In this manner

---

85. Also interesting is Arnold Ehrhardt's discussion of "beginning." Anaximander introduced it as a cosmological concept. Pythagoras argued for a static beginning originating from a numerical value, while Plato believed it to be an event, a "beginning of motion." Ehrhardt, *The Beginning*, 28–68, 87–106.

86. A good example of its influence is Philo's *De opificio mundi*. Cf. Sedley, *Creationism*, 96; and Jonathan D. Worthington, *Creation in Paul and Philo* (Tübingen: Mohr Siebeck, 2011), 29–45.

87. Possible allusions to Plato and the *Timaeus* include Justin Martyr, *The First Apology* 59–60, 67; Theophilus, *Autolycus* (hereafter *Autol.*) 2.4–5; and Irenaeus, *Adversus Haereses* (hereafter *Haer.*) 3.25.5. For a good assessment of second-century Christian understandings of creation, see Peter C. Bouteneff, *Beginnings: Ancient Christian Readings of the Biblical Creation Narratives* (Grand Rapids, Mich.: Baker Academic, 2008), 55–87.

the priest creates a historical period prior to that described in existing Greek myths into which new events may be inserted, the primary of these events being the attack by the great sea power Atlantis against Europe and Europe's salvation by Athens (*Tim.* 24e). This selfless act of heroism on the part of Athens is itself relativized, in that we are then told that subsequent earthquakes and floods wiped out both Athens and Atlantis (*Tim.* 25d). Allowing for a period before Homer and Hesiod also raises the question, voiced by Socrates, of what story they should adopt to explain the creation of the universe. Homer and Hesiod presume the existence of Earth and Sky without explaining whether they had a beginning. Timaeus rises to the challenge and provides the story behind the story, an account of creation itself. Some early Christian apologists were quite aware of this difference between Plato's account of creation and that of early Greek myths. Theophilus of Antioch, for example, writing in the second century AD, critiques the myths of Homer and Hesiod for failing, unlike Plato, to provide an explanation of the creation of the world (*Autol.* 2.5; cf. 2.7–8). All they provide, asserts Theophilus, are accounts of the origins of the gods.[88]

Timaeus's theology of creation is summarized in *Timaeus* 28–29, in which he argues that god, whom he describes as the Cause of everything and the Being, constructed "Becoming and the All" (Plato, *Tim.* 29d). In this scenario, time came into existence with the creation of the heavens (*Tim.* 38c). God, who caused the heavens and time, is thus placed outside of time, as one for whom there is no past nor future—no *Becoming*, only *Being*.[89] Timaeus recounts in detail how this timeless god created all that is Becoming: the seven planets,[90] the stars, the lesser created gods, the world, and all living creatures—everything that is in a state of becoming and subject to time. This emphasis on the timeless creator created a problem for Jewish and early Christian interpreters, for whom the six days of the biblical creation account now seemed entirely superfluous. Their

---

88. Bouteneff, *Beginnings*, 69–73.

89. Cf. Philo, *Opif.* 13, 26–28.

90. Plato, *Tim.* 38c. The seven planets, according to Plato, include the sun, moon, and five other stars, known as "planets" (lit. "wanderers"), most likely a reference to Mercury, Venus, Mars, Jupiter, and Saturn, all visible to the naked eye. While we recognize today that the moon and these five visible planets are not stars, but rather objects that reflect the light of our sun, the ancients would not have known this.

response was to allegorize the six days, or demonstrate the unique symbolism of the number six.[91]

We move to the act of creation itself. The creator god is, for Timaeus, a good god who, through a rational and orderly process, crafts out of chaotic matter a good and perfect world—a perfect sphere surrounded by a spherical heavens modeled on an eternal Form (*Tim.* 28c–29b; 33b–34b; 51d–e).[92] Later interpreters differed over whether Plato implied a creation ex nihilo or a shaping of preexistent matter. The cosmos that god creates is based upon a perfect model.[93] We have a divine master craftsman combining and shaping material, the four basic building blocks being fire, earth, water, and air (*Tim.* 31b, 32b), according to his master plan.[94] This concept of the model or plan is not too different, suggests Jonathan Worthington, from Paul's belief that God had a pre-creational plan for the glory of His creation.[95] Returning to Plato, his resultant cosmos becomes the receptacle in which the divinely created soul is housed, resulting in a cosmos that is rational and living (*Tim.* 30b). Thus, suggests Sedley, we are to understand "the benefits that intelligence has bestowed in imposing order, by describing what matter would be like even today *if* it were left entirely to its own devices (cf. 53a7–b5)."[96]

A second stage of creation involves the completion of the creation of humanity. In order to avoid making man immortal, god delegates the design and construction of the human body to lesser, created gods, who are neither wholly mortal nor immortal (*Tim.* 41a–c).[97] God creates humanity's souls. The lesser gods design the human body as a housing or receptacle for these souls in the same way that

---

91. Cf. Philo, *Opif.* 13–15, 89–110; Origen, *De Principiis* 4.3.1.

92. There is an internal inconsistency to Plato's account in that time began with the creation of the world and the celestial clock and yet before this there was chaotic motion, implying time, in the material "receptacle" before creation (cf. *Tim.* 37c6–38c3; 51d2–53c3). Many early (and later) readers of *Timaeus* rejected the idea that Plato implies that the world had a beginning. Aristotle, though he accepted Plato's concept of the cosmic soul, did not like the fact that for Plato the world has a beginning but not an end. Later Epicureans, such as Lucretius, questioned the origins of different creation accounts. There has been much discussion as to whether or not Aristotle actually understood Plato. Cf. Ehrhardt, *The Beginning*, 107–40; and Sedley, *Creationism*, 140.

93. So too Philo, *Opif.* 19, 36, 129–30.

94. Early Christian apologists debated as to whether God created *ex nihilo*. For various positions, see Bouteneff, *Beginnings*, 77.

95. Worthington, *Creation in Paul and Philo*, 45–75.

96. Sedley, *Creationism*, 118.

97. The involvement of other beings in the creation of humanity is addressed in Philo, *Opif.* 72, 75.

god created the cosmos to house the world's soul.[98] Souls are, however, subject to degradation. This occurs when they fail to master negative emotions through the application of reason (*Tim.* 42a–b).[99] As souls degrade, male bodies are correspondingly degraded into female bodies in which to house such degraded souls.[100] And so the process continues, as souls may move down the natural scale, first from men to women, and then from women to quadrupeds, from quadrupeds to legless animals such as snakes, and finally to fish. Promotion is also possible, with the highest possible state being the disembodied soul.[101] These stages of transmutation correspond to the appropriate regions of the world. Punishment occurs in Tartarus, moving up to incarnation in fish, to land-dwelling creatures like ourselves, to "the privileged inhabitants of the aether, whose life is close in purity and beauty to a totally discarnate one."[102] This is a teleological world designed to benefit souls. There is purpose, permitting us to make value judgments. Through his creation myth, quite different from that of Empedocles, Plato was the first to introduce the idea of one species transmuting into another by physical adaption to the degrading or promotion of souls.

Plato's creation account represents a combination of Socrates's conviction that man is a divinely privileged species with Pythagoras's belief in the transmigration of the soul.[103] The human rational soul was modeled by the creator god after the world's soul and housed in our approximately spherical heads in imitation of the way in which the world's soul is housed in the heavens, which are, like our heads, thought to be spherical in shape.[104] The design of our heads indicates that while creation is well designed, it has inbuilt compromises. In an oft-cited example, Plato suggests that the human head would have benefited from being surrounded by a protective

---

98. Sedley, *Creationism*, 98–99, 122–27.

99. Cf. Philo, *Opif.* 79–81.

100. In the initial act of creation, the gods created only man. Philo, *Opif.* 66, 152, 156, lays the blame for the introduction of iniquity into a perfect creation at the feet of woman, both in the pleasure she incites in man and for her failure to withstand the serpent.

101. Plato does not explicitly state that women must become men, though it is implied in *Timaeus* 91a–92c.

102. Sedley, *Creationism*, 94.

103. In contrast to Pythagoras, Socrates, and Plato, who all believed in an immortal soul, the Epicureans argued that the soul is mortal and an integral part of the material body (e.g., Lucretius, *De Rerum Natura* 5.126ff). See Guthrie, *In the Beginning*, 49, 59.

104. So too Philo, *Opif.* 69. See Sedley, *Creationism*, 98.

fatty layer of flesh, as with our thighs (*Tim.* 74e1–75c7).[105] This would have resulted, however, in a loss of sensitivity. As such, hair is a necessary compromise, providing protection without reducing sensitivity. Plato was quite aware of compromise, imperfection, and suffering within nature. For him, however, this was not evidence of a "fallen" world. The world in its current form is, despite imperfections, as intended, in that imperfect forms are required to house imperfect souls. As long as "imperfect" nature is performing its intended goal—the transformation of imperfect souls—it may be said to be perfect.

Plato sought, in contrast to Empedocles, to re-engage myth with philosophy because he rejected the rationalist Anaxagoras's conclusion that the empirical cosmos was "good" and the world the best possible world.[106] Plato believed that applying ethical terms such as "good" based purely on scientific premises could not be justified. He thus sought to re-engage with myth in order to provide a surer foundation for ethics. This came at the cost, according to Arnold Ehrhardt, of conclusiveness, resulting in a "very open system."[107] His account constantly varies between scientific description and metaphor, leading to a never-ending debate as to whether the whole account should be taken literally or metaphorically.[108] Aristotle reacted against Plato's vision of creation by replacing Plato's divine craftsman with his own self-absorbed meditative god, a god isolated from his creation.[109] Aristotle's world, in contrast to that of Plato, has no beginning, and yet it manifests design and purpose.[110] Essentially, we have purpose but without god. For Sedley, Aristotle wanted to retain "all the explanatory benefits of creationism without the need to postulate any controlling intelligence."[111]

---

105. Cf. Aristotle, *Parts of Animals* 2.10.656, who suggests that our lack of padding is to keep our heads cool. See Sedley, *Creationism*, 120.

106. This is just one of a number of disagreements Ehrhardt lists between Plato and his philosophical predecessors; see Ehrhardt, *The Beginning*, 108.

107. Ibid.

108. Harold Cherniss, *Aristotle's Criticism of Plato and the Academy* (New York: Russell and Russell, 1962), 476–78; Leonardo Taran, "The Creation Myth in Plato's Timaeus," *The Society for Ancient Greek Philosophy Newsletter* 252 (1966); and Sedley, *Creationism*, 98–107.

109. This is expressed, for example, in his description of natural processes as operating independently of the divine in Aristotle, *Phys.* 192b.20-30.

110. Philo criticises such a position in *Opif.* 1.7–11.

111. Sedley, *Creationism*, xvi–xvii.

COMPARISON WITH THE NEW TESTAMENT

The mechanics of how the world and humanity were created vary greatly in the creation accounts of Empedocles and Plato. The rejection of the Gigantomachy on the part of natural philosophers opened up opportunities for fresh retellings of creation shaped by more immediate concerns. How does this generally dismissive stance of the natural philosophers toward earlier poetic accounts compare with New Testament authors' attitudes to their own Genesis creation account?

Mayor suggests that philosophers lacked a naturalistic explanation of fossil finds with which to counter the Gigantomachy and so they avoided—with, as far as we know, the exception of Theophrastus—discussion of "giant" bone finds.[112] At one level, New Testament writers parallel the natural philosophers in that we find an equivalent lack of desire to engage with the pre-Flood world of giants (cf. *hoi gigantes*, Gen. 6:4, LXX). This should not surprise us, in that the driving purpose of New Testament writers was not to make sense of collections of giant bones but rather to comprehend the absence of bones from a certain Palestinian tomb.

Also, like the natural philosophers who reframed earlier creation accounts, New Testament writers expand on the Genesis creation account in light of the life of Jesus. This is clearly the case, for example, in John 1:1–5, in which the creation events associated with the "in the beginning" of Genesis 1:1 are refocused around Jesus as the Word ("In the beginning *was the Word*," John 1:1, emphasis added). In the seven-day time sequence of John 1:19–2:12, the evangelist creates an understanding of who Jesus is through an unfolding series of christological titles and statements.[113] Light breaks through the darkness as the reader is led on a journey of discovery concerning the identity and mission of Jesus. In Luke 24:30–31, after Jesus had

---

112. Mayor, *Fossil Hunters*, 212.

113. Herman Servotte, *According to John: A Literary Reading of the Fourth Gospel* (London: Darton, Longman and Todd, 1994), 9–15. Cf. J. Painter, "Rereading Genesis in the Prologue of John?," in *Neotestamentica Et Philonica: Studies in Honor of Peder Borgen*, ed. David E. Aune et al. (Leiden: Brill, 2003), 179–201; Maarten J. J. Menken, "Genesis in John's Gospel and 1 John," in Menken and Moyise, *Genesis in the New Testament*, 83–98; and Anthony M. Moore, *Signs of Salvation: The Theme of Creation in John's Gospel* (Cambridge: James Clark, 2013). Also see the comprehensive discussion of this point in Wilson Paroschi, *Incarnation and Covenant in the Prologue to the Fourth Gospel*, EUS (Frankfurt: Peter Lang, 2006), 19-60. For cautions regarding the six or seven day sequence in these verses see Edward W. Klink III, *John*, ZECNT (Grand Rapids, Mich.: Zondervan, 2016), 160–162.

taken, blessed, broken, and given bread to Cleopas and his fellow disciple, their eyes were "opened" and they "knew" Him (*autōn de diēnoichthēsan hoi ophthalmoi kai epegnōsan auton*). This followed Jesus's wide-ranging exposition of how the Scriptures relate to Himself as the crucified Christ.[114] Luke is signaling that through Scripture and the breaking of bread, the reader's eyes may be "opened" in a positive manner that reverses that first terrible occasion when the first man and woman ate from the tree of knowledge and their eyes were "opened" and they "knew" they were naked (*kai diēnoichthēsan hoi ophthalmoi tōn dyo, kai egnōsan*, Gen. 3:7, LXX).[115] A re-creation process is underway. Many more such examples could be provided from the New Testament, in which the Genesis creation account is alluded to in relation to the story of Jesus.

In contrast, however, to the natural philosophers who radically revised earlier Greek creation accounts, the New Testament authors accepted the Genesis creation account as a description of actual events.[116] Such a reading of the Genesis account, affirmed by Jesus Himself, is reflected in His references to God creating man and woman at the "beginning of creation" (Mark 10:6–7; cf. Matt. 19:4–5) and to the "days of Noah" (Matt. 24:37–38; Luke 17:26–27; cf. 1 Pet. 3:19–20).[117] In summary, like the natural philosophers, the earliest Christians expended little energy on explaining the phenomenon of giant bones. Unlike such philosophers, however, they accepted their own creation account as a description of actual events.[118]

---

114. For creation/Genesis allusions in Luke-Acts, see Minear, *Christians and the New Creation*, 1–61; and Peter Mallen, "Genesis in Luke-Acts," in Menken and Moyise, *Genesis in the New Testament*, 60–82. Also see the chapter in this volume by Kim Papaioannou.

115. Luke Timothy Johnson, *The Gospel of Luke* (Collegeville, Minn.: Liturgical Press, 1991), 396–97; N. T. Wright, *The Resurrection of the Son of God* (London: SPCK, 2003), 652; N. T. Wright, *Luke for Everyone* (London: SPCK, 2004), 296–98; and Dale C. Ortlund, "'And Their Eyes Were Opened, and They Knew': An Inter-Canonical Note on Luke 24:31," *JETS* 53, no. 4 (2010): 717–28.

116. So too Josephus, *Ant.* 1.27–51. For Jewish and early Christian interpretations of Genesis 1–3, see Andrew J. Brown, *The Days of Creation: A History of Christian Interpretation of Genesis 1:1–2:3* (Blandford Forum, Dorset: Deo Publishing, 2014), 17–18; and Jacques T. A. G. M. van Ruiten, "Genesis in Early Jewish Literature," in Menken and Moyise, *Genesis in the New Testament*, 7–26, esp. 9–11.

117. Ekkehardt Mueller, "Creation in the New Testament," *JATS* 15, no. 1 (2004): 47–62, esp. 52–57.

118. For the various allegorical, literal, and theological readings of Genesis 1–3 by the church fathers, see Brown, *Days of Creation*, 16–59. Brown suggests that early Christians expected all genres of the Old Testament to "function prophetically," the result being that the seven-day week of Genesis 1:1–2:3 was "ripe" for "prophetic interpretation" (21).

CREATING NEW MYTHS: ARISTOPHANES IN PLATO'S SYMPOSIUM

In Plato's *Symposium*, dated to the early part of the fourth century BC, the creation of man and woman is radically revised to include the creation of homosexuals and lesbians. The narrative setting is one in which an Apollodorus, not the author of *Library*, recounts how Aristodemus joined Socrates on the way to a meal in honor of Agathon. Socrates dramatically delays his entrance for half of the meal and then, upon entering, jests with Agathon, the host. It transpires that Agathon and his other guests have spent the previous day in heavy drinking and in light of this, they decide to seek their after-dinner entertainment in conversation rather than drink (Plato, *Symposium* [hereafter *Symp.*] 176e). One Eryximachus starts things off by raising a complaint of Phaedrus as to why no hymn has been written in praise of the god of love. In comparison, countless hymns have been produced for other gods (*Symp.* 177a–b). He then proposes that each guest make a speech in turn, from left to right, "praising Love as beautifully as he can" (*Symp.* 177d). Apollodorus then confesses that Aristodemus remembered only the memorable parts of the speeches and that his own memory is also partial (*Symp.* 178a). This provides the setting for the various speeches, one of which is delivered by Aristophanes.

Aristophanes was arguably the greatest poet of the Old Attic Comedy of the Athenian deme. He wrote numerous plays in which he satirized leading figures in Athenian society. In *Clouds* he mercilessly ridicules his younger contemporary, Socrates, as a corrupt teacher of rhetoric, an unshod charlatan (Aristophanes, *Nubes* [hereafter *Nub.*] 100), one who, for example, debates important topics as to whether gnats buzz through their mouth or their rump (*Nub.* 163), and who hangs in a basket from the ceiling in order to better discern celestial mysteries (*Nub.* 218). Plato is quite aware of Aristophanes's satirical portrayal of Socrates in that he quotes from Aristophanes's own description in *Clouds* of Socrates as one who walks "strutting our streets like a proud marsh-goose, with ever a side-long glance" (Aristophanes, *Nub.* 362, quoted in Plato, *Symp.* 221b). Plato does not join Aristophanes, however, in ridiculing Socrates. Quite the opposite. By the end of the *Symposium*, Socrates has been established to be unlike any other man, ancient or modern, the greatest of wonders (Plato, *Symp.* 221c). Although much of what he says may seem ridiculous at a surface level, his words contain divine truths nowhere else found (*Symp.* 221e–222a). In this context, it is quite difficult to know how to take Plato's characterization of Aristophanes. In *Symposium* 185c, he presents Aristophanes as unable to take his turn in making a speech due to a bout of hiccups. When he finally speaks, are we to take his speech as worthy of serious consideration, as with the previous speeches? Or is this Aristophanes the comedian speaking? Plato leaves the decision to his reader. We turn to the speech itself.

ORIGINALLY THREE GENDERS

As in the preceding speeches, Aristophanes emphasizes same-sex relationships as the ideal expression of love. His contribution is to ground this love in a retelling of earlier creation accounts that focus on the two sexes, male and female. Aristophanes begins his lesson on love by calling our attention to the nature of man and his development. He asserts that our current nature is by no means what it originally was. Initially there were "three kinds of human beings, not merely the two sexes, male and female, as present" (Plato, *Symp.* 189e). There was male, female, and male-female. The third kind had an equal share of male and female. All three kinds were round in shape with four arms and four legs. Normally they would walk upright on their four legs. Whenever they wanted to move at great speed, they would whirl like acrobats, using all eight limbs to propel themselves along. All three kinds also had two faces on a cylindrical neck and two sexual organs (*Symp.* 190a). The differences between the three sexes reflects the fact that the male was the offspring of the sun, the female the offspring of the earth, and the male-female the offspring of the moon (*Symp.* 190b). Their globular shapes reflect the shapes of their parents.

In contrast to earlier Greek creation accounts in which intrigue, jealousy, murder, and strife are present from the opening moment of creation, there is nothing in this account to suggest that there was anything initially wrong with the three kinds of human beings. Thus, we can speak, as in the biblical account, of a "fall." What caused their fall? The following account provides the answer:

> Now, they were of surprising strength and vigour, and so lofty in their notions that they even conspired against the gods; and the same story is told of them as Homer relates of Ephialtes and Otus, that scheming to assault the gods in fight they tried to mount high heaven. (*Symp.* 190b–c)

Here Aristophanes is drawing a parallel between a rebellion against the gods by the three sexes and Homer's account of a similar rebellion in which the giants Ephialtes and Otus sought to stack Mounts Pelion, Ossa, and Olympus on top of each other in order to reach the gods in heaven and make war with them. In Homer's account, Apollo killed both of them before they could put their plan into action (*Od.* 305).[119] In comparison, the gods respond to the rebellion of the three sexes by holding a council of the gods, led by Zeus, at which the decision is taken not to slay them as in the case of the giants (Plato, *Symp.* 190c). Instead, they would be spared in order to enable their continued worship of the gods. Zeus proposes to slice each of the eight-limbed creatures in half so that where there was respectively an eight-limbed round being, there would now be two semicircular beings, each with only two legs and two arms. This plan is put into effect, resulting in the eight–limbed male being sliced in two, creating two men, the eight-limbed female being cut in two, to create two women, and the male-female being cut into two, to create a man and woman. After Apollo does some reworking with the resultant forms, moving the heads and limbs around a little, stretching and tucking the skin here and there, we end up with men and woman as we know them today. Zeus threatens to slice them in two again if they continue in their rebellion, in which case they would each have only one leg and one arm (*Symp.* 190d–91a).

THE GREAT SPIRIT

How does all this relate to love? The result of being split in two has created, in the words of Aristophanes, a "human sore," which men and women try to heal by finding their original partners (Plato, *Symp.* 191c–92a). Those men who were originally one half of one of the eight-limbed male beings seek to be reunited with their original male counterpart. These are today's male homosexuals. The same applies to women who were once part of one of the original eight-limbed female forms. They, too, seek their other half; these are today's lesbians. Men who were originally part of a male-female form commit adultery and are "women-courters," as they seek to be reunited in their original form. The same holds true for those women who hunger after men, an expression of their desire for the human sore to be healed. Aristophanes then expands in detail as to how, when two men lie together, locked in embrace, they are expressing

---

119. Cf. Homer, *Il.* 5.385–87.

their innermost desire to be reunited in their original form. This, for Aristophanes, is the highest form of love (*Symp.* 193a).

In this context, both divine judgment and restoration play out in the human sphere. Aristophanes states that as a result of our sins (*dia tēn adikian*, *Symp.* 193a), Zeus has separated and dispersed us. Present judgment involves being separated from our previous halves and dispersed throughout the world. Future judgment is not a given, but may occur if humanity continues to be disorderly toward heaven. If required, this judgment will involve humans, who have already been cut in half, being quartered (*Symp.* 193a–b). Restoration occurs when one finds one's original partner, whether it be in a male-to-male, female-to-female, or male-to-female relationship. Affirmation of this process is confirmed through the sexual union of previously separated partners. Aristophanes sums up the process thus: "The way to bring happiness to our race is to give our love its true fulfilment: let everyone find his own favourite, and so revert to his original nature" (*Symp.* 193c). Love (*Erōtos*) is the god who brings this about in response to our reverent duty to the gods (*Symp.* 193d). The experience of salvation is deeply sexual and is directed less toward the god-man relationship than the various relationships within humanity. This is not to say that humanity's relationship to the gods is unimportant. If we reconcile ourselves with the gods, we shall have the fortune of discovering our proper favorites (*Symp.* 193b). Reconciliation with the gods is secondary, however, to seeking our own personal reunification.

COMPARISON WITH OTHER CREATION ACCOUNTS

How does this account compare with the earlier works of Homer and Hesiod and their later retelling in Apollodorus's *Library*? Three differences suggest themselves. First, Aristophanes provides a creation account that fundamentally challenges the Gigantomachy.[120] Gone are the Titans, giants, and heroes. Instead we are provided with a highly anthropocentric account of creation. He was by no means the first to do this. He was, in fact, following a well–worn path previously trod by Anaximander, Parmenides, Anaxagoras, Empedocles, and

---

120. Palaephatus, a friend and follower of Aristotle, provides a lengthy rereading of the Gigantomachy in *On Unbelievable Tales*, in which he rationalizes away the stranger traditions about heroes and monsters. The Epicurean Lucretius argues against the Gigantomachy's account of the destruction of the giants, suggesting that giant animals died out as a result of a lack of food (*De Re. Nat.* 4.726–43; 5.93–294, 787–933). See Mayor, *Fossil Hunters*, 216–17, 221.

Democritus, who, in their own ways, undertook the "rational separation of philosophy and mythology."[121] Second, in Apollodorus's account, the male–female distinction is presented as normative (as in the New Testament; cf. Mark 10:6–9). In contrast, Aristophanes projects back onto creation the origins of homosexual and lesbian relationships. They are affirmed as being as equally valid as the original male-female relationship. This should not surprise us, as Aristophanes is addressing a group of mostly homosexual philosophers (Socrates, who was married, also had male lovers). Third, in Apollodorus's account, the creation of the first woman, Pandora, was an act of divine punishment against the first man for colluding with Prometheus in his slighting of Zeus. The male-female relationship was bitter from the start. Inter-sex strife results not by accident nor from a fallout between the first man and woman. It is the result of a determined and defined divine intention to punish man, Pandora being the means of that punishment. In contrast, Aristophanes presents all genders as equally responsible for, and under, divine judgment. There is no singling out of the woman as the means of punishment. In this reading, the heterosexual male is morally no better off than the heterosexual woman or his homosexual and lesbian counterparts.

These differences illustrate the degree of freedom exhibited on the part of Aristophanes in framing creation. Has he replaced the mythic monsters of the Gigantomachy with his own new cast of strange creatures simply for comedic effect? This is difficult to judge. On two occasions Aristophanes exhorts Eryximachus not to make comic sport or to mock his speech (Plato, *Symp.* 193b, d). The response he receives from his auditors is largely positive. Eryximachus confesses to having enjoyed the speech and favorably compares the eloquence of Aristophanes to that of Socrates and Agathon (*Symp.* 193e). Agathon delivers his speech on the character and benefits of the god Love, a speech in which (and this may well also apply to Aristophanes's speech) he seeks to "mingle amusement with gravity" (*Symp.* 179d). At no point does Agathon criticize Aristophanes. Socrates starts his speech by complimenting the previous speakers for their "fine assortment of eloquence," although he comments that they got better toward the close (*Symp.* 198b). He singles out Aristophanes for gentle criticism when he has an interlocutor

---

121. Ehrhardt, *The Beginning*, 107.

argue that love is not about making the halves into a whole (*Symp.* 205e). Aristophanes picks up on this allusion but does not have the opportunity to defend himself (*Symp.* 212c). Noteworthy is the fact that Socrates's criticism relates to Aristophanes's understanding of the nature of love rather than to his creation account per se. He is certainly not criticized for his expansion of the creation account.

With the rejection of the accepted myth of creation, creation is now a pawn to be used for the promotion of personal agendas. This provides a salutary warning to those who would seek, especially in the context of contemporary Christian communities, to overturn the New Testament's acceptance of the Genesis creation account as a description of actual events. Reject Genesis, and the door is opened to an influx of competing accounts, each serving the personal agenda of its respective proponent. In our final comparison, to which we now turn, we will see a remarkable convergence between the world of the philosophers, popular Stoic culture, and the New Testament, centering on a shared belief in an intelligent designer.

THE ARGUMENT FROM DESIGN: XENOPHON'S *MEMORABILIA*

Xenophon was an aristocratic contemporary of Plato and fellow student of Socrates. In *Memorabilia*, written sometime after 371 BC, Xenophon presents a series of conversations involving Socrates and various interlocutors aimed at defending Socrates against the charges that he disrespected the gods, introduced strange deities, and corrupted the youth of Athens (*Memorabilia* 1.1.1).[122] In these conversations, the Gigantomachy is quietly ignored and replaced by a generic intelligent designer of the natural world. We also find little speculation as to the nature of the creation process itself.

Our sources indicate that the argument from design was, despite the protestations of the Atomists, widely held and accepted by the early Christian era. The Atomists, the most famous of whom was Epicurus, reduced the animate to the inanimate, arguing that there is nothing except atomic particles moving in infinite space.[123] They

---

122. Xenophon, *Mem.* 3.5, seems to cover events following the Spartan defeat at the battle of Leuctra in 371 BC.

123. The first atomists were Leucippus and Democritus. On the nature of the atom, see Diogenes Laertius, *Vitae Philosophorum* 10.42; Lucretius, *On the Nature of Things* 1.520, 615. For Paul's hostile attitude to the Epicureans, see Norman W. DeWitt, *St. Paul and Epicurus*

sought to free humanity from the religious consequences of believing in a creator god who keeps his creation under a supposedly hostile form of divine surveillance. Epicurus believed that just as there are an infinite number of atoms, so there must be an infinite number of worlds, similar to some of the multiverse theories proposed today.[124] In opposition to these views, the arguments for an intelligent designer were widely held in antiquity and were further developed prior to the New Testament period by the self-declared Socratic philosophers, the Stoics.[125] Their arguments for intelligent design are reflected, whether intentionally or not, by both Jewish and early Christian writers, and as such, deserve our consideration.[126]

IN THE "ABSENCE" OF SPECIAL REVELATION

In general, Xenophon's Socrates is highly skeptical of humanity's ability to discern the ways of heaven. As such, he avoids discussion of

---

(Minneapolis, Minn.: University of Minnesota Press, 1954); and Abraham J. Malherbe, "Anti-Epicurean Rhetoric in 1 Thessalonians," in *Light from the Gentiles: Hellenist Philosophy and Early Christianity; Collected Essays, 1959–2012, by Abraham J. Malherbe*, ed. Carl R. Holladay et al. (Leiden: Brill, 2014), 367–75.

124. Diogenes Laertius, *Vit. Phil.* 10.45, 74. See also Sedley, *Creationism*, 133–66. On multiverses, see Brian Green, *The Hidden Reality: Parallel Universes and the Deep Laws of the Cosmos* (New York: Knoff, 2011). For critique and defense, see George F. R. Ellis, "Does the Multiverse Really Exist?," *Scientific American*, August 2011, 38–43; and Alexander Vilenkin and Mark Tegmark, "The Case for Parallel Universes," *Scientific American*, July 19, 2011, https://www.scientificamerican.com/article/multiverse-the-case-for-parallel-universe. Rubenstein, *Worlds without End*, 17, suggests that the motivation behind modern multiverse theories is the desire to explain away a Creator God. She states, "We are reduced neither to saying, 'We're here because we're here' nor to postulating a benevolent, omnipotent, transcendent creator who must have set everything just right so that life might emerge in the universe. After all, if there are an infinite number of worlds that take on all possible parameters throughout infinite time, then strange as our specific parameters may seem, they were bound to emerge at some point." For a discussion as to whether God is the best explanation of a multiverse, see Klaas J. Kraay, ed., *God and the Multiverse: Scientific, Philosophical, and Theological Perspectives* (New York: Routledge, 2014).

125. Some credit Diogenes of Apollonias as the first to develop the argument from design. See Sedley, *Creationism*, 75–78. The Stoics were well aware of problems with their monistic view of creation. If the divine logos and matter are the same thing, we are still left wondering what caused matter; see Ehrhardt, *The Beginning*, 155–62.

126. E.g., Theophilus, *Autol.* 1.5–6; Athenagoras, *Legatio Pro Christianis* 15; Irenaeus, *Haer.* 9; and Athanasius, *Contra Gentes* 3.35–38, 47. Parallels extended well beyond intelligent design. For early Christian indebtedness to Stoic moral teaching (epistolary paraenesis, description of the "wise man," ancient psychagogy, the *Haustafeln*, diatribe, *topoi*, virtues, and vices), see Abraham J. Malherbe, "Hellenistic Moralists and the New Testament," in Holladay et al., *Light from the Gentiles*, 675–749. Malherbe notes that "Celsus could, not without cause, throw it up to the Christians that their system or morals was shared by the philosophers, and that there was nothing especially impressive or new about it, a charge with which Christians could not completely disagree" (677). Troels Engberg-Pedersen, *Paul and the Stoics* (Louisville, Ky.: Westminster John Knox, 2000), 301–4, overstates the case when he argues that Paul is more Greek Stoic than Christian Jew.

the nature of the universe and the "Cosmos of the Professors," topics so favored by other philosophers (Xenophon, *Mem.* 1.1.11). Speculation in such matters should be eschewed, according to Socrates, as man "cannot solve these riddles" (*Mem.* 1.1.13). For these views he has been described as an "anti-scientific creationist," someone who rejected the attempt on the part of natural philosophers to reconstruct divinely created mechanisms based on reason alone.[127] Our inability to perceive heavenly matters, argues Socrates, results in a plethora of opinions concerning the nature of the universe. "Some hold that 'What is' is one, others that it is infinite in number: some that all things are in perpetual motion, others that nothing can ever be moved at any time: some that all life is birth and decay, others that nothing can ever be born or ever die" (*Mem.* 1.1.14).

In the "absence" of divine revelation relating to heavenly matters (*hoi ta theia, Mem.* 1.1.15), the best we can hope for is to understand those things relating to the human experience (*peri tōn anthrōpeiōn, Mem.* 1.1.16). These include such things as "what is godly, what is ungodly; what is beautiful, what is ugly; what is just, what is unjust; what is prudence, what is madness; what is courage, what is cowardice; what is a state, what is a statesman; what is government, and what is a governor" (*Mem.* 1.1.16). The absence of divine revelation is not, as most believe, because the gods do not know everything. Rather, so asserts Socrates, it is because the gods know everything but choose to reveal only those things directly relating to humanity (*peri tōn anthrōpeiōn pantōn, Mem.* 1.1.19). Such arguments indicate a desire on the part of Socrates to shift philosophy away from cosmological speculation and toward personal ethics.[128]

In this context, Xenophon presents two conversations in which Socrates defends his belief in a creator godhead (*Mem.* 1.4.2). Socrates's motive is not to understand creation as a standalone object, but rather to appreciate the creator god's bond to humanity.[129] He hopes that, as a result, his readers will adopt an attitude of piety toward god. This reflects a wider shift in the purposes of philosophy. Ehrhardt observes that after the cataclysm of classical Greece, philosophy became much more practical. By the New Testament era,

---

127. Sedley, *Creationism*, 78.

128. In contrast, Tom Sorell, *Scientism: Philosophy and the Infatuation with Science* (New York: Routledge, 1991), argues that modern philosophy has abandoned metaphysics in favor of scientific empiricism.

129. Sedley, *Creationism*, 78–86.

speculation on the nature of the origin of the world needed to be justified in terms of how it enhanced one's general happiness (that is, *eudaemonism*). Except in the field of mathematics, it was no longer a goal in and of itself to understand our origins. Its importance as a question was "derived from the fact that an answer might provide an insurance against the unexpected."[130]

THE FIRST CONVERSATION: SOCRATES AND ARISTODEMUS

The first conversation Xenophon recounts is one he overheard between Socrates and Aristodemus, the so-called dwarf (*Mem.* 1.4.2–18). Socrates's purpose, unique in comparison both to Plato and Aristotle, was to argue for piety as the appropriate response to the gods and the supreme deity in light of their intentional design of a world in which the needs of humanity are provided for. Socrates's opening gambit is to question which is greater—something created by chance, or something created by design? (*Mem.* 1.4.4). Aristodemus concedes that things designed for a specific purpose are greater. Socrates then asserts that it is possible to guess the purpose of an animal based upon its design. As this is so, so his argument goes, we may conclude that god had a purpose in creating man because he endowed him with eyes to see, ears to hear, a nose with which to smell, and the ability to discriminate in taste between bitter and sweet (*Mem.* 1.4.5).

Socrates's focus is on our natural endowments. Each part of man's anatomy has a purpose, an indication of intentional design. Socrates then takes Aristodemus on a guided tour of the physical body, pointing out the respective purposes of the eyeball, eyelid, eyelashes, ears, incisor teeth, mouth, anus, and mental perception or self-consciousness (*Mem.* 1.4.6, 8). Aristodemus acknowledges that this apparent design seems to be the handiwork of a "wise and loving creator" (*sophou tinos dēmiourgou kai philozōou*, *Mem.* 1.4.7), "the contrivances of one who deliberately willed the existence of living creatures" (*Mem.* 1.4.7). Aristodemus's response is not to question the existence of such a creator god; this he concedes. His objections are that such a creator godhead is too great to need our service (that is, piety), and that the gods "do not pay any heed to man," removing the obligation on the part of man to offer them worship (*Mem.* 1.4.10). Evidence of design proves the existence of a creator. It does not, according to

---

130. Ehrhardt, *The Beginning*, 154.

Socrates, tell us whether such a deity cares for his creation and thus whether worship succeeds in securing his benefaction.

Socrates's response is to return to the design argument. He insists that the gods do indeed heed the concerns of man. Evidence of this is the unique design of the human body. Its upright design gives us a wider field of vision and thus helps us avoid injury (*Mem.* 1.4.11). Hands enable us to accomplish so much more than those animals forced to walk on all fours. The human tongue is unique in that it enables us to communicate in ways different from other animals. Further blessings include intelligence and non-seasonal sex (*Mem.* 1.4.12). These unique design capabilities, which enable man to care for himself, should be taken, according to Socrates, as evidence of divine care (*Mem.* 1.4.14). The gods have demonstrated their care for us by designing us to care for ourselves. Aristodemus's riposte is to declare that he will believe they care when they send "counsellors" to tell us, "Do this, or avoid that" (*Mem.* 1.4.15). Socrates's reaction is to affirm that the gods communicate through divination and portents. As such, he appeals to Aristodemus to try serving the gods and see whether they respond personally (*Mem.* 1.4.18).

THE SECOND CONVERSATION: SOCRATES AND EUTHYDEMUS

Xenophon claims to have also overheard a second conversation, this time between Socrates and Euthydemus (*Mem.* 4.3.3–17). This conversation opens with Socrates asking whether Euthydemus has ever reflected "upon the care the gods have taken to furnish man with what he needs?" (*Mem.* 4.3.3).[131] Euthydemus, most helpfully for the plot as it turns out, has not reflected on such matters. Socrates then identifies a series of physical needs and the manner in which they have been addressed by the gods. They have supplied light in order for us to see with our eyes. Our need for rest is met by their provision of nighttime. They have provided the stars and the moon to enable us to mark off the passage of time. They have made the earth in a way that it provides food to calm our appetite and water to enable life. Fire has been given as a defense against cold and as an aid in the pursuit of art (*Mem.* 4.3.7). The sun is set within just the right orbit that it provides the exact amount of heat necessary to promote rather than destroy life (*Mem.* 4.3.8).

---

131. Cf. Philo, *Opif.* 10.

Euthydemus interjects throughout this list of divine blessings with affirmations that such acts indicate divine loving kindness (*philanthrōpa*, *Mem.* 4.3.5) and forethought (*pronoētikon*, *Mem.* 4.3.6). He concludes that the earth seems to have been created for the sake of humankind and doubts whether "the gods are occupied in any other work than the service of man" (*Mem.* 4.3.8–9). As in the first conversation, Socrates moves from design to revelation and affirms that the gods communicate with men. However, these revelations do not always occur when needed. This is not, warns Socrates, an excuse for desisting in the worship of the gods. Worship and praise them because you see their works even while, he encourages Euthydemus, you wait for them to appear to you (*Mem.* 4.3.13). Though the gods and the supreme deity are unseen (*aoratos*, so too Rom. 1:20), and remain so in order to avoid overwhelming us, they may be known through their works (*Mem.* 4.3.14–17).

LATER EXPRESSIONS OF THE ARGUMENT FROM DESIGN

According to Sedley, the argument from design was held by the majority of Greco-Roman intellectuals from Plato onward, exceptions being the Epicureans and Atomists.[132] By the New Testament period, the Stoics had developed Socrates's design argument to such an extent that we find in Cicero's *De natura deorum* (hereafter *Nat. d.*) the equivalent of William Paley's "monkey on a typewriter producing the works of Shakespeare" argument. Cicero argues against those who would have us believe that "solid and indivisible particles," borne along by gravity, fortuitously collided to produce this "elaborate and beautiful world" (*Nat. d.* 2.93). He critiques them in this manner:

> I cannot understand why he who considers it possible for this to have occurred (i.e., the creation of the world out of the chance collision of atoms) should not also think that, if a countless number of copies of the one-and-twenty letters of the alphabet, made of gold or what you will, were thrown together into some receptacle and then shaken out on to the ground, it would be possible that they should produce the Annals of Ennius, all ready for the reader. I doubt whether chance could possibly succeed in producing even a single verse! (*Nat. d.* 2.93–94)[133]

---

132. Sedley, *Creationism*, 205–38.

133. Cf. Cicero's comparison of the Epicureans and Stoics in *Nat. d.* 1.43–44 and his description of the teachings of the Stoics Chrysippus and Cleanthes in *Nat. d.* 2.13–15.

Paley famously used a watch to infer the existence of a watch-maker.[134] The pantheist Stoics had already developed a more sophis-ticated version of this argument 2,100 years earlier. In the third century BC, Archimedes created a famous sphere that was said to reproduce the cycles of the sun, moon, and planets.[135] A later version was said to have been made by the Stoic philosopher Posidonius in the early first century BC.[136] The discovery in 1900 of the Antiky-thera mechanism on the sea bed near the Aegean island of Antiky-thera provided further evidence of ancient engineering marvels able, in this particular case, to correlate all the major lunar and solar cycles, eclipses, and the four-year cycle of the Olympian games. Such machines, far more complex than Paley's watch, were used by Stoics to argue for design in nature. Cicero supposes that were

> a traveller to carry into Scythia or Britain the orrery recently constructed by our friend Posidonius, which at each revolution reproduces the same motions of the sun, the moon and the five planets that take place in the heavens every twenty-four hours, would any single native person [*barbari*] doubt that this orrery was the work of a rational being? (*Nat. d.* 2.88)

Cicero protests against those who think more highly of Archime-des in making a model of the firmament than of nature, "although the perfection of the original shows a craftsmanship many times as great as does the counterfeit" (*Nat. d.* 2.88). Reliance on the argu-ment from design was open to challenge. Lactantius recalls how "the Academics, when arguing against the Stoics, often ask why, if god

---

134. William Paley, *Paley's Natural Theology with Illustrative Notes* (London: Charles Knight, 1836), 1–20. Cf. David Hume, *Dialogues Concerning Natural Religions* (London: 1779, 2nd ed.), in which, through a Socratic dialogue, he argues against the argument from design. His chief criticisms are that: (1) we know a house was built by a builder because we have observed it, but we have never observed the origin of a world; (2) there is no reason to assume that there is a single creator God, just as there is no reason to assume that a single builder built a house; (3) there is no reason to assume that intelligence, rather than heat, attraction, repulsion, or refraction, is the first cause of creation; and (4) positing a creator God still leaves us with the problem of explaining the origin of God. Cf. Rubenstein, *Worlds without End*, 8–11. Richard Dawkins, *The Blind Watchmaker: Why the Evidence of Evolution Reveals a Universe without Design* (New York: W. W. Norton, 1997), 4–6, criticizes Hume for failing to offer an alternative to intelligent design. He offers random mutation and natural selection as an alternative.

135. See *The Republic of Cicero* 1.14.22; Lactantius, *Divinarum Institutionum* 2.5.18; and Claudian, *Carmina Minora* 51.68 (ca. AD 394–95 onwards). Cf. Derek de Solla Price, "Gears from the Greeks: The Antikythera Mechanism: A Calendar Computer from ca. 80 B.C.," *Transactions of the American Philosophical Society* 64, no. 7 (1974): 1–70, esp. 57–60.

136. See Cicero, *De Natura Deorum* 2.88. Cf. Sedley, *Creationism*, 207.

made everything for the sake of man, many things are also found in the sea and on land which oppose, attack and plague us" (*De Ira Dei* 13.9–10).[137] The Stoic response was to assert that the intended usefulness of such things is still to be discovered.

DESIGN, PIETY, AND PAUL

It seems highly likely that Paul presumes the argument from design promulgated by the Stoics of his day in the first chapter of his epistle to the Romans. Paul alludes to three forms of revelation: (1) the gospel, which reveals the power and righteousness of God (Rom. 1:16–17); (2) the wrath of God, revealed from heaven in response to all ungodliness and unrighteousness (Rom. 1:18); and (3) knowledge of God, revealed through His creation of the world (Rom. 1:19–20). With respect to this third form of revelation, he states,

> For what can be known about God is plain to them, because God has shown it to them. Ever since the creation of the world his eternal power and divine nature, invisible though they are, have been understood and seen through the things he has made. So they are without excuse; for though they knew God, they did not honour him as God or give thanks to him, but they became futile in their thinking, and their senseless minds were darkened. (Rom. 1:19–21, NRSV)

Paul's argument is that God's unseen attributes (*ta aorata*, 1:20) are made visible through the things He has made. Robert Jewett demonstrates in his influential commentary on Romans that the concept that invisible attributes were made manifest through creation was common to Stoicism and Hellenistic Judaism.[138] A minority in Hellenistic Judaism believed that Gentiles were unable to discern the Creator through His creation (e.g., Wis. 13:1).[139] In contrast, argues Jewett, Paul fuses the biblical concept of the beginning of creation with the "Greco-Roman doctrine of divinity visible in the natural world."[140] For Paul, this revelation is so clear, in fact, that there is now no excuse for those who, despite knowing God through His creation, refuse to honor Him, preferring, according to Romans 1:22–23, to worship images of

---

137. Quoted in Long and Sedley, *Hellenistic Philosophers*, 330.

138. Robert Jewett, *Romans: A Commentary on the Book of Romans* (Minneapolis, Minn.: Fortress, 2007), 155.

139. Cf. Wis. 13:5; *Ep. Arist.* 132.

140. Jewett, *Romans*, 154–55. So too James D. G. Dunn, *Romans 1–8*, WBC 38A (Grand Rapids, Mich.: Zondervan, 1988), 71.

created things rather than the Creator Himself. The idea that God is known through His creation is, of course, equally well attested in the Old Testament (e.g., Ps. 19:1–6; 104). Nevertheless, Paul's selection of terms has much in common with Stoic terminology and may well reflect an intention on his part in this portion of the epistle to use terms highly familiar to Gentiles to describe their own predicament.[141]

CONCLUSION

This study has compared a number of Greco-Roman creation accounts with the New Testament's approach to creation. While the New Testament era was broadly Stoic in outlook, what strikes the reader is the variety of views that correspond to theories of origin promoted today. These include speculations relating to paleontological discoveries, natural selection, cyclical ages of creation and destruction, multiverses, and intelligent design. Early Christians faced no less a complex environment in which to promote their message as that facing Christians today.

At a popular level, early Greek cosmological myths enjoyed an enduring appeal right into the New Testament era. These myths, reflected in Apollodorus's *Library*, promoted the idea of the progressive physical degradation of the world. Paleontological discoveries testified to an earlier era in which giants and heroes once roamed the earth. These myths also affirmed, however, that the current moral state of the world is one that has existed from the very beginning. Death, strife, war, and destruction are integral elements of creation. This bleak and hopeless outlook contrasts sharply with the New Testament's affirmation of God's good creation, the Fall, and His plan for the moral and physical restoration of humanity and the rest of creation.

Challenges to these earlier myths on the part of the natural philosophers did not result in an agreed alternative. Rather, they resulted in a plethora of competing and contradictory accounts, each driven by its author's own personal agenda. More positively, this pluralistic context offered fertile points of contact that enabled New Testament authors to enrich their apologetic endeavors. Positive points

---

141. Aristotle, *de Mundo* 399a–b; Epictetus, *Diatribe* 1.6.19–20. See also Dio Chrysostom, *De dei cognitione* 12.29, 34, 36, 37; Plutarch, *Isis and Osiris* 76–77; *Moralia* 382A; Jewett, *Romans*, 155; and Keener, *Romans*, 31–34.

of contact between the New Testament and Stoic proponents of the argument from design present us with the problem of determining whether or not New Testament authors were actively influenced by such arguments. It is beyond question that New Testament authors were familiar with their wider Hellenistic environment. The Gospels, for example, are essentially Greco-Roman biographies written in the style of Old Testament narratives.[142] Paul's familiarity with Greco-Roman philosophical traditions is signaled by his citation in Acts 17:28 of a tradition attributed to the Cretan holy man Epimenides (ca. 600 BC)—"For in thee we live and move and have our being"—and the Cicilian Stoic poet Aratus of Soli (ca. 315–240 BC)—"For we are also his offspring" (*Phaenomena* 7).[143] Paul also shows awareness of rabbinic rules of interpretation and Hellenistic techniques of moral exhortation throughout his epistles.[144]

While we should acknowledge such cultural points of contact, we should avoid the danger of naively assuming that "similarity indicates genealogy," that arguments common to the New Testament and Greco-Roman traditions indicate intentional dependence. Yes, New Testament authors could utilize Greco-Roman ideas when they were in agreement with the biblical worldview. Yes, they used them when it served their apologetic goals. Their use of such traditions was not motivated, however, out of a desire to validate these ideas or teachings. Rather, their primary goal was to tell the story of Jesus in light of the Genesis account of creation and the Fall, Israel's history of kingdom and exile, and their own experience of Jesus's ministry, death, and resurrection. Theirs is a thoroughly Jewish-Christian narrative that stands in sharp contrast to the dominant views of creation of their day.

---

142. Richard A. Burridge, *What Are the Gospels?: A Comparison with Graeco–Roman Biography* (Grand Rapids, Mich.: Eerdmans, 2004).

143. Aratus is also quoted by Cleanthes (331–233 BC) in *Hymn to Zeus*, line 4. For a discussion, see Colin J. Hemer, "The Speeches of Acts II: The Areopagus Address," *TynBul* 40, no. 2 (1989): 239–59; and Richard I. Pervo, *Acts: A Commentary*, Hermeneia 65 (Minneapolis, Minn.: Fortress, 2009), 438-439.

144. Cf. Malherbe, "Anti-Epicurean Rhetoric"; and Malherbe, "Hellenistic Moralists."

Jan A. Sigvartsen, PhD

Theologische Hochschule
Friedensau Möckern, Germany

CREATION IN THE SECOND TEMPLE PERIOD

INTRODUCTION

In the Second Temple period, there was great interest in the account of origins found in Genesis 1–3. Echoes, allusions, references, and quotes appear throughout the Apocrypha, Pseudepigrapha, Philo, Dead Sea Scrolls, New Testament, Josephus, Targumim, and the literature of early Rabbinic Judaism. They demonstrate that the writers during this vibrant literary period were aware of the many real interpretative challenges in the biblical text and recognized gaps in these accounts that needed to be filled. They carefully searched the Hebrew Bible for answers to their interpretative questions—attempting to make plain what was implied and what was inferred. Important aspects of Judaism were accounted for in some of these writings, either as a part of the creation week (e.g., angels, the garden of Eden) or as something that predated it (e.g., Torah, repentance, the garden of Eden, gehenna, the throne of glory, the temple, and the name of the Messiah). Thus, during the Second Temple period, the accounts in Genesis 1–3 were not considered complete by some writers, as they did not provide a full account of the creation; nor were they considered obvious, as several statements needed to be explained by writers of this period.

Some of the interpretative questions noted by Second Temple period writers are also familiar to modern biblical scholars: Should Genesis 1–3 be understood literally or be read allegorically? Are the stories in these chapters scientific, theological, philosophical, ethical, religious, symbolic, or some combination of these? What was created during the creation week? Did God create *ex nihilo* or did something exist prior to the creation week? And when did the creation week take place? There was also a question regarding how the accounts of Genesis 1:1—2:4a and 2:4b—3:24 relate to each other—whether they should be read consecutively or if Genesis 2–3 expands upon and provides additional details to the Genesis 1 narrative. Regarding Genesis 1, there was significant interest in how the light of the first day related to the lights of the fourth day. Also, these writers addressed what it meant to be created in God's image and likeness and how to understand the "us" and "our" in the context of the creation of human beings. There were questions relating to the nature of the first human couple, most particularly to the description in the Eden narrative (Gen. 2–3). Were they mortal or immortal, an androgyne who was later separated into male and female, or was Adam created first and then Eve from one of his ribs at a later point in time? Questions were also raised regarding the serpent, the meaning of the tree of "good and evil," the Fall and its consequences, as well as the length of time Adam and Eve were in the garden prior to their expulsion.

Due to the substantial amount of material, this study will not present an exhaustive discussion regarding creation in the Second Temple period. Instead, it will provide the reader a brief overview of the creation material found in Philo, Josephus, the Apocrypha, and the Pseudepigrapha. The great complexity of this topic allows for the exploration of only a few of the interpretative questions noted by Second Temple period writers in an attempt to help the reader more fully appreciate the context of creation references in the New Testament.[1] This study will conclude by discussing the role Wisdom-Torah held in the context of creation within this literature and will consider some of its ramifications in New Testament scholarship.[2]

---

1. This study is an overview of the findings of a much larger study, currently being undertaken by the author, that provides a comprehensive look at the creation and re-creation language in Second Temple period literature and how it relates to Genesis 1–3.

2. For a comprehensive list of references to Genesis 1–3 in the Second Temple literature, see Tables 1 and 2 in the Appendix.

PARALLEL CREATION ACCOUNTS

There are five complete Second Temple period parallel accounts to the creation narrative of Genesis 1:1—2:4a.[3] The oldest parallel account is found in the book of Jubilees, "a midrashic rewriting of Genesis-Exodus" dated to the mid-second century BC, written by a Jew living in Palestine.[4] James VanderKam writes, "It seems best to say, in view of all the evidence, that the author composed *Jubilees* in the period between 160–150 BC. One cannot exclude a slightly earlier date, but it was probably not written at a later time."[5] The longest and most philosophical account was written by Philo (ca. 20 BC–ca. AD 50), a Jewish philosopher from Alexandria.[6] Another account was written by Josephus (AD 37–ca. 100), a Jewish writer and historian born in Jerusalem.[7] Although Josephus follows the seven-day pattern of the Genesis 1:1—2:4a narrative closely, Thomas Franxman notes that Josephus introduced numerous changes.[8] The fourth creation account appears in 4 Ezra, a composition of Jewish origin, dated to the late first century AD.[9] It is the only account that

3. See Table 3 in the Appendix. The Sibylline Oracles 1:7–64 presents an abbreviated account of the two creation accounts (Gen. 1–3); however, it is not included in Table 3 as it does not use the "day" formula of Genesis 1:1—2:4a. This text is a Jewish composition, most likely dated to the turn of the common era (see J. J. Collins, "Sibylline Oracles: A New Translation and Introduction," in *The Old Testament Pseudepigrapha*, ed. James H. Charlesworth, 2 vols. [New York: Doubleday, 1983–1985], 1:331–32).

4. Craig A. Evans, *Ancient Texts for New Testament Studies: A Guide to the Background Literature* (Peabody, Mass.: Hendrickson, 2005), 46. For provenance and dating, see also James C. VanderKam, "Jubilees," in *Dictionary of New Testament Background*, ed. Craig A. Evans and Stanley E. Porter (Downers Grove, Ill.: InterVarsity, 2000), 600–603; and O. S. Wintermute, "Jubilees: A New Translation and Introduction," in Charlesworth, *The Old Testament Pseudepigrapha*, 2:43–45.

5. James C. VanderKam, *The Book of Jubilees* (Sheffield: Sheffield Academic Press, 2001), 21.

6. For a brief introduction on Philo, see David T. Runia, *On the Creation of the Cosmos According to Moses: Introduction, Translation and Commentary*, Philo of Alexandria Commentary Series 1 (Atlanta: Society of Biblical Literature, 2001), ix–xvi; David M. Scholer, "Foreword: An Introduction to Philo Judaeus of Alexandria," in *The Works of Philo: Complete and Unabridged*, trans. C. D. Yonge (Peabody, Mass.: Hendrickson, 1995), xi–xx; and G. E. Sterling, "Philo," in Evans and Porter, *Dictionary of New Testament Background*, 789–93.

7. See Table 3 in the Appendix; L. H. Feldman, "Josephus: Interpretative Methods and Tendencies," in Evans and Porter, *Dictionary of New Testament Background*, 590–96. Flavius Josephus, *The Works of Josephus: Complete and Unabridged*, trans. William Whiston (Peabody, Mass.: Hendrickson, 1987), ix.

8. Thomas W. Franxman, *Genesis and the Jewish Antiquities of Flavius Josephus*, Biblica et Orientalia 35 (Rome: Biblical Institute, 1979), 37.

9. Regarding dating and provenance, see John J. Collins, *The Apocalyptic Imagination: An Introduction to Jewish Apocalyptic Literature*, 2nd ed., The Biblical Resource Series (Grand Rapids, Mich.: Eerdmans, 1998), 195–96; David A. deSilva, *Introducing the Apocrypha: Message, Context, and Significance* (Grand Rapids, Mich.: Baker Academic, 2002), 329–30; B. M. Metzger, "The Fourth Book of Ezra," in Charlesworth, *The Old Testament Pseudepigrapha*,

does not mention the Sabbath as a part of the creation week. The fifth and final creation account appears in 2 Enoch, which Craig Evans suggests was composed by an Egyptian Jew toward the end of the first century AD.[10] Table 3 in the Appendix includes a sixth creation account from Targum Pseudo-Jonathan, an Aramaic translation (not an independent account) of the Genesis creation narrative. This account was added because it includes some important additions to the Genesis narrative.[11] However, it was not counted as a Second Temple period parallel account because it is a translation. Evans writes, "Scholars are divided over the question of this Targum's origin and relation to the other Targumim."[12] Philip Alexander suggests this Palestinian Targum contains "a highly mixed tradition, an amalgam of interpretations from widely different periods. It has been argued that it contains at once some of the earliest and some of the latest dateable targumic material," adding it "is the most paraphrastic of all the Pentateuchal targumim: it is estimated to be about twice the length of the original Hebrew."[13]

ENTITIES THAT PREEXISTED CREATION

When comparing these Second Temple period parallel accounts, three accounts suggest there were entities that existed prior to the creation (4 Ezra, 2 Enoch, and Targum Pseudo-Jonathan), while the other three suggest the beginning of the cosmos took place on the first day of creation week (Jubilees, Philo, Josephus). This difference reflects the ambiguity in the Genesis creation narrative regarding

1:519–20; Jacob M. Myers, *1 and 2 Esdras*, AB 42 (Garden City, N.Y.: Doubleday, 1974), 115–19; Michael E. Stone, *Fourth Ezra: A Commentary on the Book of Fourth Ezra*, Hermeneia (Minneapolis: Fortress, 1990), 1–9; J. E. Wright, "Esdras, Book of," in Evans and Porter, *Dictionary of New Testament Background*, 337–40.

10. Evans, *Ancient Texts*, 30, see also F. I. Andersen, "2 (Slavonic Apocalypse of) Enoch: A New Translation and Introduction," in Charlesworth, *The Old Testament Pseudepigrapha*, 1:94–97; J. J. Collins, "Enoch, Books of," in Evans and Porter, *Dictionary of New Testament Background*, 316–17.

11. Philip S. Alexander, "Jewish Aramaic Translations of Hebrew Scriptures," in *Mikra: Texts, Translation, Reading & Interpretation of the Hebrew Bible in Ancient Judaism & Early Judaism*, ed. Martin Jan Mulder and Harry Sysling (Peabody, Mass.: Hendrickson, 2004), 217–54; R. Buth, "Aramaic Language," in Evans and Porter, *Dictionary of New Testament Background*, 90–91; B. D. Chilton, "Rabbinic Literature: Targumim," in Evans and Porter, *Dictionary of New Testament Background*, 903–5; and Martin McNamara, "Interpretation of Scripture in Targumim," in *A History of Biblical Interpretation*, ed. Alan J. Hauser and Duane F. Watson, vol. 1 of 3, *The Ancient Period* (Grand Rapids, Mich.: Eerdmans, 2003), 167–97.

12. Evans, *Ancient Texts*, 188.

13. Alexander, "Jewish Aramaic Translations," 219.

how Genesis 1:1–2 relates to Genesis 1:3–5 and indicates that authors in the Second Temple period understood the Genesis account in different ways—some seeing support for preexisting matter, while others did not.[14]

THE INTELLIGIBLE COSMOS

The creation accounts of Philo and 2 Enoch both suggest the cosmos existed in God's mind (intelligible cosmos) prior to Him making it a reality (sense-perceptible cosmos). According to the writer of 2 Enoch, the process from an intelligible cosmos to a physical cosmos started prior to the creation week when God established the foundation of the earth (2 En. 24:2—27:4). This is a detailed description of the process itself, in contrast to Philo's

---

14. The syntactical question regards the first word, $b\check{e}r\bar{e}'\check{s}\hat{\imath}t$ ("in [the] beginning"), as the definite article is missing in the Hebrew word. The first option is to understand the first word to be in the absolute state, thus reading the first three verses as independent sentences. This is the traditional view and is reflected in the following translation: "In the beginning God created the heavens and the earth. Now the earth was formless and empty, darkness covered the surface of the watery depths, and the Spirit of God was hovering over the surface of the waters. Then God said, 'Let there be light,' and there was light" (Gen. 1:1–3, HCSB). It could be argued that this reading is supported by Genesis 2:1, which implies that heaven and earth were also created during the period as described in Genesis 1, and in Exodus 20:11, which states, "For the LORD made *the heavens and the earth*, the sea, and everything in them *in six days*; then He rested on the seventh day. Therefore the LORD blessed the Sabbath day and declared it holy" (HCSB, emphasis added). However, in regard to the missing definite article, there are examples in Hebrew Scripture when a word in absolute state appears without the article (e.g., Isa. 46:10). Unless otherwise noted, all Scripture quotations in this chapter are the author's own translation.

The second option is to understand it to be in the construct state, thus reading it as a part of verse 3, the first independent sentence in the narrative. This view is reflected in the following translation: "When God began to create heaven and earth—the earth being unformed and void, with darkness over the surface of the deep and a wind from God sweeping over the water—God said, 'Let there be light'; and there was light" (Gen. 1:1–3, JPS).

If the interpreter follows the latter interpretation, there is no *creatio ex nihilo* ("creation from nothing"), since the earth would already have existed as unformed and covered by water when God started the first creative act. The purpose of the creation week, therefore, was to bring order to the chaos, to make the earth a place fit for life.

There is also the question of how to read the *waw* at the beginning of verses 2 and 3: should it be viewed as a conjunctive or disjunctive? Based on the syntax, the *waw* at the beginning of verse 2 is disjunctive as it prefixes a noun rather than a verb. As such, verse 2 could be read in contrast to verse 1, thereby introducing a shift in focus from the creation of heaven to the creation of the earth, interpreting verses 3–5 as God's creative activities during the second half of the first day. An alternative option is to understand verse 1 as the initial creation of the universe while verse 2 describes the condition of the earth when God started His creation acts. In this scenario, there would be an unspecified time gap between verse 1 and verse 2, while the description of God's creative activities of day one begins in verse 3. Accordingly, Genesis 1:1–2 functions as a general introduction to the cosmogony narrative.

For further reading regarding the syntactical ambiguities of Genesis 1:1–5, see Richard M. Davidson, "The Genesis Account of Origins," in *The Genesis Creation Account and Its Reverberations in the Old Testament*, ed. Gerald A. Klingbeil (Berrien Springs, Mich.: Andrews University Press, 2015), 59–129.

philosophical and theological argument (Philo, *Opif.* §§15b–25). David Runia provides the following summary of Philo's explanation: "When God decides to found the cosmos, he first forms the intelligible cosmos as plan and then executes it, using the plan as model. Where, then, is the plan located? Where else than in the divine Logos. That is the only place where God's powers in their fulness can be located."[15] In Philo's version, the creation of the master plan is the creation act of the first day, while the process of making this plan a reality began on the second day.[16] However, Philo states that although the world was made in six days, it was not because "the Creator stood in need of a length of time (for it is natural that God should do everything at once, not merely by uttering a command, but by even thinking of it); but because the things created required arrangement; and number is akin to arrangement; and, of all numbers, six is, by the laws of nature, the most productive" (Philo, *Opif.* §13).[17] Runia observes the great prominence of number symbolism in Philo's commentary, stating, "The schema of the seven days in Moses' creation account" takes up "a quarter of the entire work."[18] It appears that all of these parallel accounts understand the days of the creation week as literal days.

THE CREATION OF ANGELS

The greatest variation between the six creation accounts appears in the first half of the week, particularly during the first and second days, while the last half of the week closely follows the elements of the Genesis account. This variation in the accounts regarding the first and second days is most likely due to the syntactical issues in the first three verses of Genesis 1. There is also the question of when the angels were created. Genesis 2:1 says, "And the heaven and the earth and all their host were finished." This statement raises the question regarding the meaning of ṣābā' ("host"), a noun that could refer to angels as reflected in God's title, YHWH ṣĕbā'ôt ("LORD of hosts," "armies," or a variation thereof). However, the noun ṣābā' ("host") does not carry the meaning of angels in other occurrences

---

15. Runia, *On the Creation of the Cosmos*, 133.

16. See Table 3 in the Appendix.

17. Philo, *The Works of Philo: Complete and Unabridged*, trans. C. D. Yonge (Peabody, Mass.: Hendrickson, 1995), 4.

18. Runia, *On the Creation of the Cosmos*, 25–26.

in the Torah.[19] It carries the meaning of angels, as in the Lord of hosts,[20] predominantly in the prophetic writings, appearing 251 times.[21] In the prophetic writings it appears 16 times in the Former Prophets, 139 times in the Latter Prophets, and 96 times in the twelve Minor Prophets.[22]

The closest parallel to Genesis 2:1 in the Pentateuch appears in Deuteronomy 4:19; 17:3, in the context of the heavenly bodies. With these passages focusing on inanimate nature, it is ambiguous whether Genesis 2:1 refers specifically to angels or to everything with which God filled heaven and earth. Be that as it may, Genesis 3:24 provides a clear reference to angels when it states, "He drove man out, and east of the garden of Eden He stationed cherubim with a flaming, whirling sword to guard the way to the tree of life." The next time the cherubim are mentioned is within the context of the ark of the covenant in the wilderness sanctuary (Exod. 25–26; 36–37). With the reference to angels in Genesis 2:1 (possible) and 3:24 (certain), their creation needed to be accounted for. Thus, Jubilees states they were created during the first day of the creation week, while 4 Ezra, 2 Enoch, and Targum Pseudo-Jonathan have them

---

19. The noun appears ninety times in the Pentateuch—four times in Genesis (2:1; 21:22, 32; 26:26), five times in Exodus (6:26; 7:4; 12:17, 41, 51), seventy-seven times in Numbers (1:3 [2x], 20, 22, 24, 26, 28, 30, 32, 34, 36, 38, 40, 42, 45, 52; 2:3, 4, 6, 8, 9, 10, 11, 13, 15, 16, 18, 19, 21, 23, 24, 25, 26, 28, 30, 32; 4:3, 23, 30, 35, 39, 43; 8:24, 25; 10:14 [2x], 15, 16, 18 [2x], 19, 20, 22 [2x], 23, 24, 25 [2x], 26, 27, 28; 26:2; 31:3, 4, 5, 6 [x2], 14, 21, 27, 28, 32, 36, 48, 53; 32:27; 33:1), and four times in Deuteronomy (4:19; 17:3; 20:9; 24:5). The predominant use is in a military context. The noun appears only a few times in reference to God's people (Exod. 6:26; 7:4; 12:17, 41, 51), in the context of the sanctuary (Exod. 38:8 [2x]; Num. 4:3, 23 [2x], 30, 35, 39, 43; 8:24 [2x], 25), and in the context of the creation (Gen. 2:1; Deut. 4:19; 17:3).

20. This understanding is supported by the narrative in 2 Kings 6:8–23, when Elisha is surrounded by the Aramean army. When Elisha's servant becomes afraid, he encourages him, saying, "'Don't be afraid, for those who are with us outnumber those who are with them.' Then Elisha prayed, 'LORD, please open his eyes and let him see.' So the LORD opened the servant's eyes. He looked and saw that the mountain was covered with horses and chariots of fire all around Elisha" (2 Kings 6:16–17, HCSB).

21. It appears only twenty-four times in the books belonging to the Ketuvim: Psalms (18x); Nehemiah (2x); and 1–2 Chronicles (4x).

22. Table 4 in the Appendix demonstrates that more than 80% of these cases appear in only four books—Isaiah (23%), Jeremiah (32%), Zechariah (18%), and Malachi (9.5%), the latter two being postexilic prophets. J. N. Oswalt, "God," in *Dictionary of the Old Testament Prophets*, ed. Mark J. Boda and J. Gordon McConville (Downers Grove, Ill.: IVP Academic, 2012), 290, speculates the reason the title *Lord of Hosts* is primarily used in the oracles against the nations by Isaiah and Jeremiah is to emphasize Yahweh's absolute power, especially "in those situations where the nation of Israel seems powerless before the other nations of the world," suggesting "this might explain the complete absence of the phrase in Ezekiel, where Judah's powerlessness is not an issue."

created on the second day.[23] R. Hanina (d. ca. AD 250) suggests that the angels were created on the fifth day, together with the winged birds, reading Genesis 1:20 in light of Isaiah 6:2 (*Gen. Rab.* 1:3). Philo and Josephus do not mention when angels were created but only that they existed prior to the creation of the humans. The author of the *Hellenistic Synagogal Prayers*, however, maintains that God "before all things made the cherubim and the seraphim, both ages and (heavenly) hosts, both powers and authorities, both rulers and thrones, both archangels and angels; and after all these" made "this world that is seen, and everything in it" (*Hel. Syn. Pr.* 12:14–15).[24] This would suggest that the author believed angels preexisted the creation of the world.

These diverse views regarding the origin of the angels is an interpretative consequence of how these authors read Genesis 1:1–3. The remainder of this study will briefly consider the views appearing in Second Temple period literature regarding the creation of concepts and physical entities prior to the creation week of Genesis 1.

CREATED BEFORE THE CREATION WEEK

There are six concepts and physical entities mentioned in Second Temple period literature as preexisting the creation week of Genesis 1. They are Wisdom, the sanctuary, the Torah, the garden of Eden, gehenna, and the name of the Messiah. Some may wonder if the Sabbath preexisted creation and should, therefore, be considered a seventh concept. The parallel creation account appearing in the book of Jubilees (Jub. 2:1–33) could leave this impression in its expansion on the seventh day, the Sabbath (Jub. 2:17–33), as it mentions that God gave all the "angels of the presence" and all the "angels of the holiness" the Sabbath to keep and, together with God, they would all abstain from working on it while in heaven and on earth (Jub. 2:17–18). A careful reading, however, leads to a different conclusion as the angels were, according to the book, created on the first day of the creation week (Jub. 2:2); thus, their observation of the Sabbath would have begun on the last day of

---

23. See Table 2 in the Appendix.

24. All quotes from the Pseudepigrapha are sourced from Charlesworth, *The Old Testament Pseudepigrapha.*

the creation week, when the Sabbath was instituted. It should also be noted that not all the angels kept the Sabbath. It was given only to the angels belonging to the two highest categories of angels and not to the angels belonging to the five lesser categories associated with the natural world (the angels of the spirit of fire; the angels of the winds that blow; the angels of the spirits of the clouds for darkness, ice, hoar-frost, dew, snow, hail, and frost; the angels of the thunder; and the angels of the spirits for cold and heat, for winter and summer, and for all the spirits of his creatures that he made in the heavens and that he made on the earth, and in every [place]). This distinction is most likely due to the functions of the natural world having to continue, even on the Sabbath. This division between the angels regarding Sabbath observance parallels the human sphere—Israel and the Gentiles. Jubilees 2:31–33 states,

> The Creator of all blessed it, but he did not sanctify any people or nations to keep the sabbath thereon with the sole exception of Israel. He granted to them alone that they might eat and drink and keep the sabbath thereon upon the earth. And the Creator of all, who created this day for a blessing and sanctification and glory, blessed it more than all days. This law and testimony was given to the children of Israel as an eternal law for their generations.

As such, the author of Jubilees seems to suggest that only God and the two highest ranked categories of angels observed the Sabbath in the period between the creation week and when the people of Israel were instructed to keep the Sabbath in the book of Exodus. This provides an answer as to why Sabbath observance is not mentioned during the primeval history or patriarchal period.[25]

There are no indications in Second Temple period literature that the sacredness of the Sabbath preexisted creation. However, there was an interest during this period as to who should keep the Sabbath. The book of Jubilees argues that it was intended only for the people of Israel (Jub. 2:31)—limited in its application. Philo, in his discussion on the creation narrative (*Opif.* §§1–172), argues that the Sabbath was intended for humankind in general—universal in its application. He states in *De Opificio Mundi* §§89,

---

25. For a detailed commentary on the Sabbath and Israel in the book of Jubilee, see VanderKam, *Book of Jubilees*, 1:193–205.

But after the whole world had been completed according to the perfect nature of the number six, the Father hallowed the day following,
the seventh, praising it, and calling it holy. For that day is the festival,
not of one city or one country, but of all the earth; a day which alone
it is right to call the day of festival for all people, and the birthday of
the world.[26]

PREEXISTENCE OF WISDOM, THE SANCTUARY, TORAH, AND THE GARDEN OF EDEN

During the Second Temple period, some writers associated the
personification of Wisdom in Proverbs 8:22–31 with the creation
narrative (Bar. 3:32—4:4; Sir. 24:9–10; Aristob. Frag. 5:9–11; Philo,
Virt. §62).[27] This link was supported by the noun "beginning" used
both in Genesis 1:1 and Proverbs 8:22,[28] the assertion being that
Wisdom was created before the earth (Prov. 8:23) and the heavens
(Prov. 8:27) were made, and the summary statements of the creation that revealed that Wisdom helped create the world (Prov.
8:24–30).[29]

---

26. Philo of Alexandria, *The Works of Philo: Complete and Unabridged*, trans. C. D. Yonge (Peabody, Mass.: Hendrickson, 1993), 13.

27. Personification is a literary device that attributes human form and characteristics to abstract concepts, geographical entities, and nature. In the Old Testament, Wisdom is personified as a woman, a link expanded upon in the Second Temple period
literature.

28. Modern readers may find such a word link coincidental, but James L. Kugel, *Traditions of the Bible: A Guide to the Bible as It Was at the Start of the Common Era* (Cambridge,
Mass.: Harvard University Press, 1998), notes that for Second Temple period interpreters,
there was a conviction "that the Bible's precise wording is both utterly intentional—that is,
nothing in the Bible is said by chance or said in vain—and infinitely significant. This means
that almost every aspect of the biblical text ought to be looked into, and that almost any sort
of interpretive subtlety was justified in explaining it" (47). See also his discussion on ancient
biblical interpretation (1–41).

29. For a discussion on Wisdom and the creation narrative, see Ángel M. Rodríguez,
"Genesis and Creation in the Wisdom Literature," in *The Genesis Creation Account and Its
Reverberations in the Old Testament*, 241–52; Alan Lenzi, "Proverbs 8:22–31: Three Perspectives on Its Composition," *JBL* 125, no. 4 (2006): 687–714; Nozomi Miura, "A Typology
of Personified Wisdom Hymns," *BTB* 34, no. 4 (2004): 138–49; Roland E. Murphy, "Wisdom
and Creation," *JBL* 104, no. 1 (1985): 3–11; Bruce V. Vawter, "Prov 8:22: Wisdom and Creation," *JBL* 99, no. 2 (1980): 205–16; and Gale A. Yee, "An Analysis of Prov 8:22–31 According to Style and Structure," *ZAW* 94, no. 2 (1982): 58–66.

Genesis 1:1	Proverbs 8:22–27
bĕrē'šît bārā' 'ĕlōhîm 'ēt haššāmayim wĕ'ēt hā'āreṣ	*YHWH qānānî rē'šît darkô qedem mip'ālāyw mē'āz* *mē'ôlām nissaktî mēro'š miqqadmê-'āreṣ* *bĕ'ên-tĕhōmôt ḥôloltî bĕ'ên ma'yānôt nikbaddê-māyim* *bĕterem hārîm hoṭbā'û lipnê gĕbā'ôt ḥôloltî* *'ad-lō' 'āśāh 'ereṣ wĕḥûṣôt wĕro'š 'oprôt tēbēl* *bahăkînô šāmayim šām 'ānî bĕḥûqô ḥûg 'al-pĕnê tĕhôm*
In the beginning God created the *heavens* and the *earth*.	The LORD made me at the beginning of His creation, before His works of long ago. I was formed before ancient times, from the beginning, before the *earth* began. I was born [or brought forth] when there were no watery depths and no springs filled with water. I was delivered [or brought forth] before the mountains and hills were established, before He made the land, the fields, or the first soil on earth. I was there when He established the *heavens*, when He laid out the horizon on the surface of the ocean.

Thus, in some Second Temple period literature, Wisdom is not only present at the creation (Wis. 9:9; Philo, *Leg.* 1.43; *QG* 4.97) but also played a central role when humans were created (Wis. 9:1–2; 2 En. J30:8; *Hel. Syn. Pr.* 3:19). Jesus ben Sirach (fl. second century BC)[30] goes a step further in Sirach 24, where he suggests that Wisdom takes up residence in the Temple of Jerusalem, among the people of Israel (Sir. 24:1–12), and identifies her with the law—the book of the covenant (Sir. 24:23–25).[31] This identification of Wisdom with the Torah is also seen in Baruch 3:32—4:1:[32]

> But the one who knows all things knows her, he found her by his understanding. The one who prepared the earth for all time filled it with four-footed creatures; the one who sends forth the light, and it goes; he called it, and it obeyed him, trembling; the stars shone in their watches, and were glad; he called them, and they said, "Here

---

30. For dating and provenance of Wisdom of Ben Sirach, see deSilva, *Introducing the Apocrypha*, 157–61; and Patrick W. Skehan and Alexander A. Di Lella, *The Wisdom of Ben Sira*, AB 39 (New York: Doubleday, 1987), 8–16.

31. Skehan and Di Lella, *Wisdom of Ben Sira*, 336–37.

32. The book of Baruch was most likely composed in Hebrew in the early second century BC in Palestine. See deSilva, *Introducing the Apocrypha*, 202–5; Carey A. Moore, *Daniel, Esther and Jeremiah: The Additions*, AB 44 (Garden City, N.Y.: Doubleday, 1977), 260–61; and J. E. Wright, "Baruch, Book of," in Evans and Porter, *Dictionary of New Testament Background*, 149.

we are!" They shone with gladness for him who made them. This is our God; no other can be compared to him. He found the whole way to knowledge, and gave her to his servant Jacob and to Israel, whom he loved. Afterward she appeared on earth and lived with humankind. She is the book of the commandments of God, the law that endures forever. All who hold her fast will live, and those who forsake her will die.[33]

James L. Kugel notes that "as a result, the idea that God created the world *by means of* wisdom came to be understood as meaning that God created the world *by means of the Torah*—as if the Torah existed even before the world was created, and God consulted it in forming the universe."[34] This view is reflected in the Targum on Genesis 3:23–24, which expands on the biblical account by noting that "two thousand years before He [God] had created the world, He created the law, and prepared Gehinnam [gehenna] and the Garden of Eden" (*Tg. Yer. II*).[35] This expansion also makes a strong allusion to the sanctuary, where the Shekina dwells between the two cherubim (Exod. 25:18–22; Num. 7:89). The preexistence of the garden of Eden is also noted in 4 Ezra 3:6 and 6:2, although this interpretation is rejected by Jubilees (Jub. 2:7) and 2 Enoch (2 En. J30:1), which have the garden created on the third day.[36] This interpretation probably derived from the word *qedem* in Genesis 2:8, which carries the geographical meaning of "east" or, in a temporal sense, as an "ancient time," or "aforetime."[37]

---

33. Howard Clark Kee, ed., *The Cambridge Annotated Study Apocrypha: New Revised Standard Version* (Cambridge: Cambridge University Press, 1994), 116–17.

34. Kugel, *Traditions of the Bible*, 69.

35. The time period of two thousand years is also mentioned in the Midrash on Psalms, Ps. 90:3. Kugel, *Traditions of the Bible*, 60, suggests this number is based on reading Proverbs 8:30 in light of Psalm 90:4, thus understanding the phrase *wā'ehyeh ša'ăšu'îm yôm yôm* ("I was a delight a day, a day") as two days—or rather two thousand years.

36. See Table 3 in the Appendix.

37. L. Coppes, "*qādam*," in *TWOT* 2:785–86. P. P. Jenson, "*qdm*," in *NIDOTTE* 3:874, writes that "about half the occurrences of *qedem* have a chronological reference. 'Before' or 'in front' can refer to the relative or the absolute past (the primeval era)." C. Rogers, Jr., "*qādam*," in *NIDOTTE* 3:872, adds "as a nom. *Qedem* can have a temporal meaning, 'ancient,' 'before time' (Deut. 33:27; Ps. 143:5; Prov. 8:22–23; Mic. 5:2[1])."

Targum Jerusalem (*Tg. Yer. II*) on Genesis 3:24	Targum Pseudo-Jonathan (*Tg. Ps.-J.*) on Genesis 3:24
And He cast out Adam, and made the glory of His Shekina to dwell at the front of the east of the garden of Eden, above the two Kerubaia [cherubim].	And He drave out the man from thence where He had made to dwell the glory of His Shekina at the first between the two Kerubaia.
Two thousand years before He had created the world, He created **the law**, and prepared **Gehinnam** [gehenna] and the **Garden of Eden**.	*Before He had created the world*, He created **the law**;
He prepared the **garden of Eden** for the righteous, that they should eat, and delight themselves with the fruit of the tree, because they had kept the commandments of the law in this world.	He prepared the **garden of Eden** for the righteous, that they might eat and delight themselves with the fruit of the tree; because they would have practised [sic] in their lives the doctrine of the law in this world, and have maintained the commandments:
For the wicked He prepared **Gehinnam** [gehenna], which is like the sharp, consuming sword with two edges. He prepared in the depth of it flakes of fire and burning coals for the wicked, for their punishment for ever in *the world to come*, who have not kept the commandment of the law in this world.	(but) He prepared **Gehinnam** for the wicked, which is like the sharp, consuming sword of two edges; in the midst of it He hath prepared flakes of fire and burning coals for the judgment of the wicked who rebelled in their life against the doctrine of the law.
For the law is the tree of life; whoever keepeth it in this life liveth and subsisteth as the tree of life. The law is good to keep in this world, as the fruit of the tree of life in *the world that cometh*.	*To serve the law is better than (to eat of) the fruit of the tree of life*, (the law) which the Word of the Lord prepared, that man in keeping it might continue, and walk in the paths of the way of life in *the world to come*.

The parallels between the garden of Eden and the earthly sanctuary were also recognized by Second Temple period interpreters, who suggested there was also a heavenly sanctuary or temple (Sir. 24:9–10; Wis. 9:8; 2 Bar. 4:3, 5; 1 En. 14:16–20; T. Levi 3:4–6; 5:1–2; Jub. 31:14) that preexisted the creation (Wis. 9:8; 2 Bar. 4:4).[38] The Jerusalem Targum identifies the tree of life with the Torah, an identification

---

38. See Richard M. Davidson, "Earth's First Sanctuary: Genesis 1–3 and Parallel Creation Accounts," *AUSS* 53, no. 1 (2015): 65–89; Lifsa Schachter, "The Garden of Eden as God's First Sanctuary," *JBQ* 41, no. 2 (2003): 73–77; and Peter Beckman, "The Garden of Eden: An Archetypical Sanctuary" (master's thesis, Dallas Theological Seminary, 2017).

further supported by the sanctuary language, God's Shekinah, and the two cherubim. It should be noted that the cherubim are always associated with the sanctuary/temple in the Hebrew Scriptures and more specifically with the Holy of Holies (e.g., Exod. 26:1, 31; 1 Kings 6:29; Ezek. 41:18–25), with the mercy seat on the ark of the covenant and God's throne (e.g., Exod. 25:18, 19–20, 22; 1 Kings 6:23–28; Ezek. 10:1–20). Thus, in the garden, they are protecting the tree of life; while in the sanctuary/temple, they are associated with the Torah, God's covenant.[39] Perhaps it was this sanctuary/temple association with the garden that caused the authors of 2 Enoch and the Targum Pseudo-Jonathan to interpret Adam's activity of *lĕʿābdāh ûlĕšomrāh* ("to work it and to guard it," Gen. 2:15) as a reference to the Torah: "And I created a garden in Edem, in the east, so that he might keep the agreement and preserve the commandment" (2 En. 31:1b) and more specifically *pəlaḥ bəʾôraytāʾ ûlmintar pīqûdāhāʾ* ("to do service in the law and to observe its commandments," *Tg. Ps.-J.* to Gen. 2:15).[40]

PREEXISTENCE OF GEHENNA

The Targum Pseudo-Jonathan also suggests that gehenna preexisted creation. This place is vividly described in Second Temple period literature: in 4 Ezra 7:36 as "the pit of torment" and "the furnace of Hell" (4 Ezra 7:36), in 4 Maccabees 12:12 as an eternal place of punishment of "intense and eternal fire and tortures" (NRSV), and in 2 Enoch J10:3 as "very cruel places of detention and dark and merciless angels, carrying instruments of atrocities torturing without

---

39. An early Rabbinic tractate, *m. Pirke Avot* 6.7 (ca. AD 190–ca. 230), gives the following description of the life-giving force of the Torah: "Great is Torah, for it gives life to those who do it in this world and in the next world, as it says: 'For they are life to those that find them, and healing to all his flesh' (Prov. 4:22); and it says, 'It will be healing for your navel, and tonic to your bones' (Prov. 3:8). And it says, 'It is a tree of life to those who hold it, and those who grasp it are happy' (Prov. 3:18). And it says, 'For they are an accompaniment of grace for your head, and a necklace for your throat' (Prov. 1:9). And it says, 'She will give your head an accompaniment of grace; with a crown of glory she will protect you' (Prov. 4:9). And it says, 'For by me your days will be multiplied, and you will be given additional years of life' (Prov. 9:11). And it says, 'Length of days is in her right hand, and in her left is wealth and honor' (Prov. 3:16); and it says, 'For length of days and years of life and peace will be added to you' (Prov. 3:2); and it says, 'her ways are ways of pleasantness, and all her paths are peace' (Prov. 3:17)" (see https://www.sefaria.org/Pirkei_Avot.6.7?lang=bi&with=all&lang2=en).

40. The book of Jubilees and the Apocalypse of Moses understand the phrase *lĕʿābdāh ûlĕšomrāh* ("to work it and guard it") literally as cultivating it, protecting it against wildlife, and harvesting and storing the food (Jub. 3:15–16) or protecting it against the devil and keeping the male and female animals separate from each other (Apoc. Mos. 15:1–3; 17:3).

piety."[41] Kugel proposes that at the foundation of this interpretation lies Isaiah 30:33,[42] which states, "Indeed! Topheth has been ready for the king *for a long time now* [*mē'etmûl*, "from before"]. His funeral pyre is deep and wide, with plenty of fire and wood. The breath of the LORD, like a torrent of brimstone, kindles it" (emphasis added). It should be noted that this verse is used as a proof text when Raba (Rabbah bar Nachmani, ca. AD 270–ca. 330) lists seven things existing before creation:

> Seven things were created before the world was created, and they are: Torah, and repentance, the Garden of Eden, and Gehinnom, the Throne of Glory and the Temple, and the name of the Messiah.
> - **Torah**, as it is written, "The LORD created me at the beginning of His way" [Prov. 8:22].
> - **Repentence**, as it is written, "Before the mountains were born and [earth] was created" [Ps. 90:2] and "You return humanity to dust" [Ps. 90:3].
> - **The Garden of Eden**, as it is written, "The LORD God planted a Garden in Eden from before" [Gen. 2:8].
> - **Gehinnom** as it is written, "The Topheth has long been ready for him" [Isa. 30:33].
> - **The Throne of Glory** as it is written, "Your throne is established of old" [Ps. 93:2].
> - **The Temple** as it is written, "Your Throne of Glory on high from the beginning" [Jer. 17:12].
> - **The name of the Messiah** as it is written, "May His name endure forever" [Ps. 72:17].[43]

---

41. The dominant anthropological view in Second Temple period literature is the immortality of the soul, a soul that is described very physically. The following literary compositions found in the Apocrypha and the Pseudepigrapha present a clear view that the wicked will receive eternal punishment, most often referred to as Hades, gehenna, or the fiery abyss: 4 Ezra; Wisdom of Solomon; Book of Watchers; Book of the Epistle of Enoch; 2 Enoch; 3 Enoch; Sibylline Oracles, Book 7 and Book 8; Apocalypse of Zephaniah; Greek Apocalypse of Ezra; Vision of Ezra; Questions of Ezra; 2 Baruch; 4 Maccabees; and Pseudo-Phocylides. Three of these compositions, Wisdom of Solomon (Wis. 8:19–20), 2 Enoch (2 En. J49:2), and 3 Enoch (3 En. 43:1, 3) present an immortality of the soul in its broadest sense, as the soul neither has a beginning nor an end. Thus, in these texts, the souls would even predate the creation itself. See Jan A. Sigvartsen, *Afterlife and Resurrection Beliefs in the Pseudepigrapha*, Jewish and Christian Texts (London: Bloomsbury T&T Clark, 2019), 210–15.

42. Kugel, *Traditions of the Bible*, 58.

43. b. Ned. 39b (author's translation and emphasis).

The parallel text, b. Pesaḥim 54a,[44] goes into a lengthy discussion regarding the fire of gehenna and whether it was created at the same time as gehenna or at a later point. If it was at a later point, the opinions offered ranged from the void of gehenna being created prior to creation while its inextinguishable fire was created on the second day of the creation week, or on Sabbath Eve, or at the conclusion of the first Sabbath.[45]

PREEXISTENCE OF THE NAME OF THE MESSIAH

Raba mentions that the name of the Messiah also preexisted the creation, referring to Psalm 72, a royal psalm. In this psalm, God blesses an unnamed king in highly idealized language, which may have led some Jewish interpreters to understand the psalm as referring to

---

44. Genesis Rabbah (AD 300–500) provides a list of six things that preexist the creation of the world. Some were created, while others were contemplated or decided upon by God for later use or purpose. The Torah and the throne of glory are in the former category while the patriarchs, Israel, temple, Messiah's name, and repentance are in the latter category. Following this list of items, the discussion turns to what came first: the Torah or the throne of glory, or perhaps even the intention of creating Israel. The concluding words of the discussion allude to Proverbs 8:22–23 when stating that the Torah came first: "Thus the Torah preceded [the creation of the world] by these six things, viz., *kedem* ('the first'), *me-'az* ('of old'), *me-'olam* ('from everlasting'), *me-rosh* ('from the beginning'), and mi-lekadmin ('or ever'), which counts as two" (*Gen. Rab.* 1.4; *Midrash Rabbah*, ed. H. Freedman and Maurice Simon [London: Soncino Press, 1939], 8).

45. *b. Pesah.* 54a–b, lists ten phenomena created "**on Shabbat eve during twilight, and they were:** Miriam's **well, and manna, and** the **rainbow, writing, and the writing instrument, and the tablets, the grave of Moses, and the cave in which Moses and Elijah stood, the opening of the mouth of** Balaam's **donkey, and the opening of the mouth of the earth to swallow the wicked** in the time of Korah. **And some say** that **even Aaron's staff** was created then with **its almonds and its blossoms. Some say** that **even the demons** were created at this time. **And some say** that **even the garment of Adam, the first** man, was created at this time, as it is stated: 'And God made for Adam and his wife garments of skins and clothed them'" (Gen. 3:21). In addition, during twilight, "**the Gemara cites that the Sages taught: Seven matters are concealed from people, and they are:** The **day of death; and the day of consolation** from one's concerns; **the profundity of justice,** ascertaining the truth in certain disputes; **and a person** also **does not know what is in the heart of another; and a person does not know in what** way he **will earn a profit;** and one does not know **when the monarchy of the house of David will be restored** to Israel; **and when the wicked** Roman **monarchy will cease to exist. The** Sages taught on a similar note: The thoughts of three matters arose in God's mind to be created, and if they did not arise in His thoughts, by right they should have arisen in His thoughts, as they are fundamental to the existence of the world. God created a world in which a corpse rots, so that it requires burial and the family does not continually suffer by seeing the corpse; that the deceased are forgotten from the heart, and the sense of pain and loss diminishes with time; and that grain will rot so that it cannot be hoarded forever, and therefore one must sell his produce. And some say: He instituted that currency will circulate so that people will accept money as a method of payment" ("William Davidson Talmud," https://www.sefaria.org/Pesachim.54a ?lang=bi, emphasis in original).

the coming Messiah.[46] Marvin Tate notes, "The psalm is a prayer for the future realization of the idealized hopes of monarchy, especially reflecting the hope of Israelites in exilic and post-exilic communities for the restoration of the Davidic dynasty and the fulfillment of the promises attendant to the Davidic kingship."[47] The final stanza (Ps. 72:16–17) is of most interest, as it mentions *šĕmô* ("His name") twice and the composite word *lipnê* ("before"), which in this context could be a reference to time, suggesting that the name of the Messiah existed before the sun, which is first mentioned on the fourth day of the creation week, although it does not mention how much earlier it existed. However, *lĕʿôlām* ("forever"), which could refer both to the past and the future, would suggest that "His name" would also predate the creation itself.

> *yĕhî **šĕmô** lĕʿôlām lipnê-šemeš (yānîn) [yinnôn] **šĕmô** wĕyitbārkû bô kol-gôyim yĕʾaššĕrûhû*

> May **his name** endure forever; as long as the sun shines [Before the sun is **his name** continued], may his fame increase. May all nations be blessed by him and call him blessed. (HCSB)

This understanding is reflected in two passages in a late Second Temple period addition to 1 Enoch, the *Book of the Parables* (1 En. 37–71).[48] The first example (1 En. 48:2–6) is found in the second parable in the book (1 En. 45–57), regarding the destiny of the sinners, while the second example (1 En. 62:7) appears in the third parable (1 En. 58–69), regarding the destiny of the righteous and the elect ones. Both these passages reveal details about the "Son of Man" (*bar ʾĕnāš*), who appears in the judgment scene in Daniel 7:13–14[49] and is one of the messianic imageries applied to Jesus in the New

---

46. Walter Kaiser, "Psalms 72: An Historical and Messianic Current Example of Antiochene Hermeneutical *Theoria*," *JETS* 52, no. 2 (June 2009): 259, notes that "surprisingly, the NT nowhere quotes from Psalm 72 as a messianic psalm."

47. Marvin E. Tate, *Psalms 51–100*, WBC 20 (Dallas: Word, 1998), 222.

48. George W. E. Nickelsburg and James C. VanderKam, *1 Enoch 2: A Commentary on the Book of 1 Enoch Chapters 37–82*, Hermeneia (Minneapolis, Minn.: Fortress, 2012), 63, date 1 Enoch 37–71 "between the latter part of Herod's reign and the early decades of the first century C.E., with some preference for the earlier part of this time span." For further discussion on the dating of the book, see ibid., 58–63.

49. For a discussion on the "Son of Man" in Daniel 7, see Markus Zehnder, "Why the Danielic 'Son of Man' is a Divine Being," *BBR* 24, no. 3 (2014): 331–47; and John E. Goldingay, *Daniel*, WBC 30 (Dallas: Word, 1998), 167–72. For a discussion on the "Son of Man" in 1 Enoch, see Gabriele Boccaccini, ed., *Enoch and the Messiah Son of Man: Revisiting the Book of Parables* (Grand Rapids, Mich.: Eerdmans, 2007), 153–262.

Testament (e.g., Matt. 26:64; Mark 14:62; Luke 22:69; John 5:27).[50]
First Enoch 48:3 seems to make the link with the fourth day of creation (Gen. 1:14–19) even stronger by adding a reference to the
moon and the stars. It also seems like the author of this passage
expands on the composite word *lipnê* ("before"), interpreting it as a
time reference to the preexistence of the Son of Man (1 En. 48:6). It
should also be noted that like Psalm 72:17, "name" is mentioned
twice (1 En. 48:2, 6). The statement that "all those who dwell upon
the earth shall fall and worship before him" (1 En. 48:5) seems to be
echoed in Revelation 13:8: "All those who live on the earth will worship him, everyone whose name was not written from the foundation of the world [*apo katabolēs kosmou*] in the book of life of the
Lamb who was slaughtered" (HCSB), which in this case is applied to
the sea beast, the antichrist.[51]

> At that hour, that Son of Man was given a name, in the presence of the
> Lord of the Spirits, the Before Time; [3] *even before the creation of the sun
> and the moon, before the creation of the stars*, he was given a name in the
> presence of the Lord of the Spirits. [4] He will become a staff for the righ-
> teous ones in order that they may lean on him and not fall. He is the light
> of the gentiles and he will become the hope of those who are sick in their
> hearts. [5] All those who dwell upon the earth shall fall and worship before

---

50. For a discussion on the "Son of Man," in the New Testament and early Christian
reception, see Leslie W. Walck, *The Son of Man in the Parables of Enoch and in Matthew*, Jewish and Christian Texts in Contexts and Related Studies 9 (New York: Clark, 2011); and Bog-
dan G. Buatr, "The Son of Man and the Ancient of Days: Observations on the Early Christian
Reception of Daniel 7," *Phronema* 32, no. 1 (2017): 1–27.

51. Regarding the interpretation of Rev 13:8b, David E. Aune, *Revelation 6–16*, WBC 52B
(Dallas: Word, 1998), 746–49, notes that the syntax of Revelation 13:8b is ambiguous as
"there are two quite different ways of understanding the meaning of this text." The first
option follows the word order and considers the phrase "from the foundation of the world" as
a modifier of the phrase "the Lamb who was slain," thus giving the following translation:
"whose name was not written in the book of life of the Lamb slaughtered from the foundation
of the world." The belief that the "lamb" was destined to die (not slain) from the beginning, is
reflected in 1 Peter 1:18–20. The second option considers the prepositional phrase "from the
foundation of the world" to be linked with the verb "written," thus giving the translation
"whose name was not written from the foundation of the world in the book of life of the Lamb
who was slaughtered." The latter option parallels Revelation 17:8 and, according to Aune, is
preferable both logically and theologically. In addition, he notes this option resonates with a
passage from the pseudepigraphic book Joseph and Aseneth, a Jewish composition from
Egypt dated between 100 BC and AD 115 (P. Ahearne-Kroll, "Joseph and Aseneth," in *Outside
the Bible: Ancient Jewish Writings Related to Scripture*, ed. L. H. Feldman, J. L. Kugel, and L. H.
Schiffman, 3 vols. [Philadelphia: The Jewish Publication Society, 2013], 3:2526, which states,
"For behold, your name [Aseneth] was written in the book of the living in heaven; in the
beginning of the book, as the very first of all, your name was written by my finger, and it will
not be erased forever" [*Jos. Asen.* 15:4]). Regardless of which option is chosen, it does not
make a difference regarding the preexistence of the Messiah.

him; they shall glorify, bless, and sing the name of the Lord of the Spirits. [6] For this purpose he became the Chosen One; he was concealed in the presence of (the Lord of the Spirits) *prior to the creation of the world, and for eternity.* (1 En. 48:2–6, emphasis added)

The preexisting aspect of the Son of Man and His concealment is also mentioned in 1 Enoch 62:7, although the name element is missing:[52] "For the Son of Man was concealed *from the beginning,* and the Most High One preserved him in the presence of his power; then he revealed him to the holy and the elect ones" (1 En. 62:7, emphasis added).

The Prayer of Joseph, most likely a late Second Temple period text,[53] mentions an additional item that preexisted creation. The writer states,

I, Jacob, who is speaking to you, am also Israel, an angel of God and a ruling spirit. *Abraham* and Isaac *were created before any work.* But, I, Jacob, who men call Jacob but whose name is Israel am he who *God called Israel* which means, a man seeing God, because I am the *firstborn of every living thing to whom God* gives life. (*Pr. Jos.* A1–3, emphasis original)

Not only does this passage state that Abraham and Isaac were created before the creation, but it also presents Jacob-Israel as the firstborn son of God (*Pr. Jos.* A2–3).[54] The passage goes on to suggest he was the highest ranked archangel, "*the first minister before the face of God*" (*Pr. Jos.* A8), who "had *descended to earth*" and "had tabernacled among men" and was called Jacob (*Pr. Jos.* A4). This tradition may be based on a literal reading of Exodus 4:22, where Moses states to Pharaoh, "This is what the Lord says: Israel is My firstborn son [*běnî běkorî yiśrā'ēl*]." This tradition may be alluded

---

52. The hiddenness aspect of the Messiah is also found in 4 Ezra 12:32; 13:25–26, 51–52, and hinted at in 2 Baruch 29:3. For a discussion on the Messiah in 1 Enoch 37–71 and 4 Ezra in light of the Dead Sea Scrolls, see Michael A. Knibb, "Messianism in the Pseudepigrapha in the Light of the Dead Sea Scrolls," *DSD* 2, no. 2 (1995): 170–80.

53. For dating and provenance, see Evans, *Ancient Texts*, 59; and Jonathan Z. Smith, "Prayer of Joseph: A New Translation with Introduction," in Charlesworth, *The Old Testament Pseudepigrapha*, 2:700; and Smith, "The Prayer of Joseph," in *Religions in Antiquity: Essays in Memory of Erwin Ramsdell Goodenough,* ed. Jacob Neusner (Eugene, Ore.: Wipf and Stock, 2004), 255.

54. The Testament of Moses, most likely a first-century composition that also contains older material (for dating and provenance, see John Priest, "Testament of Moses: A New Translation and Introduction," in Charlesworth, *The Old Testament Pseudepigrapha,* 1:920–22), mentions that Moses preexisted the creation. It states, "But he [God] did design and devise me [Moses], who (was) prepared from the beginning of the world, to be the mediator of his covenant" (*T. Mos.* 1:14).

to in Jesus's dialogue with the "Jews" in John 8:48–59, when Jesus states, "I assure you: Before Abraham was, I am [*Amēn amēn legō hymin, prin Abraam genesthai, egō eimi*]" (John 8:58), thereby claiming He preexisted not only Abraham but the creation itself.

PREEXISTENCE AND THE NEW TESTAMENT

The New Testament, like the literature of the Second Temple period, also mentions several items that preexisted the creation, or existed before the foundation of the world. Ekkehardt Mueller draws the distinction between the phrase *apo katabolēs kosmou* ("*from* the foundation of the world") and *pro katabolēs kosmou* ("*before* the foundation of the world"). The first phrase appears seven times in the New Testament (Matt. 13:35; 25:34; Luke 11:50; Heb. 4:3; 9:26; Rev. 13:8; 17:8), while the latter appears three times (John 17:24; Eph. 1:4; 1 Pet. 1:20). A third and related phrase, *pro chronōv aiōniōn* ("*before* time began"), appears two times (2 Tim. 1:9; Titus 1:2). Mueller writes,

> The phrase "from the foundation [*apo katabolēs*] of the world" (Matt. 25:34; Luke 11:50) and the related phrase "before the foundation [*pro katabolēs*] of the world" (John 17:24) used by Jesus occur also in other places in the NT. The word *katabolē* can be translated as "foundation," "beginning," and to some extent as "creation." The phrase "from the foundation of the world," focuses on events which have taken place since creation. With the phrase "before the foundation of the world" events are described prior to the creation of the world.[55]

Based on a careful consideration of the New Testament passages in which these three terms appear, there seem to be five persons and entities that can be posited as existing before the foundation of the world: the plan of salvation, the Messiah, God's purpose/will for His people, God's Word, and God's throne.[56] These five persons and entities are listed at the end of this paragraph with their New Testament

---

55. Ekkehardt Mueller, "Creation in the New Testament," *JATS* 15, no. 1 (Spring 2004): 53.

56. It should be noted that the term "Throne of God" in some cases carries the general meaning of heaven (Matt. 5:34; Acts 7:49; cf. Isa. 66:1), in contrast to the specific throne of God (Heb. 1:8; 8:1; 12:2; Rev. 4:2–11; 22:3), but "heaven" and "throne" could also be used as synonyms (Matt. 23:22); see O. Schmitz, "*thronos*" in *TDNT* 3:160–67. For a discussion on throne imagery in the book of Revelation, see Charles Homer Giblin, "From and before the Throne: Revelation 4:5–6a Integrating the Imagery of Revelation 4–16," *CBQ* 60 (1998): 500–513.

textual references. Although the preexistence of the temple/sanctuary is not specifically stated in the New Testament and is therefore not included in the following list, its existence is implied. Thus, consideration for it being a sixth item that existed prior to the creation week should be made. The New Testament states there is a temple in heaven that was "not made with hands" and thus is "not of this creation" (Heb. 9:11; cf. Heb. 9:23–24). While this heavenly temple preexisted the earthly temple, this does not at first glance imply a pre-creation origin. However, assuming that the eternal God rules from His heavenly temple as stated in Revelation 11:19; 15:5–8; and 16:1, 17, and that He sits on His everlasting heavenly throne (*Ho thronos sou ho theos eis ton aiōna tou aiōnos*, Heb. 1:8), one could infer equally, like God's throne, that the heavenly temple could also predate the creation.[57]

Thus, the New Testament list closely resembles the items appearing in Second Temple period literature, which were considered previously in this study.

---

57. This assumption may be supported by the relationship between the heavenly and the earthly sanctuary/temple. If the earthly sanctuary/temple is patterned after the heavenly temple and elements of the earthly reflect the heavenly, it could be argued that because the earthly sanctuary/temple was made so God could dwell among His people (Acts 7:44; cf. Exod. 25:8–10; 2 Sam. 7:1–29), the heavenly counterpart would also serve as God's dwelling place. This suggests it may have existed prior to the creation of this world—as God preexisted the creation week of Genesis 1. Alternatively, it could be argued this relationship between the sanctuary/temple and God's throne is flawed as the book of Revelation states there will be no sanctuary/temple in the new Jerusalem (Rev. 21:22), although His throne will be located in the city (Rev. 22:3) and He will dwell in their midst (Rev. 21:3). Instead, the Apocalypse states "the Lord God the Almighty and the Lamb are its sanctuary" (Rev. 21:22, HCSB), drawing a parallel between Lord God and Jesus with that of the earthly sanctuary/temple. However, a case could also be made that the city itself parallels the Holy of Holies, as this is the only biblical architectural structure described as a perfect cube (Rev. 21:16; cf. Exod. 26; 1 Kings 6:20; Ezek. 41:4). The holy of holies in the wilderness sanctuary is smaller than the holy of holies in Solomon's Temple and in Ezekiel's vision (10x10x10 cubits versus 20x20x20 cubits, both also perfect cubes). Thus, if the cubic new Jerusalem could be considered the holy of holies, the city itself would be the integral part of the temple structure and it would not make sense to have a temple within it. For further reading, see R. E. Averbeck, "Tabernacle," in *DOTP*, 807–27; George W. MacRae, "Heavenly Temple and Eschatology in the Letter to the Hebrews," *Semeia* 12 (1978): 178–200; and Gert J. Steyn, "'On Earth as It Is in Heaven...': The Heavenly Sanctuary Motif in Hebrews 8:5 and Its Textual Connection with the 'Shadowy Copy' [ὑποδείγματι καὶ σκιᾷ] of LXX Exodus 25:40," *HvTSt* 67, no. 1 (April 2011), Art. #885, 6 pages. DOI: 10.4102/hts.v67i1.885. For a study on the heavenly temple in the Hebrew Bible and in the ancient Near East, see Elias Brasil de Souza, *The Heavenly Sanctuary/Temple Motif in the Hebrew Bible: Function and Relationship to the Earthly Counterparts*, ATSDS 7 (Berrien Springs, Mich.: Adventist Theological Society, 2005).

Plan of Salvation	Messiah	God's Purpose/ Will for His People	Word of God	God's Throne
1 Cor. 2:7–8	John 1:1–14,	Eph. 1:4–5	John 1:14a	Heb. 1:8
1 Pet. 1:18–23	18; 17:5, 24b	2 Tim. 1:9		
Rev. 14:6	1 Cor. 8:6	Titus 1:2		
	Col. 1:15–18			
	Heb. 1:1–14			
	1 John 1:1–2			
	Rev. 3:14			

Jesus, the Messiah of the New Testament, provides perhaps the most interesting parallel with the Wisdom/Torah theme in Second Temple period literature. Similar to Wisdom/Torah, the New Testament indicates that the Messiah/Jesus preexisted the creation and was with God from the beginning (John 1:1–14, 18; 17:5, 24b; 1 Cor. 8:6; Col. 1:15–18; Heb. 1:2; 1 John 1:1–2; Rev. 3:14), that the world was created through the Messiah/Jesus (John 1:3, 10a; Col. 1:16; Heb. 1:1–3, 10–12; 2:10; 3:4–6[58]), and that following His ways leads to life everlasting (John 6:51–59; 14:6; 17:3; Rom. 10:4–11; cf. Deut. 30:11–16a; 1 John 5:11–12).

CONCLUSION

The literature of the Second Temple period shows great interest in Genesis 1–3. This study noted several interpretative issues raised in this literature, focusing on Genesis 1:1–3, and briefly compared the parallel creation accounts. Then it considered the items that the Second Temple literature suggests preexisted the Genesis creation, and which also have parallels in New Testament texts, such as the Prologue of John (John 1:1–18). While much discussion about the creation story occurs in this intertestamental literature, it is clear that sources that repeat the creation story in whole assume that the days of creation were literal days. Because the New Testament writings arose in this milieu of ideas, the default position regarding the New Testament view of creation should be the same.

---

58. For a discussion on the texts from the book of Hebrews, see Felix H. Cortez, "Creation in Hebrews," *AUSS* 53, no. 2 (2015): 279–320.

Michael G. Hasel, PhD

Southern Adventist University
Collegedale, Tennessee, USA

BIBLICAL IMPLICATIONS OF ACCEPTING A NONLITERAL VIEW OF CREATION

INTRODUCTION

The creation account in Genesis 1–3 is foundational for the major historical and theological concepts found in Scripture, providing the key philosophical definitions of reality. Foundational biblical concepts include: an absolute beginning and movement through historical time and place (Gen. 1:1; John 1:1–4), the nature of God as transcendent Creator (Gen. 1:1—2:25), the triune Godhead as expressed in His plurality of creative activity (Gen. 1:1–2, 26–28; John 1:1–4), the loving character of God and His pursuant nature toward humanity (Gen. 1:1–3; 2:9), the origin and nature of humanity (Gen. 1:26–28; 2:7, 20–25), the institution of marriage (Gen. 1:26–28; 2:20–25), the institution of the law and the Sabbath (Gen. 2:1–3; Exod. 20:8–11), the reestablishment of a covenant relationship (Gen. 3:9–15), the origin and nature of sin (Gen. 3:1–15), the origin and plan of redemption (Gen. 3:15), the great controversy between good and evil (Gen. 2:9, 16–17; 3:1–7), and the restoration of God's plan for a perfect creation in the second coming.[1] In short, from a biblical

---

1. On these foundational concepts, see Gerhard F. Hasel, "The Meaning of 'Let Us' in Genesis 1:26," *AUSS* 13 (1975): 58–66; John T. Baldwin, "Progressive Creationism and Biblical Revelation: Some Theological Implications," *JATS* 3 (1992): 105–19; Michael G. Hasel, "In the

perspective, the flow of human history originates in creation and ends in re-creation; protology is the key to eschatology.[2]

However, with the presuppositions of the Enlightenment and the historical-critical method came the impetus for the emerging evolutionary hypothesis of the nineteenth century.[3] Accommodation to the evolutionary hypothesis in biblical studies became increasingly common in the twentieth century, causing a shift in the interpretation of the creation account of Genesis 1–3 from a historical, factual, and literal creation by divine fiat—*creatio ex nihilo*—a few thousand years ago, to a nonliteral interpretation.[4] The first form-critical scholar to suggest that Genesis should not be understood as history, but rather as "legend" was Hermann Gunkel, who clearly articulated that "many things reported in Genesis . . . go directly against our better knowledge."[5] By "our better knowledge" he meant the naturalistic evolutionary interpretation of scientific data, which should take precedent and inform our biblical exegesis. Evolutionary theory should be taken as the authoritative norm over the Genesis account. Subsequently, different

Beginning," *Adventist Review* (October 25, 2001), 24–27; Norman R. Gulley, "What Happens to Biblical Truth if the SDA Church Accepts Theistic Evolution?," *JATS* 15, no. 2 (Autumn 2004): 40–58; Randall W. Younker, "Consequences of Moving Away from a Recent Six-Day Creation," *JATS* 15, no. 2 (Autumn 2004): 59–70; E. Edward Zinke, "Theistic Evolution: Implications for the Role of Creation in Seventh-day Adventist Theology," in *Creation, Catastrophe and Calvary*, ed. John T. Baldwin (Hagerstown, Md.: Review and Herald, 2000), 159–71; Daniel K. Bediako, "Genesis 1:1—2:3 as a Historical Narrative Text Type," *Valley View University Journal of Theology* 1 (2011): 18–36; Richard M. Davidson, "The Genesis Account of Origins," in *The Genesis Creation Account and Its Reverberations in the Old Testament*, ed. Gerald A. Klingbeil (Berrien Springs, Mich.: Andrews University Press, 2015), 59–130; Wayne Grudem, "Theistic Evolution Undermines Twelve Creation Events and Several Crucial Christian Doctrines," in *Theistic Evolution: A Scientific, Philosophical, and Theological Critique*, ed. J. P. Moreland et al. (Wheaton, Ill.: Crossway, 2017), 783–837; John D. Currid, "Theistic Evolution Is Incompatible with the Teachings of the Old Testament," in Moreland et al., *Theistic Evolution*, 839–78; and Guy Prentiss Waters, "Theistic Evolution is Incompatible with the Teachings of the New Testament," in Moreland et al., *Theistic Evolution*, 879–926.

2. Michael G. Hasel, "The Relationship between Protology and Eschatology," in *The Cosmic Battle for Planet Earth*, ed. Ron du Preez and Jiří Moskala (Berrien Springs, Mich.: Seventh-day Adventist Theological Seminary, 2003), 17–32; and Bruce Norman, "The Restoration of the Primordial World of Genesis 1–3 in Revelation 21–22," *JATS* 8, nos. 1–2 (1997): 161–69.

3. Todd S. Beall, "Contemporary Hermeneutical Approaches to Genesis 1–11," in *Coming to Grips with Genesis: Biblical Authority and the Age of the Earth*, ed. Terry Mortenson and Thane H. Ury (Green Forest, Ariz.: Master Books, 2008), 131–62.

4. Concerning the Hebrew term *bārā'* and other exegetical arguments in favor of creation *ex nihilo*, see Paul Copan and William Lane Craig, *Creation Out of Nothing: A Biblical, Philosophical, and Scientific Explanation* (Grand Rapids, Mich.: Baker, 2004).

5. Hermann Gunkel, *The Legends of Genesis: The Biblical Saga and History* (New York: Schocken, 1964), 7 (see also 1–7).

nonliteral genres of interpretation[6] suggested for Genesis include "saga,"[7] "cultic liturgy,"[8] "hymn,"[9] "metaphorical narration,"[10] "doctrine,"[11] "story,"[12] "poetry,"[13] "theology,"[14] "metaphor/parable,"[15] "vision,"[16] "mythology" based on ancient Near East parallels,[17] "liturgy/worship,"[18] and "analogy."[19] This plethora of interpretations in itself raises some serious issues concerning the modern trajectory of form-critical genre studies: (1) There appears to be no major scholarly consensus on the literary genre of the creation account in Genesis, even though it appears certain that the form-critical approach aims to remove Genesis 1 from the category of history. (2) Form-critical approaches that reassign the text to a genre other than history still allow for a literal grammatical interpretation of "days" in Genesis 1.[20]

---

6. Steven W. Boyd, "The Genre of Genesis 1:1—2:3: What Means This Text?" in Mortenson and Ury, *Coming to Grips with Genesis*, 163–92.

7. Jerome Hamer, *Karl Barth* (Westminster, Md.: Newman Press, 1962), 119–22.

8. S. H. Hooke, *Middle Eastern Mythology* (Baltimore, Md.: Penguin Books, 1963), 119–21.

9. Gordon J. Wenham, *Genesis 1–15*, WBC 1 (Waco, Tex.: Word, 1987), 10.

10. John H. Stek, "What Says Scripture?," in Howard J. Van Till et al., *Portraits of Creation: Biblical and Scientific Perspectives on the World's Formation* (Grand Rapids, Mich.: Eerdmans, 1990), 236.

11. Gerhard von Rad, *Genesis: A Commentary* (Philadelphia: Westminster, 1972), 65.

12. J. A. Thompson, "Genesis 1–3. Science? History? Theology," *TR* 3 (1966): 25.

13. Walter Brueggemann, *Genesis: A Biblical Commentary for Teaching and Preaching* (Atlanta: John Knox, 1982), 26–28; and Bill Arnold, *Encountering the Book of Genesis* (Grand Rapids, Mich.: Baker, 1998), 23.

14. Conrad Hyers, *The Meaning of Creation: Genesis and Modern Science* (Atlanta: John Knox, 1984); Bruce R. Reichenbach, "Genesis 1 as a Theological-Political Narrative of Kingdom Establishment," *BBR* 13, no. 1 (2003): 47–69; and Davis Young, *Creation and the Flood: An Alternative to Flood Geology and Theistic Evolution* (Grand Rapids, Mich.: Baker, 1974), 86–89.

15. John C. L. Gibson, *Genesis*, 2 vols., Daily Study Bible (Edinburgh: Saint Andrew Press, 1981), 1:55–56.

16. P. J. Wiseman, *Creation Revealed in Six Days* (London: Marshall, Morgan, and Scott, 1948), 33–34; and Duane Garrett, *Rethinking Genesis: The Sources and Authority of the First Book of the Pentateuch* (Grand Rapids, Mich.: Baker, 1991), 192–94.

17. Hermann Gunkel, *Schöpfung und Chaos in Urzeit: Eine religionsgeschichtliche Untersuchung über Gen 1 und Ap Joh 12* (Göttingen: Vandenhoeck and Ruprecht, 1985); Brevard S. Childs, *Myth and Reality in the Old Testament*, SBT, 27 (London: SCM, 1962), 31–50; and Peter Enns, *Inspiration and Incarnation* (Grand Rapids, Mich.: Baker, 2005), 50.

18. Terence E. Fretheim, "Were the Days of Creation Twenty-Four Hours Long? YES," in *The Genesis Debate: Persistent Questions about Creation and the Flood*, ed. Ronald F. Youngblood (Grand Rapids, Mich.: Baker, 1990), 26.

19. C. John Collins, *Genesis 1–4: A Linguistic, Literary, and Theological Commentary* (Phillipsburg, N.J.: P&R, 2006), 125.

20. Gerhard F. Hasel, "The 'Days' of Creation in Genesis 1: Literal 'Days' or Figurative 'Periods/Epochs' of Time," *Origins* 21, no. 1 (1994), 17.

Other approaches suggest that the structure of the creation account in Genesis 1 provides merely a literary framework,[21] that the days of creation should be interpreted as (day-age) symbolism,[22] or that the creation narrative depicts a cosmic temple inauguration.[23] What is common to all these nonliteral views is the assumption that the Genesis account of origins is not a straightforward historical account of material creation. Since these ideas are making an increasing impact on evangelical and even Adventist theology,[24] the task of this study is to observe some of the recent trends and discuss important questions and implications of accepting a nonliteral view

---

21. N. H. Ridderbos, *Is There a Conflict between Genesis 1 and Natural Science?*, trans. John Vriend (Grand Rapids, Mich.: Eerdmans, 1957); Meredith G. Kline, "Because It Had Not Rained," *WTJ* 20 (1958): 146–57; Kline, *Genesis: The New Bible Commentary: Revised* (Downers Grove, Ill.: InterVarsity, 1970); Henri Blocher, *In the Beginning: The Opening Chapters of Genesis* (Downers Grove, Ill.: InterVarsity, 1984), 49–59; Lee Irons with Meredith G. Kline, "The Framework View," in *The Genesis Debate: Three Views on the Days of Creation*, ed. David G. Hagopian (Mission Viejo, Calif.: Crux Press, 2001), 217–56; W. Robert Godfrey, *God's Pattern for Creation* (Phillipsburg, N.J.: P&R, 2003), 52–53; D. F. Payne, *Genesis One Reconsidered* (London: Tyndale, 1964); and Bruce Waltke, *Genesis: A Commentary* (Grand Rapids, Mich.: Zondervan, 2001), 73–78.

22. Broad concordists believe the seven days represent longer periods; see, e.g., Derek Kidner, *Genesis: An Introduction and Commentary*, TOTC (Downers Grove, Ill.: InterVarsity, 1967), 54–58; Hugh Ross and Gleason L. Archer, "The Day-Age View," in Hagopian, *The Genesis Debate*, 123–63; and Vern S. Poythress, in *Three Views on Creation and Evolution*, ed. James P. Moreland and John Mark Reynolds (Grand Rapids, Mich.: Zondervan, 1999), 92. The "progressive-creationist" view sees each day as opening a new creative period of indeterminate length; see Robert C. Newman and Herman J. Eckelmann Jr., *Genesis One and the Origin of the Earth* (Downers Grove, Ill.: InterVarsity, 1977), 64–65; cf. Moreland and Reynolds, *Three Views*, 104. Gerald L. Schroeder, *Genesis and the Big Bang: The Discovery of Harmony between Modern Science and the Bible* (New York: Bantam, 1990) tries to harmonize the week into billions of years of "cosmic time"; see Schroeder, *The Science of God: The Convergence of Scientific and Biblical Wisdom* (New York: Free Press, 1997); and Schroeder, *God According to God: A Physicist Proves We've Been Wrong About God All Along* (New York: Harper One, 2009).

23. John H. Walton, *The Lost World of Genesis One: Ancient Cosmology and the Origins Debate* (Downers Grove, Ill.: InterVarsity, 2009); cf. Walton, *Genesis 1 as Ancient Cosmology* (Winona Lake, Ind.: Eisenbrauns, 2011). For a critique of Walton's views that Genesis speaks only of *functional* origins and not *material* origins, see Richard E. Averbeck, "The Lost World of Adam and Eve: A Review Essay," *Them* 40, no. 2 (2015): 226–39; and essays in *AUSS* 49, no. 1 (2011).

24. Ivan T. Blazen, "Theological Concerns of Genesis 1:1—2:3," in *Understanding Genesis: Contemporary Adventist Perspectives*, ed. Brian Bull, Fritz Guy, and Ervin Taylor (Riverside, Calif.: Adventist Today, 2006), 72, writes, "What we have in Genesis 1 is theological affirmation rather than scientific delineation." Fritz Guy, "The Purpose and Function of Scripture: Preface to a Theology of Creation," in Bull, Guy, and Taylor, *Understanding Genesis*, 94, maintains that "what Genesis gives us is not scientific cosmology but profound theology (even if it utilizes ancient perceptions of the world)." Larry G. Herr, "Genesis One in Historical-Critical Perspective," *Spectrum* 13, no. 2 (December 1982): 59, 61, states, "Genesis 1 is theological in intent and scientists need not attempt to harmonize the ancient cosmology with the cosmology of modern science" and "the chapter uses the common ancient Near Eastern cosmology in expressing what it takes to be the *theological* (or cosmogonic) truth."

of the creation account for biblical hermeneutics. In other words, what is at stake in terms of biblical theology when reinterpreting the creation account in Genesis as merely theology, story, or something other than a historical and literal account?

ISSUES OF BIBLICAL AUTHORITY, UNITY, AND INSPIRATION

Many major Old Testament scholars affirm that the writer of Genesis 1 meant the creation account to be taken literally.[25] James Barr, regius professor of Hebrew at the University of Oxford and one of the most important Hebrew scholars, chides evangelicals for their nonliteral interpretation of Genesis while they simultaneously affirm the infallibility of Scripture. He writes, "In fact the only natural exegesis is a literal one, in the sense that this is what the author meant."[26] Gerhard von Rad, the foremost Old Testament scholar of the twentieth century, writes, "What is said here [Gen. 1] is intended to hold true entirely and exactly as it stands."[27] "Everything that is said here [in Gen. 1] is to be accepted exactly as it is written; nothing is to be interpreted symbolically or metaphorically."[28] Von Rad is even more specific regarding the literal creation week: "The seven days [of the creation week] are unquestionably to be understood as actual days and as a unique, unrepeatable lapse of time in the world."[29] If a sequential period of seven literal and consecutive twenty-four-hour days is what the lexicography, grammar, syntax, terminology, and time boundaries of "evening and morning" demand,[30] then a nonliteral view of the creation account raises serious implications for the authority of Scripture as the inspired word of God. It assumes that the

---

25. This was the primary theological position taken by theologians through history until the time of the early Reformers; see James R. Mook, "The Church Fathers on Genesis, the Flood and the Age of the Earth," in Mortenson and Ury, *Coming to Grips with Genesis*, 23–52; David W. Hall, "A Brief Overview of the Exegesis of Genesis 1–11: Luther to Lyell," in Mortenson and Ury, *Coming to Grips with Genesis*, 53–78; and James Barr, "Luther and Biblical Chronology," *Bulletin of the John Rylands University Library* 72 (1990): 65.

26. James Barr, *Fundamentalism*, 2nd ed. (London: SCM Press, 1981), 40.

27. Von Rad, *Genesis*, 47.

28. Gerhard von Rad, "The Biblical Story of Creation," in *God at Work in Israel* (Philadelphia: Fortress, 1984), 99.

29. Ibid, 65; von Rad does make a distinction between *Historie* and *Heilsgeschichte*, or salvation history. See Michael G. Hasel, "History, the Bible, and Hermeneutics," in *Biblical Hermeneutics: An Adventist Approach*, ed. Frank M. Hasel (Silver Spring, Md.: Biblical Research Institute, 2020), 101–125; and Frank M. Hasel and Michael G. Hasel, *How to Interpret Scripture* (Nampa, Idaho: Pacific Press, 2019).

30. Gerhard F. Hasel, "'Days' of Creation," 21–28.

Bible is not a reliable source of information about origins and the beginning of this world and universe. It suggests that the first chapters of Genesis be relegated into categories that contain spiritual and theological meaning but not actual *Historie* based on actual events.[31] Is this nonhistorical view congruent with the views of the writers of the Old and New Testaments? And if not, how does this affect the unity of Scripture? What is the impact on the authority of Scripture if modern naturalistic presuppositions and conclusions are accepted as more authoritative than the biblical account and then superimposed upon the creation account?

The biblical writers unanimously reference the people and events of Genesis 1–11 as if they actually occurred the way the Bible describes.[32] Moses, for example, consistently affirms a literal seven-day creation sequence in Exodus. This includes: (1) the manna falling on six days but not on the Sabbath (Exod. 16:4–6, 21–23); (2) the fourth commandment, where God created in six days and rested on the seventh as an example for all of creation (Exod. 20:9–11); and (3) affirming the Sabbath as a sign for "in six days the LORD made the heavens and the earth, and on the seventh day he abstained from work and rested" (Exod. 31:16–17).[33] What would happen to these statements if God did not create in six days? The unity of Scripture would be compromised. Jesus states that "Scripture cannot be broken" (John 10:35)[34] and Paul affirms in 2 Timothy 3:16 that "all Scripture is given by inspiration of God, and is profitable for doctrine, for reproof, for correction, for instruction in righteousness." If only certain parts of Scripture are reliable sources of history and truth, then were the writers of the rest of Scripture, as well as Jesus and Paul, mistaken? Who decides what is historical and what is not?[35]

---

31. Michael G. Hasel, "History, the Bible, and Hermeneutics."

32. Exod. 20:9–11; Pss. 33:6, 9; 89:12; 104; Isa. 40:28; Matt. 19:4–5; 23:35; 24:37–39; Mark 10:6–9; 13:19; Luke 1:70; 3:34–38; 11:50–51; 17:26–27; John 1:1–3, 10; 8:44; Acts 3:21; 4:25; 14:15; 17:24, 26; Rom. 1:20; 5:12, 14–19; 8:20–22; 16:20; 1 Cor. 6:16; 11:3, 7–9, 12; 15:21, 22, 38–39, 45, 47; 2 Cor. 4:6; 11:3; Gal. 4:4, 26; Eph. 3:9; 5:30–31; Col. 1:16; 3:10; 1 Tim. 2:13–15; Heb. 1:10; 2:7–8; 4:3–4, 10; 11:4–5, 7; 12:24; James 3:9; 1 Pet. 3:20; 2 Pet. 2:4–5; 3:4–6; 1 John 3:8, 12; Jude 6, 11, 14–15; Rev. 2:7; 3:14; 4:11; 10:6; 12:1–4, 9, 13–17; 14:7; 17:5, 18; 20:2; 21:1, 4; 22:2–3. See articles in Klingbeil, *Genesis Creation Account.*

33. Gulley, "Theistic Evolution," 54.

34. Unless otherwise indicated, Scripture quotations in this chapter are taken from the New King James Version®. Copyright © 1982 by Thomas Nelson. Used by permission. All rights reserved.

35. See essays in James K. Hoffmeier and Dennis R. Magary, eds., *Do Historical Matters Matter to Faith? A Critical Appraisal of Modern and Postmodern Approaches to Scripture* (Wheaton, Ill.: Crossway, 2012).

Biblical authority, unity, and the very nature of inspiration would be undermined.

THE CHARACTER OF GOD AND MORAL ACCOUNTABILITY

The relationship between creation and the incarnation of Christ is revealed in the parallel between Genesis 1:1, "In the beginning God created the heavens and the earth," and John 1:1–4, "In the beginning was the Word, and the Word was with God, and the Word was God. He was with God in the beginning" (NIV). Christ is revealed as the agent of creation. "All things were made through Him, and without Him nothing was made that was made" (John 1:3; cf. Col. 1:15–16; Heb. 1:1–2). Christ spoke matter into existence at the beginning as "the Spirit of God moved over the face of the waters" (Gen. 1:2, my translation). Psalm 33:9 reaffirms, "For he spoke, and it came to be; he commanded, and it stood firm," for "by faith we understand that the universe was formed at God's command, so that what is seen was not made out of what was visible" (Heb. 11:3, NIV). God said, "Let Us make man in Our image" (Gen. 1:26). The triune Godhead is found implicitly in Genesis 1, powerfully working to create an ecosystem for life and to fill that ecosystem with perfect harmony, breathtaking beauty, and diversity. God repeatedly declared this to be "good," until finally He "saw everything that He had made, and indeed it was very good" (Gen. 1:31). The order and perfection of creation reveals the order and perfection of God. It establishes His creative activity as the basis for worship (Exod. 20:8–11; Rev. 4:11; 14:7).

If God started the process billions of years ago by simply forming matter and allowing it to evolve through the naturalistic processes of evolution, what would this mean for the nature of God? How would we need to reinterpret the character of God? And how would humans respond to such a God? A nonliteral view of creation that allows for a hybrid form of theistic evolution or progressive creation has serious implications.[36]

---

36. Others point out that naturalistic evolution and theistic creation are mutually exclusive ideas that have no common beginning or ending. Evolution presents a process from simple to complex, from partial to complete, or from less perfect to near perfect—in short, progress. Creation presents the opposite trajectory: from a perfect world to a broken world, from harmony to disharmony and strife, from love to a world where the thoughts of humanity were "only evil continually" (Gen. 6:5)—in short, a degression. One is based on philosophical naturalism that excludes any outside intervention; the other is based on theism that assumes that God interacts in His creation. See Stephen Dilley, "How to Lose a

First, the truth about God would be distorted. He would be robbed of His power to speak fully formed elements and creatures into existence *ex nihilo*. This has implications for Christ's power to change the water into wine; to say to the paralyzed man at Bethesda, "Rise, take up your bed and walk" (John 5:8); to say to Jairus's daughter, "Little girl, I say to you, arise" (Mark 5:41); or to say, "Lazarus, come forth!" (John 11:43). It is by the same power of the word that Jesus demonstrates His creative power to heal and to raise the dead. "To accept His creative power during His life on earth necessitates accepting His creative power in the Genesis record, for both are equally supernatural, and both are given to us through divine revelation."[37]

Second, it would mean that God created matter in the beginning but allowed animals and humans to compete through millions of years of torture and death in a holocaust of survival of the fittest. How is this congruent with a God who warned Adam of the evil of death (Gen. 2:17), who notices when a sparrow falls (Matt. 10:29), or who came to give life (John 3:16)? The idea that life originates from death is a pagan view of origins.[38] In the Atrahasis Epic, man is created from the flesh and blood of a slaughtered god mixed with clay, but "no hint of the use of dead deity or any other material of a living one is found in Genesis."[39] The cycle of death and rebirth is so intrinsic to Egyptian ideology that death itself is seen as part of the normal order of creation. On a funerary papyrus of the Twenty-First Dynasty, a winged serpent is standing on two pairs of legs with the caption "Death the great god, who made gods and men."[40] This is "a personification of death as a creator god and an impressive visual idea that death is a necessary feature of the world of creation, that is, of the existent in general."[41] This is the opposite of the God who

---

Battleship: Why Methodological Naturalism Sinks Theistic Evolution," in Moreland et al., *Theistic Evolution*, 593–631.

37. Gulley, "Theistic Evolution," 50.

38. See Gerhard F. Hasel and Michael G. Hasel, "The Unique Cosmology of Genesis 1 against Ancient Near Eastern and Egyptian Parallels," in Klingbeil, *Genesis Creation Account*.

39. Alan R. Millard, "A New Babylonian 'Genesis' Story," *TynBul* 18 (1967): 3–18. See p. 10 for the quotation.

40. Papyrus of Henuttawy (BM 10018), Siegfried Schott, *Zum Weltbild der Jenseitsführer des Neues Reiches*, NAWG 11 (Göttingen: Vandenhoeck and Ruprecht, 1965), 195, plate 4; see also Karol Myśliwiec, *Studien zum Gott Atum*, 2 vols., HÄB 5 (Hildesheim: Gerstenberg, 1978), 1:103.

41. Erik Hornung, *Conceptions of God in Ancient Egypt* (Ithaca, N.Y.: Cornell University Press, 1982), 81.

creates animals and humanity in a perfect world and blesses them (Gen. 1:22, 28).

Third, a God who intricately forms the miracle of life so that it can be studied in nature through the complexity of the cell, or the tiny seed that produces a tree, or a bird caring for and feeding her chicks inspires the desire to worship and invokes an innate sense of moral accountability. Paul spoke to the Athenians, "God, who made the world and everything in it . . . now commands all men everywhere to repent, because He has appointed a day on which He will judge the world in righteousness by the Man whom He has ordained" (Acts 17:24, 30–31). In Romans 1:20, people are "without excuse" for having witnessed the wonders of creation. A nonliteral view of the Genesis account removes this accountability because nature as we know it today would have evolved over millions of years without much or any divine design or providence. "Within the theistic evolution system, the complexity of living things no longer leaves unbelievers 'without excuse' (Rom. 1:20)."[42] Naturalistic evolution has a major impact on moral issues in society such as euthanasia, animal and human rights, purpose, and the divine origin of ethics.[43] In the end, humanity is left without a direct, divine origin, removing human dignity and a moral compass.[44]

THE NATURE OF "ADAM AND EVE" AND THE ORIGIN OF HUMANITY

The nature of humanity, as created by God in His image, places all human beings in a unique place at the apex of creation. The triple emphasis in God's creative act (*bārāʾ*) in Genesis 1:27 reinforces the supreme regard humans have in God's special design. Other biblical writers trace the origin of all human beings back to the first two humans, Adam and Eve. The amplification of the creative means in Genesis 2 conveys the personal attention God gives to this intimate act[45] as He carefully fashions the man out of the dust of the earth and

---

42. Grudem, "Theistic Evolution Undermines," 832.

43. Stephen Bauer, *Moral Implications of Darwinian Evolution for Human Preference Based in Christian Ethics: A Critical Analysis and Response to the "Moral Individualism" of James Rachels* (unpublished PhD diss., Andrews University, 2006).

44. Ibid., 114–20; and James Rachels, *Created from Animals: The Moral Implications of Darwinism* (Oxford: Oxford University Press, 1991), 125.

45. On the relationship of Genesis 1–2 as complementary and as one of amplification, see Jacques B. Doukhan, *The Genesis Creation Story: Its Literary Structure*, AUSDDS 5

breathes into him the breath of life.[46] God's special creation of Eve is marked by His divine reflection, "It is not good that man should be alone; I will make him a helper comparable to him" (Gen. 2:18). He builds (*bānāh*) woman from Adam's rib and brings her to him (Gen. 2:21–22). They are instructed, "Be fruitful and multiply; fill the earth and subdue it; have dominion over the fish of the sea, over the birds of the air, and over every living thing that moves on the earth" (Gen. 1:28). Humans were created to care for God's creation and fill the planet with families that would honor God and what was created.[47] Adam's historical nature is reaffirmed in Genesis 5:1–5:

> In the day that God created man, He made him in the likeness of God. He created them male and female, and blessed them and called them Mankind in the day they were created. And Adam lived one hundred and thirty years, and begot a son in his own likeness, after his image, and named him Seth. After he begot Seth, the days of Adam were eight hundred years; and he had sons and daughters. So all the days that Adam lived were nine hundred and thirty years; and he died.

Not only is the terminology *bārā'* repeated three times here in connection with the creation of Adam, but the text twice refers to "in the day" that God created him. An evolutionary process is absent here. The text mentions specific years of Adam's life before Eve bore Seth and a total number of years just like the other antediluvian men in Genesis 5. This assumes a historical existence and a reaffirmation of Genesis 1–2.[48]

The idea of a historical Adam and Eve as humanity's first ancestors is challenged by a nonliteral interpretation of Genesis 1–3 in

---

(Berrien Springs, Mich.: Andrews University Press, 1978); O. T. Allis, *The Five Books of Moses* (Philadelphia: Presbyterian and Reformed, 1943); U. Cassuto, *The Documentary Hypothesis*, trans. I. Abrahams (Jerusalem: Magnes, 1961); I. M. Kikawada and A. Quinn, *Before Abraham Was: The Unity of Genesis 1–11* (Nashville, Tenn.: Abingdon, 1985); R. N. Whybray, *The Making of the Pentateuch: A Methodological Study* (Sheffield: Sheffield Academic Press, 1987); Randall W. Younker, "Genesis 2: A Second Creation Account?" in Baldwin, *Creation, Catastrophe and Calvary*, 69–79; and Currid, "Theistic Evolution," 863–70.

46. The dust from the ground is the material from which Adam is made and the material to which all humans return; see Vern S. Poythress, *Did Adam Exist?* (Phillipsburg, N.J.: P&R, 2014), 16.

47. Jo Ann Davidson, "Creator, Creation, and Church: Restoring Ecology to Theology," *AUSS* 45 (2007): 101–22.

48. On the chronogenealogies of Genesis 5 and 11, see Gerhard F. Hasel, "The Genealogies of Gen 5 and 11 and Their Alleged Babylonian Background," *AUSS* 16 (1978): 361–74; Gerhard F. Hasel, "Genesis 5 and 11: Chronogenealogies in the History of Beginnings," *Origins* 7 (1980): 23–37; and Gerhard F. Hasel, "The Meaning of the Chronogenealogies of Genesis 5 and 11," *Origins* 7 (1980): 53–70.

several ways. First, if God created only matter in the beginning and then left naturalistic evolution to continue the process, then there were thousands of ancestors for the human race. Francis S. Collins states that our species "descended from a common set of founders, approximately 10,000 in number, who lived about 100,000 to 150,000 years ago."[49] Denis Alexander writes, "The founder population that was the ancestor to all modern humans . . . was only 9,000–12,000 reproductively active people."[50] In other words, the gene pool for our first ancestors was not one man and one woman. This means that Adam and Eve were not really created by God but were born from human parents. This is in direct conflict with Genesis 2, which states that God directly "formed man of the dust of the ground, and breathed into his nostrils the breath of life" (Gen. 2:7) and that God "built" Eve from a rib taken from Adam's side (Gen. 2:20–25). Luke affirms this in the genealogies when he writes, "Seth, the son of Adam, the son of God" (Luke 3:38). Paul also states implicitly that Adam had no parent when he writes of "the first man Adam" (1 Cor. 15:45). "But if Adam had a human father, then he would not be the first man."[51] Likewise, how could Genesis 3:20 refer to Eve as "the mother of all living" when there were thousands of others living before her?

Second, the order and sequence of creation—in which Adam is created first and then later Eve, to fully complement the first human parents—would no longer be necessary. N. T. Wright suggests that "God chose one pair from the rest of early hominids for a special, strange, demanding vocation. This pair (call them Adam and Eve if you like) were to be representatives of the whole human race."[52] Likewise, John H. Walton suggests that Adam and Eve should be understood as "archetypes" representing "Everyman" who "embodies all others in the group"[53] (the human race). Walton states that the Bible "makes no claims" regarding "biological human origins," for Genesis "talks about the *nature of all* people, not the unique *material*

---

49. Francis S. Collins, *The Language of God: A Scientist Presents Evidence for Belief* (New York: Free Press, 2006), 126.

50. Denis Alexander, *Creation or Evolution: Do We Have to Choose?*, 2nd ed. (Grand Rapids, Mich.: Monarch, 2014), 265.

51. Grudem, "Theistic Evolution Undermines," 798–99.

52. N. T. Wright, "Excursus on Paul's Use of Adam," in John H. Walton, *The Lost World of Adam and Eve: Genesis 2–3 and the Human Origins Debate* (Downers Grove, Ill.: InterVarsity, 2015), 177–78.

53. Walton, *Lost World*, 74.

origins of Adam and Eve."[54] For Walton, Adam merely had a "visionary experience" when he saw "himself being cut in half and the woman being built from the other half."[55] But nowhere in the text is any terminology used for a visionary experience.

Denis Lamoureux is more explicit: "Adam never existed"[56] and "Holy Scripture makes statements about how God created living organisms that in fact never happened" since "real history in the Bible begins roughly around Genesis 12 with Abraham."[57] Peter Enns argues along a historical-critical process[58] when he writes that Adam is Israel: "Maybe Israel's history happened first, and the Adam story was written to reflect that history. In other words, the Adam story is really an Israel story placed in primeval time. It is not a story of human origins but of Israel's origins."[59] Enns articulates his position more fully, asserting that "a literal reading of the Genesis creation stories does not fit with what we know of the past. The scientific data do not allow it."[60] After placing Israel and Adam side by side, he concludes that "the Adam story mirrors Israel's story from exodus to exile."[61]

But do these explanations correspond to what Genesis actually says concerning the material creation and origin of Adam and Eve; the order of creation as Paul reaffirms when he writes, "For Adam was formed first, then Eve" (1 Tim. 2:13); or what Jesus explicitly states in His confirmation of this special creation?[62] Jesus remarks most succinctly, "He who made them at the beginning 'made them male and female'" (Matt. 19:4). Jesus affirms the Genesis account that the first human parents were made "at the beginning"—not some billions of years after He created matter. Jesus affirms that God made

---

54. Ibid., 181.

55. Ibid., 78–79.

56. Denis Lamoureux, "No Historical Adam: Evolutionary Creation View," in *Four Views on the Historical Adam*, ed. Matthew Barrett and Ardel B. Caneday (Grand Rapids, Mich.: Zondervan, 2013), 58.

57. Ibid., 56, 44.

58. See discussion in the section of this study titled "The Origin of the Seventh-day Sabbath," 105.

59. Peter Enns, "Adam Is Israel," BioLogos, March 2, 2010, https://biologos.org/articles/adam-is-israel.

60. Peter Enns, *The Evolution of Adam: What the Bible Does and Doesn't Say about Human Origins* (Grand Rapids, Mich.: Brazos, 2012), 79.

61. Ibid., 65–66.

62. In fact, Enns makes no mention of Jesus's important discourse in Matthew 19:3–9 (Mark 10:2–9), emphasizing only Paul's statements. He also does not mention Revelation 22:1–5, where God ultimately undoes the effects and consequences of sin once and for all; see Norman, "Restoration of the Primordial World."

them "male and female" and that "what God has joined together, let not man separate" (Matt. 19:4–6). Jesus's statement in response to the Pharisees upholds a literal understanding of the Genesis account. Reinterpreting Genesis would require reinterpreting Jesus and Paul. Thus Enns sets out "to properly address Genesis as ancient literature and Paul as an ancient man,"[63] ultimately placing (with Walton and others) Genesis as ancient premodern literature that requires reinterpretation in the modern world of naturalistic science.

THE ORIGIN OF THE SEVENTH-DAY SABBATH

The seventh-day Sabbath finds its origin at creation.[64] It has been argued that it is the final goal of the creation narrative.[65] What happens to the concept of the Sabbath when a nonliteral view of creation is adopted that reinterprets creation week into a mere framework, or that sees each day as representing longer epochs of time encompassing millions of years? How is the Sabbath to be understood in light of the fourth commandment, where God instructs humanity to remember the Sabbath day by pointing back to creation week, "For in six days the Lord made the heavens and the earth, the sea, and all that is in them, and rested the seventh day. Therefore the Lord blessed the Sabbath day and hallowed it" (Exod. 20:11)? This same phrase is alluded to again in Revelation, where humanity at the end time is to "worship Him who made heaven and earth, the sea and springs of water" (Rev. 14:7).[66] Does the concept of providing this mutual day of rest and worship for Creator and creature have any meaning if the event itself

---

63. Enns, *Evolution of Adam*, xvii.

64. Gerhard F. Hasel, "The Origin of the Biblical Sabbath and the Historical-Critical Method: A Methodological Testcase," *JATS* 4, no. 1 (1993) 17–46; Gerhard F. Hasel, "The Sabbath in the Pentateuch," in *The Sabbath in Scripture and History*, ed. Kenneth A. Strand (Washington, D.C.: Review and Herald, 1982); Mathilde Frey, "The Sabbath in the Pentateuch: An Exegetical and Theological Study" (PhD diss., Andrews University, 2011); H. Ross Cole, "The Sabbath and Genesis 2:1–3," *AUSS* 41, no. 1 (2003): 5–12; Richard M. Davidson, *A Love-Song for the Sabbath* (Hagerstown, Md.: Review and Herald, 1988); and Sigve K. Tonstad, *The Lost Meaning of the Seventh Day* (Berrien Springs, Mich.: Andrews University Press, 2009).

65. Oswald Loretz, *Schöpfung und Mythos: Mensch und Welt nach den Anfangskapiteln der Genesis* (Stuttgart: Katholisches Bibelwerk, 1968), 70, says, "The goal of the whole creation and of man is God's Sabbath. The creation of the world reaches its completion only through the Sabbath, the seventh day." See also Gerhard F. Hasel, "The Sabbath in the Pentateuch," 23; and Jiří Moskala, "The Sabbath in the First Creation Account," *JATS* 13, no. 1 (2002) 56–58. This is also reflected in Jesus's statement, "The Sabbath was made for man, and not man for the Sabbath" (Mark 2:27).

66. John T. Baldwin, "Revelation 14:7: An Angel's Worldview," in Baldwin, *Creation, Catastrophe and Calvary*, 19–39.

never took place as described in Genesis? Two interpretations high-light the historical-critical or theistic evolutionary view of the Sabbath.

The historical-critical approach denies a priori the claim of the Mosaic authorship of the Pentateuch and would date the Sabbath passages in Genesis and Exodus to later Israelite tradition or to various schools.[67] For Willy Rordorf then, the Jewish Sabbath of Genesis 1 and 2, Exodus 20, and Deuteronomy 5 "originated after the occupation of Canaan and that the evidence is to be found in documents which date from the early monarchical period" but that "credit for such an invention has not been given to the Israelites."[68] With the dismissal of creation as the origin for the Sabbath, scholars have searched for Sabbath origins outside of Israel, assuming that it was borrowed from some other ancient civilization, be it Babylonian, Kenite, Arabic, Ugaritic, or sociological. "In spite of the extensive efforts of more than a century of study into extra-Israelite sabbath origins, it is still shrouded in mystery. No hypothesis . . . commands the respect of a scholarly consensus."[69] Still, historical-critical scholars would not attribute the Sabbath to a divine origin but rather would limit it to a human invention. This would have some major implications for the Sabbath's authority.

More recently, as a proponent of theistic evolution, N. T. Wright argues that "linear time (which was part of God's good creation) continues, but it is now intersected with a new phenomenon, a new kind of time. . . . So time seems now capable of being telescoped together and then pulled apart again. One might call this 'Spirit-time'. . . . All of

---

67. Both Genesis 1:1–2:3, containing the creation Sabbath, and Exodus 16:22–30, dealing with the Sabbath and manna, are attributed by source critics to the P(riestly) source that is dated either to the exilic or postexilic periods, or later editors and redactors; see Werner Schmidt, *Die Schöpfungsgeschichte der Priesterschrift*, 2nd ed., WMANT (Neukirchen-Vluyn: Neukirchner Verlag, 1976), 154–59; Gnana Robinson, *The Origin and Development of the Old Testament Sabbath*, BBET (New York: Peter Lang, 1988), 225–27; and Niels-Erik Andreasen, *The Old Testament Sabbath: A Traditio-Historical Investigation*, SBLDS 7 (Missoula, Mont.: Scholars, 1972), 63–67. Source critics often view the Sabbath commandment in Deuteronomy 5:12–15 as earlier than the Genesis and Exodus references, based on their date of the D source or the DtrH. On the date of D and DtrH, see Michael G. Hasel, *Military Practice and Polemic: Israel's Laws of Warfare in Near Eastern Perspective* (Berrien Springs, Mich.: Andrews University Press, 2005), 2–5, 21–49.

68. Willy Rordorf, *Sunday: The History of the Day of Rest and Worship in the Earliest Centuries of the Christian Church* (Philadelphia: Westminster, 1968), 18–19.

69. Gerhard F. Hasel, "Sabbath," *ABD* 5:851.

this is focused on Jesus Christ."[70] For Wright, "now that heaven and earth have come together in Jesus Christ, and now that the new day has dawned, we live (from that point of view) in a perpetual sabbath."[71] The Sabbath, as the seventh day or the first day or any specific day, has ceased to exist and has become part of the Christian "story." The Sabbath is transposed into a principle of rest that is separated from the specific (historical) day that God designated. This has implications for the eschatological nature of the Sabbath and its relation to last-day events as prophesied in Scripture. The Sabbath loses its special character as a divine test and sign of the Sabbath-keeping remnant living just before Jesus returns (Rev. 12:17; 14:12; cf. Ezek. 20:12), since it is transformed from a specific time to a "perpetual sabbath" devoid of time altogether. In this way, we see that when literal time, as defined biblically, is removed from creation, so it is also removed from the Sabbath.

The Sabbath's origin at creation as a divine act of God has major implications: (1) Since the Sabbath is rooted in God's design and not man's, only God has the authority to change its time and meaning. (2) Since the Sabbath originated at creation, before Hebrews or Jews existed, it is not to be limited to a particular people, time, or place. It is universal in application. (3) Since the Sabbath was instituted at creation, it is a creation memorial and model established in the creation order. To change this institution is to interfere with God's design, will, and purpose, not that of humanity. (4) To change, remove, alter, or abolish the seventh-day Sabbath would undo what God has ordained. (5) God Himself provides the example of Sabbath observance in establishing the rhythm of creating the world in six days and resting on the seventh. (6) God sanctified the Sabbath and made it holy. Humans do not do this by keeping a day. (7) Just as the Sabbath is linked to the universality of creation, so is the universality of the Sabbath linked to all of humanity.[72] The challenge before us is to acknowledge the seventh day of the week as the biblical day of rest that God instituted at creation and upheld throughout Scripture. We are called to "keep the commands of God [including the fourth commandment] and the faith of Jesus" (Rev. 14:12) and thus

---

70. N. T. Wright, *Scripture and the Authority of God: How to Read the Bible Today* (New York: HarperCollins, 2011), 162–63.

71. Ibid., 167.

72. Gerhard F. Hasel, "Origin of the Biblical Sabbath," 19–20.

keep the Sabbath in such a way that it gives honor to the Creator God who is also our Savior.

MARRIAGE AND THE FAMILY

The basis for marriage between a man and a woman finds its origin as an institution of creation.[73] "God was the author of this union."[74] If Sabbath is the final goal of creation, humanity and marriage is the climax.[75] More space is devoted to the creation of humanity than any other aspect of creation in Genesis 1:1—2:3. "In the image of God He created him; male and female He created them" (Gen. 1:27). In Genesis 2, this emphasis is enlarged and expanded. Eve is "built" by God of the rib taken from Adam's side. Adam declares, "This is now bone of my bones, and flesh of my flesh; She shall be called Woman, because she was taken out of Man" (Gen. 2:23, NASB 1995). Marriage requires that "a man shall leave his father and mother and be joined to his wife, and they shall become one flesh" (Gen. 2:24). For what reason is marriage to take place? Woman was taken out of man—his very flesh and bone. The created complementarity of both man and woman is unequivocal biologically so that this one-flesh relationship is to take place between a man and a woman.[76] This union is further clarified in the instruction given to the earth's first parents: "Then God blessed them, and God said to them, 'Be fruitful and multiply; fill the earth and subdue it'" (Gen. 1:28).

---

73. J. Kerby Anderson, *Moral Dilemmas: Biblical Perspectives on Contemporary Ethical Issues*, Swindoll Leadership Library (Nashville, Tenn.: Word, 1998), 165, observes, "Foundational to a Christian understanding of sexuality is God's plan in creation found in Genesis 1 and 2." On the divine institution of marriage at creation, see Ron du Preez, "The God-Given Marital Mandate: Monogamous, Heterosexual, Intrafaith," *JATS* 10, nos. 1–2 (1999): 23–40; Calvin B. Rock, "Marriage and the Family," in *HSDAT*, 725; and Richard M. Davidson, *Flame of Yahweh: A Theology of Sexuality in the Old Testament* (Peabody, Mass.: Hendrickson, 2007), 15–19.

74. Geoffrey W. Bromiley, *God and Marriage* (Grand Rapids, Mich.: Eerdmans, 1980), 3.

75. Gordon J. Wenham, *Genesis 1–15*, WBC 1 (Waco, Tex.: Word, 1987), 37, states that the creation of humans in the image of God is "the climax of the six days' work. But it is not its conclusion." Pointing to seven exegetical indicators within the text, Bruce A. Ware, "Male and Female Complementarity and the Image of God," in *Biblical Foundations for Manhood and Womanhood*, ed. Wayne A. Grudem (Wheaton, Ill.: Crossway, 2002), 72, refers to the creation of humanity as "the pinnacle of God's creative work."

76. On the biological counterpart-complement concept of pairing between male and female as part of God's design, see Robert A. J. Gagnon, "The Scriptural Case for a Male-Female Prerequisite for Sexual Relations: A Critique of the Arguments of Two Adventist Scholars," *Homosexuality, Marriage, and the Church: Biblical, Counseling, and Religious Liberty Issues*, ed. Roy E. Gane, Nicholas P. Miller, and H. Peter Swanson (Berrien Springs, Mich.: Andrews University Press, 2012), 65–70; and Gagnon, *The Bible and Homosexual Practice: Texts and Hermeneutics* (Nashville, Tenn.: Abingdon, 2001), 58–62.

In this way, the foundation of humanity and society on earth is defined in God's creative life-giving work in the beginning. The assurance of humanity's future is based on following His design. The human race is to be perpetuated from each father and mother, also a man and woman. The gift of God's marriage union is His final act in the physical creation. The institution of the Sabbath in time brings this union into communion with the divine agent of creation, Jesus Christ. Our creation in God's image forms the intended identity we have in Jesus Christ and our acknowledgement of identifying with Him comes in our worshiping on His seventh-day Sabbath. The loving relationship of the Creator with the family is to be perpetuated from the husband and wife to their children, on through the generations of history. There is a sacred trust given to the nuclear family as the basis for the rest of culture and society. As their relationship with God and with each other goes, so goes earth's history. Perhaps it is for this reason that the fifth, seventh, and tenth commandments address the sanctity of marriage in the honor bestowed to parents, ending with the instruction not to covet a neighbor's wife (Exod. 20:17).

In the New Testament, Jesus and the apostles reaffirm the institution of marriage. Jesus responds to an inquiry about divorce from the Pharisees by quoting specifically from Genesis 1 and 2. He says, "Therefore what God has joined together, let not man separate" (Matt. 19:6). Jesus affirms Scripture, and Genesis in particular, by stating that the joining together of man and woman came from God and that which God has divinely ordained should not be separated by humans.

Paul specifically addresses the foundational nature of Genesis in Romans 1:20–28. Beginning with creation, Paul affirms that all humanity through nature could come to understand the reality of the existence of God. But Paul goes on to state that "they exchanged the truth of God for the lie, and worshiped and served the creature rather than the Creator" (v. 25). This choice to believe in a lie led them to their practice: "For this reason God gave them up to vile passions" (v. 26) and what follows is the description of same-sex behavior both between two females and between two males. For Paul, biblically defined sexuality between a man and a woman is "natural" and intrinsic to the very nature of human beings who are created in the image of God (Gen. 1:27). It is the refusal to accept the Creator by exchanging His worship with that of the creature that causes them to be handed over to their lusts. Sexuality then should not be limited merely to behavior and activity; rather, it should be understood within a biblically defined concept of created humanity in totality that provides the framework to reinforce moral behavior.

The nonliteral interpretation of the Genesis creation account has consequential implications for the definition of marriage. The unique gift of marriage between a man and a woman has recently witnessed major attempts at deconstruction and redefinition. Many nations of the world have approved same-sex marriages, overturning previous laws that protected the family structure comprised at its center of one man and one woman. This is an unprecedented development in many respects, raising new questions about the institution of marriage, the separation of church and state, and the sanctity of marriage and the family as defined in Scripture.[77] It raises important questions for Christians. Is marriage, a religious institution that is defined by the Bible, biologically necessary for the creation of life, or is it a personal preference relegated to the sphere of individual human and civil rights? In short, is marriage a human institution defined by culture and society, or is it a biblical institution defined by God? How Christians have responded to these questions has determined the direction of their churches amidst increased cultural pressure. In 2009 the Evangelical Lutheran Church in America and The Episcopal Church USA both, independently, voted to approve homosexual clergy. Lutherans recently elected a practicing gay bishop in California (2013), and the Presbyterian Church USA welcomes practicing homosexuals as ministers and leaders (2011). In Europe, the Scottish Episcopal Church approved same-sex unions in 2017.

What arguments do these churches use to approve same-sex marriage in traditionally Christian countries around the world? Recent books on this subject indicate the key issues in biblical interpretation. These issues involve (1) a redefinition of Genesis 1–2 that emphasizes the culture and setting of the biblical stories, (2) a reinterpretation of key passages in Scripture that have historically

---

77. On religious liberty issues, see Alan Reinach, "Wake Up and Smell the Equality: Same-Sex Marriage and Religious Liberty," in Gane, Miller, and Swanson, *Homosexuality, Marriage, and the Church*, 229–264; and Nancy Pearcey, *Love Thy Body: Answering Hard Questions about Love and Sexuality* (Grand Rapids, Mich.: Baker, 2018).

been seen as prohibiting homosexual behavior, and (3) an application of passages on love and acceptance that take precedence over
clearer passages on the subject.

Those who affirm same-sex relationships reinterpret Genesis in
several ways. Matthew Vines suggests that God needed to provide
Adam with a woman because they were the first parents and were
required to procreate in order to fill the earth but implies that this is
not a necessity today in our world of overpopulation.[78] He subsequently suggests that Genesis 2 does not emphasize Adam and Eve's
differentness, but "their *similarity* as human beings."[79] But while it is
true that Adam speaks of Eve as "bone of my bone and flesh of my
flesh," this is in comparison with all of the different animal species. It
then does not follow that sameness and companionship was all that
mattered, for they also "became one flesh" and here the complementary nature of God's design in making this physically possible
becomes a key element.[80] They were the perfect anatomical match
for each other. Procreation is an essential purpose for marriage
(Gen. 1:27) and, even though not all couples are able to have children, the parental role of a husband and wife is also assumed in the
fifth commandment.

Others suggest that Genesis is merely descriptive and not prescriptive or proscriptive—that it describes what God did but that
God did not make marriage between a man and a woman normative
nor exclude other relationships.[81] But to this we must again appeal
to the fifth commandment, which is certainly proscriptive; to the
laws in Leviticus; and to Jesus and Paul, who both affirm the creation
order as ordained by God and, therefore, natural. In fact, after God
finished the apex of His creation, man and woman, on the sixth day,
He "saw everything that He had made, and indeed it was very good"
(Gen. 1:31). His design was perfect. There was no need in Genesis 1

---

78. Matthew Vines, *God and the Gay Christian* (New York: Convergent, 2014), 45–47; cf.
Jay Michaelson, *God vs. Gay: The Religious Case for Equality* (Boston: Beacon Press, 2012).

79. Vines, *God and the Gay Christian*, 46.

80. Much more than physical union is implied here. In Genesis 4:1 "Adam knew Eve his
wife" and she bore him a son. The term *yāda'* ("to know") can also mean "to experience, to
understand," and "to care about" (Rock, "Marriage and the Family," 725; cf. Pearcey, *Love
Thy Body*, 138: "The reference to *physical* unity was intended to express joyous unity on all
other levels as well—including mind, emotion, and spirit. Scripture offers a stunningly high
view of physical union as a union of the whole person across all dimensions."

81. John R. Jones, "'In Christ There Is Neither . . . ': Toward a Unity of the Body of Christ,"
in *Christianity and Homosexuality*, ed. David Ferguson, Fritz Guy, and David Larson (Roseville,
Calif.: Adventist Forum, 2008), Part 4, 3–42.

and 2 for proscriptive statements. It was only after the introduction of sin that such proscriptions were required.

In the end, a nonliteral view of creation or one that minimizes its normative role in Genesis has major implications for the institution of marriage and this, in turn, has significant effects on other doctrines of Scripture, including the unity and harmony of Scripture, the doctrine of humanity, grace, the church, the great controversy, and the character of God.[82]

THE ORIGIN OF SIN, DEATH, AND THE PLAN OF REDEMPTION

The world was created in perfect order. This is indicated by God's six declarations during the creation narrative that what He created was "good" (Gen. 1:4, 10, 12, 18, 21, 25) and the seventh time when "God saw all that he had made . . . was very good" (Gen. 1:31, NIV).[83] There is no indication that death existed before the Fall, as indicated by several important parameters.[84] Animals and humans are both given a vegetarian diet, eliminating the need to kill (Gen. 1:29–30). God warns Adam and Eve of the tree of the knowledge of good and evil and that the consequences of eating from that tree would be death (Gen. 2:16–17). This happens *before* the serpent tempts Eve (Gen. 3:1–4).[85] When Eve and then Adam eat of the tree of the knowledge of good and evil (Gen. 3:6–7), the perfect

---

82. Richard M. Davidson, "Homosexuality and the Bible: What is at Stake in the Current Debate," in Gane, Miller, and Swanson, *Homosexuality, Marriage and the Church*, 187–208.

83. Several patterns of seven are found in Genesis 1:1—2:3: (1) the seven consecutive days, (2) God's seven affirmations that what He created was good and then very good, and (3) the repetition of the word *bara'* seven times.

84. Hans Madueme and Michael Reeves, eds., *Adam, the Fall, and Original Sin: Theological, Biblical and Scientific Perspectives* (Grand Rapids, Mich.: Baker Academic, 2014).

85. For the identification of the serpent in the Fall account of Genesis 3 and the fall and role of Satan before humanity's disobedience, see José M. Bertoluci, *The Son of the Morning and the Guardian Cherub in the Context of the Controversy between Good and Evil* (ThD diss., Andrews University, 1985); Norman R. Gulley, *Systematic Theology*, vol. 3, *Creation, Christ, Salvation* (Berrien Springs, Mich.: Andrews University Press, 2012), 137–39; Gulley, *Systematic Theology*, vol. 2, *Prolegomena* (2003), 191–92, 390–453; Walter C. Kaiser Jr., *The Messiah in the Old Testament* (Grand Rapids, Mich.: Zondervan, 1995), 38–42; C. F. Keil and F. Delitzsch, "The First Book of Moses (Genesis)" in *Biblical Commentary on the Old Testament* (Peabody, Mass.: Hendrickson, 2006), 57–59, 62–64; and Kenneth A. Mathews, *Genesis 1–11:26: An Exegetical and Theological Exposition of Holy Scripture*, NAC (Nashville, Tenn.: Broadman and Holman, 1996), 232–35.

creation is undone by the entrance of sin.[86] Several consequences result from their disobedience.[87] Their eyes are opened (Gen. 3:7). They recognize that they are naked and are filled with shame, sewing fig leaves to cover themselves (Gen. 3:7). They hide from God (Gen. 3:8). Adam blames Eve and Eve blames the serpent for the Fall (Gen. 3:12–13). God pronounces a curse and the result of sin, which will bring with it pain and suffering (Gen. 3:14–19). God drives Adam and Eve from the garden (Gen. 3:22–23). Cherubim are placed to guard the entrance, indicating a separation (Gen. 3:24). Cain murders his brother Abel in the very next chapter (Gen. 4:1–8).

The New Testament reaffirms a literal understanding of Adam and the origin of sin and death.[88] Paul attributes the responsibility of sin to Adam and refers to him specifically as "one man." "Sin entered the world through one man, and death through sin, and in this way death came to all people" (Rom. 5:12, NIV). Adam's act in Genesis 3 seals the fate of humanity in the transgression of God's command.[89] "Death reigned from Adam to Moses, even over those who had not sinned according to the likeness of the transgression of Adam, who is a type of Him who was to come" (Rom. 5:14). Just to make it perfectly clear, Paul reiterates, "As through one man's offense *judgment came* to all men, resulting in condemnation, even so through one Man's righteous act *the free gift came* to all men, resulting in justification of life" (Rom. 5:18). Norman Gulley writes, "It was Adam and not His Creator who brought death to this planet. It was Christ who came to die to put death to death and liberate the fallen race (Rom. 4:25). It was the one act of the first Adam that caused this death-condemnation, and the one act of the second Adam's death that provided salvation (Rom. 5:18). Christ did not use death to create humans in Eden, He died to save humans at Calvary."[90]

---

86. Niels-Erik A. Andreasen, "Death: Origin, Nature, and Final Eradication," in *HSDAT*, 318–19; Jacques B. Doukhan, "'When Death Was Not Yet': The Testimony of Biblical Creation," in Klingbeil, *Genesis Creation Account*, 329–42.

87. On several essential consequences to the Fall and sin, see Moskala, "Genesis 3 as a Model for Understanding the Nature of Sin and Salvation," *JATS* 27, nos. 1–2 (2016): 134–42.

88. On the New Testament analysis of these passages and their direct link to a literal creation of Adam as the first man, see J. P. Versteeg, *Adam in the New Testament: Mere Teaching Model or First Historical Man?*, 2nd ed., trans. Richard B. Gaffin Jr., (Phillipsburg, N.J.: P&R, 2012); and Guy Prentiss Waters, "Theistic Evolution is Incompatible with the Teachings of the New Testament," in Moreland et al., *Theistic Evolution*, 879–926.

89. John M. Fowler, "Sin," in *HSDAT*, 241–42.

90. Gulley, "Theistic Evolution," 48.

Paul affirms this when he says, "The wages of sin is death, but the gift of God is eternal life in Christ Jesus our Lord" (Rom. 6:23). This promise of the Messiah is already given in Genesis 3:15, inaugurating for humanity the plan of salvation.[91] "Actually the major premise of all of Scripture is that death is an abnormal state connected with human moral guilt and not connected with an evolutionary past (Pss. 6:5; 30:9; 55:15; Prov. 5:5; 7:27; 12:28; Isa. 28:15; Jer. 21:8; 1 Cor. 15:43; Rev. 21:8)."[92]

What, then, are the implications of a nonliteral view of creation that assumes millions of years of naturalistic evolution? An evolutionary perspective would have death present for millions of years prior to the arrival of human beings. Death would be a necessary element of the process to life as thousands of species attempt to be the fittest to survive. The mythical worldview sees death and life as inseparable. In some ideologies, like ancient Egypt, death is where life originates.[93] There is an incessant cycle of death and life,[94] and conflict and violence are a necessary source of life in the mythical idea of continuity.[95] This has serious implications for the biblical view of a transcendent God who created everything perfect and for the origin of sin and its result: death. To separate death as the consequential result of sin, scientists and theologians must reinterpret the first chapters of Genesis and Paul's teachings in light of modern theories of naturalism. Hugh Ross writes, "There is nothing in Scripture that compels us to conclude that none of these entities [decay, work, physical death, pain,

---

91. Kaiser, *Messiah in the Old Testament*, 38–42; Afolarin O. Ojewole, *The Seed in Genesis 3:15: An Exegetical and Intertextual Study*, ATSDS (Berrien Springs, Mich.: Adventist Theological Society, 2002), 126–34; and Wenham, *Genesis 1–15*, 72–91.

92. William Edgar, "Adam, History, and Theodicy," in Madueme and Reeves, *Adam, the Fall, and Original Sin*, 313.

93. Gerhard F. Hasel and Michael G. Hasel, "Unique Cosmology," 27–29; cf. Ángel M. Rodríguez, "Biblical Creationism and Ancient Near Eastern Evolutionary Ideas," in Klingbeil, *The Genesis Creation Account and Its Reverberations in the Old Testament*, 293–328.

94. John N. Oswalt, *The Bible among the Myths: Unique Revelation or Just Ancient Literature?* (Grand Rapids, Mich.: Zondervan, 2009), 61–62.

95. Ibid., 59. E.g., in the Babylonian *Enuma Elish*, Tiamat, the mythical Babylonian monster and goddess of the primeval world ocean, is slain by the creator god Marduk in combat; see George A. Barton, "Tiamat," *JAOS* 15 (1893): 1–27; Gunkel, *Schöpfung und Chaos*; Thorkild Jacobsen, "The Battle between Marduk and Tiamat," *JAOS* 88 (1968): 104–8; and Mary K. Wakeman, *God's Battle with the Monster: A Study in Biblical Imagery* (Leiden: Brill, 1973), 16–22. Likewise, in the Atrahasis Epic, humanity is created from the flesh and blood of a slaughtered god mixed with clay, but "no hint of the use of dead deity or any other material of a living one is found in Genesis" (Millard, "'Genesis' Story," 10. See also Gordon H. Johnston, "Genesis 1 and Ancient Egyptian Creation Myths," *BSac* 165 [2008]: 187); and see Gerhard F. Hasel and Michael G. Hasel, "Unique Cosmology," 16–18, 22–23.

and suffering] existed before Adam's first act of rebellion against God. On the other hand, God's revelation through nature provides overwhelming evidence that all of these aspects did indeed exist a long time period previous to God's creating Adam."[96] Likewise, John Walton argues that death was a part of the non-ordered world before the archetype Everyone, Adam, came to the world.[97]

If death were present before Adam, then what would be the implications for Christ's substitutionary death on the cross and the plan of redemption? Was Christ's death on the cross truly to pay the legal price for our sin and to eradicate death once and for all? Is His death not the fulfillment of Genesis 3:15, when He becomes the serpent for us though He never sinned (John 3:14–15)? The theological implications of this should not be underestimated.[98] As Richard B. Gaffin Jr. has titled his book *No Adam, No Gospel*,[99] to remove death as the wages of sin strikes at the heart of the gospel. If death is not related to sin, then the wages of sin is not death, and Christ would have had no reason to die on the cross of Calvary for our sins.[100] To remove a literal creation together with a literal Adam and Eve, made in the image of God, would remove our hope that we might someday be restored to that image by the one who died to pay the ultimate price for our sins.

THE OLD CREATION AND THE HOPE OF A NEW CREATION

The second advent of Christ is a cherished hope of every believer. In the Old Testament God promises, "Behold, I create new heavens and a new earth" (Isa. 65:17) and it "shall remain before me" (Isa. 66:22). The new earth will be a place of peace and life restored for "the wolf and the lamb shall feed together, the lion shall eat straw like the ox" (Isa. 65:25). The very terminology of "heavens" and "earth" together with the same verb *bārā'*, now as an imperfect and

---

96. Hugh Ross, *Creation and Time* (Colorado Springs, Colo.: NavPress, 1994), 69.

97. Walton, *Lost World of Adam and Eve*, 93.

98. Zinke, "Theistic Evolution," 164–65; Gregg R. Allison, "Theistic Evolution is Incompatible with Historical Christian Doctrine," in *Theistic Evolution*, 940–41.

99. Richard B. Gaffin Jr., *No Adam, No Gospel: Adam and the History of Redemption* (Philadelphia: P&R, 2015).

100. Marco T. Terreros, *Theistic Evolution and Its Theological Implications* (Medellín: MARTER Editions, 2002); Terreros, "Is All Death the Consequence of Sin? Theological Implications of Alternative Models," *JATS* 14, no. 1 (2003): 150–75; and Reinhard Junker, *Leben durch Sterben? Schöpfung, Heilsgeschichte und Evolution*, 2nd ed. (Neuhausen/Stuttgart: Hänssler-Verlag, 2004).

future reality, harkens back to the beginning of Genesis 1–2. Isaiah's statements indicate that the new creation is intimately bound up with the first—one where no violence was present and where animals could live together in harmony without fear, for "there shall be no more curse" (Rev. 22:3).

The biblical view of history is linear, moving forward with a purpose and goal in mind.[101] Jesus is affirmed as "Him who is from the beginning" (1 John 2:14), and in Revelation three times as "the Alpha and the Omega" (Rev. 1:8; 21:6; 22:13), twice as "the Beginning and the End" (Rev. 21:6; 22:13), and once as "the First and the Last" (Rev. 22:13). Christ, who set time in motion for human existence in the beginning, will set in place "a new heaven and a new earth, for the first heaven and the first earth had passed away. . . . And God will wipe away every tear from their eyes; there shall be no more death, nor sorrow, nor crying. There shall be no more pain, for the former things have passed away" (Rev. 21:1–4). Once again this new act of creation experienced at the resurrection will be instantaneous at the sound of the voice of Jesus when all will "be changed in a moment, in the twinkling of an eye, at the last trumpet" (1 Cor. 15:51 –52). Jesus, speaking of the new earth, says, "Behold, I am making all things new. . . . Write, for these words are faithful and true" (Rev. 21:5). God promises a new creation that is just as perfect as the first—a place where "there shall be no more death, neither sorrow, nor crying, neither shall there be any more pain: for the former things are passed away" (Rev. 21:4, KJV). There will be no more sin (Rev. 21:7) and no more curse (Rev. 22:3).[102]

But even if a perfect heaven were possible in view of millions of years of naturalistic evolution or progressive creation, what hope would there be for a "new" creation? Would God take another six hundred million years to let it evolve? It is interesting to look again at the views of some of the leading proponents of a nonliteral creation in Genesis. For historical-critics and neoorthodox theologians like Bultmann, the presuppositions of modernism could not support a literal view of heaven.[103] N. T. Wright, who believes in theistic

---

101. Michael G. Hasel, "History, the Bible, and Hermeneutics."

102. Roberto Badenas, "New Jerusalem—The Holy City," in *Symposium on Revelation— Book II*, ed. Frank B. Holbrook, Daniel and Revelation Committee Series 7 (Silver Spring, Md.: Biblical Research Institute, 1992), 249–56; and Kenneth Mathews, *Revelation Reveals Jesus*, 2 vols. (Greeneville, Tenn.: Second Coming, 2012), 2:1081–32.

103. Rudolph Bultmann, *Myth and the New Testament* (London: SCM, 1960), 20–21.

evolution and does not believe that Adam and Eve were literal people, also does not believe in a literal second coming or a literal heaven. Thus when Paul speaks of the Lord descending in 1 Thessalonians, "he is finding richly metaphorical ways of alluding to three other stories that he is deliberately bringing together . . . the reality to which it refers is this: Jesus will be personally present."[104] Again as with the Sabbath and with a literal Adam and Eve, the writings of the Old Testament and New Testament on the important issue of the second coming and heaven need to be reinterpreted to accommodate a naturalistic worldview that limits what the writers themselves affirm as their hope and reality.[105]

CONCLUSION

For the biblical writers, Christ's resurrection, ascension, and promises were evidence for this hope. Belief in creation gives us the assurance of a new creation that is close at hand. It encourages us to nurture our environment. It gives us the incentive to endure the trials and tribulations of today (2 Cor. 4:16–17) and live pure and upright lives that give us the joy and certainty of our reward tomorrow (Matt. 5:12). It is in this certainty, and as a memorial to the first creation, that we worship every Sabbath. It is this truth that assures us of Christ's soon return. For He has promised, "I go to prepare a place for you. And if I go and prepare a place for you, I will come again and receive you to Myself; that where I am, there you may be also" (John 14:2–3). Jesus was going to heaven and invited His disciples and us to spend eternity with Him, when all will be restored again to what He created in the beginning.

---

104. N. T. Wright, *Surprised by Hope: Rethinking Heaven, the Resurrection, and the Mission of the Church* (New York: HarperOne, 2008), 132–33.

105. Most preterist and idealist interpreters of Revelation argue that the new Jerusalem is not a literal city but representative of either (1) the people of God (see G. K. Beale, *The Book of Revelation*, NIGTC [Grand Rapids, Mich.: Eerdmans, 1999], 1062; and David E. Aune, *Revelation 17–22*, WBC 52C [Waco, Tex.: Word, 1982], 1187) or (2) the victory of God (see J. Massyngberde Ford, *Revelation*, AB 38 [Garden City, N.Y.: Doubleday, 1975], 366).

Kayle B. de Waal, PhD

Avondale University College
Cooranbong, New South Wales,
Australia

CREATION, NEW CREATION, AND RESURRECTION

INTRODUCTION

This chapter studies the biblical concepts of creation, new creation, and resurrection and how they interact and intersect with each other theologically and intertextually. This study is conducted in the framework of biblical theology, which is concerned with developing a theology from the whole Bible, both Old and New Testaments, that takes seriously the self-consistency of Scripture and the unified message Scripture conveys in the person and work of Jesus Christ. According to Gerhard Hasel, "biblical theology employs the theological-historical method which takes full account of God's self-revelation embodied in Scripture in all its dimensions of reality."[1]

Creation introduces the biblical narrative and is critical for understanding human beginnings. Aspects of the Genesis creation story will be examined to provide the theological foundation for the New Testament aspect of the study. The specific term "new creation" (*kainē ktisis*) does not occur in the Septuagint and occurs only twice

---

1. Gerhard Hasel, "The Future of Biblical Theology," in *Perspectives on Evangelical Theology*, ed. K. Kantzer and S. Gundry (Grand Rapids, Mich.: Baker, 1979), 184. See the important contribution of Scott Hafeman, ed., *Biblical Theology: Retrospect and Prospect* (Downers Grove, Ill.: InterVarsity, 2002).

in the New Testament (2 Cor. 5:17; Gal. 6:15), but its witness perme-
ates Scripture (Ps. 51:10; 104:29–30; Matt. 19:28; John 3:1–8; Acts
3:21; Rom. 6:4; 2 Cor. 4:16; Eph. 2:15; 4:23–24; Titus 3:5; 2 Pet.
3:13).[2] This study argues that the subject of new creation in the New
Testament references passages in the latter part of Isaiah and, to a
lesser extent, Jeremiah and Ezekiel. These promises, in part, shape
the New Testament belief in resurrection that will form the latter
part of this chapter.

CREATION AND THE IMAGE OF GOD

God—eternal, infinite, and supernatural—created this world *ex
nihilo* (Ps. 90:2; Isa. 44:24; 45:18; 48:12–13; Rom. 4:17; Heb.
11:3).[3] Yet, despite His eternality, God acts in a temporal way in
human history, through sequential acts intended to bring about His
purposes.[4] God created a perfect world for human beings to enjoy
(Gen. 1–2). That enjoyment was to take place in the direct presence
of God in the garden of Eden (Gen. 2:15–25; 3:8). Since God is envel-
oped in light (Ps. 104:2; 1 Tim. 6:16), Adam and Eve, in their perfect
state, were likely cloaked in light too (Ps. 8:5). God called Adam to
steward the garden (Gen. 2:15). This stewardship must be understood in the context of God's image and the first "great commission"
in Genesis 1:26–28.[5] The commission involves the following elements: (1) "God blessed them," (2) "be fruitful and increase," (3) "fill
the earth," (4) "subdue it," and (5) "rule over."[6] Because Adam and
Eve were made in God's image, they governed the creatures and the
world that God had created for them.[7] Walter Brueggemann argues

---

2. Moyer V. Hubbard, *New Creation in Paul's Letters and Thought*, SNTSMS 119 (Cambridge: Cambridge University Press, 2002), 1.

3. See the discussion in Norman R. Gulley, *Creation, Christ, Salvation*, vol. 3 of *Systematic
Theology* (Berrien Springs, Mich.: Andrews University Press, 2012), 33–38; see also discussion regarding creation *ex nihilo* in Ekkehardt Mueller, "Creation in the New Testament," 11,
and in Félix H. Cortez, "Creation in Hebrews," 323, in this present volume.

4. Gulley, *Systematic Theology: Creation, Christ, Salvation*, 3:xxi, 6.

5. G. K. Beale, *A New Testament Biblical Theology: The Unfolding of the Old Testament in
the New* (Grand Rapids, Mich.: Baker, 2011), 57.

6. Unless otherwise indicated, Scripture quotations in this chapter are taken from the
Holy Bible, New International Version®, NIV®. Copyright © 1973, 1978, 1984, 2011 by
Biblica, Inc.™ Used by permission of Zondervan. All rights reserved worldwide. www.
zondervan.com The "NIV" and "New International Version" are trademarks registered in
the United States Patent and Trademark Office by Biblica, Inc.™

7. According to John H. Walton, *Genesis*, NIVAC (Grand Rapids, Mich.: Zondervan, 2001),
130, in Mesopotamian culture the importance "of the image can be seen in the practise of

that while it is a mandate of power and responsibility to govern, it is power used for service to the created order.[8] Furthermore, he contends that being made in God's image points to the freedom and authority that human beings have over creation.

In the ancient Near East, the king, as the image of the god, was understood as a royal figure who "represents the god by virtue of his royal office and is portrayed as acting like the god in specific royal ways."[9] Norman Gulley argues that *"male and female together* were to share in this co-rule, even as each member of the Trinity shares in their co-rule."[10] As royal rulers, Adam and Eve represented God. One of their tasks was to pass on the image of God to their posterity. While they could not create, they were nonetheless to procreate and fill the earth.[11] Just as God divided the waters and brought light from darkness, showing His rulership, so Adam and Eve were to rule over the creatures of the world. The phenomenon of sin entered the human story when Adam and Eve chose to rebel against God's will. Sin broke relationships (Gen. 3:10), severed trust (Gen. 3:12), and fostered animosity (Gen. 3:17–19). The cosmic conflict that began in heaven (Rev. 12:4) descended to the earth. Eve was enticed and deceived by the serpent and believed and obeyed his words rather than the words of God. After Adam and Eve sinned, they made fig-leaf aprons for themselves (Gen. 3:7). The light of God's presence was no longer evident and they had to cover their shame. However, God made garments of skin for Adam and Eve (Gen. 3:21), effectively portraying the death of Jesus Christ that was still to come (1 Cor. 5:7). One of the consequences of sin, pertinent for this study, is that while the image of God remains within human beings (Rom. 2:15; 1 Cor. 11:7a; James 3:9), it has been damaged and distorted (Rom. 5:12–21).

With its themes of creation, loss, and the promise of restoration, the Genesis creation story becomes the archetypal story that serves

---

kings setting up images for themselves in places where they want to establish their authority."

8. Walter Brueggemann, *Genesis*, Interpretation (Atlanta: John Knox, 1982), 32.

9. J. Richard Middleton, *The Liberating Image: The Imago Dei in Genesis 1* (Grand Rapids, Mich.: Brazos, 2005), 12; and Catherine McDowell, *The Image of God in the Garden of Eden: The Creation of Humankind in Gen. 2:5–3:24 in Light of mīs pî pīt pî and wpt-r Rituals of Mesopotamia and Ancient Egypt*, Siphrut 15 (Winona Lake, Ind.: Eisenbrauns, 2015), 136–37.

10. Gulley, *Systematic Theology: Creation, Christ, Salvation*, 3:89. See also Andrew Reid, *Salvation Begins: Reading Genesis Today* (Sydney: Aquila, 2000), 9.

11. Walton, *Genesis*, 137, suggests that the image also refers to human dignity, responsibility, and the capacity to mirror our Creator.

as the typological foundation for the rest of God's divine activity in Scripture.[12]

Cycles of Typology within Biblical History				
Genesis/new creation	Exodus and new creation through the Red Sea	Exodus and new creation through the Jordan River (Red Sea)	Exodus and new creation through the return from Babylonian exile	Heightened new exodus and new creation through Christ's life, death, and resurrection

These biblical patterns suggest that typology involves a historical event that is repeated at a higher level—a wider application—in a later parallel historical event. This typological understanding and pattern would indicate that when the later prophets and New Testament writers think typologically, they are in fact taking the Genesis 1–2 creation account as historical in nature. Aspects of these cycles will be addressed in the following discussion.

NEW CREATION IN ISAIAH

God's Word reveals knowledge and truth progressively (Prov. 4:18). In fact, God is faithful to His promise even after generations have passed. The new creation motif emerges explicitly in Isaiah (42:9; 43:16–19; 48:6; 65:17–25; 66:22). Yahweh's prophetic power is evident when He says "See, the former things have taken place, and new things I declare; before they spring into being I announce them to you" (Isa. 42:9).

Isaiah develops the concepts of newness and renewal once more in chapters 65 and 66, where God declares His intention to "create new heavens and a new earth" (Isa. 65:17). This act of God involves a

---

12. The table is adapted from Beale, *New Testament Biblical Theology*, 60. Typological interpretation is central to both the Old and New Testament. See, e.g., Dale Allison, *The New Moses: A Matthean Typology* (Minneapolis, Minn.: Fortress, 1993), in which he provides ample Old Testament examples. Further, E. Ellis, *History and Interpretation in New Testament Perspective*, Biblical Interpretation Series 54 (Leiden: Brill, 2001), 115, states that "typological interpretation expresses most clearly the basic approach of earliest Christianity toward the Old Testament." For a comprehensive analysis of the typological interpretation of the Old Testament in the New Testament, see L. Goppelt, *Typos: The Typological Interpretation of the Old Testament in the New* (Grand Rapids, Mich.: Eerdmans, 1982). See also Richard M. Davidson, *Typology in Scripture: A Study of Hermeneutical Structures* (Berrien Springs, Mich.: Andrews University Press, 1981).

complete restructuring of life. It is a whole new order of reality and existence. It is so new that the past is forgotten completely (Isa. 65:19–20, 23–25). The existence of God's people will no longer be insecure, but safe (Isa. 65:22). It will be full of joy (v. 18), fulfilling work (v. 22b), fellowship with God (vv. 23–24), and peace (v. 25).[13] This would have brought hope to the Jewish nation, whose sin threatened to destroy its hope in God. The hopelessness of the exile was replaced by the promise of a renewed covenant and the establishment of God's kingdom on earth.

The new creation motif is also connected to other prophetic hopes, like a new Davidic king (Isa. 11:1–6; Ezek. 34:23; Mic. 5:1–5), a new covenant (Jer. 31:31–34), and the reception of God's Spirit (Ezek. 36:26–27).[14] Furthermore, alongside the concept of new creation is that of new exodus (Isa. 40:3; 43:16–19). The concepts of new creation and new exodus are integrated in Isaiah.[15] Michael Bird contends that "Isaiah explains that the *new exodus* that awaits the exiles in Babylon will be on such a scale of grandeur that the only way to properly describe it is with the imagery of a *new creation*."[16]

NEW CREATION IN PAULINE THOUGHT

The Jewish longing for a future solution to their existential problems found its fulfillment in the Messiah, Jesus Christ (Matt. 1:21–22). Paul acknowledges that the age of end-time fulfillment has been inaugurated with Christ's first coming (2 Cor. 4:4; Gal. 1:4; Eph. 2:7).[17] He understands Christ to be the fulfillment of the basic plan and intent of the whole Old Testament. Christ is the center of history and key to interpreting Scripture (1 Cor. 10:13).[18] Further, Paul acknowledges that the Christian's experience is based on a

---

13. Barry Webb, *The Message of Isaiah* (Downers Grove, Ill.: InterVarsity, 1996), 245.

14. T. Ryan Jackson, *New Creation in Paul's Letters: A Study of the History and Social Setting of a Pauline Concept*, WUNT, 2nd ser., vol. 272 (Tübingen: Mohr Siebeck, 2010), 18–32. See also Richard M. Davidson, "New Testament Use of the Old Testament," *JATS* 5/1 (1994): 14–39.

15. See similar comments in Scott J. Hafemann, *2 Corinthians*, NIVAC (Grand Rapids, Mich.: Zondervan, 2000), 243.

16. Michael F. Bird, *Evangelical Theology: A Biblical and Systematic Theology* (Grand Rapids, Mich.: Zondervan, 2013), 152.

17. For a complete discussion of this concept, see G. Ladd, *A Theology of the New Testament*, rev. ed. (Grand Rapids, Mich.: Eerdmans, 1994), 54–68.

18. G. K. Beale, *John's Use of the Old Testament*, JSOTSup 166 (Sheffield: Sheffield Academic Press, 1998), 45, 127.

tension between the "already" and the "not yet." In Christ, Christians have already crucified the flesh (Gal. 5:24) yet are told to put to death the deeds of the body (Rom. 8:13). Christians are already transformed (2 Cor. 3:18; 4:16–17) yet are called to be transformed (Rom. 12:2). In the same way, God unfolds the new creation within an "already/not yet" perspective. The new creation is now with us. For "if anyone is in Christ, the new creation has come: The old has gone, the new is here!" (2 Cor. 5:17). Yet we await its final and complete establishment: "But in keeping with his promise we are looking forward to a new heaven and a new earth, where righteousness dwells" (2 Pet. 3:13; see also Rom. 8:1–11).

For Paul, the new creation is inaugurated in and through the death and resurrection of Jesus Christ. However, the exact meaning of "new creation" (*kainē ktisis*) in Paul's writings is debated in the academic literature. Paul Minear argues that new creation can be interpreted anthropologically and eschatologically.[19] Richard Hays and Thomas Schreiner contend that the term must be interpreted from a cosmic eschatological perspective.[20] Moyer Hubbard argues that the term refers to a soterio-anthropological reality rather than a soterio-cosmological one.[21] Taking these perspectives into account, this study argues that the *kainē ktisis* has rich ontological, communal, eschatological, experiential, pneumatological, and evangelistic dimensions.

This study will examine the use of the phrase "new creation" in Galatians and Corinthians. The combined insights gathered from the analysis of the passages and a consideration of their Old Testament background will be brought to bear on the reading of the phrase "new creation." The Galatian texts are briefly examined first:

> Those who want to impress people by means of the flesh are trying to compel you to be circumcised. The only reason they do this is to avoid being persecuted for the cross of Christ. Not even those who are circumcised keep the law, yet they want you to be circumcised that they may boast about your circumcision in the flesh. May I never

---

19. Paul Sevier Minear, *Christians and the New Creation: Genesis Motifs in the New Testament* (Louisville, Ky.: Westminster John Knox, 1994), 6.

20. Richard Hays, *The Moral Vision of the New Testament: Community, Cross, New Creation: A Contemporary Introduction to New Testament Ethics* (San Francisco, Calif.: HarperSanFrancisco, 1996), 19–21; and Thomas R. Schreiner, *Galatians*, ZECNT (Grand Rapids, Mich.: Zondervan, 2010), 385–86.

21. Hubbard, *New Creation*, 238.

boast except in the cross of our Lord Jesus Christ, through which the world has been crucified to me, and I to the world. Neither circumcision nor uncircumcision means anything; what counts is the new creation. Peace and mercy to all who follow this rule—to the Israel of God. (Gal. 6:12–16)

This passage is a fitting end to Paul's letter. Ben Witherington suggests that it builds upon a series of antitheses between Paul's position and that of the troublemakers: living under the old age or as part of the new creation, boasting in circumcision or the cross, and accepting or rejecting persecution.[22]

Judaizers were concerned about outward conformity to the law. They could boast about the rite of circumcision, since they belonged to the covenant community.[23] F. F. Bruce points out, however, that "boasting belonged to the old order of law (cf. Rom. 2:23) and flesh (cf. Phil. 3:4); it is excluded from the new order of faith," especially with regard to boasting as a means of attaining salvation.[24] Paul's point is that circumcision as an attempt to outwardly conform to the law provides no grounds for confidence; only Christ's death on our behalf is sufficient (Gal. 6:12–14). Moreover, if circumcision means nothing anymore, so too does uncircumcision. Martinus De Boer contends that "the religious, ethnic, and cultural distinctions caused by a world divided into circumcision and uncircumcision have, in Paul's view, been violently replaced by a 'new creation' (kainē ktisis)."[25] Paul holds that the Judaizers want to boast about their outward conformity to the law as a means to impress people and avoid being persecuted for the cross of Christ.[26] It is this very cross in which Paul boasts. The cross was an ignoble object of unrivalled shame in the ancient world. The ancients viewed it with great

---

22. Ben Witherington III, *Grace in Galatia: A Commentary on Paul's Letter to the Galatians* (Grand Rapids, Mich.: Eerdmans, 1998), 445.

23. R. Alan Cole, *Galatians*, TNTC (Grand Rapids, Mich.: Eerdmans, 1997), 234. Cf. Mark D. Nanos, *The Irony of Galatians: Paul's Letter in First-Century Context* (Minneapolis, Minn.: Fortress, 2002), 223, who understands the Judaizers, so termed in traditional scholarship, as influencers who "do not want to suffer status disapproval and the loss of legal rights and privileges that they have gained."

24. F. F. Bruce, *Commentary on Galatians*, NIGTC (Grand Rapids, Mich.: Eerdmans, 1982), 270.

25. Martinus C. De Boer, *Galatians*, NTL (Louisville, Ky.: Westminster John Knox, 2011), 402. Similarly, see Charles B. Cousar, *Galatians*, Interpretation (Richmond, Va.: John Knox, 1982), 155.

26. Richard Longenecker, *Galatians*, WBC 41 (Dallas: Word, 1990), 293.

disdain and loathing. Yet, Paul boasts in the cross for it contains the wisdom and power of God (1 Cor. 1:17–18).[27]

Hence, Paul can emphatically state in Galatians 6:15, "Neither circumcision nor uncircumcision means anything; what counts is the new creation." Verse 16 reveals that this has indeed the force of a principle or a rule: "Peace and mercy to all who follow this rule [kanōn]—to the Israel of God." In Paul's logic, the death and resurrection of Christ stands parallel with the new creation. Death inaugurates life—not just any death, but the death of the Son of God, the Creator (Col. 1:16–17; Heb. 1:1–3). Only the Creator can bring life out of death.

The new creation motif points to the status of the genuine Christian that Paul is articulating for the imprudent Galatians. The old creation is characterized by life in the flesh (Gal. 1:1, 10–12; 2:16; 6:1). The flesh is weak, flawed, morally decadent, and sinful. The new creation takes place when a person identifies with and participates in Christ's death by faith (Gal. 6:14).[28] The flesh—the old life— is crucified with Christ. The new creation is fundamentally christological and cruciform (Gal. 5:24).

There is an ontological transformation that occurs when a person receives new life through faith. Paul writes, "I have been crucified with Christ and I no longer live, but Christ lives in me. The life I now live in the body, I live by faith in the Son of God, who loved me and gave himself for me" (Gal. 2:20). Christ exchanges the old life of sin and provides His own life in its place. The believer is now found "in Christ" (Gal. 3:26–28) and they belong to Him (Gal. 3:29; 5:24). They are no longer under the lordship of Adam, but are now under the lordship of Christ. "So in Christ Jesus you are all children of God through faith" (Gal. 3:26). The apostle boldly declares that everyone who believes in Jesus is now a son (or daughter) of the living God. The believer's identity has been radically changed.

Furthermore, pneumatological restoration takes place in the life of the believer. The believer is possessed by the Spirit (Gal. 3:3; 4:6). Galatians 3:3 reads, "Are you so foolish? After beginning by means of the Spirit, are you now trying to finish by means of the flesh?" The phrase "beginning by means of the Spirit" refers to the beginning of the believer's new life in Christ, at which time the gift of the Spirit is

---

27. Bruce, *Commentary on Galatians*, 271.
28. James D. G. Dunn, *The Epistle to the Galatians*, BNTC (London: Black, 1993), 341.

received.[29] The believer lives a life of dependence on and submission to the Spirit as a child of God (Gal. 5:16–18; 6:8).

Galatians 6:15 must be understood in the context of Galatians 5:6.

Galatians 6:15	Galatians 5:6
"Neither circumcision nor uncircumcision means anything; what counts is the new creation."	"For in Christ Jesus neither circumcision nor uncircumcision has any value. The only thing that counts is faith expressing itself through love."

Bringing these two verses together adds a new layer of meaning to the concept of new creation. New creation also refers to "faith expressing itself through love." Faith does not express itself in isolation. The phrase refers to loving service for others done through faith. This service is rendered in and through the Israel of God— Jews and Gentiles in the Galatian community of faith who have accepted Christ as Lord and Savior.

These radical Galatian images that combine to define *kainē ktisis* include an experiential faith encounter with Jesus Christ that fundamentally alters the person. This encounter transforms the believer's interior life and exterior perspective (Gal. 5:22–24). According to Paul's theology, God has broken into human time and space (Gal. 1:4) and brought the eschatological promise of salvation into the present age.

Paul's comments in relation to the new creation in 2 Corinthians 5:17 have similar theological and hermeneutical connections, but differences will also be demonstrated.

> So from now on we regard no one from a worldly point of view. Though we once regarded Christ in this way, we do so no longer. Therefore, if anyone is in Christ, the new creation has come: The old has gone, the new is here! All this is from God, who reconciled us to himself through Christ and gave us the ministry of reconciliation: that God was reconciling the world to himself in Christ, not counting people's sins against them. And he has committed to us the message of reconciliation. (2 Cor. 5:16–19)

Most scholars suggest that in verse 16 Paul takes as his point of departure the death and resurrection of Jesus and its effects upon

---

29. Longenecker, *Galatians*, 103. See also Dunn, *Epistle to the Galatians*, 156; and Bruce, *Commentary on Galatians*, 150.

believers.[30] Paul will no longer regard others from a worldly point of view because of the death of Christ (v. 14). This death has purchased freedom for all who accept it by faith and has fundamentally changed how Paul views the world.

Humanity for Paul is either in Adam or in Christ. Paul uses the "in Christ" motif and related phrases over one hundred times in his writings.[31] A rich range of soteriological blessings is found in Christ, as depicted in New Testament writings (Rom. 3:24; 6:11, 23; 1 Cor. 1:4, 30; Gal. 3:14, 26; Eph. 2:10; 4:32). The "in Christ" soteriological elements of justification, holiness, redemption, sanctification, and others are all experiential and personal.[32] In the same way, the "new creation" in the immediate literary context of 2 Corinthians 5:17 refers to the experiential and personal reality of being in Christ. G. K. Beale argues on the basis of the verbal parallels of "old" (*ta archaia*), "behold" (*idou*), and "new" (*kaina*), as well as thematic parallels of restoration and new creation, that Paul is alluding to Isaiah 43:18–19.[33] He argues "that reconciliation in Christ is Paul's way of explaining that Isaiah's promises of restoration from the alienation of exile have begun to be fulfilled by the atonement and forgiveness of sins in Christ."[34] Paul applies a promise made to Israel to the Gentile Christians in Corinth. In this way, Paul is contending that the death and resurrection of Jesus have inaugurated true Israel—the church—into the presence of God.[35]

Paul clarifies for his audience that the old way of looking at the world is gone, as are the people who live in that world. The implication is that the old way of thinking, relating, and perceiving is gone.

---

30. Hafemann, *2 Corinthians*, 241; Murray J. Harris, *The Second Epistle to the Corinthians: A Commentary on the Greek Text* (Grand Rapids, Mich.: Eerdmans, 2005), 424; Ralph P. Martin, *2 Corinthians*, WBC 40 (Dallas: Word, 1986), 151; Colin Kruse, *2 Corinthians*, TNTC (Grand Rapids, Mich.: Eerdmans, 1991), 124; and Paul Barnett, *The Message of 2 Corinthians* (Nottingham: InterVarsity, 1988), 111.

31. Ivan Blazen, *In Christ: Union with Him as Saviour and Lord in Paul* (Silver Spring, Md.: Biblical Research Institute), 3.

32. Ibid., 4.

33. G. K. Beale, "The Old Testament Background of Reconciliation in 2 Corinthians 5–7 and Its Bearing on the Literary Problem of 2 Corinthians 6.14–7.1," *NTS* 35 (1989): 550–81, esp. 553. For the centrality of Isaiah 40–55 in early Christianity, see Joseph Blenkinsopp, *Isaiah 40–55: A New Translation with Introduction and Commentary*, AB 19A (New York: Doubleday, 2002), 87–92. The term "behold" (*idou*) to which Beale refers in 2 Corinthians 5:17 is in the last phrase in Greek ("behold, the new is here"), but is left untranslated in the NIV.

34. Beale, "Old Testament Background," 556.

35. Ibid., 558.

The "old" includes interior realities and external perspectives. By the same token, the "new" relates to all of these things as well. However, Paul extends the meaning of "new creation" by stating that it compels the believer to enter into a ministry of reconciliation. Just as the new creation in Galatians was to be experienced among the Israel of God, so too the new creation was to be lived out in the context of the Corinthian church. The new creation reality is not just experienced among God's people, but individual Christians are indeed the temple of God (1 Cor. 6:19).

RESURRECTION AND RENEWAL

Earlier in this study, a case was made for the "already/not yet" perspective for interpreting the New Testament. We have examined the "already" reality and now turn to the future dimension. The resurrection of Jesus and other "last things" will now be explored in more detail as they add further depth and richness of meaning to the concept of new creation.

Jesus connected resurrection and renewal when He declared, "I am the resurrection and the life. The one who believes in me will live, even though they die" (John 11:25). Jesus emphatically declares that He has power over death. This power is inherent in His person. It is this power over death that Jesus gives to those who have faith in Him. The New English Bible provides a deeper probe of what Jesus means when it states, "If a man has faith in me, even though he die, he shall come to life" (John 11:25, NEB).[36]

Paul declares that Jesus "was delivered over to death for our sins and was raised to life for our justification" (Rom. 4:25). In Romans 4, Paul argues that just as God called forth Isaac from Abraham, whose body was "as good as dead" at that time in his life, so God called Jesus from a sealed tomb and dead believers from sin into newness of life. This concluding verse has the parallelism of "death to sin—raised to righteousness."[37] A number of commentators argue that it is an early Christian formula or confession.[38] If Romans was written

---

36. C. H. Dodd, *The Interpretation of the Fourth Gospel* (Cambridge: Cambridge University Press, 1953), 365; and C. K. Barret, *The Gospel According to St. John: An Introduction with Commentary and Notes on the Greek Text*, 2nd ed. (London: SPCK, 1978), 395.

37. James R. Edwards, *Romans*, NIBCNT (Peabody, Mass.: Hendrickson, 1992), 129.

38. Ibid. and Robert Jewett, *Romans, A Commentary*, Hermeneia (Minneapolis, Minn.: Fortress, 2007), 342. James D. G. Dunn, *Romans*, WBC 38A (Dallas: Word, 1988), 240–41,

around AD 55, then this is one of the earliest Christian confessions pointing to the centrality of Jesus's resurrection to the theological understanding and development of the early Christians.

Many first-century Jews believed that God would raise the faithful at the end of history (John 11:24). God brought the resurrection forward in the resurrection of Jesus. The new creation began with the resurrection of Jesus, the firstborn from the dead (Col. 1:15, 18). His resurrection is the firstfruits and guarantee of the future resurrection (Rom. 8:29; 1 Cor. 15:20; Rev. 1:5).[39] Jesus's resurrection heralds the beginning of a new world since material existence was radically altered by what Jesus accomplished.[40] An aspect of that new world was a new understanding of the Old Testament Scriptures. New Testament writers applied well-known Old Testament passages about God delivering Israel from exile to what Jesus accomplished through His resurrection.[41]

Jesus's resurrection impacted not only early Christian theology but also eschatology. They understood that His resurrection guarantees the resurrection of the saints at His second coming (1 Cor. 15:51–52; 1 Thess. 4:16). The physical realities of the new creation will become tangible at the second coming of Christ (John 14:3; Heb. 9:28). At the second coming of Jesus, believers will be raised bodily from the dead (John 5:28–29; 1 Cor. 15:12–25) and those who are alive will be transformed (Phil. 3:20–21; 1 John 3:2).[42] This

---

suggests that it is an early Christian confession used in worship but also does not discount the possibility that Paul developed the formula himself. Earlier in this study it was argued that the concept of new creation must be understood against the Old Testament backdrop of Isaiah. Commentators like Edwards, Jewett, and Dunn contend that the language and ideas in Romans 4:25 come from Isaiah 53. Here is another subtle connection between the idea of resurrection, new creation and Isaiah.

39. John Brunt, "Resurrection and Glorification," in *HSDAT*, ed. Raoul Dederen (Hagerstown, Md.: Review and Herald, 2000), 348.

40. Bird, *Evangelical Theology*, 440–41.

41. Leon Morris, *New Testament Theology* (Grand Rapids, Mich.: Baker, 1986), 162; G. W. Buchanan, *The Gospel of Matthew*, 2 vols. (Lewiston, N.Y.: Mellen Biblical, 1996), 2:1014–15; Ajith Fernando, *Acts*, NIVAC (Grand Rapids, Mich.: Zondervan, 1998), 103; Ben Witherington III, *Matthew*, SHBC (Macon, Ga.: Smith and Helwys, 2006), 521; R. H. Gundry, *Matthew: A Commentary on His Handbook for a Mixed Church under Persecution* (Grand Rapids, Mich.: Eerdmans, 1994), 576; R. E. Brown, *The Death of the Messiah: From Gethsemane to the Grave; A Commentary on the Passion Narratives in the Four Gospels*, 2 vols. (New York: Doubleday, 1994), 2:1123, 1140; and Young S. Chae, *Jesus as the Eschatological Davidic Shepherd: Studies in the Old Testament, Second Temple Judaism, and in the Gospel of Matthew*, WUNT, 2nd. ser., vol. 216 (Tübingen: Mohr Siebeck, 2006), 95–172.

42. Brunt, "Resurrection and Glorification," 348, states that "in this new state of immortality and eternal fellowship with God believers do not shed their material bodies, but enjoy the kind of bodily existence God originally intended before the entrance of sin into the

transformation will give believers new bodies—bodies with a new motivating force, that are spiritual and perfect, imperishable and immortal (1 Cor. 15:51–55; Phil. 3:20–21).[43] These new bodies will complement the new heart (Jer. 31:31–34) and new Spirit (Ezek. 36:26–27) believers received when they entered the new creation at their new birth (John 3:6–8; 1 Pet. 1:23). Glorification culminates the moment of justification and the journey of sanctification in the believer's life. The New Testament advocates the ultimate re-creation of the heavens and the earth at the close of history (2 Pet. 3:13; Rev. 21:1–5).

After the millennium (Rev. 20), the new Jerusalem—the home of the redeemed—will descend on the earth made new (Rev. 21:2). Believers will not be disappointed at the new creation just as Adam and Eve were not disappointed with what they found at creation. Roy Naden comments that "it is certain that no matter how graphically John may have painted the picture, with our limited minds we cannot even imagine how magnificent it will be."[44] The redeemed community has direct access to God and they shall see His face. This is the promise of promises. All through Scripture, we read that no one can see the face of God and live (Exod. 33:20, 23; John 1:18). Yet in the new Jerusalem, believers will see God face-to-face just as Adam and Eve did before the Fall.[45]

Revelation 21:3 reads, "And I heard a loud voice from the throne saying, "Look! God's dwelling [*skēnē*] place is now among the people [*anthrōpōn*], and he will dwell [lit. "tabernacle"] with them. They will be his people [lit. "peoples"], and God himself will be with them and be their God." The term *skēnē* recalls God's redemptive presence in Israel's ancient tabernacle (Exod. 25:8) and in the incarnation of Jesus (John 1:14). Hans LaRondelle states that "the promise of the New Jerusalem connects the glory of God with the glory of Christ and assures the church that God will come to dwell among men in

---

world." See also Andrew Johnson, "Turning the World Upside Down in 1 Corinthians 15: Apocalyptic Epistemology, the Resurrected Body and the New Creation," *EvQ* 75 (2003): 291–309.

43. Ralph P. Martin and Gerald F. Hawthorne, *Philippians*, rev. ed., WBC 43 (Nashville Tenn.: Thomas Nelson, 2004), 233–234.

44. Roy Naden, *The Lamb among the Beasts* (Hagerstown, Md.: Review and Herald, 1996), 292.

45. Simon Kistemaker, *Exposition of the Book of Revelation*, New Testament Commentary (Grand Rapids, Mich.: Baker, 2001), 582.

fulfillment of His covenant promise."[46] The promises of not only Isaiah but of all the prophets finally come to fruition in the new Jerusalem (Isa. 2:2–4; 60:3; Jer. 3:17; Zech. 8:21–23).[47]

CONCLUSION

The Bible is a book of hope. This hope is woven into the very fabric of its concepts and narratives. Because of sin, human beings lost the direct fellowship and presence of God. However, in Eden, God demonstrated His great love when He came looking for Adam and Eve after they had sinned (Gen. 3:6) and when He provided them with coats of skin (Gen. 3:21). God also promised that the enemy who led the Edenic couple into sin would be punished and that a Deliverer would come to restore creation (Gen. 3:15). Jesus is the fulfillment of that promise.

Paul understands Jesus as the perfect image of God (Col. 1:15). The word "image" (*eikōn*), meaning copy or likeness, expresses Christ's deity. This word involves more than a resemblance or representation. Christ is fully and unreservedly God. Although He took on human form, He has the exact nature of the Father (Heb. 1:3). In the new creation, the *imago dei* is being fully restored and renovated in the life of the believer through the power of the risen Jesus.[48] What was lost in the old creation is restored by faith in the new creation, not to the measure of Adam, but to that of Christ, the Last Adam.

In the new creation, believers find rich ontological, communal, eschatological, experiential, pneumatological, and evangelistic dimensions. Ontologically, the new creation provides a new heart (Jer. 31:31–34). Pneumatologically, the new creation provides a new Spirit (Ezek. 36:26–27). Communally, the new creation provides a new humanity in a new community to worship God, fellowship with one another, and serve the world (2 Cor. 5:18; Gal. 6:16). Experientially, the new creation provides the fellowship of the Son and the Spirit (Matt. 28:20; John 14:23). Physically, the new creation will provide a

46. Hans LaRondelle, *How to Understand the End-Time Prophecies of the Bible: The Biblical-Contextual Approach* (Sarasota, Fla.: First Impressions, 1997), 478.

47. Ranko Stefanovic, *Revelation of Jesus Christ: Commentary on the Book of Revelation* (Berrien Springs, Mich.: Andrews University Press, 2002), 591. This section is adapted from Kayle B. de Waal, *Ancient Words Present Hope* (Melbourne: Signs, 2015), 147–48.

48. Ross Clifford and Philip Johnson, *The Cross Is Not Enough: Living as Witnesses to the Resurrection* (Grand Rapids, Mich.: Baker, 2012), 51.

new body (Phil. 3:20–21). Eschatologically, the new creation provides hope for a new world and a new home (John 14:1–3). The new creation is present in this evil age in and through the power of the Spirit. This new creation is the outworking of the plan of God to fully restore the image of God in humankind, a plan to be consummated in the new earth (Rev. 21:1–5).

Laszlo Gallusz, PhD

Newbold College of Higher Education
Bracknell, England

RADICALLY NEW BEGINNING, RADICALLY NEW END: CREATION AND ESCHATOLOGY IN THE NEW TESTAMENT

INTRODUCTION

The term "eschatology," derived from the Greek adjective *eschatos* ("last, final"), has many meanings.[1] Essentially, it designates the doctrine about "last things." Brian Daley observes that the core of eschatology is "faith in final solutions," and therefore the concept of hope is inherent to it.[2] He points out that eschatology appeals to "the hope of believing people that the incompleteness of their present experience of God will be resolved, their present thirst for God fulfilled, their present need for release and salvation realized."[3] Thus, eschatology reflects fundamental Christian convictions about God, the world, and human existence. It deals with God's final, decisive acts toward His creation in which His created order becomes

---

1. Markus Mühling, *T&T Clark Handbook of Christian Eschatology*, trans. J. Adams-Massmann and D. A. Gillard (London: Bloomsbury T&T Clark, 2015), 3–14, names at least five different ways the term is used in scholarly discussion, and calls our attention to the linguistic confusion that led to uncertainty in scholarly circles regarding the actual object of eschatology.

2. Brian E. Daley, *The Hope of the Early Church: The Handbook of Patristic Eschatology* (Cambridge: Cambridge University Press, 1991), 1.

3. Ibid.

renewed, His kingdom comes, and His will is done "on earth as it is in heaven" (Matt. 6:10).[4]

This study sets out the thesis that the concept of creation is of fundamental significance for New Testament eschatology. Without the creation, we would have no categories to think about the eschaton at all. As Miroslav Volf notes, "the eschaton is an eschaton of the creation, or it is no eschaton at all."[5] Movement toward the eschatological goal is one of the major themes in the biblical storyline, since His "making all things new" is essential to God's promises (Rev. 21:5). His major interventions in history follow a consistent pattern of transformation, according to which the Creator God brings disorder to order, establishing His kingly rule. Such a pattern was repeated from time to time in salvation history, being characteristic of God's mighty acts (the Creation, the Flood, the Exodus, and the return from Babylonian exile) by which His creative power was demonstrated.[6] Since the Old Testament plotline provides the substructure for New Testament theology,[7] and since God is consistent in dealing with His creation, this study argues that the theme of creation is integral to New Testament eschatology. William Dumbrell, Charles Scobie, and Matthew Emerson argue for the prominence of creation as one of the key theological themes in the biblical canon,[8] while Beale advances

---

4. G. C. Berkouwer, *The Return of Christ*, Studies in Dogmatics (Grand Rapids, Mich.: Eerdmans, 1972), 9, points out that the goal of eschatology is "not to deal with unrelated, independent events that are yet to take place; instead, it focuses on the concentration of all these events in the promise of Him who is the Last." He acknowledges that the last things center on the future return of Christ, a decisive moment for all creation. Unless otherwise indicated, Scripture quotations in this chapter are from the New Revised Standard Version Bible, copyright © 1989 the Division of Christian Education of the National Council of the Churches of Christ in the United States of America. Used by permission. All rights reserved.

5. Miroslav Volf, "Eschaton, Creation, and Social Ethics," *CTJ* 30 (1995), 130–43. The quotation is from p. 134.

6. For God's consistency and creativity in working according to this pattern in salvation history, see Jon Paulien, *Meet God Again for the First Time* (Hagerstown, Md.: Review and Herald, 2003).

7. The Old Testament is not only a preliminary stage to the New Testament, but its major biblical-theological notions and thought framework also exercised a formative influence on the theological thinking of the New Testament authors. This has been convincingly demonstrated in, e.g., C. H. Dodd, *According to Scriptures: The Sub-Structure of New Testament Theology* (London: Nisbet, 1952); and Peter Stuhlmacher, *Biblische Theologie des Neuen Testaments*, 2 vols. (Göttingen: Vandenhoeck and Ruprechts, 1992–1999).

8. William J. Dumbrell, *The End of the Beginning: Revelation 21–22 and the Old Testament* (Eugene, Ore.: Wipf and Stock, 2001); Charles H. H. Scobie, *The Ways of Our God: An Approach to Biblical Theology* (Grand Rapids, Mich.: Eerdmans, 2003); and Matthew Y. Emerson, *Christ and the New Creation: A Canonical Approach to the Theology of the New Testament* (Eugene, Ore.: Wipf and Stock, 2013).

the thesis that creation is the single central theme of both Testaments.[9] Engaging this discussion is beyond the scope of this study, since the focus of the examination will be on the relationship between creation and eschatology in the New Testament documents.

For this investigation it is of critical importance to explore, first of all, how the New Testament authors understood the concept of the "end time": what was their eschatological outlook? After laying down the foundation for this enterprise, this study will identify and discuss three cardinal components of New Testament creation theology that are integral to the eschatological thinking of the New Testament authors. The analysis of these three components will reveal the points of contact between creation and eschatology within New Testament theology. Finally, the relation between protology and eschatology will be explored from a canonical perspective, maintaining the presupposition that the Bible narrates a unified, coherent meta-narrative of God's ongoing work in creation, therefore providing an inspired ground for doing biblical theology.

THE ESCHATOLOGICAL NATURE OF THE NEW TESTAMENT

Scholarly research of the last hundred years has amply demonstrated that eschatology cannot be relegated to a mere epilogue of theology.[10] This is mainly because the message of the New Testament as a whole is deeply eschatological in character, since the framework of thought of the early Christians, for whom the basic standpoint for understanding the gospel was salvation history, was also eschatological. Their basic conviction, expressed in the earliest preaching, worship, and confessions of faith, was that the end-time predictions of the Old Testament have begun the process of fulfillment in Jesus

---

9. G. K. Beale, *A New Testament Biblical Theology* (Grand Rapids, Mich.: Baker Academic, 2011).

10. The eschatological character of early Christianity began to be more fully recognized only in the early twentieth century, due to the work of Johannes Weiss and Albert Schweitzer, New Testament scholars whose views evoked heated discussions. As a result, a number of different eschatological models have been developed to interpret Jesus's message (consistent eschatology, realized eschatology, proleptic eschatology, and models de-emphasizing eschatology). For a critical evaluation of the different approaches to Jesus's eschatology, see A. L. Moore, *The Parousia in the New Testament* NovTSup 13 (Leiden: Brill, 1966), 35–79. Somewhat later, in the second part of the twentieth century, Jürgen Moltmann, *Theology of Hope*, trans. James W. Leitch (London: SCM, 1967) and Wolfhart Pannenberg, *Systematic Theology*, trans. Geoffrey W. Bromiley, 3 vols. (Grand Rapids, Mich.: Eerdmans, 1991–1998), emphasized in their influential studies the fundamental significance of eschatology for understanding New Testament thought and Christian faith.

Christ.[11] They believed that in Jesus's ministry, death, and resurrection the history of salvation reached its climax and the foundation stone was laid for establishing the kingdom of God. For this reason, our inquiry needs to start with the figure and message of Jesus of Nazareth, who is "the starting point and focus of the New Testament proclamation, and without an adequate understanding of him we cannot arrive at an adequate interpretation of the New Testament kerygma."[12]

Jesus's proclamation was an eschatological proclamation. Even though the Gospels record sayings that have no eschatological significance, the main mode of Jesus's preaching was undeniably eschatological. His focal message was that His appearance announced the arrival of the kingdom of God (Mark 1:15)—the old era is passing away because in His person and ministry a new era, the time of salvation, has dawned. His healings and exorcisms acted as the visible manifestation of the in-breaking of the power of God's kingdom into the earthly reality: "But if it is by the finger of God that I cast out the demons, then the kingdom of God has come to you" (Luke 11:20). Jesus's kingdom sayings reveal His conviction that the eschaton was already effective in His own person and ministry. His eschatological language, as observed by N. T. Wright, heralded the arrival of the climax of Israel's history, the fulfillment of the Old Testament eschatological expectations that became realized in defeating the rule of evil itself.[13] While the cross and the resurrection were the key moments in achieving the decisive victory, the full "implementation" of the effects of the Christ-event is still in the future. Therefore, essential to Jesus's eschatological paradigm is a tension between "already" and "not yet," which implies a dynamic process: God's kingdom is inaugurated, yet not consummated. The old age and the new age overlap—the first is still present, while the second has been brought by the first advent of the Messiah. While the eschatological kingdom has invaded history in the person of

---

11. The celebration of the Lord's Supper, held in remembrance of the death and resurrection of Jesus, has a significant eschatological emphasis in the passages describing its celebration (Matt. 26:29; Mark 14:25; Luke 22:18; 1 Cor. 11:26; Did. 9:4).

12. Hans Schwarz, *Eschatology* (Grand Rapids, Mich.: Eerdmans, 2000), 68.

13. N. T. Wright, *Jesus and the Victory of God*, vol. 2 of *Christian Origins and the Question of God* (Minneapolis, Minn.: Fortress, 1996), 202–9.

Jesus, bringing people freedom in the age of sin and death, the full consummation is in the future.[14]

The authors of the New Testament wrote with the conviction that the ministry of Jesus was the climactic fulfillment of Old Testament prophecies, and they embraced Jesus's typological thinking, according to which the "time of the antitypes had arrived" in Him.[15] Consequently, their writings present Jesus as a messianic figure whose ministry has redemptive significance imbued with eschatological concepts. Likewise, they present the outpouring of the Holy Spirit as a fulfillment of Old Testament eschatological promises, the sign of the eschatological age in which salvation is granted to all who call on the name of the Lord (Acts 2:1–21; cf. Joel 2:28–32). Hans LaRondelle notes that "the whole New Testament is essentially characterized by the typological and eschatological application of the Old Testament, motivated and directed by the Holy Spirit."[16] It is a testimony about the fulfillment of God's promises concerning the coming of God's kingdom, the realization of Israel's hope about God's decisive intervention in history. Oscar Cullmann considers the transformative ministry of Jesus as the eschatologically interpreted "center of time," which essentially redefined the meaning of history.[17] A. L. Moore builds on this insight when he argues, "From the centre, Jesus Christ, the line of salvation history runs backwards through the covenant to creation and beyond, and forwards through the church and its mission to the Parousia and beyond."[18] Thus, biblical eschatology is grounded in Jesus and focused on His person, and it acts in relation to God's creation.

---

14. For the "already but not yet" tension in Jesus's proclamation, see Joachim Jeremias, *The Parables of Jesus*, trans. S. H. Hooke (London: SCM, 1954); Werner G. Kümmel, *Promise and Fulfillment: The Eschatological Message of Jesus*, trans. D. M. Barton, 3rd ed., SBT 23 (London: SCM, 1961); and George E. Ladd, *Jesus and the Kingdom: The Eschatology of Biblical Realism* (London: SPCK, 1966).

15. Hans K. LaRondelle, *Israel of God in Prophecy: Principles of Prophetic Interpretation*, Andrews University Monographs—Studies in Religion 13 (Berrien Springs, Mich.: Andrews University Press, 1983), 37. LaRondelle claims that typology and prophecy are twin sisters, both pointing forward to the same realities in the future. He explains their internal connection by referring to Fritsch: "Typology differs from prophecy in the strict sense of the term only in the means of prediction. Prophecy predicts mainly by means of word, whereas typology predicts by institution, act or person" (C. T. Fritsch, "Principles of Biblical Typology," *BSac* 104 [1947]: 215).

16. Ibid., 38.

17. Oscar Cullmann, *Christ and Time: The Primitive Christian Conception of Time and History*, trans. Floyd V. Filson (Philadelphia: Westminster, 1950), xx.

18. Moore, *Parousia*, 90.

In light of the salvation-historical standpoint of the early Christians, it is not surprising that the New Testament authors perceived the beginning of Christian history as the beginning of the end times. The phrase "latter days" and its synonyms appear approximately thirty times in the New Testament, rarely referring to the very end of history but rather to the era starting with Jesus's ministry in the first century.[19] As G. K. Beale argues, the "end-times" phrases of the New Testament have their roots in the language in the Old Testament, even though eschatological expectations are sometimes expressed in the Old Testament without using the vocabulary of "latter days," "end-times," and similar phrases. He concludes:

> The New Testament repeatedly uses precisely the same phrase "latter days" as found in the Old Testament prophecies. And the meaning of the phrase is identical, except for one difference: in the New Testament the end-days predicted by the Old Testament are seen as beginning their fulfilment with Christ's first coming. All that the Old Testament foresaw would occur in the end-times has begun already in the first century and continues on into our present day.... The establishment of His kingdom have [sic] been set in motion by Christ's life, death, resurrection and formation of the Christian church.[20]

Ample textual evidence demonstrates that the end times are not limited to a future point in history, but that they extend throughout the entire Christian era. The first occurrence of the expression "last days" in the New Testament is found in Acts 2:17 (*en tais eschatais hēmerais*, "in the last days"), where Peter interprets the experience of speaking in tongues at Pentecost as the fulfillment of Joel's end-time prophecy: "Indeed, these are not drunk.... No, this is what was spoken through the prophet Joel: 'In the last days it will be, God declares, that I will pour out my Spirit upon all flesh'" (Acts 2:15–17). In 1 Corinthians 10:11, at the end of a section in which Paul refers typologically to the events of Exodus (1 Cor. 10:1–11),[21] he

---

19. For an in-depth study on the question, see G. K. Beale, "The Eschatological Conception of New Testament Theology," in *"The Reader Must Understand": Eschatology in Bible and Theology*, ed. Kent E. Brower and Mark W. Elliott (Downers Grove, Ill.: Apollos, 1997), 11–52. For a shorter version of this essay, see Beale, "The New Testament and New Creation," in *Biblical Theology: Retrospect and Prospect*, ed. Scott J. Hafemann (Downers Grove, Ill.: InterVarsity, 2002), 159–73.

20. Beale, "Eschatological Conception," 14.

21. For an argument in favor of the typological character of this passage, see Richard Davidson, *Typology in Scripture: A Study of Hermeneutical ΤΥΠΟΣ [TYPOS] Structures*, AUSDDS 2 (Berrien Springs, Mich.: Andrews University Press, 1981), 193–297.

instructs the Corinthian Christians about the manner of their life with an exhortation that upon them "the ends of the ages have come" (*ta telē tōn aiōnōn*). In Galatians 4:4 Paul speaks of the "fullness of time" (*to plērōma tou chronou*), referring to the time of Jesus's birth, while in Ephesians 1:10 the expression about "fullness of time" (*tou plērōmatos tōn kairōn*) designates the time when He began His rule over the cosmos as a consequence of His resurrection. These last two almost identical expressions in Greek point to a God who has control over the flow of time, appointing major events in history according to His divine plan.

The "fullness of time," therefore, refers to the climax of all earthly times, the approaching of the eschatological time of Christ, in which God's purposes became realized and revealed. In 1 Timothy 4:1 the expression "later times" (*hysterois kairois*) is related to the apostasy in the church, while in 2 Timothy 3:1 reference to the "last days" (*en eschatais hēmerais*) comes in the context of the problem of deception. In these two texts, the eschatological expressions refer to the time when these problems arose in the life of the early church. That this first-century context is in mind is confirmed by the fact that in the same epistles ample evidence is found concerning the presence of deceptive teaching and apostasy (1 Tim. 1:3–7, 19–20; 4:7; 5:13–15; 6:20–21; 2 Tim. 1:15; 2:16–19, 25–26; 3:2–9). Hebrews 1:2 relates the ministry of Jesus to the beginning of the "last days" (*eschatou tōn hēmerōn*), when God spoke to humanity and acted through His Son, while Hebrews 9:26 similarly states that "he has appeared once for all at the end of the age" (*epi synteleia tōn aiōnōn*).

Peter reflects the same salvation-historical thinking when he refers to Christ's death and resurrection as an event that took place "at the end of the ages" (*ep' eschatou tōn chronōn*, 1 Pet. 1:20). He also warns the church that "in the last days scoffers will come, scoffing and indulging their own lusts" (2 Pet. 3:3). That the phrase *ep' eschatōn tōn hēmerōn* ("in the last days") refers to his time is evident from the fact that Peter speaks openly about the threat of scoffers spreading heresies in the church he is addressing (2 Pet. 2:1–22; 3:16–17). Likewise, fighting the deception of false teaching in his churches, John qualifies his time with an expression carrying a strong eschatological overtone: "Children, it is the last hour! As you have heard that antichrist is coming, so now many antichrists have come. From this we know that it is the last hour" (*eschatē hōra*, 1 John 2:18).

In addition to these eschatologically charged texts that refer to the present as the time of the end, a number of texts deal with the coming "last day" as the *eschaton* ("end, last") and with the events related to it. Thus, it is stated that the eschatological end will be preceded by the last plagues (Rev. 15) and it will bring the annihilation of death as the "last enemy" (*eschatos echthros*, 1 Cor. 15:26), the resurrection of the dead, the last judgment and salvation (John 6:39–40, 44, 54; 11:24; 12:48 [*en tē eschatē hēmera*, "in the last day"]; 1 Pet. 1:5 [*en kairō eschatō*, "in the last time"]), and also the destruction of the present cosmos (2 Pet. 3:10–12).

The discussion in this section has demonstrated that the fulfillment of the end times predicted in the Old Testament began with the Christ-event, which accounts for the eschatological nature of the New Testament. The concept of creation, as will be shown below, has a significant role in developing the New Testament eschatological outlook. In the following we will indicate how three basic aspects of New Testament creation theology are integral to the New Testament's eschatological perspective: (1) Christ's resurrection as the initiation of the new creation; (2) the creation of a new humanity that advances God's eschatological purposes in the world; and (3) the consummated new creation, the final realization of God's endeavors to create all things new. We will explore these aspects under separate headings. In discussing the eschatological character of salvation, it is striking that the New Testament authors reached back to the theme of creation to express their ideas. This fact gives a cosmic perspective to salvation and ties together the biblical concepts of creation lost and creation restored.

CHRIST'S RESURRECTION: THE INITIATION OF THE NEW CREATION

The New Testament presents Christ's death and resurrection as the turning point of salvation history. These two events together initiate God's new creation and define the basis of Christian faith and hope. Christ's death and resurrection are the climax of all the Gospel accounts, feature as key elements in Pauline theology, and hold preeminent place also in other New Testament writings. The significance of Christ's resurrection is most clearly articulated by Paul: "and if Christ has not been raised, then our proclamation has been in vain and your faith has been in vain" (1 Cor. 15:14). During the two thousand years of the Christian era, much ink has been spilled over the question of Christ's resurrection. It has often been demonstrated that precisely this belief was the focal point of early Christianity.[22] And it continues to keep faith alive to this day. Discussing the various aspects of Christ's resurrection is beyond the scope of this study, since our inquiry is focused on the relation of Christ's life, death, and resurrection to the creation theme.

The death of Jesus on the cross is the appropriate starting point for understanding His resurrection. Christ's death "carries connotations of the beginning destruction of the old world which paves the way for the new."[23] That His death is not just an ordinary death becomes clear particularly during the last three hours of the crucifixion. The supernatural events at Golgotha (darkness, earthquake, resurrection of dead believers, dividing of the temple curtain) indicate that the moment has arrived for God's major, unparalleled intervention in salvation history. For our purposes, the darkness lasting from noon to three o'clock (Mark 15:33) is particularly significant. The Egyptian plague of darkness (Exod. 10) and the cosmic judgment language of Amos 8:9 have both frequently been suggested as Old Testament events illuminating what happens in the darkness at Golgotha.

In light of these passages, the phenomenon of the crucifixion darkness has usually been interpreted as the mark of God's displeasure and judgment.[24] While we acknowledge these connections, Dane Ortlund and G. K. Beale's suggestion also merits attention. They argue that "from the broadest perspective, Mark 15:33 culminates a trajectory that is launched not in Amos or even in Exodus but in Gen 1."[25] Thus, the darkness descending at noon, together with the return of light at the resurrection, seems to echo the creation narrative in which the darkness of disorder is overcome by the dawning of God's light (Gen. 1:3–4). This background suggests that

---

22. For an overview of recent discussions on the topic, see George Hunsinger, "The Daybreak of the New Creation: Christ's Resurrection in Recent Theology," *SJT* 57 (2004): 163–81.

23. Beale, "Eschatological Conception," 20.

24. See, e.g., Morna D. Hooker, *The Gospel According to Saint Mark*, BNTC (London: Black, 1991), 375–76; and R. T. France, *The Gospel of Mark: A Commentary on the Greek Text*, NIGTC (Grand Rapids, Mich.: Eerdmans, 2002), 651.

25. Dane C. Ortlund and G. K. Beale, "Darkness Over the Whole Land: A Biblical Theological Reflection on Mark 15:33," *WTJ* 75 (2013): 221–38. The quotation is from p. 224.

the darkness over Golgotha is a phenomenon of de-creation because crucifying the incarnated Son of God, an act of utmost evil, is the expression of disorder, the reflection of the fact that humanity's relationship with their Creator is fractured. The light returning symbolically in Jesus's resurrection heralds the inauguration of the new creation, since light in the Genesis creation narrative appears not only as an abstract brightness, but also as the personification of God's creating power, by which He brings order.[26] The kingdom of God dawned when Jesus fundamentally defeated Satan and his kingdom. The effect of this act is that "the darkness is passing away and the true light is already shining" (1 John 2:8). God was doing something new through the events of the death and resurrection of Christ, echoing the creation account.

Jesus's resurrection from death was more than a public acknowledgement that God accepted His sacrifice as a ransom for sin. It was the key event signaling the dawning of the age that brought qualitative newness to God's creation. As the beginning of the new creation, the resurrection was the indicator of the renewal of everything, like the spring flowers whose appearance reveals that "the time of singing has come" (Song of Sol. 2:12).[27] In New Testament creation theology, Christ appears as "the firstborn of all creation" (Col. 1:15), through whom God reconciles to Himself "all things, whether on earth or in heaven" (Col. 1:20). The resurrection event was, therefore, no mere revivification of Jesus's dead body but the manifestation of divine power in an act comparable to the creation of the world. The world began with God's act of creation out of disorder (Gen. 1:2). Similarly, God's raising of Jesus from death was an act of announcing a new beginning after the tragedy that was the consequence of rejecting God's rule (Gen. 3). Thus, resurrection and creation belong together. Since in the new creation God's original purposes come to completion, His creation is being restored and extended.

The significance of Christ's resurrection for the theological perspective of the early church cannot be overemphasized. As Wright notes, the early followers of Jesus, in light of His rising from the dead,

---

26. In contrast to this position, ibid., 221–38, relate the motif of the returning of light to the passing of the darkness after Jesus's death. However, none of the Gospels contain a reference to light returning on Friday afternoon, after Jesus's death.

27. Berkouwer, *The Return of Christ*, 102.

reshaped "their worldview around the resurrection as the new central point."[28] This outlook is formulated clearly in Galatians 6:14–16, where Paul stresses the reality of the new creation as the principle of utmost significance:

> May I never boast of anything except the cross of our Lord Jesus Christ, by which the world has been crucified to me, and I to the world. For neither circumcision nor uncircumcision is anything; but a new creation is everything! As for those who will follow this rule—peace be upon them, and mercy, and upon the Israel of God.

This passage highlights the transformative effect of Jesus's death and resurrection, which define the future of the world, but also the nature of Christian discipleship. It emphasizes that as the result of the Christ-event the world became a different place, and therefore the question concerning the distinction between Jews and non-Jews ceases to be relevant. In the background of Paul's argument lies the Genesis creation account, since he appeals to the one Creator God, who by His creative activity exercises sovereignty over all against the disorder in the world.[29]

Christ's resurrection was an event of not only historical but also eschatological significance. The eschatological aspect is evident in at least three ways: First, the resurrection as the climax of salvation history was the foundational act for the re-creation of the world into its true form. As "the great turning point from death to life, for all men and for all creation," it was an act initiating the era leading toward perfect and eternal creation (Rev. 21:1–8).[30] Second, the events of that resurrection morning marked the difference between the old and new creations. Christ's resurrection constitutes the "borderline"[31] between the two realities, which will exist side by side until the parousia, when the old age will be terminated.[32] The believers, therefore, live in an eschatological tension—in a sense the end is already present, but it is also yet to come in the future, because

28. N. T. Wright, *The Resurrection of the Son of God*, vol. 3 of *Christian Origins and the Question of God* (Minneapolis, Minn.: Fortress, 2003), 27.

29. Ibid., 223–24.

30. Martin Franzmann, *The Word of the Lord Grows* (St. Louis, Mo.: Concordia, 1961), 15.

31. Hans Burger, *Being in Christ: A Biblical and Systematic Investigation in a Reformed Perspective* (Eugene, Ore.: Wipf and Stock, 2009), 553.

32. For a comparison of the New Testament view of the two ages with the Jewish apocalyptic views of history, see Jon Paulien, *What the Bible Says about the End-Time* (Hagerstown, Md.: Review and Herald, 1994), 65–83.

the old age is still here. Third, a fundamental consequence of the resurrection is the ultimate coming of the kingdom of God in the parousia. The expectation of that day, repeatedly presented in the New Testament in positive terms, is the major hope of Christians, endowing their life with new meaning (e.g., Titus 2:11–14). Herman Ridderbos notes the close relation between Jesus's resurrection and His parousia, arguing that in one sense they form a unity: "His announcement of the *parousia* of the Son of Man is . . . provisionally fulfilled in his resurrection."[33] Thus, the resurrection of Christ provides the basis for an ultimate, lasting eschatological hope that comes from the assurance of Christ's second coming and from the fact that the new creation has already been initiated.

The new creation is also closely tied to the concept of salvation achieved by Christ. In the Old Testament, God is presented in strictly monotheistic terms, as a Lord whose supremacy in heaven and on earth is seen in the fact that He is the Creator (e.g., Ps. 96:4–5). A basic conviction of Old Testament writers, and also first-century Jews, was that God not only created the world but also works actively within it. Wright notes that the Old Testament picture of God presupposes not only "creational" but also "providential" and "covenantal" monotheism.[34] These modifiers point to the fact that Israel's God is not intrinsically detached, but that He is involved within His creation. He is not indifferent toward evil in the world, but He has a plan according to which He acts decisively to eliminate it and restore His created order. The New Testament writings unanimously point to Jesus of Nazareth as the divine restorer promised to the first couple in Eden (Gen. 3:15), who overcame evil with His sacrifice on the cross, opening the door of salvation for humanity. By His resurrection from death He Himself became the center and goal of the new creation because in Him the barriers between humanity and God are knocked down; "in him, things in heaven and things on earth" are made one (Eph. 1:10).[35]

---

33. Herman Ridderbos, *The Coming of the Kingdom*, trans. H. de Jongste (Philadelphia: P&R, 1962), 468.

34. N. T. Wright, *The New Testament and the People of God*, vol. 1 of *Christian Origins and the Question of God* (Minneapolis, Minn.: Fortress, 1992), 248–52.

35. Paul in Romans 8 shows that God's redemption is not limited only to an individual's salvation but includes the totality of God's creation, because both are subjected to frustration from the presence of sin ("the whole creation has been groaning in labor pains until now"; v. 22). This is a statement about the worth of creation, which stresses the fact that the world is not merely an unimportant material, but a reality made by God, belonging to Him.

However, the effect of salvation is not merely to undo the work of evil and return to the "good old days"; it is to strive toward a new and unprecedented reality defined by God's creative activity. Schwarz notes that the eschatological promises act as a "driving force" for the vision of salvation because "salvation calls for a totally new creation."[36] In Jesus, therefore, in whom a completely new world came, "the hope of humanity was realized toward something final and absolute, namely, toward a new creation."[37]

The new creation started with Christ's resurrection, which was, together with His death, the foundational event in God's work of healing the world. No wonder, then, that the early Christians considered these events the central point of history that reshaped their perception of reality. God's creative activity, however, extends beyond the cross and the resurrection of Jesus. It involves the church, which is called to experience the work of the new creation and participate in its realization. The following section will discuss this aspect of God's creative activity, which came as a direct consequence of the initiation of the new creation through the Christ-event.

CREATION OF A NEW COMMUNITY: LIVING AS THE PEOPLE OF GOD

According to the witness of the New Testament, the interval between Jesus's ascension and His parousia is an eschatological end-time period in which the work of Christ continues by extending on earth the kingdom that was inaugurated in His earthly ministry. This is an era characterized by the presence and work of the Spirit on earth. Significantly, Acts presents the outpouring of the Spirit as a sign of the end, "a gift of the end time,"[38] and the eschatological fulfillment of the Old Testament promises of God (Acts 2:15–21; cf. Joel 2:28–32).[39]

As John G. Gibbs, *Creation and Redemption: A Study in Pauline Theology*, NovTSup 26 (Leiden: Brill, 1971), 34–35, observes, "The two realities are bound together by the one redemptive purpose at work in both, as evidenced by the 'hope' which is characteristic of both creation and Christians (8:20, 24)."

36. Schwarz, *Eschatology*, 160.

37. Ibid., 161.

38. Jerry L. Sumney, "'In Christ There is a New Creation': Apocalypticism in Paul," *PRSt* 40 (2013): 35–48. The quotation is from p. 40.

39. Pentecost also marked the starting point of Jesus's messianic reign. His enthronement is described in the throne room scene of Revelation 5, and the outpouring of the Spirit at Pentecost was the visible confirmation of His rule in the end-time messianic age. Ellen G. White, *The Acts of the Apostles* (Nampa, Idaho: Pacific Press, 2005), 38, states, "The Pentecostal

The Spirit's primary office is revealing and mediating the presence of Christ to people. As Neill Hamilton notes, "The Spirit is the Spirit of Christ because his office is to communicate the benefits of Christ's work."[40] As a result of His work, people who are open to His influence experience radical transformation: they receive "resurrection life in the present"[41] in anticipation of the final resurrection at the parousia. Like Christ's resurrection, the "resurrection life" of believing Christians is the work of God's new creation, since "new creation is in mind wherever the concept of resurrection occurs."[42] The link between Christ's resurrection and the Christian experience of inner transformation is explicit: our Lord's resurrection serves as the foundation for believers' experience of new creation.[43] At the same time, the link between the Genesis creation account (Gen. 1–2) and the experience of salvation is also strong. Namely, the power of the creator God, who "spoke, and it came to be" at the beginning of earth's history (Ps. 33:9), is manifested in a similarly dramatic fashion in the life of an individual when he or she experiences the transformation brought by the Spirit who was "hovering over the face of the waters" (ESV) at the original creation (Gen. 1:2).

The identification of the inner transformation with the new creation is clearly made in a number of New Testament texts. Although the phrase *kainē ktisis* ("new creation") occurs only twice in the New Testament (2 Cor. 5:17; Gal. 6:15), the motif of newness in Christ pervades the atmosphere of the New Testament writings (the adjective *kainos*, "new," occurs forty-nine times across sixteen New Testament writings).[44] As pointed out above, Galatians 6:15 highlights the

---

outpouring was Heaven's communication that the Redeemer's inauguration was accomplished. According to His promise He had sent the Holy Spirit from heaven to His followers as a token that He had, as priest and king, received all authority in heaven and on earth, and was the Anointed One over His people." For an extended argument that the event in Revelation 5 is Christ's enthronement in the heavenly temple, see Ranko Stefanovic, *The Background and Meaning of the Sealed Book of Revelation 5*, AUSDDS 22 (Berrien Springs, Mich.: Andrews University Press, 1996), 206–25.

40. Neill Q. Hamilton, *The Holy Spirit and Eschatology in Paul* (Edinburgh: Oliver and Boyd, 1957), 15.

41. Wright, *Resurrection*, 304.

42. Beale, "Eschatological Conception," 19.

43. Paul expresses the relation between the resurrection of Christ and that of the believers by using a metaphor and a typological correspondence: firstfruits offerings and Adam (1 Cor. 15).

44. For an in-depth study on the theological significance of the motif of newness in biblical literature, see Nikola Hohnjec, *Novo stvaranje: teologija novosti u Svetom pismu i njezin odraz u crkvi*, Biblioteka riječ 37 (Zagreb: Kršćanska sadašnjost, 2000).

major significance of the principle of new creation, which fundamentally defines the thinking and lifestyle of Christians. Somewhat differently, 2 Corinthians 5:17 directly states that the personal renewal of an individual in Christ is an act of new creation: "So if anyone is in Christ, there is a new creation: everything old has passed away; see, everything has become new!" The terms "old" (*archaios*), "behold" (*idou*), and "new" (*kainos*) also appear together in Isaiah 43:18–19 (LXX), which lies in the background of the passage in 2 Corinthians. Paul's argument echoes the Isaianic promise of restoration, in which the renewal is related to the motif of new creation.[45] The whole language of creation, however, is rooted first of all in the Genesis creation narrative (Gen. 1–2).

The term *palingenesia* ("regeneration, rebirth") occurs twice in the New Testament, and, like *kainē ktisis* ("new creation"), refers to the concept of new creation. It designates the future renewal of the world in Matthew 19:28, but for our purposes it is more significant that in Titus 3:5 *palingenesia* is related to the spiritual and moral renewal of an individual. The inner change is the result of the work of the Spirit who "re-creates" the individuals for new life in Jesus Christ. Similarly, *anagennaō* ("regenerate, bring to birth again") also occurs twice in the New Testament, and in both references designates the "new birth" experienced by believers. These references appear in the same context: first it is stated that believers are given the experience of new birth by God, due to the resurrection of Jesus as an event which opened up vistas of hope (1 Pet. 1:3), while later it is pointed out that this experience takes place "through the living and enduring word of God" (1 Pet. 1:23). The term *anakainoō* ("renew, make new"), which also occurs twice in the New Testament, likewise refers to the renewal of the "inner nature [person]" (2 Cor. 4:16), the "new self" modeled on "the image of its creator" (Col. 3:10). For delineating God's work of new creation in believers, attention also needs to be given to texts in which His activity is referred to using *ktizō* ("to create") without an adjective, applied clearly to renewal in Jesus Christ (Eph. 2:10; 4:24). While in the Genesis creation account *poieō* is used to designate God's creation in the Septuagint (Gen. 1:1, 21, 27; 2:4),

---

45. Isaiah 65:17 and 66:22 are also seen as forming the background to the Pauline text. See, e.g., Peter Balla, "2 Corinthians," in *Commentary on the New Testament Use of the Old Testament*, ed. G. K. Beale and D. A. Carson (Grand Rapids, Mich.: Baker Academic, 2007), 753–83. It seems, however, that these texts refer not to a "new exodus" but to a new creation of a different sort—to the cosmic new creation at the end of history.

this fact does not discount the significance of *ktizō*, which is also utilized in the New Testament for God's creative activity.

The divine work of transformation also lies in the background of a number of texts that lack an explicit reference to creation. These include the *kainos* ("new") texts and those pointing to the qualitative newness in the Christian's life. A good example of the latter is 2 Corinthians 4:6, "For it is the God who said, 'Let light shine out of darkness,' who has shone in our hearts to give the light of the knowledge of the glory of God in the face of Jesus Christ." This text is a reference to the Genesis story of creation. Paul emphasizes his point by drawing a parallel between the creation "in the beginning," and the transformation brought by the light of the gospel into the hearts of those who receive Christ. Thus, in light of the Old Testament background, experiencing the inner renewal needs to be interpreted in terms of God's creative activity. Also, Paul's *en christō* ("in Christ") language implies living in a new world, in the reality of the new creation, since as R. H. Strachan points out, "there is a new creation whenever a man comes to be in Christ."[46] Paul's death-life symbolism, the idea of dying to a certain way of life and living to God (e.g., Rom. 6:1–11; Gal. 2:20), serves the same purpose. Moyer Hubbard observes that this concept functions as "part of the interpreting framework for his new-creation statements."[47]

The people experiencing God's work of new creation make up a new, transformed community. Their life is characterized by a qualitative newness, since their former relationship to the world has ended: the old man belongs to the time "before Christ" and "without Christ."[48] The difference between old and new is emphasized by different analogies: the old yeast should be cleaned out because a new batch is prepared (1 Cor. 5:7); the old self must be crucified that we may live in newness to God in a "resurrection life" (Rom. 6:1–11). The visible testimony to the realization of God's new creation work is baptism, in which believing Christians clothe themselves "with Christ" (Gal. 3:27), becoming part of a "new" community that seeks to live in "newness of life" as people of God (Rom. 6:4).

---

46. R. H. Strachan, *2 Corinthians*, MNTC (London: Hodder and Stoughton, 1935), 113. Similarly, Jeffrey A. Gibbs, "Christ is Risen, Indeed: Good News for Him, and for Us," *CTQ* 40 (2014): 113–31. On p. 126 Gibbs points out that the "in Christ" status of the believers reflects their "participation in the new creation."

47. Moyer V. Hubbard, *New Creation in Paul's Letters and Thought*, SNTSMS 119 (Cambridge: Cambridge University Press, 2002), 89.

48. Hohnjec, *Novo stvaranje*, 61.

The mission of the church is defined by its horizon of newness and the horizon of the end times it exists in. As an eschatological community, the church is called to proclaim to all the nations the prospect of a "transition from suffering and fragmentariness to fulfilment and completeness" in Christ.[49] This task is eschatological in nature because the church serves in the eschatological era of the end times, but even more so because in its mission the eschatological hopes of the Old Testament are realized through the gathering of the scattered remnant of Israel.[50] By the proclamation of the gospel, God's work of new creation is being extended because the number of those accepting Christ's lordship and experiencing transformation multiplies. Thus, the church becomes an agent in God's new creative work, but the realization of its mission is made possible only through the generative power of the Spirit, who makes the kingdom of God present (Acts 1:8). At the same time, the church continues to be the recipient of God's transforming creation, since He never ceases to work on the inner renewal of believers' lives, and by so doing He enables them to remain faithful in their call and commission (2 Cor. 4:16–18).

In a similar way to the resurrection of Jesus, in God's creative work of redemption a clear transformative pattern can be discerned. The lives of those "without Christ" are referred to as lives of darkness, which are transformed by God's intervention as He calls them "out of darkness into his marvelous light" (1 Pet. 2:9). The life of darkness is described in Titus 3:3 in terms of moral and existential disorder. However, the description is followed by God's saving intervention, resulting in "rebirth" and "renewal":

> For we ourselves were once foolish, disobedient, led astray, slaves to various passions and pleasures, passing our days in malice and envy, despicable, hating one another. But when the goodness and loving kindness of God our Savior appeared, he saved us, not because of any works of righteousness that we had done, but according to his mercy, through the water of rebirth and renewal by the Holy Spirit. (Titus 3:3–5)

The experience of "rebirth" (*palingenesia*) is followed by the realization of God's kingship in the lives of transformed people, which is the essence of Jesus's concept of the kingdom of God; in Pauline

---

49. Schwarz, *Eschatology*, 208.
50. For an argument, see, e.g., LaRondelle, *Israel of God*, 98–123.

terminology the new life is life "in the Spirit" (e.g., Rom. 8:9). Since the gift of the Spirit is essential to God's new creational work in the eschatological messianic era, it is significant that the events at Pentecost in Acts 2 are presented in terms of an antithesis to the Babel story (Gen. 10).[51] The confusion of languages at Babel is in antithetical parallelism with the order that came as the result of the Spirit's work: understandable languages. The antecedent of the Babel story is a rebellion against God, while the results of Pentecost are renewed lives in Christ: three thousand people confessing faith in Christ and being baptized in one day (Acts 2:41). The reversal highlights the radical newness of the eschatological messianic era, in which God made provision for the turnaround from disorder to His kingship through His work of new creation.

All the new creation language related to the experience of salvation is rooted theologically in the Genesis creation-fall narrative (Gen. 1–3). The foundational nature of the creation narrative for the biblical storyline resurfaces constantly in the biblical narrative, since God's interventions in human history presuppose a historical creation and a historical fall, which necessitate a fundamental divine involvement in restoring what had been made good and perfect but was distorted by a wrong human decision. New creation, which has been inaugurated in Christ's ministry and continues to take place in the eschatological messianic era through the ministry of the Spirit, will extend forward until it reaches completion at the very end of history, when the "old age" will be terminated. We turn now to the exploration of the third cardinal aspect of this divine creative work, in which God makes "all things new" (Rev. 21:5).

THE CONSUMMATED NEW CREATION: MAKING ALL THINGS NEW

The goal of God's new creation work is the restoration of life on earth. Human beings were created from earth to live on the earth. They belong to the earth and the earth was given to them as a

---

51. For scholars viewing Acts 2 as the reversal of the Babel story, see Jud Davis, "Acts and the Old Testament: The Pentecost Event in Light of Sinai, Babel and the Table of Nations," *CTR* 7 (2009): 29–48, esp. 30n3. For an analysis of the parallels and differences between the two stories, see Barna Magyarosi, "Etnicitás és etnocentrizmus Bábel és pünkösd fényében," in *Keresztény egyetemesség és nemzettudat*, ed. Tibor Tonhaizer (Pécel: Adventista Teológiai Főiskola, 2015), 9–29.

territory to "fill," "subdue," and "have dominion over" (Gen. 1:28). It was on earth that Christ was born and crucified, on earth He experienced resurrection, and it is on earth that the people of God experience deliverance from evil and the final resurrection. Clearly, God did not give up the earth as a lost territory; He works on its restoration, which will culminate in creating a "new earth" (Rev. 21:1; cf. 2 Pet. 3:13). This will not come as a renewal through a process of gradual transformation but will be the result of an act of creation, analogous to the original creation of Genesis 1–2, following a cosmic destruction (Rev. 20:11). This major creative act of God will be, however, preceded by the millennium, starting with Christ's second coming. During this time, the saints, who came alive at the first resurrection, will reign with Christ and participate in judgment (Rev. 20).[52]

The qualitative distinction between the two worlds is indicated by the use of *kainos* ("new"), which designates newness in nature and qualitative superiority, while *neos* signifies newness in time ("what was not there before," "what has only just arisen"), though the two terms are sometimes synonymous.[53] The contrast between "first" (old) and "second" (new) expresses a qualitative antithesis in other texts of Revelation as well, indicating contrast between incompleteness and completeness.[54] However, in spite of the sharp discontinuity between the two creations, continuity will also be maintained to some degree, since "the new cosmos will be an identifiable counterpart to the old cosmos and a renewal of it, just as the body will be raised without losing its former identity."[55] Assurance of this is given in the recognition by the disciples of the resurrected Jesus (e.g., Matt. 28:9; John 20:19–20, 26–29).

God's eschatological intervention will bring redemption for the nonhuman creation as a whole, which suffers the effect of sin and God's judgment. The renewing of the moral order and the natural order are closely connected, since human evil has consequences regarding not only humans but also the rest of God's creation on the

---

52. On the interpretation of Revelation 20, which has generated much discussion and conflict in the Christian era, see, e.g., Joel Badina, "The Millennium," in *Symposium on Revelation: Book 2*, ed. Frank B. Holbrook, DARCOM 7 (Silver Spring, Md.: Biblical Research Institute, 1992), 225–42; Peter M. van Bemmelen, "The Millennium and the Judgment," *JATS* 8 (1997): 150–60; and Eric Claude Webster, "The Millennium," in *HSDAT*, 927–46.

53. E.g., Matt. 9:17.

54. G. K. Beale, *Revelation*, NIGTC (Grand Rapids, Mich.: Eerdmans, 1999), 1006, 1040.

55. Ibid., 1040.

earth. While in the Old Testament a series of passages depicts all the creatures offering praise to their Creator (e.g., Ps. 148), at the same time, in a number of passages the mourning of the earth because of the effect of human wrongdoing is referred to (e.g., Jer. 12:4; Hosea 4:1–3; Joel 1:10–12, 17–20).[56] In the New Testament this Old Testament image is taken up in Romans 8:18–23, which makes reference to Genesis 3. The connection indicates that "because of human sin, God set creation on course for un-creation."[57] According to Paul, creation's deliverance from corruption will happen at the second coming of Christ, when the children of God will attain their full salvation in the glory of the resurrection (Rom. 8:21–23).

With the consummation of the new creation, God's program of restoration reaches its culmination. The most detailed portrayal of the renovated universe occurs in the final vision of Revelation (21:1—22:5), in which the new Jerusalem appears as the reversal of sin, death, agony, futility, and discord. The vision is an appropriate conclusion not only to the book of Revelation but also to the story of the entire Bible. Dumbrell demonstrates in his insightful biblical-theological study that major theological ideas of the biblical storyline—such as the new Jerusalem, new temple, new covenant, new Israel, and new creation—find their ultimate fulfillment in the panoramic concluding vision of the biblical canon.[58] With the transformation of the universe, redemption is complete and everything that does not serve God's glory is terminated. Thus, a state of universal *shalōm* is established.

The cosmic new creation involves a fundamental reshaping of the structure of the universe. Not only a "new earth" but a "new heaven" is also created, since the governmental center of the universe is relocated from heaven to the new earth (Rev. 21:1–5; 22:1–5). Throughout the book of Revelation, the thrones of God, the Lamb, and His allies are located exclusively in the heavenly realm, whereas the thrones of God's adversaries are limited to the earth. The new creation terminates this pattern, since evil is "no more" and "the first things have passed away" (Rev. 21:4). The transfer of the center of space and time to the earth clearly indicates the disappearance of the distance between God and humanity, and the establishment of a

---

56. Strikingly, the mourning is directed to God, similar to praising (Jer. 12:11).

57. Richard Bauckham, *Bible and Ecology* (London: Darton, Longmann, and Todd, 2010), 97.

58. Dumbrell, *The End of the Beginning*.

new order in the universe. This development seals God's victory and stands as a lasting reminder of the vindication of His reputation.[59]

The structure of the new Jerusalem vision is linear. It is introduced by a thematic statement of the new creation (Rev. 21:1–8), which is followed by its description in terms of a temple-city of new Jerusalem, a holy of holies in which God lives (Rev. 21:9–27), and finally the city center is portrayed as the new garden of Eden (Rev. 22:1–5). The language of the vision is drawn first of all from Old Testament prophetic literature, primarily from the eschatological passages of Isaiah and Ezekiel 40–48.[60] Revelation 22:1–5 adds garden of Eden imagery, which ties the description of the renovated cosmos to the creation–Fall narrative (Gen. 1–3). Five parallels can be established between the creation–Fall narrative and the new garden of Eden vision. First, the river of the water of life (*potamon hydatos zōēs*, Rev. 22:1) recalls the river (*potamos*, Gen. 2:10, LXX) flowing out of Eden. Second, the tree of life (*xylon zōēs*, Rev. 22:2; *xylon tēs zōēs*, Gen. 2:9, LXX) appears in both contexts. Third, the curse (*katathema*, Rev. 22:3) is banished from the new Jerusalem, while in the Fall narrative it appears as a consequence of sin (*epikataratos*, Gen. 3:14, 17, LXX). Fourth, the promise of seeing God's face (Rev. 22:4) reflects the undoing of the Fall's consequence of banishment from the divine presence (Gen. 3:23). Fifth, the promise of the reign of the saints (*basileusousin*, Rev. 22:5) reflects Adam's original commission to rule over (*archete*, Gen. 1:28, LXX) the created world. The five allusions do not have equal strength. Whereas the first two are supported by verbal parallels, the other three reflect only thematic correspondence. John does not identify the new creation with the garden of Eden but describes the new Jerusalem in the language of paradise (a term meaning "garden" used to describe Eden in Genesis 2 and 3). Such an approach is not new, since in the Old Testament and particularly in the Jewish apocalyptic literature, garden of Eden imagery and the motif of an eschatological temple/city are related to one another.[61]

---

59. For the macrodynamic of the throne motif's development in Revelation, see Laszlo Gallusz, *The Throne Motif in the Book of Revelation*, LNTS 487 (London: Bloomsbury T&T Clark 2014), 257–68.

60. For a detailed study of intertextual links, see Jan Fekkes, *Isaiah and Prophetic Traditions in the Book of Revelation: Visionary Antecedents and their Development*, JSNTSup 93 (Sheffield: JSOT, 1994); and Jeffrey M. Vogelgesang, "The Interpretation of Ezekiel in the Book of Revelation" (PhD diss., Harvard University, 1985).

61. In the Jewish literature, just as it is stated that the earth shall return to a state of primeval disorder, the new Jerusalem is sometimes linked with paradise itself, not only

The purpose of adding garden of Eden imagery as a fresh symbolic element in the final scene of the vision, which functions as the conclusion to all of Revelation 21, lies in generating a sense of climax. The climactic tone not only of the new Jerusalem vision but also of the entire book of Revelation is generated first of all by the emphasis on the centrality of the throne of God and the Lamb in the new creation (Rev. 22:1, 3). The throne imagery here points to the fact that the new Jerusalem functions as the governmental center of the new creation. No less significantly, it is also made clear that God's kingship is a life-giving reality (the throne is closely related to two images of life: the "water of life" and the "tree of life"). Setting the divine throne in the context of the garden of Eden emanates a rhetorical energy that makes it a fitting conclusion to the book. As Celia Deutsch points out, paradise functions as "the symbol of primeval completeness, a completeness which follows the defeat of chaos. Thus, it is only fitting that the perfection of a restored or new order be symbolized by the image of Paradise. End-time has become primeval time, assuring communities under crisis of the ultimate victory of life and order."[62]

In this cosmic renewal of the universe, the same transformative pattern can be discerned as in the case of the two previously discussed cardinal aspects of God's new creation: Christ's resurrection and the transformation of human lives into "resurrection life" in the present age. The consummated new creation takes place because of the disorder in God's created world, which culminates in the moral chaos of Babylon's dominion and the anarchy following its collapse (Rev. 17–18). God establishes a new order because human sin brought His creation to the verge of collapse. The degradation caused by evil on the earth is clearly expressed in the judgment series of the seven trumpets (Rev. 8:6—11:18), which pictures the course of human history in terms of progressive de-creation.[63] Destruction is followed

---

with the new creation (2 Bar. 4:1–7; 1 En. 90:33–36). In the description of the consummation of the ages in Testament of Dan 5:12, Eden and the new Jerusalem are set in parallel: "Saints shall refresh themselves in Eden; the righteous shall rejoice in the New Jerusalem." It is also said that paradise was sometimes hidden, only to be revealed in the future (2 Bar. 59:8; 4 Ezra 7:123; 8:52; 2 En. 8:1–6).

62. Celia Deutsch, "Transformation of Symbols: The New Jerusalem in Rv 21.1–22.5," *ZNW* 78 (1987): 106–26. The quotation is from p. 117.

63. Jon Paulien, *Decoding Revelation's Trumpets: Literary Allusions and the Interpretation of Revelation 8:7–12*, AUSDDS 11 (Berrien Springs, Mich.: Andrews University Press, 1987), 229–30; Roy C. Naden, *The Lamb among the Beasts: Finding Jesus in the Book of Revelation* (Hagerstown, Md.: Review and Herald, 1996), 141–42; and Hans K. LaRondelle,

by renewal, and the result is the establishment of a new cosmos oriented toward God's throne, which is located in the center of the temple-city, a location where His people will worship Him and "see his face" (Rev. 22:4). The theocentricity of heaven pictured in Revelation 4 and 5 comes into focus again in the new Jerusalem vision, but this time the location is the new earth and God's people are pictured as participating in His rule: "For the Lord God will be their light, and they will reign forever and ever" (Rev. 22:5). The reign of the saints will be, however, freed from all associations of human rule, since it materializes in service in perfect freedom and in seeking God's glory. Thus, seeing God's face and ruling by serving "will be the heart of humanity's eternal joy in their eternal worship of God."[64]

PROTOLOGY AND ESCHATOLOGY

The biblical storyline starts with creation (Gen. 1–3) and ends with the descent of the new Jerusalem, signaling the consummation of the new creation (Rev. 21–22). These two great events serve as two related poles of the biblical meta-narrative. The connecting link is not only the theme of creation but also the motif of God's presence. The story ends with a vision of God who moves His governmental center from heaven to the new earth, coming to dwell with redeemed humanity in the new Jerusalem. The beginning of the biblical narrative resembles this picture. Genesis opens by portraying the creation of the earth, which was designed to be a place where God meets with His people. For this reason, both Eden and the new Jerusalem are pictured in terms of a temple: as a temple-garden and a temple-city.[65]

Since the divine plan was disrupted due to the disobedience of the first couple, humanity lost the privilege of enjoying God's presence directly. The complex story that follows in the biblical narrative

How to Understand the End-Time Prophecies of the Bible (Sarasota, Fla.: First Impressions, 1997), 176.

64. Richard Bauckham, *The Theology of the Book of Revelation*, New Testament Theology (Cambridge: Cambridge University Press, 1993), 142.

65. For Eden as the first earthly sanctuary, see Gordon J. Wenham, "Sanctuary Symbolism in the Garden of Eden Story," in *Proceedings of the Ninth World Congress of Jewish Studies, Division A: The Period of the Bible* (Jerusalem: World Union of Jewish Studies, 1986), 19–25. For the new Jerusalem as a temple, see G. K. Beale, *The Temple and the Church's Mission: A Biblical Theology of the Dwelling Place of God*, New Studies in Biblical Theology 17 (Downers Grove, Ill.: InterVarsity, 2004), 23–26, 365–73.

centers on God's redemptive mission, due to which the earth will be turned into a place where God and humanity can dwell together again. So, the biblical story is structured around the movement from creation to new creation, and the process of redemption is seen as a means leading to restoration of the original creation. The original creation is, therefore, "the assumption in the Old Testament from which all theological movement proceeds," and its restoration is the final goal toward which everything eventually moves.[66] The strong link between the two ends of the canon suggests that these passages frame the entire biblical narrative, and therefore serve as two poles with critical interpretive significance for all biblical material. Consequently, everything in the biblical canon is to be seen as having its roots in Genesis 1 to 3, and also moving toward the final goal in Revelation 21 and 22.[67]

The relation of Genesis 1 to 3 to Revelation 21 and 22 reflects the well-known *Urzeit–Endzeit*, or protology-eschatology schema. As David Aune notes, the essence of this pattern of thought is that "the conditions of eschatological salvation are usually conceptualized as a *restoration* of primal conditions rather than an entirely new or utopian mode of existence with no links to the past."[68] The conception that the end is recapitulating the perfect and paradigmatic beginning is foundational for the apocalyptic worldview.[69] The point of the parallel lies in emphasizing the restoration of the blessings of an earlier idyllic period. At the eschaton a new order is set up in a new environment, but it is the original creation fulfilled and restored to its Edenic origins. Still, John does not identify the new creation with the garden of Eden but rather describes the new Jerusalem in the language of paradise. While in his vision the end resembles the beginning, a significant change is also evident: in Genesis the earth is presented as a site in which some "building" (creative human activity) is expected to occur, while Revelation presents a city descending to earth.[70] The city

---

66. Dumbrell, *The End of the Beginning*, 189.

67. Beale, *Biblical Theology*, 59.

68. David E. Aune, "Eschatology (Early Christian)," *ABD* 2:594–609. The quotation is from pp. 594–95.

69. For the *Urzeit–Endzeit* pattern in Jewish apocalyptic tradition, see David E. Aune, "From the Idealized Past to the Imaginary Future: Eschatological Restoration in Jewish Apocalyptic Literature," in *Apocalypticism, Prophecy and Magic in Early Christianity*, WUNT 199 (Tübingen: Mohr Siebeck, 2006), 13–38, esp. pp. 31–34.

70. T. Desmond Alexander, *From Eden to the New Jerusalem: Exploring God's Plan for Life on Earth* (Nottingham: InterVarsity, 2008), 14.

imagery by no means suggests that the endeavors of humanity "build" an idyllic future. This holy city comes from heaven, from the divine sphere, "in the sense that all good comes from God."[71] In the ancient world, the ideal city was a motif with a strong rhetorical force embodying the ideas of security and prosperity; it was pictured as a place with the divine in its midst.[72] Thus, both creation and the eschaton flow freely from God, and His sovereignty is manifested in both events in which His creative activity is at work.[73]

CONCLUSION

Creation and eschatology are intrinsically interconnected in New Testament theology. To address one without the other risks distorting both topics. It is impossible to separate creation and eschatology since both are part of the same process by which God brings order out of disorder by turning it into an enjoyable place for His people. Moreover, the historicity of the creation narrative (Gen. 1–2) and the eschatological end (Rev. 19:11—22:5) are inherently related. Without acknowledging the historicity of the protology, the reality of the eschatological vision of the world would remain unsubstantiated. And if this were the case, then those who profess the Christian faith and embrace the Christian hope would be, as the apostle Paul claims, "of all people most to be pitied" (1 Cor. 15:19).

It has been demonstrated in this study that the end times were launched by Christ's death and resurrection, the pivotal events of salvation history. These events were the laying of the foundation stone of the new creation, which was a necessity because evil was so ingrained in the present order that a new creation was the only means of dealing effectively with it. Thus, in the eschatological messianic era, God is involved in the world through His new creational work, directing the course of history toward the ultimate and comprehensive restoration at the very end. In this study an argument has been offered in favor of the suggestion that God's new creational activity is being realized through three cardinal works that follow a chronological order: (1) Christ's resurrection as the initiation of the

---

71. Bauckham, *Theology*, 135.

72. For an extended argument, see Eva Räpple, *The Metaphor of the City in the Apocalypse of John*, SBL 67 (New York: Lang, 2004), 139–78.

73. Eric W. Baker, *The Eschatological Role of the Jerusalem Temple: An Examination of the Jewish Writings Dating from 586 BCE to 79 CE* (Hamburg: Anchor Academic, 2015), 31.

new creation; (2) the creation of a new humanity, which is the recipient of, but also the agent in, God's new creational endeavors; and (3) the consummated new creation, which leads to the final restoration of the earth to its original pristine state. In all three events, the same transformative pattern can be observed, revealing consistency in God's work with His creation. Also, all three events are eschatological because they occurred/occur/will occur in the eschatological era of the end times and because they are events of eschatological significance as major milestones in advancing God's work of "making all things new" (Rev. 21:5). The fact that the biblical storyline starts and ends with creation accounts (Gen. 1–2; Rev. 21–22) gives an eminent role to creation as a major theme in biblical theology. While in the New Testament the theme of new creation dominates the creation theology of biblical authors, it was developed having roots in the Old Testament with the conviction that God has spoken "and it came to be; he commanded, and it stood firm" (Ps. 33:9).

BIBLICAL STUDIES

Clinton Wahlen, PhD

Biblical Research Institute
Silver Spring, Maryland, USA

MATTHEW AND THE GENESIS CREATION

INTRODUCTION

The depth to which the Gospel of Matthew interacts with Scripture is difficult to fully appreciate because it operates on so many levels. "Matthew's language and imagery are from start to finish soaked in Scripture."[1] This is no less true of this Gospel's interaction with the book of Genesis and, in particular, the Genesis creation account. Among the hundreds of quotations and allusions made to Scripture, references to Genesis are frequent.[2] In fact, the Gospel's first two words (*biblos geneseōs*) seem to be a deliberate allusion to Genesis, perhaps even to the entire book.[3] Matthew's

---

1. Richard B. Hays, *Echoes of Scripture in the Gospels* (Waco, Tex.: Baylor University Press, 2016), 109; cf. David P. Scaer, "Matthew as the Foundation of the New Testament Canon," *CTQ* 79 (2015): 242–43: "Matthew's great, singular, and unmatched accomplishment is that he drew the entire Old Testament into his Gospel so that on one hand it is forever affirmed as the word of God, but its character is now forever fundamentally changed."

2. Donald Senior, "The Lure of the Formula Quotations: Re-assessing Matthew's Use of the Old Testament with the Passion Narrative as a Test Case," in *The Scriptures in the Gospels*, ed. Christopher M. Tuckett (Leuven: Leuven University Press, 1997), 89, counts sixty-one quotations and 294 implicit citations. Listed in NA[28] are three direct quotations and twenty-four allusions to Genesis.

3. Further, see the section of this study titled "Matthew 1:1," 165. The title *Genesis* already appertained to the first book of the Bible by the time Matthew was written, as evidenced by references to it in Philo (d. AD 50), *Post.* 127; *Abr.* 1; *Aet.* 19. The word *genesis*

eventual placement at the beginning of the New Testament canon,[4] just as Genesis begins the whole Bible, suggests an early recognition of the foundational importance of these two books within their respective canons, as well as, perhaps, the close connection between them. In addition to the Gospel's opening words, there are direct quotations of the creation account itself (Matt. 19:4–5) and clear allusions to other portions of Genesis.[5] Mention of "the beginning" in reference to creation (Matt. 19:8), "the foundation of the world" (Matt. 25:34), and equivalent expressions (Matt. 13:35; 24:21), as well as references to the Sabbath, "heaven and earth," and some instances of *ginomai* (which can mean "come into existence"),[6] implicitly allude to the Genesis creation account. Furthermore, the anticipation of a re-creation, the *palingenesia* (Matt. 19:28), presupposes God's original creation of the world. While the individual significance of these elements in relation to the Genesis creation account might not be immediately apparent, taken together they reinforce the importance of the creation as described in Genesis for understanding Jesus's proclamation of the kingdom of God in Matthew.

(Heb. *tôlĕdôt*) appears fifteen times in the LXX of Genesis with various nuances, including "origin" (2:4; 5:1?), "birth" (31:13; 32:10 [ET 9]; 40:20 [Heb. *hulledet*]), and "generations" or "genealogy" (5:1?; 6:9 [ET 10]; 10:1, 32; 11:10, 27; 25:12, 19; 36:1, 9; 37:2 [ET 1]). See Takamitsu Muraoka, *A Greek-English Lexicon of the Septuagint* (Leuven: Peeters, 2009), 127.

4. Peter M. Head, in private correspondence, indicates that, among all Greek manuscripts, all but one (from the sixteenth century) place Matthew first. According to Eldon Jay Epp, "Issues in the Interrelation of the New Testament Textual Criticism and Canon," in *The Canon Debate: On the Origins and Formation of the Bible*, ed. Lee Martin McDonald and James A. Sanders (Peabody, Mass.: Hendrickson, 2002), 506, of the many ancient extant collections of the Scriptures, including ancient versions, all but four arrangements (often in a single witness) place Matthew first. See P. M. Bogaert, "Ordres anciens des évangiles et tétraévangile en un seul codex," *RTL* 30 (1999): 297–314.

5. E.g., the genealogy (Matt. 1:2–16), references to "the tempter" and serpents (4:3; 10:16), the murder of Abel (23:35), Noah and the flood (24:37–39), Sodom and Gomorrah (11:24), Abraham and the binding of Isaac (1:2; 3:17), the twelve patriarchs (1:2), and Rachel (2:18).

6. W. Bauer, F. W. Danker, W. F. Arndt, and F. W. Gingrich, *A Greek-English Lexicon of the New Testament and Other Early Christian Literature*, 3rd ed. (Chicago, Ill.: University of Chicago Press, 2000), 197. Biblical quotations, when accompanied by the Greek or Hebrew text, are the author's translation. Otherwise, they are from the ESV® Bible (The Holy Bible, English Standard Version®). ESV® Text Edition: 2016. Copyright © 2001 by Crossway, a publishing ministry of Good News Publishers. The ESV® text has been reproduced in cooperation with and by permission of Good News Publishers. Unauthorized reproduction of this publication is prohibited. All rights reserved. All italicized words in biblical quotations are this author's emphasis.

MATTHEW 1:1

There has been much disagreement over the precise purpose of the opening words of Matthew.[7] It is increasingly recognized, however, that they may pertain not just to the initial genealogy or chapter but to the whole book.[8] The very first words of the Gospel could be translated "the Book of the History [Gk. *genesis*] of Jesus Christ."[9] The minds of readers familiar with the Greek Septuagint would thus be drawn to consider the relation of Matthew to the first book of the Bible. The word *biblos* is used ten times in the New Testament, always in the sense of "book" as a whole document,[10] and similarly in the Septuagint.[11] The first two words of Matthew (*biblos geneseōs*) appear twice in Genesis (Gen. 2:4; 5:1, LXX) and *nowhere else* in biblical literature. The first instance of the phrase appears at a crucial transition point in the Genesis creation account, which summarizes the seven-day creation week as "the generations of the heavens and

---

7. Dale C. Allison Jr., "Matthew's First Two Words (Matt 1:1)," in *Studies in Matthew: Interpretation Past and Present* (Grand Rapids, Mich.: Baker, 2005), 158–60, lists six views: (1) introduce the genealogy (reflected in English versions and Greek lexicons); (2) introduce the entire first chapter; (3) introduce the infancy narrative, 1:2–2:23; (4) introduce the first narrative block, 1:1–4:16; (5) represent the title of the entire Gospel; (6) combining the previous views, 1:1 is "telescopic" so that it captures an increasingly larger portion of the narrative that ultimately includes the whole gospel—the view argued by Allison and W. D. Davies (cf. n. 13 in this study) and followed here.

8. Further, see W. D. Davies and Dale C. Allison Jr., *A Critical and Exegetical Commentary on the Gospel According to Matthew*, 3 vols., ICC (Edinburgh: T&T Clark, 1988–1997), 1:149–60; Ulrich Luz, *Matthew 1–7: A Commentary*, trans. James E. Crouch, Hermeneia (Minneapolis, Minn.: Fortress, 2007), 69, and literature cited in 69n3; similarly, J. L. Leuba, "Note exégétique sur Matthieu 1.1a," *RHPR* 22 (1942), 56–61; and R. T. France, *The Gospel of Matthew*, NICNT (Grand Rapids, Mich.: Eerdmans, 2007), 26, 26n1. Alternatively, Nolland argues that 1:1 is related to Genesis only tangentially, connecting Jesus with the history of God's people by way of the genealogy and, in 1:18–25, showing how Jesus entered that history; see John Nolland, *The Gospel of Matthew: A Commentary on the Greek Text*, NIGTC (Grand Rapids, Mich.: Eerdmans, 2005), 71.

9. So Herman C. Waetjen, "The Genealogy as the Key to the Gospel according to Matthew," *JBL* 95, no. 2 (1976): 214; similarly, Luz, *Matthew 1–7*, 69, a modification of his previous position reflected in the comment on the verse in the German edition (Allison, "First Two Words," 160n7). Luz, *Matthew 1–7*, 70, rejects that Matthew could be introducing "a theology of the new creation through Christ," because Jesus is not "creator" but "part of creation" (ibid., 70n11)—a contention that overlooks the larger perspective of the book, which is, to some extent, developed here (see the section of this study titled "Jesus's Power over Creation," 178).

10. "The book of Moses" (Mark 12:26); "the book of the words of Isaiah the prophet" (Luke 3:4); "the book of Psalms" (Luke 20:42; Acts 1:20); "the book of the prophets" (Acts 7:42); "books" of magic (Acts 19:19); "the book of life" (Phil. 4:3; Rev. 3:5; 20:15).

11. E.g., God's "book" (Exod. 32:32); "the book of the law" (Josh. 1:8; 2 Chron. 17:9); "the book of the living" (Ps. 69:28); "the words of the book which Jeremiah sent" (Jer. 36:10); "the books were opened" (Dan. 7:10).

the earth when they were created" (Gen. 2:4), before describing in detail the creation of human beings (Gen. 2:5–25). The second instance introduces "the book of the generations of Adam" (Gen. 5:1) up to the time of Noah (Gen. 5:1–32), who "saved" the human race through the building of an ark.

Matthew parallels this dual usage. The use of the phrase in 1:1 introduces "the Christian 'Book of Genesis,' the beginning of the New Creation,"[12] ushered in through the incarnation of Jesus Christ.[13] Matthew's second use of *genesis* (v. 18) connects the genealogy of Jesus with the account of His "beginning" as a human being (that is, His birth),[14] preparing readers to appreciate the epochal significance of the birth of Jesus, who "will save his people from their sins" (1:21).[15] His being named Jesus (Heb. *yeshua'*, "Yahweh saves") is important because it corresponds to His work as Savior.[16] The role of the Holy Spirit in Matthew, at Jesus's birth (1:18, 20) and baptism (3:16), "harkens back to the Spirit's activity at creation [Gen. 1:2]."[17]

The genealogies of Genesis 5 and 11:10–26 function as a timeline, providing a chronology back to the creation of the world and forward to the time of Abraham.[18] The genealogy in Matthew has a theological purpose corresponding to these early genealogies of Genesis in that they link Jesus as "the Son of Abraham," who was the father of the Hebrews (Gen. 14:13), to the heritage of Israel.[19] As "the Son of David, the Son of Abraham," Jesus is also linked to the covenants God made

---

12. Frank W. Beare, *The Earliest Records of Jesus* (New York: Abingdon, 1962), 30.

13. So Davies and Allison, *Matthew*, 1:154, cf. 159. Following J. C. Fenton, *The Gospel of St. Matthew*, Pelican Gospel Commentaries (Baltimore: Pelican, 1963), 36, they consider 1:1 as a "telescopic" reference that comprehends within it progressively larger portions of the gospel narrative.

14. Use of the term in this sense does not deny the preexistence of Jesus, which is already implicit in Matthew in part through his narration of the virgin birth (cf. n. 9 in this study). In the New Testament, *genesis* appears just three more times (Luke 1:14; James 1:23; 3:6).

15. Recognizing this parallel is Raik Heckl, "Der biblische Begründungsrahmen für die Jungfrauengeburt bei Matthäus: Zur Rezeption von Gen. 5,1–6,4 in Mt 1," *ZNW* 95 (2004): 176, though his attempt to connect descriptions of the supernatural birth of Jesus and the birth of the "giants" as the supposed product of sexual relations between angels and human beings (citing *m. Sanh.* 10.3, *Gen. Rab.* 26.5, and relevant passages in 1 Enoch) is unpersuasive.

16. So Waetjen, "Genealogy," 230.

17. Jonathan T. Pennington, *Heaven and Earth in the Gospel of Matthew* (Grand Rapids, Mich.: Baker, 2007), 213.

18. Gerhard F. Hasel, "Genesis 5 and 11: Chronogenealogies in the Biblical History of Beginnings," *Origins* 7, no. 1 (1980): 23–37, esp. 25.

19. On the dissimilarity between the genealogies in Matthew and Luke, see Clinton Wahlen, *The Gospel of Matthew*, Seventh-day Adventist International Bible Commentary (Nampa, Idaho: Pacific Press, forthcoming); Clinton Wahlen, *The Gospel of Luke*, Andrews Bible Commentary (Berrien Springs, Mich.: Andrews University Press, forthcoming).

with them. The suggestion has even been made that the order of Abraham to David to Christ or Messiah (Matt. 1:17), using the initial Hebrew consonants of each name (*'dm*), may present Jesus as the new "Adam" (cf. Rom. 5:14). While not impossible in view of a similar correspondence between the number fourteen and the sum of the letters of David's name in Hebrew (*d* [4] + *w* [6] + *d* [4] = 14), it seems unlikely since Adam goes unmentioned in Matthew (but cf. Luke 3:38). The fact that Matthew's "title" in 1:1 (Jesus-David-Abraham) reverses the normal chronological order of genealogies exalts "Jesus as the goal and fulfillment" of the Hebrew Bible.[20] The seven interruptions in the rhythm of "X begot Y, Y begot Z" in Matthew's genealogy signals in each instance a major development in the fulfillment of God's promise.[21] These interruptions to the genealogical pattern reference "a significant act of God which leads Israel beyond a threat to the promise and finally to the age of the Messiah."[22] As in the beginning a miracle was required to create life, so in the final link of the genealogy a miracle birth brings the story to its climax (Matt. 1:18–25). "It is entirely the work of the Spirit," who effects the incarnation of Jesus as a human being "by a direct act of creation."[23] In the life of Jesus, "creation and history are fulfilled."[24]

More broadly, these early references to Genesis indicate an appreciation of that book as a historical account. Passing mention of the creation in the phrases "from the beginning" (Matt. 19:4, 8) or "from the beginning of the world" (24:21) and "the foundation [*katabolē*] of the world" (Matt. 13:35;[25] 25:34; cf. John 17:24),[26] likewise indicates that

---

20. Robert H. Gundry, *Matthew: A Commentary on His Handbook for a Mixed Church under Persecution*, 2nd ed. (Grand Rapids, Mich.: Eerdmans, 1994), 13.

21. As rendered in the NKJV, 1:2 ("Jacob begot Judah and his brothers"), 3 ("Judah begot Perez and Zerah by Tamar"), 5 ("Salmon begot Boaz by Rahab" and "Boaz begot Obed by Ruth"), 6 ("David the king begot Solomon by her who had been the wife of Uriah"), 11–12 ("Josiah begot Jeconiah and his brothers about the time they were carried away to Babylon. And after they were brought to Babylon . . . "), 16 ("Jacob begot Joseph the husband of Mary, of whom was born Jesus who is called Christ").

22. Charles Thomas Davis, "The Fulfillment of Creation: A Study of Matthew's Genealogy," *JAAR* 41, no. 4 (1973): 523, counting only five interruptions (1:3, 5, 6, 11–12, 16).

23. Waetjen, "Genealogy," 224.

24. Davis, "Fulfillment of Creation," 535.

25. While important textual witnesses omit *kosmou*, "of the world," other impressive manuscript evidence supports it (א*2 C D L W Θ f13 lat syph co TR) and both major edited Greek texts (GNT4, NA28) include it within brackets. See Bruce M. Metzger, *A Textual Commentary on the Greek New Testament*, 2nd ed. (New York: United Bible Societies, 1994), 28.

26. Temporal reference to the creation of the world in the sense of "beginning" is made in this way (Eph. 1:4; Heb. 4:3; 9:26; 1 Pet. 1:20; Rev. 13:8; 17:8). The word *katabolē* can also refer to conceiving life in the womb (Heb. 11:11) or simply to "creation" (*Let. Aris.* 129).

the Genesis creation account was assumed to be historical.[27] Jesus's casual mention that God "makes his sun rise on the evil and on the good" (Matt. 5:45, emphasis added) affirms that God created the sun and oversees its operation. Additional indications of the perceived historicity of Genesis are Jesus's references to Abel and Noah as historical persons (23:35; 24:37–38) and to the Flood as a historical event (24:38–39).[28] The historicity of the Genesis creation and the Flood as a global cataclysmic event is the basis for the conception of the coming of the Son of Man as a similarly global and cataclysmic event in the future (24:27, 37, 39),[29] not only in the teaching of Jesus in Matthew but also elsewhere in the New Testament (2 Pet. 3:3–7; Rev. 14:7, 14–20).

USE OF *GINOMAI* IN MATTHEW

In addition to the explicit allusion to the book of Genesis (and, less directly, to creation) in Matthew 1:1, reference to the language of the Genesis creation account may also be hinted at in the first Gospel through the frequent use of *ginomai* ("become, come into existence"). Its past tense (aorist) form, *egeneto*, which occurs twenty times in Genesis 1 alone and twice more in Genesis 2,[30] appears in Matthew in connection with miracles involving nature: Jesus calming the sea (8:24, 26),[31] the transfiguration (17:2), the three hours of darkness at midday while Jesus was on the cross (27:45), and the earthquake at His resurrection (28:2).[32] Seven times *ginomai* refers to the fulfillment of God's word (1:22; 5:18;

---

27. Ekkehardt Mueller, "Creation in the New Testament," 11, in this volume.

28. Ibid., 19: "When reading these short passages we get the clear impression that according to Jesus, Noah and Abel were not mythological figures but real human beings, that Genesis 3–11 is a historical narrative that should not be understood symbolically, and that a global flood actually happened (Gen. 6–8)."

29. See the discussion of *palingenesia* in this study in connection with "heaven and earth" in Matthew, 174.

30. In the LXX: Gen. 1:3, 5 (2x), 6, 8 (2x), 9, 11, 13 (2x), 15, 19 (2x), 20, 23 (2x), 24, 30, 31 (2x); 2:4, 7. While *ginomai* is common in the Old Testament, the aorist form *egeneto* is less frequent but occurs 116 times in Genesis—more than double the occurrences in the remaining books of the Pentateuch combined and far more than any other single Old Testament book. Furthermore, its twenty occurrences in Genesis 1 are striking, as no other chapter of the book has more than six occurrences, and in twenty chapters it does not occur at all.

31. For further discussion on the so-called "nature" miracles performed by Jesus, see the section of this study titled "Jesus's Power over Creation," 178.

32. This usage is merely suggestive rather than allusive, as the majority of occurrences in Matthew simply mean "it happened."

21:4; 24:6, 34; 26:54, 56), reminding readers of the active nature of the divine word to accomplish His purpose (Ps. 33:7; Isa. 55:11).[33] A closely related idea appears when "the tempter" suggests to Jesus that if He is really the Son of God (Matt. 3:17; cf. 1:21),[34] He should have a similar divine capacity simply to "speak" (*eipe*) so that the stones would become loaves of bread (4:3). Jesus is being encouraged to use the spoken word to perform a "creative" miracle, like that which provided manna to Israel in the wilderness, but He responds by quoting the Scripture that affirms the necessity of living "by every word that comes from the mouth of God" (Matt. 4:4; cf. Deut. 8:3).[35]

The imperative passive form of *ginomai*, echoing the creation account in which God says, "Let there be . . . " (Gen. 1:3, 6, 14, LXX), is extremely rare; yet five of the eight New Testament occurrences are in Matthew.[36] Two of these are in prayer. In Gethsemane, as Jesus commits Himself to *finishing* the work of redemption, He prays, "your will be done" (Matt. 26:42; cf. Gen. 2:1; John 19:30). The Lord's Prayer includes the same petition, "your will be done"— "be made a reality" (*genēthētō*)—"on earth as it is in heaven" (Matt. 6:10), looking forward to the earth's eschatological transformation.[37] The other three Matthean occurrences are in connection with "re-creative" healing miracles, whereby faith in Jesus's creative power enables miraculous healings to be done (8:13; 9:29; 15:28)

---

33. So Ernst Lohmeyer, *Das Evangelium des Matthäus*, 4th ed., KEK (Göttingen: Vandenhoeck and Ruprecht, 1967), 56. Accomplishing a similar purpose are the twelve fulfillment quotations (Matt. 1:23; 2:6, 15, 18, 23; 4:15–16; 8:17; 12:18–21; 13:14–15, 35; 21:5; 27:9–10).

34. The first class condition in Greek does not indicate the reality of the condition but that the possibility of it being true is accepted for the purpose of the argument. Several times in Matthew this type of condition is clearly believed to be false (Matt. 12:26–27; 27:40, 43). See James L. Boyer, "First Class Conditions: What Do They Mean?" *Grace Theological Journal* 2, no. 1 (1981): 75–114.

35. This shortening by Jesus of the last phrase of the Deuteronomic admonition compared with the LXX (a phrase not found in Luke 4:4) emphasizes even more strongly the divine origin (and concomitant authority) of God's word, which appears to be a significant theme for Matthew (1:22; 4:15; 15:4).

36. It also appears in Acts 1:20 (quoting Psalms 69:25 and 109:8 as fulfilled), Romans 11:9 (quoting Psalm 69:22–23 as fulfilled) and 1 Peter 1:15 ("be holy in all your conduct," only possible through re-creation). Outside of the Genesis creation account, the form occurs in the LXX thirty-two times, usually as a "divine passive" describing or anticipating God's direct action (e.g., Gen. 9:27; Exod. 9:9; 10:21; Judg. 6:39 [2x]; Ps. 30:19 [ET 18]; Jer. 18:22).

37. Davies and Allison, *Matthew*, 1:606–7. In my chapter, apart from direct quotations, "heaven" refers to earth's "sky" (which includes the atmosphere and perhaps also the starry heavens) while "Heaven" refers to the place where God resides, where His perfect will is done.

and spirits or demons to be cast out "with a word" (8:16).[38] In fact, in most of the miraculous healings recorded by Matthew, the word of Jesus effects the change, "recalling the power manifest at creation."[39] Other uses of *ginomai* in Matthew implying that God's creative power is at work include references to certain of Jesus's "greatest miracles" (11:20),[40] transformation to become like little children (18:3; cf. 23:26), and asking in faith to move a "mountain" (21:21). There is even a reference to what might be called "de-creative" power in connection with judgment (21:19).

THE SABBATH IN MATTHEW

The Sabbath, which points back to the creation of the world in six days and God's rest on the seventh day (Gen. 2:1–3) as recited in the fourth commandment (Exod. 20:8–11), is explicitly mentioned in Matthew eleven times in four separate passages.[41] The Sabbath disputes in Matthew are not over *whether* the Sabbath should be kept, but *how*.[42] The importance of Sabbath observance, which two successive

---

38. H. H. Esser, "Creation," *NIDNTT* 1:384. W. Grimm, "θεραπεύω [*therapeuō*]," *EDNT* 2:144, considers healing by the word characteristic of Jesus's "power as creator": "The spoken word is enough by itself; it is 'immediately' (*euthys, parachrēma*) turned to reality, in analogy to the creative word that overcame chaos" (citing Genesis 1–2 and Matthew 9:8, 13 among other passages).

39. Clinton Wahlen, "Healing," in *Dictionary of Jesus and the Gospels*, ed. Joel B. Green, Jeannine K. Brown, and Nicholas Perrin, 2nd ed. (Downers Grove, Ill.: InterVarsity Academic, 2013), 367; cf. the chart on p. 364 in which, when the means is mentioned, nine of thirteen healings recorded in Matthew (with resurrection counted as a "healing") involve the word spoken by Jesus. Interestingly, while the percentage of Jesus's healings done through the word are similar across the Synoptics (about seventy percent of the cases in which the means is mentioned), in all four healings recorded in John Jesus effects transformation by His word.

40. According to A. T. Robertson, *A Grammar of the Greek New Testament in the Light of Historical Research* (Nashville, Tenn.: Broadman, 1934), 670 (b), use of "the true superlative" is probable here.

41. Matthew 12:1, 2, 5 (2x), 8; 12:10, 11, 12; 24:20; 28:1 (2x). The second occurrence in 28:1, usually translated "week," literally means "the first day leading up to the Sabbath." See Clinton Wahlen, "The First Day of the Week in the New Testament," in *The Sabbath in the New Testament and in Theology: Implications for Christians in the Twenty-First Century*, ed. Ekkehardt Mueller and Eike Mueller (Silver Spring, Md.: Biblical Research Institute, forthcoming).

42. F. Scott Spencer, "Scripture, Hermeneutics, and Matthew's Jesus," *Int* 64, no. 4 (2010): 371: "By no means does Jesus (or Matthew) abrogate the Sabbath; the point is clarifying the boundaries of acceptable activity on this sacred day." Similarly, Robert K. McIver, "The Sabbath in the Gospel of Matthew: A Paradigm for Understanding the Law in Matthew?" *AUSS* 33 (1995): 232–33; Davies and Allison, *Matthew*, 2:307; and Phillip Sigal, *The Halakhah of Jesus of Nazareth According to the Gospel of Matthew* (Lanham, Md.: University Press of America, 1986), 192. Note, in connection with the Sabbath controversies, Jesus's defense of the disciples' plucking of grain on the Sabbath as guiltless (Matt. 12:7) and the concern with what is lawful (Matt. 12:10).

passages in chapter 12 underscore (Matt. 12:1–8, 9–14), rests on Jesus's insistence that the law is inviolable (5:17) but also on His revelation of the law's deeper significance (5:21–48) and the overarching principles in Sabbath observance of mercy (12:7) and doing good (12:12).[43] The admonition to pray about not having to flee danger on Sabbath (24:20) fits well within the same overall picture of continued Sabbath observance among the Christians to whom Matthew wrote.[44]

Looking a little more broadly within Matthew, the verses immediately preceding the Sabbath controversies of chapter 12 refer to "rest" (11:28–29), an aspect inherent in the Sabbath itself. Significantly, Jesus's invitation to come and find rest is preceded by a prayer to God as His Father, whom He addresses as "Lord of heaven and earth" (*kurie tou ouranou kai tēs gēs*). This title, used only twice more in the New Testament (Luke 10:21; Acts 17:24; cf. 4 Bar. 5:32), "recalls God's act of creation"[45] (Gen. 1:1; Isa. 37:16; Jer. 10:11) and should be understood in light of Jesus's claim in the larger overall context to be "lord of the Sabbath" (Matt. 12:8). Creation week culminated in God's setting apart of the seventh day as the Sabbath as a reminder to human beings that the whole earth and all life on it belongs to God (Gen. 2:4; cf. Exod. 20:11; 31:17) because He is the Creator (Ps. 24:1–2; cf. Jer. 10:11–12).[46] Matthew 11:25 has an additional element relevant for consideration here: a phrase unique to Matthew ("at that time/season"),[47] used also to introduce 12:1–14, further suggesting that the entire block (11:25—12:14) has the Sabbath as a unifying theme.[48]

---

43. McIver, "The Sabbath in the Gospel of Matthew," 241–243.

44. The interpretation of this verse by Graham H. Stanton, *A Gospel for a New People: Studies in Matthew* (Louisville, Ky.: Westminster John Knox, 1992), 203–5, which presupposes a context of extremely strict Sabbath observance among the persecutors of the Gospel's recipients, besides being an example of special pleading, ignores the fact that saving life was widely recognized as acceptable activity on the Sabbath long before the time Matthew was written (1 Macc. 2:29–41).

45. Davies and Allison, *Matthew*, 2:274, citing also LXX Tob. 7:17; Jdt. 9:12 (which has *despota* in place of *kyrios*). 1QapGen ar XXII:16, 21, quotes the title in Gen. 14:19, 22 as "the Lord of heaven and earth" (Aram. *mrh shmy' w'r'*), though, as Joachim Jeremias, *New Testament Theology* (London: SCM, 1971), 187 n.1, points out, the ambiguous Hebrew participle *qoneh* means "Creator"; cf. Gen. 14:19, 22, LXX: *hos ektisen ton ouranon kai tēn gēn*, "who created the heaven and the earth."

46. Walter Brueggemann, *Old Testament Theology: An Introduction* (Nashville, Tenn.: Abingdon, 2008), 76.

47. Gk. *en ekeinō tō kairō*, elsewhere only in 14:1.

48. The linking phrase is noted by Samuele Bacchiocchi, "Matthew 11:28–30: Jesus' Rest and the Sabbath," *AUSS* 22 (1984), 291, but rather than seeing the Sabbath as a unifying

The offer of rest (Matt. 11:28–29) alludes to God's promise in Exodus 33:14 that His "presence" (Heb. *panay*, "My face") will give rest to Moses.[49] The larger Old Testament context is God's revelation of Himself and of His character to Moses, the second giving of the Decalogue on tables of stone, the renewal of the covenant, and Israel's anticipated entrance into Canaan (Exod. 33:7—34:35). Jesus is the Prophet like Moses (Deut. 18:15–18),[50] who, as the Son, knows the Father intimately (cf. Exod. 33:11, 21–23; Num. 12:8; Deut. 34:10), reveals Him to others (Matt. 11:25–27 par.), and offers God's promised "rest." This rest embraces Israel's restoration,[51] their implied deliverance described elsewhere in terms of "salvation."[52] The Sabbath established at creation is the Edenic spring from which these ideas flow.[53] Based on a similar reference in the Apocrypha (*Sir.* 51:23–27), the "yoke" has often been identified as the teaching of Jesus, who represents God's wisdom, in contrast to strict Pharisaic traditions of Sabbath observance (cf. Acts 15:10; Gal. 5:1).[54] However, besides this interpretation of the yoke being unlikely in view of Jesus's earlier insistence on a righteousness that exceeds that of the scribes and Pharisees (Matt. 5:20), the image of Israel placed under a yoke (Heb. *'ōl*) in the Hebrew Bible consistently refers to a yoke of service—whether to God, the king, or a foreign power.[55] Thus, in the immediate context of Matthew 11, it is more

---

theme, he sees the connection more in terms of "the contrast between *rejection* and *revelation*" with regard to Christ's "mighty works" (emphasis original).

49. Davies and Allison, *Matthew*, 2:287.

50. Dale C. Allison, *The New Moses: A Matthean Typology* (Minneapolis, Minn.: Fortress, 1993). On pp. 218–233, the parallel based on Matt. 11:25–30 is drawn; similarly, Fenton, *Matthew*, 187.

51. B. Charette, "'To Proclaim Liberty to the Captives': Matthew 11:28–30 in the Light of OT Prophetic Expectation," *NTS* 38 (1992): 293–94.

52. Donald A. Hagner, *Matthew 1–13*, WBC 33A (Nashville, Tenn.: Thomas Nelson, 1993), 324; and M. Eugene Boring, *The Gospel of Matthew: Introduction, Commentary, and Reflections*, NIBC 8 (Nashville, Tenn.: Abingdon, 1994), 275.

53. The complicated issue of the Pentateuch's composition is not germane to our purposes here, on which see Richard M. Davidson, "The Genesis Account of Origins," in *The Genesis Creation Account and Its Reverberations in the Old Testament*, ed. Gerald A. Klingbeil (Berrien Springs, Mich.: Andrews University Press, 2015), 60n4 and the literature cited there.

54. E.g., Davies and Allison, *Matthew*, 2:289–90; and Bacchiocchi, "Matthew 11:28–30," 303.

55. It refers to Israel's service in Egypt (Lev. 26:13; Jer. 2:20), under kingly rule (1 Kings 12:4, 10–11, 14; 2 Chron. 10:4, 10–11, 14), and foreign domination (Isa. 10:27; 14:25; 47:6; Jer. 30:8; Ezek. 34:27), as well as to serving or obeying God within the terms of the covenant (Jer. 5:5).

likely that Jesus is inviting people into service in God's kingdom under His leadership as the Father's unique representative.

HEAVEN AND EARTH IN MATTHEW

Interestingly in Matthew, the kingdom Jesus proclaims is usually described more precisely as "the kingdom of *heaven*" (emphasis added).[56] Unlike the limited fulfillment of the promises to Israel of an earthly kingdom ruled by a Davidic king, Jesus, as the Messiah greater than Solomon (the "son of David") and greater than the temple (Matt. 12:6, 42), is able to offer rest now because it is available to citizens of a higher kingdom.[57] Matthew's frequent description of God's kingdom as a heavenly kingdom is highly significant as it is found nowhere else in the New Testament.[58] Paired references to heaven and earth occur over twelve times in Matthew,[59] more than any other New Testament book except Revelation. Reference to "heaven and earth" as a single unified whole, frequent in the Old Testament, occurs in Matthew only three times.[60] Two of these are similar and seem to refer to the earth and sky (5:18; 24:35) because the second of these indicates that "heaven and earth will pass away"—presumably at the eschaton when the Isaianic promise of a new heaven and new earth will be fulfilled (Isa. 65:17; 66:22; cf. 2 Pet. 3:13; Rev. 21:1). The other reference has Jesus praying to the "Father, Lord of heaven and earth" (Matt. 11:25; Luke 10:21; cf. Acts 17:24), a form of address with affinities to Old Testament expressions.[61] The dominion

---

56. This usage, which occurs thirty-two times, is unique to Matthew, showing that it is an important emphasis of this Gospel. It is not simply reverential avoidance of the divine name because "the kingdom of God" also occurs (Matt. 6:33; 12:28; 19:24; 21:31, 43).

57. In fact, "kingdom" (*basileia*) in Matthew occurs fifty-five times, which is more than Mark (twenty times) and Luke-Acts (fifty-four times), and represents more than a third of all New Testament references.

58. The phrase occurs thirty-two times and is part of a larger contrast between earthly ways and kingdoms and God's kingdom, as evidenced by the use of "heaven(ly)" in Matthew (eighty-nine times) compared to Luke (thirty-six times), and Mark and John (both eighteen times). See Robert Foster, "Why on Earth Use 'Kingdom of Heaven'?: Matthew's Terminology Revisited," *NTS* 48 (2002): 487–99; and Pennington, *Heaven and Earth*, esp. 193–216. Additionally, of the nine occurrences of "heavenly" in the New Testament seven are in Matthew.

59. See Matthew 5:18; 6:10; 11:25; 16:19 [2x]; 18:18 [2x], 19; 23:9; 24:30, 35; 28:18. Cf. Pennington, *Heaven and Earth*, 193.

60. Ibid., 200, noting use of the set phrase "article-heaven-*kai*-article-earth" with singular verb (Matt. 5:18; 11:25; 24:35); cf. p. 176, on Old Testament usage.

61. See also n. 45 in this study. More common than titles is the affirmation that God made the heaven and the earth (Gen. 1:1; 2:4; Exod. 20:11; 31:17; 2 Kings 19:15; 2 Chron. 2:12; Pss. 115:3, 15; 121:2; 124:8; 134:3; 146:6; Isa. 37:16; 51:13; Jer. 32:17; cf. Acts 4:24;

here referred to may likewise be no broader than the earth and sky, but based on the Old Testament references to God as "Lord of heaven and earth," the exalted tone of Jesus's speech, and the cosmic perspective generally found in Matthew, in 11:25 "heaven and earth" more likely refers to the entire universe. This would fit the Gospel's emphasis on the antithetic contrast between the earthly realm with its unrighteous inhabitants, outward piety, and fading rewards and the heavenly realm of the Father, who knows His people's needs and who promises incorruptible and eternal riches.[62] "Heaven is a place where the Father's will is loyally enacted but on the earth it is contested," and it is only through "access to the strength of heaven" that Jesus's disciples can fulfill the righteousness characterized by the kingdom of heaven (cf. Matt. 7:21).[63]

However, earth will not forever be in opposition to heaven. In the eschaton, when "heaven and earth will pass away" (Matt. 24:35; cf. 5:18), referring to earth and sky, there will be a re-creation (*palingenesia*) as the culmination of God's redemptive plan (19:28).[64] Although the exact nature of this transformation is not further described, it apparently refers to the time of the resurrection (22:23–33; cf. 28:6–7),[65] when judgment is entrusted to the righteous (20:21; cf. Dan. 7:22; 1 Cor. 6:2–3; Rev. 20:4–6) and they receive their reward. This apocalyptic culmination of history is frequently compared with the Isaianic depiction of a new heavens and a new earth (Isa. 65:17; 66:22),[66] which presumes the creative power of God to remake this planet to be the eternal home it was

---

Rev. 10:6; 14:7; similarly, Josephus, *Ant.* 4.40; 8.107). Jesus may show familiarity with the first benediction of the *Tefilla* (which quotes Gen. 14:19, 22; see Jeremias, *Theology*, 187, 187n1, indicating that the Heb. participle "*qōnē* means 'Creator', but in Judaism it was understood as 'Lord'").

62. Ibid., 201, 209–210.

63. Foster, "Why on Earth Use 'Kingdom of Heaven'?" 498.

64. David C. Sim, "The Meaning of παλιγγενεσία in Matthew 19.28," *JSNT* 50 (1993): 11, cites its presence in multiple Jesus traditions and attestation elsewhere in the New Testament (2 Pet. 3:10; Rev. 21:1; cf. 1 Cor. 7:31; 1 John 2:17) as evidence that the idea that "the present cosmic order has a finite existence" derives from Jesus Himself. The only other biblical use of *palingenesia* refers to the new birth (Titus 3:5; cf. John 3:3, 5–7; 2 Cor. 5:17). In Philo, *Mos.* 2:65 (also 1 Clem. 9:4), it is used in reference to the new world that greeted the inhabitants of the ark after the flood. Its single use in Josephus, *Ant.* 11.66, refers to the restoration of Israel at the time of Zerubbabel.

65. Ulrich Luz, *Matthew 8–20: A Commentary*, trans. James E. Crouch, Hermeneia 61B (Minneapolis, Minn.: Fortress, 2001), 517, noting its use in Philo, *Post.*, 124; *Cher.*, 114; and *Embassy*, 325.

66. So Craig Keener, *The IVP Bible Background Commentary: New Testament* (Downers Grove, Ill.: InterVarsity, 1993), 98; Craig L. Blomberg, *Matthew*, NAC 22 (Nashville, Tenn.:

originally intended to be. It is "the consummation of God's work" in Jesus Christ that began at creation.[67]

MATTHEW 19:3–9

The most explicit reference to the Genesis creation in Matthew is in connection with a question some Pharisees ask Jesus once He returns to Judea after completing His Galilean ministry (Matt. 19:3).[68] The issue, which was vigorously debated at the time of Jesus,[69] concerns the grounds for divorce. According to the Mosaic law, divorce was permitted if a husband "found some indecency" in his wife (lit. "nakedness of a thing," Heb. *'erwat dābār*, Deut. 24:1). The school of Shammai maintained that "nakedness" referred to sexual immorality (cf. use of *porneia* in Matt. 5:32) and various immodest acts,[70] while the school of Hillel argued essentially for an "any cause" divorce.[71] Jesus initially ignores the Pharisees' allusion to the Deuteronomic legislation,[72] referring them back to creation by quoting from two sections of the Genesis creation account.

The first quotation (verbatim from Gen. 1:27, LXX; cf. Gen. 5:2) is introduced by the substantive aorist participle (*ho ktisas*).[73] Although it could be understood as a title, "The Creator" (Matt. 19:4; cf. Isa. 45:8, LXX; Rom. 1:25), it literally means "He who created" and stresses God's creative activity. The prepositional phrase

---

Broadman, 1992), 300–301; and R. T. France, *Matthew: An Introduction and Commentary*, TNTC 1 (Downers Grove, Ill.: InterVarsity, 1985), 291.

67. Jonathan T. Pennington, "Heaven, Earth, and a New Genesis: Theological Cosmology in Matthew," in *Cosmology and New Testament Theology*, ed. Jonathan T. Pennington and Sean M. McDonough (London: T&T Clark, 2008), 43. According to Revelation 20–21, this re-creation of the earth will take place after the millennium.

68. Jewish pilgrims typically crossed over to the east side of the Jordan in order to avoid traveling through Samaria (Matt. 19:1). See Blomberg, *Matthew*, 289.

69. David Instone-Brewer, *Divorce and Remarriage in the Bible: The Social and Literary Context* (Grand Rapids, Mich.: Eerdmans, 2002), 134.

70. E.g., going in public with hair unfastened or armpits uncovered and bathing in the same place as men. See John P. Meier, *Law and History in Matthew's Gospel: A Redactional Study of Mt 5:17–48*, Analecta Biblica 71 (Rome: Biblical Institute Press, 1976), 143–44, 144n44.

71. See Instone-Brewer, *Divorce*, 91–93; *m. Git.* 9:10 interprets "indecency in anything" to include "if she spoiled a dish for him," and "no favour in his eyes" to mean "if he found another fairer than she" (Herbert Danby, trans., *The Mishnah* [London: Oxford University Press, 1933], 321).

72. Jesus's response also finesses the political implications that might have pertained to their question in the wake of John the Baptist's death (France, *Matthew*, NICNT, 716).

73. The majority text and other witnesses (א C D (L) W Z f¹³ 𝔐 lat sy) read *poiēsas* ("made") to harmonize it with the main verb (Metzger, *Textual Commentary*, 38).

(*ap archēs*, "from the beginning") links the creation of human beings on the sixth day of creation week (Gen. 1:26–31) to the very beginning of earth's history (cf. Gen. 1:1, LXX, *en archē*).[74] All three uses of the phrase *ap archēs* in Matthew refer to creation week—two in this passage (19:4, 8) and the other referring to "the beginning of the world" (24:21). As with references to "the foundation of the world" (13:35; 25:34; see previous discussion on 1:1), this language indicates that the Genesis creation account was assumed to be historical. Jesus's assertion that the Creator made them "male and female" stresses the complementarity of human beings, that from the beginning "God created the two genders for each other."[75] By continuing uninterrupted with the second quotation, from Genesis 2:24,[76] Jesus attributes the words in this verse to the Creator. In this way, while it is not obvious from the original context of Genesis, Jesus makes clear that it is God Himself who created the institution of marriage for the first couple.[77] Additionally, the word "therefore," which in Genesis follows Adam's statement about Eve being "bone of my bones and flesh of my flesh" (Gen. 2:23), is included by Jesus in order to explicitly link the creation of human beings as male and female (Gen. 1:27) to the divinely created institution of marriage (Gen. 2:24). Thus, the fact of the man leaving his parents and cleaving to his wife is not merely an explication of the marriage process but fulfills the divine command—meaning that, in accordance with the divinely established creation order, the marriage institution is designed for one man and one woman.[78] In short, by juxtaposing these two quotations, Jesus defines twin

---

74. Whether "from the beginning" modifies *ktisas* ("created") or *epoiēsen* ("made") is immaterial for our purposes, as is the issue of whether the creation of the earth is to be understood as beginning in Genesis 1:1 or 1:2.

75. Craig L. Blomberg, "Marriage, Divorce, Remarriage, and Celibacy: An Exegesis of Matthew 19:3–12," *TJ* 11, no. 2 (1990): 166. CD IV, 21 refers to "the principle of creation" in Genesis 1:27 of "male and female" to establish the divine intention that excludes polygamy and/or divorce.

76. While "and said" could be understood as Matthew's editorial work, it is more natural to understand it as a continuation of Jesus's quotation of the Creator (so, e.g., ESV, NAS95, NIV11, NKJV, NRSV), as argued by France, *Matthew*, NICNT, 726n4.

77. Cf. Ernest G. Clarke, trans., *Targum Pseudo-Jonathan: Deuteronomy*, ArBib 5B (Collegeville, Minn: Liturgical Press, 1998), 105, regarding Deuteronomy 34: "He [God] taught us to join grooms and brides because of his having united Eve with Adam." The two institutions created for human beings (the Sabbath and marriage) bracket the creation of the man and woman in Genesis 2 (vv. 1–3, 24).

78. On Jesus's exclusion of polygamy, see Sigal, *Halakhah of Jesus*, 116.

principles for marriage based on the creation order: complementarity and monogamy.

The use of the future tense ("shall leave," "shall cleave") is rare in the creation account. Throughout Genesis 1 a command form is used to describe God's design in creation,[79] but in matters where provision is made for human choice the future tense is used.[80] Accordingly, marriage is not obligatory, which may fit with Matthew's inclusion of Jesus's somewhat enigmatic statement about those who are "eunuchs for the sake of the kingdom of heaven" (19:12), apparently referring to those who remain single (cf. 1 Cor. 7:7, 25–35).[81] However, when marriage is entered into, human obedience to the Creator's command is expected. The Greek word for "cleave" (*kollēthēsetai*, as with Heb. *dābaq*) refers to "gluing," as in "something stuck to another," such as bone to flesh and flesh to skin (Job 19:20).[82] Used metaphorically of various human relationships,[83] it becomes a technical term for Israel's permanent covenant bond to the Lord.[84] Such examples illustrate the closeness comprehended in the divine intention that "the two shall become one flesh." This statement describes the divine possibility of total oneness and unity open to the couple, which their sexual union represents,[85] as well as the permanence of marriage. By quoting these two passages in Genesis, Jesus excludes divorce from the divine intention (cf. Mal. 2:14–16).[86]

The point that the marriage institution originated with the Creator is stressed by Jesus further in the next verse by His adding, "So they are no longer two but one flesh. *What* therefore *God has joined together*, let not man separate" (Matt. 19:6, emphasis added).[87] His making two people "one flesh" is an act of creation, of joining (lit.

---

79. See in the LXX: Genesis 1:3, 6 (2x), 9 (2x), 11, 14 (2x), 15, 20, 22 (4x), 24, 26, 28 (5x).

80. See in the LXX: Genesis 1:29; 2:16, 17, 19, 23, 24 (2x).

81. See Grant R. Osborne, *Matthew*, Zondervan Exegetical Commentary on the New Testament (Grand Rapids, Mich.: Zondervan, 2010), 707–8; France, *Matthew*, NICNT, 725–26; and Keener, *Bible Background*, 97.

82. France, *Matthew*, NICNT, 717, 726n20.

83. E.g., Ruth clinging to Naomi (Ruth 1:14) and Solomon clinging to foreign wives (1 Kings 11:2).

84. Richard M. Davidson, *Flame of Yahweh: Sexuality in the Old Testament* (Peabody, Mass.: Hendrickson, 2007), 45, citing (in n. 119) Deut. 10:20; 11:22; 13:5 (ET 4); Josh. 22:5; 23:8; 2 Sam. 20:2; 2 Kings 18:6. See also Jer. 13:11, which underscores the conditional element.

85. Blomberg, "Marriage," 167.

86. Sigal, *Halakhah of Jesus*, 112.

87. The word *chōrizō* ("separate") appearing in this verse is used by Paul in the sense of "divorce" (1 Cor. 7:10–11), on which see Jerome Murphy-O'Conner, "The Divorced Woman in 1 Cor. 7:10–11," *JBL* 100 (1981): 601–6.

"yoking") together in marriage,[88] which is referred to as an institution by the neuter singular pronoun "what" (*ho*). Since, in accordance with reading Genesis 1 and 2 as a unified creation account,[89] this marriage union occurred on the sixth day, Jesus's teaching on marriage is predicated on a literal understanding of the Genesis creation account. When challenged by the Pharisees regarding the Mosaic provision for divorce, Jesus differentiates this accommodation to human "hardness of heart" from the original divine intention by again referring to what was established "from the beginning" (Matt. 19:7–8).

JESUS'S POWER OVER CREATION

While all four Gospels include stories that illustrate Jesus's power over creation (so-called "nature miracles"),[90] Matthew has the most such stories and especially emphasizes Jesus's "mighty works" (*dynameis*).[91] Matthew's narration of nature miracles consistently includes details not found in the parallels, thereby underscoring this power. After the very first nature miracle, in which Jesus stills the storm, the disciples wonder among themselves "Who" [Gk. *tis*] Jesus is that He has such power, but in Matthew their awe is heightened by their asking, "What sort of man [Gk. *potapos*] is this, that even winds and sea obey him?" (8:27). Such power over nature can belong only to the Creator (Job 38:8–11, 24; Pss. 89:9; 107:29), which is no doubt why the disciples' musings remain in the form of a question. At this point in the narrative they are not yet able to grasp fully

---

88. Typically used thus also in Josephus (*Ant.* 1.314, 319, 338; 6.309; *J.W.* 1.484).

89. So William H. Shea, "The Unity of the Creation Account," *Origins* 5, no. 1 (1978): 33. Some who refer to separate "accounts" in Genesis 1 and 2 still find significant connections between them that suggest it represents a unified composition of a single author. See Jacques Doukhan, *The Genesis Creation Story: Its Literary Structure*, Andrews University Seminary Doctoral Dissertation Series 5 (Berrien Springs, Mich.: Andrews University Press, 1978), 245, referring to the "profound unity" of these chapters; and Davidson, "Genesis," 116–18.

90. Turning water into wine (John 2:1–11); miraculous catches of fish (Luke 5:1–11; John 21:1–13); stilling the storm (Matt. 8:23–27; Mark 4:35–39; Luke 8:22–25); raising of Jairus's daughter (Matt. 9:18–19, 23–26; Mark 5:21–24, 35–43; Luke 8:40–42, 49–56); five thousand fed (Matt. 14:13–21; Mark 6:32–44; Luke 9:10–17; John 6:1–15); walking on water (Matt. 14:22–33; Mark 6:45–52; John 6:16–21); four thousand fed (Matt. 15:32–39; Mark 8:1–10); raising the widow of Nain's son (Luke 7:11–17); paying the temple tax from a fish's mouth (Matt. 17:24–27); and raising of Lazarus (John 11:1–44).

91. Of the ten nature miracles, Matthew includes six, while Mark, Luke, and John each have five (see n. 90). Also, four of the seven occurrences of *dynameis* (excluding its unusual usage in reference to "the powers of the heavens" in Matt. 24:29; Mark 13:25; Luke 21:26; cf. Rom. 8:38; 1 Pet. 3:22) are unique to Matthew (7:22; 11:20, 23; 13:58 [but cf. use of the singular form *dynamin* in Mark 6:5]). The other shared occurrences are in Matt. 11:21/Luke 10:13; Matt. 13:54/Mark 6:2; Matt. 14:2/Mark 6:14.

Jesus's divine identity. In the account of the raising of Jairus's daughter, the girl is already dead by the time Jesus is approached (Matt. 9:18; cf. Mark 5:23; Luke 8:41–42), making it not a request for healing, but for resurrection,[92] another divine prerogative (Isa. 25:8; 26:19; Hos. 13:14). Just before Jesus feeds the five thousand (a nature miracle preserved in all four Gospels), He not only teaches the crowds but heals their sick (Matt. 14:14).[93] When Jesus walks on the Sea of Galilee and comes to the aid of the disciples who are struggling to keep the boat afloat during a storm, only in Matthew does Peter join Him in walking on the water in response to Jesus's command (14:28–31). In feeding the four thousand, Matthew makes clear, unlike Mark,[94] that the number fed was substantially more than that by indicating that the number did not include women and children (15:38). Matthew also includes another nature miracle not found in any other Gospel—Jesus's instruction for Peter to pay the temple tax using a coin found in the mouth of the first fish he catches (17:27).[95]

All of these miracle stories portray Jesus as having power over nature, thus implicitly pointing to creation.[96] Being able to raise the dead presumes the power to give life, which belongs only to the Creator (Gen. 2:7; Job 33:4). Multiplying the loaves and fish in order to feed thousands is akin to the creation of life in Genesis 1, while miraculous healings showcase Jesus's restorative power of re-creation. Christ's walking on water and His enabling of Peter to do the same recalls the description of the Creator treading on the sea (Job

---

92. Clinton Wahlen, *Jesus and the Impurity of Spirits in the Synoptic Gospels*, WUNT ser. 2, no. 185 (Tübingen: Mohr Siebeck, 2004), 115.

93. In Mark, Jesus just teaches (6:34). Luke also includes both teaching and healing (9:11), but this may be in dependence upon the other two Gospels.

94. Cf. Mark 8:9, which has the masculine form of the substantival adjective "thousand" (Gk. *tetrakischilioi*). While this could strictly refer to men only, in view of Mark 6:44 specifying "five thousand men" (*pentakischilioi andres*), it should probably be understood generically ("people"). So James R. Edwards, *The Gospel According to Mark*, PNTC (Grand Rapids, Mich.: Eerdmans, 2002), 231.

95. To fulfill the command, Peter is to use a "hook" (Gk. *ankistron*, only here in the New Testament), rather than a net, so that it might be clearly the "first" fish caught. Frequently, commentators observe that the miracle is not actually narrated. However, while the miracle story form normally includes narration of the miracle's accomplishment to confirm its occurrence, there is no reason rigidly to insist that it must always be present; this episode may qualify as a miracle story since readers are expected to assume that Peter did as instructed and that the miracle occurred.

96. While Elisha performed some of these miracles (e.g., 2 Kings 4:32–37, 42–44), from Matthew's perspective his ministry foreshadowed the messianic work of Jesus (Matt. 3:1–3), who was preceded by John the Baptist just as Elijah preceded Elisha (Matt. 11:14; 17:10–12).

9:8; cf. Gen. 1:2; Ps. 104:3) and parting the waters for Israel to pass over (Exod. 14:21–22). Jesus's stilling the storm (Matt. 8:26) shows the obedience of "even winds and sea" (v. 27) to the voice of Him who from the original watery world created a life-filled earth (Gen. 1:2–10, 20–23). Although such characteristics are explicitly synthesized only in John into a coherent portrait of Jesus as the Creator of the world "in the beginning" (John 1:1–3, 14),[97] their sum total in Matthew implicitly conveys the same message. The question "What sort of man is this . . . ?" (Matt. 8:27) can only accurately be answered with the affirmation made by believers in Him that Jesus is not just a man, but the "Lord,"[98] the initial occurrences of which refer to God Himself (Matt. 1:20, 22, 24; 2:13, 15, 19; 4:7, 10; 5:33).[99]

CONCLUSION

Beginning with its first two words, the Gospel of Matthew draws the attention of readers to the book of Genesis and, in particular, to the creation account. The unrepeated miracle by which life on earth was created is mirrored in Matthew by the unprecedented and unrepeatable miracle of Jesus being born of a virgin. As the Spirit of God moved upon the waters, so the Holy Spirit moves upon Mary at the incarnation, ushering in a new creation through which Jesus will fulfill the covenants that God made to Abraham and David and save His people from their sins.

As at creation, so in Jesus's ministry, the divine word fulfills itself by accomplishing what it says. The word spoken by Jesus is the means of miraculous healings and the casting out of demons, echoing the power of God's spoken word displayed at Creation. Most New Testament occurrences of "Let there be . . . " are found in Matthew, including the petition that God's will would become a reality "on earth as it is in heaven" (6:10)—pointing to the ultimate goal of a

---

97. See Jon Paulien, "Creation in the Gospel and Epistles of John," 225, in this volume.

98. The word *kyrios* used in addressing Jesus occurs nineteen times in Matthew (8:2, 6, 8, 21, 25; 9:28; 14:28, 30; 15:22, 25, 27; 16:22; 17:4, 15; 18:21; 20:30, 31, 33; 26:22), compared to just once in Mark (7:28, but cf. 16:19). While Luke also has nineteen occurrences, the concentration in Matthew (with 18,363 words) is slightly greater than in Luke (with 19,495 words).

99. Unlike Mark (1:3; 2:29), which may be one reason for the NRSV's translation of *kyrios* in Mark 7:28 as "Sir" but as "Lord" in Matthew 15:27. Luke's use of *kyrios* is similar to Matthew's in that the early occurrences refer to God (Luke 1:6, 9, 11, 15–16, 25, 28, 32, 38, 45–46, 58, 66, 68; 2:9, 15, 22–24, 26, 39; 4:6, 12), with some notable exceptions (Luke 1:17, 43, 76; 3:4; cf. Matt. 3:3).

new world. The Sabbath, as the culmination of creation week, also figures prominently in Matthew. Jesus, in addressing the Father as the Creator of heaven and earth, invites all to come and find rest. Jesus acts to free the Sabbath from restrictive Pharisaic traditions. Thus He claims authority over the Sabbath equal to that of the Creator (12:8). Matthew uniquely describes God's kingdom as a heavenly kingdom and looks forward to the resurrection and a re-creation (19:28), which is predicated upon God's power to remake the world just as He had power to create it in the beginning.

The clearest and most explicit reference to the Genesis creation in Matthew is in connection with a question about divorce brought to Jesus by the Pharisees. Rather than entering into a debate with them about the relevant Mosaic legislation, Jesus goes back to the very beginning, connecting God's creation of human beings as male and female (Gen. 1:27) with the marital union of Adam and Eve in Eden (Gen. 2:24), claiming that it is God Himself who joined them together as husband and wife (Matt. 19:4–6). Thus Jesus confirms the historicity of the Genesis creation account and affirms the twin principles of complementarity and monogamy based on the creation order and excludes divorce from the divine intention. His teaching on marriage would be incomprehensible apart from a literal understanding of the Genesis creation account.

Descriptions of Jesus's power over nature in Matthew (e.g., stilling the storm, walking on water, and giving life to the dead) echo the exercise of divine power described in Genesis 1 and 2, as well as in other Old Testament passages, and include unique details that highlight the "mighty deeds" done by Jesus. The cumulative effect of Matthew's quotations and allusions to Genesis is not merely to connect the new work of God in Jesus with the Genesis creation account but to identify Jesus as the divine "Lord" whose life, death, and resurrection opens the way for the ultimate realization of the divine plan in the re-creation at the eschaton (19:28). Jesus's life shows that God's powerful word is able to restore lives now, and also, at the end of time, to reconstitute elements from the ground into resurrected human bodies not unlike the creation of the first human beings (Gen. 2:7, 21–22) and to totally remake the earth to fulfill His original intention not only for our world but for each individual human being.

Thomas R. Shepherd, PhD, DrPH

Andrews University
Berrien Springs, Michigan, USA

CREATION IN THE GOSPEL OF MARK

INTRODUCTION

This study describes the creation theology and its implications and interconnections to other theological ideas found in the Gospel of Mark. The approach will be to discuss passages in Mark individually and then conclude by summarizing the theology of creation in the Gospel of Mark. Four passages in either allude to creation or explicitly refer to it (Mark 1:1; 2:27–28; 10:5–9; 13:18–20). We will deal with each, beginning with the passages with the clearest links to Genesis 1–2. We will also note how Mark 1:12–13 and 4:35–41 may allude to creation.

This study's presupposition is that Mark was written by John Mark, an occasional traveling companion of Paul and Barnabas (Acts 12:25; 13:1–13; 15:36–39) who left them on their first missionary journey but who eventually was reconciled to Paul (Col. 4:10; 2 Tim. 4:11; Philem. 24) and also served Peter (1 Pet. 5:13). This study views Scripture as the inspired word of God and uses the grammatical–historical method of exegesis.

MARK 2:27–28: THE SABBATH (GEN. 2:2–3)

kai elegen autois; to sabbaton dia ton anthrōpon egeneto kai ouch ho anthrōpos dia to sabbaton; hōste kyrios estin ho huios tou anthrōpou kai tou sabbatou.

And He said to them, "The Sabbath was made for Man[1] and not Man for the Sabbath. So then, the Son of Man is Lord also of the Sabbath." (Mark 2:27–28)[2]

INTRODUCTION

Mark 2:23–28 is the fourth in a series of five stories of controversy in Mark 2–3. The five stories are in a concentric pattern. This means a key concept or word links a story with the previous story, another key concept or word connects it to the next story,[3] and the final story circles back and links to the first story. In Mark 2:23–28, the link to the previous story (the controversy over food and fasting, Mark 2:18–22) is food and the link to the next story (healing a man on the Sabbath, Mark 3:1–6) is the Sabbath. Mark 2:23–28 deals with the question of Sabbath breaking, and 3:1–6 deals with the issue of Sabbath keeping.

In Mark 2:23–28, the Pharisees charge Jesus' disciples with breaking the Sabbath. Even though the specific infraction is not mentioned, it likely had to do with the disciples plucking and eating grain from a field as they passed by. According to the list of prohibited activities for the Sabbath, later codified in the Mishnah, the disciples could likely be accused of reaping (by plucking the grain),

---

1. The term "Man" is used in translation here only because of the play on words that occurs between "Man" in verse 27 and "Son of Man" in verse 28. The Greek term is *anthrōpos*, a generic term for humanity in many cases, as it is here. However, because "Son of Man" is the well-known translation for the title Jesus uses to refer to Himself, to express the word play in English the term "Man" is used. The reason for the capitalization is because of the link to the creation of the first humans, as will be explained below.

2. All New Testament translations are the author's. Old Testament quotations are from the ESV® Bible (The Holy Bible, English Standard Version®). ESV® Text Edition: 2016. Copyright © 2001 by Crossway, a publishing ministry of Good News Publishers. The ESV® text has been reproduced in cooperation with and by permission of Good News Publishers. Unauthorized reproduction of this publication is prohibited. All rights reserved.

3. See Joanna Dewey, *Markan Public Debate: Literary Technique, Concentric Structure, and Theology in Mark 2:1—3:6*, Society of Biblical Literature Dissertation Series 48 (Chico, Calif.: Scholars Press, 1980). Mark 2:1–12 deals with healing and sin; 2:13–17 with sin and food; 2:18–22 with food; 2:23–28 with food and the Sabbath; and 3:1–8 with the Sabbath and healing.

threshing (by rubbing it in their hands), and winnowing (by blowing away the chaff).[4]

Jesus defends His disciples by referencing the story of David, when he received holy bread from Ahimelech at the sanctuary at Nob (1 Sam. 21). The Lord argues by typological analogy that just as David and his men were approved to eat the holy bread without guilt, so can He (the Son of David, according to Mark; see Mark 10:46–52) authorize His disciples to eat grain from a field as they pass along.[5]

This brings us to Mark 2:27–28, a further teaching on the issue of the Sabbath. Whereas Mark 2:23–26 deals with the specific case of what Jesus's disciples were doing, verses 27–28 present a general maxim regarding the Sabbath that covers all of humanity. Jesus thus moves from the specific to the general in this passage.

THE REFERENCE TO CREATION

The reference to creation occurs in verse 27, when Jesus says, "The Sabbath was made for Man and not Man for the Sabbath." The structure of the verse is a simple chiasm:

$$\begin{array}{cc} \textbf{A} & \textbf{B} \\ \text{The \textbf{Sabbath} was made for \textbf{Man}} \end{array}$$

$$\begin{array}{cc} \textbf{B}' & \textbf{A}' \\ \text{not \textbf{Man} for the \textbf{Sabbath}} \end{array}$$

In such a chiastic structure, the emphasis falls on the central element, in this case Man (humanity), indicating that the focus of the Sabbath command is the benefit of humanity.

This is a reference to creation, not simply to the Sabbath commandment in Exodus 20. The reason for this assertion is found in two aspects of Mark 2:27. The first aspect is the use of the verb *ginomai* ("to be, to come to be"). We could translate this verse, "The Sabbath came into existence for Man not Man for the Sabbath."

This leads to the question: when did the Sabbath come into existence? Some argue it was created by God at Sinai. But to do so is

---

4. See *m. Šabb.* 7:2.

5. There is no question here of stealing the food. In Israel as you passed by your neighbor's field you could pluck and eat to satisfy your hunger, but you could not bring a basket to fill (see Lev. 19:9; 23:22; Deut. 23:25). Jesus's argumentation here is somewhat unusual because questions of law were typically settled by reference to commands in the law, not via stories in the Old Testament.

completely against the text and theology of the book of Exodus. The Sabbath is referenced before Sinai in Exodus 16, so it had to exist before Sinai. But more importantly, the Sabbath commandment itself points to creation as the origin of the Sabbath:

> Remember the Sabbath day, to keep it holy. Six days you shall labor, and do all your work, but the seventh day is a Sabbath to the LORD your God. On it you shall not do any work, you, or your son, or your daughter, your male servant, or your female servant, or your livestock, or the sojourner who is within your gates. For in six days the LORD made heaven and earth, the sea, and all that is in them, and rested on the seventh day. Therefore the LORD blessed the Sabbath day and made it holy. (Exod. 20:8–11)

The commandment gives God's creative work in making the world as the reason for rest in a clear reference to Genesis 1:1—2:3. Furthermore, it notes that as a result of creation, the Lord "blessed" (Heb. *bērak*) the Sabbath day and "made it holy" (Heb. *yĕqaddĕšêhû*, in the *piel* here). These same two verbs are used in Genesis 2:3 to indicate that God blessed and consecrated the seventh day. It is clear from these details that the Sabbath was established at creation and not at Sinai.[6]

Mark 2:27 also points in the same direction. The verb "to come to be, come into existence" (*ginomai*) is linked not only to the Sabbath but also to humanity. The second half of verse 27, "not Man for the Sabbath," simply lacks the verb. But clearly the intent is the same verb as in the first half of the verse. Thus, it would read, "Man did not come into existence for the Sabbath." It is a clear allusion to the creation account of Genesis 1:26–31, where the first humans were created. Jesus's statement, therefore, takes for granted the historical veracity of the creation account, since the very keeping of the Sabbath is based on the seven-day weekly cycle, without which the reason for keeping the Sabbath disappears.

THE SABBATH AND CREATION

Genesis 2:2–3 indicates four actions that God took on the seventh day of creation: He finished His work, He rested, He blessed the day,

---

6. While the noun "Sabbath" (*šabbāt*) is not used in Genesis 2:1–3, the verb form *šābat* ("to stop, rest") is used to refer to God's activity. The linkage to Exodus 20 via the verbs *berak* and *qaddĕše* and the wording of the commandment make it clear that the Sabbath is in mind in Genesis 2:1–3.

and He consecrated it. The first two actions describe what God did as a matter of history—stopping and resting. But the last two actions are expressions of God's will, indicating the purpose of the Sabbath. He blessed the day and set it apart for a holy purpose. When God blesses something in Scripture, it is meant for growth and fruitfulness (cf. Gen. 1:28–31). So it is striking that He blesses a day when everything and everyone is to stop and rest. But it is that rest that pulls people aside from the daily toil of life to pause and contemplate and connect with God.

In Mark 2:27–28, Jesus reacts to the focus on legalities that blunts the emphasis on connection to God for which the Sabbath was intended. He indicates that the Sabbath was meant as a conduit for human growth, not as a barrier to it.

One might reason that because the Sabbath was the conclusion of creation week, it was the ultimate focus. But the depiction of God's will in blessing and setting the Sabbath aside for a holy purpose suggests that relationships were involved. And indeed, this is the pattern of the use of *bārak* ("to bless") and *qādaš* ("to consecrate, dedicate") in the Old Testament. They involve relationships—between God and humans and between people, either as individuals or as groups.[7] *Qādaš* is also used in reference to things consecrated to God, but these dedicated items are used in the worship of God by people, linking the worshipers to God.[8] And days and years set apart for God are consecrated as part of the relationship between God and people. Thus, Jesus's teaching in Mark 2:27 is not at variance with Old Testament patterns. Rather, He restores what has been lost sight of.

Mark 2:28 involves a play on words paralleling "Man" with "Son of Man." The shift that takes place between these terms parallels a shift from recipient of the Sabbath in verse 27 to Lord of the Sabbath in verse 28.[9] So, as Lord of the Sabbath, Jesus can explain how it is to be kept. His general statement of the Sabbath's role in blessing humanity is based on His role as Lord. Verse 28 indicates that He is

---

7. On *bārak*, cf. Gen. 1:28; 12:2–3; 14:19–20; 22:18; Exod. 20:24; Lev. 9:22–23; Deut. 7:13; 24:13; 26:15; 30:16; 1 Sam. 25:33; 2 Sam. 7:29; Neh. 8:6; Pss. 28:9; 67:1; Isa. 51:2. On *qādaš*, cf. Exod. 19:10, 14; 28:41; 29:43–44; Lev. 11:44; 22:32; 25:10; 2 Chron. 35:6; Job 1:5; Isa. 29:23; Ezek. 28:25; 36:23.

8. Interestingly, the use of *qādaš* in Joshua 20:7, setting apart the cities of refuge, is a more secular use of the term but continues to express relationships between people, here the tribes of Israel providing for the rescue of the innocent.

9. Cf. the explanation in Robert H. Gundry, *Mark: A Commentary on His Apology for the Cross* (Grand Rapids, Mich.: Eerdmans, 1993), 144–145.

Lord *also* of the Sabbath. The "also" implies that He is Lord of something else as well. Within the context of the passage, the logical conclusion is that He is Lord of all creation.[10] The usage of the term "Lord" in this setting corroborates this assertion since it is a typical appellation for God.

MARK 10:5–9: CREATION AND MARRIAGE
(GEN. 1:27; 2:24)

ho de Iēsous eipen autois; pros tēn sklērokardian hymōn egrapsen hymin tēn entolēn tautēn. apo de archēs ktiseōs arsen kai thēly epoiēsen autous; heneken toutou kataleipsei anthrōpos ton patera autou kai tēn mētera [kai proskollēthēsetai pros tēn gynaika autou,] kai esontai hoi dyo eis sarka mian; hōste ouketi eisin dyo alla mia sarx. ho oun ho theos synezeuxen anthrōpos mē chōrizetō.

And Jesus said to them, "He [Moses] wrote this commandment for you because of the hardness of your heart. But from the beginning of creation 'He made them male and female. For this reason, a man shall leave his father and mother [and be joined to his wife] and the two will become one flesh.' So, they are no longer two but one flesh. Therefore, what God has joined together a person should not separate." (Mark 10:5–9)[11]

INTRODUCTION

In Mark 10:1–9, Jesus has a dispute with the Pharisees about divorce. Afterward, in verses 10–12, the disciples continue the discussion in private to get more clarification. In the time of Jesus, two schools of interpretation, the School of Shammai and the School of Hillel, taught different views on divorce.[12] The School of Shammai

---

10. Some commentators suggest that the "also" along with "Son of Man" reminds the reader of Mark 2:10, where Jesus claims the authority to forgive sins (cf. e.g., Adela Collins, *Mark* Hermeneia (Minneapolis, Minn.: Fortress Press, 2007), 204–205. However, we argue that one need not go so far afield to understand the "also." The reference to "man" in 2:27 alludes to Adam and Eve in Genesis 1–2, and in that context, the creation of the Sabbath was the culmination of God's creative work and hence a representation or capstone of all His creative power. Consequently, Jesus being Lord of the Sabbath implies that He is Lord of all creation "also."

11. The words in brackets are excluded by important early manuscripts (ℵ, B) but found in many others.

12. See *m. Giṭ.* 9:10 for the positions of the Schools of Shammai and Hillel and the even more liberal Rabbi Aqiba.

was more conservative and divorce was harder to obtain; the School of Hillel was more liberal and divorce was easier to obtain (though Hillelite court proceedings were generally slower).[13] Both groups took for granted that divorce was acceptable.

Their question to Jesus in verse 2 is whether it is lawful to divorce one's wife. Jesus responds with a question as to what Moses commanded (v. 3). They respond that Moses permitted that a bill of divorce be written for the wife.

THE REFERENCE TO CREATION

Jesus responds in a somewhat similar approach as in Mark 2, where He invokes original design and purpose. Here in Mark 10 He states that Moses gave the command for divorce because of the hardheartedness of the people (Mark 10:5). This implies that God's original plan did not include divorce. Jesus proceeds to fill in the missing sense of God's intention by quoting from the creation accounts of Genesis 1 and 2.

Jesus quotes from Genesis 1:27 with a focus on the creation of the two sexes on the sixth day of creation. However, He goes further, using the terminology "from the beginning of creation" (Mark 10:6) to indicate that this pattern of sexual differentiation, prominent in the Genesis 1 account, continues into the present world.

This differentiation, then, becomes the basis, according to Jesus, for marriage. He quotes from Genesis 2:24, "Therefore a man shall leave his father and his mother and hold fast to his wife, and they shall become one flesh."[14] The word "therefore" in the original context of Genesis 2:24 is a deduction from the story of the creation of the first woman. In that story, beginning in Genesis 2:18, God says, "It is not good that the man should be alone; I will make him a helper fit for him." Strangely, the next scene has God bringing all the animals to

---

13. Both the School of Shammai and the School of Hillel accepted four grounds for divorce: childlessness, material neglect, emotional neglect, and marital unfaithfulness. Their question to Jesus was about a particular text, Deuteronomy 24:1–4. They were likely seeking to trap Him so they could accuse Him to Herod Antipas, who had divorced his wife and married his sister-in-law Herodias (Mark 6:14–29). See discussion in David Instone-Brewer, *Divorce and Remarriage in the Bible: The Social and Literary Context* (Grand Rapids, Mich.: Eerdmans, 2002), 81–132. See also David W. Chapman, "Marriage and Family in Second Temple Judaism," in *Marriage and Family in the Biblical World*, ed. Ken M. Campbell (Downers Grove, Ill.: InterVarsity, 2003), 183–239. Mishnaic references that discuss these matters include *m. Ketub.* 5:5–8; *m. Git.* 9:8–10 and *m. 'Arak.* 5:6.

14. The direct quotation from Genesis 1:27 and 2:24 in Mark 10 agree with the Septuagint text of Genesis.

the man for him to name, as though these could be possible "helper[s] fit for him." But none is found.[15]

The story proceeds with the first anesthesia, as God puts the man to sleep, removes a rib, closes the place with flesh, and then forms a woman from the rib. He then brings the woman to the man and the man proceeds to deliver the first love poem (Gen. 2:23):

> This at last is bone of my bones
> > and flesh of my flesh;
> she shall be called Woman,
> > because she was taken out of Man.

Then follows Genesis 2:24, with its expression of "therefore" as a conclusion from the story in verses 18–23. In Genesis, it seems the story focuses on the union or common linkage of the man and woman ("bone of my bones and flesh of my flesh") as the basis for marriage, placing a strong emphasis on the relational nature of marriage, whereas in Mark 10, Jesus seems to focus on the distinction between male and female as the basis of marriage (quoting from Genesis 1:27, "male and female he created them").

However, we must remember that Jesus is speaking in a polemical setting in which the issue of discussion is not union but divorce. His discussion of marriage begins with two physically separate and distinct individuals (Gen. 1) then moves to their union in marriage (Gen. 2). His point is not disunion, as the two schools of the Pharisees seem to be focused on. His emphasis is on the union that occurs in marriage.[16] By highlighting that the individuals were once two and now are one flesh, Jesus emphasizes that this union is something God has brought about and people should not separate what God has joined together (Mark 10:8). Thus, Jesus is consistent with the underlying teaching of Genesis 2, even as He illustrates the contrast between Genesis 1 and 2.

We can go further. Jesus gives every indication that He considers Genesis 1 and 2 to depict historical events with real people and that the patterns set up there concerning sexual differentiation and

---

15. The strange process of the naming of the animals at this point in the narrative of Genesis 2 has the effect of creating in Adam a sense of need in a perfect world. No appropriate helper was found for him. The fact that Adam sensed his need is illustrated in Genesis 2:24 when he exclaims "At last!" as Eve comes on the scene.

16. It is clear from this passage in Mark 10 and Jesus's quotation of the Genesis 1–2 account that the biblical standard for marriage is one man and one woman married for life.

marriage relationships are lasting and binding in the present world. Jesus speaks of God being active in the story of Adam and Eve, both setting their sexual identity and blessing their union in marriage. As ongoing responsibilities and relationships concerning the Sabbath in Mark 2 arise from creation, so we see the same here arising in sexual identity and marriage relationships.

MARK 13:19–20: GREAT TRIBULATION (GEN. 1–2)

esontai gar hai hēmerai ekeinai thlipsis hoia ou gegonen toiautē ap archēs ktiseōs hēn ektisen ho theos heōs tou nyn kai ou mē genētai. kai ei mē ekolobōsen kyrios tas hēmeras, ouk an esōthē pasa sarx; alla dia tous eklektous hous exelexato ekolobōsen tas hēmeras.

For those days will be such a tribulation as has not happened since the beginning of creation which God created up until now and never will be. And unless the Lord had shortened the days, no one at all would be saved. But for the sake of the elect whom He chose, He shortened the days. (Mark 13:19–20)

INTRODUCTION

Mark's last reference to Genesis 1 and 2 occurs within Jesus's eschatological discourse on the Mount of Olives, opposite Herod the Great's beautiful temple, which dominated the city of Jerusalem in the first century AD. In Mark 13:2, Jesus makes the startling prediction that it all will be torn down. Four of His disciples—Peter, James, John, and Andrew—approach Him on the Mount of Olives and ask when these events will take place. Jesus explains in a lengthy discourse, covering events from His lifetime to His return in the clouds of glory.

THE REFERENCE TO CREATION

The eschatological discourse is found in Matthew 24, Mark 13, and Luke 21. Differences between these accounts are not the subject of our investigation. We are interested in the setting of the reference to creation in Mark 13. This chapter can be divided into three main parts: verses 1–18, dealing with the events surrounding the destruction of the temple and Jerusalem; verses 19–27, dealing with the lengthy time from the fall of Jerusalem to the second coming; and finally, verses 28–37, dealing with lessons to draw from these predictions.

Verses 19–20, the subject of our inquiry, occur at the transition between the focus on the first century and the period of time that extends into the future from there. The clearest marker of the shift in focus is the change from the use of the words "this" and "these" (Gk. *houtos*) to the use of "that" and "those" (*ekeinos*). "This" and "these" predominate in the first part of the discourse (Mark 13:1–18) and "that" and "those" in the latter part of the discourse (Mark 13:19–27).[17] It is significant that the reference to creation occurs at the shift. In verse 19, Jesus refers to "*those* days"—marking the shift to a later, more distant perspective in regard to persecution.

When Jesus shifts to speak of more distant events in the future, He mentions creation as a distant reference point in the opposite direction. The redundancy in the expression "since the beginning of creation which God created" simply emphasizes the factuality of creation as a marker and anchor in the context of the horrific nature of the tribulation to come that is so unsettling.[18] Nothing has ever occurred like this before, nor will it in the future. The merism of distant past and distant future points to the stark reality of the tribulation to come.[19] Covering the entire history of the world, Jesus refers to creation, to the present, and to the distant future, all in verse 19.

If creation were some vague myth or based on long evolutionary trial and error with much suffering, pain, and death, it would be illogical to reference it in relation to the tribulation to which Jesus refers. That is to say, a long evolutionary process of suffering, pain, and billions of years of death would far outweigh the pain of the tribulation to which Jesus refers. Consequently, Jesus's statement implies a literal fiat creation coming from the Creator's hand without long evolutionary periods of development.

---

17. *Houtos* appears in Mark 13:2, 4, 8, 11, 13, 29–30; *ekeinos* appears in Mark 13:11, 17, 19, 24, 32. Interestingly, this shift helps explain the conundrum of Mark 13:30–32 and the phrase "this generation." In verse 30 Jesus predicts that "this generation" will not pass away "until all *these things* take place" (emphasis supplied). In verse 32 He refers to "*that* day or hour" (emphasis supplied). Verse 30 refers to the events in 13:1–18 where *houtos* predominates, and verse 32 clearly refers to the parousia in verses 26–27, in the section where *ekeinos* predominates.

18. The parallel in Matthew 24:20 has "from the beginning of the world until now, no, and never will be." Luke 21 does not have a parallel phrase to that found in Mark 13:19.

19. That this tribulation cannot simply be the fall of Jerusalem, as terrible an event as that was, is supported by the fact that, unfortunately, many worse events have occurred since then. The horrific nature of what Jesus predicts is significantly related to the *length of time* involved in the tribulation—centuries of persecution of the people of God.

MARK 1:1: THE BEGINNING (GEN. 1:1)

Archē tou euangeliou Iēsou Christou huiou theou.

The beginning of the gospel of Jesus Christ, the Son of God. (Mark 1:1)

INTRODUCTION

The Gospel of Mark begins with an incomplete sentence, spanning from verse 1 to verse 3. Some scholars suggest that the first verse is actually a title for the book of Mark, but that seems less likely since verse 2 begins with *kathōs* ("just as"), which continues what is said in verse 1.[20] The terminology here, "the beginning of the gospel," likely refers to the events in the prologue of the book extending from verse 1 to 13.[21]

With these details in mind, it is not surprising that some scholars do not see any allusion to the creation account here, since the focus is on Jesus's ministry. However, three elements of Mark 1:1 and the wider context of the entire book suggest an allusion to Genesis 1:1 (or at least an echo of it): the position of "beginning" (*archē*) in the sentence, the monadic usage of "beginning," and, more widely, the usage of the phrase "from the beginning" in Mark 10:6 and 13:19. We will look at each of these ideas in turn.

THE POSITION OF "BEGINNING"

The term "beginning" (*archē*) is the first word in Greek in Mark 1:1, much as "in the beginning" (*en archē*) appears first in the Greek text of the Septuagint in Genesis 1:1 (cf. the same format, *en archē,*

---

20. Cf., for instance, Vincent Taylor, *The Gospel According to St. Mark*, 2nd ed. (London: Macmillan, 1966), 152; and Adela Collins, *Mark*, AB (Minneapolis, Minn.: Fortress, 2007), 134. Counter the titular concept, see Robert A. Guelich, *Mark 1–8:26*, WBC (Dallas: Word, 1989), 6–7. R. T. France, *Mark*, NIGTC (Grand Rapids, Mich.: Eerdmans, 2002), 50, notes that *kathōs* ("just as") normally links to that which precedes it, not what follows, except for the occasional situation where *houtōs* "thus, so, in this manner" follows it. *Houtōs* does not follow *kathōs* here. See also his discussion on pp. 49–53.

21. The verses that comprise the prologue are disputed. Some scholars maintain that it consists of Mark 1:1–8, others Mark 1:1–13, and others Mark 1:1–15. For a discussion of the different positions, see Robert Gundry, *Mark: A Commentary on His Apology for the Cross* (Grand Rapids, Mich.: Eerdmans, 1993), 29–33. The present study takes the middle position because Mark 1:1–8 leaves out the important baptism of Jesus as part of the initiation of His ministry. This study also maintains that Mark 1:14–15 starts a new section, particularly with the use of John's and Jesus's names, indicating the shift from the ministry that includes John to that which focuses on Jesus. However, the transition in Mark 1:14–15 has links back to the prologue proper.

in John 1:1). The Hebrew text of Genesis 1:1 uses *bĕrē'šît*, most commonly translated "in the beginning."

However, there is a difference between the form found in Mark 1:1 and the one in Genesis 1:1. Whereas Mark has the nominative case of *archē*, simply "beginning" or usually translated "the beginning," Genesis 1:1 has "*in* the beginning." The usage in Genesis 1 is adverbial, indicating the timing of the events narrated in the text—they happened "in the beginning."

In contrast, the term *archē* in Mark 1:1 is a nominative absolute: grammatically, it stands independent from the rest of the sentence.[22] Daniel Wallace indicates that this usage is typical of book titles, listing Matthew 1:1 and Mark 1:1 as examples.[23] This seems appropriate for Matthew 1:1, since there is no verb present in the sentence and the next verse begins "Abraham begat. . . ." However, in Mark, as previously noted, verse 2 begins with *kathōs* ("just as"), indicating a connection between the first and second verses. Therefore, while Mark 1:1–3 is not a complete sentence and thus *archē* can still be seen as a nominative absolute, verse 1 does seem to be connected to what follows, serving less as a title and more as a marker of the initial events of the gospel story.

In this first verse, the usage of *archē* appears to be temporal in nature. There was a time prior to the gospel events. But now, at the appropriate time, when the prophecies quoted in verses 2–3 are coming to fulfillment, *that is the time*, "the beginning of the gospel of Jesus Christ, the Son of God."[24] Thus *archē* in Mark 1:1 points to a dividing line in time. There was a "before" and now there is a "beginning" of gospel events. As the prologue and opening passages of Mark (1:14–15) will show, the beginning of the gospel of Jesus Christ occurs when a key component of the prophecy of Daniel 9:24–27 comes to fulfillment—the baptism of Jesus, where He is anointed with the Holy Spirit as Messiah—and when the prophecies of Exodus, Isaiah, and Malachi are fulfilled.[25]

---

22. See Daniel B. Wallace, *Greek Grammar: Beyond the Basics* (Grand Rapids, Mich.: Zondervan, 1996), 49–51.

23. Ibid.

24. Mark 1:2 refers to the prophecy of Isaiah only (Isa. 40:3), even though the text has parallels to Exodus 23:20 and Malachi 4:1. The reason for the focus on Isaiah is because the evangelist wants that text to stand out in our mind more than the others for what he will share in the coming verses.

25. At the baptism the Holy Spirit descends on Jesus as a dove, anointing Him for His gospel ministry, much as Daniel 9:24–27 describes the coming of the Messiah, the "anointed

The question is: Is there a connection to creation in all of this?[26] In Genesis 1:1 the first word, *bĕrē'šît* ("in the beginning"), has the appearance of a construct form (no article with the noun "beginning"). But construct forms are followed by the head noun they go with, which has the article (such as "the king *of Judah*" where "Judah" would be the head noun with the article). But *bĕrē'šît* is followed by a verb in Genesis 1:1: "In the beginning, God created. . . ." Thus, it seems to point toward the timing of events—the period of time when the creation occurred.[27]

In a similar way in Mark 1:1, the *beginning* of the gospel story is about the timing of events as set by the prophecies of Exodus, Isaiah, Malachi, and Daniel coming to fulfillment in the ministry of Jesus Christ. The power of Jesus's ministry is set within the temporal framework of the Old Testament prophecies now coming to fulfillment. Just as God was active in the creation events of Genesis 1–2, so He is active again in the beginning of the gospel, when Jesus begins His ministry. As God spoke the world into existence in Genesis 1, so here in Mark 1 He speaks to His Son before the incarnation (Mark 1:2–3), in the words of the prophets in Exodus, Isaiah, and Malachi, and again at the baptism (Mark 1:11), where the Holy Spirit descends on Jesus in the form of a dove, anointing Him for His ministry and fulfilling the messianic prophecy of Daniel 9:25–26.[28]

THE MONADIC USAGE OF "BEGINNING"

The Greek language has a definite article but no indefinite article like English. The Greek article or its absence is a major subject in the

---

one." Cf. Acts 10:38.

26. Most commentators do not see a link to creation here. Guelich, *Mark 1–8:26*, 8, notes the parallel but rejects it as focusing on a different event, the beginning of the gospel story. I am not suggesting that "the beginning" here in Mark is the same beginning as in Genesis 1:1 but that the literary pattern of starting the book with a similar temporal marker echoes the Genesis 1 account and invokes it conceptually. Note Strauss' words, "Mark may also be consciously echoing the opening phrase of the LXX (Gen 1:1 LXX: ἐν ἀρχῇ [*en archē*] 'in the beginning'; cf. John 1:1; 1 John 1:1) and in this way marking the beginning of the new creation through the salvation available in Jesus Christ." Mark Strauss, *Mark* ZECNT (Grand Rapids, Mich.: Zondervan, 2014), 59.

27. See the extensive discussion in Richard M. Davidson, "The Genesis Account of Origins," in *The Genesis Creation Account and Its Reverberations in the Old Testament*, ed. Gerald A. Klingbeil (Berrien Springs, Mich.: Andrews University Press, 2015), 61–69.

28. Notice in Acts 10:37–38 how Peter describes Jesus's baptismal scene as being "anointed with the Holy Spirit." Also note Jesus's words in Mark 1:14–15, where He notes that "the time is fulfilled"—pointing back to Daniel 9:24–26.

study of Koine Greek grammar.[29] The article was originally a demonstrative pronoun—"this/that"—indicating that it had the force of pointing out or specifying one thing as opposed to another. As Wallace notes, it *conceptualizes* something.[30] Take the adjective "all" (*pas*): when the article is added, it becomes a noun "the whole" (*ho pas*). The article also serves as an identifier and at times makes an object definite.[31]

The absence of the article would typically have the contrary effect, indicating quality instead of specificity. However, the meaning of the absence of the article ranges from something indefinite, to something qualitative, and all the way to something definite.[32] In the case of Mark 1:1, the use of *archē* is monadic, which means that this "beginning" is one of a kind in nature.[33] That is to say, there is only one beginning for the gospel story—one period in time in which it occurs. In the same way, there was only one beginning for creation as in Genesis 1:1. The stage was set temporally by "in the beginning."

Admittedly, the connection between Mark 1:1 and Genesis 1:1 in this regard is only related by kind of expression—that is, both verses present the time period when the events there narrated began. They are different events, but both are beginnings. However, the Jewish milieu of biblical ideas within which Mark was written, combined with the fact that both Genesis and Mark have these words in the very first verse of their books, strengthens the connection. Also, in both books the beginning is connected with the action of God.

"BEGINNING" IN MARK 10:6 AND 13:19

The term *archē* is used four times in the Gospel of Mark (1:1; 10:6; 13:8, 19). Two of these uses specifically refer to the Genesis creation (10:6 and 13:19).[34] In Mark 10:6, the Lord speaks of how "from the beginning of creation God made them male and female." Quoting from Genesis 1:27, Jesus presents His teaching regarding

---

29. Wallace, *Greek Grammar*, 208, has eighty-five pages on the topic of the article, noting that "there is no more important aspect of Greek grammar than the article to help shape our understanding of the thought and theology of the NT writers."

30. Ibid., 209.

31. Ibid., 209–210.

32. Ibid., 243–245.

33. Ibid., 248–249.

34. Mark 13:8 focuses attention on the destruction of Jerusalem and refers to the buildup of tensions and violence before that event, calling that buildup the "beginning of the birth pains."

marriage and bases it on the creation order going all the way back to "the beginning of creation."[35]

In Mark 13:19, the Lord is describing what will happen after the fall of Jerusalem, and He speaks of great tribulation such "as has not happened since the beginning of creation which God created up until now and never will be."[36] The purpose of referencing creation at this point is to emphasize the severity of the suffering to take place. It is placed within a cosmic setting, stretching all the way back to the creation of the world and looking forward in this eschatological discourse to the consummation of all things at the Lord's return. In other words, the trouble Jesus describes is the worst suffering that has ever happened or ever will occur in our world.

What is interesting about the usage in Mark 10:6 and 13:19 is the way "beginning" is tied to the cosmic event of creation. The evangelist may have had a sense of the word "beginning" that is linked to origins, roots, backgrounds, and thus "the beginning of the gospel of Jesus Christ" (1:1) would be a cosmic event as well, not unlike the event of creation itself.

In sum, Mark 1:1 is about the beginning of the gospel. It may allude to or echo the creation account of Genesis 1–2. Several details noted above suggest this: the use of "beginning" (*archē*) as the first word in the Gospel of Mark, even as *en archē* is first in Genesis 1:1 in the Septuagint; the noun *archē* used monadically, pointing to a specific, unique time period when God is active, parallel to Genesis 1; and finally, the concept of "beginning" in Mark 10:6 and 13:19, tied to creation, suggesting a mental concept of "beginning" in Mark 1:1 tied to creation concepts.

Several other passages in Mark may also allude to creation concepts or motifs. Mark 1:12–13 refers to Jesus in the wilderness with the wild animals. This picture may be linked to Genesis 1–2, with the creation of the animals and Adam naming them. Mark 4:35–41 relates a striking story of a storm on the Sea of Galilee, when Jesus rebukes the wind and waves and they obey Him, reminiscent of the Genesis 1 account of all creation being subservient to God and appearing at His command.

---

35. See the discussion above regarding this passage in the section titled "Mark 10:5–9: Creation and Marriage (Gen. 1:27; 2:24)."

36. See the discussion regarding this passage, especially regarding "this/these" and "that/those," in the section above titled "Mark 13:18–20: Great Tribulation (Gen. 1–2)."

MARK'S THEOLOGY OF CREATION

We have noted four passages where the evangelist clearly references or may allude to creation: Mark 2:27–28, regarding the creation of humans and the gift of the Sabbath; Mark 10:5–8, regarding marriage and its Edenic origin; Mark 13:18–20, utilizing creation as part of a merism used to describe the horrific nature of tribulation for the people of God; and Mark 1:1, a more allusive reference, regarding the concept of "beginning" (and possibly Mark 1:12–13 and 4:35–41). Having studied these passages, we ask what they tell us about Mark's theology of creation. Let me sketch briefly some of the theological ideas that flow from Mark's description and usage of creation imagery.

CREATION TIED TO THEOLOGY

The opening of Mark's Gospel focuses on the action of God (theology proper). The shift that takes place as the Messiah enters the world was foretold by the prophets. When He arrives on the scene, God speaks, affirming His Son. It is a beginning not unlike the beginning in the creation account where God is active and brings about change. So the gospel story starts with God actively touching the world through His Son. This allusion to creation imagery may be extended to when Jesus is in the wilderness with wild beasts (Mark 1:12–13) and when He calms the stormy sea (Mark 4:35–41).

COSMIC EVENT

Mark presents creation as a cosmic event that stands at one end of a merism that encompasses all of history. Creation thus takes on a stabilizing and epochal nature in the Markan narrative. It focuses attention thereby on the opposite end of the merism, the eschaton. If a literal creation in the past is rejected or taken metaphorically, so is the eschaton. The importance of creation is thus established and emphasized by the evangelist.

CREATION AND ETHICS

Two of the passages, Mark 2:27–28 and 10:5–8, make specific reference to creation events—the creation of the Sabbath and the establishment of the first marriage. Jesus argues that the Sabbath was made with people in mind, for their benefit. He further argues that marriage is protected by taking creation seriously. What God has brought together should not be destroyed or broken by people. It is striking that the gifts we have from the Garden of Eden—the Sabbath and marriage—are defended by Jesus on the basis of creation theology. That is to say, creation theology matters for ethical behavior in a world taken captive by the enemy.

THE HISTORICITY OF CREATION

Throughout these passages in Mark that describe creation or allude to it, and throughout Jesus' discourses on these issues, it is clear that both the evangelist and the Christ he portrays believe in and take creation seriously. Jesus speaks of creation as a real event brought about by God. If He were not to take such a position, His argumentation on both marriage and the Sabbath would be unconvincing, unrealistic, and likely dismissed.

Jesus uses creation as a marker in the past with a counterpart—the eschaton—in the future. Without the historicity of the past event, the veracity of the future event would be called into question. Furthermore, the point He makes in Mark 13:19–20, placing suffering within a cosmic setting, would be robbed of its broader field of understanding.

Here we may respond to John Walton's argument in his carefully written *The Lost World of Genesis 1*.[37] Walton argues that the Genesis 1–2 account is about functional origins, not material ones. He says the text is not about when and how the universe originated; rather, the stories help explain the functions of nature that we observe around us.[38] Some interpreters may feel that the way Mark describes creation and makes use of the creation story fits well within Walton's thesis—that Mark uses creation texts to affirm Sabbath observance and marriage, to encourage endurance in the face of trial, and to point to the beginning of the gospel ministry of Jesus. In their view, this fits within a functional perspective, dealing with and explaining the activities of people's lives. However, we demur.

We note that Jacques Doukhan affirms that some references to Genesis 1–2 in the Old Testament clearly have functional aspects.[39] That is,

---

37. John H. Walton, *The Lost World of Genesis 1* (Downers Grove, Ill.: IVP Academic, 2010).
38. Ibid., 23–46.
39. See Jacques B. Doukhan, "A Response to John H. Walton's *Lost World of Genesis 1*," *AUSS* 49, no. 1 (2011): 197–205.

these particular texts in the Old Testament (e.g., Job 38–41; Ps. 104; Prov. 8:22–36) allude to or quote Genesis 1–2 with the purpose of explaining or guiding functions in human life or in nature. But Doukhan goes on to explain the purpose of such allusions or quotations:

> These texts are not just using the motif of creation for their own functional purpose; the way they allude or refer to the event of creation, the words, the syntax, and the structure of these texts denote clearly that they all refer to a single literary source as recorded in Genesis 1–2. This way of pointing back to the prior document presupposes the event of creation. It is not the idea of function—the experience of salvation or newness—that has produced and, therefore, preceded the idea of creation, but the other way around. Creation is already assumed to be a past event, and it is on the basis of this reference that the functional idea has been generated and elaborated.[40]

As previously noted, in the references to creation in the Gospel of Mark, the very literal nature of the creation events is crucial to the evangelist's point. If Genesis 1:1 is alluded to in Mark 1:1, it is to show a historical event at the beginning of the world that parallels a historical event at the beginning of the gospel. In referring to creation in the dispute over the Sabbath in Mark 2:23–28, Jesus talks about both the Sabbath and humanity coming into existence, the one made for the benefit of the other. If they did not come into existence in a creative event at the beginning of our world within one day of each other, then the reason for keeping the Sabbath and its benefit for humanity disappears.

Similarly, in arguing for the unity and permanency of marriage (Mark 10), Jesus is dependent on a real Adam and a real Eve, created on the sixth day of creation. Otherwise, His argument fails to convince. And finally, without a historical creation, those going through the tribulation Jesus predicted (Mark 13) would have no comfort if the events did not happen as narrated in Genesis 1–2, and their hope for the future eschaton would also be dashed.

CONCLUSION

While Mark's Gospel refers to or alludes to creation only a handful of times, these references make it clear that the evangelist takes the

---

40. Ibid., 199.

subject seriously. Creation serves as a paradigm for his presentation of the beginning of the gospel story. It is tied to central concepts of the ethics of Jesus, the Sabbath and marriage, His eschatological understanding of where the world is headed, and His participation in the Creator's power. Creation concepts display theology proper in Mark with God continuing to act in His world to bring salvation. The historicity of the creation events and the Genesis 1–2 creation account are assumed within Mark's Gospel. If not for the historical nature of the events, then the argumentation, ethics, and eschatology would lose their force, and, indeed, the christology would be diminished. It is clear that creation theology and the historicity of the creation account are important to the truth and effectiveness of the Gospel of Mark.

Kim Papaioannou, PhD

Cyprus Region of Seventh-day
Adventists

CREATION THEOLOGY IN LUKE AND ACTS

INTRODUCTION

Luke and Acts have long been believed to be the work of a single author,[1] Luke.[2] Luke was a medical doctor (Col. 4:14) and close companion of Paul (Col. 4:14; 2 Tim. 4:11; Philem. 24). Though there is no absolute consensus, the dominant opinion is that he was a Gentile by birth,[3] a Greek or a Hellenized Syrian[4] from the city of

---

1. Donald Juel, *Luke-Acts* (Richmond, Va.: John Knox, 1983), 3. David J. Williams, *Acts*, New International Biblical Commentary (Peabody, Mass.: Hendrickson, 1990), 2, asserts that "it is almost an axiom of New Testament scholarship that whoever wrote the Third Gospel was also the author of Acts."

2. Juel, *Luke-Acts*, 5. Regarding internal and external evidences of authorship, see Charles W. Carter and Ralph Earle, *The Acts of the Apostles* (Grand Rapids, Mich.: Zondervan, 1959), xi–xii; and Eduard Schweizer, *The Good News According to Luke* (Atlanta: John Knox, 1984), 6–7. See also John B. Polhill, *Acts*, NAC 26 (Nashville, Tenn.: Broadman and Holman, 1992), 23, who writes that "scholars of all persuasion are in agreement that the third Gospel and the Book of Acts are by the same author."

3. Everett F. Harrison, *Introduction to the New Testament* (Grand Rapids, Mich.: Eerdmans, 1971), 198. David L. Tiede, *Luke*, ACNT (Minneapolis, Minn.: Augsburg, 1988), 9–21, tries to strike a balance between those who view Luke as a Gentile and a Hellenist and those few who see him as a Jew. He opines that Luke was probably a Gentile who, at some point, may have converted to *the faith of Israel*. This would explain why Luke, after he became a Christian, exemplified such familiarity with and respect for the Old Testament. The possibility that Luke may have been attached to a synagogue before becoming a Christian should not be discounted. Nonetheless, Colossians 4:10–17, in the present author's view, precludes the possibility that he became a full convert to Judaism at any point in his life.

4. Harrison, *Introduction to the New Testament*, 198. François Bovon, *Luke 1*, Hermeneia (Minneapolis, Minn.: Fortress, 2002), 8, describes Luke as "a Greek by birth, who turned to

Antioch on the Orontes.[5] Both his profession and ancestry make him unique among New Testament writers and have a strong bearing on any discussion of creation. His profession signifies a thorough non-Jewish education, which is something none of the other apostles seem to have had[6]—not even the polymath Paul.[7] Luke's Gentile background could suggest that he did not grow up with knowledge of the creation story but rather with any of the various creation or even evolution myths prevalent in the Hellenistic world.[8] Both Luke and Acts are addressed to a person named Theophilus (Luke 1:3; Acts 1:1). Though there is no consensus on Theophilus's identity, the majority view is that he was a high official in the Roman Empire, and a Gentile either sympathetic to Christianity or a full convert.[9]

This brief background information is helpful in ascertaining the importance of the creation story in the early church. Initially, the majority of Christians were of a Jewish background. Persecution in Jerusalem, the conversion of Paul and his subsequent missionary journeys, and the other apostles' missionary work meant that within a few decades the church had become predominantly Gentile. Since both Luke and Theophilus were likely of Gentile background, Luke's theology of creation may indicate the importance of creation even among Gentile believers who had not grown up with it.

The evidence from Luke-Acts unambiguously displays the centrality of belief in a literal six-day creation. The narrative-historical nature of both works does not lend itself to a systematic treatment of the topic. Nonetheless, Luke contains four clear references and many more allusions to creation, underlining both his familiarity and belief in the topic. Indeed, creation serves as a launching pad for Luke to develop other important theological themes—especially his view of the universal sovereignty of God and the brotherhood of humanity.

Judaism early in life."

5. D. A. Carson, Douglas J. Moo, and Leon Morris, *An Introduction to the New Testament* (Grand Rapids, Mich.: Zondervan, 1992), 115. See also Williams, *Acts*, 3.

6. Carson, Moo, and Morris, *Introduction to the New Testament*, 114.

7. Carter and Earle, *Acts of the Apostles*; cf. Donald T. Rawlinson, *Introduction to New Testament Study* (New York: Macmillan, 1956), 108–9.

8. I. Howard Marshall, *Luke: Historian & Theologian* (Downers Grove, Ill.: IVP Academic, 1988), 53–76. See also Cedric E. W. Vine, "Greco-Roman Creation Accounts and the New Testament," 31, in this volume.

9. Carson, Moo, and Morris, *Introduction to the New Testament*, 115. See also Robert H. Stein, *Luke*, NAC 24 (Nashville, Tenn.: Broadman and Holman, 1992), 65; and Alfred Plummer, *Luke*, ICC (New York: T&T Clark, 2014), 5.

This study will examine the topic of creation theology in Luke and Acts in three steps. First, we will discuss briefly Luke's view of the historical reliability of the creation story. Even a simple perusal of the evidence strongly indicates that Luke considered the Genesis story to be fully historical and accurate. This is evidenced by repeated references to persons, events, and the creation text (usually in passing) in a way that indicates that both he and his audience considered them as historically true.

Second, we will explore allusions and echoes to the creation event. These might be words or themes that often become springboards for Luke to develop important theological themes.

Third, we will discuss four pericopes where Luke makes clear, unambiguous references to the creation event. These constitute the fullest Lukan discussion of the creation account and confirm his familiarity and belief.

CREATION AS HISTORY

Luke was very familiar with the creation story and the Scriptures that narrate it. In his Gospel, there are a multitude of quotations from and allusions to the Old Testament, the Pentateuch and Genesis in particular.[10] This suggests that Luke was fully conversant with the Hebrew Scriptures, or at least the Septuagint, and accepted them as true and historically reliable.

Eight times in the Gospel (Luke 2:22; 5:14; 16:29, 31; 20:28, 37; 24:27, 44) and ten times in Acts (Acts 3:22; 6:11, 14; 13:39; 15:1, 5, 21; 21:21; 26:22; 28:23) Moses is explicitly or implicitly acknowledged as the author of the Pentateuch. In Acts 7:2–50, Stephen gives a prolonged account of the history of Israel, with references to Genesis in particular and the Pentateuch and the Old Testament in general, all accepted as true.

In Luke 11:42–52, Jesus pronounces a series of six woes on the Pharisees and lawyers. In the fifth woe, He condemns them for having killed the prophets of God "from the foundation of the world . . . from the blood of Abel to the blood of Zechariah, who perished between the altar and the sanctuary" (Luke 11:50–51).[11] The Hebrew

---

10. Tiede, *Luke*, 26, calls Luke "a scriptural commentary," "midrash," and "hermeneutical project."

11. Unless otherwise indicated, Scripture quotations in this chapter are from the The ESV® Bible (The Holy Bible, English Standard Version®). ESV® Text Edition: 2016.

Scriptures contain the same books as our Old Testament but in a different order, ending with 2 Chronicles.[12] The last person 2 Chronicles mentions to have died for his faith is Zechariah, son of Jehoiada (2 Chron. 24:20–21). Abel is the first martyr (Gen. 4:8). By mentioning these two individuals with the words "from . . . to . . ." Jesus (and Luke) indicate acceptance of the Hebrew Scriptures as an authoritative and historically accurate account of the history of God's people. By tying "the foundation of the world" to Abel, Luke also demonstrates that he accepts the Genesis creation account, with which Abel is associated, as accurate history.[13]

In Luke 3:23–38, the evangelist gives the genealogy of Jesus. We will discuss this passage in more detail below. Suffice it to say here that Luke traces backwards Jesus's genealogy, culminating with Adam, who was "the son of God" (Luke 3:38),[14] indicating he accepts the genealogy as historically valid.[15] Luke presents Adam as a real, historical person.

The many quotations and allusions, the ascription of the Pentateuch to Moses, the prolonged defense of Stephen, the reference to the martyrs Abel and Zechariah, and the genealogy of Jesus all constitute conclusive evidence that Luke was both fully conversant with and fully believed in the Hebrew Scriptures in general and the creation account in particular.

---

12. John Nolland, *Luke 9:21–18:34*, WBC 35B (Dallas: Word, 1993), 668–69, states that "this is the earliest indication that, as was true later, 2 Chronicles . . . already came last in the Hebrew OT." R. C. H. Lenski, *The Interpretation of St. Luke's Gospel* (Columbus, Ohio: Wartburg, 1946), 668, notes that in using the phrase, Jesus "confines himself to the Scriptures and refers to its first and its last book." Cf. William Hendriksen, *Luke*, New Testament Commentary (Grand Rapids, Mich.: Baker, 1978), 643.

13. The term *katabolēs kosmou*, translated as "foundation of the world," requires some comment. *Katabolē* appears eleven times in the New Testament (Matt. 13:35; 25:34; Luke 11:50; John 17:24; Eph. 1:4; Heb. 4:3; 9:26; 11:11; 1 Pet. 1:20; Rev. 13:8; 17:8). With the exception of Hebrews 11:11, it is accompanied by the substantive *kosmou* as a reference to creation. On the significance of the expression in salvation history, see Friedrich Hauck, "*katabolē*," TDNT 3:620–21.

14. The LXX inserts one extra name in relation to the Masoretic Text: Kenan, son of Arphaxad (Gen. 11:12). Luke follows the LXX.

15. For a brief discussion of the seriousness with which Luke takes the genealogy, see Nolland, *Luke 1–9:20*, 171. See also Bovon, *Luke 1*, 133–36, who, while not accepting the historical accuracy of Luke's genealogy, explains eloquently how important accurate genealogies were for both Luke and the early church.

ECHOES OF THE CREATION STORY

Moving beyond the historicity of the creation account, we will now explore some linguistic elements in Luke through Acts that suggest that Luke picks language from the creation story and uses it as a base to develop important theological themes. There are many such elements—some more prominent, some more subtle—and they are presented here in thematic order, each standing on its own.

CREATION LANGUAGE RELATING TO DEATH AND RESURRECTION

The language Luke uses to describe death and resurrection is of interest to this study. In Luke 23:46, just before He dies, Jesus calls out with a loud voice, "Father, into your hands I commit my spirit!" Immediately after this, "he breathed his last." The Greek verb here is *ekpneō*, literally "to breathe out."[16] It is only used here and in the parallel passage of Mark 15:37, 39—nowhere else in the New Testament or the LXX. The noun "spirit" (*pneuma*) comes from *pneō* and *pnoē* ("to breathe"[17] and "breath,"[18] respectively). The raising of Jairus's daughter is recorded similarly in Luke 8:49–56. Jesus commands her to "arise," and Luke records that immediately "her spirit [breath] returned" (*kai epestrepsen to pneuma autēs*, Luke 8:55).[19]

In Acts 5:1–11, Luke records the deaths of Ananias and Sapphira. In relation to both deaths, he uses the word *exepsyxen*, meaning to "breathe out" from the preposition *ek* and the verb *psychō*.[20] The same verb is used to describe the death of Herod Agrippa I in Acts 12:23 but occurs nowhere else in the New Testament. It is very rare even in the LXX (only in Judges [A] 4:21 and Ezekiel 21:7). In Acts 20:10, after Eutychus has fallen from a window and died, Paul declares, "Do not be alarmed, for his life [*psychē*, "breath"] is in him." Likewise, Acts 17:25 depicts God as the one who gives *zōēn kai*

---

16. "*Ekpneō*," LSJ 517; "*ekpneō*," BDAG 308.

17. "*Pneō*," LSJ 1424–25; "*pneō*," BDAG 837.

18. "*Pnoē*," LSJ 1425.

19. Stein, *Luke*, 263, assumes that the return of the spirit indicates a distinct entity that would survive the death of the physical body. Bovon, *Luke 1*, 340–41, likewise observes that the soul of a dead person was believed to remain for three days in the vicinity of the corpse. Nolland, *Luke 1–9:20*, 422, more correctly observes that this text should be understood in light of the Hebraic rather than Hellenistic view of human nature and that the spirit that returned "may be nothing much more than the life force, which is what is intended by the use of נֶפֶשׁ, *nepeś* (Greek: ψυχή [*psychē*]), in 1 Kings 17:21–22."

20. "*Psychō*," LSJ 2028–29.

pnoēn—"life and breath," two words that probably function here as a hendiadys.[21]

The idea of death being the process of the breath leaving the body and resurrection as the breath coming back into the body is more pronounced with Luke than other New Testament writers[22] and clearly points back to the account of the creation of Adam. According to Genesis 2:7, God formed man from the dust of the earth and then "breathed [*enephysēsen*, LXX] into his nostrils the breath [*pnoēn*, LXX] of life, and the man became a living creature [*psychēn zōsan*, LXX]." Apart from validating the veracity of the creation account, Luke's use of creation motifs in his description of death probably serves an anthropological function. To a Greek audience, whose belief in the immortality of the soul was almost a *sine qua non* of their worldview, Luke counters by describing life in conditional terms as a gift of God, given at a specific time through the gift of breath and able to be withdrawn, leaving man as what he once was: dust.

CREATION LANGUAGE AND CHURCH GROWTH

Another echo of creation is found in Luke's description of the growth of the early church. When God created Adam and Eve, He told them to "be fruitful [*auxanesthe*, LXX] and multiply [*plēthynesthe*, LXX] and fill the earth" (Gen. 1:28). The same command/promise was given to the sea creatures and birds of the air created on the fifth day (Gen. 1:22). Henceforth, the two verbs *auxanesthe* and *plēthynesthe* become almost a standardized formula of God's blessings, either promised or attained. Thus, God commands the living creatures that have come out of Noah's ark after the Flood, as well as Noah and his sons, to "be fruitful and multiply" (Gen. 8:17; 9:1, 7).

Jacob also receives this promise (Gen. 35:11; 48:4). It is fulfilled by the growth of the children of Israel in Egypt (Exod. 1:7) and it is promised to them anew (Lev. 26:9). The promise is again given in Jeremiah 23:3, in regard to the return of Israel from the Babylonian exile and with a clear messianic hue.[23] It is worth noting that of the ten times these verbs appear together in the Old Testament, Genesis

---

21. R. C. H. Lenski, *The Interpretation of the Acts of the Apostles* (Minneapolis, Minn.: Augsburg, 1934), 727, sees the two as distinct—"life in its essence" and "its continuance in our bodies," respectively—though the distinction is minute.

22. Cf. *SDABC*, 5:771; cf. William F. Arndt, *Luke*, Concordia Classic Commentary Series (St. Louis, Mo.: Concordia, 1956), 243–48.

23. Andrew W. Blackwood Jr., *Commentary on Jeremiah* (Waco, Tex.: Word, 1977), 172.

contains seven, while Exodus, Leviticus, and Jeremiah have one each. Jeremiah appears to reflect the promises of Genesis—Israel's abundance, after its reconstitution. We can safely conclude that it is primarily a pentateuchal formula and closely tied to God's creative and redemptive work.

In the New Testament, the two verbs appear together only three times, all in the book of Acts (Acts 6:7; 7:17; 12:24). In Acts 7:17 Stephen recounts the growth and multiplication of the children of Israel in Egypt and reflects back on Exodus 1:7.[24] In Acts 6:7, however, Luke uses these two verbs to describe the rapid growth of the early Christian church.[25] Given that Acts is the only book that contains these two verbs, the usage is not incidental. In describing the growth of the church in terms of fruitfulness and multiplication, Luke clearly envisages the fulfillment of the command/promise given to Adam and Eve, then to Noah, then to Jacob as the father of the nation of Israel, and finally to the returning exiles. While by Luke's time the world is already filled with people, he envisages a spiritual fulfillment—the world is not simply to be filled with people, but with people who love and fear God.

In Acts 12:24, Luke offers a fresh dimension to the promise to be fruitful and multiply. Now it is the word of God that is fruitful and multiplies. Whether Luke is referring to the numerical increase of the church or simply to the increased manifestation of power from God is not altogether clear; maybe both are in view.[26] The statement comes immediately after the description of the death of Herod Agrippa I, who, when praised as a god by the Tyrians and Sidonians, did not reject the praise but gloated in it.[27] Luke records that "an angel of the Lord struck him down, because he did not give God the glory" (Acts 12:23). As such, the fruitfulness and multiplication appears to refer to God's powerful intervention in human affairs.[28]

It is obvious that of all New Testament writers, Luke is alone in adopting the creation command/promise "be fruitful and multiply"

---

24. Cf. C. K. Barrett, *The Acts of the Apostles*, ICC (Edinburgh: T&T Clark, 1994), 1:352.

25. Lenski, *Acts*, 248, rightly observes that the use of the imperfect tense of the two verbs indicates "steady continuation," as the church "continued to grow."

26. Barrett, *Acts of the Apostles*, 1:595, understands the phrase to mean that "the word of God increased in effectiveness and in effect, so that the number of believers multiplied."

27. Gerard A. Krodel, *Acts*, ACNT (Minneapolis, Minn.: Augsburg, 1986), 222–23.

28. Lenski, *Acts*, 488–89, ties the death of Herod to the growth of the church and concludes that this is a pattern of persecution: the persecutor dies, and the church continues to grow.

and applying it to the growth of the early church and the divine inter-ventions that made such growth possible. As he looks at the early church, he sees the promise of Genesis 1:28 becoming a reality.

CREATION LANGUAGE AND PETER'S VISION

A further and somewhat unexpected echo of creation appears in Acts 10:9–16 and again in 11:5–10. While praying on a housetop in Joppa, Peter receives a vision of a great sheet containing "all kinds of animals and reptiles and birds of the air" (Acts 10:12). This state-ment is repeated with slight variation in 11:6. The language draws from Genesis 1:21, 24, 30. A comparison of the Greek makes this obvious:

> ... ta tetrapoda kai herpeta tēs gēs kai peteina tou ouranou. (Acts 10:12)

> ... ta tetrapoda tēs gēs kai ta thēria kai ta herpeta kai ta peteina tou ouranou. (Acts 11:6)

> ... zōōn herpetōn, ... kai pan peteinon pterōton ... (Gen. 1:21)

> ... tetrapoda kai herpeta kai thēria tēs gēs ... (Gen. 1:24)

> ... kai pasi tois thēriois tēs gēs kai pasi tois peteinois tou ouranou kai panti herpetō ... (Gen. 1:30)

Using language from Genesis informs us that the living crea-tures Peter saw reflect the whole created order of animals. Peter later explains that the sheet with the animals represents the peo-ple of the world, toward whom "God shows no partiality, but in every nation anyone who fears him and does what is right is accept-able to him" (Acts 10:34–35).[29] As such, the vast created order of animals represents the vast number of nations, tribes, kindreds, and languages in the world, in which God has people He wants to reach with the gospel. The language of Genesis serves to highlight the universality of the appeal of the gospel.

The creation language used is inclusive, listing both clean and unclean animals.[30] This is also indicated by the phrase "all kinds of

---

29. Rudolf Stier, *The Word of the Apostles* (Minneapolis, Minn.: Klock and Klock, 1981), 159, insightfully observes that the four corners from which the heavenly sheet was upheld may symbolically encompass the four corners of the world.

30. Luke T. Johnson, *The Acts of the Apostles*, SP 5 (Collegeville, Minn.: Liturgical Press, 1992), 184, correctly observes that the listing of living beings follows Genesis 1:24 and not Leviticus 11:1–47 and includes both clean and unclean animals. Everett F. Harrison, *Acts: The Expanding Church* (Chicago: Moody Press, 1975), 167. Dennis Gaertner, *Acts*, The College

animals" (Acts 10:12).[31] Peter could not eat either because while the unclean animals were forbidden by divine command (Lev. 11:1–47), the clean animals were forbidden by Jewish tradition, according to which clean food could become "common" (*koinon*) if associated with anything considered a source of defilement (cf. Matt. 15:11, 18, 20; Mark 7:2, 5, 15, 18, 20, 23; Acts 21:28; Rom. 14:14).[32] This is evident in Peter's reply to the angel who ordered Peter to eat: "By no means, Lord, for I have never eaten anything that is common [*koinon*] or unclean [*akatharton*]" (Acts 10:14).[33]

The angel then replies to him, "What God has made clean, do not call common" (Acts 10:15). The angel is telling Peter that within the sheet encompassing all the animals created by God, there are some animals which God has declared clean and therefore legitimate for consumption but which Peter, in line with Jewish tradition but wrongly in God's eyes, calls "common"—that is, unfit to eat. He is telling Peter that there is agreeable food in that sheet, but Jewish tradition is blinding him to that fact. God never does away with His distinction of clean and unclean; rather, He pushes aside human tradition. He invites Peter to select that which is clean. This is reflected in Peter's interpretation of the vision. He does not say that all people are clean; he says God accepts from "every nation anyone who fears him" (Acts 10:35).[34]

Luke's use of creation language in the narration of Peter's vision serves to highlight the universality of the gospel call and help inform

---

Press NIV Commentary (Joplin, Miss.: College Press, 1993), 171, describes Peter's vision as a "mixture of . . . unclean animals with the clean." By contrast, Darrell L. Bock, *Acts*, BECNT (Grand Rapids, Mich.: Baker Academic, 2007), 388–89, mistakenly concludes that the sheet contains only unclean animals. He cites Peter's refusal to eat as evidence, but fails to note that Peter's response entails two categories of refusal: refusal to eat unclean animals and refusal to eat *koinon*, literally "common" animals (Acts 10:14).

31. Cf. Lenski, *Acts*, 402.

32. Michael J. Wilkins, *Matthew*, NIVAC (Grand Rapids, Mich.: Zondervan, 2004), 536–38; David E. Garland, *Mark*, NIVAC (Grand Rapids, Mich.: Zondervan, 1996), 271–86; Ajith Fernando, *Acts*, NIVAC (Grand Rapids, Mich.: Zondervan, 1998), 554; and Douglas J. Moo, *Romans*, NIVAC (Grand Rapids, Mich.: Zondervan, 2000), 459–60.

33. Johnson, *Acts of the Apostles*, 184, considers the distinction redundant, though he does admit that "the term *koinos* is sometimes used for things considered ritually 'unclean'" and cites 1 Maccabees 1:47, 62 and Josephus, *Ant.* 3.181, 11.346, and 12.320. However, Johnson provides no New Testament evidence, which is both clearer and more abundant.

34. There is a certain contradiction entailed by commentators who assert that through the vision God made all animals clean and the statement here that while the gospel is available to all, not all are worthy of it. Bock, *Acts*, 398, correctly notes that according to Acts 10:35, for a person to be acceptable to God two requirements need to be in place: (1) the person must fear God and (2) the person must "do right" or "perform righteousness" (*ergazomenos dikaiosynēn*).

contemporary exegesis and interpretation of the implications of the vision in relation to clean and unclean animals.

CREATION LANGUAGE HYPOCRISY

In Luke 11:40 we have another echo of creation. Jesus is invited to a meal at a Pharisee's house and shocks His host by not washing His hands prior to the meal, as is Pharisaic tradition.[35] Jesus uses this opportunity to point out their hypocrisy: they care for outside cleanliness but disregard inward impurity. Jesus asks the rhetorical question, "You fools! Did not he who made the outside make the inside also?" (Luke 11:40). The statement may appear to refer to cups and dishes, since this is what Jesus has been addressing in Luke 11:39. However, it does not. Jesus switches and now begins to talk about the human being. Therefore the "he" who made both the inside and the outside is none other than God, and the "made" (*poiēsas*)[36] refers to the creation of humans. The implication is that even though Pharisees may wash the outside (hands), the inside of their being may be impure. This means they are culpable. God, who created them, sees both the outside and the inside; they cannot hoodwink Him by their outer show of cleanliness.

CREATION LANGUAGE AND GOD'S CARE FOR NATURE

In Luke 12, we see a further echo of creation in the description of the processes of nature. Jesus gives four examples from nature to assure His audience of God's ongoing care. The first example is the sparrows sold in the markets of Israel for two pennies. They may seem valueless to most people, yet Jesus assures us that not one of them is forgotten by God (Luke 12:6). He then adds a second example from nature, stating that even the hairs of a person's head are numbered (Luke 12:7). The implication of both statements is that God is the Creator of both humans and sparrows. How else would He know the number of hairs on the head of each person? Why else would He care for each one of the seemingly valueless sparrows?

---

35. The corresponding statement in Matthew 23:26 appears to begin from the position of the School of Hillel—cleanse the inside of the cup since the cleanliness of the inside is all that matters—though it continues differently, with the cleansing of the inside securing that of the outside. Cf. C. F. Evans, *Saint Luke* (Philadelphia: Trinity, 1990), 504.

36. The participle *poiēsas* is a form of the verb *poieō*, used repeatedly of God's creative acts in the Greek text (LXX) of the creation story (Gen. 1:1, 7, 11, 12, 16, 21, 25, 26, 27[3x], 31; 2:2[2x], 3, 4, 18).

In Luke 12:22–32, Jesus mentions two more examples from nature. The first is the ravens who "neither sow nor reap" (12:24), yet the heavenly Father takes care of them. The second is the lilies and grass of the fields, which, though blossoming one day and gone the next, are nonetheless more beautiful in their raiment than even the glorious Solomon in all his riches (12:27). The implication is that if God cares for these seemingly least valuable of nature's plants and animals, then He will surely care for human beings, who should therefore not worry or fret.

CREATION LANGUAGE AND JESUS'S CONTROL OVER NATURE

A somewhat fainter echo is found in Luke 8:22–25. During a night crossing of the Sea of Galilee, Jesus and the disciples are caught in a storm. The disciples fear for their lives and awaken Jesus, who was peacefully sleeping. Jesus calms the sea and the storm, then rebukes the disciples for their lack of faith. They wonder in amazement, "Who then is this, that he commands even winds and water, and they obey him?" (Luke 8:25). Though lacking clear linguistic parallels, this incident probably reflects back on God's rulership over the primeval state of the earth when it was covered in water (Gen 1:2) and/or the Flood. Indeed, raging waters symbolized chaos and the uncontrollable forces of nature to the Jews.[37] This explains their amazement at Jesus's power to calm the storm. As such, this incident is a subtle pointer to the divinity of Jesus.[38]

CREATION LANGUAGE AND THE DEFEAT OF SATAN

In Luke 10:19, we find another echo of creation. Earlier in the chapter, Jesus sends the seventy-two disciples to visit the towns He was planning to visit and prepare the way (Luke 10:1). In verse 17 the disciples return with joy, declaring, "even the demons are subject to us in your name!" Jesus then replies, "I saw Satan fall like lightning from heaven" (Luke 10:18) and adds, "Behold, I have given you authority to tread on serpents and scorpions, and over all the power of the enemy, and nothing shall hurt you" (Luke 10:19).

The authority to tread over serpents and scorpions has a dual application. First, there is the physical application that offers the

---

37. Justo L. González, *Luke*, Belief: A Theological Commentary on the Bible (Louisville, Ky.: Westminster John Knox, 2010), 107.

38. Evans, *Saint Luke*, 382.

disciples a level of protection from the dangers of nature. A fulfill-ment of this promise is in Acts 28:4–6, when, after the shipwreck in Malta, Paul is bitten by a venomous snake. The locals assume that divine judgment has come upon him for something evil he certainly must have done before, but Paul shakes off the snake into the fire and suffers no harm. Seeing this, the locals recognize divine power at work.

Three elements in Luke 10:18–19, however, suggest a second, spiritual application. First, in Luke 10:18 and in response to the report of the seventy-two disciples' ministry, Jesus declares that He "saw Satan fall like lightning from heaven." The fall of Satan is associated with his defeat,[39] which was accomplished through "the original expulsion of Lucifer from heaven, the collapsing of his kingdom of darkness as it was being shaken by [Jesus's] ministry and that of His disciples, and the certainty of the devil's ultimate ruin which would be accomplished by His atoning death on the cross."[40] It is not the disciples' ministry that defeats Satan; rather, in ministry the disciples become coworkers in the plan of salvation and covictors with Jesus.[41] Second, both in the Bible and in non-biblical Jewish writings, Satan is associated with the serpent.[42] Third, in Luke 10:19 Jesus declares, "I have given you authority [*exousia*] to tread on serpents." The noun *exousia*, especially as used by Luke, suggests here adminis-trative and particularly spiritual authority.[43] Here *exousia* appears with the article and is therefore definite. Jesus has a specific, spiri-tual *exousia* in mind. To have this *exousia* over serpents means hav-ing spiritual authority over the powers of Satan. This implication is confirmed by the additional statement "and over all the power of the enemy" (Luke 10:19)—clearly over the power of Satan. The idea of treading on serpents as a sign of spiritual authority over the power

---

39. Arndt, *Luke*, 285.

40. Frank B. Holbrook, "The Great Controversy," in *HSDAT*, 977.

41. C. Marvin Pate, *Luke*, Moody Gospel Commentary (Chicago: Moody, 1995), 232. Commenting on Luke 10:18, Trent C. Butler, *Luke*, Holman New Testament Commentary (Nashville, Tenn.: Broadman and Holman, 2000), 177, posits that "with God exercising his power through the followers of Jesus, Satan has lost."

42. See Gen. 3:1–15; Rev. 12:1–17.

43. For spiritual authority, see: Luke 4:6, 32, 36; 5:24; 9:1; 12:5; 20:2, 8, 20; 22:53; Acts 1:7; 8:19; 26:18. For administrative authority, see: Luke 7:8; 12:11; 19:17; 23:7; Acts 5:4; 9:14; 26:10, 12.

of Satan harkens back to the promise of Genesis 3:15, where the Seed, a symbol of Jesus, would bruise the serpent's head.[44]

CREATION LANGUAGE AND PARADISE

A further echo of the creation story may be seen in the use of the word "paradise." In the creation story in the Septuagint, paradise (*paradeisos*) is the name of the garden God planted for Adam and Eve (Gen. 2:8, 9, 10, 15, 16; 3:1, 2, 3, 8, 10, 23, 24). In the New Testament, the name appears only three times, in Luke 23:43, 2 Corinthians 12:4, and Revelation 2:7. In Luke 23:43 it is part of the promise to the thief on the cross that he would be with Jesus in paradise. In 2 Corinthians 12:4 it is part of the description of Paul's heavenly trip/vision, where he saw things beyond description.[45] Revelation 2:7 looks forward to the inheritance of the saints. The term "paradise" therefore reflects back to the story of creation and looks forward to the restoration of the created order after the consummation of this age.[46]

CREATION LANGUAGE AND THE ORIGIN OF EVIL

Another echo of the creation story may be detected in the use of the adjective *ponēros* ("evil"). In the creation story, the forbidden tree is called the tree of the knowledge of "good and evil" (*kalon kai ponēron*, Gen. 2:9, 17; 3:5, 22). The adjective *ponēros*, though common throughout the LXX, is less so in the New Testament: there is one occurrence in Revelation, none in Peter or Jude, two in James, three in John's Gospel, eight in John's epistles, thirteen in Paul's

---

44. James McKeown, *Genesis*, THOTC (Grand Rapids, Mich.: Eerdmans, 2008), 39.

45. Paul's statement in 1 Corinthians 2:9 could be added here: "no eye has seen, nor ear heard, nor the heart of man imagined, what God has prepared for those who love him." Though often used to refer to what is being prepared for the saved in the new heaven and new earth, contextually it seems to apply to the wisdom of the plan of salvation, unseen by unbelievers but revealed by God to His people; see, e.g., John E. MacArthur, *1 Corinthians*, MacArthur New Testament Commentary (Chicago: Moody, 1984), 61. While this observation has some validity, the application to the new heavens and new earth should not be discounted. There are pointers in the text that admit as much. In 1 Corinthians 2:6, Paul speaks of "the rulers of this age, who are doomed to pass away." Then in 1 Corinthians 2:7, he contrasts them with believers: "But we impart a secret and hidden wisdom of God, which God decreed before the ages for our glory." The phrase "for our glory" probably looks not only at the present experience of believers, which in many ways was anything but glorious, but at the future culmination of this age and the restoration of the new heavenly order that will indeed result in glory for believers. Moreover, the fact that Paul writes to believers yet describes something they have not yet been able to fully fathom indicates that a future, much grander reality is at least partly in view.

46. Arndt, *Luke*, 470–71; and Henry B. Swete, *Commentary on Revelation* (Grand Rapids, Mich.: Kregel, 1977), 28–30.

epistles, and two each in Hebrews and Mark. By contrast, Matthew has twenty-six and Luke-Acts twenty-one. Matthew and Luke's choice of *ponēros* over other synonyms may be a deliberate attempt to connect the evil of their generation with Adam and Eve's choice to partake of the forbidden fruit—evil's point of entry into the world. However, this is just a tentative suggestion; the evidence does not allow for decisive conclusions.

CREATION LANGUAGE AND THE SABBATH

Last but not least, we have an echo of creation in Luke's references to the Sabbath. Paul has two references, Matthew eleven, Mark twelve, and John thirteen. Luke has twenty in the Gospel and another ten in Acts—making a total of thirty. More importantly, Luke is the only New Testament author who mentions the fourth commandment specifically. Speaking of the women who prepared spices for the entombment of Jesus, he writes, "Then they returned and prepared spices and ointments. On the Sabbath they rested according to the commandment" (Luke 23:56). The reference to the commandment obviously points back to Exodus 20:8–11 (cf. Deut. 5:12–15), where the command to remember and keep the Sabbath holy is directly linked to the fact that God created the world in six days and rested on the seventh. Luke's reference to the Sabbath commandment also indicates that he recognized Sabbath-keeping as a divine command.

Another clear reference to the fourth commandment—and, implicitly, the creation account—is in Luke 13:14: "There are six days in which work ought to be done. Come on those days and be healed, and not on the Sabbath day." Here Luke quotes a synagogue ruler who was complaining that Jesus was healing on the Sabbath. His zeal is misplaced. Jesus replies that healings are perfectly legitimate on the Sabbath: "You hypocrites! Does not each of you on the Sabbath untie his ox or his donkey from the manger and lead it away to water it? And ought not this woman, a daughter of Abraham whom Satan bound for eighteen years, be loosed from this bond on the Sabbath day?" (Luke 13:15–16). Jesus does not object to Sabbath keeping but argues that works of loosening the power of Satan are in harmony with the spirit of the Sabbath. Indeed, upon His reply His adversaries are put to shame and the people rejoice (Luke 13:17).

Interestingly, the phrase *hēmera tou sabbatou*, used in both the synagogue ruler's statement (Luke 13:14) and in Jesus's reply (Luke 13:16), first appears in the LXX in Exodus 20:8 in the context of the fourth commandment. Subsequently, it is found mostly in legal texts. In the New Testament, it is used only by Luke.

Luke contains three more references to the fourth commandment—two direct quotations and one allusion (Acts 4:24; 14:15; 17:24). These will be discussed in more detail later in this study. We can conclude that the text of the fourth commandment, which closely ties together the Sabbath with the creation story, plays a prominent role in Luke's writings.

CLEAR REFERENCES TO THE CREATION STORY

In this final section of this study, we will discuss four passages that contain the clearest references to creation.

THE GENEALOGY OF JESUS

The first is Luke 3:23–38, already briefly discussed in relation to Luke's acceptance of the historicity of the creation story. Here we will explore the theological implications. Luke 3:23–38 contains the genealogy of Jesus. A comparison with Matthew's genealogy is useful. Writing primarily for Jews and Jewish Christians, Matthew begins his genealogy with Abraham (Matt. 1:2), the father of the Hebrew nation, and arranges the list of names in groups of fourteen generations (Matt. 1:17), possibly in order to highlight God's rulership and guidance over the history of Israel.[47] By contrast, Luke begins with Jesus (Luke 3:23) and moves backwards, past Abraham and the patriarchs to Adam and God (Luke 3:38).[48] Since Adam is the father of all nations, Luke's genealogy gives a more universal outlook to the person of Jesus: He is the Savior of all peoples. This is in line with Luke's more universal outlook and interest in outsiders,

---

47. Wilkins, *Matthew*, 56–57. R. T. France, *The Gospel of Matthew*, NICNT (Grand Rapids, Mich.: Eerdmans, 2007), 29–31, points out that Matthew likes to arrange his material in numerical groups, usually three or seven, and that fourteen is "twice seven." Moreover, fourteen is the sum of the numerical value of the letter of the name David in Hebrew. Each of the three periods Matthew lists ends with something related to David: period 1, the Davidic dynasty established; period 2, the Davidic dynasty abolished with the destruction of Jerusalem and the Babylonian exile; and period 3, the Davidic dynasty restored in Jesus.

48. Tiede, *Luke*, 96, notes that there are seventy-seven names in Jesus's genealogy, which could imply a pattern of eleven sets of seven. Jesus would be the beginning of the twelfth set, and also the first of the seventh cycle from David.

the poor and oppressed, sinners, tax collectors, Samaritans, women,[49] and even Gentiles.[50]

The genealogy of Luke 3:23–38 also has important implications for the concept of sonship. Throughout Luke and Acts, sonship of God is used primarily of Jesus and relates to His heavenly, divine origin (Luke 1:31–32, 35; 3:22; 4:3, 9, 41; 8:28; 10:22; 22:70; Acts 9:20; 13:33). However, in Luke 3:38, by calling Adam "son of God" Luke gives another dimension to sonship. Human beings, by virtue of having been created by God through the creation of Adam, are also "sons of God"—albeit not in the same sense or with the same authority as Jesus. In harmony with this, Luke 6:35 promises that those who follow Jesus will be "sons of the Most High." This promise probably pertains to the restoration of all things, when the sonship experienced by Adam is fully restored,[51] though a present dimension should not be excluded.[52] In Luke 16:8, Jesus calls believers "sons of light" (*huios tou phōtos*), a reference to believers being God's sons,[53] or at least walking in the light revealed by Jesus. In Luke 20:36, glorified believers after the resurrection are called "sons of God" and are said to be "equal to angels." This, in turn, reminds us of Psalm 8:6, where man was created a little lower than the angels.

It seems that for Luke, God's creation of Adam ascribes to him and his descendants a special status as sons of God. This sonship is not on a par with the sonship of Jesus. It is a glorious status that is, in some sense, experienced now but awaits ultimate fulfillment at the resurrection, when glorified believers will be put on the same level of glory as angels.

THE PAEAN OF PRAISE TO THE CREATOR

The next direct Lukan reference to creation appears in Acts 4:24, in the context of a paean from believers (Acts 4:23–31) after the

---

49. Mark L. Strauss, *Four Portraits, One Jesus* (Grand Rapids, Mich.: Zondervan, 2007), 286–87.

50. Tiede, *Luke*, 97, opines that though the genealogy of Jesus may identify him with the Gentiles, Luke does not develop the theme. While it is true that the Gospel does not develop the theme fully, if one looks at Luke-Acts as a two-volume work, then it becomes evident that the gospel to the Gentiles plays a prominent role in Luke's outlook.

51. Bock, *Luke*, 191.

52. *SDABC*, 5:749.

53. In Luke 2:32, "light" is almost personified in the person of Jesus, in which case the "sons of light" could be understood as sons of God or of Jesus.

release of Peter and John from the Sanhedrin (Acts 4:1–22). Their praise begins, "Sovereign Lord, who made the heaven and the earth and the sea and everything in them" (Acts 4:24). The words come directly from the LXX of Exodus 20:11, as a simple comparison demonstrates:

> *ton ouranon kai tēn gēn kai tēn thalassan kai panta ta en autois . . .*
> (Exod. 20:11)
> *ton ouranon kai tēn gēn kai tēn thalassan kai panta ta en autois . . .*
> (Acts 4:24)

The aim of this quotation is undoubtedly to highlight the sovereignty of God over the affairs of earth. Since God created everything in the heavens, the earth, and the sea, He is Lord over these. This is why the praise begins with "Sovereign Lord" (*despota*). What follows confirms this. The believers' praise continues (Acts 4:25–26) with a quotation from Psalm 2:1, describing how nations have risen against the Anointed of God, and then interprets accordingly the actions of Herod and then Pilate, who, together with the Gentiles and the Jews, try to destroy Jesus and the disciples but fail (Acts 4:27–31). The creation event therefore serves as a launching point for a paean on the sovereignty of God over all the created order, historical events, and the well-being of His people.

RETURN TO THE CREATOR

The third direct reference to creation comes in the context of Paul's ministry in Lystra (Acts 14:8–18). After Paul heals a lame man, the pagans of the city assume him and Barnabas to be gods and want to offer sacrifice to them. Alarmed, the two apostles tear their clothes, rush to the middle of the adoring crowd, and give a short speech highlighting the uniqueness of the Creator God against all other gods. The key verse is Acts 14:15, where Paul declares, "you should turn from [*epistrephō*] these vain things [idols] to a living God, who made the heaven and the earth and the sea and all that is in them." As with Acts 4:24, the latter part of the statement comes directly from the fourth commandment in Exodus 20:11:

> *epoiēsen kurios ton ouranon kai tēn gēn kai tēn thalassan kai panta ta en autois . . .* (Exod. 20:11)
> *hos epoiēsen ton ouranon kai tēn gēn kai tēn thalassan kai panta ta en autois.* (Acts 14:15)

The Greek for "turn from" (*epistrephō*) has the idea of "returning."[54] Paul's invitation that the nations "return" to God implies that they once were with God—probably at creation and soon thereafter, before they scattered and followed their own ways. Paul further asserts that even when the nations went their own way and lived estranged from God, He nonetheless still witnessed to them, sending rains in due season and giving them food and gladness (Acts 14:17). Therefore, the invitation to return to God is presented as the logical thing to do; by returning to God, nations are returning to their roots. The picture of God that we get from Paul's words is that through creation God establishes Himself as a type of Father figure who not only brings the world and its people into existence but continues to care for them even when they walk according to their own wishes, worshiping things that are not gods.

THE CREATOR PREACHED IN ATHENS

The last clear reference to creation appears in the context of Paul's speech to the Areopagus in Athens (Acts 17:22–31). Within this pericope, there are several references to God's creative acts. Verse 24 mentions "the God who made the world and everything in it." The word for "world" is *kosmos* and alludes back to Genesis 2:1, the only Old Testament text where this word is used in relation to creation. The phrase "everything in it" is a quotation/allusion to the fourth commandment (Exod. 20:11). As in Acts 4:24, God's creative work is the source of His authority. Paul, therefore, declares that by virtue of creation God is "Lord of heaven and earth" (Acts 17:24). The word "Lord" (*kyrios*) also draws from the fourth commandment (Exod. 20:11).

In Acts 17:25, Paul declares that this heavenly God who is Lord of heaven and earth gives "to all mankind life [*zōēn*] and breath [*pnoēn*] and everything." The mention of *zōēn* and *pnoēn* points back to *pnoēn zōēs* in Genesis 2:7, whereby Adam became alive when God breathed into his nostrils the breath of life.

In Acts 17:26–27, Paul moves on to explain what this means in practice. He states, "And he made from one man [*ex enos*] every nation of mankind to live on all the face of the earth, having determined allotted periods and the boundaries of their dwelling place that they should seek God, and perhaps feel their way toward him

---

54. "*Epistrephō*," *LSJ* 661; and "*epistrephō*," *BDAG* 382.

and find him." There is an important textual variant in Acts 17:26, where in place of *ex enos* ("from one [man],") some manuscripts read *ex enos haimatos* ("from one blood").[55] Theologically, the difference is not major since both readings point back to the creation of the first person, from whom all nations have sprung into being. Textually, "from one man" fits better not only because of better manuscript support but also because the creation account speaks of the creation of man, without specific references to blood.

The implication of the creation reference is twofold. First, since God created all people from one person, all people are His children and He wants all of them to know the plan of salvation. It is for this reason that God has allotted "periods" and "boundaries." These work to enlighten the nations. Second, by virtue of creation, God is Lord. Therefore, it is He who has allotted periods and boundaries—that is, He oversees the flow of the history of nations.

Paul continues to highlight God's lordship by stating that "in him we live and move and have our being" (Acts 17:28). These words possibly reflect the sayings of Epimenides of Knossos, a sixth-century BC Greek writer.[56] Paul may add them to confirm his teaching about creation using a source with which his Greek audience at the Areopagus would be familiar. He then adds a quotation from another Greek source, Aratus of Soli, a third-century BC writer from Soli in Cilicia: "For we are indeed his offspring" (Acts 17:27).[57] The idea of humans being the offspring of God in the context of Luke-Acts no doubt harkens back to Adam and all his descendants being in a sense sons of God, as previously discussed (cf. Luke 3:38; 6:35; 16:8; 20:36).[58]

---

55. Bruce M. Metzger, *A Textual Commentary on the Greek New Testament*, 2nd ed. (New York: United Bible Societies, 1994), 404–5, reviews the evidence typically given in favor of "from one blood" (*ex enos haimatos*) and notes that while this reading has support from the Western text, various early versions, and patristic witnesses, the external evidence of highly respected manuscripts weighs in favor of excluding the word "blood" (*haimatos*).

56. The statement by Epimenides comes from his work *Cretica* and is extant in a Syriac manuscript of the ninth century, a commentary on Acts by Ishodad of Merv, bishop of Hdatta. The manuscript was translated (back) into Greek, and also into English, by James R. Harris and is discussed in a series of articles, chiefly James R. Harris, "The Cretans Always Liars," *The Expositor* 2, no. 4 (1906): 305–17.

57. Krodel, *Acts*, 336; Aratus of Soli, *Phaenomena*, line 5. Aratus's work *Phaenomena*—a poem probably based on two earlier prose works, *Phaenomena* and *Enoptron*, both by Eudoxus of Cnidus—is an introduction to the constellations and was a popular work among the Greeks and Romans at the time of Paul.

58. Originally the statement of Aratus does not reflect on the creation as described in Genesis, having been written in a pagan context. Paul, and Luke, who quotes him, nonetheless use this pagan quote as a springboard to connect the Athenian audience to the biblical worldview and to the one true God as the Creator of everyone, as evidenced in Paul's

Paul concludes his sermon before the Areopagus with a call to repentance in light of the coming judgment (Acts 17:29–31). Since God is the Creator, He is entitled to expect a certain outlook from His creatures. And while He is willing to overlook ignorance, He will by no means fail to hold people accountable for their behavior.

CONCLUSION

This brief study on the theme of creation in Luke and Acts has revealed a number of important points. While there is no systematic treatment of the topic, Luke's writings reverberate with creation language and allusions that form the background for a number of important theological themes. Furthermore, Luke consistently assumes the full historical reliability of the creation account. This is evident in his acknowledgment that Moses was the author of the Pentateuch, in the numerous references to pentateuchal stories that clearly assume them to be true, and, not least, in his repeated allusions to the creation account.

Theologically, perhaps the most important point that comes out of Lukan creation material is the rulership and lordship of God. It is the act of creation that places God above every other authority and gives Him the right to expect a certain mode of conduct from humanity. This theme comes out most clearly in our discussion of Acts 14:1–18 and 17:22–31. As ruler of everything that takes place in the human sphere, God intervenes in history and guides it so His purposes are fulfilled and His people prosper. This is clearly the implication in Acts 4:23–31. His power over human affairs is symbolically displayed in Jesus's calming of the storm (Luke 8:22–26). God's rulership means that eventually He will hold all people to account at the designated "day" of judgment. While this theme is not prominent in Lukan creation theology, it is implied in God's rulership and discussed explicitly in Acts 17:22–31.

Another very important theological theme is the sense of brotherhood and care for all nations that creation implies. Adam, the "son of God" (Luke 3:38), is also the father of all peoples, who in turn are also God's "offspring" (Acts 17:26–28) and, though they suffer now,

---

theological apologetic: "The God who made the world and everything in it" (Acts 17:24). The fact that God created everyone makes Him the Father of all and therefore ties in with Luke's sonship theology elsewhere in his writings.

await their full restoration to sonship at the resurrection (Luke 20:36). This was also evident in Acts 4:8–18, where God's rulership over the earth means that He is the one who tenderly provides for the needs of all His creatures. The universal fatherhood of God is also evident in the use of creation language in Peter's vision of the sheet containing all kinds of animals (Acts 10:12; 11:6). Since the vision is intended to refer to people, the use of inclusive creation language likewise points to inclusivity of people: God shows no partiality and has His people "in every nation" (Acts 10:34–35).

God's care for the created order extends beyond humans—to other living creatures and even the plants. This is evident in Jesus's statement about the sparrows that do not fall to the ground without God's knowledge, the number of hairs on the head, and God's care for the ravens and even the lilies of the field and the grass (Luke 12:6–31).

Beyond the two important themes of God's rulership over creation and God's care for all creation, there are other secondary themes found in this study of Luke's creation theology. The repeated references to breath as a constituent component of life, and its departure as the reality of death, point us back to the creation of Adam in Genesis 2:7. Such imagery reinforces the unity of the human being (as opposed to Hellenistic dualism and the distinction between body and soul) and the nature of death as the complete cessation of life. Luke's allusion to the promise of Genesis 1:28 to "be fruitful and multiply" (Acts 6:7; 12:24) and his application of this promise to the early church give an ecclesiological dimension to Luke's creation theology. God is not interested in simply filling the earth with people, but with people who love and obey Him. Therefore, the growth of the early church was a direct fulfillment of God's purpose expressed in Genesis 1:26.

We also noted how Luke's frequent use of the adjective *ponēros* could be a hint pointing back to the tree of knowledge of good and evil, suggesting that all that goes wrong in this world can be traced back to that first act of disobedience.

Finally, we noted that Luke's creation theology is closely linked to the seventh-day Sabbath. Luke is the only New Testament writer who uses the expression *hēmera tou sabbatou* ("the day of the Sabbath," Luke 13:14, 16; 14:5), which comes directly from the fourth commandment and links the Sabbath to creation. He is the only New

Testament writer who directly references the fourth commandment (Luke 23:56). Luke also refers to God's creative acts by twice quoting a part of the fourth commandment (Acts 4:24; 14:15), and once by alluding to it and to God's creation rest of Genesis 2:1 (Acts 17:24). Such interest in the creation Sabbath becomes even more fascinating given that he is the only Gentile writer in the New Testament, writing to a Gentile audience. Or perhaps this helps explain his interest. Being from a Gentile background, the creation origin of the Sabbath was the key factor demonstrating that the Sabbath was not simply a Jewish institution but a universal blessing for all peoples.

While Luke's writings contain no systematic, theological treatment of creation, his quotations and allusions offer a wealth of beautiful creation theology.

Jon Paulien, PhD

Loma Linda University
Loma Linda, California, USA

CREATION IN THE GOSPEL AND EPISTLES OF JOHN

INTRODUCTION

There is a relative paucity of scholarly literature on the subject of creation in the Johannine writings.[1] For almost any topic related to the Gospel of John, you can find hundreds of commentaries, monographs, scholarly articles, and more that address the topic in one way or another. But direct attempts to address creation in the Gospel of John are few,[2] and the scholarly task becomes like a scavenger hunt, looking for hints of creation in studies on other topics. And when it comes to the Johannine epistles, the author of

---

1. Brian J. Tabb, review of *Signs of Salvation: The Theme of Creation in John's Gospel*, by Anthony M. Moore, *RBL* (2015), https://www.sblcentral.org/home/bookDetails/9555. The theme of creation has received attention in Pauline scholarship but "little formal treatment" in studies of John; see Jeannine K. Brown, "Creation's Renewal in the Gospel of John," *CBQ* 72, no. 2 (April 2010): 275–76. Many scholars find little reference to creation even in the Prologue; see Jan A. du Rand, "The Creation Motif in the Fourth Gospel: Perspectives on Its Narratological Function within a Judaistic Background," in *Theology and Christology in the Fourth Gospel: Essays by the Members of the SNTS Johannine Writings Seminar*, ed. G. Van Belle, J. G. Van der Watt, and P. Mantz, BETL 184 (Leuven: Leuven University Press, 2005), 21.

2. Among the few are Brown, "Creation's Renewal"; Moore, *Signs of Salvation*; Mary L. Coloe, "Theological Reflections on Creation in the Gospel of John," *Pacifica* 24 (2011): 1–12; Abraham Terian, "Creation in Johannine Theology," in *Good News in History*, ed. E. L. Miller (Atlanta: Scholars, 1993): 45–61; and Pierre Trudinger, "The Seven Days of the New Creation in St. John's Gospel: Some Further Reflections," *EvQ* 44 (1972): 154–58.

the present study did not find a single scholarly item that focused directly on creation.[3]

Of special interest for our current discussion, no single piece of scholarship suggests any link between the Johannine literature and the theme of origins. In fact, John has been accused of "emphatically" passing over in silence the fact that "the world is a divine creation."[4] Scholars seem to agree that when John[5] makes reference to creation he is doing so with spiritual intent, rather than describing how or when the world was created.[6] Creation in the beginning becomes a metaphor for revelation[7] and/or for the "new creation" that Jesus establishes through His life, death, and resurrection.[8] Spiritual issues are no less real than scientific ones; they are just of a different kind.

This study begins by identifying the key passages in the Gospel of John where scholars believe creation is most clearly in view. It then offers a quick survey of the "new creation" theme in the Old Testament

---

3. Agreeing with this is Ekkehardt Mueller, "Creation in the New Testament," *JATS* 15, no. 1 (2004): 47–62. See also the first chapter of this volume by Ekkehardt Mueller (p. 11), which is an updated version of his article in *JATS*. Scholarship does, however, recognize that creation is emphasized much more in the Gospel of John than in the Synoptic Gospels; see J. Duncan M. Derrett, "New Creation: Qumran, Paul, the Church, and Jesus," *RevQ* 13 (1988): 607.

4. Hans-Ulrich Wiedemann, "The Victory of Protology over Eschatology? Creation in the Gospel of John," in *Theologies of Creation in Early Judaism and Ancient Christianity*, ed. Tobias Nicklas and Korinna Zamfir in cooperation with Heike Braun, DCLS 6 (Berlin: De Gruyter, 2010), 299; quoting Jürgen Becker, *Das Evangelium nach Johannes*, ÖTK, 4th ser., vol. 1 (Gütersloh: Gütersloher Verlagshaus, 1991), 93.

5. Mainstream scholarship debates the authorship of the Gospel and Epistles attributed to John. In a paper of this length we cannot address such issues. We recognize the disciple John, the son of Zebedee and brother of James, as the author of both the Gospel and Epistles of John. Since all the relevant texts for our topic are in the Gospel of John, any distinction between the Gospel of John and the Epistles of John does not materially affect the outcome of this study.

6. Thomas Barrosse, "The Seven Days of the New Creation in St. John's Gospel," *CBQ* 21, no. 4 (October 1959): 516; and Terian, "Creation in Johannine Theology," 45. From the beginning, the Gospel of John was recognized as a "spiritual gospel." According to the early Christian historian Eusebius (*Hist. eccl.* 6.14.7), Papias, who wrote within twenty-five years of the Fourth Gospel's publication, uses that phrase to describe it.

7. Elaine Pagels, "Exegesis of Genesis 1 in the Gospels of Thomas and John," *JBL* 118, no. 3 (Fall 1999): 489.

8. Although creation in the Gospel of John is a relatively neglected topic, there are a few scholars who believe creation is the Gospel's central theme or underlying structure: Brown, "Creation's Renewal," 277; Mary L. Coloe, "Structure of the Johannine Prologue," *ABR* 45 (1997): 40–55; Ernst Käsemann, *The Testament of Jesus: A Study of the Gospel of John in the Light of Chapter 17*, trans. Gerhard Krodel (Philadelphia, Pa.: Fortress, 1968), 62–63; and Moore, *Signs of Salvation*. In fact, G. K. Beale, "The Eschatological Conception of New Testament Theology," in *Eschatology in Bible and Theology: Evangelical Essays at the Dawn of a New Millennium*, ed. Kent E. Brower and Mark W. Elliott (Downers Grove, Ill.: InterVarsity, 1997), 11–52, goes so far as to suggest the new creation is "a plausible and defensible centre for New Testament theology."

and in Hellenistic Judaism, which helps us make sense of John's later references to creation. Then a careful study of each of the identified Johannine texts is presented in the order of their importance to the theme. After a brief exploration of the epistles of John, the study ends with a double conclusion: first, summarizing what we have learned about John's theology of creation, and its spiritual implications; and finally, concluding with an overview of the apocalyptic implications of creation in the Fourth Gospel and how they point to John's belief that the original creation was literal, real, and produced by the spoken word of God. This conclusion provides additional biblical support for belief in a recent, six-day creation.

SCHOLARSHIP ON CREATION IN THE GOSPEL OF JOHN

Scholars universally agree that the clearest references to creation in the Gospel of John are found in the Prologue (John 1:1–18).[9] The second most widely cited creation text in the Gospel is John 20:22: "He breathed on them and said, 'Receive the Holy Spirit.'"[10] This is generally believed to be an allusion to Genesis 2:7. Scholars suggest other allusions to creation in the last four chapters of the Gospel that are more or less related to this reference.[11] A smaller, but still significant, number of scholars see creation as a major theme in the Sabbath healings,[12] which elaborate on the life and light that the Word brought at creation (John 1:4–5). At the pool of Bethesda, Jesus brings life to a man paralyzed for thirty-eight years. And in chapter 9, Jesus brings light to the man born blind.

Finally, and more speculatively, a number of scholars argue that the seven days of creation are repeated sequentially in the Gospel narratives. Most frequently, they refer to the seven-day period between John 1:19 and the wedding at Cana (John 2:1–11). But others suggest that the seven days of creation can be seen in chapters

---

9. Brown, "Creation's Renewal," 277. Käsemann believes the Prologue is the only place in the Gospel where creation appears; nevertheless, he feels it is the hermeneutical key to the Gospel's christology (as outlined in Wiedemann, "Victory of Protology," 300–301, 303).

10. All biblical quotations are the author's translation unless otherwise indicated.

11. Tabb, review of Moore, *Signs of Salvation;* Wiedemann, "Victory of Protology," 321.

12. Paul Sevier Minear, *Christians and the New Creation: Genesis Motifs in the New Testament* (Louisville, Ky.: Westminster John Knox, 1994), 87–95; Jon Paulien, *John: Jesus Gives Life to a New Generation,* Abundant Life Bible Amplifier (Nampa, Idaho: Pacific Press, 1995), 124–25; Terian, "Creation in Johannine Theology," 53–59; and Weidemann, "The Victory of Protology," 314–18. See also above n2 in this chapter.

1–5, in the seven major miracles of Jesus,[13] and in other sequences in the Gospel. Various scholars also argue for more minor allusions to creation throughout the Gospel, but these are usually too speculative to concern us here.[14]

HOW JOHN VIEWS THE CREATION STORY

Before looking at the Gospel of John itself, it will be helpful to see how earlier Jewish literature utilizes the creation story. We will begin in Genesis, work our way briefly through the Old Testament, and then look at Jewish literature from the time between the testaments. We will notice a trend: the further a writing gets from the time of creation, the more one sees creative and spiritual applications of the original creation. John is not the first writer to recall the creation story. To a large degree, he views that story through lenses provided by many of his predecessors. Significant scholarship seeks to trace parallels to John's use of creation in the Old Testament and particularly in Hellenistic Judaism between the Testaments.[15]

Through the Lens of the Old Testament

The creation story in the Old Testament is grounded in the first three chapters of Genesis. God calls forth that which does not yet exist by His spoken word or command. Creation is a divine act, done by God/Yahweh. Before there was any creature, there was the Creator. And, according to Genesis, the power of God in creation is the basis for His power in history. Because of the Fall in Genesis 3, however, creation is in need of renewal.[16]

The capstone of the Fall narrative in Genesis is the Flood story. This is evident in that the Flood is described in the language of the creation account. The Flood is seen as a reversal or piece-by-piece undoing of the original creation, followed by a rebuilding of that creation, in fairly literal terms.[17]

---

13. Moore, *Signs of Salvation*, 131–95.

14. See, e.g., Brown, "Creation's Renewal," 278, 287–88, 290.

15. Jacques B. Doukhan, *The Genesis Creation Story*, AUSDDS 5 (Berrien Springs, Mich.: Andrews University Press, 1978), 81–117; Masanobu Endo, *Creation and Christology: A Study on the Johannine Prologue in the Light of Early Jewish Creation Accounts* (Tübingen: Mohr Siebeck, 2002), 227; and Gerald A. Klingbeil, ed., *The Genesis Creation Account and Its Reverberations in the Old Testament* (Berrien Springs, Mich.: Andrews University Press, 2015).

16. Based on du Rand, "Creation Motif," 32–33.

17. Richard M. Davidson, "The Genesis Flood Narrative," *AUSS* 42, no. 1 (2004): 49–77; Warren Austin Gage, *The Gospel of Genesis: Studies in Protology and Eschatology* (Winona

The Exodus story, on the other hand, uses specific creation language in creative or even figurative ways (Exod. 14:22–23).[18] The counterpart of a water-covered earth (Gen. 1:2; 8:1) is Israel's enslavement in Egypt.[19] Instead of a global flood, there is a localized body of water (the Red Sea). Where the Genesis story describes human beings in the image of God, in Exodus the role of Adam and Eve is played by the nation in covenant relationship with God. Adam's dominion over the animals and the earth is replaced by Israel's dominion over the land of Canaan. Instead of a tree of life, Israel is sustained by the manna. Both narratives mention serpents, but in Genesis, the serpent tested Adam and Eve with poisonous words, while in the desert the Israelites were tested with poisonous snake bites.[20]

The Old Testament prophets see the return from exile in terms of both a new creation and a new exodus.[21] After the return from Babylonian and Assyrian captivity, God would make a new covenant with a new Israel, writing His laws in their hearts (Jer. 31:31–34; Ezek. 36:26–28).[22] That renewal would be so great that it could be described in terms of a new creation (Isa. 65:17; 66:22).[23]

Isaiah grounds the redemptive work of Yahweh in His work in creation. He is the One who "made all things," who uses His creative word to redemptively build the temple and populate Jerusalem by drying up the river of Babylon (Isa. 44:24–28). Over and over in Isaiah, the language of redemption is woven into the framework of

---

Lake, Ind.: Carpenter, 1984); Jon Paulien, *Meet God Again for the First Time* (Hagerstown, Md.: Review and Herald, 2003), 25–27; Paulien, *What the Bible Says About the End-Time* (Hagerstown, Md.: Review and Herald, 1994), 45–46; and Paulien, *The Deep Things of God: An Insider's Guide to the Book of Revelation* (Hagerstown, Md.: Review and Herald, 2004), 35–39.

18. Calum M. Carmichael, *The Story of Creation: Its Origin and Its Interpretation in Philo and the Fourth Gospel* (Ithaca, N.Y.: Cornell University Press, 1996), 39; Paulien, *Deep Things of God*, 39–42; and Paulien, *Meet God Again*, 33–34.

19. The author of this study deliberately avoids the common designation of "pre-creation chaos" on account of Roberto Ouro, "The Earth of Genesis 1:2: Abiotic or Chaotic? Part I," *AUSS* 36, no. 2 (1998): 259–76.

20. Richard Davidson, "Earth's First Sanctuary," *AUSS* 55, no. 1 (2015): 65–89, summarizes recent scholarship, which also sees strong connections between the Israelite sanctuary and the garden of Eden.

21. Barrosse, "Seven Days," 508; du Rand, "Creation Motif," 35; Paulien, *Deep Things of God*, 45–53; Paulien, *What the Bible Says*, 55–62; and Paulien, *Meet God Again*, 46–52. Doukhan, *The Genesis Creation Story*, 110–14, notes that in the Hebrew Jeremiah repeatedly echoes the opening phrase of the Hebrew Old Testament (Gen. 1:1, *běrē'šît*; cf. Jer. 26:1; 27:1; 28:1; 49:34–35). It is also found one time in the Greek (Gen. 1:1, LXX, *en archē*, cf. Jer. 33:1, LXX).

22. Sandra M. Schneiders, "The Raising of the New Temple: John 20:19–23 and Johannine Ecclesiology," *NTS* 52 (2006): 345.

23. The book of Revelation expands the Isaianic vision typologically to include the whole earth and all humanity. See also n24.

creation (Isa. 46:8–13; 48:12–15). The past actions of the Creator provide confidence that He can restore and renew still today.[24]

In chapters 65 and 66, Isaiah speaks explicitly about the creation of a new heaven and a new earth. In the new Jerusalem that God will create, His people will live long lives with great joy, the wild and domestic animals will be at peace with each other (Isa. 65:17–25), and the whole human race will worship God (Isa. 66:22–23).[25] The new creation will transcend the old creation (Isa. 42:9; 43:18–19; 48:6–7). Isaiah's new creation is significant for its spiritual dimension and for its restoration of the conditions of the original creation.[26]

The Old Testament wisdom literature also expands on the original creation story. While in Genesis, God simply spoke and things happened, in Psalm 33 we see the "Word of the LORD" (Heb. *děbar YHWH*; Gk. *tō logō tou kyriou*) described as an agent of creation (Ps. 33:6). Since Psalm 33:6 is often alluded to in early Jewish creation accounts, this shift appears to have been very influential.[27] In Proverbs 8:22–31, "Wisdom" personified (named in Prov. 8:1; Heb. *ḥokmāh*; Gk. *sophia*) existed with Yahweh before creation (vv. 22–26) and worked as an artisan alongside Yahweh in the process of creation (v. 30).[28] This is certainly an important background to

---

24. Du Rand, "Creation Motif," 34; and Endo, *Creation and Christology*, 215.

25. This picture contains elements (Isa. 65:10; 66:24) that are in some contrast with the picture of Revelation 21 and 22. These make sense in the context of the return from Babylon in Isaiah's relatively immediate future. While inspired by God and containing elements that would be expanded and clarified typologically by later revelation, Isaiah's view of that future was grounded in his time and place. God's people were largely a single ethnic group and the faith was geographically centered in old Jerusalem. For us today this picture is "what might have been," a future that God would build gradually over time (cf. Deut. 28:1–14). This "new heaven and new earth" pictures the restoration of Judah to Jerusalem after the exile, rather than the renewal of the whole earth. It is only between the testaments that a radical change between the present and future ages becomes the norm. See discussions in Jon Paulien, "Will There Be Death on the New Earth? Isaiah 65:20," in *Interpreting Scripture: Bible Questions and Answers*, ed. Gerhard Pfandl, Biblical Research Institute Studies 2 (Silver Spring, Md.: Biblical Research Institute, 2010), 225–27; Paulien, *What the Bible Says*, 55–71; and "The Role of Israel in Old Testament Prophecy," in *The Seventh-day Adventist Bible Commentary*, ed. Francis D. Nichol, 7 vols. (Washington, D.C.: Review and Herald, 1955), 4:25–38.

26. Derrett, "New Creation," 598–99.

27. Jub. 12:4; *Sib. Or.*, books 1 and 3; 4Q381, 422; 2 Bar. chs. 21, 48, 54; *Apoc. Ab.* 9:3; 22:2; Sir chs. 33 and 39. See Endo, *Creation and Christology*, 210. Other significant allusions to creation can be found in Pss. 8, 104, 139, and 148.

28. Coloe, "Structure of the Johannine Prologue," 46; and Richard M. Davidson, "Proverbs 8 and the Place of Christ," *JATS* 17, no. 1 (2006): 44–48. Endo, *Creation and Christology*, 211, on the other hand, questions whether the text of Proverbs 8 sees Wisdom as a co-creator.

John's use of creation in the Prologue.[29] An often overlooked account of creation can be found in God's challenge to Job in Job 38–41 (creation is especially mentioned in Job 38:4–11; 40:15, although the whole four chapters imply God as Creator). In Job, however, the accounting of creation is fairly straightforward; it is not applied to a new creation, as is the case in the Prophets.

Intertestamental and Hellenistic Judaism[30]

Most Protestant Christians do not believe that the Apocrypha and other Jewish writings between Malachi and Matthew are inspired. Nevertheless, such documents help us in at least two ways. First, they help us understand what Jewish New Testament writers were aware of, the questions some Jews were asking, and how they read the Bible. Second, there is evidence in the New Testament that its authors were aware of such literature. A brief exploration of how intertestamental writers used the creation theme will prove interesting for our study of John.

The Qumran community (keepers of the "Dead Sea Scrolls"), for one, believed they were the first steps in a new creation that God would perform at the time of judgment. That new creation would not only restore the social and political order but would also be signaled by people converting to the rules of the community.[31] In the coming new creation, the faithful ones would keep the Torah perfectly.[32] And God's power in creation was seen to have direct implications for the Qumran community.

Along similar lines was the Hellenistic Jewish novella *Joseph and Aseneth*, which recounts the conversion of Aseneth and her marriage to the patriarch Joseph (an expansion of Gen. 41:45).[33] The document presents this conversion as an act of creation. The same God "who creates all things and brings all things to life" (*Jos. Asen.* 8:3, 9; 12:1; recalling Gen. 2:7) completes His original act of creation in her.[34] The thought is that while there is only one original creation,

---

29. According to Charles H. Talbert, *Reading John: A Literary and Theological Commentary on the Fourth Gospel and the Johannine Epistles* (New York: Crossroad, 1992), 68, both the *Logos* (Word) and Wisdom are preexistent: they are with God, divine in some sense, and agents of creation.

30. See also Jan A. Sigvartsen, "Creation in the Second Temple Period," 71, in this volume.

31. This conclusion is based on 1QS 8:7–8; 1QH 6:26–27; 7:8–9; 4Q164 1:2–3; 4Q 174:6.

32. Derrett, "New Creation," 599–600.

33. Wiedemann, "Victory of Protology," 328.

34. Ibid., 329.

pagans do not have a full share in it; they can achieve that only by conversion to Judaism (*Jos. Asen.* 15:5; 27:10).[35] It was after Aseneth's conversion that "the dead became alive" (*Jos. Asen.* 20:7). Aseneth was "dead" until she came in contact with the life-giving God in conversion.[36] In a similar vein, Sirach 39:16–18 builds on Psalm 33:6, 9 to link the motif of God's word in creation to the mighty works of His salvation.

Apocalyptic texts like 4 Ezra and 2 Baruch build on various texts from Isaiah to show that the very Word of God that did acts of creation in the beginning will act in the same way at the end.[37] This new creation would occur at the end of the old age and set the stage for the age to come (4 Ezra 7:75; 2 Bar. 32:6; 44:12; 57:2; Apoc. Ab. 17).[38] Not only this, but the apocalyptic writers also personify the Word (4 Ezra 6:38, 43; 2 Bar. 54:3; 56:4) in ways similar to the *logos* of John's Gospel.

Philo's use of creation is also important for our purpose. Philo does not discount the plain meaning of the biblical text, including the direct acts of God in creating the world, but he seeks further significance in those actions, much as John appears to do.[39] For Philo, the creation described in Genesis is attributed to the *logos* (Word), who is an intermediary with God. This seems to amplify earlier Jewish tradition in which the word is that which God speaks (Sirach and Qumran) before every creative act.[40] Genesis 1, and its elaboration in personified Wisdom (Prov. 8:22–31) seems to have provided biblical grounds for Philo's adoption of the Platonic *logos* concept.[41]

The biblical concept of God's word went through interesting developments in the Aramaic paraphrases of the Hebrew Bible (the Targums).[42] There, a common designation for God is "The Word (Aram. *memra*) of the Lord." This phrase became a synonym for God's name. For example, where the Hebrew reads "the voice of God," the Targums often render it "the voice of the *memra* of God."[43]

---

35. Ibid., 330.

36. Ibid., 331–32.

37. Endo, *Creation and Christology*, 215.

38. Du Rand, "Creation Motif," 36.

39. Carmichael, *Story of Creation*, 36.

40. Terian, "Creation in Johannine Theology," 46.

41. Ibid., 47.

42. Most Targums come from a period after the New Testament but contain traditions that go back to earlier times. See John J. Collins, "Targum, Targumim," *Eerdmans Dictionary of Early Judaism* (Grand Rapids, Mich.: Eerdmans, 2010), 1278–81.

43. Ibid., 48.

This identification of the *memra* with God also has similarities with the Prologue of the Gospel of John.[44]

CREATION TEXTS IN THE GOSPEL OF JOHN

Three topics in John have special links to creation. The most obvious is the first, the Prologue in which the evangelist refers to the *logos* as the Creator. The death and resurrection of Jesus in chapters 19 and 20 also have a tentative link. Finally, the Sabbath miracles in John 5 and 9 carry this link as well.

THE PROLOGUE

The Gospel of John opens with the phrase "in the beginning" (*en archē*; John 1:1).[45] This is a clear allusion to the opening of Genesis in the LXX (*en archē*; Gen. 1:1).[46] While John 1:3 makes it clear that this opening alludes to Genesis, the unique phraseology in verse 1 by itself would still point to the first phrase of the Old Testament. The Word in John 1:1 was with God[47] and was fully God in quality (anarthrous predicate nominative).[48] The use of *logos* ("Word") in 1:1 is probably an interpretation and replacement of the phrase "and God said" (Gen. 1:3, cf. Ps. 33:6).[49]

---

44. Coloe, "Structure of the Johannine Prologue," 50; and Terian, "Creation in Johannine Theology," 49, 61.

45. Endo, *Creation and Christology*, 206. This phrase is often found in ancient Jewish contexts where reference is made to God's work of creation (Prov. 8:22; Sir. 24:9; Jub. 2:2; 4 Ezra 3:4; 6:38; 2 En. 24:2; Matt. 19:4; Mark 10:6; 2 Pet. 3:4). According to Raymond T. Stamm, "Creation and Revelation in the Gospel of John," in *Search the Scriptures*, ed. J. M. Myers (Leiden: Brill, 1969), 13, by this opening, the Gospel of John has become "the New Testament counterpart of the Old Testament Genesis."

46. George R. Beasley-Murray, *John*, WBC 36 (Waco, Tex.: Word, 1987), 10; Brown, *The Gospel According to John I–XII: A New Translation with Introduction and Commentary*, AB 29A (Garden City, N.Y.: Doubleday, 1966), 4; Coloe, "Structure of the Johannine Prologue," 53; Du Rand, "Creation Motif," 38; Endo, *Creation and Christology*, 206; Craig S. Keener, *The Gospel of John: A Commentary*, 2 vols. (Peabody, Mass.: Hendrickson, 2003), 1:365; Minear, *Christians and the New Creation*, 82; John Painter, "Theology, Eschatology and the Prologue of John," *SJT* 46 (1993): 30; and Paulien, *John*, 42. In the New Testament there are only two other examples of *en archē*: in Acts 11:15 and Philippians 4:15.

47. The Greek translated "with" in verse 1 is literally "toward" (*pros*) God. This implies a dynamic relationship, one that is "in motion." The relationship between the Word and God was an ever-expanding relationship. Brown, *The Gospel According to John I–XII*, 5; and Stamm, "Creation and Revelation," 18.

48. Wiedemann, "Victory of Protology," 304. The articular and anarthrous forms also serve to distinguish the Father and the Son in 1:1, making the parallel with 1:18 even closer.

49. John Painter, "Rereading Genesis in the Prologue of John?" in *Neotestimenica et Philonica: Studies in Honor of Peder Borgen* (Leiden: Brill, 2003), 179–201, esp. 179–80; and Painter, "Theology, Eschatology and the Prologue of John," 31–32. By replacing "Wisdom"

"Word" and "God" in this text parallel "Son" and "Father" in the concluding verse of the Prologue (John 1:18). Verse 1 describes the relationship between Jesus and His Father in eternity, verse 18 describes their relationship after the *logos* entered human history (note also the first use of "Father" in v. 14).[50] The Prologue makes it clear that the Creator has now come in human form. His miracles in the Gospel, therefore, are pointers to His creative power.

The most indisputable reference to creation in the Gospel of John is found in John 1:3: "All things [*panta*] were made [*egeneto*] through [*di'*] him, and without him was not anything made that was made" (ESV).[51] The focus here is universal ("all things," Gk. *panta*), not just planetary. This is the creation of the whole reality outside of God.[52] By way of contrast, in verse 10, the evangelist repeats the statement but substitutes "world" (Gk. *kosmos*) in place of "all things" (*panta*).[53] The words translated "made" three times in 1:3 are from the Greek root *ginomai*. The fact that the Greek Old Testament (called the Septuagint or LXX) of Genesis 1 never uses the usual Greek word for "create" (*ktizō*, see, e.g., Col. 1:15–16) makes this significant for our study.[54] Instead, it uses the Greek words for "made" (*poieō*, Gen. 1:1, 7, 16, 21, 25–27, 31) and "came to be" (*egeneto*, aorist form of *ginomai*, Gen. 1:3, 6, 8–9, 11, 13–15, 19, 23–24, 30–31). By using *egeneto* three times in John 1:3 and again in 1:10, the evangelist makes it clear that his reference to creation is an allusion to the first chapter of Genesis.[55]

(*sophia*) with "Word" (*logos*), the resonance with Genesis, where God spoke and it was done, is increased. See Brown, "Creation's Renewal," 277; Coloe, "Structure of the Johannine Prologue," 46; Mueller, "Creation in the New Testament," 58; and Paulien, *John*, 40. Since "Word" in Judaism was another way of saying Torah, Jesus is understood in John 1 as the true Torah, which is spelled out in John 1:17.

50. Brown, *The Gospel According to John I–XII*, 5; Coloe, "Structure of the Johannine Prologue," 42; du Rand, "Creation Motif," 37; and Paulien, *John*, 42.

51. It is interesting how God the Father fades into the background in verse 3; the Creator here is the *logos*, not *theos*. See Wiedemann, "Victory of Protology," 308.

52. Edwin C. Hoskyns, *The Fourth Gospel*, ed. Francis Noel Davey (London: Faber and Faber, 1947), 142. In verse 10 the focus moves from creation of the universe to creation of the world (*kosmos*). See Weidemann, "Victory of Protology," 307–8. This focus on the universe enhances the power of the Word exponentially. Note a similar universal emphasis in Colossians 1:15–20.

53. Terian, "Creation in Johannine Theology," 50.

54. Mueller, "Creation in the New Testament," 49–51.

55. Brown, *The Gospel According to John I–XII*, 6; du Rand, "Creation Motif," 39–40; and Terian, "Creation in Johannine Theology," 50.

An important side note can now be made. John 1:1 is probably the clearest assertion of the deity of Jesus Christ in the entire New Testament. While in Genesis 1:1, "in the beginning" focuses on what God did at that time, John 1:1 begins before "the beginning." There is a sharp contrast between the threefold expression of *ginomai* ("became, made") in verse 3 and the threefold expression of *ēn* (ongoing past existence, "was") in verses 1 and 2. Before the beginning of creation the *logos* was already in continuous existence. The *logos* is not only Creator; He also existed long before creation. It is the creation that "comes into being," not the *logos*.[56] John 1:1 declares that the Word existed before creation, was with God (the Father) in creation, and was fully God in quality.

John's agenda for his use of creation becomes clear in his further use of *ginomai*. This crucial creation word is repeated three more times in the last half of the Prologue. In verse 12, "as many as received Him, to them He gave the right to become [*genesthai*] children of God" (NASB 1995). It is the power of creation that transforms people into children of God. For John, being a child of God is the goal of creation.[57] In verse 14, "the Word became [*egeneto*] flesh," signaling that the Logos had moved from "was" (John 1:1–2, *ēn*) to "became" (*egeneto*).[58] The Mediator of creation became the Mediator of re-creation at the incarnation.[59] In verse 17, Moses and the Law (Torah) were part of the first creation, and "grace and truth came [*egeneto*] through [*dia*] Jesus Christ" (NIV). The salvific work of Jesus Christ in the Gospel of John is a new creation, grounded in His power as Creator.[60] So the creation statement in verse 3 stands in the service of the salvation

---

56. Note the discussion on this in du Rand, "Creation Motif," 38–39.

57. Recall the earlier discussion in this study of *Joseph and Aseneth*, 231. See also Weidemann, "Victory of Protology," 304.

58. Du Rand, "Creation Motif," 39, 42.

59. Carmichael, *Story of Creation*, 37–38; and du Rand, "Creation Motif," 24, 42. The concept "mediator of creation" is perhaps most clearly expressed in 1 Corinthians 8:6. There Paul expands on the Shema, the fundamental confession of Hebrew monotheism: "Hear, O Israel: the Lord our God, the Lord is one" (Deut. 6:4, NIV). Paul ties the Shema to creation when he says, "for us there is but one God, the Father, *from whom all things came* [*ex hou ta panta*] . . . and there is but one Lord, Jesus Christ, *through whom all things came* [*di' hou ta panta*]" (1 Cor. 8:6, NIV, emphasis added). Jesus is here included in the one God of Judaism. While all things come from the Father, it is through Jesus ("the Lord") that all things are made. See also Col. 1:16; Heb. 1:2.

60. Du Rand, "Creation Motif," 43; and Hoskyns, *The Fourth Gospel*, 147. Regarding John's view of the historicity of Genesis, see the section of this study titled "John, Apocalyptic, and Implications for Religion and Science," 246.

statements in verses 12, 14, and 17.[61] John expresses a spiritual and theological agenda in the language of the original creation.

A third reference to creation in the Prologue is found in verses 4 and 5. By itself, the reference to light would not certify an allusion to Genesis. But the combination of light, life, and darkness with the language of creation (*egeneto*) in verse 3 makes this a strong reference to creation as well.[62] The light is not the Word Himself but is brought by the Word.[63] In ancient Judaism, light is more than just literal. It has an ethical and religious sense, implying the revelatory activity of God (Isa. 2:3–5; 51:4; Sir. 17:11; 2 Bar. 17:4; 59:2; 77:13, 16; Wis. 18:4; T. Levi 14:4; 1QS).[64]

When the light appears, it shines in the darkness and is not overcome by it (John 1:4–5). Since the first state of creation in Genesis was darkness (Gen. 1:2), the great creative act of the first day was the word "Let there be light!" But the darkness was not completely dispelled; rather, it was brought under God's control and ordered into day and night.[65] Unlike Genesis, however, in the Prologue the light met with stunning failure, at least before the incarnation of Christ (John 1:14). It "encountered opposition and incomprehension (1:5); second, lack of recognition (1:10); and finally outright rejection (1:11)."[66] The Word came to His own creation (*idia*), yet His own people (*idioi*) rejected Him (John 1:11).[67] John, however, will not end on this negative note. In 1:12–13, he notes how as many as received Him received authority to become children of God.

---

61. Weidemann, "Victory of Protology," 304–7. There are three other statements in the New Testament where Christ is co-Creator with God: 1 Corinthians 8:6, Colossians 1:16–20, and Hebrews 1:2–3. See Hoskyns, *The Fourth Gospel*, 142. In each of these, the mediator of creation is likewise the mediator of salvation. So John's Prologue is one of four crucial creation texts in the New Testament.

62. Brown, "Creation's Renewal," 277; and Pagels, "Exegesis of Genesis 1," 481. The Greek word for life (*zōē* and its derivatives) is used in the LXX of Genesis 1:20–21, 24, 30, and 2:7; so Genesis 2, as well as 1, is alluded to in the Prologue. See Endo, *Creation and Christology*, 216.

63. David G. Deeks, "The Prologue of St. John's Gospel," *BTB* 6, no. 1 (February 1976): 68.

64. Du Rand, "Creation Motif," 40; and Endo, *Creation and Christology*, 219, 226.

65. Painter, *Rereading*, 195. While we will see in "Creation in the Epistles of John, 245, that John weaves a cosmic conflict motif into the Prologue, that motif is missing in Genesis 1.

66. Pagels, "Exegesis of Genesis 1," 481, 489, 494. Pagels believes that John 1:11 refers to the time before the incarnation, which is clearly introduced in John 1:14 ("the Word became flesh"). But the point in the main text would not be invalidated if John 1:9–11 included the incarnation, as many scholars believe. In several ways the "light" has been resisted. See Wilson Paroschi, *Incarnation and Covenant in the Prologue to the Fourth Gospel (John 1:1-18)*, EUS (Frankfurt: Peter Lang, 2006), 75–95.

67. Du Rand, "Creation Motif," 42; and Pagels, "Exegesis in Genesis 1," 489–90.

It is fair to conclude that the author of the Fourth Gospel takes the straightforward narrative of Genesis and applies it to the salvific work of Jesus Christ in His incarnation, life, death, and resurrection.[68] The physical categories of Genesis 1 lie behind "the spiritual dimensions of John 1."[69] "The prologue subtly convinces its readers to interpret the Word as both the light of creation and the light of salvation."[70]

THE DEATH AND RESURRECTION OF JESUS

The Passion Narrative has two parts tied to creation themes. These are found in chapters 19 and 20. However, because chapter 20 is taken as more clear, it is addressed first.

John 20

The Prologue of John (1:1–18) builds mostly on the first chapter of Genesis. The latter part of the Gospel builds particularly on the second chapter of Genesis. The most widely recognized allusion to creation in the latter half of the book is found in John 20:22.[71] The scene climaxes with Jesus giving the Spirit to His disciples. He delivers the Spirit (*pneuma*) by breathing on (*enephysēsen*) them (John 20:22). This recalls Genesis 2:7, where God breathes (*enephysēsen*) into Adam the breath (*pnoēn*) of life (Gen. 2:7).[72] The outcome of the cross, therefore, is described as a spiritual "bringing to life," a new creation through the power of the Holy Spirit.[73] It results in the forgiveness of sins (John 20:23).[74] Just as Adam received life from God in the old

---

68. Endo, *Creation and Christology*, 229.

69. R. W. Thomas, "'Life' and 'Death' in John and Paul," *SJT* 21 (1968): 201, quoted in Terian, "Creation in Johannine Theology," 45.

70. Du Rand, "Creation Motif," 40.

71. Beasley-Murray, *John*, 380; Brown, "Creation's Renewal," 279, 282; du Rand, "Creation Motif," 33; Edith M. Humphrey, "New Creation," in *Dictionary for Theological Interpretation of the Bible*, ed. Kevin J. Vanhoozer (Grand Rapids, Mich.: Baker Academic, 2005), 536; Keener, *Gospel of John*, 2:1204; Tabb, review of Moore, *Signs of Salvation*; and Terian, "Creation in Johannine Theology," 58.

72. See also Brown, "Creation's Renewal," 282; du Rand, "Creation Motif," 45, esp. n72; and Paulien, *John*, 270.

73. Brown, "Creation's Renewal," 282–83; Brown, *The Gospel According to John XIII–XXI: A New Translation with Introduction and Commentary*, AB 29B (Garden City, N.Y.: Doubleday, 1966), 1022–23, 1037; and Wiedemann, "Victory of Protology," 323–24. In the LXX of Ezekiel 37:9 the breath (*emphysēson*) of Yahweh re-creates His people from a valley of dry bones. See also Beasley-Murray, *John*, 380–81; and Brown, *The Gospel According to John XIII–XXI*, 1037.

74. The Spirit as the instrument of creation and re-creation was widespread in the Apocrypha and Pseudepigrapha (Jdt. 16:14; Wis. 1:7; 12:1; 2 Bar. 21:4; 23:5). The

creation, so the disciples receive life from Jesus in the new creation.[75] Jesus's resurrection is the sign of the new creation (John 2:18–22).

Several scholars notice that the event preceding the upper room appearance occurs at the tomb (John 20:1–18) and that the tomb was located in a garden (*kēpos*, John 19:41). In fact, the entire passion story began in a garden (*kēpos*, John 18:1). While John 20:1–18 does not again mention the garden, the reader is reminded of that fact by Mary Magdalene's assumption that Jesus could be the gardener (*kēpouros*, John 20:15). The mention of this detail is, perhaps, a pointer to the role of Adam in the original garden.[76]

A problem with this thesis is that the LXX of Genesis 2:8 uses a different Greek word for garden (*paradeison* instead of *kēpos*, John 18:1, 26; 19:41).[77] Nevertheless, these two Greek words for garden are used as synonyms in the Septuagint.[78] So it is not surprising that two other ancient Greek Old Testaments, Aquila (Gen. 2:8; 3:2) and Theodotion (Gen. 3:2), use *kēpos* rather than *paradeisos* to translate the Hebrew *gan* (garden) in Genesis. And in the LXX of Ezekiel 36:35, the Hebrew reference to Eden (*gan*) is translated *kēpos* rather than *paradeisos*.[79] Since *paradeisos* in the New Testament refers to the future reward of the righteous (Luke 23:43; 2 Cor. 12:4; Rev. 2:7), *kēpos* is a more appropriate word for John 20.[80] So an allusion to creation is certainly possible, even likely, in the tomb story.[81]

---

re-creation is also associated with cleansing from sin (Ezek. 36:25–27; 1QS 3:7; 4:20–21; cf. Acts 2:38; 1 Cor. 6:11; Titus 3:5; 1 Pet. 1:23; 2:1). So the basic concept of a future re-creation is not strange in early Judaism. What was different in John is applying it to the present in the context of the work of Jesus Christ. See du Rand, "Creation Motif," 46.

75. Brown, *The Gospel According to John XIII–XXI*, 1037; James D. G. Dunn, *Baptism in the Holy Spirit* (Naperville, Ill.: Allenson, 1970), 180; and Wiedemann, "Victory of Protology," 325, 329.

76. Nicolas Wyatt, "'Supposing Him to Be the Gardener' (John 20,15): A Study of the Paradise Motif in John," *ZNW* 81 (1990): 24. See also Brown, "Creation's Renewal," 279; R. H. Lightfoot, *St. John's Gospel: A Commentary* (Oxford: Clarendon Press, 1956), 321; John N. Suggit, "Jesus the Gardener: The Atonement in the Fourth Gospel as Re-Creation," *Neot* 33 (1999): 166–67; Tabb, review of Moore, *Signs of Salvation*; N. T. Wright, *John for Everyone*, 2 vols. (Louisville, Ky.: Westminster John Knox, 2004), 2:102; and Ruben Zimmermann, "Symbolic Communication between John and His Reader: The Garden Symbolism in John 19–20," in *Anatomies of Narrative Criticism: The Past, Present, and Futures of the Fourth Gospel as Literature*, ed. Tom Thatcher and Stephen D. Moore, Society of Biblical Literature Resources for Biblical Study 55 (Atlanta: Society of Biblical Literature, 2008), 221–35.

77. Brown, *The Gospel According to John XIII–XXI*, 943.

78. Brown, "Creation's Renewal," 280 (see Eccles. 2:5; Sir. 24:30–31).

79. Brown, "Creation's Renewal," 280. For a detailed listing of the Old Testament data, see Moore, *Signs of Salvation*, 68–71.

80. Suggit, "Jesus the Gardener," 166.

81. See the detailed argument for this in Moore, *Signs of Salvation*, 58–93.

John 19

A number of scholars note the theme of "God's work coming to completion" in Jesus at the cross (John 19:28–30).[82] In Genesis 2:1, it tells us that the heavens and the earth were "completed" (*synetelesthēsan*, LXX). In verse 2, the Hebrew rewords the same: "God completed [*synetelesen*, LXX]. . . . *His works* which He made" (*ta erga autou, ha epoiēsen*, LXX, emphasis added). The word "made" (*epoiēsen*) is used repeatedly in the first chapter (Gk. root *poieō*, Gen. 1:1, 7, 16, 21, 25–27, 31). But a new word is introduced in the second chapter: "works" (Gk. *erga*). Three times in Genesis 2:1–3, it speaks of God's works. First, it says that God "completed His works" (Gen. 2:2). Then, twice it says that He "rested from all His works" (Gen. 2:2–3).

Although the Gospel of John does not use the exact Greek word for "completed" (*teleioun*) used in Genesis 2 (*syntelein*), this adjustment corresponds to the Johannine tendency to avoid compound verbs.[83] With this in mind, a strong case can be made for a creation allusion also at the cross. Jesus's last words on the cross echo Genesis 2: "It is finished" (*tetelestai*, John 19:30). Two verses earlier in the narrative, the text reports Jesus's awareness that since "all was now completed" (*tetelestai*, John 19:28) the Scriptures were also being "fulfilled" (*teleiōthē*).[84] So both the Scriptures and the ministry of Jesus were "completed" at the cross. For John, the full meaning of Genesis 2:1–3 is achieved in the events of the cross and the resurrection.[85]

An allusion to Genesis 2 at the cross is bolstered by the mention of the Sabbath immediately after Jesus's statement "it is finished."[86] In John 19:31, the Jews ask Pilate to break Jesus's legs so that His body would not remain on the cross over the Sabbath (*sabbatou*). It is significant that John mentions Sabbath here and not Passover. Twice in Genesis 2:2–3 it is mentioned that God had "finished" His work and rested on the seventh day. While the word "Sabbath" is not mentioned in Genesis 2, the cognate verb (*šābat*) does appear

---

82. Brown, "Creation's Renewal," 284; cf. Coloe, "Structure of the Johannine Prologue," 54.

83. Wiedemann, "Victory of Protology," 314, esp. n50.

84. John could have used a different word to express the "fulfillment" when writing John 19:28 (*plēroun* instead of *teleiōthē*, see John 19:36). The use of *teleiōthē* is consistent with an allusion to Genesis 2.

85. Martin Hengel, "Die Schriftauslegung des vierten Evangeliums auf dem Hintergrund der christlichen Exegese," in Martin Hengel, *Jesus und die Evangelien: Kleine Schriften V*, WUNT 211 (Tübingen: Mohr Siebeck, 2007), 640; and Wiedemann, "Victory of Protology," 321–22. See also Coloe, "Reflections," 5–6.

86. Brown, "Creation's Renewal," 286; and Hengel, *Kleine Schriften*, 5:640.

(Gen. 2:2), and Exodus 20:8–11 makes clear the connection between the seventh day, creation, and the Sabbath. The crucifixion account, therefore, most probably alludes to the creation account of Genesis 2:1–3.[87]

We see the full significance of these allusions when we discover that Jesus completing God's "works" (*erga*) is not limited to the cross. It also plays a major role in the ministry of Jesus in the Gospel of John.[88] In John 4:34, Jesus describes His ministry to the Samaritan woman as serving "to complete His [God's] work" (*teleiōsō autou to ergon*).[89] In the broadest sense, Jesus's ministry was to complete (*teleiōsō*) the works (*erga*) the Father had given Him to do (John 5:36). Jesus's miracles are the "works" of God (John 9:3–4). When Jesus is challenged to prove that He is the Messiah (John 10:24), He responds three times with reference to the works that the Father gave Him to do (John 10:25, 32, 37). With Genesis 2:1–3 in mind, it seems evident that John portrays Jesus's ministry and miracles as a completion of God's works in creation (see also John 14:10–12; 15:24).[90] Jesus's earthly ministry was a new creation, restoring what was lost at the Fall.

THE SABBATH

Unlike the healings on the Sabbath in the Synoptic Gospels, the Johannine Sabbath miracles are unique to John and related to the theme of creation. In the Prologue, it tells us that the Word was the bringer of life and light (John 1:4–5), reminiscent of the original creation (Gen. 1:3–5, 11–12, 20–28). In the two Sabbath miracles of the Gospel of John, Jesus brings life (chapter 5) and light (chapter 9) to two hapless men. The new creation that Jesus brings, therefore, is associated with the Sabbath, just as much as the first creation was (Gen. 2:1–3).[91]

The first of these miracles was performed by the spoken word (John 5:8, 19; cf. "And God said," Gen. 1), and the second by handling

---

87. Hengel, *Kleine Schriften*, 5:639–40. At the cross is an allusion to Genesis 2:1–3 (John 19:28–30); after the resurrection is an allusion to Genesis 2:7 (John 20:22). So the commissioning of the disciples was an extension of the new creation that was "completed" at the cross.

88. Wiedemann, "Victory of Protology," 319–20.

89. Coloe, "Structure of the Johannine Prologue," 54; and Wiedemann, "Victory of Protology," 315.

90. Brown, "Creation's Renewal," 285; and Wiedemann, "Victory of Protology," 319–20.

91. Painter, "Theology, Eschatology and the Prologue of John," 35; and Terian, "Creation in Johannine Theology," 53–54.

the dust of the earth (John 9:6, 32, cf. Gen. 2:7).[92] The two Sabbath healings, therefore, not only tie together the themes of light and life that were introduced in the Prologue (John 1:4–5)[93] but also allude to details in the creation narratives of Genesis 1 and 2.

John 5

In the miracle at the pool of Bethesda (John 5:1–15), Jesus does creative work on the Sabbath (John 5:17).[94] This miracle is given theological elaboration in John 5:19–30.[95] There we learn that Jesus is able to impart life to whoever hears His voice (John 5:21, 25–26, 28). In verse 21 Jesus repeats the key verb spoken at the pool (*egeirei*).[96] In John 5:8 He commands the paralytic to "rise up" (*egeire*). In verse 21 it is the Father who "raises up" (*egeirei*) the dead and gives them life (*zōopoiei*). Likewise, the Son gives life (*zōopoiei*) to whomever He wishes (John 5:27). But Jesus also defends His healing action in 5:17: "My Father is working until now, and I am working" (ESV).[97] The force of "working" (*ergazomai*) derives from its Septuagintal use (in noun form) in Genesis 2:1–3 to refer to all that God did in creation.[98] So the Sabbath healing at Bethesda anticipates the climax of Jesus's works of creation in John 19:28–30 (cf. John 4:34; 5:36).[99] The healing of the paralytic in John 5 is as much an act of creation as the events recorded in the narratives of Genesis.

In John 5:19 Jesus says that He only does what He sees His Father doing (*poiounta*). This is an echo of Genesis 1, where it repeatedly

---

92. Terian, "Creation in Johannine Theology," 54.

93. Minear, *Christians and the New Creation*, 92; and Terian, "Creation in Johannine Theology," 55, 57.

94. Wiedemann, "Victory of Protology," 316. Systematic theologians draw a distinction between God's work of creation and His work of sustaining that creation. Although that language may be helpful in explaining John 5:17, for example, such a distinction is probably not in John's mind as he records this incident in the life of Jesus.

95. Terian, "Creation in Johannine Theology," 54–55.

96. Minear, *Christians and the New Creation*, 87.

97. The idea that God continues to work on the Sabbath was widespread in Jewish traditions of the time. So Jesus is claiming divine prerogative to do what His Father does on the Sabbath, rather than what humans are permitted to do. Acts of creation and re-creation are permissible on the Sabbath. See Brown, "Creation's Renewal," 285–86.

98. Minear, *Christians and the New Creation*, 87, 92; and Wiedemann, "Victory of Protology," 314. At this point the Greek philosophical mind is tempted to ask: Who actually created? The Father or Jesus? John does not attempt to answer these questions in Greek philosophical terms. His Hebrew philosophical answer would simply be yes. In the words of Minear, the Father and the Son are "co-creators."

99. The Sabbath was approaching when Jesus said, "It is finished." See Brown, "Creation's Renewal," 285.

says, "and God made" (*poieō*, Gen. 1:1, 7, 16, 21, 25–27, 31). The echo undergirds the point that the healing of the paralytic was an act of creation.[100] But that kind of action is only the beginning of the new creation. In John 5:21–30, Jesus's acts of creation come in two phases. There is a "now is" phase (John 5:21–25), in which people like the paralytic are as good as dead but are raised to eternal life spiritually as well as physically (5:24–25). Eternal life is the present gift of the new creation. Jesus gives life to the existentially dead.[101] The second phase of the new creation "is coming" (John 5:28). In the end-time phase, those who now reside in tombs will hear His voice and come out of the tombs (5:28–29). This is a clear statement of future eschatology—rare in John but nevertheless real.[102] While John normally prefers to emphasize the present eschatology in His earthly ministry, this glimpse of future eschatology will be revisited at the end of this chapter and that will lead to further implications.

John 9

The setting for the second Sabbath miracle is the theme of light. Jesus is the "light of the world" (John 9:5)—a phrase that builds on John 1:4–5, 9–11. Those who follow the Light of the World will never walk in darkness (John 8:12, cf. 1:5). This second miracle also builds on the concept of "God's work." The daylight is the time when God's works should be done (John 9:4, cf. 11:9).[103] God from the first had a purpose for the blind man, and that purpose was the new creation performed by Jesus Christ.[104] John's awareness of the new creation implications can be seen in 9:32, where the formerly blind man declares that "never since the world began" has such an act occurred as has just happened to him.[105]

Jesus spitting on the ground, making clay, and placing it on the eyes of the blind man (John 9:6) is strongly reminiscent of Genesis 2:7, where God makes Adam from the dust of the ground.[106] Jesus making mud points to the new creation He was effecting. The sight the man

---

100. Minear, *Christians and the New Creation*, 88.

101. Paulien, *John*, 124.

102. Ibid., 124–25.

103. Terian, "Creation in Johannine Theology," 55, 59.

104. Minear, *Christians and the New Creation*, 91; and Wiedemann, "Victory of Protology," 318.

105. Minear, *Christians and the New Creation*, 92, 94.

106. Ibid., 93.

receives is the fulfillment of John 1:9, which speaks of the Word as the "true Light which was coming into the world."[107] But in his blindness, the man also served as a symbol of the spiritual darkness of those who resist the "Light of the World" (John 9:39–41).[108]

DAYS OF CREATION

A number of scholars argue that the seven days of creation are repeated in sequence in the narrative of the Gospel.[109] Most frequently, they refer to the seven-day period between John 1:19 and the wedding at Cana (John 2:1–11).[110] But others suggest the seven days of creation can be seen in the Prologue (John 1:1–18),[111] chapters 1–5,[112] and in the seven major miracles of Jesus.[113]

Of these proposals, the two most promising see the days of creation in the seven major signs of the Gospel and over the seven days running from John 1:19 to John 2:11. The seven "signs" in the Gospel are usually listed as follows: (1) turning water into wine (2:1–11), (2) healing the official's son (4:46–54), (3) healing the paralytic at Bethesda (5:1–15), (4) feeding the five thousand (6:1–15), (5) walking on water (6:16–21), (6) healing the blind man at the pool of Siloam (9:1–7), and (7) raising Lazarus from the dead (11:1–44).[114] We have already noted many allusions to creation in the healing at Bethesda and the healing of the blind man.

Calum Carmichael sees a number of allusions to creation in the wedding at Cana (John 2:1–11).[115] He sees the wedding story mirroring the activity of the third day of creation (Gen. 1:9–13). The water in the stone pots (John 2:6) is equivalent to the union of water

---

107. Terian, "Creation in Johannine Theology," 57–58.

108. Minear, *Christians and the New Creation*, 95.

109. These observations are based largely on speculative echoes of creation in the Gospel, rather than explicit allusions.

110. The originator of this view appears to be M. E. Boismard, *Du baptême à Cana (Jean 1,19–2,11)* (Paris: Editions du Cerf, 1956), esp. 133–59; see also Carmichael, *Story of Creation*, 35n6. See also cautious approval by Brown, *The Gospel According to John I–XII*, 105–6.

111. Bruno Barnhart, *The Good Wine: Reading John from the Center* (Mahwah, N.J.: Paulist Press, 1993), 303–4.

112. Carmichael, *Story of Creation*, 36.

113. Brown, "Creation's Renewal," 287; Brown, *The Gospel According to John I–XII*, cxxxix, 429–30; and Moore, *Signs of Salvation*, 131–95.

114. Compare the list in Brown, "Creation's Renewal," 287.

115. Carmichael, *Story of Creation*, 68.

and earth on the third day of creation.[116] The abundance of wine recalls the appearance of vegetation in Genesis 1:11–12. Wine and the third day of creation are associated in Psalm 104:14–15.[117] According to 2 Esdras 6:42–44, water was gathered on the third day from six of the seven parts of the world, the six becoming dry land. Carmichael associates this with the six empty water pots of John 2:6.[118] He also notes that the name "Cana" may derive from the Hebrew word for creation (*qanah*).[119] This approach is unquestionably creative, but the evidence cited seems largely circumstantial. While there is some evidence of the miracles in John being related to creation, it is far from clear that they deliberately echo the days of creation in order.[120]

The most promising of the "days of creation" schemes sees the seven days of creation in John 1:19–2:11. On the first day (1:19–28), John is questioned by religious leaders, presumably from Jerusalem. On the next day (1:29), he sees Jesus and bears witness to Him (1:29–34). On the following day (1:35), John encourages two of his disciples to follow Jesus (1:35–42). On the day after that (1:43), Jesus encounters Philip and Nathanael (1:43–51). The wedding at Cana then takes place on "the third day" (2:1), making up a week of six or seven days (depending on the scheme), climaxing with a wedding.[121] This could recall the original creation week in which the first

116. Ibid., 69.

117. Ibid., 70–71.

118. Ibid., 72–73.

119. Ibid., 74. Carmichael also sees significance in the presence of Jesus's mother on this occasion (ibid., 74–76).

120. For much more on the wedding at Cana, see Jocelyn McWhirter, *The Bridegroom Messiah and the People of God: Marriage in the Fourth Gospel* (Cambridge: Cambridge University Press, 2006). See also Moore, *Signs of Salvation*, 137–98, summarized in Tabb, review of Moore, *Signs of Salvation*. For Moore the wedding at Cana (John 2:1–11) is a theological parallel to the creation of light; the healing of the official's son (4:46–54) corresponds to the creation of the firmament; the healing at the pool (5:1–15) corresponds to the separation of land and sea; the feeding of the multitude (6:1–15) represents the creation of sun, moon, and stars; walking on the water (6:16–21) represents the creation of sea creatures and birds; giving sight to the blind man reminds of the creation of humans and other creatures on the sixth day; and the raising of Lazarus (11:1–44) proves that God is still at work on the Sabbath. As can be seen from this summary, the connections seem more speculative than persuasive. See Tabb's critique.

121. See Barnhart, *Good Wine*, 58–59; and Brown, *The Gospel According to John I–XII*, 105–6. If one uses inclusive reckoning, the "third day" is reckoned to include the "fourth day" of the sequence in John 1 (vv. 43–51), making a total of six days beginning with 1:19. If the third day sequence begins the day after the encounter with Nathanael and adds three days to the four in chapter one, it makes a total of seven days beginning with John 1:19. Trudinger, "Seven Days," 154–58, discusses at length the division of days.

wedding occurred at the end of the sixth day or the beginning of the seventh (Gen. 2:21–25).[122]

Thomas Barrosse attempts to find detailed connections between each of these days in John and the respective days of creation.[123] But these attempts are evocative rather than based on verbal and structural parallels.[124] In any case, assuming some reference to Genesis with these successive days, the wedding at Cana is the climax of the new creation week. The fact that Jesus's mother is called "woman" could also be a reflection of that first wedding in Genesis (Gen. 2:22–23). So at Cana you have the climax of a week that begins with John 1:19—a wedding, the mention of "woman," and a miracle based on Jesus's creative word. All of these hints of creation, coming right after the Prologue, bring an allusion to creation into the realm of possibility.

If all this was in John's mind as he wrote out the wedding story, Jesus used His creative word (John 2:7) to inaugurate a new creation in which the mighty works of the original creation (1:3) were echoed by miraculous actions in the present. It is important to remember that there are no narrative parables in the Gospel of John.[125] It is the stories in the Gospel, particularly the miracle stories, that become "living parables" of the new creation Jesus was bringing about.

CREATION IN THE EPISTLES OF JOHN

Although scholarship does not appear to address the theme of creation in the epistles of John, there are strong echoes of the Prologue to the Gospel of John in 1 John 1:1–3.[126] Instead of "in the

---

122. In Jewish reckoning the change of day occurs at sunset, so the first Sabbath would have begun at dusk on the sixth day (note the "evening and morning" sequence throughout the Genesis creation account: Gen. 1:5, 8, 13, 19, 23, 31).

123. Barrosse, "Seven Days," 508–15.

124. So also Brown, *The Gospel According to John I–XII*, 106. An example of Barrosse's creativity is the addition of an extra day (he divides it between verses 40 and 41, even though there is no "on the next day" marker in the text; see Barrosse, "Seven Days," 510–11). He also divides days between the Philip and Nathanael accounts (between verses 44 and 45) and essentially ignores the reference to "on the third day" in John 2:1 (ibid., 512–14). Trudinger, "Seven Days," 154–58, seems to do a little better, but the author of the present study still finds the suggestions more evocative than solid.

125. There are a number of "aphoristic" parables in John. See Wilson Paroschi, "Signs, Parables, and the Writing of John's Gospel," in *Biblical Parables: Essays in Honor of Robert M. Johnston*, ed. Thomas R. Shepherd and Ranko Stefanovic (Berrien Springs, Mich.: NT Dept., Seventh-day Adventist Theological Seminary, Andrews University, 2016), 185–98.

126. Coloe, "Structure of the Johannine Prologue," 46; du Rand, "Creation Motif," 38; and Minear, *Christians and the New Creation*, 99.

beginning" (John 1:1), the epistle opens with "from the beginning" (*ap' arches*, 1 John 1:1; cf. 1 John 2:7; 3:11; 2 John 1:5). In 1 John, as in the Fourth Gospel, the true light dispels the darkness (1 John 1:5; 2:8–11).[127] The Son is sent into the world just as the light was in the Prologue (1 John 4:9; John 1:9–11, 14). While there is an allusion to the Cain and Abel narrative (1 John 3:12–15),[128] there is no direct allusion to the creation story of Genesis itself (Gen. 1–3). So the epistles do not seem to draw on creation as a basis for theology; they merely use language that echoes the Prologue of the Gospel more directly and Genesis more indirectly.

CONCLUSION ON THE THEOLOGY OF CREATION IN JOHN

The theme of creation in the Gospel of John is primarily found in the Prologue (John 1:1–18), in the events surrounding the cross and the resurrection of Jesus (John 19:28–30; 20:11–22), and in the two Sabbath healing stories (John 5:1–30; 9:1–41). Already in the Old Testament (descriptions of the exodus and the return from exile) and in Intertestamental Judaism (particularly at Qumran and in the story of Joseph and Aseneth), creation was taken as a pointer to further truth. John, for his part, sees a spiritual new creation in the ministry of Jesus (John 1:12, 14, 17) that is modeled on Jesus's role in the reality of the original creation. John expresses his own spiritual and theological agenda in the language of the original creation. The author of the Gospel assumes the straightforward narrative of Genesis and applies it to the incarnation, life, death, and resurrection of Jesus. The physical characteristics of Genesis 1 become the spiritual dimensions of John 1. While this approach to creation is clear enough in the Prologue to the Gospel, it is further undergirded by the narratives of the first Easter weekend (John 19:28–30; 20:11–22) and the Sabbath healings of John 5 and 9.

JOHN, APOCALYPTIC, AND IMPLICATIONS FOR RELIGION AND SCIENCE

Does the Gospel of John have anything to say to contemporary issues of science, design, and creation? The general consensus of Johannine scholarship offers a definitive answer to that question:

---

127. Hoskyns, *The Fourth Gospel*, 141.
128. Minear, *Christians and the New Creation*, 100.

the Fourth Gospel has nothing to say regarding the science of origins.[129] The author of the present study does not share that view but rather believes John's use of Genesis can give us at least some insight into the question.

The first three verses of John clearly build on Genesis 1:1.[130] Then John moves from the creation of "all things" (Gk. *panta,* John 1:3) to the creation of this world (Gk. *kosmos,* John 1:10). John's argument in the Prologue makes sense only if he believes that the account of Genesis reflects a literal creation. For him, the power of the gospel is its ability to transform human lives through the creative power of God. Belief in creation, therefore, is essential to the power of the gospel. In the words of Rudolf Bultmann, John 1:3 clearly states that "everything without exception has been made by the *logos.*"[131] In the realm of biblical theology, John's view of the original creation's reality is an important part of one's assessment of the meaning of Scripture. Something similar can be said about Jesus's use of creation in John 5 as well as His statements in the Synoptic Gospels.

But one can say even more than this on the basis of the Fourth Gospel. John's subtle use of apocalyptic has further implications for the theme of creation. The Gospel of John does not tell an explicit story of either the cosmic conflict (Rev. 12:7–12) or apocalyptic eschatology (Rev. 19:11–21). But the author seems familiar with both. First of all, as we have seen, John 1:3 describes the creation of not only the world but of the entire universe (John 1:3, cf. 1:10).[132] This is supported by verse 4, where "the light" is used in an absolute sense, of which "the light of men" is just one manifestation.[133] The first hint of cosmic conflict is found in John 1:5, where it says, "The light shines in the darkness, and the darkness has not overcome it" (ESV). The Greek word behind "overcome" (*katelaben*) can have two distinct meanings. It can mean to "grasp with the mind," in the sense

---

129. See, e.g., Stamm, "Creation and Revelation," 14.

130. The combination of "in the beginning" (*en archē,* John 1:1) with "all things were made" (*panta egeneto,* John 1:3).

131. Rudolf Bultmann, *The Gospel of John: A Commentary,* trans. G. R. Beasley-Murray (Oxford: Basil Blackwell, 1971), 37. The original text reads, "Mit Nachdruck wird also gesagt, daß *alles, ohne Ausnahme, durch den Logos geschaffen ward;* über das Wie un Wann aber fehlt jede Reflexion" (emphasis added). According to Bultmann, John accepts the reality of the original creation but does not get into the how or when. See Rudolf Bultmann, *Das Evangelium des Johannes* (Gottingen: Vandenhoeck and Ruprecht, 1964), 20.

132. Wiedemann, "Victory of Protology," 300.

133. Ibid., 310.

of to understand or to comprehend. But it can also mean "grasp with the hand," in the sense of seize with hostile intent to conquer or destroy.[134] It is the latter meaning that is most likely in verse 5.[135]

As was the case in Genesis (Gen. 1:2), the darkness in John was there before the light (John 1:5). Darkness is not depicted as a hostile entity in Genesis 1; it is simply there. God does not destroy it in creation but rather orders it and makes it part of the harmony of His creation (Gen. 1:3–6).[136] In contrast, however, the Prologue of John sees the darkness as an aggressive force that resists and opposes the light. It seeks to "overcome" (seize with hostile intent) the light, but fails to do so (John 1:5). In the very beginning of the Gospel, there is a cosmic perspective and a sense of hostile powers that resist the Word's work of creation[137]—the bringing of light and life. Hans-Ulrich Wiedemann goes so far as to see "an underlying trans-historical power of evil" implied in verse 5.[138] There is a universal dualism between good and evil in view here, and such a dualism is a core feature of apocalyptic theology.[139] Since dualism in the biblical perspective is not permanent, the dualism expressed here implies a future resolution, even though that is not explicitly stated.[140]

This echo of primordial conflict is brought to earth when describing the resistance received by the light from "His own" (*idioi*, John 1:11). Since some did receive Him (John 1:12–13), the primordial battle continues on earth and particularly in the ministry of Jesus. The "glory" of the incarnation of the Word shines grace and truth into that darkness (John 1:14), to do battle with it.

While the Prologue makes no direct reference to future events or judgments, this is worked out in the body of the Gospel.[141] The healing at the pool of Bethesda provokes the first demonstration of

---

134. Hoskyns, *The Fourth Gospel*, 143.

135. Mary L. Coloe, *God Dwells with Us: Temple Symbolism in the Fourth Gospel* (Collegeville, Minn.: Liturgical Press, 2001), 136, 184.

136. See Painter, "Rereading," 196.

137. In further support of this point is the fact that "overcome" is in aorist indicative while "shines" (*phainei*) in the first part of the verse is in present tense. The attempt to overcome was a specific historical event of resistance. See Coloe, "Structure of the Johannine Prologue," 47.

138. Wiedemann, "Victory of Protology," 310.

139. John does not belong to the literary genre of apocalyptic, but there is an apocalyptic dimension to his Gospel in the struggle between light and darkness. See Painter, "Theology, Eschatology and the Prologue of John," 33–34; and Painter, "Rereading," 194.

140. Painter, "Theology, Eschatology and the Prologue of John," 32–33.

141. Ibid., 40.

hostility against Jesus on the part of "the Jews."[142] This hostility was anticipated in the darkness of John 1:5 and the resistance of "His own" in 1:11. This provokes from Jesus the most apocalyptic passage in the Gospel. As we have seen, in John 5:21–30 the new creation (5:17, 19, 21) occurs in two phases:[143] the first in Jesus's present acts of healing and salvation (5:21–25), and the second in the final physical resurrection of both righteous and wicked (5:26–29). The latter passage is grounded in recognizable apocalyptic tradition. It uses "Son of Man" without the article, just like Daniel 7:13–14. And the judgment in the passage is very reminiscent of Daniel 12:1–2.[144] So for John, the Son of Man is an apocalyptic figure with a central role in the final judgment (John 5:22–23, 27–29).

In John 8:44, the cosmic dimension appears in the person of a devil who was a liar and a murderer "from the beginning" (John 8:44), a clear echo of the Genesis story (Gen. 3:1–6; 4:1–15) and also of the darkness that resisted the light in John 1:5.[145] In John 12:31, there is a "ruler of this world" who needs to be judged and cast out (see also John 14:30; 16:11).[146] This echoes the theme of cosmic conflict central to Revelation 12:7–10. In John 14:1–3, Jesus promises to return from His Father's house at some point in the future. And in John 17:5, Jesus speaks of the glory He had with His Father "before the world existed" (cf. John 17:24).[147] The climax of this apocalyptic conflict in John comes in the words "It is finished" at the cross (John 19:30) and the act of new creation in John 20:22.

There are two key points that arise from these observations. First, the salvation that John sees in the present and foresees in the future is meaningful only if there is an interventionist God in the past. It is the power of God in creation that is exercised both in the miracles of

---

142. Paulien, *John*, 119–20.

143. Minear, *Christians and the New Creation*, 88.

144. Paulien, *John*, 120–21. The language of John 5:27–29 is much more like Daniel's than it is like the language of Jesus in the Synoptic Gospels. See Painter, "Theology, Eschatology and the Prologue of John," 40–41.

145. Minear, *Christians and the New Creation*, 96.

146. This is a cosmic and universal judgment; see Paulien, *John*, 201. That the ruler of this world and the devil are one and the same in Johannine thought is evident from John 8:39–44, where the devil is the one who rules in the hearts of those seeking to kill Jesus. The work of God is "making alive" (John 5:21); the "works" of the devil involve putting to death (John 8:40). See Wiedemann, "Victory of Protology," 312, 317.

147. Mueller, "Creation in the New Testament," 48, sees John 17:24 as a significant creation text but does not mention John 17:5, which is quite similar. Part of John's apocalyptic foundation is the conviction that Jesus (the *Logos*) existed before creation and that everything that now exists was made by Him.

the earthly Jesus and the ultimate destruction of death in the future.[148] Second, John's eschatology clarifies his understanding of creation.[149] The eschatological defeat of "darkness" and death is assumed to be real and located at the end of history. The underlying assumption is that the story of creation is as real and tangible as Jesus's mighty acts in the present and in the envisioned future. Jesus is portrayed as having the authority to create anew,[150] but if the past creation is not material and tangible, the present salvation is an illusion and the future salvation offers no hope.[151]

CONCLUSION

The scholarship on creation in John is correct in seeing the new creation primarily in spiritual terms; the textual evidence is overwhelming. Jesus's ministry of healing and salvation is a new creation as real as the original creation but experienced at a spiritual level much more than on a visibly spectacular one. The Gospel of John also exhibits an underlying apocalyptic dimension that points forward to the cataclysmic new creation at the end of history. This future creation points back to the reality at the dawn of history as well. The new creation has meaning only if the original one is real. It is true that John does not emphasize that aspect of his theme as much, but it is equally clear that a real creation is necessary to his theological use of that creation.[152]

---

148. See Brown, "Creation's Renewal," 276; and Endo, *Creation and Christology*, 227.

149. This idea was triggered by a reading of Wiedemann, "Victory of Protology," 302.

150. Derrett, "New Creation," 608.

151. According to Painter, "Theology, Eschatology and the Prologue of John," 34, John assumes the original creation is the material expression of the language of God. It manifests God's grace in bounty for all—food to sustain life but also to delight the palate. There is not only eyesight, but the beauty of nature and human artistic creativity. There is not only hearing, "but Bach, Beethoven, and even the Beatles." In other words, for John, the original creation is real, not just a great story.

152. Derrett, "New Creation," 603, sees a similar way of engaging creation at Qumran.

Richard A. Sabuin, PhD

Northern Asia-Pacific Division
Seventh-day Adventist Church

CREATION THEOLOGY IN THE PAULINE LITERATURE

INTRODUCTION

As a well-educated Jew, Paul was well acquainted with the Old Testament Scriptures. He was familiar with the Pentateuch[1] and the Prophets.[2] Thus, Paul had a good knowledge of God's creative work that marks the beginning, depicted in Genesis 1 and 2.[3] This explains why Paul often makes direct references to the creation account. In his writings, Paul uses several terms to describe the creation motif. He uses the verb *ktizō* ("to make, create") in its various forms,[4] the

---

1. Paul, as Jesus does, often uses the phrase "it is written" in referring to the Old Testament Scriptures (Rom. 1:17; 2:24; 3:4, 10; 4:17; 8:36; 9:13, 33; 10:15; 11:8, 26; 12:19; 14:11; 15:3, 9, 21; 1 Cor. 1:19, 31; 2:9; 3:19; 9:9; 10:7; 14:21; 15:45; 2 Cor. 4:13; 8:15; 9:9; Gal. 3:10, 13; 4:22, 27). He refers to the the writings of Moses (Rom. 9:15; 10:5, 19; 1 Cor. 9:9), and specifically indicates that the writings of Moses were still read in Paul's time (2 Cor. 3:15).

2. See, e.g., Rom. 1:2; 3:21.

3. So also, e.g., Roy E. Ciampa and Brian S. Rosner, "1 Corinthians" in *Commentary on the New Testament Use of the Old Testament*, ed. G. K. Beale and D. A. Carson (Grand Rapids, Mich.: Baker, 2007), 733–34; Ben Witherington III, *Conflict and Community in Corinth: A Socio-Rhetorical Commentary on 1 and 2 Corinthians* (Grand Rapids, Mich.: Eerdmans, 1995), 170; G. K. Beale "Colossians," in *Commentary on the New Testament Use of the Old Testament*, ed. G. K. Beale and D. A. Carson (Grand Rapids, Mich.: Baker, 2007), 851–54; and James Dunn, *Colossians and Philemon*, NIGTC (Grand Rapids, Mich.: Eerdmans, 1996), 90–91.

4. The verb is used in indicative mood (1 Cor. 11:9; Eph. 2:15; Col. 1:16[2x]; 1 Tim. 4:3), substantival participle *ho ktisantōn* ("He who creates, the creator," Rom. 1:25; Eph. 3:9; Col. 3:10); adjectival passive participle *ktisthentōn* ("being created," Eph. 2:10; 4:24).

noun *ktisis* ("creation, what is created, created order, creature," Rom. 1:20, 25; 8:19, 20, 21, 22, 39; 2 Cor. 5:17; Gal. 6:15; Col. 1:15, 23), the noun *ktisma* ("what is created, creature," 1 Tim. 4:4), the noun *katabolē* ("beginning, creation," Eph. 1:4), the verb *plassō* ("to mold, form, create," Rom. 9:20; 1 Tim. 2:13), and the noun *plasma* ("what is molded," Rom. 9:20).

This study connects Paul's epistles with the creation account of Genesis 1 and 2. Although creation terminologies are also found in other Old Testament books, such as Isaiah and Jeremiah,[5] this study focuses only on Paul's use of Genesis 1 and 2. The following table contains the direct references Paul makes in his epistles to the creation account of Genesis 1 and 2:[6]

Creation Direct References	Genesis 1 and 2	Pauline Writings
Heaven and earth	"In the beginning God created the heavens and the earth" (1:1)	"For by Him all things were created that are in heaven and that are on earth" (Col. 1:16; cf. 1 Cor. 8:6)
Existence of light	"Let there be light" (1:3)	"Let light shines out of darkness" (2 Cor. 4:6, NIV)
The image of God	"God created man in His own image" (1:27)	"The new man who is renewed in knowledge according to the image of Him who created him" (Col. 3:10)
Man and woman	"She shall be called Woman, because she was taken out of Man" (2:23)	"For man is not from woman, but woman from man" (1 Cor. 11:8) "For Adam was formed first, then Eve" (1 Tim. 2:13)

---

5. See, e.g., Reed Lessing, "Yahweh versus Marduk: Creation Theology in Isaiah 40–55," *ConJ* 36, no. 3 (Sum. 2010): 234–44; Richard J. Clifford, "The Hebrew Scriptures and the Theology of Creation," *Theological Studies* 46, no. 3 (Sept. 1985): 507–23; Ben C. Ollenburger, "Isaiah's Creation Theology," *Ex Auditu* 3 (1987): 54–71; Jonathan Moo, "Romans 8.19–22 and Isaiah's Cosmic Covenant," *New Testament Studies* 54, no. 1 (Jan. 2008): 74–89; and Martin Klingbeil, "Creation in the Prophetic Literature of the Old Testament: An Intertextual Approach," *JATS* 20, nos. 1–2 (2009): 19–54.

6. This table excludes mere mentions of creation objects in Pauline writings without an obvious context of creation. Unless otherwise indicated, Scripture quotations in this chapter are taken from the New King James Version®. Copyright © 1982 by Thomas Nelson. Used by permission. All rights reserved.

Creation Direct References	Genesis 1 and 2	Pauline Writings
Adam from the dust	"And the LORD God formed man of the dust of the ground" (2:7)	"The first man was of the dust of the earth" (1 Cor. 15:47, NIV)
Adam becoming a living being	"And man became a living being" (2:7)	"The first man Adam became a living being" (1 Cor. 15:45)
Everything was good	"Then God saw everything that He had made, and indeed it was very good" (1:31; cf. vv. 4, 10, 12, 18, 21, 25)	"For everything God created is good" (1 Tim. 4:4, NIV)
Adam and Eve becoming one flesh	And they shall become one flesh" (2:24)	"The two will become one flesh" (1 Cor. 6:16, NIV; cf. Eph. 2:15; 5:31)

In addition to the direct references presented above, there are also possible indirect references to the creation story of Genesis 1 and 2 in the Pauline writings:

Creation Indirect References	Genesis 1 and 2	Pauline Writings
Association of "light" with "day" and"darkness" with "night"	"God called the light Day, and the darkness He called Night" (1:5)	"You are all sons of light and sons of the day. We are not of the night nor of darkness" (1 Thess. 5:5)
Separation of light from darkness	"God divided the light from the darkness" (1:4)	"And what communion has light with darkness?" (2 Cor. 6:14)
Vegetation	"The LORD God planted a garden eastward in Eden, . . . And out of the ground the LORD God made every tree grow" (2:8–9)	"I planted the seed, . . . but God has been making it grow" (1 Cor. 3:6, NIV)
Different kinds of seeds and plants	"The herb that yields seed according to its kind" (1:12)	"But God gives it a body as He pleases, and to each seed its own body" (1 Cor. 15:38)

Creation Indirect References	Genesis 1 and 2	Pauline Writings
Instruction on food	"Every seed-bearing plant ... every tree that has fruit with seed ... they will be yours for food" (1:29, NIV)	"To abstain from foods which God created to be received" (1 Tim. 4:3)
Heavenly bodies	"The greater light to rule the day, and the lesser light to rule the night. He made the stars also" (1:16)	"One glory of the sun, another glory of the moon, and another glory of the stars" (1 Cor. 15:41)
Fishes and birds	"So God created great sea creatures ... and every winged bird according to its kind" (1:21)	"Animals and creeping things" (Rom. 1:23) "Another of fish, and another of birds" (1 Cor. 15:39)
Animals and creeping thing	"Livestock, the creatures that move along the ground, and the wild animals, each according to its kind" (1:24, NIV)	"Animals and creeping things" (Rom. 1:23)

This study will analyze the theological contexts of the Pauline writings that use creation terms and that mention the creation objects of Genesis 1 and 2. The purpose is to see Paul's perspective on creation and understand the ideas Paul establishes in connection to creation.

PAUL AND THE HISTORICITY OF CREATION

Paul not only builds his theology upon what is written in the Old Testament but also assumes the historicity of the Old Testament. For example, his statement in 1 Corinthians 10:11 clarifies his belief that the account of Israel in the Pentateuch is not merely a written story but something that really happened. In this context, Moses, the people of Israel, the crossing of the Red Sea, the manna, water coming out of the rock, and the people killed by snakes were all real people and events in history (1 Cor. 10:2–10). The events *happened* . . . as examples, and they were *written* for our admonition" (1 Cor. 10:11, emphasis added). Before further discussing the theological use of Genesis 1 and 2 in the Pauline writings, it is necessary to see whether Paul believes creation really happened in the timeline of history.

One of the arguments for the historicity of the creation account is based on Paul's usage of the prepositions *apo* ("from") and *pro* ("before"), in connection with phrases referring to creation, such as "foundation of the world" (Eph. 1:4),[7] "the beginning of the ages" (Eph. 3:9; Col. 1:26),[8] and, of course, "the creation of the world" (Rom. 1:20). Eleven of the eighty-eight occurrences of the preposition *apo* in the Pauline writings denote temporal meaning.[9] Paul uses the preposition to describe: what happened from the time of Adam to the time of Moses (Rom. 5:14); his admonition to the Corinthians concerning what to do from now on once they receive his letter (2 Cor. 5:16); his desire to visit the Christians in Rome many years before he wrote to them (Rom. 15:23); a certain period of time within which the Macedonians desired to donate money (2 Cor. 8:10; 9:2); his partnership with the Philippians, from the first day he met them until the time he wrote them the epistle (Phil. 1:5); and the proper training received by Timothy from his childhood until the time he received Paul's last letter (2 Tim. 3:15). Paul talks about real places that exist, living persons, and events that were taking place during his missionary journeys. Therefore, Paul must be referring to a real event that took place in history when he uses *apo* in the temporal sense to modify "the creation of the world" (Rom. 1:20) and "the beginning of the ages" (Eph. 3:9; Col. 1:26). For Paul, creation was real and took place in history.

---

7. The meaning of *katabolē* cannot be traced in the Hebrew Bible because the word does not exist there. However, the only occurrence of this word in the LXX may give a hint for the meaning: "For as the master builder of a new house must be concerned with the whole construction [*katabolē*], while the one who undertakes its painting and decoration has to consider only what is suitable for its adornment, such in my judgment is the case with us" (2 Macc. 2:29, RSV). See also Plutarch, *Mor.* 956a, who uses *katabolē* to refer to the "foundation of the world." With these clues, the translation of *katabolē* as creation in the New Testament makes sense, since creation is similar to construction. Also, the phrase *katabolē kosmou* ("[the] foundation of the world") always refers to the creation account of Genesis in the context of all but one of its occurrences in the New Testament (Matt. 13:35; 25:34; Luke 11:50; John 17:24; Eph. 1:4; Heb. 4:3; 9:26; 1 Pet. 1:20; Rev. 13:8; 17:8). The word *katabolē* itself occurs eleven times in the New Testament. Interestingly, it is found only once, in Heb. 11:11, without the genitive *kosmou* ("of [the] world," though in Matt. 13:35 a textual variant also excludes *kosmou*). In Heb. 11:11 *eis katabolēn* is translated "to conceive" by most English Bible versions. This meaning connotes a concept of beginning.

8. It is evident that *apo tōn aiōnōn* ("from the ages" or "from the beginning of the ages," Eph. 3:9; Col. 1:26), means "from the creation." In both places where the phrase occurs, either the verb *ktizō* or the noun *ktisis* also occurs in the context.

9. Rom. 1:20; 5:14; 15:23, 2 Cor. 5:16; 8:10; 9:2; Eph. 3:9; Phil. 1:5; Col. 1:26; 2 Tim. 3:15.

Another hint to the historicity of creation in the Pauline writings is Paul's use of the phrase "from ages and from generations, but now has been revealed to His saints" (Col. 1:26). Here, Paul uses the term *apo tōn aiōnōn* ("from the ages"; cf. Eph. 3:9). He also mentions *ta telē tōn aiōnōn* ("the end of the ages," 1 Cor. 10:11). Therefore, although *aiōn* can mean "eternity," *apo tōn aiōnōn* should not be translated as "from eternity." Otherwise, there must be "the end of eternity." In this light, *apo tōn aiōnōn* refers to a point of beginning in the past ages. Thus, for Paul it points to creation. Moreover, in Ephesians 3:9 and Colossians 1:26, this phrase is used in the connection with the verb *ktizō*. Interestingly, in Colossians 1:26, after mentioning "from the ages" (which is "from the creation"), Paul mentions "from generations, but now . . . ." Paul seems to be expressing the idea of "from the creation through the various generations until the present generation." Since generations are real and inseparably attached to the history of humankind, creation must also be real and inseparably attached to history.

Notably, for Paul, there is no generation before Adam; the first generation was Adam. That is why, in explaining that death is caused by sin, Paul states that "death reigned from Adam to Moses" (Rom. 5:14). Before Adam there was no sin, and "through one man sin entered the world" (Rom. 5:12). In fact, sin entered the world not only through one man but through "the first man Adam" (1 Cor. 15:45). By referring to Adam as the first generation, Paul must have in mind the creation of Adam on the sixth day of creation week (Gen. 1:26–27; 2:7). Thus, since the generations are real and inseparably attached to history, the creation of Adam must also be attached to history. Therefore, it suffices to say that the creation account of Genesis 1 and 2 is attached not only to history but also to the beginning of the history of humanity. In fact, for Paul, without creation, there is no history.

Having established the historicity of the creation account of Genesis 1 and 2, this study will now discuss Paul's usage of creation terms, with direct and indirect references, in connection to his theology.

CREATION AND THE CREATOR

Paul presents God as the Creator (Rom. 1:20–21, 25; Eph. 3:9; 1 Tim. 4:3). Christ, being the image of God, is also presented as the

Creator, as described in Colossians 1, where the creation terms in Colossians appear (vv. 15, 16[2x], 23). This passage has been seen as "a christological hymn with an interesting structure."[10] Here, Jesus is presented as the image of the invisible God, "the firstborn over all creation" (v. 15). He is qualified for these titles because (*hoti*) "by Him all things were created that are in heaven and that are on earth, visible and invisible, whether thrones or dominions or principalities or powers. All things were created through Him and for Him" (v. 16). Because He is the Creator of all things, the term "the firstborn over all creation" does not mean Jesus was created, but rather that He holds preeminent status as the Creator.[11] In fact, the *hoti* clause of Colossians 1:16 begins and ends with the same verb, *ktizō* ("For by Him all things were created.... All things were created through Him and for Him." *hoti en autō ektisthē ta panta ... ta panta di' autou kai eis auton ektistai*),[12] just as the complete creation narrative of Genesis begins and ends with a phrase including the verb "to create," (*bārā'*, Gen. 1:1; 2:3).[13] In between the two references to *ktizō*, Paul lists what Jesus has created: "all things were created that are in heaven and that are on earth, visible and invisible, whether thrones or dominions or principalities or powers" (Col. 1:16). Likewise, in between the two uses of *bārā'* (Gen. 1:1; 2:3), the author of Genesis presents the complete narrative of creation. It seems that Paul uses the creation narrative of Genesis as a reference point to argue that Jesus is not a created being but the Creator Himself.[14]

Furthermore, Colossians 1:16 clarifies what Paul means by *ktisis* in verse 15. In verse 15, Paul speaks about *pasēs ktiseōs*, "all creation." Then in verse 16, he mentions that "by Him all things were created

---

10. Ekkehardt Mueller, "Creation in the New Testament," Biblical Research Institute, 11, https://adventistbiblicalresearch.org/sites/default/files/pdf/CreationNT.pdf. He presents a chiastic structure of Colossians 1:15–20 in which Christ is presented as the Creator (ibid., 13).

11. See David Pao, *Colossians & Philemon,* ZECNT (Grand Rapids, Mich.: Zondervan, 2012), 95.

12. Notice the chiastic structure of this inclusio in verse 16: *ektisthē ta panta ... ta panta ... ektistai.*

13. See Matilde Frey, "The Sabbath in the Pentateuch: An Exegetical and Theological Study" (PhD diss., Andrews University, 2011), 22–23. According to Frey, the usage of the double framing clause *bārā' 'ĕlōhîm* in Genesis 1:1 and 2:3 indicates the literary unity of the first account.

14. Genesis 1 and 2 present two accounts of one creation. The first account is Genesis 1:1–2:3 and the second account is Genesis 2:4–24. In a sense, the second account is an elaboration of the first account especially on the sixth day of creation. For further clarification about the connection between the two accounts, see Jiří Moskala, "A Fresh Look at Two Genesis Creation Accounts: Contradictions?," *AUSS* 49, no. 1 (Spring 2011): 45–65.

that are in heaven and that are on earth." This sounds like Genesis 2:1, "Thus the heavens and the earth, and all the host of them, were finished." Both passages use merisms to describe the totality of creation. It is clear that Paul presents Christ as the Creator of the six-day creation. Paul continues clarifying that Christ created the "visible and invisible"—something that does not have a verbal link to Genesis 1 and 2. Then Paul presents two pairs of "whether . . . or" phrases attached to the "visible and invisible"—namely, "thrones [and] dominions" and "principalities [and] powers." It seems that by using "all creation," Paul goes beyond the six-day creation account. His emphasis is that there are neither thrones nor dominions, neither principalities nor powers that exceed the power of Christ. There is no power above Christ. This negates the claim that Christ was created and then performed the six-day creation. He is the Creator Himself and "He is before all things, and in Him all things consist" (Col. 1:17).

Now, when the noun *ktisis* reappears in Colossians 1:23, it no longer refers to the heavens and the earth and all that is in them. It refers to all creatures "under heaven," to whom the gospel is proclaimed. It seems that Paul is referring to human beings as the target of the gospel proclamation in this verse. Hence the *ktisis* in verse 15 has a much larger scope than the referent in verse 23.

By highlighting that Jesus was not created, Paul demonstrates that our Savior is God and the Creator Himself, "in whom we have redemption through His blood, the forgiveness of sins" (Col. 1:14), and that "in Him all the fullness should dwell, and by Him to reconcile all things to Himself, by Him, whether things on earth or things in heaven, having made peace through the blood of His cross" (Col. 1:19–20). The presentation of Jesus Christ as the one who died for us is connected to Him being our Creator. Thus, He who died for us is the one who created us.

CREATION AND SIN

Paul builds his theology of salvation on references and allusions to creation. In Romans 1, the terms *ktizō* and *ktisis* appear in the context of God's wrath upon the wickedness of humanity (Rom. 1:18–32). Paul begins with the statement "For the wrath of God is revealed from heaven against all ungodliness and unrighteousness of men, who suppress the truth in unrighteousness" (v. 18). God's wrath comes because although the knowledge of God is manifest and shown to them, they do not glorify Him as God (vv. 19, 21).[15] Then Paul clarifies that what was manifested to them are the things God has made since the creation of the world (v. 20).[16] Although they knew God as the Creator (v. 21), these wicked humans did not glorify Him. Instead, they changed "the glory of the incorruptible God into an image made like corruptible man—and birds and four-footed animals and creeping things" (v. 23).[17] Instead of glorifying God, they glorified images of the creatures made on the fifth and sixth days (Gen. 1:20–28).[18] This is the first exchange that the wicked made.[19]

Paul describes another two exchanges: They "exchanged the truth of God for the lie, and worshiped and served the creature rather than the Creator" (Rom. 1:25). Based on the context of the passage, "the truth of God" is the fact that God is the Creator who made all things, God to whom the glory belongs, and the one who is worthy of honor and worship. In the book of Romans, the expression *hē alētheia* ("the truth") is first introduced in 1:18, which is the introduction to verses 18–32, and refers to the truth that the unrighteous suppress (v. 18). The exchanging of the truth for the lie, and the worship of the creature rather than the Creator, may refer implicitly to the entry of sin in the garden of Eden. Instead of holding the truth of God (Gen. 2:16–17), Adam and Eve believed in the deceptive words of the serpent (Gen. 3:1–6); they worshiped and served the creature rather than the Creator.[20]

---

15. This statement is followed by the use of the causal conjunction *dioti* ("because, for") twice (Rom. 1:19, 21), suggesting the reasons for God's wrath.

16. The phrase *apo ktiseōs kosmou tois poiēmasin* ("since the creation of the world in the things that are made" [author's translation]) sounds like an allusion to Genesis 2:1–2, where the word *kosmos* appears for the first time in the LXX, and the verb *poieō* ("to make") appears three times.

17. The genitive construction *tēn doxan tou aphthartou theou* may be seen as an objective genitive in which the incorruptible God receives the act of glorifying. This is evident in the context, since Paul uses the *theon edoxasan*, "they glorify God" (v. 21), in which God is the object.

18. Birds were created on the fifth day (Gen. 1:20–23); humans, four-footed animals, and creeping things were created on the sixth day (Gen. 1:24–28). In Romans 1:23 Paul uses the same words used by the LXX for birds (*peteinos*, cf. Gen. 1:20), four-footed animals (*tetrapous*, cf. Gen. 1:24), and creeping things (*herpeton*, Gen. 1:24).

19. For more details on creation in Romans 1, see the chapter by Wilson Paroschi, "Intentional Design and Innate Morality: Creation in Romans 1–2," 275, in this volume. Paul uses the verb *allassō* ("change, exchange," Rom. 1:23) and the verb *metallassō* ("exchange," Rom. 1:25, 27) to convey the idea of exchange.

20. The serpent in Genesis 3:1 is called more crafty than any other beast *ḥayyâ* ("living being"). The LXX uses the term *thērion* ("beast"), pointing to something made on the sixth day of creation (Gen. 1:24–25).

In Romans 1:18–32 the unrighteous also exchange "natural relations for unnatural" (v. 26, RSV), in which women had unnatural relations and men "burned in their lust for one another, men with men committing what is shameful" (v. 27). This was against God's original plan and instruction at creation: "Therefore a man shall leave his father and mother and be joined to his wife, and they shall become one flesh" (Gen. 2:24).

The usage of *ktizō* and *ktisis* in Romans 1:18–32 demonstrates that Paul is familiar with the creation account of Genesis 1 and 2. In explaining the wrath of God toward a wicked generation, he refers to the entry of sin into Eden, where there was neither Jew nor Greek. He contrasts God's ideal in Eden with the immorality of human beings. He illustrates sin as the opposite of God's perfect ideal described in Genesis 1 and 2. In a sense, Paul even connects sin to the transgression of the law (cf. 1 John 3:4).[21] Because of sin, both the Jew and the Greek are subject to judgment and punishment.

Paul also sees that the transgression of humanity affects creation (*ktisis*).[22] He demonstrates this by comparing creation (*ktisis*) and humanity in Romans 8:18–30:[23]

The Creation	Humanity
"the creation eagerly waits [*apekdechetai*] for the revealing of the sons of God" (v. 19)	"we ourselves . . . eagerly waiting [*apekdechomenoi*] for the adoption" (v. 23)
"in hope [*helpidi*] that the creation itself also will be set free" (vv. 20–21, NAS)	"For we were saved in this hope [*helpidi*]" (v. 24)
"the whole creation groans [*systenazei*]" (v. 22)	"We ourselves groan [*stenazomen*] inwardly" (v. 23)
"suffers the pains of childbirth together until now [*synōdinei achri tou nyn*]" (v. 22, NAS)	"sufferings of this present time [*ta pathēmata tou nyn*]" (v. 18)

21. Even before Paul uses the term *nomos* nineteen times in the next chapter of this epistle (Rom. 2:12[2x], 13, 14[4x], 15, 17, 18, 20, 23 [2x], 25[2x], 26, 27[2x]), where he includes the second, seventh, and eighth commandments (Rom. 2:21–23), he has connected in Romans 1:18–32 at least four of the Ten Commandments to the creation account: the first (vv. 20–21), second (v. 23), seventh (vv. 26–27), and ninth (v. 25).

22. After the occurrence of *ktisis* in Romans 1, it appears again five times in chapter 8 (vv. 19, 20, 21, 22, 39), this time in the context of the comparison between the present sufferings and the future glory, except the use in verse 39.

23. Since the word *ktisis* appears as a key term in verses 18–30, this passage could be considered a unit. See the more extensive discussion of this passage in the chapter by Wilson Paroschi, "Intentional Design and Innate Morality: Creation in Romans 1–2," 279, in this volume.

The table above demonstrates that whatever is experienced by humanity is also experienced by the creation, and vice versa: Humanity waits for the adoption as sons of God, a reality that the creation has been eagerly awaiting. Humanity expects the hope of redemption of their bodies (Rom. 8:23–24), which is, at the same time, the hope of the creation for liberation from bondage. Both have been suffering until the present time (*achri tou nyn*).

The rebellion of human beings takes place in the created world. However, in Romans 8:18–30 the creation has been suffering the result of that rebellion (Rom. 1:18–32). It is obvious that the suffering of the creation is "not by its own choice" (Rom. 8:20, NIV). In fact, it is humanity who, "although they knew God, . . . did not glorify Him as God" (Rom. 1:21)—who "changed the glory of the incorruptible God into an image made like corruptible man" (Rom. 1:23) and "exchanged the truth of God for the lie" (Rom. 1:25). This concept echoes God's statement to Adam declaring that because of his disobedience, the ground (earth), not by its own choice, was cursed by God (Gen. 3:17).

In explaining sin, and its wages and consequences, it is important for Paul to refer to creation so that he can better explain restoration and salvation. Otherwise, it is impossible for him to introduce the concept of the restoration of the image of God or the image of Christ.

CREATION AND THE RESTORATION OF GOD'S IMAGE

In Romans 8, Paul presents what has to be done to and by wicked people, as he does in Romans 1:18–32. Paul is now talking about the same *ktisis*—all created beings including, but not limited to, human beings. It seems there is a frame that Paul establishes by using the creation motif in chapters 1 and 8. The *ktisis* worshiped by humanity (Rom. 1:25) has been suffering up to the present time (Rom. 8:22). Now humanity, who exchanged "the glory of the incorruptible God [for] an image made like corruptible man" (Rom. 1:23), in the redemption experience has to be "conformed to the image of His Son" (Rom. 8:29).[24] It is the exchange of God's image into man's image that causes the suffering of the creation. Therefore, it is humanity's positive response to God's calling that allows them to be conformed to the image of His Son and creation to be restored. While

---

24. Interestingly enough, Paul uses the term *eikōn* only twice in his epistle to the Romans (1:23; 8:29).

in Romans 1:23 there is suffering of the creation, in Romans 8:18 there is hope of incomparable glory to be revealed to humanity.[25]

The concept of transformation into the image of the Creator is also presented in Colossians 3:10. The substantival participle *tou ktisantos* ("the creator") in Colossians 3:10 should be understood as referring to Jesus. This has been the emphasis earlier in the epistle (Col. 1:16); thus the phrase "image of Him [the Creator]" in Colossians 3:10 refers to the image of Jesus the Creator.[26] Given this concept, the restoration of the old man into a new man is according to the image of Jesus. Colossians 3:10 contains the only occurrence of the phrase *kat' eikona* ("according to the image") in the New Testament. This phrase is mostly used in the Old Testament in connection to the creation of man and woman by God the Creator (Gen. 1:26–27; 5:1, 3).[27]

The use of *eikōn* in Romans 8:29 and Colossians 3:10 may refer back to Genesis 1:26–27, describing the creation of human beings according to God's image. This shows Paul's acquaintance with the creation account of Genesis 1 and 2. It also indicates the incredible significance of the creation account to Paul in establishing his concept of the restoration of God's image in humanity. If not for the creation account, Paul may not have been able to picture the image of God into which human beings are to be conformed. Moreover, by presenting Jesus as the image of God, Creator, and Savior, Paul

---

25. See also Steven J. Kraftchick, "Paul's Use of Creation Themes: A Test of Romans 1–8," *Ex Auditu* 3 (1987): 82–84. He says that the frame created by Romans 1 and 8 "involves the relationship between the creation and the Creator as it is manifested in the human response to its created status. It is especially the case that the idea of rebellion can be seen in chap. 1. As a result of the human refusal to recognize the creation as God's, and itself as part of the created order, the human removes itself from proper relationship to God and the created order. It is in this state of rebellion where the Christ encounters us (chap. 5), and it is from this state of rebellion from which we will ultimately be redeemed (chap. 8). In chap. 1 the creation is the arena in which the opportunity for the rebellion occurs, but as chap. 8 makes clear, the creation is also subjected to frustration, from which it cannot be released until the final redemption of the rebellious ones is a fact. Hence there is an interesting symbiotic relationship between creation and human beings. We are intrinsically part of the problem for creation and necessary for its final release from bondage. It was in the revelation of God's power and godliness to humans that the creation had its purpose. Now, it is the redemption of humans for which creation awaits so that it may obtain its freedom. In the former case the creation is for the service of humanity, in the latter it depends upon humanity for its redemption" (ibid., 84).

26. Paul presents God as the Creator (Rom. 1:25; Eph. 3:9; 1 Tim. 4:3–4) and Jesus also as the Creator (1 Cor. 8:6; Col. 1:15–16; 3:10). This is not to suggest that the Father and Jesus Christ the Son are the same member of the Godhead but rather that both are divine.

27. In the Old Testament the phrase occurs five times: four times in Genesis (1:26, 27; 5:1, 3), and once in Hosea 13:2. The first four are used in connection to God the Creator and the other one is used in connection to idols.

emphasizes that the work of salvation is the work of bringing back into humanity the image of our Creator and Savior.

CREATION AND SALVATION

In pronouncing judgment on wicked people (Rom. 1:18–32), Paul argues that they have no excuse for ignoring God, because His power and character have been revealed to all since creation (vv. 19–20). Interestingly, Paul does not present creation only to highlight men's wickedness, the suffering of the creation, and the wrath of God (Rom. 1:18–32). In fact, Paul discusses the connection between creation and salvation after introducing the gospel of Christ, which is "the power of God to salvation for everyone who believes, for the Jew first and also for the Greek" (Rom. 1:16).[28] By referring to the creation account, Paul argues that both salvation and punishment apply the same way to everyone, both the Jew and the Greek (Rom. 2:9–10).

By emphasizing the equality between Jews and Gentiles in receiving the privilege of salvation, Paul explains that salvation is for all. He uses the argument of creation to remind the Jews in particular that they are the clay and God is the Potter (Rom. 9:20–21). Paul uses *plassō* ("to mold, form, create"), a verb that clearly refers to the creation of man and woman.[29] Paul goes beyond referring to Abraham and Isaac (Rom. 9:7–9), Jacob and Esau (vv. 10–13), Moses and Pharaoh (vv. 15–18), Hosea (vv. 25–26), and Isaiah (vv. 27–30) in emphasizing God's prerogative, extending the offer of salvation to

---

28. The connection between Romans 1:16–17 and Romans 1:18–32 is evident. In Romans 1:17 Paul speaks of the God's righteousness revealed in the gospel. In Romans 1:18 God's wrath is revealed against ungodliness. This is presented in a chiastic structure:
   dikaiosynē *gar theou en autō*
   apokalyptetai . . .
   Apokalyptetai
   gar **orgē** *theou ap' ouranou epi pasan asebeian kai adikian anthrōpōn.*
The author appreciates his colleague, Thomas Shepherd, for pointing out this chiasm in Romans 1:17–18.

29. There is no question that Romans 9:20 quotes, more or less, Isaiah 29:16. However, it could also be argued that Paul, in using the verb *plassō* ("to mold, form, create"), might be referring to Genesis 1 and 2 for at least three reasons: First, this is exactly the verb that describes God forming humankind at creation (Gen. 2:7–8). The LXX uses *plassō* in parallel with *poieō* ("I make") (see, e.g., Job 10:8; Ps. 73:17, LXX [ET 74:17]; 94:5, LXX [ET 95:5]; 118:73, LXX [ET 119:73]; Isa. 29:16; 43:7; Jer. 40:2). Second, in Romans 9:20–21, Paul uses an analogy of a potter forming the clay—a motif that is first implied in Genesis 2:7. Job 10:9 gives a hint that clay and dust are interchangeable. Thus, although Genesis 2:7 mentions dust instead of clay, it can be understood that forming the clay refers also to the creation of humankind. Finally, 1 Timothy 2:13 mentions the forming of Adam and Eve in the same order as presented in Genesis 1:27 and 2:7, 22. For Paul, therefore, the verb *plassō* is a creation term.

everyone. For Paul, God can do this because He is the Potter, the Maker, and the Creator, and human beings are His creation.

Paul further relates salvation to creation in his epistle to the Ephesians. Paul uses the verb *ktizō* four times in Ephesians (2:10, 15; 3:9; 4:24). In Ephesians 2:10 he says, "For we are God's handiwork, created in Christ Jesus to do good works, which God prepared in advance for us to do" (NIV). Here the verb *ktizō* appears in the context of a comparison between being dead in transgression (Eph. 2:1–5) and being alive in Christ (vv. 5–10). This division of the passage may be marked by the use of the preposition *en* ("in"). In the first part (vv. 1–5), Paul describes his situation and that of his audience before Christ saved them: in transgressions and sins (v. 1) and in the lusts of flesh (v. 3). In the second part of the passage (vv. 5–10), Paul depicts their situation after Christ saved them: in the heavenly realms in Christ Jesus (v. 6). The expression *en Christō Iēsou* ("in Christ Jesus") is even repeated three times (vv. 6, 7, 10). The contrast between the past and the present is demonstrated by two opposite concepts. The concept of being dead in transgressions is repeated twice with similar expressions: "dead in trespasses and sins" (v. 1) and "we were dead in trespasses" (v. 5). Paul contrasts this with "made us alive together with Christ" (v. 5)[30] and "raised us up together" (v. 6). Therefore, when Paul uses the verb *ktizō* in verse 10, he is reemphasizing the making alive or raising of the dead. This creation term is used here in addition to the resurrection term in order to describe the understanding of salvation by grace through faith (v. 8): the dead person cannot make himself alive, but God makes him alive; the dust molded into the shape of a man had no life in it, but God breathed into it and made it a living being (Gen. 2:7).

There are indications that, in using the verb *ktizō* in Ephesians 2:10, Paul refers to the creation of humanity in Genesis 2:7. This is evident from the use of the word *poiēma* ("what is created or made"). The cognate verb of this noun, *poieō* ("I create, make"), appears significantly in the creation account of Genesis 1 and 2 (1:1, 7, 16, 21, 25, 27[3x], 31; 2:2[2x], 3, 4, 18, LXX), and it appears most frequently in the description of God creating Adam and Eve on the sixth

---

30. In the New Testament, the verb *syzōopoieō* ("to make alive together") occurs only twice (Eph. 2:5; Col. 2:13). However, the verb *zōopoieō* ("to make alive") occurs eleven times (John 5:21[2x]; 6:63; Rom. 4:17; 8:11; 1 Cor. 15:22, 36, 45; 2 Cor. 3:6; Gal. 3:21; 1 Pet. 3:18), eight of which are used in the context of resurrection of the dead.

day—five times (1:26, 27[3x]; 2:18). Another hint of Paul's reference to Genesis 1 and 2 in Ephesians 2:1–10 is his use of the verb *syzōopoieō* (Eph. 2:5), a synonym of *zōopoieō* ("to make alive"). This echoes the statement of Genesis 2:7, "And man became a living being." Paul himself suggests this parallel when he says in another context, "And so it is written, 'The first man Adam became a living being.' The last Adam became a life-giving spirit [*pneuma zōopoioun*]" (1 Cor. 15:45; cf. Gen. 2:7).[31] Therefore, with these parallels in view, this study argues that Paul uses the creation of humanity to strengthen his concept of salvation by grace through faith and that he does not have any other creation account in mind than the one in Genesis 1 and 2. These he takes literally and historically.

Using resurrection to illustrate the concept of salvation by grace is enlightening. Adding to it the illustration from the creation account even makes the concept clearer. Just as humans did not originate in themselves but were created by God, so they cannot save themselves but are redeemed by God's grace through faith in Jesus Christ.

Paul also uses creation to illustrate salvation in terms of change of character. This is demonstrated by his similar and complementary usage of the verb *ktizō* in Ephesians and Colossians.[32] The verb *ktizō* in Colossians 3:10 ("the new self, which is being renewed in knowledge in the image of its Creator" [NIV]) conveys a similar meaning as in Ephesians 4:24 ("the new self, created to be like God in true righteousness and holiness" [NIV]). The verb describes a change from an "old man [person]" (Col. 3:9; cf. Eph. 4:22) to a "new man [person]" (Col. 3:10; cf. Eph. 4:24). The characteristics of the old person are "immorality, impurity, lust, evil desires and greed" (Col. 3:5, NIV), "anger, wrath, malice, blasphemy, [and] filthy language out of your mouth" (Col. 3:8). The characteristics of the new person are "tender mercies, kindness, humility, meekness, longsuffering" (Col. 3:12), "bearing with one another, and forgiving one another" (Col. 3:13), "love" (Col. 3:14), "peace of God," and gratefulness (Col. 3:15). In the structure of Colossians 3:1–17, the mention

---

31. In Romans 4:17 Paul connects this verb with both resurrection and creation: "God, who gives life [*zōopoiountos*] to the dead and calls those things which do not exist as though they did."

32. Scholars notice a great resemblance between Ephesians and Colossians. See, e.g., D. A. Carson et al., *An Introduction to the New Testament* (Mandaluyong: OMF Literature, 1998), 311: "These two letters [Ephesians and Colossians] resemble each other more than any other two in the Pauline corpus."

of the renewing power of the Creator appears in between the lists of the old man's characteristics and those of the new man. Interestingly, in Ephesians 4:17–5:21, the phrase "the new man [person] which was created according to God" (Eph. 4:24) is presented in the context of a change from darkness to light: "For you were once darkness, but now you are light in the Lord" (Eph. 5:8). Paul uses the verb *ktizō* to describe this change. It is also the Creator who performed the seven-day creation when "the earth was without form, and void; and darkness was on the face of the deep . . . . Then God said, 'Let there be light'; and there was light" (Gen. 1:2–3). This suggests that in using the verb *ktizō* Paul refers to the creation account of Genesis 1 and 2, in which the creative power belongs only to God/Christ.

Paul also refers to the creation account when he says *ta de panta ek tou theou* ("but all things are from God"). In its two occurrences in the Pauline epistles (1 Cor. 11:12; 2 Cor. 5:18), this phrase is related to either *ktizō* or *ktisis*. This pair of creation terms and creation phrases is utilized by Paul to present two different applications: the ancient creation (1 Cor. 11:8, 12) and the new creation—the "[being] in Christ" or salvation in Christ (2 Cor. 5:17–18).[33] It seems that Paul wants to add one more message in building this connection. By this construction, Paul argues that just as creation is possible only by the creative power of God, so too is salvation, as all things are from God.

It has been demonstrated that it is impossible to separate Paul's teaching on salvation from his understanding of the historical narrative of creation in Genesis 1 and 2. Salvation is literal and real, just as creation is. Blurring the historicity and the literal account of creation will weaken the reality of salvation by Jesus Christ, the Creator and Savior.

CREATION AND ECCLESIOLOGY

The preceding discussion sheds light on the use of the creation verb *ktizō* in Ephesians 2:15. Paul has not yet gone far from verse 10, where he makes reference to the creation of humanity, and he now adds one more hint to his reference to the creation account of Genesis 1 and 2 in the phrase "to create in Himself one new man from the two"

---

33. The term *kainē ktisis* ("new creation") appears twice in the New Testament, only in Pauline writings (2 Cor. 5:17; Gal. 6:15). Besides this, a similar expression also occurs with *kainon anthrōpon* ("new person," Eph. 2:15; 4:24) and *ton neon* ("the new [man]," Col. 3:10).

(Eph. 2:15).[34] In this context the verb *ktizō* may be seen as an act of uniting two parties into one. In this case, it is the uniting of the Jews and the Gentiles in Christ. This may fit well with Genesis 2:24, where God unites Adam and Eve to become one flesh. This suggestion is not remote from the context of the epistle because a similar reference is made again in Ephesians 5:31: "For this reason a man shall leave his father and mother and be joined to his wife, and the two shall become one flesh." It seems that Paul has in mind a clear sequence of the creation account of Genesis 2: God created man, He created woman, and then He made the two become one.[35]

Although the concept of two becoming one is applied differently in Ephesians 2:15 and 5:31, there are some thematic parallels: (1) The allusion in Ephesians 2:15 is applied to the unity in Christ between the Jews and the Gentiles; the one in Ephesians 5:31 is between Christ and His church. (2) The one in Ephesians 2:15 deals with intra-unity within the church; the one in Ephesians 5:31 is inter-unity between Christ and His Church. (3) In both instances, it is only God/Christ who can bring that unity, for creative power belongs only to God. Hence the creation term *ktizō* also carries ecclesiological significance.

Paul also uses the argument from creation to deal with some interpersonal and cultural issues in the church. The verb *ktizō* in 1 Corinthians 11:9 appears in the context of Paul's advice to the women in the Corinthian church to cover their heads. Paul supports his advice by highlighting the relationship between man and woman. For Paul, the best reference for this relationship is creation (vv. 6–9). In fact, Paul seems to allude to Genesis 2:21–23. This is supported by the resemblance between the phrase "but woman [is] from man" (1 Cor. 11:8) and Adam's statement, "This is now bone of my bones and flesh of my flesh; she shall be called Woman, because she was taken out of Man" (Gen. 2:23). Moreover, Paul's use of the verb *ktizō* confirms that he is referring to the creation in Genesis 1 and 2.

When dealing with the issue of head covering, Paul uses the argument of creation to highlight the relationship between man and

---

34. The verb *ktizō* in Ephesians 4:24 is also used in connection with the making of a new person (*kainon anthrōpon*) in Christ.

35. Paul also makes a direct reference to Genesis 2:24 in 1 Corinthians 6:16: "The two will become one flesh" (NIV). He utilizes this reference to discourage his audience from being involved in sexual immorality: "He who is joined to a harlot is one body with her" (NKJV).

woman and the distinctions between them in their roles (1 Cor. 11:2–16). The interpretation of this passage is highly controverted.[36] Rather than taking sides in the contentious debate regarding the roles of men and women, our interest here is to illustrate how the passage references the creation narrative of Genesis 1 and 2 and its theology and historicity. It should be understood that the issue of head covering is a local issue for the Corinthian church. This issue, according to Paul, should be settled in light of the principle God established at creation: "For man is not from woman, but woman from man. Nor was man created for the woman, but woman for the man" (1 Cor. 11:8–9).

After Paul presents the creation argument that woman is from man, he counterbalances it with this statement: "Nevertheless, neither is man independent of woman, nor woman independent of man, in the Lord. For as woman came from man, even so man also comes through woman; but all things are from God" (1 Cor. 11:11–12). In verses 9–10 Paul presents the distinction between man and woman based on creation: woman is from (*ek*) man. In verses 11–12 he presents the equality between man and woman: both are from (*ek*) God and both groups within the church have experienced the new creation. He also emphasizes that man and woman are interdependent (v. 11), because woman is from (*ek*) man and man comes through (*dia*) woman, "but all things are from God" (1 Cor. 11:12). These woman-*from*-man and man-*through*-woman relationships suggest the interdependence of man and woman. But the use of different prepositions to describe the relationships suggests different roles of man and woman. However, the fact that both come from (*ek*) God confirms that they are equal in the Lord (v. 11).[37]

Paul also uses the creation argument in 1 Timothy 2:8–15 to clarify the relationship between man and woman and their respective roles. Although Adam was created first and then Eve, both were

---

36. See also the discussion of this passage in the chapter by Dominic Bornand, "Cosmology and Creation in First and Second Corinthians," 251, in this volume; Matthew L. Tinkham Jr., "Neo-Subordinationism: The Alien Argumentation in the Gender Debate," *AUSS* 55, no. 2 (2017): 237–90; Edwin Reynolds, "Biblical Hermeneutics and Headship in First Corinthians" (presentation, meeting of the Theology of Ordination Study Committee, Baltimore, July 22, 2013), 1–46; and Richard M. Davidson, "Headship, Submission, and Equality in Scripture," in *Women in Ministry: Biblical and Historical Perspectives*, ed. Nancy Vyhmeister (Berrien Springs, Mich.: Andrews University Press, 1998), 259–95.

37. See also William J. Webb, "Balancing Paul's Original-Creation and Pro-Creation Arguments: 1 Corinthians 11:11–12 in Light of Modern Embryology," *WTJ* 66 (2004): 280–81.

created by God; although it was not Adam but Eve who was deceived, both fell into transgression and both needed salvation. Salvation is possible for both because *"there is* one God and one Mediator between God and men, *the* Man Christ Jesus, who gave Himself a ransom for all" (1 Tim. 2:5–6). God "desires all men to be saved" (v. 4), and women also "will be saved" (v. 15). Paul uses the argument of creation to emphasize that while man and woman are both created by God, both have fallen into sin but may receive salvation.

CREATION AND OTHER ISSUES

Paul also refers to the creation narrative of Genesis 1 and 2 in relation to some other issues. In 1 Timothy 4:3 Paul uses the verb *ktizō* while counterattacking false doctrines that forbid marriage and command abstinence from the food God has created. These teachings were forms of asceticism, a practice introduced possibly by Proto-Gnosticism that considered "matter to be corrupt, or evil, and only spirit to be good."[38] Although Gnosticism was fully developed later in the second century, it is possible its influence was entering Ephesus when Paul wrote his letters to Timothy,[39] instructing him to battle against this teaching.[40]

Against these false teachings, Paul refers to the creation narrative of Genesis 1 and 2. God gave instruction about marriage and food just after He created Adam and Eve (Gen. 1:28–29). In fact, Paul mentions marriage and food in the same order they are presented in Genesis 1: first marriage (Gen. 1:28), and then food (Gen. 1:29). In 1 Timothy 4:4 Paul uses the noun *ktisma* ("created being, creature") in explaining why the teachings are false: "For every creature [*ktisma*] of God is good, and nothing is to be refused if it is received with thanksgiving." Here Paul adds one more reference to the creation narrative, referring to Genesis 1:31: "Then God saw everything that He had made,

---

38. Gordon D. Fee, *1 and 2 Timothy, Titus*, NIBC (Peabody, Mass.: Hendrickson, 1988), 99. See also Ekkehardt Mueller, "Marriage and Food in 1 Timothy 4:1–5," Biblical Research Institute, 1, https://adventistbiblicalresearch.org/sites/default/files/pdf/Marriage%20and%20Food%20in%201%20Timothy%204.pdf

39. Robert Black and Ronald McClung, *1 & 2 Timothy, Titus, Philemon: A Commentary for Bible Students* (Indianapolis, Ind.: Wesleyan, 2004), 21. For further study on the influence of pre-Gnostic ideas in Ephesus as described in the Paul's letters to Timothy, see P. H. Towner, "Gnosis and Realized Eschatology in Ephesus (of the Pastoral Epistles) and the Corinthian Enthusiasm," *JSNT* 31 (1987): 95–124.

40. Fee, *1 and 2 Timothy, Titus*, 161.

and indeed it was very good." With this additional reference, Paul in 1 Timothy 4:3–4 not only refers to the creation narrative of Genesis 1 and 2 but also presents it in the sequential order of Genesis 1:28–31: marriage, food, everything created is good.

It seems there is no better reference Paul could have used to counterattack these false teachings. By referring to the most ancient historical narrative in Scripture, Paul lays a solid foundation and example on how to deal with false teachings related to food and marriage.

ALLUSIONS TO THE DAYS OF CREATION

The preceding discussion of Paul's use of creation terms has noted many references to Genesis 1 and 2. However, the Pauline writings contain many more allusions to the creation narrative—both direct and indirect—which will be dealt with in this section.

THE FIRST DAY OF CREATION

Paul obviously refers to Genesis 1:3 when he presents God's command: "Let light shine out of darkness" (2 Cor. 4:6, NIV). By referring to the first day of the literal creation, Paul wants to illustrate the power of the gospel. In 2 Corinthians 4, Paul twice mentions similar expressions in connection to light: "the light of the gospel of the glory of Christ, who is the image of God" (v. 4) and "the light of the knowledge of the glory of God in the face of Jesus Christ" (v. 6). It seems that Paul understands "the glory of Christ, who is the image of God" parallel to "the glory of God in the face of Jesus Christ." This suggests another parallel: the gospel and the knowledge. Paul illustrates the work of God as shining into hearts via the light of the gospel by referring to His power in creating light and separating it from the darkness on the first day of creation (Gen. 1:3).[41]

Although Paul does not always explicitly indicate the meaning of light as the gospel (2 Cor. 4:4, 6), he always associates light with

---

41. Paul consistently sees light in contrast to darkness, an ancient concept introduced in Genesis 1:4: "And God saw the light, that it was good; and God divided the light from the darkness." Genesis never calls darkness evil or bad. However, Paul places light and darkness in contrast to each other. Perhaps Paul adds the Greco-Roman concept of light and darkness to establish this contrast. That is why Paul always puts *phōs* ("light") and *skotos* ("darkness") as opposite poles. For example, Paul says, "So let us put aside the deeds of darkness and put on the armor of light" (Rom. 13:12, NIV); "Or what fellowship can light have with darkness?" (2 Cor. 6:14, NIV); "For you were once darkness, but now you are light in the Lord. Live as children of light" (Eph. 5:8, NIV); "You are all children of the light and children of the day. We do not belong to the night or to the darkness" (1 Thess. 5:5, NIV).

salvation. Light means salvation (Rom. 13:12);[42] light means being in Christ (2 Cor. 6:14).[43] In Ephesians 5:8 it is associated with being in the Lord, abandoning all evil deeds. Light also apparently means being awake and ready for the coming of the Lord (1 Thess. 5:5). By directly referring to the creation of light (2 Cor. 4:6; cf. Gen. 1:4), Paul conveys a message about the power of God for salvation. He is not spiritualizing the literal light created on the first day of creation, but he uses it as an illustration to portray God's power in bringing salvation. Just as by His power God created light, it is by His power that He brings salvation through Jesus Christ, the heart of the gospel itself. The gospel of Christ is "the power of God to salvation for everyone who believes" (Rom. 1:16).

THE THIRD DAY OF CREATION

Paul does not make a direct reference to what God created on the third day of creation. However, he mentions God's power to make things grow: "God has been making it grow" (1 Cor. 3:6, NIV); "but only God, who makes things grow" (v. 7, NIV). On the third day of creation God's creative power made the earth bring forth vegetation (Gen. 1:11–12). Also, "the LORD God planted a garden. . . . And out of the ground the LORD God made every tree grow" (Gen. 2:8–9). Paul uses an agricultural analogy to compare what he and Apollos can do (plant and water the seed) and what no one but God can do (make it grow). The apostle emphasizes that creative power belongs only to God. He uses this argument to soothe the conflict within the Corinthian church about who the founder of the church is—who their leader is (1 Cor. 3:3–5). Paul reminds his audience that just as God was able to make trees grow from the earth, the same God is also able to make the church grow. Thus Paul uses the third day of creation to emphasize missiological significance: the importance of outreach and God's blessing on it.

---

42. This is based on a parallel between the phrase "our salvation is nearer [*engyteron*]" (Rom. 13:11) and "the day is at hand [*ēngiken*]" (v. 12). Thus, he uses day or light to refer to salvation.

43. 2 Corinthians 6:14–16 presents five questions that contrast two opposite elements, entities, or individuals: "What fellowship has righteousness with lawlessness? And what communion has light with darkness? And what accord has Christ with Belial? Or what part has a believer with an unbeliever? And what agreement has the temple of God with idols?" In this series of contrasts, the contrast between Christ and Belial is placed at the center. This suggests that Paul is giving two options: being in/with Christ or being in/with Belial. Thus light means being in Christ.

THE THIRD, FOURTH, FIFTH, AND SIXTH DAYS OF CREATION

Paul also mentions other creation objects, such as humankind, animals, fish, birds, sun and moon, and stars (1 Cor. 15:39–44), which some scholars connect to what God created on the third, fourth, fifth, and sixth days.[44] To this observation it should be added that Paul not only refers to the objects created on those days but presents them in reverse order. Paul begins by mentioning humanity and animals, created on the sixth day (v. 39). He continues by presenting birds and fish, created on the fifth day (v. 39). Then he mentions the sun, moon, and stars, which God created on the fourth day (v. 40). In verses 42–44 Paul presents an agricultural analogy alluding to the third day of creation (cf. vv. 37–38).

Paul also presents in sequential order objects created within those creation days: birds first, and then fish on the fifth day (v. 39; cf. Gen. 1:20–23); the sun first, the moon next, and then the stars on the fourth day (v. 40; cf. Gen. 1:14–19). One possible reason Paul presents humans first and then animals in verse 39 could be the resurrection as Paul's main theme in 1 Corinthians 15. That is why after presenting these creation objects in a reverse sequence, Paul brings his argument to a climax with what happens to humanity at the resurrection—at the coming of the Lord (vv. 45–54). Paul presents this creation argument in response to some of the Corinthians who say there is no resurrection (1 Cor. 15:12). In particular, he defends resurrection against those who see it as a complicated and impossible thing by asking, "How are the dead raised up? And with what body do they come?" (v. 35). Paul argues that the God who is able to create the heavens and the earth is the same God who is able to resurrect the dead. Nothing is too complicated or chaotic for God

---

44. See, e.g., Raymond F. Collins, *First Corinthians*, SP (Collegeville, Minn.: Liturgical, 1999), 563–64: "The living beings cited in the second analogy (v. 39) are divided into categories that reflect God's work of creation on the fifth and sixth days (Gen 1:20–28). The three categories of celestial bodies cited in the third analogy (vv. 40–41) reflect the work of the fourth day of creation (Gen 1:14–19). Since the second and third analogies so clearly reflect the Priestly author's story of creation it is not unlikely that Paul's agricultural analogy alludes to the creation of seeds and plant life on the third day of creation (Gen 1:11–13). The biblical story of God's creation of agriculture uses the verb 'to sow' (*speirein*, 'yielding' in the NRSV translation of Gen. 1:11) and 'seed' (*sperma*), two of the key words in Paul's agricultural metaphor (cf. vv. 42–45)." So also Gordon D. Fee, *The First Epistle to the Corinthians*, NICNT (Grand Rapids, Mich.: Eerdmans, 1987), 782. David Prior, *The Message of 1 Corinthians: Life in the Local Church*, The Bible Speaks Today, ed. John R. W. Stott (Leicester: InterVarsity, 1985), 272, sees a connection with God the Creator.

to put in order.[45] Also, by referring to the creation account in a somewhat reversed order in his argument of resurrection, Paul seemingly wants to suggest the idea that just as death is a reversal of creation (cf. Gen. 2:7; Eccles. 12:7), so also resurrection is the reversal of death. That is why after presenting his complete argument for resurrection Paul rejoices, saying, "Death is swallowed up in victory. O Death, where is your sting? O Hades, where is your victory?" (1 Cor. 15:54–55; cf. Isa. 25:8; Hos. 13:14).[46]

In fact, Paul speaks about what will take place at the second coming of Christ (1 Cor. 15:51–52). The apostle explains that the resurrection and the mortal body's change into immortality will take place "in a moment, in the twinkling of an eye" (v. 52). Using the creation narrative of Genesis 1 and 2 as an illustration, even referring to the specific objects created on the single days of creation to illustrate resurrection and the instantaneous change at the second coming, Paul must not have been thinking about a creation that would take place over millions of years. Just as the resurrection and the change will take place "in a moment, in the twinkling of an eye," so did creation. It must have taken place instantaneously when God said, "Let there be," and it came to be.

CONCLUSION

Paul is clearly familiar with the creation account of Genesis 1 and 2. He presents God and Jesus Christ as the Creator who performed the work of creation in a week's time. From Paul's consistent use of the creation account of Genesis 1 and 2 in his argumentation, we surmise that he takes it to be a historical narrative that describes what really took place in the history of humankind. In fact, it was the beginning of time and history. Believing in the six-day creation, Paul

---

45. The concept that God is a God of order is not first presented in 1 Corinthians 15. It is indicated by Paul earlier in this epistle. He presents the sequential steps for growth: seed planting, watering, and growing (1 Cor. 3:6–7); the materials for a foundation from the most to the least glorious (gold, silver, costly stones, wood, hay or straw; 1 Cor. 3:12); the regulations about the practice of the gift of tongues and an orderly worship (1 Cor. 14:26–40): "Let all things be done decently and in order" (v. 40).

46. Craig S. Keener, *1–2 Corinthians*, New Cambridge Bible Commentary, ed. Ben Witherington III (New York: Cambridge University Press, 2005), 132, states, "Paul may have preferred to prove the resurrection from a Pentateuchal text, like Pharisees often did against Sadducees, even if its connection to resurrection was less than obvious; but Jewish midrashic exegesis naturally linked Genesis 2:7 with resurrection by God's Spirit/breath in Ezekiel 37."

makes specific references to the objects God created on those six days. He does so not in an attempt to defend creation—for he assumes that his audience already believes in creation—but rather to highlight important theological themes.

For Paul, creation and salvation are two inseparable themes. Just as God is able to create the heavens and the earth, by His grace He is also able to save human beings. He does not discriminate between people because at creation there was neither Jew nor Gentile, male nor female. Paul also uses creation for ecclesiastical significance. The God who brought Adam and Eve into one flesh is also able to unite the church with Christ. As He made plants grow, He and only He is the one who is powerful enough to make the church grow. There is nothing too complicated or impossible for God. Paul argues that the God who created the heavens and the earth and put everything in order is also able to do what is considered impossible: resurrection of the dead. To conclude, if references to the creation account were to be removed from the Pauline literature, many theological themes presented by Paul would crumble for lack of support. All these details point together to Paul's acceptance of the historicity of the creation account in Genesis 1 and 2.

Wilson Paroschi

Southern Adventist University
Collegedale, Tennessee, USA

INTENTIONAL DESIGN AND INNATE MORALITY: CREATION IN ROMANS 1–2

INTRODUCTION

Romans is the Pauline letter that most frequently refers to the creation and fall accounts of Genesis 1–3. There are no fewer than twenty individual references (Rom. 1:20, 23, 25–27; 2:14; 4:17; 5:12, 14–19; 8:19–22, 39; 11:36; cf. Gen. 3:15 in Rom. 16:20). This study focuses on Romans 1:18–2:16,[1] which introduces the first major section of the letter (1:18—3:20). After the conventional epistolary salutation (1:1–7) and note of thanksgiving (vv. 8–15), Paul announces the theme of Romans: the "good news" (*euangelion*) of what God has done through Jesus Christ to save us (vv. 16–17). Then in the lengthy passage that follows, running to 3:20, the apostle describes the extent of the human predicament and so the reason we all need God's salvation. The point is clear: the whole world stands accountable before God and liable to divine punishment (cf. 1:32; 3:19). The argument moves from the utter depravity of the Gentiles (1:18—2:16)[2] to the concurrent guilt of

---

1. For discussion of the theology of creation in the Pauline literature, see Richard A. Sabuin, "Creation Theology in the Pauline Literature," in the present volume.

2. Since Paul never explicitly uses the term *ethnē* ("Gentiles") in Romans 1:18–32, some more recent scholars tend to see in this first part of the argument a reference to all

the Jews (2:17—3:8) and closes with the universal sinfulness of humankind (3:9-20). Creation is referred to in connection to the Gentiles. Contrary to the Jews, who have broken God's written law (cf. 2:12-13, 17-23, 25-27), the Gentiles are guilty for having violated the creation prescript, which was made known to them both objectively, through the things they could see (1:19-20), and

---

humanity (including Jews), rather than just to the Gentiles. Paul calls them "people" (*anthropoi*, Rom. 1:18; cf. "women," vv. 26–27, and "men," v. 27) and the language—so it is argued—is reminiscent of the OT description of the fall (Gen. 2–3) and of the golden calf apostasy (Exod. 32), suggesting that the Jewish people were also in the scope of the apostle's discussion. Further evidence would be the use of the indicative aorist throughout the passage (Rom. 1:19b–27), implying a reference to the original sin of rebellion against the Creator, and the "therefore" at the beginning of 2:1, which seems to indicate that those represented by Paul's hypothetical interlocutor—supposedly the Jews (cf. vv. 17–29)—would be included in 1:18–32. In this case, Paul's argument would move from the general (all humans) in chap. 1 to the specific (the Jews) in chap. 2 (e.g., James D. G. Dunn, *Romans 1–8*, WBC 38A [Dallas: Word, 1988], 53; Bruce W. Longenecker, *Eschatology and the Covenant: A Comparison of 4 Ezra and Romans 1–11*, JSNTSup 57 [Sheffield: *JSOT*, 1991], 173; Robert Jewett, *Romans: A Commentary*, Hermeneia [Minneapolis, Minn.: Fortress, 2006], 152). Despite the plausibility of some of these points, most scholars still favor a reference to Gentiles: not only do the language and sins specified—idolatry, immorality, homosexuality— match the ones first-century Jews would typically use in their denunciation of pagans, but also the knowledge of God alluded to in the passage comes solely through natural revelation (Rom. 2:19–20) (e.g., Ernst Käsemann, *Commentary on Romans*, trans. G. W. Bromiley [Grand Rapids, Mich.: Eerdmans, 1980], 33; F. F. Bruce, *The Epistle of Paul to the Romans: An Introduction and Commentary*, 2nd ed., TNTC [Grand Rapids, Mich.: Eerdmans, 1985], 81–2; Joseph A. Fitzmyer, *Romans: A New Translation with Introduction and Commentary*, AB 33 [New York: Doubleday, 1993], 270; Raymond E. Brown, *Introduction to the New Testament*, ABRL [New York: Doubleday, 1997], 566; Arland J. Hultgren, *Paul's Letter to the Romans: A Commentary* [Grand Rapids, Mich.: Eerdmans, 2011], 88; Grant R. Osborne, *Romans: Verse by Verse*, ONTC [Bellingham, Wash.: Lexham, 2017], 37). There is no question, however, that many Jews, especially the Israelites before them, were guilty of the same sins (cf. 2:9, 17–24), and from this perspective Paul's indictment would also to some degree be applicable to them (cf. C. E. B. Cranfield, *The Epistle to the Romans*, ICC, 2 vols. [Edinburgh: T&T Clark, 1975], 1:105–6). Their situation, however, was wholly different and Paul holds them accountable specifically for not having obeyed the revelation they had been given in the law (cf. 2:17–29; cf. vv. 12–13) (Douglas Moo, *The Letter to the Romans*, 2nd ed., NICNT [Grand Rapids, Mich.: Eerdmans, 2018], 108). With regard to Romans 2:1–16, these verses are often understood as a reference to Jews, and so the beginning of the new section that stretches to 3:8. More recently, however, several scholars have concluded that the passage makes more sense as a continuation of the argument in 1:18–32, meaning that Paul's imaginary interlocutor (cf. 2:1–5) is actually a Gentile who felt himself morally superior (see Stanley K. Stowers, *A Rereading of Romans: Justice, Jews, and Gentiles* [New Haven, Conn.: Yale University Press, 1994], 37; Runar M. Thorsteinsson, *Paul's Interlocutor in Romans 2: Function and Identity in the Context of Ancient Epistolography*, ConBNT 40 [Stockholm: Almqvist & Wiksell, 2003], 188–94; Ben Witherington III, *Paul's Letter to the Romans: A Socio-Rhetorical Commentary*, with Darlene Hyatt [Grand Rapids, Mich.: Eerdmans, 2004], 73–7; Frank J. Matera, *Romans*, Paideia [Grand Rapids, Mich.: Baker, 2010], 57–60). As Witherington remarks, in 2:1–16 Paul condemns those who do the same things listed in 1:18–32 (cf. 2:3), refers to "those who sin without the law" (v. 12), which can apply only to Gentiles, and explicitly comments about Gentiles (vv. 14–15; Witherington, *Paul's Letter to the Romans*, 76).

subjectively, as an innate moral sense implanted in their hearts (2:14–15).[3]

NATURAL REVELATION

Paul begins the passage by bringing up the other side of God's saving righteousness just mentioned (Rom. 1:17)—namely, His divine wrath, which "is [also] being revealed" in the present (*apokalyptetai*) "against all ungodliness and unrighteousness of men" (v. 18).[4] The two sides are closely connected, as they represent two inseparable attributes of God—His love and His justice.[5] It has been argued that the revelation of God's wrath, like the revelation of His righteousness, takes place in the preaching of the gospel (v. 16), as it is the cross that shows how abundant God's grace is toward sinners and at the same time how harsh His condemnation of their sins.[6] Despite being theologically true, this interpretation is unlikely on exegetical grounds, as the prepositional phrase *en autō* ("in it"), present in verse 17, is absent here. In this case, rather than having verse 16 as its point of reference, verse 18 explains (introductory *gar*) why only "the one who is righteous by faith shall live."[7]

---

3. It has been argued that those referred to in 2:14–15 are Gentile believers who now have the law written in their hearts as part of the new covenant promise (Jer. 31:33), and who now are able to obey the law's requirements because of the indwelling Spirit (cf. Rom. 8:4) (e.g., Cranfield, *The Epistle to the Romans*, 1:155–159). This is unlikely, however, as Paul's statement in verse 14 that "these, not having the law, are a law to themselves" can hardly be a description of Christians, who also had access to the written law (Craig S. Keener, *Romans*, NCCS [Eugene, Ore.: Cascade, 2009], 45). It has also been argued that the obedience Paul refers to in these verses is merely hypothetical, as only perfect obedience brings righteousness and such obedience is not really possible (e.g., Bruce, *The Epistle of Paul to the Romans*, 90; Frank Thielman, *Theology of the New Testament: A Canonical and Synthetic Approach* [Grand Rapids, Mich.: Zondervan, 2005], 352). As Richard N. Longenecker correctly points out, however, both interpretations entirely miss the point of Paul's argument, which is "that obedient Gentiles shame disobedient Jews" (*The Epistle to the Romans*, NIGTC [Grand Rapids, Mich.: Eerdmans, 2016], 275).

4. All biblical quotations are the author's translation, unless otherwise indicated.

5. Wrath is not the counterpart of love. As James P. Ware explains, love belongs to God's very nature, while wrath is consequent upon human sin and rebellion (cf. Eph. 2:3; 5:6; Col. 3:6). Wrath is the necessary response of a just and holy God to evil (*Paul's Theology in Context: Creation, Incarnation, Covenant, and Kingdom* [Grand Rapids, Mich.: Eerdmans, 2019], 33). Also, Osborne, *Romans*, 38.

6. So, Cranfield, *The Epistle to the Romans*, 1:110; Collin G. Kruse, *Paul's Letter to the Romans*, PNTC (Grand Rapids, Mich.: Eerdmans, 2012), 87.

7. This author supports the adjectival reading of *ek pisteōs* ("by faith") in the sentence *ho de dikaios ek pisteōs zēsetai* ("but the one who is *righteous by faith* shall live"), rather than the adverbial one ("but the one who is righteous *shall live by faith*") for the following reasons: (1) the immediate context (1:16) talks about righteousness by faith; (2) the larger context (3:21—4:25) emphasizes righteousness by faith; (3) other passages in Romans

The end of verse 18, which summarizes the whole section, points in the direction that Paul's argument now moves. God's wrath is being inflicted upon those "who by their unrighteousness suppress [*katechō*] the truth." The implication is that the truth was made manifest to them, and yet they did not respond as they should. The compound verb *katechō*, which prefixes the preposition *kata* to *echō*, means to hinder something by hiding or removing it from sight.[8] In this passage, it describes a continuous (present tense), deliberate (active voice) action. In what follows (1:19–21), Paul makes three basic points concerning the truth he is talking about: (1) it refers to "what can be known about God" (*to gnōston tou theou*)—that is, to "His invisible attributes" (*ta aorata autou*) that are further specified as "His eternal power and divine nature" (*hē . . . aidios autou dynamis kai theiotēs*); (2) such attributes have been "clearly seen" (*kathoraō*) and "understood" (*noeō*) by all humans "since the creation of the world" (*apo ktiseōs kosmou*); and (3) the medium through which God has made those attributes "known to them" (*autois ephanerōsen*)[9] is exactly "the things that have been made" (*ta poiēma*).

Despite some difficulties Paul's language entails,[10] there is no question that he conceives the universe (*kosmos*) as having been

---

affirm righteousness by faith (4:11, 13; 5:1; 9:30; 10:6); and (4) Galatians 3:11 uses the same Habakkuk quotation (Hab. 2:4b) as a proof text for righteousness by faith (i.e., against righteousness by works of the law). See Hultgren, *Paul's Letter to the Romans*, 78–9.

8. BDAG 532–3.

9. On the semantic equivalence between *apokalyptō* in verses 17–18 and *phaneroō* in verse 19, see L&N 28.36, 38.

10. The terms *kathoraō* and *theiotēs* occur only here in the entire NT, while *aidios* and *poiēma* each occur twice, the other occurrences being, respectively, in Jude 1:6 and Ephesians 2:10. The precise meaning of *kathoraō* is disputed. It derives from *horaō* ("to see") and the preposition *kata*, which in this case serves to intensify the verb, thus the translation "clearly seen." The verb *horaō* is also the root of the subject of the sentence, *ta aorata* ("invisible things/attributes"). Though in Greek literature *kathoraō* is sometimes used in the sense of inward or intellectual perception (BDAG 493), Cranfield argues that the deliberate oxymoron in verse 20 (*ta aorata . . . kathoratai*) requires *kathoraō* to denote "physical sight" (*The Epistle to the Romans*, 1:115). The verb *noeō*, in turn, goes beyond physical sight and denotes the ability "to grasp or comprehend someth[ing] on the basis of careful thought" (BDAG 674). It is used thirteen other times in the NT always expressing some type of comprehension or understanding (Matt. 15:17; 16:9, 11; 24:15; Mark 7:18; 8:17; 13:14; John 12:40; Eph. 3:4, 20; 1 Tim. 1:7; 2 Tim. 2:7; Heb. 11:3). Paul's phrase *nooumena kathorai*, therefore, would convey both ideas: external observation of data and inner apprehension of that data—similar to the use of *horaō* and *noeō* in Matthew 24:15, Mark 13:14, and John 12:40 (Longenecker, *The Epistle to the Romans*, 208). With regard to syntax, the adverbial participle *nooumena* preceding *kathoratai* could express the reason God's attributes have been clearly seen—"*because they are perceived* through the things that have been made"—or, more likely, the manner through which they have been clearly seen—"*being*

created by God at a specific point in time. Neither Paul nor any other NT writer ever entertains a different creation concept other than the one found in the Hebrew Scriptures. In the NT the *ktisis* ("creation") word group (*ktistēs*, "Creator"; *ktisma*, "creature"; *ktizō*, "to create") always refers to God's creation.[11] The noun *poiēma* in Romans 1:20 also denotes "that which is made" (cf. Eph. 2:10). In Jewish and early Christian literature, this term is frequently used "of the works of divine creation."[12] The related verb is *poieō* ("to make"), which is rather common both in the LXX and in the NT to describe God's creating (e.g., Gen. 1:1, 7, 16, 21, 25–27, 31; 2:2, 4; Pss. 94:5 [95:5 LXX]; 95:5 [96:5 LXX]; Isa. 41:20; 42:5; 2 Macc. 7:28; Mark 10:6; Acts 4:24; 17:26; Rom. 9:20; Heb. 1:2, 7; Rev. 14:7).[13] About the temporal aspect of creation, Paul conveys this idea through the prepositional phrase *apo ktiseōs kosmou* ("from the creation of the world"), which also occurs elsewhere in the NT (Mark 10:6; 13:19; 2 Pet. 3:4; cf. Matt. 19:4). This phrase always designates time, though it also portrays creation as a finished product. The same applies to two other parallel NT expressions: *apo katabolēs kosmou* ("from the foundation of the world"; Matt. 13:35; 25:34; Luke 11:50; Heb. 4:3; 9:26; Rev. 13:8; 17:8)[14] and *ap'archēs kosmou* ("from the beginning of the world"; Matt. 24:21).[15]

---

understood through the things that have been made" (cf. NASB, NIV, NKJV, NRSV) (see Jewett, *Romans*, 155). As for the noun *kosmos*, the reference certainly transcends this world as the dwelling place of humans (e.g., Rom. 1:8; 4:13; 1 Tim. 1:15) to encompass the entire universe (e.g., Acts 17:4; Eph. 1:4; Phil. 2:5; BDAG 561–63).

11. Moisés Silva sees 1 Peter 2:13 as an exception to this rule ("*ktizō*," *NIDNTT* 2:758–66). This, however, does not enjoy broad consent. See, for example, W. Foerster, "*ktizō*," *TDNT* 3:1034–5; J. N. D. Kelly, *The Epistles of Peter and Jude*, BNTC (Peabody, Mass.: Hendrickson, 1969), 108; Peter H. Davids, *The First Epistle of Peter*, NICNT (Grand Rapids, Mich.: Eerdmans, 1990), 98–9; John H. Elliott, *1 Peter*, AB 37B (New Haven, Conn.: Yale University Press, 2007), 489.

12. BDAG 842.

13. In the creation narrative of Genesis (1:1—2:4), the LXX uses *poieō* to render both *'āśāh* (e.g., Gen. 1:7, 25–26) and *bārā'* (1:1, 21, 27). The same equivalence is found in Isaiah 41–45 (Moisés Silva, "*poieō*," *NIDNTT* 4:77–81). It should be noted that the Hebrew verb *bārā'*, which is also rendered in the LXX as *ktizō* ("to create"), though less frequently and never in Genesis, is used in the OT only for God's creative actions (W. Foerster, "*ktizō*," *TDNT* 3:1008).

14. In Matthew 13:35, the word *kosmou* is textually suspect, but the meaning remains the same. The NT also uses *pro katabolēs kosmou* ("before the foundation of the world"; John 17:24; Eph. 1:4; 1 Pet. 1:20), which, irrespective of the subject matter, also underscores the historical beginning of God's creation. "Both phrases [*apo/pro katabolēs kosmou*] are attested so far only in the NT and in texts dependent upon it" (O. Hoffius, "*katabolē*," *EDNT* 2:255–6).

15. There is also *ap'archēs* ("from the beginning"; Matt. 19:4, 8; John 8:44; 1 John 3:8), though the reference is not so much to the creation of the universe as it is to the beginning

Most importantly, however, is the role Paul assigns to creation; it is this role that legitimizes the disclosure of God's wrath. In Romans 1:20 Paul claims that the created things in the universe plainly testify of the existence of a personal and powerful Creator ("His eternal power and divine nature").[16] Regardless of its precise scope, this claim is not to be taken in absolute terms, since Paul knows, on one hand, that God's essential being will always remain far beyond human grasp (Rom. 11:33–36; Eph. 1:19; 4:6; 1 Tim. 1:17) and, on the other, that God has provided further and more specific revelations about Himself (Rom. 16:25–26; Eph. 1:3–10; 3:1–3, 7–11; Col. 1:25–28; cf. Heb. 1:1–3). Yet, he does say that God can be known through creation. "Creation is a visible disclosure of the invisible God, an intelligible disclosure of the otherwise unknown God."[17] In theological terms, Paul is defending the concept of natural revelation—not to be confused with natural theology, which is the attempt to prove the existence and attributes of God through observation of nature and the use of human reason, without appealing to any divine revelation. The natural theology concept goes back to classic Greek philosophy (e.g., Plato) and also existed in some Jewish circles in Paul's time. Philo, for example, believed that by contemplating nature a person could (mentally) ascend to heaven and form a conjectural conception of God through reason.[18] Space precludes full discussion of this matter here; suffice it to say that, for Paul, "what can be known about God" has been made known by God Himself (Rom. 1:19), instead of being the result of human observation and reasoning.[19] Hence, it is even more true that the Gentiles were "without excuse" (v. 20). They "knew God," and yet "they did not glorify/honor him as God." Instead, "they became futile in their thinking, and their

---

of human history—whether or not both occurred at the same point in time (the supposed time interval between Gen. 1:1–2 and the following verses) is not relevant to our purposes here. In John's letters, *ap'archēs* is also used in connection to the beginning of the gospel events and message (1 John 1:1; 2:7, 13, 14; 2:24; 3:11; 2 John 1:5, 6).

16. This is a recurrent theme in Scripture (Job 36:22–25; Pss. 8:1, 3; 19:1–6; 104:1–32; 139:14; Isa. 6:3; 40:26; cf. Acts 14:17; 17:24–27) and in extrabiblical Jewish literature (Wis. 13:1–9; *Sib. Or.* 3.15–16).

17. John R. W. Stott, *Romans: God's Good News for the World* (Downers Grove, Ill.: InterVarsity, 1994), 73.

18. Philo, *Praem.* 7.43. For discussion of relevant texts both Greco-Roman and Jewish, see Charles H. Talbert, *Romans*, SHBC (Macon: Smyth & Helwys, 2002), 59–62, 72–73. For a Christian approach to natural theology, see Alister E. McGrath, *Re-Imagining Nature: The Promise of a Christian Natural Theology* (Chichester: Wiley & Sons, 2016).

19. Markus Bockmuehl, *Jewish Law in Gentile Churches: Halakhah and the Beginning of Christian Public Ethics* (Edinburgh: T&T Clark, 2000), 130.

foolish hearts were darkened" (v. 21 ESV). Whatever they knew about God, it was enough to condemn them.[20] Some ancient philosophers (e.g., Socrates, the Stoics) thought that true knowledge leads to godliness.[21] So did Paul (cf. 1 Cor. 15:34; Eph. 1:17; 4:1; Phil. 1:9–10; esp. Col. 1:9–10; Titus 1:1). And it is exactly because knowledge did not lead (Gentiles) to godliness (cf. *asebeia* in Rom. 1:18) that knowledge is now grounds for (their) indictment.[22]

ARGUMENT FROM DESIGN

The idea of divine design in nature was well known in antiquity.[23] It seems to have been first advocated by Diogenes of Apollonias in the fifth century BC[24] and further developed by the Stoics during (and after) the last three centuries prior to the NT era. In fact, this was the standard view. A dissenting voice was that of the Atomists (e.g., Epicurus, Lucretius), so called because they maintained that everything that exists, life included, is the result of the random collision of atoms.[25] Most Greco-Roman intellectuals, however, rejected any nontheistic or naturalistic explanations for the origin of the universe. Though there was no agreement on how creation occurred, the belief that the world was created by a divine agency and that purpose and design are inherent to creation dominated the scene. It

---

20. Similarly, Wis. 13:8–9; 2 Bar. 54.17–19; *Sib. Or.* 3.8–45.

21. For an introductory discussion, see Mark McPherran, "Socrates and Plato," and Tad Brennan, "The Stoics," both in *Ancient Philosophy of Religion*, vol. 1 of *The History of Western Philosophy of Religion*, ed. Graham Oppy and N. N. Trakakis (New York: Routledge, 2009), resp. 53–78, 105–18.

22. See also Ephesians 1:17; 4:1; Colossians 1:9–11. There is a question of whether the infinitive *peripatēsai* ("to walk") at the beginning of Colossians 1:10 indicates result or purpose. Either way, the passage clearly links the knowledge of God's will with appropriate conduct. See Scot McKnight, *The Letter to the Colossians*, NICNT (Grand Rapids, Mich.: Eerdmans, 2018), 115.

23. See esp. David Sedley, *Creationism and Its Critics in Antiquity*, SCL 66 (Berkeley, Calif.: University of California Press, 2007). Additional studies include: Arnold Ehrhardt, *The Beginning: A Study in the Greek Philosophical Approach to the Concept of Creation from Anaximander to St. John* (Manchester: Manchester University Press, 1968); Robert W. Sharples, "Threefold Providence: The History and Background of a Doctrine," *Ancient Approaches to Plato's Timaeus*, Bulletin of the Institute of Classical Studies, Supplement, 78 (London: University of London, 2003), 107–27; Andrew Gregory, *Ancient Greek Cosmogony* (London: Duckworth, 2007), 140–202; and Mary-Jane Rubenstein, *Worlds without End: The Many Lives of the Multiverse* (New York: Columbia University Press, 2014), 40–69.

24. Sedley, *Creationism and Its Critics in Antiquity*, 75–8. I am indebted to Sedley, as well as to Keener (*Romans*, 32–3), for some of the following references. See also Cedric Vine, "Greco-Roman Creation Accounts and the New Testament," 31, in this volume.

25. On Atomism, see Sedley, *Creationism and Its Critics in Antiquity*, 133–66.

was argued, for example, that the complex structure of things, from small organisms to celestial systems, indicates design, not chance,[26] and that design is even more evident in the case of human beings, their anatomy, skills, and especially their intellect.[27] For many philosophers, human intellect, in all its intricacy and potentiality, cannot be properly explained apart from design.[28] They also exalted the astonishing beauty and harmony of the universe as elements of divine contemplation, affirming that the deity is present in and can be known through his works, provided that we possess the faculty of seeing and a grateful disposition.[29] In language that resembles that of Paul, some even acknowledged that the deity, yet "invisible [*atheōrētos*] to all mortal nature, . . . is seen [*theōreitai*] through his works."[30] And, like Paul, they also insisted that one can learn much about the deity's (or the deities') attributes from creation, particularly his (or their) care for people.[31]

It is obvious that the Stoics' theology of creation cannot be equated with that of Paul,[32] notwithstanding the more monotheistic outlook of some philosophers (cf. Acts 17:23).[33] Even if it could, it is

---

26. Epictetus, *Disc.* 1.6.7; and Cicero, *Nat. d.* 2.34–35. In the second century AD, scientist and philosopher Galen would maintain, for example, that all the anatomical decisions of the creator were, without a single exception, not only intelligent and good, but the best possible decisions he could have made (*On the Usefulness of Parts* 2.154–162).

27. Cicero, *Nat. d.* 2.58–61; Seneca, *Ben.* 6.23.6–7; and Epictetus, *Disc.* 1.6.14–15; cf. Cicero, *Fin.* 5.12.35–36 (cf. *Let. Aris.* 156–157).

28. Cicero, *Nat. d.* 2.59, 61; and Porphyry, *Marc.* 26.410–11. Criticism of those who did not recognize divine providence in nature could become rather harsh, even ludicrous at times. "Amazing shamelessness and stupidity!" exclaims Epictetus (*Disc.* 1.16.8). See also Cicero's caustic description of the Epicureans (*Nat. d.* 1.43) or his satirical argument of an epic poem being randomly produced by gold molds of the alphabet letters thrown together into some receptacle and then shaken out on to the ground (*Nat. d.* 2.37).

29. See Epictetus, *Disc.* 1.6.1–2, 23–24 (cf. Josephus, *C. Ap.* 2.190, 192).

30. Pseudo-Aristotle, *Mund.* 399b. Similarly, Epictetus, *Disc.* 1.6.19: "God has introduced man to be a spectator of god and of his works." Epictetus emphasizes that both "the visible things and the faculty of seeing" demonstrate the creator, and criticizes those who, "being blinded to the giver," do not acknowledge their benefactor.

31. The same Pseudo-Aristotle claims that, by observing "the whole ordering of life" in the universe, "we must think of god, who in might is most powerful, in beauty most fair, in time immortal, in virtue supreme" (*Mund.* 399b). Cf. Paul's speech on the Areopagus, Acts 17:22–31.

32. The Stoics believed, for example, that god (or the intelligent cause of the world) was nothing but a divinity immanent in the world, which makes the world itself a divine living being (e.g., Seneca, *Ep.* 65.2; cf. Sedley, *Creationism and Its Critics in Antiquity*, 209–10). Some also argued that the divine nature must be spherical because this is the perfect shape (Cicero, *Nat. d.* 2.17).

33. Most Greeks and Romans were polytheists, but many Stoic philosophers came to believe in one main god above all others. See, for example, Diogenes Laertius 7.1.134 (cf. Heraclitus in Diogenes Laertius 9.1.1). Michael Frede explains: "The Platonists, the

not within our power to determine whether or not Paul's indictment of Gentiles applied to the Stoics. That it did not necessarily apply to *all* Gentiles seems clear from Romans 2:6–11, according to which, as James Dunn points out, "Jews as well as Gentiles will be counted among 'those who do evil,' just as Gentiles as well as Jews will be counted among 'those who do good.'"[34] And in verses 14–15, Paul explicitly says that *some* Gentiles (*ethnē* without the article),[35] despite not knowing the law, do comply with the basic tenets of the law (*ta tou nomou*). They do this, he explains, "by nature" (*physei*),[36] due to their having that which the law requires (*to ergon tou nomou*) inscribed on their hearts (v. 15a), something that can be the work of only the Creator Himself.[37] That is, for Paul, as well as for some philosophers of his time, humans have an innate sense of morality[38] and

---

Peripatetics, and the Stoics do not just believe in one highest god, they believe in something which they must take to be unique even as a god. For they call it 'god' or even '*the* god,' as if in some crucial way it was the only thing which deserved to be called 'god' [e.g., Plotinus, *Enn.* 6.8.19; cf. lines 1, 6]. If, thus, they also believe that there are further beings which can be called 'divine' or 'god,' they must have thought that these further beings could be called 'divine' only in some less strict, diminished, or derived sense" ("Monotheism and Pagan Philosophy in Late Antiquity," in *Pagan Monotheism in Pagan Antiquity*, ed. Polymnia Athanassiadi and Michael Frede [Oxford: Oxford University Press, 1999], 43).

34. Dunn, *Romans 1–8*, 104.

35. John D. Harvey, *Exegetical Guide to the Greek New Testament: Romans* (Grand Rapids, Mich.: Baker, 2017), 60.

36. Though some interpreters think that the dative *physei* modifies the preceding participial phrase ("Gentiles who *by nature* do not have the law") (e.g., Cranfield, *The Epistle to the Romans*, 1:156; and Jewett, *Romans*, 214), important syntactical considerations have convinced others, including all major translations (ESV, NASB, NIV, NJB, NKJV, NRSV), that it modifies the main verb that follows ("do *by nature* things required by the law"; e.g., Dunn, *Romans 1–8*, 98; Witherington, *Paul's Letter to the Romans*, 82; Longenecker, *The Epistle to the Romans*, 274–75; Moo, *The Letter to the Romans*, 159–60; see also A. Andrew Das, *Paul, the Law, and the Covenant* [Grand Rapids, Mich.: Baker, 2001], 178–82).

37. Klyne R. Snodgrass is correct in tying this natural sense of morality to the activity of the Holy Spirit ("Justification by Grace—to the Doers: An Analysis of the Place of Romans 2 in the Theology of Paul," *NTS* 32 [1986]: 81). Even if the Spirit is God's special gift in the new covenant era (e.g., Isa. 44:3–4; Ezek. 11:19–20; 36:26–27; Joel 2:28–29; cf. Acts 2:32–33, 38–39; 19:2; 2 Cor. 3:6; Eph. 1:13–14), it is precarious to deny that the Spirit was active before that, even among Gentiles (cf. Gen. 6:3; Exod. 14:3; Jon. 3:5).

38. Greco-Roman philosophers also conceived in a variety of ways a moral law that could be understood through nature. Socrates, for example, speaks of "unwritten laws" that are common everywhere, such as that children should "honor parents" (Xenophon, *Mem.* 4.4.19). Aristotle refers to laws based on nature that never change (*Rhet.* 1.15.6), and Cicero defines a law of nature as "a kind of innate instinct," which includes religion, gratitude, retaliation, reverence, and truth (*Inv.* 2.22.65; 2.53.161). Seneca praises the qualities that are naturally found in every human person. "Nature bestows upon us all this immense advantage," he says, "that the light of virtue shines into the minds of all alike; even those who do not follow her, behold her" (*Ben.* 4.17.4). For additional examples, see Jacqueline A. Laing and Russell Wilcox, eds., *The Natural Law Reader* (Chichester: Blackwell, 2014), 11–79.

those (Gentiles) who conform themselves to it will be reckoned as righteous by God (cf. Rom. 2:13, 26–27; also Peter in Acts 10:34–35).[39] In relation to this, however, four observations are in order: (1) in 2:14–15, Paul is not talking about God's will as expressed in the Mosaic law, and thus he cannot be referring to the same kind of obedience that is required from both Jews and Christians;[40] (2) Paul's argument here is not to be understood within the framework of his faith-versus-works discussion, which presupposes acquaintance with the Mosaic law (cf. Acts 13:38–39; Rom. 3:20, 28; 10:1–4; etc.); (3) the obedience Paul has in mind (in the context of Romans 1–2) is but a reverent response to the knowledge of God attained through natural revelation,[41] which means it would to some extent be equivalent to "the obedience that comes from faith" (Rom. 1:5 NIV) as the intended result of the gospel message (cf. Eph. 2:10; Titus 2:12) and the inner work of the Holy Spirit (cf. Rom. 8:4, 13; Gal. 5:16);[42] and (4) Paul never assumes that such obedience is perfect, as he recognizes an inner struggle on the part of those morally responsive Gentiles (Rom. 2:15–16), meaning they are still sinners (cf. 3:9–19, 23) and their final salvation will still rest on a knowledge of God and His grace made possible through Jesus Christ (3:23; 5:10, 18–21; 2 Cor. 5:18–19; Titus 2:11).

APOSTASY AND PUNISHMENT

Paul's concern in Romans 1:18–32, however, is not those Gentiles who lived up to the knowledge they had but rather those who did not. After mentioning their rejection of God's self-revelation through

---

39. So, Dunn, *Romans 1–8*, 98–106; C. K. Barrett, *A Commentary on the Epistle to the Romans*, 2nd ed., BNTC (London: Black, 1991), 41–52, 58; Terence L. Donaldson, *Paul and the Gentiles: Remapping the Apostle's Convictional World* (Minneapolis: Fortress, 1997), 146–7; Mark A. Seifrid, "Natural Revelation and the Purpose of the Law in Romans," *TynBul* 49 (1998): 115–29; Bockmuehl, *Jewish Law in Gentile Churches*, 131; Troels Engberg-Pedersen, *Paul and the Stoics* (Louisville, Ky.: WJK, 2000), 203; Hultgren, *Paul's Letter to the Romans*, 117–18; Osborne, *Romans*, 64–5. For arguments that 2:14–15 can hardly refer to Gentile Christians or that the obedience Paul has in mind is but merely hypothetical, see n. 2 above in the present study.

40. Longenecker, *The Epistle to the Romans*, 274–76.

41. See Dunn, who argues that doing what the law requires, when the law itself is unknown, is possible only when the knowledge of God (Rom. 1:19, 21) "is the basis of conduct" (*Romans 1–8*, 98–9).

42. So, the common discussion of whether Paul believes that Gentiles who do not know the gospel will be justified by works (e.g., Thomas Schreiner, "Did Paul Believe in Justification by Works? Another Look in Romans 2," *BBR* 3 [1993]: 131–58) does not really seem appropriate.

nature (vv. 19–21), he goes on to describe the devastating results of their apostasy (vv. 22–27). Paul builds his argument around a three-fold repetition of two key verbs: *allassō* (or *metallassō*, "to exchange") in verses 23, 25, and 26b, and *paradidōmi* ("to give over") in verses 24, 26a, and 28. In each instance, the Gentiles deliberately put away the truth about God and replaced it with their own perverted notions and practices, thus supporting the verdict that they were "without excuse" (v. 20). As a result, God sentences them to their own sinful ways. The argument can be structured as such:

1. The Gentiles "exchanged [*ēllaxan*] the glory of the immortal God for images of mortal creatures" (v. 23). Therefore, God "gave [them] over" (*paredōken*) to their "lustful desires to dishonor their own bodies among themselves" (v. 24).
2. They "exchanged" (*metēllaxan*) God's truth for idolatrous worship (v. 25). Therefore, God "gave [them] over" (*paredōken*) to "degrading passions" (v. 26).
3. They "exchanged" (*metēllaxan*) natural relations for unnatural (vv. 26b–27). And just as they did not acknowledge God, He "gave [them] over" (*paredōken*) to a worthless mind and indecent behavior (v. 28).

Arland J. Hultgren argues that the pattern is to be taken not as a sequence of steps but as one dynamic process of rebellion expressed in three different ways.[43] Yet, it would be preferable to say that for Paul the fall into idolatry is the cause of the sinful behavior he mentions, all the more so because the whole point is exactly the Gentiles' unwillingness to acknowledge God (cf. vv. 20–21).[44] In this passage, Paul draws from biblical texts and extrabiblical traditions. In the OT, idolatry—in this case, of Israel—is already described in terms of an exchange (cf. *allassō* in Ps. 105:20 [106:20 LXX] and Jer. 2:11 LXX). Also, that which the Gentiles substituted for the true God—birds, animals, and reptiles (Rom. 1:23; cf. v. 25)—corresponds to the threefold division in the animal kingdom of the creation account (Gen. 1:20, 24, 26; cf. Deut. 4:16–18). And the tracing of the pagans' moral sins to idolatry is plainly taught in Second Temple Jewish

---

43. Hultgren, *Paul's Letter to the Romans*, 93.

44. Witherington, *Paul's Letter to the Romans*, 68. Similarly, C. K. Beale: "Paul sees idolatry to be the root of and the essence of sin" (*A New Testament Biblical Theology: The Unfolding of the Old Testament in the New* [Grand Rapids, Mich.: Baker, 2011], 370).

literature. Wisdom of Solomon, for example, reads, "The idea of making idols was the origin of fornication [*porneia*], their discovery corrupted life" (14:12 NJB). Later in the same chapter it adds, "The worship of idols with no name is the beginning, cause, and end of every evil" (v. 27 NJB; cf. vv. 16, 22–26), and Paul also provides a broad list of sins that originate from human renunciation of God (Rom. 1:29–31; cf. Eph. 4:19).

God's response to the Gentiles' defiant apostasy is expressed as a giving over (*paradidōmi*). In the LXX, this verb is frequently used for God delivering rebellious Israel into the hands of their enemies (e.g., Judg. 2:14; 6:13; Ps. 105:41 [106:41 LXX]; Jer. 32:4).[45] In Romans, God delivers wicked Gentiles to their own wicked ways. It has been suggested that this is to be understood as a mere acquiescence on God's part, a tacit assent to let people follow the course of their sinful inclinations.[46] The context, however, suggests a positive act of judgment whereby God condemns them to the very sins they embrace.[47] This would explain Paul's reference in 1:18 to God's wrath as being revealed (*apokalyptetai*) in the present time, which is to be distinguished from the definitive, irrevocable infliction of the divine wrath in the future (cf. 2:5, 8; 3:5; 4:15; 5:9; 9:22; 12:19; Col. 3:6; 1 Thess. 1:10). The wrath that is now at work, says Douglas Moo, is the giving over "of human beings to their chosen way of sin and all its consequences."[48] The concept echoes Wisdom of Solomon: "In return for their foolish and wicked thoughts, which led them astray to worship irrational serpents and worthless animals, you sent upon them a multitude of irrational creatures to punish them, so that they might learn that one is punished by the very things by which one sins" (11:15–16 NRSV). The reference is to the Egyptians at the time of Exodus. God afflicted them with the very creatures they worshiped—the instrument of sin becoming the instrument of punishment (cf. Wis. 12:23, 27a; 16:1; 18:4). Paul's argument seems to imply a vicious circle (cf. Rom. 1:21c–d, 24, 28b–c). The more

---

45. The formula *paradidōmi eis (tas) cheiras* or *en (tē) cheiri* ("deliver into the hand[s]") occurs in the LXX over 120 times (esp. in Joshua and Judges). "The subj. of the vb. is almost always God, and in practically every case it implies handing over to ruin, to defeat, to annihilation, to death" (Moisés Silva, "*paradidōmi*," *NIDNTT*, 3:622–3).

46. So, Wiard Popkes, "*paradidōmi*," *EDNT* 3:20; and Osborne, *Romans*, 43.

47. "God is not the initiator," Michael P. Middendorf remarks, "humanity's act, 'exchanged,' came first (1:23)" (*Romans 1–8*, ConcC [Saint Louis, Mo.: Concordia, 2013], 132).

48. Moo, *The Letter to the Romans*, 112.

humans delved into sin, the more their senses were corrupted, thus requiring additional levels of satisfaction to quench their passions. And so the more they sinned, the more they were punished with sin.

HOMOSEXUAL RELATIONS

Paul focuses on homosexuality, which he sees as a major deviation from God's creative purpose. One of the many sexual practices Jewish people often denounced as typical of Gentile behavior,[49] same-sex relations were rather common in ancient Greco-Roman societies,[50] though there were some critics as well, notably among the Stoics.[51] Paul refers to such relations as "unnatural" or "contrary

---

49. For Jewish parallels connecting idolatry to sexual perversions, see *Sib. Or.* 3.8–44, 586–600; 4.24–39; *T. Jos.* 4.5–6; *T. Naph.* 3.3–4; and Wis. 14:22–28. For additional texts and comments, see William Loader, *The Pseudepigrapha on Sexuality: Attitudes Towards Sexuality in Apocalypses, Testaments, Legends, Wisdom, and Related Literature*, with a contribution by Ibolya Balla (Grand Rapids, Mich.: Eerdmans, 2011); idem, *Philo, Josephus, and the Testaments on Sexuality: Attitudes Towards Sexuality in the Writings of Philo and Josephus and in the Testaments of the Twelve Patriarchs* (Grand Rapids, Mich.: Eerdmans, 2011). Also useful is William Loader, *The Septuagint, Sexuality, and the New Testament: Case Studies on the Impact of the LXX in Philo and the New Testament* (Grand Rapids, Mich.: Eerdmans, 2004).

50. Among Greeks, there was a widespread and long-established acceptance of homosexual relations, especially during the transition from childhood to adulthood. The practice of older men mentoring the youth quite often turned into a sexual relationship. Since it was a basic form of homoerotic affectivity between adult men and boys, it was known as pederasty (Gk. *paiderastia*, "love for boys"). In some circles, this relationship was even held as essential for personal development and society cohesion, though it was expected to stop once the young men reached marrying age, around thirty, which means it would normally not conflict with the pursuit of a heterosexual marriage. Homosexual activity between men, as well as between women, was sometimes justified on the grounds of being preordained by the gods or by the zodiac sign. Roman law (*Lex Scantinia*) criminalized sexual assaults (*stuprum*) against a freeborn male minor, but it seems to have also been used to prosecute adult male citizens who willingly took the passive role in homosexual relations; they were thought to lack *virtus*, the quality that distinguished a man (*vir*). Roman virility was not compromised in the case of sex with males of lower status, such as slaves or foreigners, provided that the Roman citizen took the active (penetrating) role. With the Roman emperors, of course, things were different, as they were not just above the law, they *were* the law. Nero, for example, in addition to having married three wives (Claudia Octavia, Poppaea Sabina, and Statilia Messalina) and a young former male slave (Sporus), is also reported to have played the role of *wife* to two husbands (Doryphoros and Pythagoras). Suetonius (*Nero* 26–35) and Cassius Dio (*Hist. rom.* 62.28—63.13) tell about this (cf. Dio Chrysostom, *Disc.* 21.6–8). See Craig A. Williams, *Roman Homosexuality*, 2nd ed. (Oxford: Oxford University Press, 2010), 96–104, 279–86. For texts, both Greek and Roman, see Thomas K. Hubbard, ed., *Homosexuality in Greece and Rome: A Sourcebook of Basic Documents* (Berkeley, Calif.: University of California Press, 2003); and Jennifer Larson, *Greek and Roman Sexualities: A Sourcebook* (London: Bloomsbury, 2012). For additional discussions, see Marilyn B. Skinner, *Sexuality in Greek and Roman Culture*, 2nd ed. (Oxford: Blackwell, 2014), and the several articles in Craig A. Williams, ed., *A Companion to Greek and Roman Sexualities* (Oxford: Blackwell, 2014).

51. Socrates, for example, condemns a man who runs after girlish boys (Plato, *Phaed.*, 239c) and compares him to a pig scratching himself against stones (Xenophon, *Mem.*,

to nature" (*para physin*; Rom. 1:26), at the same time that he describes sexual relations between a man and a woman as "natural" (*physikos*) (v. 27). The choice of words is not without significance. It matches the overall emphasis on creation in the argument and accounts for the singling out of homosexuality from among all other sexual sins. Paul understands the male-female relationship of the Genesis creation story (Gen. 2:24) to be normative for humans. And this is something that can be grasped simply from observation of human anatomy and procreative function. So, even if the Gentiles did not have the benefit of Moses's writings, Robert Gagnon correctly indicates that "same-sex intercourse represents one of the clearest instances of conscious suppression of revelation in nature by gentiles, inasmuch as it involves denying clear anatomical gender differences and functions."[52] This explains Paul's strong stance on homosexual activity.[53] It all goes back to the same point: "Although

---

1.2.30). Plato, who first believed that homoerotic relationship between an older and a younger man was noble and essential for personal development (*Symp.* 211b; cf. Xenophon, *Symp.* 8.23), came in later works to argue that sex was only for procreation and that inter-male or inter-female sexual relationship was contrary to nature (*Leg.* 838e–39a). Diodorus of Sicily refers to heterosexual intercourse between man and woman as natural (32.10.4–9). Cicero castigates Roman citizens who accept the passive role in a homoerotic relation (*Phil.* 2.44–45). Seneca despises the sexual exploitation of slaves (*Ep.* 47.7). Plutarch defends heterosexual marriage and considers pederastic relationship as against nature (*Amat.* 751c–e). And Ovid argues that no man should lessen his status to that of a woman and be penetrated by another, and that inter-female sexual relations do not occur even in the animal world (*Metam.* 9.728–34; cf. *Am.* 2.683–84). Some of these examples are taken from Martti Nissinen, *Homoeroticism in the Biblical World: A Historical Perspective*, trans. Kirsi Stjerna (Minneapolis, Mo.: Fortress, 2004), 79–88.

52. Robert A. J. Gagnon, *The Bible and Homosexual Practice: Texts and Hermeneutics* (Nashville, Tenn.: Abingdon, 2001), 264. Among the Stoics, Cicero (*Fin.* 3.62) and Hierocles (502.15–20) maintain that "nature intends human beings to reproduce and that the shape of the genitals indicates this goal, but they also argue that friendship is the primary goal of sexual activity, quite apart from its reproductive function" (Kathy L. Gaca, *The Making of Fornication: Eros, Ethics, and Political Reform in Greek Philosophy and Early Christianity* [Berkeley, Calif.: University of California Press, 2003], 97). Assuming that passion could harm the soul of the offspring, some authors came to advocate that sexual intercourse should be limited to procreative purposes. This was the case, for example, of Plato in his later writings (*Leg.* 838e–39a; cf. 636c), though after some years of marriage, when the couple has produced the requisite number of children (ideally two, one of each sex) or exceeded the main age for reproduction (averaging about ten years), moderate non-procreative sexual activity is permissible (*Leg.* 784e–85a). Musonius (*Lect.* 13a) and Seneca (*Frag.* 27, 84; in Jerome, *Ep. Jov.* 1.49) favor sexual relations only within marriage and for the sole purpose of producing children. See discussion by Gaca, *The Making of Fornication*, 59–93.

53. Commenting on Romans 1:26–27, Jewett quotes Bernadette J. Brooten (*Love between Women: Early Christian Responses to Female Homoeroticism* [Chicago: Chicago University Press, 1996], 241) to argue that "it is clear . . . that 'natural intercourse means penetration of a subordinate person by a dominant one,' a female by a male" (*Romans*, 176). In view of the reciprocity and symmetry conveyed in 1 Corinthians 7:2–4, however, it is unlikely that Paul would have shared the hierarchical understanding of marital sex that was common in his

they knew God, they did not honor [*doxazō*] him as God or give thanks [*eucharisteō*] to him, but they became futile in their thinking, and their foolish hearts were darkened. Claiming to be wise, they became fools" (Rom. 1:21–22 ESV).

RECENT INTERPRETATIONS

Some have tried to interpret Paul's statements as if the people being condemned are heterosexuals engaging in sexual activity that is contrary to their nature.[54] It is doubtful, however, that Paul would hold such a customized notion of nature. When read in light of the immediate context, as well as of the OT and other contemporary Jewish polemics against Gentile vice, it becomes readily evident that the terms *physis* and *physikos* refer to the natural order as God made it.[55] In addition, the reference to "male" (*arsēn*) and "female" (*thēlys*) in verses 26–27 most likely "is intended to reflect the creation of

---

days, as if sex were "the husband's privilege and the wife's obligation" (Gordon D. Fee, *The First Epistle to the Corinthians*, rev. ed., NICNT [Grand Rapids, Mich.: Eerdmans, 2014], 311). On another note, this passage also lends some support, yet incidental, to the idea of a divinely established pattern for marriage. By rejecting the Corinthians' suggestion of abstinence within marriage as a solution to sexual immorality (1 Cor. 7:1; cf. 6:12–20), Paul emphasizes the mutual indebtedness that exists between married couples, and in so doing he speaks of marriage as about a male husband (*anēr*) and a female wife (*gynē*). This does not seem to be without a reason. Roy E. Ciampa and Brian S. Rosner also argue that Paul's use of the plural *porneias* ("sexual immoralities") in Romans 7:2 would comprise all sexual offenses that he speaks against in chapters 5–7; namely, incest (5:1), adultery, homosexuality (6:9), prostitution (vv. 15–16), and presumably premarital sex, which Paul sees as a possible temptation for some (7:9; 36–37) (*The First Letter to the Corinthians*, PNTC [Grand Rapids, Mich.: Eerdmans, 2010], 276). A divine pattern for marriage (and sexual behavior as a whole), then, can be positively assumed.

54. James E. Miller argues that the reference in verse 26 is not to homosexual sex but to unnatural (non-procreative) heterosexual relations ("The Practices of Romans 1:26: Homosexual or Heterosexual?" *NovT* 37 [1995]: 1–11). Building on Miller's argument, Gareth Moore contends that in verse 27 Paul is talking not about egalitarian homosexuality but about men with "a feminizing submission to a desire to play the role of the woman in sexual intercourse with a man" (*A Question of Truth: Christianity and Homosexuality* [London: Continuum, 2003], 98–9). For Jeramy Townsley, Paul's reference to unnatural sex is related not to modern categories of homosexuality but to the cross-gender behavior and subversion of the masculine sexual roles through castration of ancient temple prostitutes ("Queer Sects in Patristic Commentaries on Romans 1:26–27: Goddess Cults, Free Will, and 'Sex Contrary to Nature,'" *JAAR* 81 [2013]: 56–79).

55. Jewish literature of Paul's time abounds in evidence that Jews considered same-sex relations as a gross violation of the natural order as God has made it. See, for example, Ps.-Phoc. 191; *T. Levi* 14.6; *T. Naph.* 3.4–5; *T. Benj.* 9.1; *T. Sol.* 4.5 (cf. 2.2–3); Philo, *Spec.* 1.325; 2.50, 170; 3.37–42; *Abr.* 135–137; *Contempl.* 60; and Josephus, *C. Ap.* 2.199; cf. *2 En.* 10:2[ms. P]; 34:1–2; and Pseudo-Phocylides, *Sent.* 190–193. For discussions, see Gagnon, *The Bible and Homosexual Practice*, 159–83; and William Loader, "Homosexuality and the Bible," in *Two Views on Homosexuality, the Bible, and the Church*, ed. Preston Sprinkle (Grand Rapids, Mich.: Zondervan, 2016), 24–30. On *physis/physikos*, see Moisés Silva, "*physis*," in *NIDNTTE* 4:630–3.

humankind as 'male and female' [*arsēn kai thēlys*] in Genesis 1:27 [LXX]."[56] In other words, for Paul "what is natural has theological status because it is how God created things to be and so it is what is right."[57] Romans 1:18–32 is a discussion not of individual behavior but of humanity's rebellion against and estrangement from their Creator.

Others argue—with some measure of overlap among the views, including the previous one—that Paul condemns only sex as a form of domination,[58] pederasty,[59] excessive self-indulgence,[60] sexual exploitation of male slaves,[61] or the sexual depravities of the Roman emperors.[62] This, however, is difficult to justify exegetically. There is nothing in verses 26–27 that limits Paul's argument to a specific kind of homosexuality. Also, the consensual character of the relationship is evident from (1) the reference to female homosexuality (v. 26), which does not fit the active and passive distinctions that exist among males;[63] (2) the active voice of both *metallassō* (v. 26)

---

56. Loader, "Homosexuality and the Bible," 39.

57. Loader, "Homosexuality and the Bible," 39. William Loader adds: "We may assume that Paul's stance towards matters sexual is informed by his Jewish heritage, not least his biblical heritage" (*The New Testament on Sexuality* [Grand Rapids, Mich.: Eerdmans, 2012], 233). See also Richard B. Hays, *The Moral Vision of the New Testament: A Contemporary Introduction to New Testament Ethics* (San Francisco: HarperSanFrancisco, 1996), 379–406; Gagnon, *The Bible and Homosexual Practice*, 254–70; and Andrie B. du Toit, "Paul, Homosexuality, and Christian Ethics," in *Neotestamentica et Philonica: Studies in Honour of Peder Borgen*, ed. David E. Aune, Torrey Seland, and Jarl H. Ulrichsen (Leiden: Brill, 2003), 92–107.

58. Brooten, *Love between Women*, 302. Mostly concerned with female homoeroticism, Brooten argues that by condemning same-sex relationships "Paul demonstrates that he is a man of the Roman world" (301); that is, Paul is both theologically and culturally conditioned by the predominant view of his time, whether Jewish or Greco-Roman, that women are "inferior, unfit to rule, passive, and weak" (ibid.), hence his categorization of sex—Brooten actually says "love"—between women as "sinful, unnatural, and shameful" (302). According to her, the same concept underscores Paul's condemnation of sex between men: it betrays his cultural bias whereby only men, by virtue of their natural superiority, can play the active role, while women, inferior as they are, are doomed to the subordinate, passive role (ibid.).

59. Robin Scroggs, *The New Testament and Homosexuality: Contextual Background for Contemporary Debate* (Philadelphia: Fortress, 1983), 109–18. See also Victor P. Furnish, *The Moral Teaching of Paul* (Nashville: Abingdon, 1979), 52–83.

60. Especially, David E. Fredrickson, "Natural and Unnatural Use in Romans 1:24–27: Paul and the Philosophic Critique of Eros," in *Homosexuality, Science, and the "Plain Sense" of Scripture*, ed. David L. Balch (Louisville, Ky.: WJK, 1999), 197–222; James V. Brownson, *Bible, Gender, Sexuality: Reframing the Church's Debate on Same-Sex Relationships* (Grand Rapids, Mich.: Eerdmans, 2013), 153–78.

61. Jewett, *Romans*, 180–81.

62. Neil Elliott, *The Arrogance of the Nations: Reading Romans in the Shadow of Empire* (Minneapolis, Minn.: Fortress, 2008), 77–83.

63. This seems to explain why some supporters of homosexuality argue that Paul is not addressing female homosexual relations in Romans 1:26, but only non-procreative heterosexual relations, such as oral and anal intercourse. See, for example, Miller, "The Practices of Romans 1:26," 11; Fredrickson, "Natural and Unnatural Use in Romans 1:24–27," 201;

and *aphiēmi* ("to leave/give up," v. 27a); and (3) the explicit reference to mutual lust (v. 27b),[64] which rules out the use of coercive
intimidation or one-sided self-gratification. Paul never distinguishes
between offenders and victims. On the contrary, he speaks of both
partners as actively "committing what is shameful [*aschēmosynē*],
and receiving in themselves the penalty of their error which was
due" (v. 27c–d NKJV).[65] The language could hardly be clearer.[66] At the
end of the passage, after mentioning additional vices (vv. 29–31),
Paul once again emphasizes the conscious and deliberate nature of
those people's behavior: they "not only do them [the aforemen-
tioned sins] but also give approval to those who do the same" (v.
32c). Such people, he says, "are worthy of death" (v. 32b),[67] a probable echo of Leviticus 20:13. Despite being aware of the depth and
full weight of their actions, they defiantly continued to do them, thus
confirming the divine verdict: "they are without excuse" (Rom. 1:20).

SEXUAL ORIENTATION

Convinced of the inadequacy of the traditional understanding of
Romans 1, supporters of homosexuality tend to resort to the social con-
ventions of the Greco-Roman world in search for alternative interpretive frameworks.[68] Common to most approaches is the depreciation,

---

Moore, *A Question of Truth*, 96–9; Thomas Hanks, "Romans," in *The Queer Bible Commentary*, ed. Deryn Guest et al. (London: SCM, 2006), 591; Brownson, *Bible, Gender, Sexuality*,
244–46; Townsley, "Queer Sects in Patristic Commentaries on Romans 1:26–27," 70–2; and
David J. Murphy, "More Evidence Pertaining to 'Their Females' in Romans 1:26," *JBL* 138
(2019): 221–40.

64. The context requires the passive *exekauthēsan* (of *ekkaiō*, "to be inflamed") to have
an active sense (Harvey, *Romans*, 45).

65. The Greek term *aschēmosynē* ("shameless/indecent act") is also used with reference to the exposure of nakedeness; that is, of the genitals; this meaning is common in the
LXX (cf. Exod. 20:26; 28:42; Deut. 23:14; Ezek. 16:8; Nah. 3:5; and particularly Lev. 18 and
20, where "to uncover the nakedness" means "to have sexual relationship with") (Moisés
Silva, "*aschēmosynē*," *NIDNTT* 1:434–6; cf. BDAG 147).

66. "As it stands, Paul's language of mutuality is unqualified and cannot be stuffed into a
more narrow type of homosexual relations" (Preston Sprinkle, "Paul and Homosexual
Behavior: A Critical Evaluation of Romans 1:26–27," *BBR* 25 [2015]: 516).

67. In Romans 1:27c ("receiving in themselves the penalty of their error which was
due"), Paul refers to the punishment that manifests itself in the very sexual intercourse as
the result of the divine *paradidōmi* (vv. 24, 26, 28), while in verse 32b the reference is to the
future encounter of God's wrath (cf. 2:2–9; 3:5; 4:15; 5:9; 9:22; 12:19). See Cranfield, *The
Epistle to the Romans*, 1:126–27, 134.

68. For a recent brief survey, see Benjamin H. Dunning, "Same-Sex Relations," in *The
Oxford Handbook of New Testament, Gender, and Sexuality*, ed. Benjamin H. Dunning
(Oxford: Oxford University Press, 2019), 573–91. As Sprinkle points out in his critique of
the excessive-lust view, the search for ancient parallels is quite often selective, being limited to that which can support the argument, while other important nonsupportive

if not rejection, of the OT and Judaism as the conceptual background of Paul's view on sexual matters. This background, however, is too obvious to ignore. If the context itself, with its deliberate and unambiguous appeal to the creation order so as to establish the guilt of the world, were not enough to demonstrate the distinctive Jewish— and theological, rather than social—character of Paul's condemnation of homosexuality, we also have his consistent use of Wisdom of Solomon throughout Romans 1:18–32.[69] At the heart of the discussion, therefore, is the hermeneutical issue of scriptural authority. Bernadette J. Brooten, for example, while being able to provide a detailed and sound exegesis of the passage, ends up criticizing Paul for his—so she thinks—cultural bias and urging the churches today no longer to consider verses 26–27 as authoritative.[70] Luke T. Johnson does not explicitly criticize Paul, but while acknowledging that from an exegetical standpoint the passage "contains little ambiguity," he argues that Paul's reasoning is culturally conditioned and should be read "in light of later experience and perception."[71] The point he tries to make is that homosexuality may not be entirely a matter of sexual sin, as it seems to Paul, but a practice "compatible with a chaste and covenantal relationship."[72]

This has become a popular argument. It is maintained that the ancients, Paul included, "did not look at same-sex eroticism with the understanding of sexual orientation that is commonplace today,"[73] and they did not do so simply because "the notion of sexual orientation was absent" in antiquity.[74] Though it is true that modern

---

evidence is left out; he provides several examples ("Paul and Homosexual Behavior," especially 501–12). See also Preston Sprinkle, "Romans 1 and Homosexuality: A Critical Review of James Browson's *Bible, Gender, Sexuality*," *BBR* 24 (2014): 523–26.

69. The parallels are well-known. Perhaps the most complete list is found in Witherington, *Paul's Letter to the Romans*, 63. As Witherington comments, the "parallels are both too numerous and too closely spaced together in both Romans and Wisdom to be coincidental" (ibid.). Longenecker clarifies that, despite borrowing some of the ideas, structure, and even language of Wisdom of Solomon, chapters 13–14, Paul gives this material his own interpretive imprint so as to make it represent his own teaching (*The Epistle to the Romans*, 226).

70. Brooten, *Love between Women*, 302. For Dunning, this is a "contentious and opaque passage," and he argues "for refusing to treat Romans 1 as any sort of prooftext on sexual issues" ("Same-Sex Relations," 586–7).

71. Luke T. Johnson, *Reading Romans: A Literary and Theological Commentary* (Macon, Ga.: Smyth & Helwys, 2001), 35.

72. Ibid.

73. Brownson, *Bible, Gender, Sexuality*, 166.

74. Ibid., 170. Additional references include: David M. Halperin, *One Hundred Years of Homosexuality and Other Essays on Greek Love* (New York: Routledge, 1990), 3–40; Nissinen, *Homoeroticism in the Biblical World*, 123–40; Dan O. Via, "The Bible, the Church, and

categories of homosexuality are more numerous and nuanced than the ones in the past, it has been repeatedly pointed out that the Greeks and Romans did talk about innate and fixed (homo)sexual orientation, which for some of them was predetermined by the gods or by stellar conjunctions.[75] It seems thus inappropriate, if not inconsistent, to just assume that Paul knew nothing about this and that Romans 1 does not, or cannot, apply to situations in which homosexual orientation is not willfully chosen. Notwithstanding, the claim that Paul is concerned not with orientation but only with behavior may not properly account for the evidence either.[76] As William Loader notes, a central feature in Paul's discussion is the perverted state of mind that precedes the exchanging of truth for error. Paul says that "they became futile in their thinking [*dialogismos*], and their foolish hearts [*asynetos kardia*] were darkened" (v. 21 ESV), which is paralleled by "God gave them up to a debased mind [*adokimos nous*] to do what ought not to be done" (v. 28 ESV). This is, to some degree, a psychological argument that focuses not only on behavior but also on the mind behind it.[77] The actions are wrong, as is the attitude that generates them.

Homosexuality," in *Homosexuality and the Bible: Two Views*, ed. Dan O. Via and Robert A. Gagnon (Minneapolis, Minn.: Fortress, 2003), esp. 15–18; Dale B. Martin, *Sex and the Single Savior: Gender and Sexuality in Biblical Interpretation* (Louisville, Ky.: WJK, 2006), esp. 93–102; L. William Countryman, *Dirt, Greek, and Sex: Sexual Ethics in the New Testament and Their Implication for Today*, rev. ed. (Minneapolis, Minn.: Fortress, 2007), 253–83; and Megan K. Defranza, "Journeying from the Bible to Christian Ethics in Search of Common Ground," in *Two Views on Homosexuality, the Bible, and the Church*, ed. Preston Sprinkle (Grand Rapids, Mich.: Zondervan, 2016), 69–101.

75. For example, Richard B. Hays, "Relations Natural and Unnatural: A Response to John Boswell's Exegesis of Romans 1," *JRE* 14 (1996): 184–215; Amy Richlin, "Not before Homosexuality: The Materiality of the *Cinaedus* and the Roma Law against Love between Men," *JHS* 3 (1993): 523–73; Brooten, *Love between Women*, 119–20, 132–7, 140; Skinner, *Sexuality in Greek and Roman Culture*, 374–5; and Sprinkle, "Romans 1 and Homosexuality," 523–6. According to Sprinkle ("Paul and Homosexual Behavior," 505n27), ancient references to concepts of innate or fixed homosexual desires include Aristotle, *Eth. Nic.* 1148b; Pseudo-Aristotelian, *Problemata* 4.26; Soranus, *On Chronic Disorders* 4.9.134; Soranus, *De morbis chronics* 4.131–132, 134; Maternus, *Matheseos libri viii* 7.25.1; and Dorotheus of Sidon, *Carmen Astrologicum* 2.7.6. Also well known is Aristophanes's attempt to trace same gender attraction to Zeus being angered at human insolence and cutting three human creatures—one male, one female, and one androgynous—in half, causing them to ever after seek their other half (Plato, *Symp.* 189–193). Philo was aware of this myth but emphatically rejected it, and he did so on the basis of Genesis 1:27, according to which God created human beings male and female, apparently implying *only* male and female (*Contempl.* 50–63).

76. For example, Sprinkle, "Paul and Homosexual Behavior," 505.

77. William Loader, "Reading Romans 1 on Homosexuality in the Light of Biblical/Jewish and Greco-Roman Perspectives of Its Time," *ZNW* 108 (2017): 130.

It is such an attitude that causes passion (*pathos*, Rom. 1:26) and desire (*epithymia/orexis*, v. 27) to express themselves in actions that violate the creation prescript—the *para physin* concept. So, the problem with these feelings is not simply their excessive or abusive character but that they arise from a corrupted mind and follow in the wrong direction,[78] which in turn only degrades their minds even more (v. 28). That is, that which begins in the mind develops into a self-feeding spiral of decadence and sin that ends up affecting several other aspects of life (vv. 29–31). It is not possible to separate the actions from the attitude that brings them about,[79] and so Paul's condemnation encompasses both because both are part of one and the same process of rebellion.[80] Yet, Paul does not consider this fundamental inability to think and decide correctly about God and His will as inevitable or irresistible but sees it as a distortion for which those who nurtured it are to be held responsible (vv. 20d, 32). In fact, given Paul's Jewish-Christian worldview, it seems difficult to conceive that a behavior that is so unanimously condemned by both the OT (cf. Gen. 19:1–28; Lev. 18:22; 20:13; Deut. 23:17–18) and the NT (cf. Acts 15:29; 21:25; 1 Cor. 6:9; 1 Tim. 1:10; Jude 1:7)[81] alike

---

78. Gagnon points out that neither *pathos* nor *epithymia* has an inherently negative connotation and that the negative valence is mandated by the context (*The Bible and Homosexual Practice*, 232–5). "For Paul passion or desire is not in itself sinful. It must however be in its rightful place in the order of God's creation as he understands it" (Loader, "Reading Romans 1 on Homosexuality," 133). With regard to *epithymia*, its neutral connotation is even more evident in light of its use elsewhere by Paul (Phil. 1:23; 1 Thess. 2:17; cf. the use of the cognate verb *epithymeō* in Matt. 13:17; Luke 15:16; 17:22; 22:15; 1 Tim. 3:1; Heb. 6:11; 1 Pet. 1:12; see Gagnon, *The Bible and Homosexual Practice*, 232–3; and Sprinkle, "Paul and Homosexual Behavior," 515). See also W. Michaelis, "*pathos*," *TDNT* 5:926–30; and Moisés Silva, "*epithymeō*," *NIDNTT* 2:241–4.

79. "This runs contrary to those who seek to retrieve a gentler Paul by arguing that only actions matter, not attitude or orientation" (Loader, "Reading Romans 1 on Homosexuality," 130).

80. Commenting on Romans 1:28, Moo says: "People who have refused to acknowledge God end up with minds that are disqualified from being able to understand and acknowledge the will of God. The result, of course, is that they do things that are 'not proper'" (*The Letter to the Romans*, 128).

81. On 1 Corinthians 6:9–10 and 1 Timothy 1:9–10, see Gagnon, *The Bible and Homosexual Practice*, 303–39. As for Acts 15:29 and 21:25 (cf. Rev. 2:14, 20), I have argued elsewhere that the four binding requirements of the so-called Apostolic Decree are most likely based on resident alien laws of Leviticus 17–18, in which case the fourth prohibition of Acts (*porneia*) would stand for all sexual sins mentioned in Leviticus 18, including same-sex relations (Wilson Paroschi, *The Book of Acts* [Nampa, Idaho: Pacific Press, 2018], 74–6). See also Amy-Jill Levine and Marac Z. Brettler, eds., *The Jewish Annotated New Testament*, rev. ed. (Oxford: Oxford University Press, 2011), 229. On the ongoing force of the Leviticus prohibition of same-sex relations, see Roy E. Gane, *Old Testament Law for Christians: Original Context and Enduring Application* (Grand Rapids, Mich.: Baker Academic, 2017), 361–5.

might be justified on the grounds of its involuntary or inborn drive.[82] Any attempt to somehow limit the scope of Paul's discussion appears unwarranted. For him, same-sex relations, irrespective of their form or motive, reflect the depths of human depravity. He regards them as concrete evidence of a deliberate rejection of God's self-revelation through nature—more specifically, as a conscious deviation from God's original plan for man and woman.[83]

CONCLUSION

Paul's canonical authority might be disputed on presuppositional grounds, but on exegetical grounds the overall meaning of his words seems beyond dispute. By the same token, Paul's appeal to creation, which is central to his argument, becomes largely irrelevant if the creation narrative in Genesis is not recognized as normative, which implies it is also truthful and reliable. For Paul, it certainly is (cf. 1 Cor. 8:6; 11:8–9; 2 Cor. 4:6; Eph. 3:9; 5:31; Col. 1:15–16; 1 Tim. 2:13; 4:4).[84] Creation in Romans 1–2 is not simply a rhetorical device intended to illustrate Paul's theological or anthropological convictions. Rather, it is the standard on the basis of which he establishes the guilt of the Gentiles for their idolatry and immorality. Relativize creation and Paul's case will be fundamentally undermined. Most importantly, however, is that for Paul the condemnation of the world is not an end in itself but a means to draw attention to the greatest need of the world—namely, the gospel of Jesus Christ. What drives Paul is not a moralizing or revengeful bias—and on this he parts company with most Jews of his time concerning the Gentiles (cf. Rom. 2:17–29)—but an earnest desire that all humans, including Jews, will eventually accept what God has done through Jesus to bring them back into full harmony with Him (Rom. 3:21–26).

---

82. Sprinkle, "Paul and Homosexual Behavior," 506.

83. "In the Bible," says Gane, "marriage is only between a man and a woman. Homosexual 'marriage' is an oxymoron. No amount of social recognition can invest gay 'marriage' with moral legitimacy for Christians whose guide is Scripture. . . . The solution for homosexuals is not to seek legitimate ways to act on their tendencies, of which there are no such ways to act, but to rely on the mighty power of Christ and the Spirit in order to live in sexual purity" (*Old Testament Law for Christians*, 364–5).

84. "For Paul the decisive indication of what would be 'natural' is the man-woman relationship as ordained by God, the Creator . . . the term 'unnatural' is here, at the deepest level, a theological judgment" (du Toit, "Paul, Homosexuality and Christian Ethics," 101).

Dominic Bornand, MA

German Swiss Conference
Zurich, Switzerland

COSMOLOGY AND CREATION IN FIRST AND SECOND CORINTHIANS

INTRODUCTION

The purpose of this study is to determine Paul's perception of cosmology and creation as presented in the Corinthian correspondence.[1] It is clear from reading 1 and 2 Corinthians that Paul sees no need to instruct on the subject of cosmology or creation per se in these letters. However, he frequently refers to cosmological or creational concepts to support his argumentation.

Taking a closer look at cosmological and creational material in Paul's letters to Corinth, there is no need to assume that Paul adopts an extracanonical cosmology. Quotations and allusions to the Mosaic creation account reveal that Paul believed the Mosaic creation account to be a reliable source regarding the origin of species.[2] He sees God as

---

1. The number of letters that Paul wrote to the Corinthian believers is disputed. In this study, mentions of the Corinthian correspondence or the Corinthian letters refer only to 1–2 Corinthians in the New Testament canon.

2. In regard to Paul's use of the Old Testament, this study follows the method and terminology suggested by G. K. Beale, *Handbook on the New Testament Use of the Old Testament: Exegesis and Interpretation* (Grand Rapids, Mich.: Baker Academic, 2012), 29, that a quote is "recognizable by its clear and unique verbal parallelism." In regard to allusions and echoes, he points out that there is no consistent use of these terms within literature, therefore he proposes to use the term allusion and further qualify it as certain, probable, or possible (ibid., 31–32).

an exclusive power, calling not only present creation into existence but also the new creation. Additionally, Paul utilizes this account when giving ethical instructions regarding sexuality and idolatry. By doing so, he implements a Greco-Roman methodology in which cosmology determines ethics. Not only does this approach imply Paul's acceptance of the Mosaic creation account, but it also reveals his presupposition that his audience accepts it as well.

First, this study will address Paul's cosmological material by analyzing his reference to a third heaven (2 Cor. 12:2). Then, Paul's creational material will be explored, constituting the majority of the study. The discussion will be presented according to the believer's three phases of new creation: creation and conversion (2 Cor. 4:6; 5:17), creation and the daily life of the believer (1 Cor. 6:12–20; 8:1—11:16), and finally, creation and the bodily resurrection (1 Cor. 15:35–49).[3] The overarching thesis of this study is that the historicity and theological teachings of Genesis 1–2 are integral and essential to Paul's theology of Christian faith.

PAUL'S COSMOLOGICAL CONCEPT

In 2 Corinthians 12:2, Paul refers to the third heaven, stating that he knows a godly man who "has been carried up to the third heaven."[4] Since the biblical canon nowhere explains numbered heavens, some suggest that Paul here adopts an extracanonical cosmology. However, it is unnecessary to postulate such an argument, as a study of the immediate context of Paul's statement will reveal.

In 2 Corinthians 12, Paul proceeds to describe the experience of this godly man. He "was carried to paradise and heard inexpressible words, which are impossible to be spoken by man" (v. 4). The word *paradeisos* ("paradise") appears only three times in the New Testament. Apart from the present text, it appears in Luke 23:42, where paradise is the dwelling place of God in heaven (see Ezek. 28:13).[5]

---

3. Note that the same divine power will also perform the creative act of transforming the bodies of those believers who are alive at the parousia (1 Cor. 15:51–53). However, in these verses, no reference to the creation account is given, which is the reason why this analysis deals exclusively with the resurrection of the dead.

4. All biblical translations are the author's.

5. In the LXX (Greek Old Testament), the word *paradeisos* ("paradise") appears thirty-four times. It can refer to general gardens or orchards (Num. 24:6; 2 Chron. 33:20; Neh. 2:8; Eccles. 2:5; Song of Sol. 4:13; Isa. 1:30; Jer. 36:5; Joel 2:3; cf. Sir. 24:30; 40:17, 27; Sus. 7, 26, 54). See "παράδισος," [*paradeisos*], LSJ 1309. More significant, however, is its use in reference

Similarly, Revelation 2:7 refers to a heavenly place where the righteous ones will receive the reward for their life. It seems likely, then, that Paul associates the third heaven with God's heavenly dwelling place, which will serve as the believer's residence after the parousia.

While the context clarifies the meaning of the third heaven, it does not provide a final explanation for Paul's cosmological conception. Scholarly literature offers two different suggestions: First, some argue that Paul adopts a cosmology from surrounding cultures, such as the Greeks or the Babylonians.[6] This suggestion finds support in the frequent numbering of heavens in Jewish extracanonical literature. However, the references to heaven significantly differ regarding quantity as well as features of each particular heaven. Some refer to 995 heavens (3 En. 48:1), others to a heaven that is tenfold (2 En. 20–22), sevenfold (3 En. 17–18; Apoc. Ab. 19:5–6; see also b. Ḥag. 11b), fivefold (3 Bar. 2–11), or threefold (T. Levi 3:1;[7] Apoc. Sedr. 2:5; Apoc. Mos. 37:5; 40:1).[8] Remarkably, the texts that promote a threefold heaven do identify the third heaven as the paradise or the place of Lord's presence.[9] However, they do not really assist in answering how Paul understands the first and second heavens. The Testament of Levi provides further remarks on the features

---

to God's dwelling place, either in heaven (Ezek. 28:13; see also Gen. 13:10; Ezek. 31:8–9; and "παράδισος" [*paradeisos*], BDAG 761) or on earth in the form of the original earthly sanctuary, the garden of Eden (Gen. 2:8–10, 15–16; 3:1–3, 8, 10, 23–24; 13:10; Isa. 51:3; Pss. Sol. 14:3). For further discussion on the garden of Eden as the original earthly sanctuary, see Richard M. Davidson, "Earth's First Sanctuary: Genesis 1–3 and Parallel Creation Account," *AUSS* 53, no. 1 (2015): 65–80.

6. Adela Yarbro Collins, *Cosmology and Eschatology in Jewish and Christian Apocalypticism*, JSJSup 50 (Leiden: Brill, 1996), 46. Besides this suggestion, Collins also considers a plausible option to be that numbering heavens in early Jewish literature results from "an inner Jewish development, based on the phrase 'heaven of heavens'" (ibid., 46), which appears in 1 Kings 8:27 and 2 Chronicles 2:6.

7. H. C. Kee, "Testaments of the Twelve Patriarchs: A New Translation and Introduction," in *The Old Testament Pseudepigrapha*, ed. James H. Charlesworth (Garden City, N.Y.: Doubleday, 1983), 1:799 n2, argues that "the vision originally included three heavens, although in some forms of the text (α) 3:1–8 has been modified and expanded in order to depict seven heavens."

8. Moyer Hubbard, "2 Corinthians," in *Romans to Philemon*, Zondervan Illustrated Bible Backgrounds Commentary 3 (Grand Rapids, Mich.: Zondervan, 2002), 194–263, points out that "in each instance . . . the point is that the one ascending has reached the *highest* heavens, the very abode of God." Therefore, 2 Corinthians 12:2 indicates that Paul's cosmology includes three heavens.

9. Second Enoch 8–10 also identifies the third heaven as paradise (chs. 8–9). However, north of the third heaven there is a place described where punishment of the evilest people takes place (ch. 10). While 2 Enoch locates ungodly people in the second, third, and fifth heaven, the righteous ones are located only in the third heaven. Third Baruch locates the place for the righteous ones in the fourth heaven (10:5).

of the first and second heaven. It points out that while the lower heaven contains God's means to punish the ungodly at the judgment day, the second heaven contains the armies needed to take vengeance on the spirits of Beliar (T. Levi 3:2–3). Nothing comparable can be found in Paul's references to heaven. Therefore, the possibility that Paul adopts a contemporaneous, extracanonical cosmology remains, but the textual data is not conclusive.

Second, some argue that while the third heaven, God's dwelling place, refers to something unrelated to creation, the first and second heaven are part of God's creation.[10] The Mosaic creation account mentions the *rāqîaʿ* ("expansion"), which is identified as the *šāmayîm* ("heavens").[11] Regarding the expansion's function, Genesis 1 states that it divides the waters *mittaḥat* ("underneath") from those *mēʿal* ("above") it (vv. 6–8). The heavenly bodies are placed *birqîaʿ* ("in") it (vv. 14–15, 17) and the birds fly over the earth *ʿal-pĕnê* ("on") it (v. 20). Based on these last two prepositional phrases, Kenneth Mathews argues that "the 'expanse' describes both the place in which the luminaries were set (vv. 14–15, 17) and the sky where the birds are observed (v. 20)."[12] Thus, it is possible that Paul understands the first heaven as the atmosphere and the second heaven as the stellar heaven. While this explanation remains unprovable, it has the advantage that it agrees with the semantic range of heaven used in the canon.[13]

PAUL'S CREATION CONCEPT

This section will investigate references to creation in order to establish Paul's understanding of it. The analysis will examine direct quotations, along with terminological and thematic allusions to Genesis 1–2 and other texts dealing with creation. Additionally, it will consider texts containing terms of the semantic field *ktizō* ("to create").

---

10. In his argumentation and conclusion, the author is indebted to Richard M. Davidson.

11. According to P. Joüon and T. Muraoka, *A Grammar of Biblical Hebrew*, 2nd ed., Subsidia Biblica 27 (Rome: Gregorian and Biblical, 2011), 252, *šāmayim* ("heavens") is not a dual, but a plural. In contrast to the Hebrew Bible, the LXX renders the plural *šāmayim* ("heavens") consistently with a singular form of *ouranos* ("heaven"; Gen. 1:1, 8–9, 14–15, 17, 20, 26, 28, 30; 2:1, 4, 19–20).

12. Kenneth A. Mathews, *Genesis 1:1–11:26*, NAC 1A (Nashville: Broadman and Holman, 1996), 150.

13. Siegfried H. Horn, "Heaven," *Seventh-day Adventist Bible Dictionary* (Hagerstown, Md.: Review and Herald, 1960) 467–68.

The discussion will be presented according to the believer's three phases of new creation: creation and conversion (2 Cor. 4:6; 5:17); creation and the daily life of the believer, which includes the discussion of three separate issues (prostitution in 1 Cor. 6:12–20, consumption of food offered to idols in 1 Cor. 8:1—11:1, and head coverings while praying and prophesying in 1 Cor. 11:2–16); and finally, creation and resurrection (1 Cor. 15:35–49).

CREATION AND CONVERSION (2 CORINTHIANS 4:6; 5:17)

In 2 Corinthians 5:11–21, Paul neither quotes nor alludes to Genesis 1–2, but he uses the word *ktisis* ("creation") to describe the believer who has experienced conversion by surrender of his or her life to God. In 2 Corinthians 5:17, Paul's statement reads, "Therefore, if anyone is in Christ, he is a new creation. The old has passed away, behold, something new has been created." This attributive adjective "new" indicates that Paul understands these individuals as part of a different creation than the one described in Genesis 1–2. The immediate context in 2 Corinthians clarifies three important characteristics regarding the new creation. First, just as He performed the creative work described in Genesis 1 and 2, God also has the creative power of the new creation. This divine characteristic becomes clear by the statement "and all things are from God" (2 Cor. 5:18). Second, Christ's death and resurrection enable the new creation. The Genesis account reports that at some point after the completion of creation, the invasion of sin and death corrupted and subjected it. This subjection to the rule of sin and death caused separation between creation and its Owner, the Creator God (see Gen. 3; Rom. 5:12–21; 1 Cor. 15:20–22). Paul understands the new creation as God's strategy to reclaim His possession. In 2 Corinthians 5:14–21, the apostle identifies Christ's death and resurrection as God's means to deliver creation from the power of sin and death, reconciling it with sin-affected humanity.[14] Since creation is under the rule of sin and death, anything that is delivered from it automatically becomes part of a new creation. Third, the new creation manifests itself when an

---

14. N. T. Wright, *Christian Origins and the Question of God*, vol. 3 of 4, *The Resurrection of the Son of God* (Minneapolis, Minn.: Fortress, 2003), 336, states that "the heart and centre of it all, then, is the defeat of death in the future, based on the proleptic defeat inflicted in the resurrection of Jesus himself; or, to put it another way, it is the final completion of the 'age to come', which was inaugurated, in the midst of the 'present evil age', through the Messiah's death and resurrection."

individual experiences deliverance from subjection to sin and death. In 2 Corinthians 5:15, Paul states that "those who live live no longer for themselves but for the one who died for them and was raised." Related statements in Romans 6:1–14, 7:1–6, and Galatians 2:19–21 indicate that Paul understands conversion to be this deliverance from subjection to sin. Therefore, conversion marks the moment in time when a person begins as a new creation.[15]

These characteristics of the new creation are implied in Paul's illustration in 2 Corinthians 4:6, which alludes to Genesis 1:3–4. The apostle points to God's creative power in speaking the words "Out of darkness, light shall shine."[16] Paul continues, saying that God "has shone in our hearts, bringing light, which is the knowledge about the glory of God in the face of Jesus Christ" (2 Cor. 4:6). The syntax not only identifies God as the subject of the action but also indicates that Paul compares the knowledge of God's glory through the person of Jesus Christ with the light. According to the Genesis account, light was the first phenomenon called into existence (Gen. 1:3–4). Similarly, Paul understands the internalization of the knowledge of Christ's glorious act for humanity—His death and resurrection—as the first of several steps in the process of new creation.[17] Applying this illustration, Paul goes beyond the three characteristics (God being the creative power of the new creation, Christ's death and resurrection enabling the new creation, and the conversion of the believer as a manifestation of the new creation) by comparing God's act of creating light with the apostolic task of winning new believers, constituting the expansion of the new creation (2 Cor. 4:5, see also 1 Cor. 3:6).[18]

---

15. Paul's concept of conversion is closely connected to the baptismal rite. This is evident in Romans 6:1–14, where he links the believer's experience of death to sin with baptism (esp. vv. 3–4; see also Col. 2:12).

16. Since Paul's statement is not exactly quoting Genesis 1:3–4, scholars suggest that Paul may have Isaiah 49:6 in mind, where it reads, "And I will put you as a light for the nations." See Ralph P. Martin, *2 Corinthians*, 2nd ed., WBC 40 (Grand Rapids, Mich.: Zondervan, 2014), 224. Richard B. Hays, *Echoes of Scripture in the Letters of Paul* (New Haven, Conn.: Yale University Press, 1989), 152–53, points out that "indeed, the only direct verbal contact between 2 Corinthians 4:6 and Genesis 1:3–4 is the juxtaposition of the terms *light* and *darkness*. This may seem like a faint echo indeed where such universal symbolic elements are concerned, but the Genesis text is so foundational for the Jewish understanding of creation that the allusion can hardly be missed."

17. This viewpoint agrees with Jesus's teaching, associating believers with light and unbelievers with darkness (John 8:12; 12:46). Paul makes use of the same association (Rom. 2:19; 13:12; 2 Cor. 6:14; 1 Thess. 5:5).

18. Rudolf Bultmann, *Exegetica: Aufsätze zur Erforschung des Neuen Testaments*, ed. Erich Dinkler (Tübingen: Mohr Siebeck, 1967), 374–75.

CREATION AS A SOURCE FOR ETHICAL AND MORAL GUIDANCE

The Corinthian correspondence bears witness to the struggle of the Corinthian believers as they become part of the new creation while still living under the sinful conditions provided by the original creation. The numerous ethical and moral issues that Paul addresses suggest that some of the Corinthian believers, while becoming a new creation, were still comfortable embracing various Roman customs that contradicted God's ethical and moral standards. For issues related to sexuality (1 Cor. 6:12–20; 11:2–16) and idolatry (8:1—11:16), Paul uses creational concepts as the authoritative source by which to define God's ethical and moral standard.

Paul's use of creation theology follows a commonly accepted Greco-Roman methodology—namely, that cosmology impacts ethical behavior. Heraclitus, the pre-Socratic cosmologist, claimed that "all human laws are nourished by one law, the divine one" (Heraclitus, *Frag.* 114). Plato's Athenian stranger argued that "reason which controls what exists among the stars" must be applied "to the institutions and rules of ethics" (Plato, *Leg.* 967e). Later, Zeno of Citium, the founder of Stoicism, defined the *telos* ("goal") of life as "a life in agreement with Nature" (Diogenes Laertius, *Lives* 7.87). Seneca states that "but of things divine the nature is one. Reason, however, is nothing else than a portion of the divine spirit set in a human body" (Seneca, *Ep.* 66.12). Thus, the Stoics, with their pantheistic perception of nature,[19] believed that natural law not only orders nature but is also incorporated as *logos* ("reason") in the human soul, giving ethical guidance to the wise individual.

The very nature of the issues addressed by Paul in the Corinthian correspondence indicates that the church members had a predominantly non-Jewish background.[20] Living in Corinth, a Roman colony, they were heavily immersed in the pagan Greco-Roman environment. For this reason, there are two important implications to Paul's method of rooting his ethical and moral instructions exclusively within the Mosaic creation account and cosmology. First, his exclusive reliance on these indicates Paul's high view of their content. This becomes

---

19. Christine Hayes, *What's Divine about Divine Law? Early Perspectives* (Princeton, N.J.: Princeton University Press, 2015), 55, argues that "for the Stoics, God was not distinct from nature. God was nature; nature was divine. Therefore the rational order or eternal reason (*logos*) of nature is none other than the eternal reason of God." See also Seneca, *Ep.* 92.30.

20. Among the most dominant ones are factions, social status, sexuality, idolatry, and resurrection.

even more evident when Paul's writings are compared to Second Temple literature, the cosmology of which is heavily influenced by surrounding cultures. Second, Paul evidently considers this strategy the most promising way to influence the ethical and moral behavior of his audience. For this reason, it is natural to conclude that his audience was familiar with the Mosaic cosmology and creation account. Beyond bare familiarity, it is likely that Paul also presumes that his audience accepts the Mosaic cosmology and creation account as exclusively as he did. This is supported by the fact that the ethical principles Paul derived from the Mosaic cosmology and creation account were contrary to non-Jewish Greco-Roman ethics. In other words, the acceptance of ethical principles rooted in the Mosaic creational account also presume acceptance of the account itself.

The Issue of Prostitution (1 Corinthians 6:12–20)

The first daily life issue Paul links to creation is the problem of prostitution (1 Cor. 6:12–20). Paul both alludes to and quotes from Genesis 2:24 when addressing the spiritual consequences for believers engaged in sexual immorality with prostitutes.[21] Their behavior is culturally influenced by Roman sexual ethics, which considers sexual intercourse with prostitutes to be ethically acceptable,[22] along with

---

21. The Greek term *porneia* can refer generally to any kind of sexual immorality or in particular to prostitution. Commentators disagree on whether in 1 Corinthians 6:12–20 Paul is addressing sexual immorality in general or prostitution in particular. For a list of supporters of each view, see Eckhard J. Schnabel, *Der erste Brief des Paulus an die Korinther*, HTA (Witten: Brockhaus; Giessen: Brunnen, 2010), 327. As the discussion indicates, although Paul specifically addresses prostitution, his argument would also be applicable to any sexual immorality.

22. Women were expected to restrict their sexual activity to their husbands. See James S. Jeffers, *The Greco-Roman World of the New Testament Era: Exploring the Background of Early Christianity* (Downers Grove, Ill.: InterVarsity, 1999), 243. Men's sexual activity was less restricted. Plautus, *Curc.* 35–37, states, "Nobody forbids anyone . . . so long as you stay away from the married woman, the widow, the virgin, the youth, and freeborn boys, love whatever you like." Thus, the Greco-Roman culture perceived adultery only in the case of a married woman having sexual intercourse outside of her marital relationship. See Everett Ferguson, *Backgrounds of Early Christianity*, 3rd ed. (Grand Rapids, Mich.: Eerdmans, 2003), 76. In the case of a married man, it was socially and morally acceptable to have sexual intercourse with slaves and prostitutes of either gender. For a more detailed discussion on the penetrating-penetrated model that dominated Roman sexuality and its consequences on practiced sexuality in regard to gender and social status, see Rebecca Langlands, *Sexual Morality in Ancient Rome* (Cambridge: Cambridge University Press, 2006), 1–36; and Amy Richlin, *The Garden of Priapus: Sexuality and Aggression in Roman Humor*, rev. ed. (New York: Oxford University Press, 1992), 220–26. Prostitution was even understood as a means of preventing men from committing adultery. A statement about Psyllus, a pimp, reads, "As keeper of common women he dissuaded young men from adultery" (*AnthLyrGreac* 7.403; see also Horace, *Sat.* 1.4.113–14; 2.7.46–71).

Roman anthropology, which attributes no ethical importance to the body, due to its mortality.[23] Their justification that "everything is lawful" (1 Cor. 6:12) proves they do not perceive their behavior as amounting to ethical failure. By alluding to and quoting from Genesis 2:24, Paul reminds the Corinthians of a completely different sexual ethic and anthropology.[24]

Genesis 2:24 presents creation's ideal of a nuptial relationship by referring to three characteristics: first, the man *ya'ăzob* ("will leave") his parents; second, he *wĕdābaq* ("will cleave") to his wife; and finally, he *wĕhāyû lĕbāśār 'eḥād* ("will become one flesh") with her. The Hebrew syntax in Genesis 2:24 indicates that these three characteristics form an intentional sequence. In 1 Corinthians 6:16–17, Paul applies only the second and third characteristics to the relationship between the believer and the prostitute and between the believer and God. He asks the Corinthians if they know that "the one who cleaves to the prostitute becomes one body." Then he adds a parallel statement, that "the one who cleaves to the Lord becomes one spirit" (v. 17). The expression *kollōmenos* ("the one who cleaves") alludes to *proskollēthēsetai* ("he will cleave to," Gen. 2:24).[25] The same can be said of the phrase "becomes one body" (1 Cor. 6:16), which alludes to

---

23. Greco-Roman philosophy maintains a dualistic anthropology, which, to a certain extent, is already visible in Homer, where the soul does not transfer into Hades unless the body is appropriately buried (Homer, *Il.* 23.69–74; Homer, *Od.* 11.51–83). While later philosophical schools do not fully agree in their views on the afterlife, they do agree that the body, due to its mortality, never plays a role in the afterlife. This characteristic is why the soul was perceived superior to the body (Plato, *Phaed.* 80a; Aristotle, *Pol.* 1254a–b; Aristotle, *Top.* 128b; Aristotle, *Part. an.* 678b; Lucretius, *De Rerum Natura.* 3.323–24; Seneca, *Ep.* 92.33). For this reason, they treat the body, for the most part, with indifference (Plato, *Phaed.* 67a; see also Seneca, *Ep.* 78.10). Stoicism teaches that as long as an individual counters the satisfaction of the bodily urges with apathy, it is acceptable to seek satisfaction of the bodily urges, such as drinking, eating, and having sexual intercourse, while still living a virtuous life. For an excellent overview on Stoic ethics, see Malte Hossenfelder, *Geschichte der Philosophie*, vol. 3.3 of 12, *Die Philosophie der Antike: Stoa, Epikureismus und Skepsis*, 2nd ed., ed. Wolfgang Röd (Munich: Beck, 1995), 45–68.

24. This becomes evident by asking them three parallel questions in relation to the body, each one starting with "Do you not know that . . . " (1 Cor. 6:15, 16, 19), thereby indicating that the content of the question was already known. See Hans Conzelmann, *1 Corinthians: A Commentary on the First Epistle to the Corinthians*, trans. James W. Leitch, Hermeneia (Philadelphia: Fortress, 1975), 98.

25. *Kollaomai* ("to cleave") and *proskollaomai* ("to cleave") are synonyms; see "προσκλίνομαι [*prosklinomai*]; κολλάομαι [*kollaomai*]; προσκολλάομαι [*proskollaomai*]; προσκληρόομαι [*prosklēroomai*]," *L&N* 34.22. Matthew 19:5 also quotes from Genesis 2:24 using *kollaomai* ("to cleave"). Ephesians 5:31 uses *proskollaomai* ("to cleave"). Scholars have widely rejected J. L. Miller's proposal that *proskollaomai* ("to cleave") has a sexual connotation, whereas *kollaomai* ("to cleave") has a more general sense. See J. L. Miller, "A Fresh Look at 1 Corinthians 6:16f," *NTS* 27, no. 1 (1980): 125–27.

"they will become one flesh" (Gen. 2:24). The change from "flesh" to "body" seems intentional in order to connect Genesis 2:24 to the issue at hand—the believer's body. Their synonymous meaning is confirmed by the added quote "the two will become one flesh" (1 Cor. 6:16; quoted from Gen. 2:24).[26]

The majority of commentators argue that "to cleave" refers to the believer's sexual intercourse with the prostitute (1 Cor. 6:16; see Sir. 19:2).[27] However, Renate Kirchhoff observes that the Greek translation of "to cleave" in 1 Corinthians 6:16 has no sexual connotation.[28] The same has been argued about the Hebrew term "to cleave" in Genesis 2:24.[29] The term often takes the Lord as a direct object,[30] describing the covenantal relationship between Israel and the Lord (Deut. 11:22; 13:5; 30:20; Josh. 22:5; 23:8). This covenantal relationship entails the reception of a new identity.[31] Because Paul uses "to cleave" with the Lord as a direct object (1 Cor. 6:17), the covenantal connotation should not be ignored when "to cleave" is used within the parallelism with the prostitute as a direct object (v. 16). Thus, describing the believer's relationship with a prostitute using "to cleave" indicates that the believer enters a covenant-like relationship, which will influence his or her identity.

---

26. In contrast to the Masoretic text, which reads *wĕhāyû lĕbāśār 'eḥād* ("and they will become one flesh"), the LXX adds *hoi dyo* ("the two"), which identifies, according to the context, the unidentified third person plural subject of the Hebrew verb as man and woman. The Samaritan Pentateuch and the Aramaic Targumim do the same (see Tg. Ps.-J. Gen. 2:24; Tg. Neof. Gen. 2:24; C. Tg. B. Gen. 2:24; not so in Tg. Onq. Gen. 2:24).

27. This comment from Robert G. Bratcher, *A Translator's Guide to Paul's First Letter to the Corinthians*, Helps for Translators 32 (London: United Bible Society 1982), 53, is a paradigmatic example: "Joins his body to a prostitute: 'has sexual relations with a prostitute.'" Similarly, Paul Ellingworth and Howard Hatton, *A Translator's Handbook of Paul's First Letter to the Corinthians*, Helps for Translators 37 (London: United Bible Society, 1985), 119, state that "joins himself here means 'has sexual relation with' and may be translated this way in certain languages."

28. Renate Kirchhoff, *Die Sünde gegen den eigenen Leib: Studien zu πόρνη und πορνεία in 1 Kor 6,12–20 und dem sozio-kulturellen Kontext der paulinischen Adressaten*, SUNT 18 (Göttingen: Vandenhoeck & Ruprecht, 1994), 159n214. Moisés Silva refers to the sexual connotation of *kollaomai* and *proskollaomai* only in relation to 1 Cor. 6:16: Moisés Silva, "κολλάω [*kollaō*], προσκολλάω [*proskollaō*]," *NIDNTTE* 2:718–20. K. L. Schmidt states that "At root this κολλᾶσθαι [*kollasthai*], like the corresponding דבק in Gn. 2:24; 34:3 . . . and 1 K. 11:2 . . . , does not have the sexual sense, but it acquires this, just as the word copulation is used particularly for marriage." K. L. Schmidt, "κολλάω [*kollaō*], προσκολλάω [*proskollaō*]," *TDNT* 3:822–23.

29. G. Wallis states "*dbq*, however, does not denote a sexual relationship" and "*dabhaq* does not connote sexual union." G Wallis, "דָּבַק דֶּבֶק דָּבֵק, [*dabaq, debeq, dābēq*]" *TDOT* 3:79–84.

30. Note that the Lord is never the subject but always the direct object of the joining. See E. Jenni, "דבק *dbq* to hang on," *TLOT* 1:325.

31. See also Kirchhoff, *Sünde*, 167–72, for a detailed discussion on the meaning of *kollaomai* ("to cleave").

"Becomes one body" or "one spirit" expresses the identity change. Paul's statements in 1 Corinthians 6:16–17 should be understood sequentially, based on the Hebrew syntax of Genesis 2:24. Thus, a person who cleaves to the Lord will undergo a change of identity by becoming one spirit with the Lord. This identity change takes place through the reception of the Holy Spirit at the moment a person surrenders to God and is publicly displayed by baptism (see 1 Cor. 12:13). Applying this sequence to 1 Corinthians 6:16 means that after cleaving to a prostitute, the new identity is received in the form of becoming one body with the prostitute. In this case, the individual is controlled by the sinful desires of the body, which find expression in the immoral sexual intercourse.[32] By juxtaposing God and the prostitute as covenantal partners of the believer, Paul indicates their mutual exclusivity.

Interestingly, throughout 1 Corinthians 6:12–20 Paul keeps to a solely theological argument.[33] His interest is neither to explain the meaning of Genesis 2:24 nor to comment on the potential effects of sexual intercourse with a prostitute on a believer's marriage. Rather, he addresses the impact of a believer's sexual immorality on the believer's relationship with God. Paul's argument indicates that he had to convince some believers of the merits of a radically different sexual ethic and anthropology. Evidently, he perceives that a reminder of the sexual ethic, as present in the Mosaic creation account, might be the most promising way to convince his audience. This indicates that, for Paul, this particular account of origin provides a normative source for ethical standards. In addition, it presumes yet again that his audience must have, to a certain degree, shared in his viewpoints on the Mosaic creation account, since the way Paul asks his questions hints at their previous exposure to the content of Genesis 2:24.

The Issue of Food Offered to Idols (1 Corinthians 8:1—11:1)

The second daily life issue Paul links to creation regards the consumption of food offered to idols (1 Cor. 8:1—11:1). Although there is no direct reference to the Mosaic creation account in 1 Corinthians 8:1—11:1, Paul still utilizes God's creative power to argue that the pagan gods differ from the Creator God (8:5–6) and to point to God's

---

32. The creational ideal of becoming one flesh in Genesis 2:24 should not be reduced to sexual intercourse; see Richard M. Davidson, *Flame of Yahweh: Sexuality in the Old Testament* (Peabody, Mass.: Hendrickson, 2007), 46–48.

33. Schnabel, *Korinther*, 348.

legitimate ownership of all creation (10:26). This is necessary because some Corinthian believers concluded, based on their own insight, that pagan gods did not exist (8:4) and they could therefore participate in pagan temple gatherings and consume food offered to idols in this context. These offerings included animals, cakes, fruits, vegetables, or incense. They were either burned, poured out, or eaten.[34] Sacrifices were usually divided into three parts: One part was offered to the deity on the altar. The second part was given to the priests or the temple, which was, in the case of a surplus, sold on the market to generate funds (see 1 Cor. 10:25).[35] The third part was returned as a godly gift to those offering the sacrifice. They either ate it during a social gathering within an assigned room of the temple or took it home for private consumption.[36]

References to God's creative power in 1 Corinthians 8:1—11:1 provide the foundation for two important points in Paul's argument. First, God's unique status as Creator and Redeemer makes Him worthy of worship. Paul acknowledges the existence of "many gods and many lords," although they are only "so-called gods."[37] He locates them within creation, "in heaven" and "on earth" (8:5), and thus hints at their condition of being created (see also Rom. 1:23, 25).[38] Paul continues the parallelism of gods and lords, moving to define the one and only God as the Father and the one and only Lord as Jesus Christ (1 Cor. 8:6). Regarding the Father, Paul states, "from whom all things are and we are for Him." Regarding Jesus Christ, he says, "through whom all things are and we are through Him." The prepositions define each one's role. In regard to the Father, *ek* ("from") identifies Him as the source of creation and *eis* ("for") as the goal of the redeemed person. In regard to Jesus Christ, *dia* ("through") identifies Him twice: as the means through which the creation happened and as the one through whom believers live for God.[39] Thus, in contrast to the pagan gods,

---

34. Jeffers, *Greco-Roman World*, 91; and Ferguson, *Early Christianity*, 188–89.

35. John T. Fitzgerald, "Food and Drink in the Greco-Roman World and in the Pauline Communities," in *Paul and Economics: A Handbook*, ed. Thomas R. Blanton IV and Raymond Pickett (Minneapolis, Minn.: Fortress, 2017), 205–44, argues that meat offered to idols was of higher quality and therefore more expensive than meat not offered to idols.

36. Dennis E. Smith, "Greco-Roman Sacred Meals," *ABD* 4:653–55.

37. Paul identifies these so-called gods as *daimonia* ("demons," 1 Cor. 10:20–21).

38. Conzelmann, *1 Corinthians*, 143; Wolfgang Schrage, *Der Erste Brief an die Korinther*, 4 vols., EKKNT 7 (Düsseldorf: Benziger; Neukirchen-Vluyn: Neukirchner, 1991–2001), 2:241n177.

39. Murray J. Harris, *Prepositions and Theology in the Greek New Testament: An Essential Reference Resource for Exegesis* (Grand Rapids, Mich.: Zondervan, 2012), 74–75. Daniel B.

God the Father and Jesus Christ are not created but are the Creator and Redeemer of humanity. According to Paul, these characteristics render this God and this Lord worthy of worship. Involvement in idolatrous practices in 1 Corinthians 10:14–22 leads to the worship of something that deserves no worship, since it is created rather than Creator (see Rom. 1:19–23).

Second, Paul points to God's unimpeachable role as the Owner of creation. He argues in 1 Corinthians 10:24–11:1 that a believer can eat any food sold in the market or served at a Gentile's home if he has no knowledge of whether it was previously offered to idols.[40] Paul sees no issue in this regard because offering food to an idol has no impact on God's ownership of creation or, by proxy, on the food itself. As scriptural proof, Paul quotes Psalm 24:1 (23:1, LXX): "The earth and its fullness is the Lord's."[41] The psalm defines God as the Owner of the earth and everything in it because He created it (Ps. 24:1–2).

Paul may not explicitly refer to the Mosaic creation account in 1 Corinthians 8:1—11:1. However, he still quotes from Psalm 24:1 (23:1, LXX), which certainly alludes to it. Therefore, it is still this unique creation account from which Paul derives the foundation for his normative, moral instruction to believers participating in idolatrous activities and consciously consuming food offered to idols. Paul's use of creational concepts in this particular argumentation reveals that he understands God to be the exclusive Creator and Owner of creation. He denies the involvement of any other force in the creation of the world.

Wallace argues that "διά [dia] + genitive is used for *intermediate* agent." See Daniel B. Wallace, *Greek Grammar beyond the Basics* (Grand Rapids, Mich.: Zondervan, 1996), 164.

40. There are two reasons why scholars understand Paul's specifications as a deviation from the strict prohibition of eating food offered to idols in the Old Testament and Acts 15. First, Acts 15:13–29 refers to a later agreement by James and others. Thus, when Paul wrote 1 Corinthians and Romans, he had no knowledge about this agreement. See Johannes Weiss, *Der erste Korintherbrief*, 9th ed., KEK (Göttingen: Vandenhoeck and Ruprecht, 1910; repr., 1970), 212–13; and Joseph A. Fitzmyer, *First Corinthians*, AB 32 (New Haven, Conn.: Yale University Press, 2008), 334–35. Second, Paul disagrees with the decision taken at Jerusalem and chooses to deviate from it. See C. K. Barrett, "Things Sacrificed to Idols," *NTS* 11 (1965): 138–53. A third view, which is preferable, denies Paul's deviation, arguing that he permits only the unconscious consumption of food offered to idols. See Alex T. Cheung, *Idol Food in Corinth: Jewish Background and Pauline Legacy*, JSNTSup 176 (Sheffield: Sheffield Academic, 1999), 152–62; and David J. Rudolph, *A Jew to the Jews: Jewish Contours of Pauline Flexibility in 1 Corinthians 9:19–23*, WUNT 2nd ser., vol. 304 (Tübingen: Mohr Siebeck, 2011), 97–101.

41. In contrast to the Hebrew Bible's usual introductory words "a Psalm by David," the LXX adds the words *tēs mias sabbatōn* ("about the first week," v. 1). This seems to provide an additional reference to the Mosaic creation account.

The Issue of Head Coverings while Praying and Prophesying (1 Corinthians 11:2–6)

The third daily life issue Paul connects to creation regards head coverings while praying and prophesying (1 Cor. 11:2–16). In 1 Corinthians 11:7–12, Paul extensively alludes to Genesis 1:26–28 and 2:21–23, providing further explanation for his argument on this issue. He begins his exposition by stating, "But I want you to understand" (1 Cor. 11:3). This indicates that what follows is new to the Corinthians.[42] After this introduction, Paul proposes that "Christ is the head of every man, but the man is the head of a woman, but God is the head of Christ" (v. 3).[43] The parallelism in 11:4–5 outlines the two different, yet related, issues at hand.[44]

---

42. Conzelmann, *1 Corinthians*, 183.

43. Matthew L. Tinkham Jr. briefly outlines two different readings of 1 Corinthians 11:3. The first reading is hierarchical, which orders the involved parties in a "*hierarchical* manner from highest to lowest levels of perceived authority: God-Christ relationship, Christ-man relationship, and man-woman relationship." This understanding reads *kephalē* metaphorically as "authority." The second reading is chronological, which orders the relationships according to the creation order: first, creation of man from Christ (Gen. 2:7); second, creation of woman from man (Gen. 2:21–25); and third, incarnation of Christ from God (John 1:1–3, 14). This reading argues for a metaphorical translation of *kephalē* as "source," or "origin," which is very rare, yet not unknown to Paul (Eph. 4:14–15; Col. 2:18–19). See Matthew L. Tinkham Jr., "Neo-Subordinationism: The Alien Argumentation in the Gender Debate," *AUSS* 55, no. 2 (2017): 237–90. Due to the extensive amount of creational material in the argument, it would be rhetorically warranted to use creational concepts in the proposition of the argument (1 Cor. 11:3). Since the issues at hand are related to head coverings (vv. 4–5), using in the proposition a very rare, but possible, semantic meaning of *kephalē* would be a brilliant wordplay, paying homage to Paul's authorial skills. A third possible reading metaphorically translates *kephalē* as "representative"; see Anthony C. Thiselton, *The First Epistle to the Corinthians: A Commentary on the Greek Text*, NIGTC (Grand Rapids, Mich.: Eerdmans, 2000), 816–20. See also David E. Garland, *1 Corinthians*, BECNT (Grand Rapids, Mich.: Baker Academic, 2003), 514–16.

44. Literature reveals numerous proposals regarding the issue at hand. Besides the view taken here, two prominent views exist: The first view interprets headship and the role of men and women in church being based on the creation order; see Edwin Reynolds, "Biblical Hermeneutics and Headship in First Corinthians" (paper presented at the Meeting of the Theology of Ordination Study Committee, Baltimore, July 22, 2013), 1–46, https://www.ad ventistarchives.org/biblical-hermeneutics-and-headship-in-first-corinthians.pdf. The exegetical reasoning for the headship view has been challenged, especially based on the creation account, by Richard M. Davidson, "Headship, Submission, and Equality in Scripture," in *Women in Ministry: Biblical and Historical Perspectives*, ed. Nancy Vyhmeister (Berrien Springs, Mich.: Andrews University Press, 1998), 259–95. The second view interprets the passage as an issue of honor and social status; see Schnabel, *Korinther*, 601–2. Based on Plutarch's statement that men "uncover their heads in the presence of men more influential than they" (Plutarch, *Quaest. rom.* 10), this view argues that believers of high social rank were not willing to give up their status in church and, therefore, did not uncover their heads while praying and prophesying. At first glance, this interpretation seems legitimate because the Corinthian correspondence indicates that the church consisted of members with different social statuses and because Paul uses honor and shame language extensively throughout the passage. However, this view seems unlikely for two reasons. First, Plutarch's

The first issue concerns male believers who dishonor their head, Christ (v. 3), by praying or prophesying with their heads covered (v. 4).[45] Regarding the issue, Plutarch asks if men should "cover the head, when they worship gods" (Plutarch, *Quaest. rom.* 10).[46] This Roman custom started with Aeneas (see also Dionysius of Halicarnassus, *Ant. rom.* 12.16). It could be done either by "covering the head, or . . . pulling up the toga to the ears" (Plutarch, *Quaest. rom.* 10).[47] With this understanding, Christian male believers who covered their heads while praying and prophesying sent syncretistic signals that dishonored Christ.

The second issue concerns female believers who dishonor their head, their husband (1 Cor. 11:3),[48] by praying or prophesying with their heads uncovered (v. 5). In contrast to the male issue, Paul adds an initial explanation as to why this is the case, stating that the

---

statement refers to encounters between men in the streets, covering their heads temporarily due to sunshine, wind, or rain, since it was uncommon for men to cover their heads in public. This does not fit the situation described in 1 Corinthians 11:2–16. Second, the issue concerning the male believers is focused on their relationship to Christ (vv. 3–4). However, an issue of status focuses more on interpersonal relations.

45. Some scholars argue that the phrase *kata kephalēs echōn* should be read as "having [something] down from the head" (v. 4) in reference to long hair (v. 14); see Jerome Murphy-O'Connor, "1 Corinthians 11:2–16 Once Again," *CBQ* 50 (1988): 265–74. However, Plutarch uses almost exactly the same expression (*kata tēs kephalēs echōn*) to describe Scipio on his inspection tour in Alexandria, stating that he "walked while having the toga covering the head," intending to remain unrecognized. However, the surrounding people "insisted that he uncover and show his face to their yearning eyes" (Plutarch, *Mor.* F200). Murphy-O'Connor argues that the reference in Plutarch offers only an unlikely possibility, since the Old Testament requires priests to make sacrifice with head covered (Exod. 28:4, 37–38; Ezek. 44:18). However, Murphy-O'Connor misses that Christ is not dishonored by the actual covering of the head but by the syncretistic signals of this act. This is especially of interest in the context of Paul's teachings in 1 Corinthians 8:1—11:1.

46. This finds wide support in Roman iconography. For a short discussion, see Cynthia L. Thompson, "Hairstyles, Head-Coverings, and St. Paul: Portraits from Roman Corinth," *BA* 51, no. 2 (1988): 99–115; and David W. J. Gill, "The Importance of Roman Portraiture for Head-Coverings in 1 Corinthians 11:2–16," *TynBul* 41, no. 2 (1990): 245–60.

47. The only exceptions Plutarch mentions are the worship of Saturn and Honor, (see Plutarch, *Quaest. rom.* 11, 13). However, these exceptions are insignificant because both cults were exclusively worshiped in Rome, see Hans-Friedrich Mueller, "Saturn," *The Oxford Encyclopedia of Ancient Greece and Rome* 6:221–222; Leonhard Schmitz, "Honor or Honos," *Smith's Dictionary of Greek and Roman Biography and Mythology* 2:512.

48. The translation for *gynē* can either be "woman" or "wife." Similarly, *anēr* can either be translated as "man" or "husband." As Bruce W. Winter, *After Paul Left Corinth: The Influence of Secular Ethics and Social Change* (Grand Rapids, Mich.: Eerdmans, 2001), 126–27, observes, the fact that Paul refers to the veil indicates Paul is exclusively talking about married women, since only married women had to veil themselves in public. The argument that *pasa* ("all") women indicates that also unmarried women had to veil themselves in prayer and prophesying is historically invalid. Because only married women had to veil themselves in public they would be the logical recipients of a rebuke for praying or prophesying unveiled. However, it should also be considered that in Roman culture, women married in their early/mid-teens.

female believer who prays or prophesies uncovered "is one and the same with the one being shaved" (v. 5). He continues that if a woman has her head uncovered, she "also should cut" her hair (v. 6). Paul then explicitly declares that a shaved woman is considered "shameful" (v. 6),[49] whereas long hair is counted an "honor" (v. 15) and having her head covered "is fitting" for her (v. 13).[50] In Roman culture, chastity and modesty were the most honorable virtues of women.[51] As a sign of these values, married women covered their heads in public.[52] A married woman unveiled in public was dishonoring her husband by signaling withdrawal from her marital relationship (see Valerius Maximus, *Of Severity* 6.3.10; Seneca the Elder, *Controv.* 2.7.6).[53] Therefore, a female believer, praying and prophesying with her head uncovered, dishonored her husband accordingly (1 Cor. 11:5).[54]

---

49. Dio Chrysostom refers to a Cyprian law that required the woman convicted of adultery to cut her hair and be like a prostitute; see Dio Chrysostom, *2 Fort.* 3.

50. A more recent trend argues that Paul's main concern was hairstyles. See Stefan Lösch, "Christliche Frauen in Corinth (1 Cor. 11:2–16): Ein neuer Lösungsversuch," *TQ* 127 (1947): 216–61. Abel Isaksson, *Marriage and Ministry in the New Temple: A Study with Special Reference to Matthew 19.13–12 [sic] and 1. Corinthians 11.3–16*, ASNU 24 (Lund: Gleerip, 1965) proposes that *akatakalyptos* should be translated as "with hair unbound," based on the LXX rendering of Leviticus 13:45. For two reasons, the viability of this interpretation may be questioned. First, Marlis Gielen, "Beten und Prophezeien mit unverhülltem Kopf? Die Kontroverse zwischen Paulus und der korinthischen Gemeinde um die Wahrung der Geschlechtsrollensymbolik in 1Kor 11,2–16," *ZNW* 90 (1999): 220–49, argues that if *kata kephalēs echōn* is understood as "to loosen long hair of men" and *akatakalyptō* "to loosen long hair of women," the *intended* antithesis of verse 4 to verse 5a no longer exists. Second, Preston T. Massey, "The Meaning of κατακαλύπτω [*katakalyptō*] and κατὰ κεφαλῆς ἔχων [*kata kefalēs echōn*] in 1 Corinthians 11.2–16," *NTS* 53 (2007): 502–23, demonstrates "that κατακαλύπτω [*katakalyptō*] is never used in any ancient Greek text suggesting that human hair is the indirect object used for covering the head. Rather, the meaning of the verb conveys a unanimous and unambiguous sense of a cloth covering."

51. Lauren Caldwell, *Roman Girlhood and Fashioning of Feminity* (Cambridge: Cambridge University Press, 2015), 15–44. The apostle is arguing biblically, referencing the creation story (Gen. 1–2) in 1 Corinthians 11:7–9, but he is interfacing Christian theology with Greco-Roman culture. The question is how to present the high moral standard of the Christian faith within a pagan culture. Taking into account Greco-Roman customs and values is part of that missional interface so that the Christian church and Christian message are not misunderstood. It is not compromise with the culture that the apostle seeks but clear communication.

52. The *stola* ("outer garment") and the *vitta* ("hair ribbon") were badges of modesty (see Ovid, *Tristia* 2:247; and Philo, *Spec.* 3.52–63, esp. 56, where he identifies the veil as the woman's symbol of modesty). For a detailed discussion, see Bieber, "Stola," PW 2/7:56–62. Similarly to the prostitute, female adulterers had to wear the *toga* ("male outer garment") instead of the *stola*. See Thomas A. J. McGinn, *Prostitution, Sexuality, and the Law in Ancient Rome* (New York: Oxford University Press, 1998), 140–215.

53. Judith Lynn Sebesta, "Symbolism in the Costume of the Roman Woman," in *The World of Roman Costume*, ed. Judith Lynn Sebesta and Larissa Bonfante (Madison, Wis.: University of Wisconsin Press, 1994), 46–53.

54. Similarly, BECNT 7 (Grand Rapids, Mich.: Baker Academic, 2003), 522.

In 1 Corinthians 11:7, Paul transitions in his explanations to the Mosaic creation account by a short but certain allusion to Genesis 1:26–27. Paul states, "a man ought not to cover the head because he is the image and glory of God" (1 Cor. 11:7). This expression "image of God" alludes to Genesis 1:26–27, where it says that God decided to make "human beings according to our image and likeness" (v. 26).[55] In the Genesis account, the image of God clearly includes male as well as female human beings (v. 27). Paul restricts the allusion in this context only to men, while stating about the women that they are the "glory of man" (1 Cor. 11:7). The word *doxa* ("glory") stands in sharp contrast to the words associated with shame in verses 5–6, which deal with worship.[56] This contrast further supports the idea that the issue regarding male worshipers was vertical, dealing with the human-divine relationship, while the issue regarding female worshipers was horizontal, dealing with the nuptial relationship.[57]

The term *eikōn* ("image") indicates that being created as the image and the likeness of God (Gen. 1:26), human beings have the greatest affinity to the Creator. In Paul's religious understanding, the trait of being the Creator or a creature determines whether worship is merited or not. Whereas the Creator merits being worshiped by creatures, no creature merits being worshiped. If a male believer, being part of the group with likeness to the Creator, worships the Creator in a similar way as pagan worshipers worship created *eikōn* ("idols"), then he dishonors God, the Creator.

The brief statement on female worshipers being the "glory of man" (1 Cor. 11:7) is explained by two explanatory parallelisms.

Structure of 1 Corinthians 11:8–9

A	*ou gar estin anēr ek gynaikos*	man is not out of the woman
A'	*alla gynē ex andros*	but woman out of man
B	*ouk ektisthē anēr dia tēn gynaika*	man is not created for the sake of woman
B'	*alla gynē dia ton andra*	but the woman for the sake of man

---

55. The expression "glory of God," is no direct allusion to creation; however, Psalm 8:5–7 mentions the Lord who "crowned him [human being] with glory and honor" (v. 6), since humanity received dominion over the works of the Lord's hand (v. 7).

56. Garland, *1 Corinthians*, 523.

57. The term "glory" (*doxa*) is used the same way in both instances in verse 7. However, in the first usage, the relationship is between God and man, whereas in the second usage the relationship is between man and woman.

Both parallelisms refer to concepts clearly rooted in the Mosaic creation account. A and A' thematically allude to Genesis 2:21–23,[58] which describes how God *wayyiben* ("built") the woman out of man, and how the man recognized the woman as "bone from my bones and flesh from my flesh" (v. 23). Besides the likeness in form, this first perception of man's fellow human being also reveals man's deep appreciation for the woman. B and B' conceptually allude to Genesis 2:18, 20,[59] which can be understood as "no helper similar to him was found" (v. 20). The term *'ēzer* ("helper") is used to indicate a beneficial relationship.[60] In fact, it is often used in reference to God preserving the life of His servants (Exod. 18:4; Deut. 33:7; Pss. 70:5; 94:17; 115:9–11 [69:6; 94:17; 113:17–19, LXX]).[61]

There are two arguments as to why the Genesis account allows for this connotation of *'ēzer* ("helper") to be used in relation to the woman, as the woman helping to preserve man's existence. First, both man and woman are included as being created in the image of God (Gen. 1:27). Second, man's aloneness is the only condition that the creation account labels as *lō'-ṭôb* ("not good," Gen. 2:18). Thus, Genesis 2 portrays man in existential need of the woman in order to reach completeness and thus guarantee human existence due to the ability to procreate (see Gen. 1:28).[62]

---

58. The thematic relation to Genesis 2:21–23 is evident by the sequence of creation. God created man first, followed by the woman. On a textual level, the Greek preposition *ek* ("from"), indicating source, is used when Adam recognizes Eve (v. 23). While it is impossible to argue for an allusion to Genesis 2:21–23 on a purely terminological level, the preposition *ek* ("from") in combination with the clear thematic parallel significantly increases the probability of an allusion to the Genesis account.

59. In this case there is no terminological connection between 1 Corinthians 11:9 and Genesis 1–2.

60. Davidson, "Headship," 262. An opposing viewpoint from Davidson's on the meaning if Genesis 2 is the view expressed by Paul S. Ratsara and Daniel K. Bediako, "Man and Woman in Genesis 1–3: Ontological Equality and Role Differentiation" (paper presented at the Theology of Ordination Study Commission, Silver Spring, Md., 23 July 2013), www. adventistarchives.org/july-2013-papers-presented.

61. Oliver Glanz, *Wenn die Götter auferstehen und die Propheten rebellieren: Glauben in einer modernen Welt* (Alsbach-Hähnlein: Stimme der Hoffnung, 2012), 52.

62. Davidson, "Headship," 261, argues that "the movement in Genesis 2, is . . . from incompleteness to completeness"; for the idea of existence, see Glanz, *Götter*, 53.

Structure of 1 Corinthians 11:11-12	
A	*plēn oute gynē chōris andros*	nevertheless, woman is not apart from man
A'	*oute anēr chōris gynaikos*	nor is man apart from woman
B	*en kyriō*	in the Lord
C	*hōsper gar hē gynē ek tou andros*	for as the woman is out of man
C'	*houtōs kai ho anēr dia tēs gynaikos*	so is also the man through the woman,
B'	*ta de panta ek tou theou*	but everything is from God

In 1 Corinthians 11:11-12, both parallelisms end with a prepositional phrase expressing divine creational activity, in *en kyriō* ("in the Lord [Christ]") (B) and in *ek tou theou* ("from God") (B').[63] Thus, Paul employs creational concepts in these parallelisms that go even beyond the level of allusion to Genesis 1-2. The preposition *en* ("in" or "by") (B) identifies the Lord as the agent who assigns man and woman their unity (see Gen. 1:26-28; 2:24).[64] The first parallel statement, "woman is not apart from man" (A), along with "nor is man apart from woman" (A') repeats the existential interdependence of both genders designed by the creator.[65] The conjunction *gar* ("for") indicates that the second parallelism clarifies the first parallelism. Regarding the statement "as the woman is out of man" (C), Paul argues with "so is also the man through the woman" (C') that every man is given birth by a mother (see Gen. 4:1).

Paul may have intended a double entendre in 1 Corinthians 11:11-12. This is indicated by the meaning of "in the Lord" (B) and "but everything is from God" (B'). The apostle often uses "in the

---

63. 1 Corinthians 11:10, in between the two structures noted in verses 8-9 and verses 11-12, deals with propriety in worship, where holy angels participate with the congregation in worshiping God, and serves as a conclusion to the prior discussion. See Thieslton, *The First Epistle to the Corinthians*, 838-41; and see also Paul Gardner, *1 Corinthians*, ZECNT (Grand Rapids, Mich.: Zondervan, 2018), 492-93. Concerning the creational language in verses 11-12, see Jill E. Marshall, "Uncovering Traditions in 1 Corinthians 11:2-16," *NovT* 61 no. 1(2019): 70-87. Regarding verses 11-12 she states, "This argument [concerning what Marshall sees as hierarchy in 11:3], however, does not work for Paul because *he envisions a new creation* that is not hierarchical but that continues to include male and female" (p. 86, emphasis added).

64. Harris translates it as "by the Lord's assignment . . . ." See Harris, *Prepositions and Theology*, 129.

65. The woman is created out of man (see A' in the table). Man cannot exist without the woman (see B' in the table).

Lord" in reference to the realm where believers exist.[66] The parallel statements of B' (1 Cor. 8:6; 2 Cor. 5:18) refer not only to God's activity in creation but also to His activity in the new creation. Whereas "the woman is out of man" (C) is a reference to Eve, "so is also the man through the woman" (C') may refer to the woman who gave birth to the promised male offspring, providing deliverance from sin for all human beings (Gen. 3:15; see also Gal. 4:4).[67]

Paul introduces creation to his argument by identifying man as the image and glory of God (1 Cor. 11:7). He understands that if men worshiped God the way that pagan men worshiped their idols, it would be an act of dishonor to God. At the same time, Paul addresses the issue related to women worshipers based on the creation of man and woman according to Genesis 2, clarifying what it means for the woman to be "the glory of man." He emphasizes that the creation order states that the woman is made for the man. The Genesis account explicitly mentions the purpose of the woman as a helper. This title illustrates her role in completing humanity, preserving its existence through procreation. Since the ethics rooted in the Mosaic creation account restricts this benefit to nuptial relationships, Paul is highly concerned with women who send signals of withdrawing from their nuptial relationships by praying and prophesying with head uncovered, dishonoring their husbands in the process.[68] Additionally, Paul's emphasis on creation order, as presented in the Mosaic account and its crucial role for Paul's argument, implies that he understands the content of the Mosaic creation account as a reliable source on origins and as the foundation of the institution of marriage.

CREATION AND RESURRECTION (1 CORINTHIANS 15:35–49)

In 1 Corinthians 15:35–49, Paul uses the idea of creation extensively in his elaborations on the bodily resurrection of the dead,

---

66. Rom. 16:8, 11–13; 1 Cor. 4:17; 7:22; 9:1–2; 16:19; Phil. 1:14; 4:1; 1 Thess. 3:8; Philem. 16.

67. Similarly, Norbert Baumert, *Woman and Man in Paul: Overcoming a Misunderstanding*, trans. Patrick Madigan and Linda M. Maloney (Collegeville, Minn.: Liturgical Press, 1996), 191–92.

68. While the action of these women has often been perceived as an intentional rebellious act, it seems more likely that the house church setting created this specific issue. Married women, when at home, usually remained unveiled. However, the church gathering in a household turned the home into a public space. Still being in a home setting, some women evidently considered the veil to be unnecessary. In doing so, they may have unconsciously dishonored their husband, demonstrating a lack of devotion to their nuptial relationship; see Winter, *After Paul Left Corinth*, 128.

which completes the new creation process for the believer who died. Some of the Corinthian believers claimed that "there is no resurrection of the dead" (1 Cor. 15:12). Part of their conclusion was their inability to explain "how the dead are going to be raised" or, more importantly, "what kind of body they will have" (v. 35). Thus, they were wrestling with the bodily aspect of the resurrection of the dead, due to the Greco-Roman concept that the soul is eternal and the body mortal.[69]

Paul explains the bodily resurrection with several analogies to nature. He points to specific features and processes regarding flora, fauna, and celestial objects (vv. 36–41), which he then compares to features and processes of the bodily resurrection (vv. 42–49).

Regarding flora, Paul refers to three aspects: First, the same plant has different *sōmata* ("bodies" or "forms") at different stages. Paul explains that "what you sow is not the body of the grown plant, but the bare seed" (v. 37). Thus, when sowing, the form of the seed is used, which transforms into the form of the plant. Second, the death of the seed is necessary in the transformation from one body to the other body—in other words, from the seed to the plant. Paul makes the comment that "what you sow is not made alive unless it dies" (v. 36). He is referring to the observation that digging up a rooted plant will reveal that the seed has ceased to exist in its original form. Third, God the Creator assigns to each seed its corresponding botanical body. Paul states that "God gives a body to each, as he has chosen, and to each seed its own body" (v. 38). Despite missing exact terminological parallels, Paul's analogy is possibly an allusion to Genesis 1:11–12.[70]

---

69. The Old Testament shows familiarity with the concept of a bodily resurrection (see Job 19:25–27; Isa. 26:19; Dan. 12:2). See Artur Stele, "Resurrection in Daniel 12 and its Contribution to the Theology of the Book of Daniel" (PhD diss., Andrews University, 1996); Jon Paulien, "The Resurrection and the Old Testament: A Fresh Look in Light of Recent Research," *JATS* 24, no. 1 (2013): 3–24; and John C. Brunt, "Resurrection and Glorification," in *HSDAT*, ed. Raoul Dederen, 7 vols. (Hagerstown, Md.: Review and Herald, 2000), 347–74. In contrast, the Greco-Roman schools of philosophy unanimously agreed that the body would have no share in the afterlife. For an extensive discussion, see Wright, *Christian Origins*, 32–60. For extensive discussion of biblical concepts on anthropology see Clinton Wahlen, ed. *"What are Human Beings That You Remember Them?": Proceedings of the Third International Bible Conference*, Nof Ginosar and Jerusalem, June 11–21, 2012 (Silver Spring, Md.: Review and Herald Publishing Association, 2015).

70. The possible allusion is seen in the idea that each plant produces a seed according to its kind. Thus, a certain kind of plant consists of a particular seed and the corresponding plant in its grown form.

Paul refers to two aspects of fauna and celestial objects. First, he points to creation's diversity, which displays God's ability as a Creator. He argues that in terms of fauna, "not every flesh is the same flesh" (1 Cor. 15:39)—namely, that humans, land animals, birds, and fish all have their unique flesh. In pointing this out, Paul certainly alludes to Genesis 1:20–31.[71] The same applies to celestial objects—in particular, the sun, moon, and stars, alluding to Genesis 1:14–19. In this case, Paul refers to their unique *doxa* ("glory" or "shine," 1 Cor. 15:41). By pointing out all the diversity on earth and in heaven, Paul portrays God as an able Creator.

Second, Paul compares earthly bodies with heavenly bodies, hinting at the superiority of the latter (1 Cor. 15:40). Earthly bodies refer to flora and fauna, whereas heavenly bodies refer to celestial objects. At this point, Paul simply attests that "there are heavenly and earthly bodies, but the glory of the heavenly ones is another than the one of the earthly ones" (v. 40). However, since earthly bodies are more perishable than the heavenly ones, Paul perceives the heavenly sphere as superior to the earthly one.[72] The evidence for his point is found in the Old Testament portrayal of the heavenly bodies. Psalm 89:37–38 (88:37–38, LXX) reveals that the heavenly bodies, particularly the sun and moon, were perceived to endure forever.[73]

Drawing an analogy between nature and the resurrection of the dead (1 Cor. 15:42), Paul answers the initial questions of "how the dead are going to be raised" and "what kind of body they will have" (v. 35). Picking up the language of *speirō* ("to sow," v. 36) and *egeirō* ("to raise," v. 35), Paul applies the three concepts of flora to the resurrection of the dead: First, he suggests that the current body will differ from the transformed body (vv. 42–49). Second, he indicates

---

71. The reversed order in comparison to Genesis 1:20–31 could function as a hint that Paul prioritizes the role of human beings; see Werner Straub, *Die Bildersprache des Apostels Paulus* (Tübingen: Mohr Siebeck, 1937), 72.

72. Schrage argues that Paul understood, based on Isaiah 40:26; 45:12; Psalm 19:2, 6; etc. and concepts found in apocalyptic literature (1 En. 18:13–15; 21; 75:3; 2 En. 29; 2 Bar. 59:11, etc.), the idea of heavenly bodies as an analogy to living beings (Schrage, *Korinther*, 4:290–93, esp. nn. 1430–31). However, the Old Testament texts do not provide support for such a conclusion. Wright, *Christian Origins*, 346, in contrast, argues that "Paul does not, then, think of 'heavenly bodies' as 'spiritual beings clothed with light.' He is not buying in to the cosmology of the *Timaeus*; indeed, the way the entire chapter is built around Genesis 1 and 2 indicates that he is consciously choosing to construct a cosmology, and within that a future hope, from the most central of Jewish sources."

73. In prophetic literature, it is part of the dramatic events, accompanying God's judgment over the unfaithful ones, when the sun and moon cease to shine (Isa. 13:9–12; Ezek. 32:7–8; Joel 2:10; 3:4; 4:15).

that the transformed body requires the end of the current body, either by decomposition after death or as a result of the transformation process for those still alive at Christ's return (vv. 50–57). Third, the passive voice of the verbs ("raised," vv. 42–44; "changed" vv. 51–52) indicates a divine passive, identifying God as the Creator of the current body as well as the transformed body. Paul also uses four antitheses to emphasize that the body in which a believer *egeiretai* ("is raised") is superior in every conceivable way to the current body, in which a believer *speiretai* ("is sown"). The current body is identified as a *sōma psychikon* ("natural body"), being perishable, dishonorable, and weak. In contrast, the transformed body is described as a *sōma pneumatikon* ("spiritual body"), being imperishable, honorable, and strong (vv. 43–44).

After describing what kind of body will be resurrected (v. 44), Paul clarifies the concept that enables a bodily resurrection. Elaborating further on the terms *psychikon* ("natural") and *pneumatikon* ("spiritual"), he quotes from Genesis 2:7: "The first human being, Adam, became a 'living being' [*psychēn zōsan*]" (1 Cor. 15:45).[74] The quotation associates Adam, being a *psychēn zōsan* ("living being"), with the *sōma psychikon* ("natural body").[75] In comparison to the first Adam, Paul introduces Jesus as "the last Adam" (v. 45), the one who became a *pneuma zōopoioun* ("life-giving spirit"). Jesus, being a *pneuma zōopoioun* ("life-giving spirit"), is not only associated with the superior *sōma pneumatikon* ("spiritual body") but is also presented as God's means of creating the spiritual body (v. 44).[76] In verses 47–49, Paul associates Adam with earth and Jesus with

---

74. Paul adds to the quote from Genesis 2 the words *prōtos* ("first") and *Adam*. Christopher D. Stanley, *Paul and the Language of Scripture: Citation Technique in the Pauline Epistles and Contemporary Literature*, SNTSMS 69 (Cambridge: Cambridge University Press, 1992), 208, argues concerning the addition of *prōtos* that "nothing in either the Greek or Hebrew textual traditions offers any reason to think that Paul might have found the word πρῶτος [*prōtos*] in his *Vorlage* of Genesis 2.7. In the context of 1 Corinthians 15, on the other hand, the addition brings to the formal expression the fundamental contrast between Adam and Christ as the πρῶτος [*prōtos*] and ἔσχατος [*eschatos*] Adam (v. 45b) that forms the backbone of the ensuing argument." Concerning the second addition of *Adam*, ibid., 208–9, he points to the fact that "none of the LXX manuscripts shows any of the Pauline wording in Genesis 2.7." However, "both Theodotion and Symmachus have ὁ Ἀδάμ ἄνθρωπος [*ho Adam anthrōpos*] at this point in their texts." Thus, he concludes "Paul may not have added the proper name Ἀδάμ [*Adam*] to his text of Genesis 2.7."

75. This inferiority was not originally intended by God (Gen. 1:31) but was a result of sin entering the cosmos (Rom. 5:12).

76. Jesus Christ is, Paul says, "a life-giving spirit." This moniker indicates that He is the one who raises the dead (cf. John 5:25–29; 1 Thess. 4:13–18).

heaven. At this point, Paul's previous comparison between earthly and heavenly bodies becomes important. Alluding again to Genesis 2:7, Paul states that "the first human being was made out of dusty soil." Adam's offspring share "the dusty image" (1 Cor. 15:48–49; see Gen. 5:3). Thus, human beings receive by default the inferior and perishable *sōma psychikon* ("natural body"). However, through faith in Jesus, who is "from heaven" (1 Cor. 15:47), believers will receive "the heavenly image" (vv. 48–49), or in other words, the superior, imperishable *sōma pneumatikon* ("spiritual body").[77] Based on God's ability to create the heavenly bodies, Paul can argue that God is also able to create an imperishable body for the resurrected ones.

The Mosaic creation account serves as a benchmark in Paul's discussion of the bodily resurrection of the dead in 1 Corinthians 15:35–49. Paul explains the unique concept of bodily resurrection through analogies to nature. However, the way he presents his analogies clearly indicates that he understands nature through the lens of the Mosaic creation account. This becomes evident in two different features of his argument: First, Paul's consistent use of the divine passive—along with his statement about God giving the plant, animal, and celestial creation their unique bodies or forms—identifies God not only as the Creator but also as the Designer of each particular seed, plant, fish, bird, land animal, human being, and celestial object. Second, the presented anthropology is based on Genesis 2:7, which understands the human body as consisting of dusty soil and the breath of the Spirit. Both of these concepts are rooted in the Mosaic creation account and are foundational for Paul's response to the Corinthian believers' doubts about the bodily resurrection.

CONCLUSION

Although Paul felt no need to explicitly teach about creation in his letters to the Corinthian church, he frequently refers to cosmological or creational concepts. Having taken a closer look at how these references function within their immediate context, it is clear that Paul was not influenced by the extracanonical cosmological

---

77. Paul clarifies the meaning of the future tense of *phoresomen* ("we shall bear") in 1 Corinthians 15:50–58, where he indicates that the bodily transformation from the current body to the future body will take place in the twinkling of an eye, when the last trumpet sounds (vv. 51–52)—in other words, at the parousia.

theories of his time. In regard to origin, Paul exclusively relies on the Genesis account.

This study has also revealed further insights into Paul's perception of the Mosaic creation account. First, in regard to the role of the Creator, Paul is certain that creation is a result of God's exclusive power to create. All things have their origin in God. There is no other power involved in the creation process. This leads Paul to conclude that God is the only one worthy of worship. Therefore, he uses creation as an argument in addressing issues related to idolatry. Based on this exclusive power of God, Paul also argues for God's exclusive involvement in the new creation—the restorative process of creation to rid the world of the invasive power of sin and death.

Second, Paul incorporates the Mosaic cosmology and creation account into his instructions on the ethics of sexual behavior, community worship, and idolatry. In doing so, he follows both typical Judaic reasoning as seen in the Hebrew Bible as well as commonly accepted Greco-Roman methodology, according to which cosmology determines ethical behavior. Since his Corinthian audience mainly consisted of people with a non-Jewish background, he believed that using ethical and moral concepts rooted in the Mosaic cosmology would be the most efficient strategy to adjust their immoral and unethical behavior. Paul's exclusive reliance on the Mosaic source indicates not only his acceptance of its content but also the presupposition that his audience had been previously exposed to its content and was willing to accept it accordingly.

Finally, in regard to the Mosaic creation account itself, Paul's discussion on the bodily resurrection indicates that he understood God to be not only the main creative force but also the Designer responsible for the vast biodiversity observed in flora, fauna, and celestial objects. By accommodating his argument to the exclusive order of creation, as presented in the Mosaic account, Paul implies that he believes the Mosaic account to be a reliable source in regard to the sequence of the origin of species.

Félix H. Cortez, PhD

Andrews University
Berrien Springs, Michigan, USA

CREATION IN HEBREWS

INTRODUCTION

The Letter to the Hebrews is certainly an important voice in any discussion on the biblical view of creation. Among the books of the New Testament, it contains more references to Genesis 1–2, and creation in general, than all but the Apocalypse.[1] It contains perhaps the most famous affirmation on the topic: "By faith we understand that the worlds were prepared by the word of God, so that what is seen was made from things that are not visible" (Heb. 11:3, NRSV).[2]

The purpose of this study is to examine the language and theology of creation in Hebrews; thus, it is both exegetical and theological in nature. This study will consider the following questions:

1. What does Hebrews say about the creation of our world?
2. What role does the creation of our world play in the broader argument of Hebrews?

---

1. There are a total of eleven references. For a list of references in the New Testament to Genesis 1–2 and creation in general, see Ekkehardt Mueller, "Creation in the New Testament," *JATS* 15, no. 1 (2004): 48. In this list, Hebrews is tied with Romans for second place, with nine references each (Revelation is first, with fourteen). However, this list does not include Hebrews 2:10 and 3:4.

2. All biblical translations are the author's, unless otherwise indicated.

3. How do the views on creation in Hebrews relate to the debate on the origin of the world in antiquity (especially to Plato, whose views held a prominent position in the intellectual landscape of the ancient Greco-Roman world)?
4. What are the implications of the views on creation in Hebrews for the current debate between creationism and evolution?

HEBREWS AND HELLENISTIC VIEWS ON CREATION

The study of the debate on the origin of the world among ancient Greek philosophers is especially important for the study of Hebrews, as it is the most Hellenistic of the New Testament documents. It seems obvious that its author was well educated and enjoyed rhetorical training;[3] his arguments and style are sophisticated. The book's Greek is excellent—"by far the best Koine to be found among New Testament writings."[4] It contains complex sentences of elevated style, carefully redacted to delight readers and evoke varying rhetorical effects.[5] The letter is not only beautifully written but also carefully argued. In fact, some consider this book to be the beginning of Christian philosophy.[6] Thus, insight into the ancient debate on the origin of the cosmos, together with a thorough knowledge of the Hebrew Scriptures (no New Testament book quotes the Old Testament as extensively as Hebrews[7]), provides the reader with the tools to reconstruct, as much as possible, the

---

3. Harold W. Attridge, *Hebrews: A Commentary on the Epistle to the Hebrews*, Hermeneia (Philadelphia: Fortress, 1989), 5.

4. Luke Timothy Johnson, *Hebrews: A Commentary*, NTL (Louisville, Ky.: Westminster John Knox, 2006), 8.

5. Attridge, *Hebrews*, 5. See also Michael R. Cosby, *The Rhetorical Composition and Function of Hebrews 11: In Light of Example Lists in Antiquity* (Macon, Ga.: Mercer University Press, 1988); David A. deSilva, *Despising Shame: Honor Discourse and Community Maintenance in the Epistle to the Hebrews*, SBLDS 152 (Atlanta: Scholars, 1995), 30–33; and Craig R. Koester, *Hebrews: A New Translation with Introduction and Commentary*, AB 36 (New York: Doubleday, 2001), 92–96.

6. See James W. Thompson, *The Beginnings of Christian Philosophy: The Epistle to the Hebrews*, CBQMS 13 (Washington, D.C.: Catholic Biblical Association, 1982).

7. See George H. Guthrie, "Old Testament in Hebrews," in *Dictionary of the Later New Testament and Its Developments*, ed. Ralph P. Martin and Peter H. Davids (Downers Grove, Ill.: InterVarsity, 1997), 841–42. George Guthrie, for example, counts thirty-six quotations and thirty-seven allusions. Compare with Pamela Michelle Eisenbaum, *The Jewish Heroes of Christian History: Hebrews 11 in Literary Context*, SBLDS 156 (Atlanta: Scholars, 1997), 90–91; and Simon Kistemaker, *The Psalm Citations in the Epistle to the Hebrews* (Amsterdam: van Soest, 1961), 16. The book of Revelation, however, has more allusions to the Old Testament than Hebrews.

appropriate chamber of resonance that will not distort its music or dampen its singular tones.

The ancient debate on the origin of the cosmos was lively and the spectrum of positions wide. Anaxagoras, Empedocles, Socrates, Plato, and the Stoics, with distinct differences and subtle nuances, championed the argument from design and found compelling evidence for a creator. Aristotle embraced teleology—that is, that the world is purposeful and contains purposeful structures—yet, he denied an active organizing intelligence (that is, no divine oversight, planning, or enforcement). The atomists, who were strict materialists, appealed to the explanatory power of infinity and accident and proposed the fundamental insight of natural selection.[8] This study will not be able to explore this wider landscape but will focus on the most prominent and influential of ancient cosmologies: Plato's *Timaeus*.

The *Timaeus* proved "from the start the most influential of all Plato's works, and probably the most seminal philosophical or scientific text to emerge from the whole of antiquity."[9] It became the basic Platonic dialogue for Middle Platonism (ca. 80 BC–AD 250)[10] and the only Platonic dialogue in general circulation in the Western Middle Ages.[11]

Scholars of the book of Hebrews have long argued that the book adopts a Platonic worldview similar to, or mediated through, that of Philo[12]—a Hellenistic Jewish philosopher who lived in Alexandria ca. 20 BC–ca. AD 50.[13] In his writings, Philo brought together Jewish

8. David Sedley, *Creationism and Its Critics in Antiquity,* Sather Classical Lectures 66 (Berkeley, Calif.: University of California Press, 2007). See also Keith Augustus Burton, "The Faith Factor: New Testament Cosmology in Its Historical Context," *JATS* 15, 1 (2004): 34–46; and Arnold Ehrhardt, *The Beginning: A Study in the Greek Philosophical Approach to the Concept of Creation from Anaximander to St John* (New York: Barnes and Noble, 1968).

9. Sedley, *Creationism and Its Critics*, 96.

10. Gerhard May, *Creatio ex nihilo: The Doctrine of 'Creation out of Nothing' in Early Christian Thought*, trans. A. S. Worrall (London: T&T Clark, 2004), 3–4.

11. See Jaroslav Pelikan, *What Has Athens to Do with Jerusalem?: Timaeus and Genesis in Counterpoint* (Ann Arbor, Mich.: The University of Michigan Press, 1997), 111–32. According to J. M. Dillon, "Plato, Platonism," in *Dictionary of New Testament Background*, ed. Craig A. Evans and Stanley E. Porter (Downers Grove, Ill.: InterVarsity, 2000), 804–5, Platonism, as a system of philosophy, is "perhaps the greatest philosophical edifice ever erected in the Western intellectual tradition" and helped shape Christian theology in its first centuries of existence. For a study of the influence of Plato's *Timaeus* on Christian theology, see Pelikan, *What Has Athens to Do with Jerusalem?*

12. See, e.g., Thompson, *Beginnings of Christian Philosophy*; and Johnson, *Hebrews*, 17–21.

13. In *Legat.* 1, 182, Philo describes himself among the "aged" and "gray-headed." It could be inferred from this that he was between sixty and seventy years old in AD 40. See Ronald Williamson, *Jews in the Hellenistic World*, vol. 1, bk. 2, *Philo*, Cambridge Commentaries on Writings of the Jewish and Christian World 200 BC to AD 200 (Cambridge: Cambridge University Press, 1989), 1.

tradition and Greek philosophy. He was especially influenced by what is known today as Middle Platonism, which is a blend of Platonic thought with Stoic and Pythagorean ideas.[14] In his study on the origin of the early Christian doctrine *creatio ex nihilo*, or creation out of nothing, Gerhard May argues that it was not until the latter part of the second century that Christianity began to respond to the challenges of philosophical theology and Platonizing Gnosticism by developing a clear doctrine of *creatio ex nihilo*.[15] Hebrews was written in the previous century, but the forces and tendencies that would shape the later debate were already taking place. By the time Hebrews was written, Plato's worldview had great influence on the thinking of Hellenistic Judaism and was beginning to have such influence in early Christian sectors as well.[16] Thus, the questions arise: What position does Hebrews favor in what would be the later debate? Does Hebrews reinterpret the Genesis account from a Platonic/Philonic point of view? If so, in what ways and to what extent?

This study comprises three main sections. The first section introduces the debate in modern scholarship regarding Plato's/Philo's influence on Hebrews. This includes a summary of Plato's views on the origin of the cosmos. The second section analyzes the references to the creation of the world in Hebrews and what role they play in the argument of their immediate contexts. Finally, the third section presents some of the implications of this study in terms of the theology of creation in Hebrews and the debate between creation and evolution.

DID THE AUTHOR OF HEBREWS HAVE A PLATONIC/PHILONIC WORLDVIEW?

There is a long history behind the view that the author of Hebrews was influenced by the Alexandrian Jewish philosopher Philo and the existential dualism of Plato. Philo was contemporary to Herod the Great, Hillel, Shammai, Gamaliel, Paul, and Jesus. He is also a prime example of a Hellenization process that occurred especially among diaspora Jews. His entire work is an attempt "to show

---

14. Ellen Birnbaum, "Philo of Alexandria," in *NIDB* 4:512.

15. May, *Creatio ex nihilo*, rejects the common notion that the concept of *creatio ex nihilo* emerged in pre-Christian Hellenistic Judaism (e.g., 2 Macc. 7:28–29) and was simply presupposed and absorbed by early Christians. He suggests that with Irenaeus this doctrine takes a settled form and the debate reaches a specific conclusion (xiv).

16. John Turner, "Plato, Platonism," in *NIDB*, 4:546–47.

that the Jewish people did not need to be ashamed of their cultural and religious heritage"[17] and it endeavors to explain the Old Testament and Judaism in terms of Greek philosophy—especially from the Platonic strand.[18] Philo influenced Christian thinkers such as Clement and Origen, and his philosophical/allegorical exegesis was continued by the Alexandrian Christian Church.[19]

In the early fourth century, Eusebius of Caesarea referred to Plato's *Republic* while commenting on Hebrews 8:5 (Eusebius, *Praep. ev.* XII). Hugo Grotius in 1646 suggested, probably for the first time, the possibility of Philonic influence on Hebrews.[20] In 1894, Eugene Ménégoz was the first to produce a thoroughgoing presentation on Philo's influence on Hebrews. He concluded that "[l'auteur de l'épître] est un philonien converti au christianisme."[21] This view dominated the first part of the twentieth century and reached its climax in Ceslas Spicq's massive commentary in 1952. Spicq evaluated vocabulary, hermeneutic techniques, psychology, and parallels with Hebrews 11 and concluded by quoting Ménégoz's view with approval, even suggesting that the author of Hebrews knew Philo personally.[22] He did not describe the author of Hebrews as a

---

17. David T. Runia, *Exegesis and Philosophy: Studies on Philo of Alexandria*, Collected Studies 332 (Aldershot: Variorum, 1990), 5.

18. It could be said that the Hellenistic literature, from the Septuagint to Philo and Josephus, had a "double purpose: to defend the Jews and Judaism from the attacks of pagans and to prove the superiority of the Jews and Judaism over other nations and their religions" (Robert H. Pfeiffer, *History of New Testament Times: With an Introduction to the Apocrypha* [New York: Harper, 1949], 197). Philo evidences a broad and penetrating knowledge of Greek culture in his writings. According to Samuel Sandmel, *Philo of Alexandria: An Introduction* (New York: Oxford University Press, 1979), 15, he quotes "some fifty-four classical authors directly and accurately." See also Peder Borgen, *Philo of Alexandria: An Exegete for His Time*, NovTSup 86 (Leiden: Brill, 1997), 3.

19. Philo influenced Christian thinkers such as Clement and Origen (J. M. Knight, "Alexandria, Alexandrian Christianity," in Martin and Davids, *Dictionary of the Later New Testament*, 36–37). Indeed, we owe the survival of Philo's works to the Christian church. Of the more than seventy treatises he wrote, the fifty that survived are essentially those in Eusebius's catalogue of Philo's work (*Hist. eccl.* 2.18.1–7). See Gregory E. Sterling, "Philo," in Evans and Porter, *Dictionary of New Testament Background*, 790. As suggested by David T. Runia, *Jewish Traditions in Early Christian Literature*, vol. 3, *Philo in Early Christian Literature: A Survey*, CRINT (Minneapolis, Minn.: Fortress, 1993), 3–7, 31–33, we could say to some extent that Philo was adopted by the Christian church.

20. For other suggestions of Philonic influence before the twentieth century, see James H. Burtness, "Plato, Philo and Hebrews," *LQ* 10 (1958), 54–55.

21. "[The author of the Epistle] is a Philonian converted to Christianity." Eugène Ménégoz, *La théologie de L'Epitre aux Hébreux* (Paris: Fischbacher, 1894), 198.

22. Ceslas Spicq, *L'épître aux Hébreux*, EBib (Paris: Gabalda, 1952), 1:91. See also Lincoln D. Hurst, *The Epistle to the Hebrews: Its Background of Thought*, SNTSMS 65 (Cambridge: Cambridge University Press, 1990), 7n5.

thoroughgoing Philonist; however, he recognized that there is a "resolute repudiation" of Philo's allegorical method in the epistle. The discovery of the Dead Sea Scrolls and the publication of an article by C. K. Barrett in 1956—which stressed that the perspective of Hebrews is eschatological and not existential dualistic—dealt major blows to the ideas championed by Spicq.[23] In 1970, Ronald Williamson wrote a comprehensive, point-by-point critique of Spicq's case, concluding that Spicq's case was groundless.[24]

However, the case for Platonic/Philonic influence continues to exert influence in the interpretation of Hebrews even today.[25] In 1982, James W. Thompson asserted that Spicq succeeded in demonstrating that Hebrews uses "the vocabulary of educated Hellenistic Jews."[26] In his opinion, the problem was that Spicq had claimed too much.[27] Thompson argued that Williamson's critique had not been able to refute the idea that Philo and the author of Hebrews belonged to a common conceptual background[28] and quite correctly identified the crux of the debate:

> The *eschatology of the Epistle* to the Hebrews has been a central issue
> for debate in discussion of the intellectual world of the author. This

---

23. See C. K. Barrett, "The Eschatology of the Epistle to the Hebrews," in *The Background of the New Testament and Its Eschatology in Honour of Charles Dodd*, ed. W. D. Davies and D. Daube (Cambridge: Cambridge University Press, 1956), 363–93.

24. Ronald Williamson, *Philo and the Epistle to the Hebrews*, ALGHJ 4 (Leiden: Brill, 1970), 576–77, states, "But it is in the realm of ideas, of the thoughts which words and O.T. texts were used to express and support, that the most significant differences between Philo and the Writer of Hebrews emerge. On such fundamental subjects as time, history, eschatology, the nature of the physical world, etc., the thoughts of Philo and the Writer of Hebrews are poles apart."

25. Johnson, *Hebrews*, 17–21, argues that Hebrews shares the worldview of Plato. Kenneth L. Schenck, *Cosmology and Eschatology in Hebrews: The Settings of the Sacrifice*, SNTSMS 143 (Cambridge: Cambridge University Press, 2007), 113–81, rejects that Hebrews adopts a Platonic/Philonic worldview, but he speculates that salvation in Hebrews is salvation from the created realm, partly on the basis of Hebrews 9:26, which declares that atonement was needed from the beginning of creation.

26. Thompson, *Beginnings of Christian Philosophy*, 8.

27. Ibid., 11, says that no amount of verbal parallelism can demonstrate that the author of Hebrews is a "philonien converti au christianisme." "The relationship between Philo and Hebrews is probably too complex to be reduced to a matter of literary dependence."

28. Ibid., 10. Thompson has softened his position, however: "The major debate in scholarship on Hebrews has been the determination of the author's intellectual worldview. We need not choose one over the other, as if the Jewish and Greek worlds existed in isolation from each other. The author lives between the world of Scripture and that of Greek philosophy. He is one among many early Jewish and Christian writers who struggled to describe their faith in the language of philosophy. . . . Like Clement of Alexandria, Origen, and other early Christian writers, he affirmed Christian convictions that could not be reconciled with Platonism while employing Platonic categories to interpret Christian existence" (James W. Thompson, *Hebrews*, Paideia [Grand Rapids, Mich.: Baker Academic, 2008], 24–25).

debate appears to result from the fact that Hebrews contains both passages which assume the spatial dualism of Plato (i.e., 8:5) and statements which assume the apocalyptic, temporal dualism of the two ages [linear apocalyptic] (i.e., 1:2; 6:4).[29]

The question, then, continues to be debated. Was the author of Hebrews influenced by Philo and Plato's views and, if so, to what extent did their views shape the book's views on the creation of the world? It is important to evaluate the evidence.

ORIGIN OF THE UNIVERSE ACCORDING TO PLATO

Plato conceives the earth as approximately spherical, located motionless at the center of the greater sphere of heaven. The surface rises in different degrees so that some sectors lie underwater, others in the air, and others rise to the upper atmosphere known as aether. Below the surface, there are underground rivers.[30] Souls are assigned to an appropriate region according to the level of their purification, ranging from punishment in Tartarus to living in beauty and purity in the upper atmosphere in a nearly discarnate state. How did this earth come to exist?

This is described in the *Timaeus*. The discourse on cosmology is, in fact, just a fragment of the *Timaeus-Critias*, which is a truncated series of monologues that includes the Atlantis story told by Critias, the relation of the origin of the world by Timaeus, and a second disposition by Critias. But the document breaks off before revealing what a third speaker, Hermocrates, would have said.[31] David Sedley lists the main highlights of Timaeus's discourse on cosmology in the following way:

- *"First principles.* After an opening prayer, Timaeus invokes a strong version of the Platonic 'two world' metaphysics, which separates a realm of intelligible being from one of perceptible becoming. . . .

---

29. Thompson, *Beginnings of Christian Philosophy*, 41, emphasis added.

30. This is described in the *Phaedo*'s closing myth (Plato, *Phaed.* 107c1–115a8). I will follow the description of Plato's cosmology by Sedley, *Creationism and Its Critics*. For further study, see Ehrhardt, *The Beginning*, 87–106; and Thomas Kjeller Johansen, *Plato's Natural Philosophy: A Study of the Timaeus-Critias* (Cambridge: Cambridge University Press, 2004).

31. For a study of the internal logic of the different sections of the *Timaeus-Critias*, see Johansen, *Plato's Natural Philosophy*, 7–23. The *Timaeus* is presented as a continuation of the *Republic*. Johansen argues that "the *Timaeus-Critias* can be seen as an extension of the concern in the *Gorgias* and the *Republic* with refuting the view that nature supports vice and undermines virtue" (ibid., 22).

- *"World design.* The product of an intrinsically good 'maker' or 'Demiurge,' our world is modelled on an eternal Form, and is itself a single, spherical, intelligent entity, consisting of the four familiar stuffs, earth, water, air, and fire, plus a soul.
- *"Materials.* The Demiurge designed the microscopic structure of the four elementary stuffs, imposing beauty and functionality on a substrate called the 'receptacle' whose motions had prior to his intervention been more or less chaotic....
- *"The world soul* was composed by the Demiurge out of a complex mixture of sameness, difference, and being, arranged in two strips—the circle of the Same and the circle of the Different—and divided into harmonic intervals. This is the structure that underlies the orderly motions of the heavenly bodies.
- *"The human rational soul.* The human rational soul, also constructed by the Demiurge, was modelled by him on the world soul, and was later housed in our approximately spherical heads in imitation of the way the world soul occupies, and rotates, through the spherical heaven. Its incarnation has disrupted its naturally circular motions, but by imitating the world soul it can aspire eventually to restore them.
- *"The human body.* Anything the Demiurge makes, including our rational souls, is thereby immortal. To avoid making human beings themselves immortal, the detailed design and construction of the human body, including the mortal soul-parts, had to be delegated to the lesser, created gods. They designed and built the human body as a suitable housing for the rational soul.
- *"Other animals.* These were created as deliberately engineered degenerations from the human archetype, designed to imprison ex-human souls for a period of punishment and redemption."[32]

Interpreters of the *Timaeus* have long debated whether Plato truly considered there was a divine craftsman who, on a specific date in the past, had built the world out of chaotic matter or if this image was employed only to describe the causal role of intelligence in a world that has existed essentially unchanged from past eternity.[33] David Sedley concludes that Plato believed in an act of creation in time and that Aristotle, the Epicureans, the Stoics, and Galen all

---

32. Sedley, *Creationism and Its Critics*, 97–98.
33. For references to studies on this debate, see ibid., 98n9.

favored a literal reading of the *Timaeus*.[34] Plato's Demiurge is a craftsman. He is not the omnipotent God of the Bible. He models the world on an eternal Form and uses preexisting matter of a previous state of chaos. He is limited to some extent, however, by the matter he uses to create, so the world he creates is less than perfect. He structures the world in order "to provide souls, through a system of punishments and rewards, with the possibility of self-purification, divinization, and eternal discarnate bliss."[35] The world is made with the soul in mind. The entire animal kingdom was modeled on one Form. The superior species are those that resemble more closely the Form—these are the immortal fiery animals (the star gods) created by the Demiurge. The lower ones are the mortal species associated with air, earth, and water and were created by the immortal fiery animals.[36]

DOES THE LETTER TO THE HEBREWS CONTAIN PLATONIC IDEAS?

Some consider the use of the terms *hypodeigma, skia, antitypos, eikōn, pragma,* and *alēthinos* to be evidence of the presence of Platonic ideas in Hebrews. A closer analysis, however, shows that this is not the case.

"*Hypodeigma* has perhaps played more of a role in the 'Platonizing' of Hebrews than any other factor."[37] This word appears in Hebrews 8:5 and has been translated as "copy" (e.g., RSV), conveying the sense that the earthly sanctuary was a "copy" of the heavenly one. Plato believed that the earthly world (perceived by the senses) is a "copy" (*mimēma* or *eikōn*) of eternal ideas (Plato, *Tim.* 48e–49a). Philo shared this view. According to him, God created the earthly world as a beautiful copy (*mimēma kalon*) of a beautiful pattern (*kalou paradeigmatos*; e.g., Philo, *Opif.* 16[38]). The comparison between the earthly and the heavenly world and between shadow and reality in Hebrews 8:5 and 9:23 made some conclude that the

---

34. The *Timaeus* has the outward form of a creation myth, but its contents switch repeatedly between myth, fable, prayer, and scientific analysis. See ibid., 97, 107.

35. Ibid., 125–26.

36. See ibid., 127–32.

37. Hurst, *Epistle to the Hebrews*, 14.

38. "For God, being God, assumed that a beautiful copy [*mimēma*] would never be produced apart from a beautiful pattern, and that no object of perception would be faultless which was not made in the likeness of an original discerned only by the intellect" (Philo, *Opif.* 16 [Colson, LCL]). See also Peder Borgen, Kåre Sigvald Fuglseth, and Roald Skarsten, *The Philo Index: A Complete Greek Word Index to the Writings of Philo of Alexandria* (Grand Rapids, Mich.: Eerdmans; Leiden: Brill, 2000), 226.

author of Hebrews was influenced by the classical dualism of Plato via Philo.[39] There are, however, several problems with this view. First, "*hypodeigma* is *not* a word characteristic of Philo."[40] He and Plato preferred *paradeigma* (e.g., Philo, *Opif.* 16). Second, *hypodeigma* does not mean "copy" but the opposite: "something *to be* copied," an "example."[41] A better translation in the context of Hebrews 8:5 and 9:23 would be "sketch" or "prototype." Third, *paradeigma* in Plato and Philo denotes the world of ideas, while in Hebrews *hypodeigma* denotes the earthly tabernacle. The use of *hypodeigma*, then, does not actually support the idea that Hebrews has a Platonic worldview.

The use of the term *antitypos* has also been understood in Platonic terms,[42] especially where the earthly tabernacle is contrasted with the heavenly one in Hebrews 9:24. *Antitypos* could mean "copy" as well as "original," and in classical Greek "occasionally means 'echo,' 'corresponding,' 'opposite,' 'reproduction.'"[43] The immediate context of this verse, however, suggests a prefiguration relationship (type-antitype) rather than a metaphysical one (original-copy; see also preceding discussion on *hypodeigma*). The only other occurrence of the term in the New Testament is found in 1 Peter 3:21, which uses *antitypos* in a type-antitype relationship as well.[44] This same relationship seems to better fit the context of Hebrews. In this sense, Moses's tabernacle is a prefiguration of something that comes later; thus, *antitypos* does not carry a Platonic sense in Hebrews 9:24.

---

39. William L. Lane, *Hebrews 1–8*, WBC 47A (Dallas: Word, 1991), 207.

40. Hurst, *Epistle to the Hebrews*, 13. *Hypodeigma* is used only four times by Philo. See Borgen, Fuglseth, and Skarsten, *The Philo Index*, 226. In fact, "Kenneth Schenck [*A Brief Guide to Philo* (Louisville, Ky.: Westminster John Knox, 2005), 84] points out that the term 'is *never* used by *any* ancient author, let alone Philo or Plato, in reference to a Platonic copy,'" (quoted in Edward Adams, "The Cosmology of Hebrews," in *The Epistle to the Hebrews and Christian Theology*, ed. Richard Bauckham et al. [Grand Rapids, Mich.: Eerdmans, 2009], 133).

41. Hurst, *Epistle to the Hebrews*, 14. In the Septuagint and in Philo, the term is used mostly in the sense of moral example.

42. For example, in Neoplatonism by Plotinus, *Enneades* 2.9.6, where *antitypos* is contrasted with *authentikon* (Hurst, *Epistle to the Hebrews*, 18). The term *antitypos*, however, was rarely used in Judaism.

43. Hurst, *Epistle to the Hebrews*, 17–18. Philo uses it only three times (*Plant.* 133; *Conf.* 102; *Her.* 181) in the sense of "resistant" or "inimical."

44. It should be noted that the order is reversed in 1 Peter. The baptism, which is the antitype, is the fulfillment, while in Hebrews the antitype is what prefigures the fulfillment. This should not have much importance since it is the type-antitype relationship in the context of the history of salvation that is important for understanding the use of the term in Hebrews (Hurst, *Epistle to the Hebrews*, 18).

The phrase *eikona tōn pragmatōn* (lit. "image of the things") in Hebrews 10:1 has been forwarded as another example of Platonic and Philonic influence on Hebrews.[45] Plato (*Crat.* 306e) and Philo (e.g., *Leg.* 3.96; *Abr.* 3f.) use *eikōn* ("image") to refer to the earthly (perceived) world. For Philo, "image" (*eikōn*) and "shadow" (*skia*) are synonymous and both refer to the earthly world of perception.[46] In Hebrews, however, "image" (*eikōn*) belongs to the heavenly world and is opposed to "shadow" (*skia*).[47] In conclusion, the terms are the same but used differently, evidencing a different conceptual background.

Finally, as Lincoln D. Hurst explains, "it has been assumed by many that ἀληθινός [*alēthinos*], used by *Auctor* [of Hebrews] in 8:2 and 9:24, relates specially to Plato's *Republic* VI.499c, and means the 'real' world of the eternal archetypes as opposed to the 'unreal' world of earthly copies."[48] The comparison in those verses, however, is not between the phenomenal sanctuary (earthly) and the ideal (heavenly) but between the symbol (Mosaic tabernacle) and the reality (heavenly tabernacle). The Greek term *alēthinos* ("true") refers in this case to "the reality to which the symbol points"[49]—namely, the heavenly sanctuary. Further examples in the New Testament of this typological argument may be found in John 6:32, Romans 2:28, and Philippians 3:3. Again, the use of *alēthinos* ("true") does not evidence that Hebrews shares a Platonic/Philonic worldview.

SHOULD WE UNDERSTAND THE VERTICAL HEAVEN-EARTH DUALITY IN HEBREWS FROM A PLATONIC POINT OF VIEW?

The presence of "vertical" patterns in Hebrews (for example, a heaven-earth duality) does not necessarily imply a Platonic or Philonic mode of thinking. The idea that Greek thought deals with space (a "vertical" cosmological framework) while Jews think in terms of time (a "horizontal" temporal framework) has been overstated.[50]

---

45. See ibid., 19.

46. *Leg.* 3.96 reads: "Bezaleel means, then, 'in the shadow of God'; but God's shadow is his Word, which he made use of like an instrument, and so made the world. But this shadow, and what we may describe as the representation, is the archetype for further creations. For just as God is the Pattern [*paradeigma*] of the Image [*eikōn*], to which the title of Shadow [*skia*] has just been given, even so the Image becomes the pattern of other beings, as the prophet made clear at the very outset of the Law-giving by saying, 'And God made the man after the image of God'" (Colson, LCL).

47. Hurst, *Epistle to the Hebrews*, 19–20.

48. Ibid., 20.

49. Ibid., 20–21.

50. Ibid., 21.

Christianity, in fact, merges both frameworks. Christianity's worldview includes the idea of the present and coming ages (horizontal temporal framework), which overlap with the heavenly and earthly domains (vertical cosmological framework). Colossians 3:1–4 is a good example of this phenomenon:

> So if you have been raised with Christ, seek the things that are above, where Christ is, seated at the right hand of God. Set your minds on things that are above, not on things that are on earth, for you have died, and your life is hidden with Christ in God. When Christ who is your life is revealed, then you also will be revealed with Him in glory.

In this text, the apostle merges vertical and horizontal frameworks. He invites his readers to look for the things above (vertical framework) so that they might be revealed in the future (horizontal framework) with Jesus in glory.

In the same way, the view of reality in Hebrews includes the overlap of vertical and horizontal dimensions. According to Hebrews 8:5, the earthly tabernacle built by Moses was a *hypodeigma* ("pattern") and *skia* ("shadow") of the heavenly sanctuary. Yes, there is a vertical dimension that involves heaven and earth, but there is also a horizontal dimension in time. Moses's tabernacle was a pattern of an eschatological reality to be fulfilled by Christ when He offered Himself as a sacrifice and ascended to heaven to minister on our behalf.[51] Thus, in the argument of Hebrews, the earthly tabernacle is not simply a shadow but a foreshadow of the heavenly one. According to Hebrews 10:1, the ritual of Moses's tabernacle pointed toward the future: "Since the law has only a shadow [*skia*] of the *good things to come* and not the true form of these realities . . . " (NRSV, emphasis added; see also Heb. 9:11–14). The contrast between the heavenly and the earthly sanctuary is then temporal ("then-now," horizontal) and spatial ("above-below," vertical).[52]

---

51. Hurst, *Epistle to the Hebrews*, 16.

52. An apparent contradiction results, however, from this horizontal (temporal) contrast between both sanctuaries. How do we understand that the earthly sanctuary is the "prefiguration" of the heavenly one (the "good things to come," Heb. 10:1) if the heavenly sanctuary was already present in Moses's time and seems to be the basis on which the earthly one was designed (Heb. 8:5)? Does not Exodus 25:40 imply that the heavenly comes first and the earthly later? Hebrews is interested in the expiatory function of the sanctuary and Jesus's priestly work in it. While the heavenly sanctuary existed from the beginning of creation as the dwelling of God and the place of His throne (e.g., Jer. 17:12), the expiatory function of the sanctuary and Jesus's priestly ministry in it began with His ascension after His death on the cross as the sacrifice for our sins. For the author of Hebrews, the Israelite

The overlap of vertical and horizontal dimensions in Hebrews is, however, a little more complex. The ritual of the earthly sanctuary pointed toward the new reality achieved by Christ, which is in heaven now but which believers will enjoy only in the future (e.g., Heb. 11). Thus, the author of Hebrews sees the future as already happening in heaven. This is a frequent occurrence in other biblical writings. For example, the future inheritance of Christians is seen as already present in heaven:

> Blessed be the God and Father of our Lord Jesus Christ! By his great mercy he has given us a new birth into a living hope through the resurrection of Jesus Christ from the dead, and into an inheritance that is imperishable, undefiled, and unfading, *kept in heaven for you.* (1 Pet. 1:3–4, NRSV, emphasis added)

Likewise, what is present in God's mind is considered as having already happened or even eternal; this concept is the essence of the Jewish thought of predestination. For example, Revelation 13:8 asserts, "All inhabitants of the earth will worship the beast—all whose names have not been written in the book of life belonging to the Lamb that was slain from the creation of the world" (cf. Eph. 1:4–5).

There are other evidences that Hebrews does not share a Platonic view of the universe. Hebrews does not exhibit the slightest trace of discomfort with the idea that God created the physical universe (Heb. 2:10; 3:4; 4:3–4; 11:3), and it does not accord the Son, who collaborated in creation, a demiurgical role (1:2–3, 10–12).[53] The heaven-earth duality in Hebrews hardly agrees with Plato's distinction between the physical world and the realm of ideas. The author

---

desert sanctuary was a foreshadow or prototype of this expiatory function of the sanctuary and the priestly work of Jesus. Hurst, *Epistle to the Hebrews*, 37–41, has a similar position. He mentions that there were four views in Judaism as to when the heavenly sanctuary was built: (1) before creation, (2) at creation, (3) when the earthly sanctuary was built, and (4) at the end of the age. Hurst argues that Hebrews should be included in the fourth view and gives several arguments: (1) Hebrews 8:2 says that the heavenly tabernacle was actually pitched by the Lord; therefore, it is not archetypically eternal in the Platonic sense. (2) Hebrews 9:8 clearly implies that the heavenly sanctuary is the "second" and the earthly is the "first." (3) Hebrews 9:23 says that the sanctuary was "purified" by Jesus's blood, which must refer to the inauguration of the sanctuary and not to the day of the atonement (see 9:15–22). (4) Finally, Hebrews 13:14 talks about the future manifestation on earth of this heavenly temple (implied in the "heavenly city"). Hurst offers 1 Enoch 90:28–29 as an example of the view that God would build a sanctuary at the end of the age. The heavenly sanctuary existed independent of the sin problem and will continue to exist after it is forever solved. However, after the Fall the sin problem had to be addressed. The book of Hebrews focuses largely on this aspect.

53. Adams, "The Cosmology of Hebrews," 130.

describes heaven as a city populated with angels, with God and Jesus at its center. In Hebrews, heaven and earth do not form an antithetical dualism. They are not polarized.[54] Finally, Hebrews announces a future destruction of the world (Heb. 12:25–27), but Plato (*Tim.* 32C, 33A) and Philo (*Aet.* 1–20) argue that the universe will last forever.

In summary, Hebrews uses "Platonic-sounding language," but this use does not suggest that its author sees the universe in Platonic dualistic terms.[55] Furthermore, the author of Hebrews is at odds with the Platonic view in regard to the inherent worthiness of the physical world and the eternal destiny of the present world.

WHAT DOES THE AUTHOR OF HEBREWS SAY ABOUT THE CREATION OF THE WORLD?

A number of texts in Hebrews refer to the creation of the world. We take them each in turn.

HEBREWS 1:2

ep' eschatou tōn hēmerōn toutōn elalēsen hēmin en huiō, hon ethēken klēronomon pantōn, di' hou kai epoiēsen tous aiōnas.

In these last days He spoke to us in a Son, whom He appointed heir of all things, through whom also He made the universe. (Heb. 1:2)

This is the first passage in Hebrews to refer to creation, raising two questions: What did God create? And how did He create it?

The passage affirms that God, through Jesus, made the *aiōnas*, which is the Greek term translated here as "universe." The Greek term *aiōn* has a long history of development, and therefore it is not strange that New Testament authors use it in different ways.[56] *Aiōn* may refer to prolonged time or eternity, both for the future and the

---

54. Ibid., 134.

55. Ibid., 138.

56. See H. Sasse, "αἰών" [*aiōn*], *TDNT* 1:197–208; J. Guhrt, "αἰών" [*aiōn*], *NIDNTT* 3:826–33. In ancient Greece, *aiōn* denoted relative time—or time "allotted to a being" (Sasse, *TDNT* 1:197-98)—in contrast to *chronos*, which denoted time itself. Thus, Homer uses *aiōn* as a parallel to life (*Il.* 16, 453), Hesiod uses it to denote a lifespan (*Frag.* 161, 1), and Aeschylus uses it to denote a generation (*Sept.* 742). Plato, however, uses *aiōn* to refer to timeless, ideal eternity in contrast to *chronos*, which is the time created with the world. Plutarch and the earlier stoics adopted Plato's views and from them the traditions of the mysteries of *aiōn* and the speculations of the Gnostics. Finally, the idea of a personal *Aiōn*—or personified *aiōnes*—became important in Hellenistic syncretism.

past—especially when used with a preposition (e.g., *ek tou aiōnos, eis ton aiōna*).[57] It may also refer to time or duration—for example, in the expression "the end of the age [*synteleia aiōnos*]" (e.g., Matt. 13:39; cf. 28:20; 1 Cor. 10:11). A third use of *aiōn* refers to the world itself and not to its time. In this sense, the meaning is not temporal but local—making *aiōn* equivalent to *kosmos*—and could be translated as "world" or "universe" (e.g., Matt. 13:22; Mark 4:19; 1 Cor. 1:20; 2:6–8; cf. 1 Cor. 3:19; 7:33).[58] Finally, this term was also used to refer to the eschatological scheme of this age and the age to come, which is found in apocalyptic and rabbinic texts and in the New Testament.[59]

The term *aiōn* appears fifteen times in Hebrews and the author uses it in all the senses previously mentioned.[60] However, the author of Hebrews is unique in the New Testament in two respects: first in the fact that here (Heb. 1:2) and in Hebrews 11:3, he refers to the object of the Son's creation activity with the term *aiōn*, and also that he uses it in the plural form.[61] This opens several possibilities regarding the meaning of this passage. Does it refer to the creation of "ages"—that is, the present and coming age[62]—or the creation of "worlds"?[63]

What would these "worlds" be that God created through the Son? Hebrews does not show any interest in a multiplicity of worlds, as is the case with later rabbinical writings.[64] Ron A. Stewart suggests that the author refers to the creation of the visible (or sense-perceptible)

---

57. See L&N 93.615; and Sasse, *TDNT* 1:198–202.

58. The temporal element, though, is not completely lost but only recedes into the background.

59. E.g., Matt. 12:32; Mark 10:30; Luke 16:8; 20:34; Eph. 1:21. See also Hermann Leberecht Strack and Paul Billerbeck, *Kommentar zum Neuen Testament aus Talmud und Midrasch*, 6 vols. (Munich: Beck, 1922–1961), 3:671–72; 4 Ezra 3:9; 8:41; Midr. Ps. 15[72b]; and Sasse, *TDNT* 1:204–7.

60. Prolonged time or eternity: Heb. 1:8; 5:6; 6:20; 7:17, 21, 24, 28; 13:8, 21. The time or duration of the world: 9:26. This age and the age to come: 6:5 (cf. 2:5; 9:9–10). World or universe: 1:2; 11:3 (see discussion below).

61. The plural of *aiōn* is common in prepositional phrases or as an attributive genitive to refer to prolonged time or eternity. In the LXX and the New Testament, it appears as the direct object of a verb only in Hebrews 1:2, 11:3, and Tobit 13:18.

62. David A. deSilva, *Perseverance in Gratitude: A Socio-Rhetorical Commentary on the Epistle "to the Hebrews"* (Grand Rapids, Mich.: Eerdmans, 2000), 87.

63. See Attridge, *Hebrews*; Paul Ellingworth, *The Epistle to the Hebrews: A Commentary on the Greek Text*, NIGTC (Grand Rapids, Mich.: Eerdmans, 1993); and Spicq, *Hébreux*.

64. Ellingworth, *Epistle to the Hebrews*, 96. Rabbinic writings refer to the creation of *'ôlām*—a word usually translated in the LXX with the plural of *aiōn*—referring to the creation of other worlds (see Strack and Billerbeck, *Kommentar*, 3:671–72).

and invisible (intellectual) worlds that sum up the entire universe,[65] but as we will see, it is unlikely that the author is using Platonic categories here or elsewhere in the epistle. Others suggest that the author refers to the spheres that comprise the universe.[66]

The context suggests that the author has a spatial meaning in mind—that he is referring to the creation of "worlds." In the immediate context, the affirmation that God created *tous aiōnas* through the Son is parallel to the affirmation that the Son inherited "all things" (*ta panta,* Heb. 1:2) and that He (the Son) sustains "all things" (*ta panta*) by His powerful word (Heb. 1:3). The expression *ta panta* is commonly used in the New Testament to express the idea that all creation is *God's* work and, therefore, there is no power independent of Him in the universe.[67] Thus, the best translation for the expression *tous aiōnas* is likely "universe."[68] In this sense, Hebrews 1:2 affirms that the Son inherits what He helped create in the first place—that is, "all things." We should understand that "all things" involves the earthly as well as the heavenly world, or "coming world," which the Son also inherits according to Hebrews 2:5 and 8:1–2.[69] It could not be otherwise, since it is the Son who created the angels inhabiting heaven (Heb. 1:7).

How did God create the universe? He created it *through* (*dia*) the Son. This idea is also attested in other New Testament writings (e.g., John 1:3, 10; 1 Cor. 8:6; cf. Col. 1:16). The author's affirmation that God created the universe "through" Jesus does not mean that Jesus is inferior to the Father, as a hammer or a saw is inferior to the builder or as the servant is inferior to the master. The context emphasizes the identification and close relationship between the Son and God (Heb. 1:3–4). Jesus is the one who enacts the purposes of the Father. Thus, without contradicting himself, the author may refer to the Son

---

65. Ron A. Stewart, "Creation and Matter in the Epistle of the Hebrews," *NTS* 12 (1966), 288. See also Ellingworth, *Epistle to the Hebrews,* 96.

66. Attridge, *Hebrews,* 41. Note that Genesis 1 refers to, among other things, the creation of the "vault," meaning the heavens. See Randall W. Younker and Richard M. Davidson, "The Myth of the Solid Heavenly Dome: Another Look at the Hebrew רָקִיעַ (*rāqîaʿ*)," in *The Genesis Creation Account and Its Reverberations in the Old Testament,* ed. Gerald A. Klingbeil (Berrien Springs, Mich.: Andrews University Press, 2015), 31–56.

67. B. Reicke, "πᾶς" [*pas*], *TDNT* 5:893–96.

68. Lane, *Hebrews 1–8,* 5. See BDF, §§ 4(2), 141(1). See analysis of the expression *epi synteleia tōn aiōnōn* in the section of this study titled "Hebrews 9:26."

69. This is further supported by the quotation of Ps. 102:26–28 (LXX) in the very next section, Hebrews 1:10–12, which refers to the creation of the earth (*gē*) and the heavens (*ouranoi*).

in Hebrews 1:10 as the "Lord" who created "the earth and the heavens." The same cannot be affirmed of a tool that is manipulated or a servant who only follows the commands of another. The creation of the universe through Jesus speaks of the "perfect accord of will and activity between Father and Son."[70]

The passage has an underlying logic that is worth noting. Before affirming the role of the Son in the creation of the universe, the author argues that the Son functions as God's word: "God, having spoken long ago in many parts and in many ways to the fathers by the prophets, in these last days spoke to us in a Son" (Heb. 1:1–2).[71] Thus, the passage affirms that Jesus is both the word of God in "these last days" and the means through which God created the universe at the beginning of time. (There is, then, a consistency in the way God acted at the beginning of time and now at the end of time.) This implicitly agrees with the Old Testament assertions that God created the universe through His word (Gen. 1:3, 6; Ps. 33:6). The next passage, Hebrews 1:3, strengthens these allusions by noting that the Son continues to sustain the universe "by his powerful word" (NRSV).

In summary, this passage refers not only to the creation of the world but also to the creation of the universe—that is, the creation of everything over which God has sovereignty. It also confirms the intimate connection between the Father and the Son in the work of creation and the implicit affirmation in Genesis that God created through His "word."

HEBREWS 1:10

The second reference to creation is found in Hebrews 1:10–12, which quotes—with some modifications—Psalm 101:26–28 (LXX).

sy kat' archas, kyrie, tēn gēn ethemeliōsas, kai erga tōn cheirōn sou eisin hoi ouranoi.

You, in the beginning, Lord, founded the earth, and the heavens are the work of Your hands. (Heb 1:10)

---

70. John Webster, "One Who Is Son: Theological Reflections on the Exordium to the Epistle to the Hebrews," in Bauckham et al., *Epistle to the Hebrews*, 84.

71. The expression *en huiō* ("in a Son") can be understood as the Son being the messenger (so NRSV, "by his Son") or as embodying the message (so NASB 1995, "in His Son"). The argument of Hebrews 2:6–10 implies not only that Jesus carries a message for humanity but that He Himself also embodies that message. He is Himself "divine speech" (Koester, *Hebrews*, 185). See also Craig R. Koester, "Hebrews, Rhetoric, and the Future of Humanity," *CBQ* 64 (2002): 103–23.

Psalm 101 (LXX) is a petitionary hymn in which the distance between the Creator and the creature is emphasized.[72] The author quotes this psalm to support his previous assertion that God created the universe "through the Son" (see above) and to emphasize the absolute superiority of the Son over the angels (Heb. 1:5–14).[73] They are created and transient (v. 7), while the Son is Creator and remains forever (vv. 10–12). In fact, the author straightforwardly calls the Son "God" in Hebrews 1:8—by means of the quotation of Psalm 44:7–8 (LXX)—and attributes to Him, in Hebrews 1:10–12, what was said of God in Psalm 101:26 (LXX). The author plainly attributes full divinity to the Son through these quotations.[74]

Two issues require attention in this passage: What "beginning" is the author referring to? Does this verse contradict the idea of Genesis that God created the world with His word?

Let us begin with the first question of what "beginning" the author refers to. The quotation of Psalm 101:26–28 (LXX) in Hebrews 1:10–12 is divided in two unequal parts. The first has to do with the actions of the Son regarding the beginning of the world: in the beginning, He "founded" the earth and made the heavens (Heb. 1:10). The second part has to do with what the Son will do at the end (vv. 11–12): He will "roll them up" and "change" them.[75] The expression *kat' archas* is a classic synonym for the expression *en archē* ("in the beginning") used in the LXX of Genesis 1:1.[76] The juxtaposition of the beginning and the end in Hebrews 1:10–12 suggests that the author has in mind a merism.[77] Similarly, the reference to the earth and the heavens is a merism used to refer to the totality of the world. The author refers to "laying the foundation" of the earth (*ethemeliōsas*) and building the heavens, which are the two farthest points of the totality of the

---

72. Johnson, *Hebrews*, 80.

73. For the relationship between Hebrews 1:1–4 and the chain of quotations in Hebrews 1:5–14, see John P. Meier, "Structure and Theology in Heb 1,1–14," *Bib* 66, (1985): 168–89.

74. See Richard Bauckham, "The Divinity of Jesus Christ in the Epistle to the Hebrews," in Bauckham et al., *Epistle to the Hebrews*, 24–26.

75. This passage is the counterpart to the quotation of Haggai 2:6 in Hebrews 12:26, where it says that God will shake the heaven and the earth in the end. They explain each other (Ellingworth, *Epistle to the Hebrews*, 126).

76. Ibid., 127. See also G. Delling, "ἀρχή" [*archē*], *TDNT* 1:478–82; and H. Bietenhard, "ἀρχή" [*archē*], in *NIDNTT* 1:165–69.

77. A merism is a figure of speech that lists two or more elements of a thing—usually its opposite extremes—to denote the totality of a thing—for example, the familiar English expression that someone "searched high and low" to mean that he searched "everywhere."

cosmos.[78] Thus, this passage affirms both that Jesus has created the totality of the world (universe) and that He has acted throughout the totality of time.

The reference to "earth" and the "heavens" is an allusion to Genesis 1:1, though in the opposite order. Hebrews changes the order of the elements with the purpose of emphasizing heaven,[79] which is the realm where angels live[80] and an important concept in Hebrews. The author emphasizes heaven again in Hebrews 12:26 when he refers to the final destruction of the world. Thus, the context in Hebrews 1 (also true of the book of Hebrews as a whole) suggests that the author has in mind the same beginning of Genesis 1:1—the beginning of the universe as a whole, also marking the beginning of time.

Does Hebrews 1:10, with its reference to God creating the heavens with His hands, contradict the assertion of Genesis that God created the heavens and earth with His word?[81] Genesis 2:7 affirms that "God formed man from the dust of the ground" (NRSV), which seems to imply the use of His hands. The expression "works of someone's hands," however, is an idiomatic expression referring to the activity of a person, not the manner in which a person does things.[82] The strength and energy of a person "are made effective through his hands" (see Heb. 2:7 [variant reading]; 8:9; 10:31; 12:12);[83] thus, the hand of God is a symbol of His power (2 Chron. 20:6) to create (Isa. 48:13), protect (Ezra 7:6; Job 5:18; Ps. 145:16; Isa. 49:16), and destroy (Exod. 7:4; 9:3; 1 Sam. 7:13). In fact, the "hands" can stand for a person (Acts 17:25). Thus, "the heavens are the work of Your [God's] hands" means simply that the heavens are the result of God's activity and power; it does not imply a contradiction to the assertion that God created the world through His word (Heb. 11:3).

---

78. There is no interest in this passage in Stoic doctrines of the foundation of the earth before its actual creation. The expression "You, Lord, laid the foundation of the earth in the beginning" (Heb. 1:10, ESV) refers simply to the act of creation and is synonymous with the foundation of the world in Hebrews 4:3 and 9:26 (see comments on those passages, especially 4:3). It does not imply that the earth is unmovable, as it will "perish" and "be rolled," "changed," or "shaken" at the end of time (Heb. 1:10–12; 12:26–27).

79. Ellingworth, *Epistle to the Hebrews,* 127.

80. Attridge, *Hebrews,* 60. Some consider that the plural refers to several heavens where different orders of angels lived; see Ellingworth, *Epistle to the Hebrews,* 126–27.

81. See also Isa. 66:2; Acts 7:50.

82. Ellingworth, *Epistle to the Hebrews,* 127. See F. Laubach, "χείρ" [*cheir*], in *NIDNTT* 2:148–50; and E. Lohse, "χείρ" [*cheir*], *TDNT* 9:424–34.

83. F. Laubach, "χείρ" [*cheir*], *NIDNTT* 2:148–50.

HEBREWS 2:10

Eprepen gar autō, di' hon ta panta kai di' hou ta panta, pollous huious eis doxan agagonta ton archēgon tēs sōtērias autōn dia pathēmatōn teleiōsai.

For it was fitting for Him, for the sake of whom are all things, and through whom are all things, in bringing many sons to glory, to perfect the champion of their salvation through sufferings. (Heb. 2:10)

The phrase "for the sake of whom are all things, and through whom are all things" is a circumlocution for God.[84] This form of reference to God is significant in two ways: First, it reminds the readers that the same God who created them is the one who will provide everything necessary to fulfill their divinely ordained plan. That original plan is described in Psalm 8, quoted in Hebrews 2:5–9, but the author of Hebrews argues that it has been brought to fulfillment only in and through Jesus.[85] Second, this circumlocution for God shows that the author has not the slightest hesitation to identify God as the agent for the creation of the physical universe. In Plato's worldview, the supremely good god could not have created the universe; instead it was a minor god (a Demiurge) and a series of derivations who created the physical universe.

HEBREWS 3:3–4

pleionos gar houtos doxēs para Mōusēn ēxiōtai, kath' hoson pleiona timēn echei tou oikou ho kataskeuasas auton; pas gar oikos kataskeuazetai hypo tinos, ho de panta kataskeuasas theos.

For Jesus is worthy of more glory than Moses, just as the builder of a house has more honor than the house itself. For every house is built by someone, but the builder of all things is God. (Heb. 3:3–4)

This passage contains the simple assertion that God is the Creator of all things. But this assertion is misleadingly simple.

In Hebrews 3:1–6, the author develops a comparison between Jesus and Moses. Both were faithful to God (3:1–2), yet Jesus has superior glory to Moses because He is a Son over the house of God

---

84. Lane, *Hebrews 1–8*, 55; and Adams, "The Cosmology of Hebrews," 125. Similarly, *megalōsynē* ("Majesty") in Heb. 1:3; 8:5.

85. See Koester, "Hebrews, Rhetoric, and the Future of Humanity," 103–23.

while Moses is a servant in the house of God (3:5–6).[86] The central element in this comparison, the axis on which the comparison turns, is the simple assertions of verses 3 and 4.[87] Verse 3 says that Jesus has superior glory to Moses, just like the builder of a house has more glory than the house he has built. The comparison of Jesus and Moses to the builder and a house is more than just a comparison. Just like the string of an instrument may produce a number of overtones along with the fundamental tone, so this comparison produces a series of important "overtones." First, it brings to mind that Jesus is the builder of the universe (Heb. 1:3, 10–12) while Moses is a created being and, therefore, part of the house built (3:5–6). Second, the author's play with different uses of the word house (*oikos*) produces another overtone.[88] In 3:1–2 the word "house" denotes God's people, Israel.[89] But the truism in 3:4 ("every house is built by someone, but the builder of all things is God" [NRSV][90]) raises the stakes. In this verse "house" denotes everything—the universe—and only God can be its builder. The affirmation that God is the builder of "all things" does not deny that Jesus is the builder of the universe (remember that in 3:3 Jesus is clearly compared to a builder); instead, it brings to mind earlier references to the divinity of Jesus (1:2–4, 8–12), who

---

86. Regarding the importance of glory or honor in the Greco-Roman culture of the first century AD, see deSilva, *Perseverance in Gratitude*, 134–37.

87. Lane, *Hebrews 1–8*, 77.

88. See discussion in Ellingworth, *Epistle to the Hebrews*, 205–6.

89. The reference to Jesus as faithful priest in Hebrews 3:1–2 also brings to mind the prophecy of 1 Samuel 2:35, where God promises to raise a "faithful priest" and build him a "sure [*pistos*, 'faithful'] house." In this case, "house" denotes a family lineage or dynasty of priests. Note that in Hebrews 10:19–23, the author refers to Jesus as a great priest over the house of God, implying that believers are a house of priests (see 13:10–16). The importance of the sanctuary and the author's concern with the inauguration of the new covenant sanctuary in heaven (9:15–23) also suggest the possibility that the author is referring to the construction of a sanctuary in Hebrews 3.

90. The expression *ho kataskeuasas*—used to refer to God as the builder of "all things"—may mean to make ready for some purpose ("make ready, prepare"), to bring a structure into being ("build, construct, erect, create"), or to furnish/equip something; see BDAG, 526–27. Hebrews uses the verb both to mean the construction of something (e.g., Noah's construction of the ark, 11:7) and to the act of furnishing something (e.g., the sanctuary for priestly service, 9:2, 6). Here, the previous assertions of Hebrews 1:3, 10–12 suggest that the author refers to the creation or construction of the universe more than its furnishing. In fact, the LXX translates the participle *bôrē'* ("creator"), from the verb *bārā'* ("to create"), with the expression *ho kataskeuasas* ("the builder"). The verb *kataskeuazō* is also used for God's creational work: in the LXX, Isa. 40:28; 43:7; 45:7, 9; Bar. 3:39; Wis. 9:2; 11:24; 13:4 (Adams, "The Cosmology of Hebrews," 126). Koester, *Hebrews*, 245, suggests that the author may have both meanings in mind in the sense that God both built the universe and furnished it so that there could be glory (Heb. 2:10), rest (4:4, 10), and a city (11:16) for His people.

participated with God the Father in the creation of the universe (1:2–3, 8–12).[91] It also brings to mind sovereignty over the universe. Jesus is the Son who is "heir of all things" (1:2, NRSV). Thus, the next verses (Heb. 3:5–6) describe Jesus as Son "over" the house of God.

In summary, this passage asserts simply that God is the Creator of the universe. But along with this assertion, it brings to mind that Jesus is co-Creator with God, divine like Him, and sovereign over the universe with the Father.

HEBREWS 4:3–4, 10

There are four references to creation in Hebrews 4. The references in verses 3, 4, and 10 will be addressed first.

eiserchometha gar eis [tēn] katapausin hoi pisteusantes, kathōs eirēken; hōs ōmosa en tē orgē mou; Ei eiseleusontai eis tēn katapausin mou, kaitoi tōn ergōn apo katabolēs kosmou genēthentōn. eirēken gar pou peri tēs hebdomēs houtōs; Kai katepausen ho theos en tē hēmera tē hebdomē apo pantōn tōn ergōn autou.

For we who have believed enter that rest, just as God has said, "As in my anger I swore, 'They shall not enter my rest,'" though His works were finished at the foundation of the world. For in one place it speaks about the seventh day as follows, "And God rested on the seventh day from all His works." (4:3–4, NRSV)

ho gar eiselthōn eis tēn katapausin autou kai autos katepausen apo tōn ergōn autou hōsper apo tōn idiōn ho theos.

For the one who has entered into his rest he also has rested from his labors just as God did from His. (4:10)

These references to creation appear in the second exhortatory section of Hebrews, found in chapters 3 and 4.[92] In this section, the author uses the language and events of Psalm 95 and Numbers 14 to call the readers' attention to the danger of disregarding God's word.[93] The author describes the readers as being in the same situation as the

---

91. See Johnson, *Hebrews*, 109.

92. See discussion in Felix Hadid Cortez, "'The Anchor of the Soul that Enters within the Veil': The Ascension of the Son in the Letter to the Hebrews" (PhD diss., Andrews University, 2008), 284–89.

93. The author introduces this section with the warning "Today, if you hear His voice, do not harden your hearts" (Heb. 3:7–8). This is a warning he repeats two other times in the section (cf. 3:15; 4:7).

wilderness generation of Numbers 14: the moment of the fulfillment of the promise, or, in other words, the moment of entering the "rest."[94] According to the argument of Hebrews, the repetition of the promise by David in Psalm 95 (94, LXX) shows that the promise was not fulfilled in the time of Joshua (Heb. 4:8). The psalm's exhortation of "Today, if you hear His voice, do not harden your hearts" (Ps. 94:7-8, LXX, quoted in Heb. 3:7-8, NRSV; cf. 3:15; 4:7) implies that the reason for the wilderness generation's failure was disobedience resulting from lack of faith (3:18-19).[95] The author then exhorts the readers to obey the voice of God by entering the "rest."[96] However, Hebrews 4:3-10 redefines the concept of "rest," which believers should "make every effort to enter" (v. 11, NRSV). The author essentially argues—though in a complex fashion—that the rest the desert generation was not able to enter, and which believers are exhorted to enter, is the rest God enjoyed on the seventh day at the completion of creation.[97] Thus, the author refers to this type of rest as a *sabbatismos*, converting Sabbath observance into a symbol of salvation—a return to Eden.

The use of the creation week Sabbath as a symbol of salvation raises some questions about the author's understanding of the nature of the creation week. Did the author of Hebrews understand

---

94. See John Dunnill, *Covenant and Sacrifice in the Letter to the Hebrews*, SNTSMS 75 (Cambridge: Cambridge University Press, 1992), 141-43. Psalm 95 refers to Meribah and Masah (Exod. 17:7; Num. 20:13). Hebrews reads Psalm 95 in relation to Numbers 14 (Heb. 3:17), where the "rest" implied is the land of Canaan (Deut. 3:20; 12:9-10; 25:19; Josh. 1:13, 15; 21:44; 22:4). Rabbi Aqiba also makes the same connection (b. *Sanh.* 110b; t. *Sanh.* 13:10; j. *Sanh.* 9.29c). See Otfried Hofius, *Katapausis: Die Vorstellung vom endzeitlichen Ruheort im Hebräerbrief*, WUNT I/11 (Tübingen: Mohr Siebeck, 1970), 41-47; Attridge, *Hebrews*, 125n33.

95. The Psalmist's exhortation refers to God's incrimination in Numbers 14:22 "[They] have tested me these ten times and have not obeyed my voice."

96. Scholars continue to debate the meaning of "rest" in Hebrews 3-4. The debated issues include whether rest is a place or a state, a present reality or a promise about the future, the heavenly temple or a Christian Sabbath. For an evaluation of the several views, see Jon Laansma, *"I Will Give You Rest": The Rest Motif in the New Testament with Special Reference to Mt 11 and Heb 3-4*, WUNT II/98 (Tübingen: Mohr Siebeck, 1997), 276-332; and Erhard Gallos, "Κατάπαυσις [*Katapausis*] and Σαββατισμός [*Sabbatismos*] in Hebrews 4" (PhD diss., Andrews University, 2011), 118n3. (Gallos understands *sabbatismos* in Hebrews 4 as a call to literal Sabbath keeping now, giving the faithful believer a weekly spiritual rest in this world.) In addition, different views regarding the religio-historical origin of the concept of "rest" have produced different solutions—for example, entry into the gnostic pleroma, liberation from foreign oppression (George Wesley Buchanan, *To the Hebrews: Translation, Comment and Conclusions*, AB 36 [Garden City, N.Y.: Doubleday, 1972], 9, 63-65, 71), entry into the eschatological temple (Hofius, *Katapausis*, 53-54), and entry into the heavenly spiritual world (Thompson, *Hebrews*, 99).

97. Harold W. Attridge, "'Let Us Strive to Enter That Rest': The Logic of Heb 4:1-11," *HTR* 73 (1980): 284.

the creation week as a historical event consisting of a literal week, as we experience it today?

Hebrews 4 implies that God's rest on the seventh day of creation was the prototypical rest into which He always desired His people to enter. The author calls this rest a *sabbatismos*. This term derives from the verb *sabbatizein*, which means "to keep the Sabbath"—just like *baptismos* ("baptism") derives from *baptizein* ("to baptize")—and refers to the Jewish and early Christian practice of keeping the seventh day of the week as a day of rest for religious purposes.[98] Erhard Gallos, after analyzing all the references to this term occurring both in Christian and non-Christian literature,[99] concludes, "We can say that *sabbatismos* is used always literally, although sometimes pejoratively, with the exception of Origen who uses the term twice figuratively as a time period in the scheme of ages and as a cessation from sin."[100]

Is *sabbatismos*—and by extension the creation week—understood in Hebrews as a historical or as a mythical event? This passage does not provide a categorical answer. There are some indications, however, that suggest the author considered creation week to be historical.

According to Hebrews 4, God's *sabbatismos* at the end of the creation week was a prototype for what God wanted His people to enjoy as a result of their faith in Him. Thus, the relationship of God's *sabbatismos* to life in the land of Canaan for Israel's desert generation is similar to the relationship between a type and an antitype—only in a more complex fashion. Israel's rest in the land of Canaan is a type of the salvation God wants to provide believers, which is at the same time described as entering the rest that God enjoyed on the Sabbath of creation week. Thus, rest in the land of Canaan is a type that points simultaneously to the future (to the salvation of God's people) and to the past (to God's rest on the Sabbath of creation). The important thing is that the relationship between rest in the land of Canaan and God's *sabbatismos* is equivalent to other type-antitype relationships in the book of Hebrews. In these, the

---

98. See discussion in Gallos, "Κατάπαυσις [*Katapausis*] and Σαββατισμός [*Sabbatismos*]," 219–25.

99. Plutarch, *Superst.* 2 (166); Justin Martyr, *Dial.* 23.3; Epiphanius, *Pan.* 30.2.2; *Martyrium Petri et Pauli* 1; *Apos. Con.* 2.36.2; Origen, *Cels.* 5.59; *Comm. Jo.* 2.27; *Or.* 27.16; *Sel. Exod.* 12.289.7; *Exc. Ps.* 17.144.31.

100. Gallos, "Κατάπαυσις [*Katapausis*] and Σαββατισμός [*Sabbatismos*]," 225.

former or earlier element on which the type-antitype relationship is anchored is always a historical event: Melchizedek's priesthood, a type of Jesus's priesthood (Heb. 7); the Mosaic sanctuary, a type of the heavenly sanctuary (8:5); the sacrifice for the inauguration of the old covenant, a type of Jesus's sacrifice inaugurating the new covenant (9:15–23); and the animal sacrifices of the old covenant, a type of Jesus's sacrifice for the cleansing of sin (10:1–18), are all historical events. This consistent pattern demonstrates that the author considers God's rest on the Sabbath of creation a historical event as well. The antitype is also historical in nature, though of a heavenly, eschatological character in Hebrews. Thus, Jesus's priesthood according to the order of Melchizedek (Heb. 7), the heavenly sanctuary inaugurated by Jesus, and His sacrifice for the transgressions committed under the first covenant (9:15–28) are all historical events or institutions.[101]

The description of God's rest at creation as a *sabbatismos* happening at the foundation of the world (*apo kataboles kosmou*) is significant in this respect. The term *katabolē*, as an extension of its original meaning of laying a foundation, is used to refer to a historical starting point.[102] The expression *apo kataboles kosmou* ("from the foundation of the world") marks the starting point of the history of our world (Matt. 13:35; 25:34; Luke 11:50; Heb. 4:3; 9:26; Rev. 13:8; 17:8). When biblical authors want to refer to events before the beginning of the history of the world, they use the expression *pro kataboles kosmou* ("before the foundation of the world," John 17:24; Eph. 1:4; 1 Pet. 1:20, NRSV). This means that God rested at the beginning of earth's history and, therefore, His rest on the seventh day of the creation week was the first *sabbatismos* ("Sabbath observance") in a succession of *sabbatismoi* ("Sabbath observances") throughout history. Thus, God's Sabbath rest at creation is the historical anchor that makes possible the description of believers' salvation as an eschatological *sabbatismos*.

---

101. Jesus's sacrifice is also heavenly and eschatological in nature. While He died on the cross outside Jerusalem, His death is considered part of the heavenly sanctuary service (Heb. 9:11–14).

102. For example, Josephus uses it to refer to the date of the beginning of a rebellion (*J.W.* 2.260); see H. H. Esser, "*katabolē*," *NIDNTT* 1:377.

HEBREWS 4:12–13

Zōn gar ho logos tou theou kai energēs kai tomōteros hyper pasan ma-
chairan distomon kai diiknoumenos achri merismou psychēs kai pneu-
matos, harmōn te kai myelōn, kai kritikos enthymēseōn kai ennoiōn
kardias; kai ouk estin ktisis aphanēs enōpion autou, panta de gymna kai
tetrachēlismena tois ophthalmois autou, pros hon hēmin ho logos.

Indeed, the word of God is living and active, sharper than any two-edged
sword, piercing until it divides soul from spirit, joints from marrow; it is
able to judge the thoughts and intentions of the heart. And before him
no creature is hidden, but all are naked and laid bare to the eyes of the
one to whom we must render an account. (Heb. 4:12–13, NRSV)

This passage culminates the exhortation to believers to enter
into the rest of God.[103] In fact, it should be considered a warning to
those who decide to ignore God's word. It was written with the
intention of producing fear in the readers by emphasizing the power
of the word of God to judge and punish human behavior and intentions. This, of course, makes the exhortation to pay attention to
God's word all the more compelling.[104] Two elements give force to
the warning: the double meaning of the expression "word of God"
and the description of the readers as "creatures."

This passage likely contains a transition from the message to the
person who gives the message. Hebrews 4:12 focuses on God's message. This message is specifically God's invitation to us in Psalm
95:7b–11 to enter into His rest. If we reject this invitation, we will
incur the judgment of God. In Hebrews 4:13, however, there is likely
a transition from the message to the person of God. The NRSV suggests this transition by translating "And before *him* no creature is
hidden" (emphasis added), rather than "before it. . . . "[105] This transition is important because it brings God and His word into close relationship. God both created the world (Gen. 1:3; Ps. 33:6, 9) and acts
in history through His "word" (the prophetic word, 1 Sam. 15:24;
Isa. 1:10; Jer. 1:4; Amos 5:1; Mic. 1:1; etc.).[106] To this word, the author

---

103. Note that the passage is introduced with the coordinating conjunction *gar* (Heb.
4:12), which effectively connects Hebrews 4:12–13 with the preceding argument.

104. deSilva, *Perseverance in Gratitude*, 170–71.

105. This would mean that God is the antecedent of *autou* twice ("before *Him*" and "in
His sight") as well as of the relative pronoun *hon* ("whom"). Peter T. O'Brien, *The Letter to
the Hebrews*, PNTC (Grand Rapids, Mich.: Eerdmans, 2010), 177n139.

106. Johnson, *Hebrews*, 132.

of Hebrews attributes the divine trait of "living,"[107] which itself is a favorite description of God in Hebrews (3:12; 9:14; 10:31; 12:22).[108]

Those subject to God's word and God's judgment are described as "creatures." This description is important because it provides the rationale for their subjection to judgment: "creatures" are subject to the judgment of their creators (see 1:10–12). In this case, the argument implies that creatures are subject to the word of God because He created them.

HEBREWS 6:7–8

gē gar hē piousa ton ep' autēs erchomenon pollakis hyeton kai tiktousa botanēn eutheton ekeinois di' hous kai geōrgeitai, metalambanei eulogias apo tou theou; ekpherousa de akanthas kai tribolous, adokimos kai kataras engys, hēs to telos eis kausin.

Ground that drinks up the rain falling on it repeatedly, and that produces a crop useful to those for whom it is cultivated, receives a blessing from God. But if it produces thorns and thistles, it is worthless and on the verge of being cursed; its end is to be burned over. (Heb. 6:7–8, NRSV)

The language of "thorns and thistles" (*akanthas kai tribolous*) is a possible allusion to Genesis 3:12–18, where God curses the earth because of human sin.[109] The cursing of the land in 3:18 is given as an example of the harsh consequences of disobedience. The language of the passage is also reminiscent of the covenantal language of Deuteronomy 30 and the song of the vineyard in Isaiah 5:1–10.

HEBREWS 9:26

epei edei auton pollakis pathein apo katabolēs kosmou; nyni de hapax epi synteleia tōn aiōnōn eis athetēsin [tēs] hamartias dia tēs thysias autou pephanerōtai.

---

107. See Deut. 4:33 (LXX); Ps. 83:3 (LXX); Isa. 37:4, 17 (LXX).

108. "Active" (*energēs*) suggests strength and effectiveness. In the New Testament, the cognates *energeia* (Eph. 1:19; 3:7; Phil. 3:21; Col. 2:12) and *energeō* (1 Cor. 12:6, 11; Gal. 2:8; 3:5; Eph. 1:11, 20; 3:2; Phil. 2:13; Col. 1:29) often refer to the work of God in the community. See Johnson, *Hebrews*, 133.

109. Attridge, *Hebrews*, 173; Johnson, *Hebrews*, 164; Koester, *Hebrews*, 316; and Lane, *Hebrews 1–8*, 143. Others emphasize the role of Isaiah 5:1–5 in the interpretation of this passage (deSilva, *Perseverance in Gratitude*, 229; and George H. Guthrie, "Hebrews," *Commentary on the New Testament Use of the Old Testament*, ed. G. K. Beale and D. A. Carson [Grand Rapids, Mich.: Baker Academic, 2007], 963).

For then he would have had to suffer again and again since the foundation of the world. But as it is, he has appeared once for all at the end of
the age to remove sin by the sacrifice of himself. (Heb. 9:26, NRSV)

We have already studied the phrase "foundation of the world"
(*apo katabolēs kosmou*) in 4:3, which refers to creation, the historical beginning of the world. Here, the reference to the foundation of
the world contrasts the reference to the "end of the age,"[110] and
together they span the whole story of the universe.

The passage contains a double comparison: first, between the multiple offerings of the high priests every Day of Atonement and the singular offering of Christ and, second, between the priest's offering of
"blood that is not his own" and Jesus's "sacrifice of himself" (9:25, 26).
The author stresses that Jesus's sacrifice is so effective that by a single
sacrifice it has removed sin. He concludes that if this were not the case,
Jesus would have had to die "again and again" (v. 26) since the foundation of the world. The argument is a *reduction ad absurdum*:[111] no
human dies "again and again," and therefore it is absurd that Jesus
would have to die again and again. It also suggests, however, the historicity of the fall of Adam and Eve in Genesis 3.[112] If Jesus's sacrifice had
been as ineffective as animal sacrifices, Jesus would have had to die
"repeatedly since the foundation of the world" because that was the
time when sin entered the world, making sacrifices necessary (see
Rom. 5:12).[113] This was not necessary, however, because Jesus's single
sacrifice is enough to provide cleansing for human sin. Jesus "has
appeared once for all at the end of the age" to solve a problem that
originated "since the foundation of the world"—that is, since the fall of
Adam and Eve. Neither event stands outside of history.

HEBREWS 11:3

*Pistei nooumen katērtisthai tous aiōnas rhēmati theou, eis to mē ek
phainomenōn to blepomenon gegonenai.*

---

110. For the importance of the contrast, see Ellingworth, *Epistle to the Hebrews*, 484.
The expression *epi synteleia tōn aiōnōn* is an allusion to Daniel 9:26–27; 11:35; 12:13; see
Attridge, *Hebrews*, 264; Ellingworth, *Epistle to the Hebrews*, 484; and Johnson, *Hebrews*, 244.

111. See Koester, *Hebrews*, 428.

112. Schenck, "The Spatial Dualism of Hebrews," ch. 5, and "The Heavenly Tabernacle in
Hebrews," ch. 6 in *Cosmology and Eschatology*, argues on the basis of this passage that the
author refers not to the entrance of sin into the world but to the fact that creation, though
not fallen, is itself a hindrance to the attainment of glory. It is not clear, however, why an
unfallen creation would need a sacrifice of purification or atonement (Heb. 9:15–28).

113. Koester, *Hebrews*, 422.

> By faith we understand that the universe was fashioned by the word of God, so that from what is not visible became what is visible. (Heb. 11:3)

This is the most important passage on creation in Hebrews, and probably the most famous biblical text on the topic in the whole New Testament. It contains an allusion to Genesis 1, where Scripture describes how God created the world through His word. It also plays on the concepts of "faith" and "sight," firmly connecting the author's assertion about creation to the larger argument on faith in the immediate context. According to Hebrews 11:1, faith has to do with things we do not see but we hope for. The author affirms that the believer can grasp them through faith,[114] then provides in the rest of Hebrews 11 a list of heroes of faith who exemplify this fact. By faith, they "saw and greeted" the promises from a distance (11:13, NRSV). By faith, they looked "ahead to the reward" (v. 26, NRSV), to a heavenly country and a heavenly city (v. 16).

The first example in the list, however, is not a hero from the past, but the believer in the present. Furthermore, what this person does not see but believes is not something in the future but an event in the past. Faith in this verse provides certainty not about the "things hoped for" (v. 1, NRSV) but about the origin of all things. According to the author, we believers understand by faith the creation of the universe. Though we were not able to see it because we were not there at creation, yet we understand it by faith. This passage's allusion to Genesis 1 implies that the believers' understanding is anchored in Scripture.

The idea that we should understand *by faith* the creation of the world was as unpopular in the world of the New Testament as it is today in academic circles. J. W. Thompson notes that "a catalogue of heroes of *pistis*, introduced as patterns of imitation, is unthinkable in any Greek tradition."[115] William Lane explains that the reason for this is that "to the formally educated person, *pistis*, 'faith,' was regarded as a state of mind characteristic of the uneducated, who believe something on hearsay without being able to give precise reasons for their belief. The willingness of Jews and Christians to suffer for the undemonstrable astonished pagan observers."[116] This passage challenged

---

114. Paul makes a similar assertion in 2 Corinthians 4:18: "Because we look not at what can be seen [*ta blepomena*] but at what cannot be seen [*ta mē blepomena*]; for what can be seen is temporary, but what cannot be seen is eternal."

115. Thompson, *Beginnings of Christian Philosophy*, 53.

116. William L. Lane, *Hebrews 9–13*, WBC 47B (Dallas: Word, 1991), 316. See also E. R. Dodds, *Pagan and Christian in an Age of Anxiety* (London: Cambridge University Press,

the original readers, as it challenges us today, to "disregard the shame" of clinging to faith in an age of reason.

However, the specific meaning of this passage regarding the creation of the world is much debated and will be explored here with two questions in mind: First, what did God create? This question is closely related to whether or not we should read this verse from a Platonic worldview. Second, how did God create? Or is there an assertion of creation *ex nihilo* here?

What Did God Create?

The Greek term *tous aiōnas* is translated "universe." It literally means "the ages" but could also have a spatial meaning, thus referring to "the worlds."[117] It has been argued that the plural "worlds" refers to the archetypal (noumenal) and phenomenal worlds of Plato's worldview. According to this view, the Platonic model of the cosmos—which distinguishes between the archetypal world perceived by the mind and a phenomenal world perceived by the senses—lies behind the formulation of this verse.[118]

This reading seems to be strengthened by the affirmation in the second half of the verse that "from what is not visible [the archetypal world?] became what is visible [the phenomenal world?]."[119] Another observation seems to further strengthen the case of a Platonic reading. According to Plato, the Demiurge fashioned the world from a preexisting mass in chaotic disorder (*Tim.* 52D2–53B5).[120] The author of Hebrews uses the Greek term *katērtisthai* to describe the work of creation by the word of God. This term literally means "to put in order" or "restore."[121] Thus, some scholars conclude that this verse argues not that God created the universe out of nothing but that He used preexisting matter in chaos to "fashion"—or "put in order"—the universe we now see. In summary, Hebrews 11:3 may be read from a Platonic perspective in this way:

1965), 120–22.

117. See the analysis in the section of this study titled "Hebrews 1:2," 336.

118. Attridge, *Hebrews*, 316; and Stewart, "Creation and Matter," 284–93.

119. E.g., Philo refers to the invisible sources of the created universe (*Opif.* 16; *Conf.* 172; *Spec.* 2.225; 4.187; *Leg.* 2.2). See also Erich Gräßer, *Der Glaube im Hebräerbrief*, Marburger Theologische Studien 2 (Marburg: Elwert, 1965), 53–54.

120. See also Williamson, "Philo and Hebrews," 377–381; and Adams, "Cosmology of Hebrews."

121. BDAG, 526; and LSJ, 910.

Pistei nooumen katērtisthai tous aiōnas rhēmati theou, eis to mē ek phainomenōn to blepomenon gegonenai

By faith we understand that the worlds [the archetypal and the phenomenal worlds] were put in order by the word of God, so that from what is not visible [archetypal world] became what is visible [phenomenal world].

This reading would probably not have seemed strange in antiquity. It is often affirmed that "contemporary Platonism helped to shape Christian theology in the first centuries AD."[122] Jewish Hellenistic figures like Philo—and later ancient Christian theologians like Justin, Tatian, Clement, and Origen—were clearly influenced by Platonism in varying degrees.[123]

A Platonic worldview, however, does not fit the text. Hebrews 11:3 would argue from this point of view that God created both the archetypal and phenomenal worlds. According to Plato, however, the Demiurge did not create the archetypal world of ideas. This world is eternal (*Tim.* 29A). Second, and more importantly, Hebrews 11:3 affirms that God created the world "from" or "out of" (*ek*) "what is not visible." Plato says, however, that the Demiurge created the world out of preexistent, visible matter in a state of chaos. Plato states, "The god took over all that was visible . . . and brought it from disorder into order" (*Tim.* 30A).[124] Though the archetypes may be visible only to the mind, the phenomenal world is built not "out of" (*ek*) them but "according" to them (*Tim.* 28C5–29B1).[125]

Furthermore, the verse may not refer to the use of preexistent matter. The term *katērtisthai* does not mean only "to put in order," "restore," etc. It is also used to refer to the act of "creating," "making," "preparing," or "furnishing" something.[126] The verb denotes the action of ordering, restoring, making, or creating something, in the sense of making it suitable or apt for use.[127] For example, this verb is

---

122. Dillon, "Plato," 805.

123. Ibid., 807.

124. See Adams, "The Cosmology of Hebrews," 128; Lane, *Hebrews 9–13*, 332; and Sedley, *Creationism and Its Critics*, 116–18.

125. Adams, "The Cosmology of Hebrews," 128

126. BDAG, 526; LSJ, 910. It is used in the LXX to translate nine different Hebrew verbs, including those meaning "to make," "to establish," and "to found" (R. Schippers, "καταρτίζω" [*katartizō*], *NIDNTT* 3:350).

127. The verb *katartizō* is a derivative of the term *artios* that means "suitable, appropriate, useful, apt"; see Schippers, *NIDNTT* 3:349; Ellingworth, *Epistle to the Hebrews*, 570.

used in Ezra to denote the building of the wall and the temple (Ezra 4:12, 13, 16; 5:3, 9, 11; 6:14, LXX) but in Psalms 73:16 (LXX) and 88:38 (LXX) for the creation of the sun and the moon. In Hebrews 11:3, *katērtisthai* is equivalent to *gegonenai*, which means "has become" or "was made." In Hebrews 10:5, *katērtisō* is used to refer to the action of God "preparing" a body for Jesus to come into the world and offer Himself as a sacrifice. Thus, the verb does not necessarily imply the use of preexistent matter by the Creator, but it does emphasize that what He created was suitable or apt for use.

Finally, this passage may not refer to the creation of "worlds." The second half of the verse helps us understand that the meaning of the expression *tous aiōnas* ("worlds") in the first half is equivalent to what is denoted by the singular *to blepomenon* ("what is visible") in the second half. This agrees with the fact that the expression *tous aiōnas* may just mean "universe," as it does in Hebrews 1:2.[128] Furthermore, the author's allusion to Genesis 1 helps us understand its meaning.[129] What God created is what is visible from the point of view of Genesis 1: "the heavens and the earth," or the universe.[130]

In summary, a Platonic worldview does not fit the assertion of the passage. This passage is talking about the creation not of Plato's noumenal and phenomenal worlds but of the universe as conceived in Genesis 1. As Edward Adams concludes, "the author's wording seems to exclude any positive influence from Platonic cosmogony; indeed, it may well be a polemic against it."[131]

How Did God Create?

Hebrews 11:3 simply affirms that what we see (the universe) came from or by[132] "what we do not see,"[133] but this can be understood in more than one way.

---

128. See the analysis in the section of this study titled "Hebrews 1:2," 336. See also Lane, *Hebrews 1–8*, 5. See BDF §§ 4(2), 141(1).

129. Johnson, *Hebrews*, 280; and Philip Edgcumbe Hughes, "The Doctrine of Creation in Hebrews 11:3," *BTB* 2, no. 1 (1972), 64. Also, Lane, *Hebrews 9–13*, 331.

130. Koester, *Hebrews*, 473. See my analysis of Hebrews 1:2 above. The variation between the plural and the singular is only stylistic; see Ellingworth, *Epistle to the Hebrews*, 569.

131. Adams, "The Cosmology of Hebrews," 128. Lane, *Hebrews 9–13*, 332, suggests that the author's aim was to correct a tendency in Hellenistic Judaism to read Genesis 1 in the light of Plato's views.

132. The preposition *ek* can denote, among other things, origin and derivation or cause; thus, the passage can be translated either "what is seen was made *from* things that are not visible" (origin) or "*by* things that are not visible" (cause, emphasis added). See BDAG, [3e] 297.

133. Since the negative (*mē*) precedes the preposition, it is possible to read it with the verb (*gegonena*). In this case the verse would affirm that what is visible was not made from

Some see in the expression "so that what is seen was made from things that are not visible" (NRSV) an affirmation that God created the universe out of nothing, a creation *ex nihilo*.[134] These interpreters equate "what is not visible" with "nothingness."[135] Thus, they would understand the passage in the following way:

Pistei nooumen katērtisthai tous aiōnas rhēmati theou, eis to mē ek phainomenōn to blepomenon gegonenai.

By faith we understand that the universe was fashioned by the word of God, so that from what is not visible [nothingness] became what is visible [universe].

The Old Greek translation of Genesis 1:2 describes the earth before God's creation activity as *aoratos* ("invisible") and *akataskeuastos* ("not built/prepared"). Jacques Doukhan makes a solid case that Genesis 1:2 refers to a creation out of nothing.[136] In this sense, what is "invisible" (*aoratos*, Gen. 1:2) or "not visible" (*mē phainomenōn*, Heb. 11:3) would be equivalent to "nothingness." In a similar fashion, 2 Enoch 25:2 equates the invisible with the nonexistent: "Before anything existed at all, from the very beginning, whatever is I created from non-being into being, and from the invisible things into the visible."[137] Romans 4:17 and some noncanonical works (2 Macc. 7:28; 2 Bar. 21:4; 48:8; 2 En. 24:2) also refer to this idea of a creation out of nonexistence (nonbeing). It is commonly understood that these assertions of creation out of "nonexistence" should be understood as affirming a creation out of nothing, *ex nihilo*. We cannot be entirely sure of this, however. The expression "nonbeing" did not necessarily mean "nothingness" to the ancient mind. For example, Xenophon asserts that "parents

---

what is visible. That is to say, the verse would deny a visible source for the universe. The order *mē ek phainomenōn*, however, is normal in classical Greek and occasional in the New Testament (BDF, §433) and has the purpose of emphasizing the negation. Thus, the verse should probably be read as an affirmation of an invisible source for the universe (see, e.g., Ellingworth, *Epistle to the Hebrews*, 569; and Hughes, "The Doctrine of Creation in Hebrews 11:3," 65).

134. E.g., Chrysostom, in *The Nicene and Post-Nicene Fathers*, series 1, ed. Philip Schaff, 14 vols. (1886–1889; repr., Peabody, Mass.: Hendrickson, 1994), 14:465; and F. F. Bruce, *The Epistle to the Hebrews*, NICNT (Grand Rapids, Mich.: Eerdmans, 1990), 279.

135. Hughes, "The Doctrine of Creation in Hebrews 11:3," 67.

136. Jacques Doukhan, "The Genesis Creation Story: Text, Issues, and Truth," *Origins* 55 (2004): 12–33.

137. James H. Charlesworth, ed., *Old Testament Pseudepigrapha*, 2 vols. (New York, Doubleday, 1983), 1:143.

bring forth their children out of non being" (*Mem.* 2.2.3).[138] It is clear that parents bring forth their children out of nonbeing, but not out of nothing.

A second view is that the expression "what is not visible" refers to the earth in an unformed state prior to the creation week.[139] The Old Greek translation of Genesis 1:2 refers to the earth as being "invisible" (*aoratos*) and "formless" (*akataskeuastos*) prior to or at the beginning of the creation week. This would mean there was a gap between the time God created the universe, including this earth in a raw state, and the beginning of the creation week. In this sense, "what is not visible" refers not to "nothingness" but to invisible and unformed matter. The passage would be translated in this way:

> *Pistei nooumen katērtisthai tous aiōnas rhēmati theou, eis to mē ek phainomenōn to blepomenon gegonenai.*

> By faith we understand that the universe was fashioned by the word of God, so that from what is not visible [raw, unformed earth, (Gen. 1:2, LXX)] became what is visible [earth after creation].

The problem with this view is that an allusion to the LXX translation of Genesis 1:2 is not strong. The LXX uses the word *aoratos* ("invisible"), but Hebrews uses *mē phainomenōn* ("not appearing").

A third view is that the expression "what we do not see" refers to the "word of God." It is argued that this passage might contain an inverted parallelism or chiasm:[140]

> *Pistei nooumen*
> **A** *katērtisthai*
>   **B** *tous aiōnas*
>   **C** *rhēmati theou*
>   **C'** *eis to mē ek phainomenōn*
>   **B'** *phainomenōn to blepomenon*
> **A'** *gegonenai*

---

138. See other examples and discussion in May, *Creatio ex nihilo*, 6–21.
139. See Adams, "The Cosmology of Hebrews," 128–29.
140. E.g., Koester, *Hebrews*, 474.

By faith we understand

    A was fashioned

      B the universe

        C **by the word of God**

        C′ **so that from what is not visible**

      B′ what is visible

    A′ became

There are important similarities between the elements of this parallelism. Both A and A′ are verbs in infinitival form that function as the main verbs of their respective clauses. The elements B and B′ are both accusative, directly related to the infinitive verbs. This suggests that C and C′ are parallel as well.

The structure suggests, then, that "what is not visible" refers not to "nothingness" but to the "word of God" because it places them as parallel elements.[141] In this sense, "what is not visible," or "the word of God," is not the material out of which the universe was created but the effective cause. If this is the case, then the second part of Hebrews 11:3 does not offer new information to the reader about how God created the world but rather explains in different words what is said in the first part of the passage: that God created the world through His word.

Scripture often associates God with invisibility (e.g., Col. 1:15; 1 Tim. 1:17). Hebrews 11:27 says that Moses "endured as seeing Him [God] who is invisible" (NKJV). Romans 1:20, a passage similar to Hebrews 11:3, affirms that the "eternal power and divine nature" (NRSV) of God are "invisible" (*aorata*) but may be "understood" (*nooumena*) from what He has created. This suggests, in agreement with the structure of the passage, that "what is not visible" in Hebrews 11:3 is the "word of God," which is another way to refer to God Himself and His power and divinity, which are invisible according to Hebrews 11:27 and Romans 1:20.[142] This view suggests that the preposition *ek* in Hebrews 11:3 refers not to the material out of which the universe ("what is visible") came to be but to the agent through which creation occurred.[143] This agrees with the fact that

---

141. Ibid.

142. See discussion in the section of this study titled "Hebrews 4:12–13," 348.

143. The preposition *ek* can denote, among other things, origin, derivation, or cause; thus, the passage can be translated either "what is seen was made *from* things that are not visible" (origin) or "*by* things that are not visible" (cause, emphasis added). See BDAG, 297.

the author refers elsewhere to the word of God in connection to the creation of the world (Heb. 1:2; 4:12–13). In summary, Hebrews 11:3 may also be read in the following way:

> *Pistei nooumen katērtisthai tous aiōnas rhēmati theou, eis to mē ek phainomenōn to blepomenon gegonenai.*

> By faith we understand that the universe [heaven and earth] was made by the word of God, so that through what is not visible [word of God/God] became what is visible [the universe].

This view faces the problem that in the Greek text, "word of God" is singular but "what is not visible" is plural. Furthermore, "word of God" is dative and clearly instrumental, but the expression "what is not visible" is governed by *ek* plus the genitive, which normally identifies source, not an instrument. So these two elements are not clear-cut parallels.[144] However, these are not insurmountable objections. The expression "what is not visible" in the original language, though plural, conveys a single idea, so therefore can be parallel to the word of God. Also, as mentioned above, *ek* plus the genitive can be translated "by" in the sense of an effective cause.[145] Finally, inverted parallelisms or chiasms are not uncommon in Hebrews.[146] One example is found in the immediate context. Hebrews 11:1 says,

> *Estin de pistis*
> **A** *elpizomenōn*
>   **B** *hypostasis*
>   **B′** *pragmatōn elenchos*
> **A′** *ou blepomenōn*

Now faith is
  A of things hoped for
    B the **assurance**,
    B′ the **conviction** of things
  A′ not seen.

---

144. The author may well be, after all, making a distinction between the "word of God" as the instrument of creation and "what is not visible as its source" (Adams, "The Cosmology of Hebrews," 128).

145. See BDAG, 297; Ellingworth, *Epistle to the Hebrews*, 569; Koester, *Hebrews*, 474; and O'Brien, *The Letter to the Hebrews*, 402.

146. E.g., Heb. 1:5; 12:6; 13:2, 14.

Note the similarities: Both A and A' are genitive plural participles whose function is to describe the elements in B and B'. Both B and B' are nouns in the nominative singular. It is probable, then, that Hebrews 11:3 is also an inverted parallelism. If this is the case, the author's intention in this passage is to drive home the idea that God created the world through His word, repeating the idea twice. It is important to the author that we understand it by faith.

In summary, though it is not entirely clear in which of the three previously mentioned ways the author intended his assertions in Hebrews 11:3 to be taken, it is clear the author is not indebted to Platonic ideas in his understanding of creation. Hebrews 11:3 also makes clear that Genesis 1 is very important for him and that he understands it to be the basis of faith and understanding on issues of creation. This study further suggests that the probable presence of the inverted parallelisms in Hebrews 11:3 and 11:1 supports the view that this passage speaks only about creation through the word of God according to Genesis 1. Whether or not this creation was *ex nihilo,* the epistle does not say.

HEBREWS 12:27

to de Eti hapax dēloi tēn tōn saleuomenōn metathesin hōs pepoiēmenōn, hina meinē ta mē saleuomena.

This phrase, "Yet once more," indicates the removal of what is shaken— that is, created things—so that what cannot be shaken may remain. (NRSV)

The question that comes to mind is: does this passage imply that there are eternal entities (that is, those not created) that will survive God's shaking of earth and heaven? In other words, is there anything that has not been created by God and is, therefore, inherently eternal?

Some commentators consider this passage to show how the Platonic worldview has been incorporated into and adapted to the argument of the author of Hebrews.[147] James W. Thompson, for example, argues that this passage contrasts the sense-perceptible world (the material world) from the intelligible world (the

---

147. Johnson, *Hebrews,* 335. Similarly, Erich Gräßer, *An die Hebräer,* EKKNT 17/1 (Zurich: Benziger Neukirchener, 1990), argues that the author of Hebrews distinguishes a lower transient heaven and earth (Heb. 1:10–12) from the eternal heavens where God and Christ abide.

nonmaterial world).[148] The first world is transitory and the author of Hebrews also refers to it as "what is visible" (Heb. 11:3), what can "be touched" (12:18, NRSV), what is "made with hands" (9:11, 24, NRSV), and what is "of this creation" (9:11, NRSV). This realm is transitory and corrupt. It is not permanent. The intelligible world, on the other hand, is the world where the "true tabernacle" is (8:2; 9:24). It is the heavenly world where Jesus has been exalted (1:3; 4:14; 7:26; 8:1; 9:24) and where we have access through faith in Him (4:14–16; 10:19–25). This realm is "true," perfect, steady, and eternal. Thompson concludes, then, that the author of Hebrews conceives a dual universe:

> He knows two worlds already possessing full reality, one of which is material, and therefore, shakable; the other is not material, and is unshakable. When the material world disappears, only the world that is presently unseen (11:1) and untouchable (12:18), remains.[149]

From this point of view, the term *pepoiēmenōn* ("created things") stands in apposition to *tōn saleuomenōn* ("what is shaken") and has the function of explaining what will be "removed." In this sense, creation will be removed because it is transient, imperfect, and corrupt. In summary, those who read this passage from a Platonic perspective understand it in the following way:

> *to de eti hapax dēloi tēn tōn saleuomenōn metathesin hōs pepoiēmenōn, hina meinē ta mē saleuomena.*
>
> This phrase, "Yet once more," indicates the removal of what is shaken [the sense-perceptible world]—that is, created things—so that what cannot be shaken [the intelligible world/the heavenly world] may remain. (NRSV)

Does the author of Hebrews hold this negative view of creation? Craig R. Koester correctly notes that in the preceding verse (Heb. 12:26), the author of Hebrews explains that God is going to "shake" both earth *and* heaven. In fact, the author places a clear emphasis on the fact that God is going to "shake" heaven.[150] Thompson responds to this objection that the author of Hebrews distinguishes between the created heavens (cosmological heaven), which belong to the

---

148. James W. Thompson, "'That Which Cannot Be Shaken': Some Metaphysical Assumptions in Heb 12:27," *JBL* 94 (1975): 580–87.

149. Ibid., 586.

150. Koester, *Hebrews*, 547.

lower, transient realm (1:10–12), and the heaven where Jesus entered and where God resides and the true tabernacle is located (axiological heaven). This "upper" realm (axiological heaven) is eternal and uncreated.[151] He argues that it is the lower (cosmological) heaven that is "shaken" and removed according to Hebrews 12:26.[152] But this distinction is not clear in Hebrews, much less in the immediate context.[153] In fact, the closest reference to heaven is found in the immediately preceding verse (12:25) and refers to God warning believers "from heaven." This heaven would clearly be the "upper" (axiological) heaven. The author makes no difference with the heaven to be "shaken" in verse 26.[154] It seems clear, then, that the "shaking" includes the heavenly realm.

Furthermore, the author does not have a negative view of creation. He does make a distinction between "this creation" and the heavenly realm in Hebrews 9:11–14, but the distinction is qualitative, not antithetical.[155] Note that the Son is highly involved in the act of creation but there is not a hint of discomfort for this fact. The author does not accord the Son a demiurgical role while emphasizing God's transcendence and distance from the act of creation. In fact, the author positively affirms God as Creator as well (2:10; 3:4; 4:3–4, 10).[156] Similarly, a negative view of creation and matter does not fit with the reference to Jesus's resurrection in Hebrews 13:20. Furthermore, the author does not have a Platonic view of the heavenly realm where God and the true sanctuary are. He states clearly that the "heavenly things"—the heavenly sanctuary where Jesus entered to appear in the presence of God—stand in need of cleansing, needing "better sacrifices" (9:23–24). A Platonic cosmology does not fit the wider argument of Hebrews.

In the previous passage, Hebrews 12:18–24, the author compares believers with the desert generation, who heard God speak at

---

151. Thompson, "That Which Cannot Be Shaken," 586. Similarly, Gräßer, *An die Hebräer.*

152. If the author refers here to a lower, transient heaven, his emphasis on the shaking of this heaven over the shaking of earth does not make sense.

153. Koester, *Hebrews,* 547.

154. The difference in number (*ouranōn* [Heb. 12:25]/*ouranon* [12:26]) is not significant. The author alternates between the singular and the plural for no apparent reason than stylistic variation. For example, he may use the plural to refer both to the created heavens (1:10) and to the realm where God lives (12:25). Conversely, he may use the singular as well to denote the place where God lives (9:24).

155. Adams, "The Cosmology of Hebrews," 129.

156. Ibid., 130.

(and shake) Mount Sinai. The author contends that the believers, who experienced a greater revelation and benefits than the desert generation (Heb. 2:1–4), are liable to a greater judgment. He concludes that if the desert generation did not escape judgment, much less will believers.

In Hebrews 12:25–27, the author of Hebrews quotes a portion of Haggai 2:6–7, 21–22 to make the point that God has announced a judgment:

> For thus says the Lord of hosts: Once again, in a little while, *I will shake the heavens and the earth* and the sea and the dry land; and I will shake all the nations, so that the treasure of all nations shall come, and I will fill this house with splendor, says the Lord of hosts. . . . Speak to Zerubbabel, governor of Judah, saying, *I am about to shake the heavens and the earth, and to overthrow the throne of kingdoms; I am about to destroy the strength of the kingdoms of the nations, and overthrow the chariots and their riders; and the horses and their riders shall fall, every one by the sword of a comrade.* (Hag. 2:6–7, 21–22, NRSV, emphasis added)

The quotation of this passage in Hebrews is very significant. The author makes some changes in his quotations to emphasize the points he wants to make.

First, Hebrews focuses on the shaking of heaven. The author does this with three changes to the text of Haggai 2:6 (cf. Hag. 2:21): (1) He deletes any reference to the sea and the dry land; only earth and heaven are important to him. (2) He changes the order of the words to put "heaven" at the end. (3) He adds "not only . . . but" to place a strong emphasis on "heaven." The author wants us to know that God will shake the "earth and the heaven" but especially, and most importantly, "heaven."[157]

Second, he emphasizes the finality of this event. This is an eschatological event that describes the end of heaven and earth as we know them. The author argues that the expression "once more" (*eti hapax*, Heb. 12:27) indicates or makes clear the removal of things that are shaken. The author has argued throughout the letter that Christ died "once" (*hapax*) to emphasize the finality of His sacrifice (9:7, 26–28; 10:2). Here, the expression carries the sense of a "once for all" (cf. *ephapax*) removal of what can be "shaken" (12:27) as in 7:27, 9:12, and 10:10. In other words, we could translate this

---

157. Cf. Matt. 24:29; Mark 13:25; Luke 21:26.

expression as "yet once more and forever." This means there will be an event of final consequences in the "earthly" realm, but especially in the "heavenly" realm, that is described as a shaking.

In the Old Testament, the shaking of the earth is a common image of the presence of God, who shows up to deliver His people.[158] Thus, shaking becomes a signal of God's judgment over the oppressors.[159] The LXX uses the verb *saleuō* ("to shake") regarding those who experience God's judgment.[160] In the Prophets, the shaking happens in the context of the day of the Lord.[161] On the other hand, what is not "shaken" is not a Platonic transcendental realm but rather the righteous person who trusts in the Lord.[162]

Haggai 2 was uttered about seven weeks after Haggai gave the leaders and the people the message that it was necessary to begin rebuilding the temple, and four weeks after they actually began doing it. The message was delivered during the Feast of Tabernacles.[163] This feast was a memorial of God's care for Israel through the desert, but also the dedication of Solomon's Temple (1 Kings 8:2). This remembrance, however, made the people think that the temple they were building was not worth the effort because it would not be even nearly as glorious as Solomon's Temple had been (Hag. 2:3). But Haggai promised that God would "shake the heavens and the earth . . . and [all] the nations" and fill this temple with glory by bringing their treasures to the temple they were building. He explains this in a following oracle pronounced two months later, on the twenty-fourth day of the ninth month (2:21–23, NRSV), when the foundation of the temple was laid (2:18). The oracle explains that the Lord will overthrow the kingdoms and their armies, establish His own king in Jerusalem from the line of David (represented by Zerubbabel), and give Him total authority—like that represented

---

158. Pss. 68:7–8; 9:27; 46:6; 60:2; 77:17–18; 97:4; 107:27; Mic. 1:4; Nah. 1:5; Hab. 3:6; Matt. 24:29; Mark 13:25; Luke 21:26; Acts 16:26.

159. E.g., Pss. 96:10 (95:10, LXX); 99:1 (98:1, LXX).

160. 2 Kings 17:20; Pss. 9:27 (MT, 10:6); 45:7 (MT, 46:6); 47:6 (MT, 48:6); 108:10 (MT, 109:10). See Lane, *Hebrews 9–13*, 481.

161. Pieter A. Verhoef, *The Books of Haggai and Malachi*, NICOT (Grand Rapids, Mich.: Eerdmans, 1987), 103. E.g., Isa. 13:1–22; 24:18; 34:1–17; Ezek. 7:1–27; 30:1–9; 38:20; Joel 2:1–11; Hab. 3:6.

162. Pss. 14:5 (MT, 15:5); 15:8 (MT, 16:8); 20:8 (MT, 21:7); 61:3 (MT, 62:2); 111:6 (MT, 112:6).

163. The precise date was the twenty-first of the seventh month (Hag. 2:1), which would be the seventh day of the Feast of Tabernacles.

by a signet ring (2:23). He will be the Plenipotentiary of the Lord.[164] According to Haggai, then, the "shaking of heaven and earth" (2:6) meant the destruction of kingdoms and thrones (2:22).

What is shaken in Hebrews? What is judged? The point is that the author of Hebrews emphasizes the shaking of heaven.[165] This refers to a judgment that includes the heavenly realm (Heb. 12:26) or "heavenly things" (9:23). The "heavenly things" that are judged ("shaken") should include the heavenly powers (angels) and believers who were just described as being with God in the heavenly Jerusalem (12:22–24).[166] Verse 27 explains that they have one thing in common: they are created beings[167] and, therefore, subject to the judgment and scrutiny of God (4:13).[168] They can be removed because they are created, but the text does not say that they are removed because they are created. Verse 25 explains that they are removed because they "turn away from the one who warns them from heaven."

This agrees with the author's emphasis throughout the exhortatory sections that believers will face a judgment,[169] that "the day"—probably the day of Christ (Phil. 1:10)—is approaching (Heb. 10:25). Thus, he announces that the enemies of the Son—who has been installed as King and Plenipotentiary of the Lord (1:5–14)[170]—will be subjected. They will be made a footstool for Jesus's feet (1:13–14; 10:11–14). These enemies include those who once received the knowledge of truth but now "willfully persist in sin" (10:26–27, NRSV; cf. 6:4–8). The result of this judgment is the final removal of

---

164. Verhoef, *The Books of Haggai and Malachi*, 148.

165. Koester, *Hebrews*, 547, suggests that the shaking of heaven in Hebrews 12:26 is related to the cleansing of heaven in 9:23.

166. Similarly, Revelation constantly describes believers as standing in heaven before the throne, and Paul also describes believers as being seated already with Christ (Eph. 2:5–6).

167. Hebrews 1:7 refers to angels as part of God's creation.

168. See Lane, *Hebrews 9–13*, 482.

169. Heb. 2:1–4; 4:12–13; 6:4–8; 10:26–31; 12:25–29.

170. The prophecy of Haggai is given in the context of the inauguration of the building of the sanctuary and in conjunction with the promise of a Davidic king who will be God's Plenipotentiary. In Hebrews, both issues are important. The book begins with the assertion that Jesus is enthroned forever at God's right hand. Jesus is identified as the Person in whom the Davidic promises of a Son who would sit on the throne forever are fulfilled. He has power over the angels of God. He has become, in fact, God's Plenipotentiary. On the other hand, the inauguration of Jesus's rule in heaven also coincides with three other events—the inauguration of Jesus's high priestly ministry, the inauguration of the heavenly sanctuary (Heb. 9:15–23; cf. 8:5–6), and the inauguration of the new covenant. Thus, just like in Haggai, the promise of a future shaking is given in the context of the inauguration of the rule of a Davidic King and the inauguration of a sanctuary.

what can be shaken. Enemies will be destroyed forever. This same word (*metathesis*) is used for the removal of the Levitical priesthood (7:12) and Enoch from the earth (11:5). In both cases the removal is not temporary. In Hebrews, what remains that cannot be shaken is Jesus Himself (1:11; cf. 13:8), His priesthood (7:3, 24), and the inheritance of the new covenant (10:34). These three things are what God invites us not to refuse. If we refuse them, we will be shaken or removed—that is, treated as the enemies of Jesus (10:27).

The next verse, Hebrews 12:28, explains that as a result of this "shaking" believers "are receiving a kingdom that cannot be shaken" (NRSV). This is probably an allusion to Daniel 7:14, 18, where the saints receive a kingdom that cannot be destroyed.[171] Interestingly, according to Daniel 7, the saints are given a kingdom as a result of a judgment in heaven. This is an allusion to a pre-advent judgment that results in the believers receiving the kingdom.

In summary, once we have understood the meaning of the quotation of Haggai 2:6 in Hebrews 12:27, we are able to read the passage in the following way:

> *to de eti hapax dēloi tēn tōn saleuomenōn metathesin hōs pepoiēmenōn, hina meinē ta mē saleuomena*

> This phrase, "Yet once more," indicates the removal of what is shaken [enemies who reject God both in heaven and earth]—as created things [as subject to God's judgment]—so that what cannot be shaken [the believer who trusts God] may remain.

So this passage does not affirm that there are uncreated things that are inherently eternal and will survive the shaking of creation at the end of time. This passage coheres with the assertions elsewhere in Hebrews that God is the Creator of all things and therefore everything is subject to His judgment ("shaking"). What remains after God's "shaking" (judgment) are not uncreated things but God's "kingdom" and believers ("we") who receive the kingdom from Him (Heb. 12:28). This passage is then parallel to Hebrews 4:12–13, where the author warns the readers that the word of God will judge them and the readers need to pay attention (3:7).

---

171. Attridge, *Hebrews*, 382; Otto Michel, *Der Brief and die Hebräer*, KEK 13 (Göttingen: Vandenhoeck and Ruprecht, 1966), 475–76; Brooke Foss Westcott, *The Epistle to the Hebrews: The Greek Text with Notes and Essays* (London: Macmillan, 1892; repr., Grand Rapids, Mich.: Eerdmans, 1984), 442.

Similarly here, the author warns the readers that they need to pay attention to Him who warns from heaven, lest they will face the judgment, or "shaking," of God.

CONCLUSION

Hebrews teaches at least seven things about creation:

1. God created the universe—that is, "all things." (Heb. 1:2, 10; 3:3–4).

2. Both the Father and the Son created (1:2, 10; 3:3–4). They are co-Creators. In the overall argument of Hebrews, the act of creation did not imply or require the subordination of one to the other but rather a perfect accord or subordination to each other. Thus, according to Hebrews, the universe was created "through" and "for" the Son (cf. 1:10) but also "through" and "for" the Father (2:10).

3. The Son created the universe ("all things") "in the beginning" and will "roll them up," "change," or "shake" them in the end, meaning that just as the Son has created the totality of things, so He has acted through the totality of time (1:10; 12:26–27).

4. God created the universe through His "word" (11:3).

5. To understand that God created the universe requires faith (11:3)—something no more popular at the time that Hebrews was written than it is today.

6. The belief that God created the universe is paradigmatic of true faith. Believers are the first listed among the exemplars of faith (11:3).

7. The belief that God created the universe is central to faith. Hebrews affirms that what God created is subject to His judgment (4:12–13; 12:26–27); therefore, God's claim to have created the world is central to His sovereignty.

It is also clear that the author of Hebrews was acquainted with the creation account of Genesis 1–3. He alludes to the creation of the universe in Genesis 1:1 (Heb. 1:10; 11:3), refers to God's rest on the seventh day of creation (Heb. 4:3–4, 10), and suggests the historicity of the fall of Adam and Eve (Heb. 9:26; possibly 6:7–8). His argument suggests that he considers Genesis 1–3 a historical account (Heb. 4:3–4; esp. 9:26).

THE INTERCHANGEABILITY OF ROLES
BETWEEN THE FATHER AND THE SON

A closer inspection of the assertions in Hebrews regarding creation shows that the roles of God the Father and the Son in creation are interchangeable. Deliberately or not, the author assigns them the same roles.

First, the Father and the Son are Creators. Several passages clearly identify God the Father as the Creator of the universe;[172] Hebrews 1:10, however, clearly ascribes to the Son the creation of the universe. In this passage, the Father says to the Son, "In the beginning, Lord, *you* founded the earth, and the heavens are the work of your hands" (NRSV, emphasis added).

Second, the Father and the Son are the agents and beneficiaries of creation. We often note the affirmation in Hebrews 1:2 that God created the universe "through" (*dia* followed by genitive) the Son and that the Son will inherit "all things" (*ta panta*). We often forget, however, that Hebrews 2:10 affirms the opposite.[173] There, the author says that everything exists "through" (*dia* followed by genitive) God the Father, and that "all things" (*ta panta*) are "on account of" or "for" (*dia hon*) Him.

Finally, the Father and the Son are both sovereign over creation and judge it. Hebrews 12:26–27 (NRSV) affirms about God,

> At that time His voice shook the earth; but now He has promised, "Yet once more I will shake not only the earth but also the heaven." This phrase, "Yet once more," indicates the removal of what is shaken—that is, created things—so that what cannot be shaken may remain.

Thus, God's sovereignty and power over creation are evident in the fact that God will "shake" in the future "heaven and earth." Hebrews 1:10–12 (NRSV) affirms the same about the Son, but in different words:

> And, "In the beginning, Lord, you founded the earth, and the heavens are the work of your hands; they will perish, but you remain; they will all wear out like clothing; like a cloak you will roll them up, and like clothing they will be changed. But you are the same, and your years will never end."

---

172. For God as Creator, see Heb. 1:2; 3:4; 4:3–4; 11:3.

173. Koester, *Hebrews*, 227.

According to this passage, the Son has the power of "rolling" the heavens and the earth "like a cloak" so that they will perish. Thus, just as God can "shake" the universe, the Son can "roll them up." In both cases, the result is their total destruction. The Son, then, has the same sovereignty over creation that the Father has.

This interchangeability of roles should not come as a surprise to the reader of Hebrews.[174] The author of this letter had already affirmed at the very beginning of his work the intimate relationship between the Father and the Son, not only in terms of their work for the salvation of believers but also in terms of the homogeneity of their essence or being (Heb. 1:1–4). Thus, the Son is straightforwardly called God (1:8) and has attributed to Him the characteristics that only God possesses (7:3; 13:8). This has strong implications for the christology of Hebrews, but we will not discuss them in this study.

CREATION AND SOVEREIGNTY

Creation in Hebrews has to do with God's sovereignty. God judges what He first created and then sustained. Though this point is very important, this study is not able to develop its implications. Gerhard May argues that the doctrine of creation out of nothing was not clearly articulated in Hellenistic Judaism before Christianity.[175] He suggests that it was not until the second century AD, in the face of the Gnostic challenge, that Christian thinkers felt obligated to articulate in clear terms that the all-powerful God who is above all is the one who created the world out of nothing, and not the ignorant Gnostic creator who originated in the fall of a higher heavenly being.[176] It became very clear for the Christian thinkers that anything that God would not have created (preexisting matter) would in reality not be under His power. Thus, in their view, a creation *ex nihilo* was an essential element of God's sovereignty.

According to Jews and Christians, two characteristics of Yhwh, the God of Israel, identified Him as unique or different from all other

---

174. The same phenomenon occurs in Paul. The doxology found in Romans 11:36 affirms that "all things" are "through" God (*dia* followed by genitive), but 1 Corinthians 8:6 affirms that "all things" are "through" Jesus (*dia* followed by genitive). Similarly, Romans 11:36 and 1 Corinthians 8:6 affirm that "all things" are "for" God (*eis* followed by accusative), but Colossians 1:16 affirms that "all things" are "for" the Son (*eis* followed by accusative).

175. May, *Creatio ex nihilo*, 1–38.

176. Ibid., 177.

reality.[177] Yʜᴡʜ was the sole Creator of all things[178] and the sole ruler of all things.[179] There is a small but important difference between these two conceptions. Jewish theology asserted that God had no helper, assistant, or servant in His work of creation. Simply, no one else had any part in it.[180] Jews believed, however, that God employs servants to rule over the universe—myriads of them, in fact. Thus, God is portrayed seated on a very high throne while the angels stand before Him, as servants in lower heavens, awaiting His command.[181] Noncanonical early Jewish writings refer to several exalted figures—principal angels and exalted patriarchs—who played an important role in God's rule of the universe. There is, however, a conscious clear difference between them and God, however exalted they may be: when the human seer mistakes the glorious angel for God and begins to worship him, this figure forbids it and directs the human to worship God only.[182] Accordingly, these exalted figures never sit on God's throne but stand before Him ready to serve. God alone rules. This defines who God is and confirms the fact that His attributes and sovereignty cannot be delegated to a creature.[183] In view of all this, Yʜᴡʜ alone can and must be worshiped. This explains why "Judaism was unique among the religions of the Roman world in demanding the *exclusive* worship of its God."[184]

---

177. Richard Bauckham, *Jesus and the God of Israel: God Crucified and Other Studies on the New Testament's Christology of Divine Identity* (Grand Rapids, Mich.: Eerdmans, 2009), 9.

178. E.g., Neh. 9:6; Isa. 40:26, 28; 42:5; 44:24; 45:12, 18; 48:13; 51:16; Hos. 13:4 (LXX); 2 Macc. 1:24; Sir. 43:33; Bel. 5; Jub. 12:3–5; Sib. Or. 3:20–35; 8:375–76; 2 En. 47:3–4; 66:4; Apoc. Ab. 7:10; Jos. Asen. 12:1–2; T. Job. 2:4.

179. Dan. 4:34–35; Bel. 5; Add. Esth. 13:9–11; 16:18, 21; 3 Macc. 2:2–3; 6:2; Wis. 12:3; Sir. 18:1–3; Sib. Or. 3:10, 19; 1 En. 9:5; 84:3; 2 En. 33:7; 2 Bar. 54:13; Josephus, *Ant.* 1.155–6.

180. Isa. 44:24; 2 En. 33:4; 4 Ezra 33:4; Josephus, *Ag. Ap.* 2.192. For example, in explaining Genesis 1:26, Philo argued that the creation of humanity was the sole exception (*Opif.* 72–75; *Conf.* 179).

181. Dan. 7:10; Tob. 12:15; 4Q530 2.18; 1 En. 14:22; 39:12; 40:1; 47:3; 60:2; 2 En. 21:1; Ques. Ezra A26, 30; 2 Bar. 21:6; 48:10; 4 Ezra 8:21; T. Ab. A7:11; 8:1–4; 9:7–8; T. Adam 2:9. See also Bauckham, *Jesus and the God of Israel*, 10.

182. Larry W. Hurtado, *Lord Jesus Christ: Devotion to Jesus in Earliest Christianity* (Grand Rapids, Mich.: Eerdmans, 2003), 46–47. Some of the examples he gives are Tobit 12:16–22, Apocalypse of Zephaniah 6:11–15, Joseph and Aseneth 15:11–12, and 3 Enoch 16:1–5. The same case is found in Revelation 19:10 and 22:8–9.

183. Richard Bauckham, "The Divinity of Jesus Christ in the Epistle to the Hebrews," in Bauckham et al., *Epistle to the Hebrews*, 17. The author of this study follows Bauckham's analysis here.

184. Richard Bauckham, "Jesus, Worship of," in *ABD* 3:816; N. T. Wright, *The New Testament and the People of God*, Christian Origins and the Question of God 1 (Minneapolis, Minn.: Fortress, 1992), 248–59; and Hurtado, *Lord Jesus Christ*, 29–53.

The author of Hebrews unabashedly refers to God's sovereignty over the universe. He introduces the letter by affirming that God created and sustains "all things" (*ta panta*) through His Son and that He has given "all things" (*ta panta*) as inheritance to the Son. These truths are why He sits on the throne over the universe and the Son sits at His "right hand." This affirmation of God's sovereignty at the beginning of the letter is essential to the argument of Hebrews and is repeated throughout the letter (Heb. 1:2–3, 13–14; 2:5, 8; 8:1–2; 10:12–13; 12:1–2). In fact, the author will explain that this is the main argument of his work (8:1–2). It is essential because it is the rationale for God's and the Son's superiority over the angels or spirits that were feared in the ancient world. Immediately after affirming the role of the Son as Creator, Sustainer, and Co-ruler of the universe in Hebrews 1:1–4, the author devotes the next section to affirm the Son's superiority over the angels (1:5–14). They are created (1:7); therefore, the angels worship the Son (1:6) and serve Him as ministers in favor of believers (1:7, 14). Since the Son is sovereign, He can both deliver and judge. This is why the readers are exhorted to "hold fast" to their confession of Jesus (4:14–16; 10:19–25; cf. 3:1), even in the face of persecution and suffering (10:32–39; 12:1–4).

It is important to note that references to creation in Hebrews are part of an affirmation of majesty/dominion (1:1–4, 10–12; 3:4), judgment (1:10–12; 4:3, 4, 10, 12–13; 12:27), or salvation (2:10; 9:26).[185] Hebrews does not try to prove that God created the world or describe how He created it; it just assumes that He did. What is important for Hebrews is that God can rule the universe, judge the wicked, and save the believers because He is sovereign, and this sovereignty has an indispensable foundation in the fact that He created "all things" (*ta panta*).

VOCABULARY AND PRESUPPOSITIONS

It is important to note that the vocabulary referring to God's act of creation in Hebrews is diverse. The author uses the verbs *poieō* ("to do, make"), *themeliō* ("to found, establish"), *kataskeuazō* ("to prepare, build, furnish"), and *katartizō* ("to put in order, restore"); the nouns *katabolē* ("beginning"), *ergon* ("work"), *ktisis* ("creature, creation");

---

185. Hebrews 11:3 is the exception. In this case, the author refers to the relationship between creation and faith.

and the participle *pepoiēmenōn* ("what is made"). Many of these terms were used by Greek philosophers in their discussion about the origin of the cosmos with very different presuppositions. As shown in this study, however, the fact that Hebrews uses some of the philosophers' vocabulary does not mean that he shares their worldviews.

Another difficulty encountered while studying Hebrews in the context of a debate about the origins of the world is the fact that its author's concerns are very different from ours today. The questions he was trying to answer were simply different. As previously mentioned, the author of Hebrews is not concerned with proving God created the world or explaining how He did it. He assumes that God created the world and uses this assumption as an important argument in his work.

This fact leads us to a second phenomenon. Some of the passages relating to creation in Hebrews provide room for a limited variety of views on creation. One example is Hebrews 11:3, which can be read in at least three different ways. While it is true that the context privileges some readings above the others, the fact is that the text is less conclusive than we may like it to be. Again, this is due to the author not sharing the same concerns as ours today.

All of this, however, does not make Hebrews or the Bible irrelevant to the modern debate about origins. The Bible provides a worldview that should inform the believer in studying the origins of our world. Any theory we may create or adopt about the origin of our world has an effect on the way we understand who God is and what He can do for us. As the believer evaluates the implications of any theory, the Bible should be allowed to provide clear counsel and direction in his or her thoughts.

FAITH WAS AS UNPOPULAR THEN AS IT IS TODAY

It was no easier for the early Christian community to have faith than it is today—particularly in a world of scientific sophistication. From the point of view of classical Greek philosophy, faith was the lowest level of cognition. "It was the state of mind of the uneducated."[186] Galen, who was relatively sympathetic to Christianity, said that Christians possessed three of the four cardinal virtues: they had courage, self-control, and justice but lacked *phronēsis* ("intellectual insight"),

---

186. Dodds, *Pagan and Christian*, 121.

which, in his opinion, was the rational basis for the other three.[187] Others were less favorable. Celsus accused them of being enemies of science. In his opinion, Christians were frauds who deceived people by saying that knowledge is bad for the health of the soul.[188] Porphyry repeated Celsus's accusation, protesting "an irrational and unexamined *pistis* [faith]"[189] and Julian blurted out, "There is nothing in your philosophy beyond the one word 'Believe!'"[190]

Hebrews, however, commends faith. It devotes an entire chapter to praising heroes of the past for their faith. It is significant that in the list of heroes of Hebrews 11, the author refers to the common believer, who accepts the biblical assertion that God created the world by His word, as the first exemplar of faith. In the author's view, to believe that God created the universe through His word will gain approval for believers (11:2). Similarly, Noah's building of the ark before rain fell (11:7), Abraham's leaving his inheritance for a land he did not know (11:8), Abraham's offering of Isaac, believing God would resurrect him (when that had never happened; 11:17–19), and Moses's refusal to be called the "son of Pharaoh's daughter" (11:23–26, NRSV) secured God's commendation for them (11:39–40).

The author of Hebrews is not naïve. He understands that the path of faith requires "disregarding its shame" (12:2) and "being publicly exposed" (10:33, NRSV), but he also understands that those who take this path follow the steps of Jesus, "the pioneer and perfecter of our faith" (12:2; cf. 13:13–14).

---

187. R. Walzer, *Galen on Medical Experience* (London: Oxford University Press, 1900), 15, referred to in Dodds, *Pagan and Christian*, 121.

188. Origen, *Cels.* 3.75, quoted in Dodds, *Pagan and Christian*, 121.

189. Porphyry, *Christ.* 1.17, quoted in Dodds, *Pagan and Christian*, 121.

190. Julian according to Gregory of Nazianzus, *Or. Bas.* 4.102 (Patrologia Gaeca 35, p. 637), quoted in Dodds, *Pagan and Christian*, 121.

Thomas R. Shepherd, PhD, DrPH

Andrews University
Berrien Springs, Michigan, USA

CREATION IN THE GENERAL EPISTLES

INTRODUCTION

This chapter describes the theology of creation and its implications and interconnections to other theological ideas found in the New Testament Epistles of James, 1–2 Peter, and Jude. It will briefly introduce the context in which the books were written, discuss individual passages in each book that relate to creation, and finally create a summary theology of creation for the four books. When discussing the individual books, each passage will be translated and its use of Genesis 1–2 in its theology described.

JAMES

The short book of James was likely written by Jesus's relative always mentioned first in the list of Jesus's brothers in the Gospels (Matt. 13:55; Mark 6:3), who became the leader of the church in Jerusalem and presided at the Jerusalem Council (Acts 12:17; 15:13; 21:18). His fiery little book has three main themes—testing (James 1:2–4, 12–18; 4:13–5:6), wisdom (James 1:5–8, 19–21; 3:1–4:12), and poverty/wealth (James 1:9–11,

22–25; 2:1–36).[1] James minces no words, outlining the need to face testing with fortitude, to ask God for wisdom, and to share resources with those in need.

James has more references or allusions to Genesis 1–2 than any of the other books covered in this chapter. Seven times the author makes allusion to the Genesis stories in six passages. It is not surprising, given the parallel to wisdom literature within the book (though written in a different style than books like Sirach, Wisdom, or the book of Proverbs).[2] Interestingly, references or allusions to Genesis 1–2 appear in all three thematic sections (testing, wisdom, wealth/poverty), suggesting that the creation theme is an important aspect of James's theology.

DESIRE, SIN, DEATH—JAMES 1:13–15 (GEN. 2:17; 3:1–6)[3]

> *mēdeis peirazomenos legetō hoti Apo theou peirazomai; ho gar theos apeirastos estin kakōn, peirazei de autos oudena. hekastos de peirazetai hypo tēs idias epithymias exelkomenos kai deleazomenos; eita hē epithymia syllabousa tiktei hamartian, hē de hamartia apotelestheisa apokyei thanaton.*

> No one should say when he is tempted, "I am being tempted by God," for God cannot be tempted by evil things, and He Himself tempts no one. Instead, each person is tempted by **his own desire** that drags him away and entices him. Then desire, after it has conceived, gives birth to **sin**, and sin when it is mature brings forth **death**!

It is a rather colorful passage with quite striking metaphors, typical of the book of James. A strong force named Desire overpowers and entices, followed by that same Desire now in the form of a woman giving birth to a daughter named Sin, who produces Desire's grandchild, Death. At first glance, there may not seem to be any allusions to the

---

1. See Peter Davids, *James*, NIGTC (Grand Rapids, Mich.: Eerdmans, 1982), 22–28. Cf. Craig L. Blomberg and Mariam J. Kamell, *James*, ZECNT (Grand Rapids, Mich.: Zondervan, 2008), 23–26.

2. Davids, *James*, 23. Cf. Proverbs 8, where Wisdom personified is linked to creation.

3. Bold text in each passage indicates references or allusions to the creation accounts of Genesis 1–2. All New Testament translations are the author's. Old Testament quotations are from the ESV® Bible (The Holy Bible, English Standard Version®). ESV® Text Edition: 2016. Copyright © 2001 by Crossway, a publishing ministry of Good News Publishers. The ESV® text has been reproduced in cooperation with and by permission of Good News Publishers. Unauthorized reproduction of this publication is prohibited. All rights reserved.

creation story in this passage.[4] Desire, sin, death—what do they have to do with creation? However, the progression from desire to sin to death is clearly reminiscent of Genesis 2:17, in which God expressly warns Adam that if he eats from the tree of the knowledge of good and evil he will surely die.[5] Further, this progression—desire, sin, death—has a clear link to the temptation and fall as described in Genesis 3:1–6. While James does not specifically quote the divine directive nor the story of the Fall (Gen. 3), his affirmation of the path and consequences of sin illustrates that his theology of sin is consistent with and rooted in the text of Genesis 2–3 as an expression of the origin of death in the world.[6]

FATHER OF LIGHTS—JAMES 1:16–18 (GEN. 1:3, 14–19)

Mē planasthe, adelphoi mou agapētoi. pasa dosis agathē kai pan dōrēma teleion anōthen estin katabainon apo tou patros tōn phōtōn, par' hō ouk eni parallagē ē tropēs aposkiasma. boulētheis apekyēsen hēmas logō alētheias eis to einai hēmas aparchēn tina tōn autou ktismatōn.

Do not be deceived, my beloved brothers. Every good gift and every perfect endowment is from above, coming down from **the Father of Lights**, with Whom there is not the slightest variation nor the trace of a shadow's turn. By His own will He gave birth to us by the word of truth so that we could be a kind of firstfruits of **His creatures**.

Again, the colorful nature of James's writing is apparent. Whereas in James 1:13–15 he describes the dire consequences of following sinful desire, here he turns to the blessings of receiving life and gifts from God. Two links to the creation story of Genesis 1 appear in the passage. The first is the characterization of God as "the Father of Lights," where God is described as the creator of the heavenly

---

4. See the discussion of an evil *yēṣer* as seen in Qumran documents and the relationship to James's discussion of evil in Benjamin Wold, "Sin and Evil in the Letter of James in Light of Qumran Discoveries," *NTS* 65, no. 1 (2019): 78–93. Wold is studying not the subject of creation but rather anthropology. He notes that external forces are at work in the Christian's life (the devil, God) and internal desires (desire, sin) in relationship to the problem of evil. But the texts that Wold refers to, 4QInstruction from cave 4 in Qumran and Ben Sira 15.14–15 (cf. Sir. 49:16; 7:30; 17:1–4; 24:81–9 [regarding Wisdom]; 43:5–6, 33), do take the Genesis creation accounts as historical events and the basis of anthropology, even as they place them within a wisdom literature setting for Ben Sira and a wisdom/apocalyptic setting for 4QInstruction.

5. See Davids, *James*, 85.

6. While James is allusive, Paul is more explicit regarding this pattern in Romans 5:12.

bodies.[7] It is a clear allusion to Genesis 1:3, which reports that God created light on the first day, and to Genesis 1:14–19, which reports His creation of the lights in the heavens—sun, moon, and stars—on the fourth day.[8] In James's theology this creation of light is tied to the blessings of good gifts from God. Light, blessing, and goodness are interconnected, suggesting that the Jacobean theology of creation sees this work of God as good, reminiscent of the creation story where all things were created "good," indeed, "very good" (Gen. 1:31). Consistency is the underlying character trait of the deity ("not the slightest variation nor the trace of a shadow's turn"), producing positive results in people who open their lives to His transforming power.[9] This leads to the conversion of people into a sample of the new creation order, in which they are firstfruits.

The reference to the firstfruits of God's creatures is the second reference in the passage to the creation account. The term for "creatures" is *ktisma*, which means "a creature" but also "that which is created," with a root in the verb *ktizō* ("to create"). The concept of created things recalls both Genesis 1 and 2, where the world's living, moving organisms are called into existence by the creator's word and act.

James places this concept of created beings within the context of new life given to people by God. While it is never described in James as "new" life, the idea of "firstfruits" suggests a move into a new setting in which redeemed people become the first evidences of a new world about to be revealed—a new creation. Parallel to Paul's description in Romans 8:18–25, James seems to indicate that not only will people be redeemed, but all of nature will share in the renewal of the world. The people are just the firstfruits of the entire harvest to be brought home by God's redemptive work. James clearly

---

7. "Of lights" is clearly an objective genitive, indicating that God is the one who created the lights. Cf. Douglas J. Moo, *James*, PNTC (Grand Rapids, Mich.: Eerdmans, 2000), 79.

8. James does not detail, nor is it our intention here to suggest, that the entire universe, including all the stars, were created in the creation week of Genesis 1. The text of Genesis 1:16 is rather laconic in regard to the stars. It simply adds "and the stars" at the end of the verse with the direct object marker before them. It could easily be translated "And He made the stars also," supplying the verb from the previous clause. This perspective could easily accommodate a viewpoint that the stars were made prior to creation week in our world, possibly long before.

9. Whereas objects in the sky such as the sun, moon, and planets move against the background of stars, and thus are "variable," God is not so. He is stable and trustworthy. Cf. Moo, *James*, 79–80; and R. T. France and George H. Guthrie, *Hebrews, James*, rev. ed., Expositor's Bible Commentary 13 (Grand Rapids, Mich.: Zondervan, 2006), 223.

sees the world in a lost state in need of redemption, but does not specify exactly how and where this trouble began. However, his statements regarding human sinfulness and redemption are all in keeping with the common biblical perspective on how sin entered our world and how the problem will be solved.

FAITH WITHOUT WORKS IS DEAD—JAMES 2:26 (GEN. 2:7)

hōsper gar to sōma chōris pneumatos nekron estin, houtōs kai hē pistis chōris ergōn nekra estin.

For just as the **body without the spirit is dead**, so also faith without works is dead.

With this verse, James concludes his lengthy discussion of the necessity to always combine faith in God with deeds of kindness and justice toward others around us (James 2:14–26). James's numerous examples (e.g., Abraham and Rahab) conclude with this famous statement comparing bodily life with Christian experience. The allusion is to Genesis 2:7, though in reverse order ("body without the spirit is dead," reversing "dust from the ground" plus "breath of life" in Genesis 2:7). This pattern in James is similar to the "de–creating" of a human being as expressed in Ecclesiastes 12:7 ("The dust returns to the earth as it was, and the spirit returns to God who gave it"). As God made the first man by combining dust and the breath of life, so the body without that breath of life or spirit is dead.[10]

This anthropological expression has a clearer tie to the Genesis story than the reference to sin previously noted. Whereas sin is an activity that people do over and over, and thus has a place in many historical events, the expression that "the body without the spirit is dead" is an anthropological truth that James presupposes and does not argue. This indicates his expectation that his readers have the same belief. The book presumes a community of faith affirming this fundamental anthropological statement. The roots of the statement are found in Genesis 2, and thus it appears quite certain that James and his readers accepted the events of that chapter as historical and above necessity to defend.

Furthermore, James uses the Genesis 2 belief to argue ethical behavior that is binding on the Christian. The moral linkage reinforces

---

10. Notice that the Greek word for "spirit" in James 2:26 is *pneuma*, which also means "wind" as per Jesus's play on words in John 3.

the historical veracity of the creation account because of its roots in anthropology. To remove the historical nature of the creation story would be to undermine the ethical teachings James propounds.

FOUR TYPES OF CREATURES—JAMES 3:7 (GEN. 1:26)

pasa gar physis thēriōn te kai peteinōn, herpetōn te kai enaliōn damazetai kai dedamastai tē physei tē anthrōpinē.

For every species of wild **beasts and birds, reptiles and also sea creatures** is tamed and has been tamed by the human species.

This verse in James 3 alludes to Genesis 1:26. The Genesis text describes the creation of humans, male and female, in the image of God and states they will have dominion over all creatures on earth. Just as Genesis 1 divides creatures into four groups—water creatures, birds, livestock, and creeping things (Heb. *remeś*, "small animal, reptile")—so James follows the same pattern of nature's order—beasts and birds, reptiles and sea creatures. James states that people are well able to tame wild animals of all sorts (the dominion described in Genesis 1:2–28).[11] But ironically, they cannot tame their own tongues and instead misuse them to mistreat others. It is a stark illustration of the problem of sin, a problem that did not exist before the events of Genesis 3.

MADE IN THE LIKENESS OF GOD—JAMES 3:9 (GEN. 1:26)

en autē eulogoumen ton kyrion kai patera kai en autē katarōmetha tous anthrōpous tous kath' homoiōsin theou gegonotas.

By it we bless the Lord and Father and by it we curse people who are **in the likeness of God**.

This text alludes directly to Genesis 1:26, in which human beings are made in the image of God, after His likeness.[12] James has been describing the untamable nature of the human tongue. One incongruity he notes is that people will bless God with their tongue while

---

11. Cf. Blomberg and Kamell, *James*, 159, who also note a parallel to God's words to Noah at the end of the Flood: "The fear of you and the dread of you shall be upon every beast of the earth and upon every bird of the heavens, upon everything that creeps on the ground and all the fish of the sea," Gen. 9:2). Cf. Davids, *James*, 144.

12. Dan G. McCartney, *James*, BECNT (Grand Rapids, Mich.: Baker, 2009), 192n25, notes, "The word for 'likeness' (ὁμοίωσις, *homoiōsis*) is found only here in the NT and is rare even in the LXX, making the allusion to Genesis 1:26 almost certainly deliberate."

at the same time cursing people who are in the likeness of God. The parallelism between God and His likeness in people stands in sharp contrast with the opposites of blessing and cursing coming from the same lips. James argues that this incongruity makes no sense and should be abandoned. Again, ethics and creation theology support each other.

This concept of respecting people because they are made in the image and likeness of God is also found in the book of 2 Enoch 44:1–5, especially in the longer J recension, coming from approximately the same time period as the book of James. Enoch is described as teaching his sons not to insult people. Verses 1 and 2 read:

> The LORD with his own two hands created mankind; in a facsimile of his own face, both small and great, the LORD created [them]. And whoever insults a person's face, insults the face of a king, and treats the face of the LORD with repugnance. He who treats with contempt the face of any person treats the face of the LORD with contempt.[13]

This parallel suggests that James's ethic was not isolated among early Christians but also a common view among Jews of the time period. The basis of this teaching in a historical creation account would also be a common heritage of both these Jewish and Christian authors.

THE SPIRIT IN US—JAMES 4:5 (GEN. 2:7)

> ē dokeite hoti kenōs hē graphē legei; Pros phthonon epipothei to pneuma ho katōkisen en hēmin?

> Or do you think that in vain the Scripture says, "He yearns jealously over **the spirit He caused to dwell in us**"?

The sixth and final passage paralleling the creation accounts is James 4:5. This passage suggests a parallel to Genesis 2:7, the constitution of the first man via the combination of the dust of the ground and the breath of life, similar to the same text alluded to in James 2:26—that is, the spirit God made to reside within humans was the breath of life that returns to God at death ("the spirit returns to God who gave it," Eccles. 12:7). If this is the case, it is consistent with James's other expressions related to creation. He takes the creation

---

13. Francis I. Andersen, "2 (Slavonic Apocalypse of) Enoch," in *The Old Testament Pseudepigrapha*, ed. James H. Charlesworth, vol. 1 of 2 (New York: Doubleday, 1983), 91–221.

account as foundational to Christian life and ethics and as historical (that God directly created the first humans).

However, other than these details, James 4:5 has a number of anomalies that make interpretation of this passage challenging. First, James indicates that he is quoting Scripture, but the passage has no certain parallel to any Old Testament text (though see below).[14] Second, it is unclear exactly what the quoted "Scripture" means. The phraseology is somewhat unusual, with a prepositional clause starting the quotation: *pros phthonon* ("toward envy"), possibly used here adverbially—thus, "jealously."[15] The central verb is *epipotheō* ("to long for, desire"), a fairly uncommon verb itself. The subject of the verb could be either God or "the spirit," being either the human spirit (cf. Gen. 2:7) or the Holy Spirit (cf. Gen. 6:3, 17). Most commentators agree that God is the subject of the verb and "spirit" is the object.[16] But we are still left with the question of whether the "spirit" refers to God's Spirit or to the human spirit or breath. If it is the Holy Spirit, then the likely reference is to the time of the Flood ("My Spirit shall not abide in man forever, for he is flesh: his days shall be 120 years," Gen. 6:3). But the problem here is the use of the verb *epipotheō* ("to long for, desire"), which does not seem to fit quite so well with the Flood story ("not abide" is not "to long for, desire"). Why would God be jealous of His own Spirit?

Thus, if Genesis 6 is excluded, Genesis 2:7 seems the more likely choice, with "spirit" referring to the breath of life God infused into humankind at creation (cf. Eccles. 12:7). But why would God yearn jealously over the spirit or breath placed in them?

Context helps us unravel the mystery. James 4:1–10 describes the necessity for Christians to live humble lives. It is a passage filled with references to turbulent human emotions—quarrels, fights, passions, and even murder. It is not likely that the church members were actually killing one another, but James speaks hyperbolically to

---

14. See Davids, *James*, 162–65 for discussion and suggested parallels. Davids makes reference to Gen. 2:2, 7; 6:3, 17; 7:15; Exod. 20:5; Job 14:15; Pss. 41:2; 83:3; 104:29–30; Ezek. 37. Davids thinks the reference is to some unknown apocryphal text. Moo, *James*, 188–90, on the other hand, argues for a clear link to Exod. 20:5, 34:14, and Zech. 8:2 and supports a link to Gen. 2:7. Craig B. Carpenter, "James 4.5 Reconsidered," *NTS*, 47, no. 2 (2001): 189–205, argues that James 4:5b–6a is an indirect discourse construction that serves as an introduction to the quotation in verse 6.

15. So Davids, *James*, 164. Cf. also Martin Dibelius, *James*, Hermeneia (Philadelphia: Fortress Press, 1975), 220–224.

16. Davids, *James*, 164; Dibelius, *James*, 223–24; and Blomberg and Kamell, *James*, 190–92.

make his point. In this context, James gives his quotation in verse 5. The more likely Old Testament background for the reference to "yearns jealously" here is Exodus 20:5, the second commandment that refers to God as a "jealous God." That is to say, He is passionate about His covenant relationship with His people (Heb. *qannā'*, "jealous, envious"). He will countenance no rivals in this relationship— "no other gods" (20:3). When we fight and quarrel with others, it illustrates that we are placing our own concepts and understandings above God, making ourselves or our feelings a god in the place of the one God we should serve.

Thus, God's yearning over the spirit He has placed in us is His insistence that we live in accordance with the principles of His law, which requires devotion only to His will and way. This suggests that in James's theology there is an intimate connection between the law of God and creation—a not incongruent perspective, given that close linkage between the Sabbath and creation in the Decalogue.

CONCLUSION ON JAMES

It is striking just how much James roots his theology in creation. We see ties to the first and fourth days of the Genesis 1 creation story in James 1:17. In 3:7 he ties his argumentation to the typical categories of animals described in the fifth and sixth days of creation. In 3:9 he clearly alludes to the creation of people in the likeness of God from the sixth day of creation. In 1:18 he alludes to the fifth and sixth days of creation with a reference to all of God's creatures.

But James also refers to the creation story of Genesis 2. In 1:13–15 he alludes to the typical chain of sin leading to death, parallel to Genesis 2:17. And twice (James 2:26; 4:5) he alludes to Genesis 2:7, with its biblical formula of holistic anthropology. It is important to note that James draws from the creation stories two great anthropological truths: people are made in the likeness of God (Gen. 1:26), and a person is a whole (a person does not *have* a soul but rather *is* a soul, Gen. 2:7).

While some may suggest that James's references to creation are allusive and general in nature, the broad and consistent parallels to both Genesis 1 and 2 point in a different direction—that James assumes the historical nature of the events described in the first two chapters of Genesis and repeatedly uses the concepts and theology of these chapters as the basis of his argumentation.

1 PETER

The epistle of 1 Peter was written to a group of Christians scattered across what is present-day Turkey. They were being pressured by the pagans around them to conform to a lifestyle the believers had left behind. Throughout history, Christians have commonly reacted to such persecution by either conforming to the culture in one way or another or by withdrawing to enclaves where they can practice their faith in peace.

What is striking about 1 Peter is that the apostle recommends neither course. He insists on high moral standards (1 Pet. 1:16, quoting from Lev. 19:2, "You must be holy because I am holy") while at the same time affirming continued contact with the world outside the church (1 Pet. 2:11–3:7; 3:13–17). In light of this continued contact with the world, 1 Peter contains a profound theology of community formation—describing the great salvation that God has brought to the believers (1:1–12) and characterizing the believers as a house or building founded on Jesus Christ as the chief cornerstone (2:4–10). The apostle sees this community as the heir to the wonderful Old Testament promises to Israel.[17] Their role is to live faithfully and thus draw others into the community of believers (2:13–3:17) and silence the slander of outsiders (2:11–12; 3:15–16).

So, it may come as a bit of a surprise that Peter has a number of references to creation in his argumentation. In fact, these references, not unlike what we saw in James, play a crucial role in the apostle's argumentation.

FOUNDATION OF THE WORLD—1 PETER 1:20 (GEN. 1–2)

proegnōsmenou men pro katabolēs kosmou, phanerōthentos de ep' eschatou tōn chronōn di' hymas

[the Lamb], on the one hand, foreknown before the **foundation of the world**, but, on the other hand, revealed in the last times for your sakes

In 1 Peter 1:13–17, the section just prior to this verse, the apostle calls for a holy lifestyle based on the amazing commitment that the Father, Son, and Holy Spirit have made in providing new birth and

---

17. This is not supersessionism but fulfillment of the promises, along the lines of Paul's theology of Israel in Romans 9–11, though expressed in different ways that do not suggest literary dependence.

salvation to the beleaguered recipients of the book (1:1–12). Peter's readers are besieged because they have become Christians and are out of step with the culture around them.[18] The apostle goes out of his way to emphasize the power of God working for them in so many ways (1:1–12, 18–21; 2:4–10, 21–25).

1 Peter 1:18–21 explains that our salvation depends solely on the great sacrifice that Christ has made for us.[19] The apostle underscores the value of this sacrifice in three ways: First, he states that Christ's blood is more precious than silver or gold (1:18–19). Second, His blood is like that of a spotless lamb without blemish (1:19). Third, a great length of time spans from when the sacrifice was planned (from "before the foundation of the world," 1:20) to the time when it was revealed ("in the last times," 1:20); thus, the cosmic view of salvation spans from before creation to the end of days.

Peter refers to the foundation of the world, its creation. The term he uses is *katabolē*, which means "foundation, beginning." The term is used only eleven times in the New Testament, ten of which link it with the creation of the world.[20] In the New Testament, the events

---

18. Cf. 1 Peter 1:1 where they are called elect/chosen strangers of the diaspora. The term "elect/chosen" (*eklektos*) is a badge of honor while "strangers" (*parepidēmos*) is a term expressing weakness and therefore shame. They are strangers because they have accepted being chosen by God.

19. Peter utilizes theology (who God is, 1 Pet. 1:15–17) and christology (who Christ is, 1 Pet. 1:18–21) as reasons why Christians must live a faithful lifestyle (1 Pet. 1:13–14, 22–25; 2:1–3).

20. Matt. 13:35; 25:34; Luke 11:50; John 17:24; Eph. 1:4; Heb. 4:3; 9:26; 11:11; 1 Pet. 1:20; Rev. 13:8; 17:8. The one exception is Hebrews 11:11, where the term is used to refer to Abraham's role in the conception of Isaac. See Craig R. Koester, *Hebrews*, AB 36 (New York: Doubleday, 2001), 487–88; and Paul Ellingworth, *Commentary on Hebrews*, NIGTC (Grand Rapids, Mich.: Eerdmans, 1993), 586–89. See also similar terminology regarding the foundation or beginning of the world in Barnabas 5:5 ("And furthermore, my brothers: if the Lord submitted to suffer for our souls, even though He is Lord of the whole world, to whom God said *at the foundation of the world*, 'Let us make man according to Our image and likeness,' how is it then, that He submitted to suffer at the hand of men? Learn!" [*The Apostolic Fathers*, ed. Michael W. Holmes, trans. J. B. Lightfoot and J. R. Harmer (Grand Rapids, Mich.: Baker, 1992), 285, emphasis added]); 1 Enoch 48:2–3, 6 (the "Son of Man was given a name, in the presence of the Lord of the Spirits, the Before-Time; even *before the creation of the sun and the moon, before the creation* of the stars, he was given a name in the presence of the Lord of the Spirits . . . he was concealed in the presence of [the Lord of the Spirits] *prior to the creation of the world*, and for eternity" [emphasis added]); 62:7 ("For the Son of Man was *concealed from the beginning*" [*The Old Testament Pseudepigrapha*, ed. James H. Charlesworth (Garden City, N.Y.: Doubleday, 1983), 1:35, emphasis added]); Testament of Moses 12:4 ("God has created all the nations which are in the world [just as He created] us. And He has foreseen both them and us *from the beginning of the creation of the world* even to the end of the age" [*Old Testament Pseudepigrapha*, 1:934, emphasis added]). These parallels illustrate how not only the terminology that Peter uses but also a number of the ideas Peter emphasizes were common in the Jewish and Christian literature of the time. See the

connected with this phraseology are said to occur either "before" (*pro*) or "from" (*apo*) the foundation of the world. "Before" points to a time prior to the creation of our world. "From" indicates the passage of time ever since the creation of our world up until the time of the event being discussed. Only three of the New Testament uses utilize "before" and in each case point toward some pivotal, crucial event taking place in God's plan of salvation, all before the creation of our world.[21] Creation, then, becomes a marker of importance for the theology Peter propounds—in the case of 1 Peter 1:20, the atonement made by Christ. The salvation of humanity was not an afterthought. It was indeed a forethought before the world came into existence. But it is interesting to ponder the role of creation here. Salvation preceded creation in God's plan. The Son of God was there, ready to make the sacrifice. Creation going wrong required that preplanned salvation to be put into effect. It is as though Peter says that before the beginning of all we know, there was the salvation of God already prepared.

EVERY CREATION—1 PETER 2:13–14 (GEN. 1–2)

> *hypotagēte pasē anthrōpinē ktisei dia ton kyrion, eite basilei hōs hyper-echonti eite hēgemosin hōs di' autou pempomenois eis ekdikēsin kakopoiōn, epainon de agathopoiōn.*

> Submit to **every creation** of a human nature because of the Lord, whether to the king as supreme or to the governors as sent by him for the punishment of evil doers but the praise of those who do good.

Peter begins a new section in 1 Peter 2:11–12, where he admonishes the Christians to eschew evil and embrace a strong moral and uplifting way of life so their witness before Gentiles will refute false accusations about the Christian faith. A major theme in this call for a holy life is the call to submission. All Christians are called to submit to governing authorities (2:13–17). Christian servants are told to submit to masters, even unscrupulous ones (2:18–20), following their great example, Jesus Christ (2:21–25), and Christian wives are told to submit to their husbands, to help win them to faith in Christ

---

discussion of "before the foundation of the world" in Jan A. Sigvarten's chapter, "Creation in the Second Temple Period Literature," 71, in this volume.

21. God gave Christ glory before the foundation of the world (John 17:24); God chose us in Christ before the foundation of the world (Eph. 1:4); and Christ was foreknown as the Redeemer before the foundation of the world (1 Pet. 1:20). Notice the christological and redemptive focus in each case (in John, glory is linked to the cross).

$(3:1-6).^{22}$ Finally, young people are instructed to submit to older Christians (5:5).

The idea of submission is viewed in Western society today as an outmoded, even dangerous concept to embrace. But Peter sets this calling within a context that gives it a meaning different from the popular conception of his day—and indeed, even that of the present time. Three underlying motifs redirect the meaning of submission while at the same time affirming its practice. We will touch on the first two briefly, since they do not directly address the question of creation, and then spend more time on the third, which relates to Peter's view of creation.

The first motif running through Peter's theology of submission is that the language of submission is always linked to the language of justice. They are never separated. That is to say, Peter teaches submission but always within a context of God's justice. God is the final arbiter of all human relationships and will set right all wrongs. Peter uses terms like "good," "evil," "kind," and "unscrupulous" to describe the character traits or actions of those with authority over Christians.[23] By using these terms, Peter elucidates the moral universe in which all actions occur. Everyone must answer to God, no matter what their position. This includes the Christians ("judgment begins from the house of God," 1 Pet. 4:17; cf. Ezek. 9:6). Evildoers will not get away with abuse. God will hold them accountable for their deeds (1 Pet. 2:11–12; 3:16; 4:5–6, 12–19).

The second motif is the example of Jesus Christ serving as the paradigm for the Christian's response to persecution. The centerpiece of this theme is the profound meditation on Christ's passion found in 1 Peter 2:21–25, where He is presented as both example and sacrifice. His cross provides the atonement for our sins that changes our outlook on life and enables us to follow in His steps of submission and self-sacrifice. Peter never wanders far from either the salvific or exemplary roles of Jesus in this book. Christ is the Savior in chapter 1, the cornerstone and example for the church in chapter 2, the victor over evil forces in chapter 3, our companion in

---

22. Submitting to a cruel, crooked, or dishonest (Gk. *skolios*) master seems counterintuitive for a Christian. What we must take into account is that Peter is describing an entire moral universe with God at the pinnacle. A morally deficient master is judged as such by the holy will of God. Everyone, including all masters, will give account to God (1 Pet. 4:17–19). See below for more discussion. Cf. John H. Elliott, *1 Peter*, AB 37B (New York: Doubleday, 2000), 517–22.

23. See 1 Pet. 2:12, 14–15, 18; 3:9, 13, 16; 4:1–6, 12–18.

suffering in chapter 4, and the chief shepherd in chapter 5. He is the center and circumference of Christian life according to this book.

The third motif is the reordering of power structures. It is the one that links particularly to creation. It is found in 1 Peter 2:13–14, in the word *ktisis* ("creation, creature"). Peter calls on the Christians to submit to every "creation of a human nature," usually translated as every "human institution." Two issues need to be resolved regarding Peter's meaning here. The first is the use of the term "human" (*anthrōpinos*). The other is what he means by "creation, creature" (*ktisis*).

Anthrōpinos is the adjectival form of the noun *anthrōpos*. The noun means "human being." While the noun *anthrōpos* is very common in the New Testament (155 uses), the adjective *anthrōpinos* ("human") is fairly rare, with only seven uses. Typically, it is tied to some object related to human life—human hands (Acts 17:25), human wisdom (1 Cor. 2:13), human day in court (1 Cor. 4:3), human temptation (1 Cor. 10:13), and the human species (James 3:7). Once it is used as an adverb, "humanly" (Rom. 6:19). And then there is 1 Peter 2:13, where the adjective is tied to a word that seems rooted in something other than human life: *ktisis*, "creation, creature." Creation or creatures are things made by God, not humans.

So, why this linkage of "human" with something normally linked to God's activity, "creation, creature"?[24] In the passages that follow, all the individuals to whom Christians are called on to submit are leaders in some realm of human life—government (1 Pet. 2:13–17), home (2:18–20; 3:1–6), church (5:5).[25] But all these leaders have three things in common: they themselves are human, they are all subservient to God, and they must all give account to Him. John Elliott, in his massive 1 Peter commentary, states regarding *ktisis* in 2:13,

> In connection with emperor and governors, *human creature* [Elliott's translation of *anthrōpinē ktisei*] has a particular salience. With this expression, imperial power is subtly but decisively demystified, desacralized, and relativized. . . . Ultimate supremacy is reserved for God the creator, and it is "because of him, the Lord," that Christians are subordinate.[26]

---

24. See Elliott, *1 Peter*, 489, for a valuable discussion of the meaning of this phraseology.

25. As Elliott points out (ibid.), the submission Peter calls for is to individuals, not to institutions. The concept of institutions such as we know in the modern world was foreign to the ancient setting.

26. Ibid.

In fact, if we step back and look at the three motifs of submission discussed here (linkage to justice, the example of Jesus, and reordering of power structures), they all have the same direction and focus: surrender to the will of God. That is to say, God is at the pinnacle of power in 1 Peter. All things, all people, and all circumstances are below Him. In the first motif, with its linkage of submission to the language of justice, it is God who is the arbiter and judge of all human affairs, the one who will administer justice and restore balance. Everyone must answer to Him. In the second motif, it is linkage to the example of Jesus that empowers the Christian to submit to human authorities through the lens of submission to the will of God ("as free . . . but as slaves of God," 1 Pet. 2:16). And in the third motif, all to whom Christians submit are creatures, below God in power, and accountable to Him for their use or abuse of their leadership position. As Peter works this out in Christian experience and theology, he fundamentally reorders the concepts of power in the Greco-Roman world. All of the Greco-Roman world leaders and people are answerable to God, as are the Christians. So, the Christians ultimately submit or answer not to Rome but to God.

Creation's role within this reordering of power is interesting. Creation is depicted in 1 Peter 2:13 as the juncture of relationship to God. Where humans in leadership in the Greco-Roman world saw themselves as pinnacles of power, Peter brings down their leadership and role to a creaturely, creation-not-creator position. Thus, the concept of creation orders the human realm by relating it to the superior role of the creator, thereby establishing limits to human power. Peter's injunction to submit to human authorities is consequently not an appeal for total subservience, since these authorities do not wield absolute and ultimate power. This elevates the subordinate and reins in human rulers. Ethics finds its roots in this relatedness to God. Since the concept of creation is representative of and integral to this relationship to God, it too is intimately tied to ethics.

FAITHFUL CREATOR—1 PETER 4:19 (GEN. 1–2)

hōste kai hoi paschontes kata to thelēma tou theou pistō ktistē paratithesthōsan tas psychas autōn en agathopoiia.

So then, those who suffer according to the will of God should also entrust their lives to the **faithful Creator** in well doing.

In this passage, the apostle concludes his discourse in 1 Peter 4:12–19 on why Christians should not be surprised by the fires of persecution. Peter contrasts the proper, upright behavior befitting the Christian and the contrary lifestyle they must avoid. Peter indicates that there is no shame but rather blessing in suffering for Christ and that the Christian should glorify God in the midst of persecution. He argues that the reason for this boldness (lack of shame) and the glorification of God is rooted in the reversal that God will bring about in the judgment. This judgment begins from the household of God (cf. Ezek. 9:6), and as Peter notes, "if the righteous scarcely is saved, where will the ungodly and sinner appear?" (1 Pet. 4:18).

This brings Peter to his conclusion in 4:19. However, a question arises with the first two words, *hōste kai* ("so then also/and"). The *hōste* ("so then") fits well as a concluding conjunction for the entire passage, but the *kai* ("also/and") is problematic. It could stand as an antithetical parallel to the *kai* that starts verse 18: "*and* if the righteous scarcely is saved, where will the ungodly and sinner appear? So then, those *also* who suffer according to the will of God should entrust their lives to the faithful Creator in well doing" (4:18–19). But that seems unlikely, since the *kai* at the beginning of verse 18 links it to what proceeds as an additional example of the fate of the wicked. Furthermore, tying the clauses of verse 19 to these ideas does not make sense of the two verses together.

Thus, it seems that the *kai* in verse 19 must link internally to the verse itself or else have some tie to the passage as a whole. The possibility that it ties to the passage as a whole does not fit well because it would suggest that the sentence in verse 19 is somehow an *addition* to the points made in the section, but suffering according to the will of God seems to be the main point of the passage, including the imperative in the concluding counsel of verse 19.

This leaves only the link internally to the verse, and there are two options here. The *kai* links to "those who suffer" or to the imperative verb "entrust." The former would suggest a translation something like, "So then, *even* those who suffer according to the will of God should entrust their lives to the faithful Creator in well doing." The latter would translate as follows: "So then, those who suffer according to the will of God should *also* entrust their lives to the faithful Creator in well doing." The first option has difficulty because it suggests that some other group earlier in the epistle had entrusted their lives to the Creator, yet this is the only use of the term "Creator" (*ktistēs*) in the book—and, in fact, in the New Testament.[27] This leaves the last option, which makes good sense of the *kai*, making it a transition note to the imperative instruction:[28] "So then, those who suffer according to the will of God should also entrust their lives to the faithful Creator in well doing."

Why does Peter introduce the concept of the Creator into his discourse on suffering? The key is found in the adjective he uses to modify "Creator." The Creator is called "faithful," One Who keeps faith or is trustworthy. Peter has been arguing that Christians should be unashamed of the suffering they experience. He contends that the confessing Christian will rejoice in glory with Christ (4:13), that the Spirit of God rests on that person (4:14), and that faithfulness bears good results in the judgment (4:17–18).[29] God's steady, unwavering character of upholding the right and the good is present through all these concepts. His faithfulness is the assurance of the Christian's hope in times of suffering (cf. 1 Pet. 1:3–9; 3:13–22). Reaching back to creation suggests to the beleaguered believer that God has *always* been faithful, from the time He created the world. Thus, creation becomes the guardian of Christian trust in God's dependability in the midst of life's trials.

There is one more crucial point regarding this passage. We are able to elucidate more clearly Peter's view of creation from his interweaving of creation theology and his teaching on suffering. Throughout the Bible, we see creation consistently presented as something that God did through His almighty power without the least difficulty.

> By the word of the LORD the heavens were made, and by the breath of his mouth all their host. . . . For he spoke, and it came to be; he commanded, and it stood firm. (Ps. 33:6, 9)

---

27. Ibid., 805. But note that the participial form of *ktizō* appears in Romans 1:25, Ephesians 3:9, and Colossians 3:10 with essentially the same meaning of "Creator" (particularly Romans 1:25).

28. Ibid. Elliott is following the suggestion of C. A. Bigg, *A Critical and Exegetical Commentary on the Epistles of St. Peter and St. Jude*, 2nd ed., ICC (Edinburgh: T&T Clark, 1902), 181–82, who sees the *kai* as balancing the thought in verse 16 about glorifying God. Thus, Christians should not only glorify God but also entrust their lives to the faithful Creator.

29. Notice that Christ is the one they have fellowship with in suffering (1 Pet. 4:13) and the Spirit of God rests upon them (1 Pet. 4:14). With the addition of the faithful Creator (God the Father) in verse 19, the Trinity is presented as being involved in this section of 1 Peter—guiding, protecting, and building up the beleaguered believers in a way not unlike their actions at the beginning of the book (see 1 Pet. 1:1–12).

Creation was instantaneous. God spoke, and there it was. There is no indication in Scripture that bringing forth life in its myriad forms on our planet took millions of years or involved evolutionary processes of death, struggle, tooth and claw. On the contrary, the biblical record is simple and direct. God created life in this world in six literal days and rested on the seventh day as a memorial of His creative power.

It is to this sense of the creative power, the inexorable authority, and unsurpassable sovereignty of God that Peter appeals in 1 Peter 4:19. Any other view of creation would bring small comfort to people facing the trials of which Peter speaks. How would creation through long eons of struggle, with death and suffering, bring comfort to people suffering persecution?[30] Thus Peter's theology of suffering, linked inextricably to his view of creation, closes the door on any view of origins that involves long ages of death and suffering.

CONCLUSION ON 1 PETER

Creation in the thought of 1 Peter has three central foci: First, it is tied to salvation. God's plan to redeem our world was fixed before the world itself was created. Second, creation is tied to the reordering of human power structures. Humanity is creature, not creator, and all human relationships are related to God, the Arbiter of all human affairs. Finally, creation is the guardian of Christian trust in God in the face of suffering. Salvation, power, and suffering—creation has much more to do with Peter's theology than first impressions might suggest. If Peter took the creation stories as anything other than literal and historical truth, it is hard to see how he could place such theological emphasis and weight on this doctrine.

2 PETER

The apostle refers to creation in only one passage in his second epistle, but it plays a major role in his argumentation.

---

30. Evolutionary concepts insist that beauty, order, and complexity have arisen from long ages of struggle, pain, and death. Such concepts may lead to wonder concerning the beauty of nature but bring no comfort to the individual experiencing pain and facing death. But a faithful Creator who brought forth creation in an instant promises hope for those suffering in the present as they look forward to restoration in the future (1 Pet. 1:3–9).

FORMED BY THE WORD OF GOD—2 PETER 3:4–7 (GEN. 1)

kai legontes, Pou estin hē epangelia tēs parousias autou? aph' hēs gar hoi pateres ekoimēthēsan, panta houtōs diamenei ap' archēs ktiseōs. lanthanei gar autous touto thelontas hoti ouranoi ēsan ekpalai kai gē ex hydatos kai di' hydatos synestōsa tō tou theou logō di' hon ho tote kosmos hydati kataklystheis apōleto; hoi de nyn ouranoi kai hē gē tō autō logō tethēsaurismenoi eisin pyri tēroumenoi eis hēmeran kriseōs kai apōleias tōn asebōn anthrōpōn.

And saying, "Where is the promise of His coming? For from the time when the fathers fell asleep, all things continue in the same way **from the beginning of creation**." But they willingly forget this one thing, that **the heavens existed long ago and the earth was formed from water and through water by the Word of God**. And through these the former world was destroyed, inundated by water. But the present heavens and the earth by this same Word are being preserved and stored up for fire in the day of judgment and destruction of ungodly people.

FOCUS OF 2 PETER

Second Peter has one basic focus: countering and defeating the false teachers who Peter says will come in the last days (3:3, cf. 2:1–2).[31] The apostle starts this short epistle with a reminder of the way God's wonderful promises protect the Christian from failure. He then lays out the sure foundation of his message in his personal experience of Christ's ministry and the reliable word of God (1:16–21). In chapter 2, he attacks the evil character of these false teachers (with such heated language that one might imagine the page to still feel warm two thousand years later). In chapter 3, he addresses

---

31. See the chapter by Laszlo Gallusz, "Radically New Beginning, Radically New End: Creation and Eschatology in the New Testament," 135, in this volume for a discussion of how the "last days" began with the resurrection of Jesus Christ. Consequently, the false teachers in 2 Peter were likely a group in Peter's day, but they may also forecast what can occur again near Christ's second coming. Also note the differentiation Gene L. Green, *Jude & 2 Peter*, BECNT (Grand Rapids, Mich.: Baker, 2008), 153, makes between the opponents in Jude and those in 2 Peter. Green maintains that in Jude the opponents were from outside, while in 2 Peter they were insiders, members of the congregations. The distinction between the two books (Jude and 2 Peter) on this point is slight. Jude 4 uses the term *pareisdynō* ("to slip in stealthily, sneak in"), while 2 Peter 2:1 uses *pareisagō* ("to bring in secretly or maliciously"). The heretics in 2 Peter are teachers, thus individuals who would have standing within the community. But "bring in" suggests an outside source. It may be that the false teachers came into leadership in the church and then from teachings similar to those of the Epicureans or Saducees, began to teach false doctrines.

directly the deceitful doctrines of the false teachers. Our passage is central to this discussion in chapter 3.

The false teachers question the second coming of Christ based on their view of the way the world developed. According to their perspective, the basic rule of nature was a type of uniformitarianism. All things since creation have continued without change. So why should one expect change in the future? In order to quell any questioning of their authority, these false teachers add ridicule to their presentation. This is illustrated by their sneering question, "Where is the promise of His coming?" (3:4). According to these teachers, the promise of the parousia transmitted through the apostles was hollow and untrustworthy. Anyone silly enough to accept such a teaching was building on false hopes. The aim of these teachers is to silence objections. Their method is intimidation and falsehood.

Peter's response takes these false teachers seriously. He spends the entire letter discussing their threat to the church. He quotes their argumentation and not only counters it but goes on to instruct the church members regarding questions raised by the false teachers' accusations. Peter had a pastor's heart and wanted to protect his flock.

The central truth discussed by the apostle in 2 Peter 3 is the second coming. But because of the false teachers' accusations and presuppositions, the subject of creation comes up as well. Protology and eschatology are thus linked in Peter's argumentation.

THE FALSE TEACHERS AND THE EPICUREANS AND SADDUCEES

The false teachers' argument bears striking similarities to the philosophies of two groups in the ancient world: the Epicureans from Greek culture and the Sadducees from Jewish culture.[32] The Epicureans were founded by the Greek philosopher Epicurus (341–270 BC). He taught that the purpose of life was to seek simple pleasures through philosophical insights, with the the absence of evil. He believed that the gods do not judge, reward, or punish—that there is

---

32. Concerning Epicureanism, see Richard Bauckham, *Jude, 2 Peter*, WBC 50 (Waco, Tex.: Word, 1983), 156–57; Green, *Jude & 2 Peter*, 150–59; and esp. Peter Davids, *The Letters of 2 Peter and Jude*, PNTC (Grand Rapids, Mich.: Eerdmans, 2006), 132–36. Concerning the Sadducees, see Everett Ferguson, *Backgrounds of Early Christianity*, 3rd ed. (Grand Rapids, Mich.: Eerdmans, 2003), 519–20; Günter Stemberger, "Sadducees," in *Eerdmans Dictionary of Early Judaism*, ed. John J. Collins and Daniel C. Harlow (Grand Rapids, Mich.: Eerdmans, 2010), 1179–81; and Davids, *2 Peter and Jude*, 132–36. Some scholars argue for a link to the Gnostics, but as Green, *Jude & 2 Peter*, 154, notes, "The heresy confronted in 2 Peter does not conform to any gnostic system known to us."

no providence. There is no life after death, no judgment, and no postmortem retribution.

The Sadducees had some similar beliefs and may have borrowed some from the Epicureans. This Jewish sect, especially linked with the temple services in Jerusalem, taught that no fate exists—there is no providence. God does not commit nor even see evil. They believed in radical free will (self-determination) and that the soul does not live on after death. There are no penalties or rewards in the under-world and no resurrection. These teachings of the Sadducees are presented in the works of Josephus, but the Gospels and Acts also give some notation of their rejection of the resurrection (Matt. 22:23–33; Mark 12:18–27; Luke 20:27–38; Acts 23:8).[33]

This is not to say that the false teachers described in 2 Peter are either Epicureans or Sadducees, but their teachings do hold certain affinities to what those groups taught. The Sadducees do not seem to have been an evangelistic group like the Pharisees (cf. Jesus's words in Matt. 23:15), so it seems unlikely that the false teachers would have direct connection to the Sadducees.[34] And while the Epicureans had widespread influence, 2 Peter never mentions this philosophical school. We note the parallels, however, because it places the description of the false teachers within the cultural milieu Peter writes from.

In our passage, Peter describes the false teachers' viewpoint on creation and then responds with his own belief. The false teachers describe a uniform view of action within the natural world and link it temporally to creation. Everything has gone on in the same way ever since creation. The false teachers see this as a predictor of the future—all things will continue into the future without change as well.[35] The reference to creation ("from the beginning of creation," 3:4) is used in a similar manner as in other New Testament texts

---

33. See Josephus, *Ant.* 13.5.9; 18.1.4; *J.W.* 2.8.14. For more details on the afterlife in Juda-ism, see Clinton Wahlen, "Greek Philosophy, Judaism, and Biblical Anthropology," in *"What Are Human Beings That You Remember Them?" Proceedings of the Third International Bible Conference, Nof Ginosar and Jerusalem, June 11-21, 2012*, ed. Clinton Wahlen (Silver Spring, Md.: Biblical Research Institute, 2015), 107-31.

34. One should note that Jesus regularly refers to the "scribes and Pharisees." The scribes were official experts in the interpretation of the law. They are linked to the chief priests in Jerusalem in Mark (Mark 14:1–2). We do not know if their linkage to the chief priests, who tended to be Sadducees, would indicate that the scribes were Sadducees as well. The Gos-pels and Josephus never state this explicitly. See Anthony J. Saldarini, "Scribes," *ABD* 5:1012–16

35. See Green, *Jude & 2 Peter*, 158, for the way this parallels Philo's idea of the inde-structibility of the world.

that use the phraseology "the foundation of the world" (Matt. 13:35; 25:34; Luke 11:50; Heb. 4:3; 9:26; Rev. 13:8; 17:8), with the crucial exception that the events in almost all these other passages deal with God's action, and the false teachers are purporting the *absence* of God's intervention since creation.[36]

This is too much for Peter. In 2 Peter 3:5–7, he responds to their argument. He will emphasize the concept of remembering or not letting something escape one's notice.[37] In verses 5–6 he recalls something the false teachers delibertly overlook: "But they willingly forget this one thing, that the heavens existed long ago and the earth was formed from water and through water by the Word of God. And through these the former world was destroyed, inundated by water."

The false teachers "willingly forget." They do not want to face the facts about God's sovereignty over the world and so they disregard it. They know the truth but are unwilling to admit it and live by it. But Peter does not let them get away with such deceptive thinking. He calls them (and his readers) back to the foundational truths of creation in Genesis. The apostle will reason from creation to the end of time, using elements of creation as his tools.

THE STRUCTURE OF PETER'S ARGUMENT

There are certain ambiguities in the Greek text of 2 Peter 3:5–6 that lead scholars to puzzle over their exact meaning.[38] Peter describes the time, object, means, and mode of creation all within one phrase in verse 5. Briefly stated, the time was "long ago," the object of creation was "the heavens . . . and the earth," the means of creation was the "Word of God," and the mode of creation was "from water and through water." But putting it this way hides many challenges within the text. We will note the ambiguities below. However, several characteristics of the passage help explain Peter's words. First is the literary structure. It can be outlined as follows:

---

36. The exceptions in the list of texts are Luke 11:50, where it is the prophets' blood poured out from/since the foundation of the world that will be required of Jesus's generation, and Hebrews 9:26, where the apostle indicates that Christ's sacrifice is not like that of an earthly high priest, otherwise He would have needed to suffer repeatedly from/since the foundation of the world. Tellingly, all the other passages use passive verbs linked with the phrase "from the foundation of the world," pointing to divine action as the causative agency (divine passive).

37. Bauckham, *Jude, 2 Peter*, 194, notes that 2 Peter is a testament—written to remind the readers of the important truths the author wants them to remember after his departure.

38. Cf. Bauckham, *Jude, 2 Peter*, 296–302; Green, *Jude & 2 Peter*, 318–23; and Lewis R. Donelson, *I & II Peter and Jude*, NTL (Louisville, Ky.: Westminster John Knox, 2010), 268–71.

A. The False Teachers' Words: 2 Peter 3:3–4
- Their status as mockers who live by their own desires
- Their question "Where is the promise of His coming?"
- Their reasoning "All things continue in the same way from the beginning of creation"

B. Peter's Response: 2 Peter 3:5–7
- Their status as forgetters
- The reality of creation from and through water
- The reality of destruction by water
- The conclusion about future destruction by fire

We notice that Peter characterizes the false teachers as mockers in verse 3 and then describes their doctrine in verse 4. This parallels his characterization of the false teachers as forgetters in verse 5a, followed by a response to their false ideas in verses 5b–7. The false teachers started with eschatology ("Where is the promise of His coming?" v. 4a), and based their doubt on the supposed uniform nature of life from the beginning (protology—"All things continue in the same way from the beginning of creation," v. 4b). Peter responds in reverse order, starting with creation in verse 5b, progressing to the Flood in verse 6, and concluding with eschatological destruction in verse 7. Thus, we have a chiastic form of the entire argumentation with introductions in parallel as follows:[39]

A Characterization Introduction (v. 3)
   B Argument from Eschatology (v. 4a)
   C Support from Creation (v. 4b)
A' Characterization Introduction (v. 5a)
   C' Support from Creation (vv. 5b–6)
   B' Support from Eschatology (v. 7)

Notice the chiasm in the B C C' B' arrangement. The value of recognizing this is realized when interpreting Peter's more opaque

---

39. See Bauckham, *Jude, 2 Peter*, 296, for a proposed chiastic structure for verses 3–10, where verse 3–4 presents the false teacher's concept of questioning the promise of the second coming with reference made to creation. Then verses 5–7 answer the question of creation, and verses 8–10 respond to the issue of the promise of Christ's return. While the author of this study agrees with this as a broad expression of the passage, two concepts lead him to see a chiasm as well in verses 3–7: the reference to the end of the world in judgment in verse 6 and the change of subject in verse 7, where Peter now calls on his readers not to forget as the false teachers do. Thus, verses 5–7 seem to answer the main argument of the false teachers, and verses 8–10 provide further instruction to Peter's readers, answering questions that may have arisen due to the false teachers' doctrines.

words about creation in verse 5b ("And the earth was formed from water and through water by the Word of God"). As we will see, Peter's argument answers the point the false teachers are making when they talk about creation in verse 4b ("All things continue in the same way from the beginning of creation"). Below, we will note another literary pattern between verses 5 and 7 that also helps narrow the interpretative options for verse 5.

THE TIME OF CREATION

Peter begins his refutation of the false teachers in verse 5b with a reference to creation and its time element. He uses the indefinite term "long ago." However, because the statement is made in relation to the words of the false teachers, who stress that "all things continue in the same way *from the beginning of creation*" (v. 4), Peter's reference to "long ago" simply plays upon their stress of continuity extending back to creation. Thus, Peter's statement of "long ago" refers to creation itself. One cannot derive from this a specific age for the earth or the universe at large. The purpose of the phrase seems to play more into the concept of God's sovereignty over creation. Peter stresses this point at the end of verse 5 by arguing that the world was created "by the Word of God." The false teachers argue for a world running like a clock, with God at a distance if there at all. Peter argues for God being present in creation and then later in the Flood (3:6).

THE OBJECT OF CREATION

Peter uses traditional biblical terminology of "the heavens and the earth" to describe what God created—though with a certain twist, as we shall see. The phrase comes from Genesis 1:1—"In the beginning, God created the heavens and the earth." The Genesis account is a simple statement of creation as to time, the actor, the action, and what was made. The time was "the beginning," God was the actor, He created, and what He made was the heavens and earth.

In contrast to ancient Near Eastern stories of creation, where the gods had a variety of struggles to make the world, the Genesis account is simple and forthright, indicating that the almighty God created with incredible power and had no difficulty whatsoever in accomplishing His task in six literal days.[40] Alluding to the Genesis 1

---

40. See Gerhard Hasel, "The Significance of the Cosmology in Genesis in Relation to Near Eastern Parallels," *AUSS* 10 (1972): 1–20, for a fascinating comparison between the

story, Peter establishes his first major point in conflict with the false teachers. Their remark, "The same [as it was] from the beginning of creation," tellingly makes no reference to the Creator. Peter will have none of it. His allusion to the Genesis account and his specific reference later in the verse to the "Word of God" establish the theological foundation of his message. God is at the center.

THE WORDING OF 2 PETER 3:5

Peter's wording in verse 5 is rather intriguing. A word-for-word translation of the Greek text would read something like this: "The heavens [plural] were/existed [plural] long ago and the earth [singular] from water and through water having congealed [singular] by the Word of God." Several points are interesting here. "Heavens" is plural, as is its accompanying verb "to be" ("were/existed"). "Earth" is singular, as is its accompanying verbal form of "to congeal" ("having congealed"). In fact, "having congealed" (*synestōsa*) here is a Greek perfect active singular participle in the nominative feminine, which agrees with "earth" (also feminine) but not with "heavens" (masculine).

Deciphering the content and intent of this phraseology is challenging. Richard Bauckham suggests that the verbs "were" and "created" (his translation of *synestōsa*) go together in a typical periphrastic construction of the verb "to be" with a participle.[41] This has some appeal because it solves the problem of the verb being plural and the participle being singular and not agreeing with the gender of one of the nouns ("heavens" is masculine in Greek and "earth" is feminine). Bauckham's solution links together "heavens and earth" in the typical merism of Genesis 1:1.

However, there are challenges with Bauckham's solution. The phraseology in Genesis 1:1 in the Hebrew text reads: *bĕrē'šît bārā' 'ĕlōhîm 'ēt haššāmayim wĕ'ēt hā'āreṣ* ("In the beginning, God created the heavens and the earth") and in the Septuagint it is: *En archē epoiēsen ho theos ton ouranon kai tēn gēn* ("In the beginning God made the heaven and the earth").

Genesis account of creation and the accounts of other Near Eastern peoples of the ancient world. Cf. Gerhard F. Hasel and Michael G. Hasel, "The Unique Cosmology of Genesis 1 against Ancient Near Eastern and Egyptian Parallels," in *The Genesis Creation Account and its Reverberations in the Old Testament*, ed. Gerald A. Klingbeil (Berrien Springs, Mich.: Andrews University Press, 2015), 9–30.

41. See Bauckham, *Jude, 2 Peter*, 296–98, for discussion of this challenging phrase. See also Green, *Jude & 2 Peter*, 318–20; and Davids, *2 Peter and Jude*, 267–70.

Four characteristics of the text of Genesis 1:1 stand in contrast to the text of 2 Peter 3:5 as follows:

1. Genesis uses the more common term for "create" (Heb. *bārā'*; Gk. *poieō*), but 2 Peter has the much more rare *synistēmi* ("combine, erect, organize, congeal, compose, condense") rather than *poieō* as in the LXX.

2. In Genesis 1:1 in both Hebrew and Greek, the terms for "heaven(s)" and "earth" have the article, whereas in 2 Peter 3:5 it is absent from both "heavens" and "earth."[42]

3. "The heavens and the earth" stand as a connected phrase in both Hebrew and Greek in Genesis 1, but in 2 Peter 3:5 the terms are separated by "long ago" (*ekpalai*).

4. The verbs in Hebrew and Greek in Genesis 1 are transitive and have direct objects ("God created **the heavens and the earth**"), but in 2 Peter the verbs are stative and intransitive, with no direct object.

This is not to suggest that Peter is talking about some process or event other than creation, but it indicates that he is speaking of it in a somewhat specialized way, as we will see below.

THE MEANING OF *SYNISTĒMI*

One of the issues of primary interest is the meaning of the verb *synistēmi* in 2 Peter 3:5. *Synistēmi* is a rather versatile verb. Its basic central meaning is "unite." It is a compound word made up of *syn* ("with") and *histēmi* ("stand"). In various contexts, it means "to unite, collect, present, introduce, demonstrate, show, put together, establish, stand with, consist, continue, endure, exist."[43] In mathematics, it meant to erect two lines on a straight line to bring them together to form a triangle.[44] In 2 Peter 3:5 it is in the active voice, suggesting that the items involved "came together" in creation. Since the verb is linked especially with the term "earth," this may point toward the appearance of dry land out of the waters covering the planet. The perfect tense of the participle suggests that the process

---

42. Interestingly, in the Hebrew of Genesis 1:1 "heavens" is plural and "earth" is singular, as in 2 Peter 3:5, whereas in the Greek Septuagint, both "heaven" and "earth" are singular in Genesis 1:1. We will note how the Greek article does appear with both "heavens" and "earth" in 2 Peter 3:7 and the significance of this fact.

43. See "*synistēmi*," BDAG 972–73.

44. See "*synistēmi*," LSJ 1718–19.

of creation came to completion at that long ago time and the world stood complete.

HEAVENS AND EARTH

As previously noted, Bauckham suggests that the verb "to be" (here plural in the imperfect tense, "were") should be linked to the participle *synestōsa* ("formed") as a periphrastic construction, in this case "were formed" or his translation "were created." However, the two words ("were" and "formed") are separated by quite a distance (eight intervening words), and each of these verbal forms agrees in number and gender with the nouns to which they are closest, as previously noted. "Were" goes with "heavens" and "formed/congealed" goes with "earth." This wide separation of the terms, the first ("were") being plural and the second ("formed") being singular, along with their linkage with different terms, suggests at least some separation of the ideas.

This emphasis on holding the terms apart is strengthened by observing the parallel structure in 2 Peter 3:7, which reads as follows:

hoi de nyn ouranoi kai hē gē tō autō logō tethēsaurismenoi eisin pyri tēroumenoi eis hēmeran kriseōs kai apōleias tōn asebōn anthrōpōn.

But the present heavens and the earth by this same Word are being preserved and stored up for fire in the day of judgment and destruction of ungodly people.

The distinction from verse 5 is fairly marked. The terms "heavens" and "earth" are drawn close together in verse 7, and each has the article. The verbal forms are all plural as well.[45]

This all suggests that Peter has something special in mind in verse 5 with the way he describes the creation process. Bauckham's suggestion of bringing the verb "was" and the participle "formed" together is valuable because of the way it resolves the problem of the hanging participle,[46] but it may be that Peter is suggesting two different processes, one for "the heavens" in contradistinction from

---

45. This does not leave out the singular "earth." Quite commonly, singular nouns are combined with plural nouns and the plural verbs subsume both. The problem we noted in verse 5 was the large distance between the verbal forms.

46. Bauckham refers to the participle being attracted to the nearest subject, which is singular, *gē*. Bauckham, *Jude, 2 Peter*, 296.

"the earth." That is, the heavens may have already existed and then the earth was brought into existence, with water playing a major role in God's creative process of the earth. This is only one of the possibilities of explaining the enigmatic phrase.[47]

WATER AND THE WORD OF GOD

One of the other key parts of Peter's presentation revolves around the term "water." He uses *ex hydatos* ("from water" or "out of water"), *di' hydatos* ("through water" or "by water"), and *hydati* ("by water") in verses 5 and 6. This phraseology is unique to 2 Peter, and thus there are challenges in determining the author's exact intent. Nevertheless, no one can doubt that "water" is very much at the heart of the discussion.

In Genesis 1, after the beautiful and succinct statement that in the beginning God created the heavens and the earth, the text goes on to state, "The earth was without form and void, and darkness was over the face of the deep. And the Spirit of God was hovering over the face of the waters" (Gen. 1:2). Note the reference to the "deep" and the "face of the waters." It seems that when the Lord first created our world, it was covered with a shoreless ocean. Up from out of this sea, the Lord brought dry land and then created vegetation and creatures.

But in 2 Peter, even this focus on water is overshadowed by the instrumentality of the Word of God both in creation and destruction. Verse 6 begins with *di' hōn* ("through which").[48] Bauckham outlines the various options for the antecedent of the phrase and concludes that it likely involves water and God's Word.[49] The main point of verse 6 is that God destroyed the world of that time by a cataclysm

---

47. As we have noted, Bauckham, *Jude, 2 Peter*, 296–98, prefers seeing the terms brought together, aligning the passage with the Genesis 1:1 creation account. Green, *Jude & 2 Peter*, 314, 319–20, on the other hand, sees the reference to the heavens as referring to creation, but the reference to the earth with *synistēmi* he sees as a reference to God sustaining the earth since creation ("by the word of God the heavens came into being long ago and the earth is sustained, having been formed out of water and through water").

48. The Nestle-Aland 28th edition has *di' hon* at the start of verse 6, which would be translated "because of which" or "on account of which." But the manuscript evidence is strongly in favor of *di' hōn* ("through which"; P⁷, ℵ, A, B, C, Ψ, 048, 5, 33, 81, 307, 436, 442, 642, 1448, 1611, 1735, 1739, 1852, 2344, 2492, Byz, lat, sy, co) versus the evidence in favor of *di' hon* ("because of which"; P, 1175, t, vg^mss). *Di' hōn*, interestingly, is what the Nestle-Aland 27th edition has. The editors of the 28th edition may have felt that *di' hon* is the harder reading and hence prior, but in the present author's opinion, the opposing manuscript evidence is too overwhelming to allow such a reading.

49. Bauckham, *Jude, 2 Peter*, 298.

of water—the Noahic Flood of Genesis 6–9. The Flood story in Genesis is a reversal of God's creative action of making the world in Genesis 1–2.[50] This is exactly Peter's point in 2 Peter 3:6: the world that was made "from water and through [out of] water" "by the Word of God" was also destroyed by the same method. It was made from water and was destroyed by water. This directly counters the false teachers' notion that "everything continues the same as it was from the beginning of creation." It is Peter's second major argument against them. First he emphasized God's sovereignty; now he emphasizes God's control and power not only in creation but also in destruction.

In 2 Peter 3:7, Peter presents the implications he draws from God's creation of the world and destruction of it in the Flood: "But the present heavens and the earth by this same Word are being preserved and stored up for fire in the day of judgment and destruction of ungodly people."

Verses 5–6 present what we might call the "lesson of water"—God is the creator and sovereign over the universe. From His great love He created the world. But He is also the impartial judge of all and destroyed the ancient world because of its wickedness. At that time, He promised to never again destroy the earth with water (Gen. 9:8–17).

Verse 7 presents what we might call the "lesson of fire"—God is preserving the present heavens and earth for the day of judgment and destruction of ungodly people by fire. The false teachers indicate that the past predicts how things will go in the future ("Where is the promise of His coming? For from the time when the fathers fell asleep, all things continue in the same way from the beginning of creation."). Likewise, Peter takes the same tack—the cataclysm of the past in the Noahic Flood is a predictor of how God will destroy the world once again, but this time with fire. Peter meets the false teachers on their own ground. They refer to creation; so does he. They indicate that things will not change; he insists that the past experience of the Flood points to the coming cataclysm of fire that will destroy the ungodly. The Word of God is the instrument of creation and destruction. It bridges the past and the future as the agency of God's action in the world.

---

50. See Richard M. Davidson, "The Genesis Flood Narrative: Crucial Issues in the Current Debate," *AUSS* 42, no. 1 (2004): 49–77, esp. 67–69.

CONCLUSION ON 2 PETER

Let us summarize Peter's argument: He responds to the false teachers' dual denial of God's intervention in the past and Christ's promise to return. The apostle accepts their premise that the past is the predictor of the future and then deconstructs their argument. God has always intervened in our world. He created the heavens and the earth, bringing the dry land out of the waters, but then destroyed the world in the judgment of the Deluge. This portends how He will intervene again with fire in the final judgment of evil. In each case, it is His Word that has the power of creation, destruction, and judgment. The false teachers are wrong because they have forgotten who God is and how involved He is with His creation. He has not lost His immanence to His transcendence.

JUDE

The brief book of Jude has only one reference that has a tie to the creation narrative, not a specific reference to creation.

SEVENTH FROM ADAM—JUDE 14–15 (GEN. 2; 5:1–24)

Proephēteusen de kai toutois hebdomos apo Adam Henōch legōn, idou ēlthen kyrios en hagiais myriasin autou poiēsai krisin kata pantōn kai elenxai pasan psychēn peri pantōn tōn ergōn asebeias autōn hōn ēsebēsan kai peri pantōn tōn sklērōn hōn elalēsan kat' autou hamartōloi asebeis.

Now Enoch, the seventh person from Adam, also prophesied about these people [the false teachers] when he said, "Behold, the Lord will most certainly come with His ten thousands of holy ones to pass judgment on all and to convict every person concerning all of their deeds of impiety that they committed impiously and concerning all of the harsh things that sinners spoke against Him in impiety." (Jude 14–15)

Verse 14 refers to Enoch being the seventh from Adam and verses 14–15 share his message regarding the ungodly, whom Jude links to the false teachers. Jude attributes this prophecy to Enoch (Gen. 5:18–24), the seventh from Adam (using Hebraic inclusive reckoning of Adam being the first generation).[51] The reference to

---

51. Jude apparently alludes to the book of 1 Enoch (1 En. 1:9), a book in the Old Testament Pseudepigrapha. Describing the relationship of the General Epistles to pseudepigraphal writings of the time period goes beyond the scope of this chapter. We simply suggest

Adam and how Jude describes Enoch's prophecy indicate quite clearly that he takes both individuals as historical figures of the ancient world and, hence, the text of Genesis 1–5 as a description of historical events.

CONCLUSION

These four brief epistles, James, 1–2 Peter, and Jude, a mere fourteen chapters in the New Testament, contain an incredible number of references to creation. Creation forms the basis of much ethical argumentation and is the foundation for understanding human nature, death, suffering, sin, and eschatology. Its principles reorder human relationships and power structures, striking at the very core of injustice and human depravity (James, 1 Peter, Jude). It reminds us of God's closeness to us and His sovereignty over us, His immanence and His transcendence (2 Peter). It speaks to the necessary connection between the human being and human action and reminds us of the obligation to treat others with grace and justice because they are created in the likeness of God (James). As a marker in time, a literal creation gives us that deep sense of beginning and points us to the great end toward which our world is moving (1–2 Peter). It tells us that God is the one faithful, trustworthy, and unchanging Being in our universe who will save His people and bring to account those who have done them wrong (James, 1–2 Peter, Jude).

If one were to remove from these books creation and the clear acceptance of a literal, historical creation event, it would be like pulling a central thread from a woven garment with the concomitant ruin of the apparel. Creation is so integral to the argument of these books that it is impossible to imagine their authors taking its historicity and veracity as anything but certain.

---

that 1 Enoch could contain traditions that go back to the historical Enoch. Cf. discussion by Davids, *2 Peter and Jude*, 75–80; and especially Green, *Jude & 2 Peter*, 26–33.

Ekkehardt Mueller, DMin, ThD

Biblical Research Institute
Silver Spring, Maryland, USA

CREATION IN THE BOOK OF REVELATION

INTRODUCTION

The book of Revelation is known for its amazing, and at times disturbing, apocalyptic imagery, which has triggered many different interpretations. Some people—particularly those who have more thoroughly engaged with the book—are intrigued by its pervasive doctrine of God, its rich Christology, and its strong ecclesiology. At first glance, it may appear that John's Apocalypse has not much to say about creation. However, one must take a closer look.

Also, scholars have asked what creation truly means,[1] relating to both creation in the past as described in Genesis and other Old Testament texts as well as the new creation found also in some Old Testament texts but especially in the last chapters of Revelation. Does Revelation's creation theme suggest that God actually created the universe, heavenly beings, and earth and filled our planet with life as described in Scripture? Does John propose that God will physically remake this earth and its immediate environment and

---

1. For a discussion of the meaning of creation in the Greco-Roman context, see the chapter by Cedric E. W. Vine, "Greco-Roman Creation Accounts and the New Testament," 31, in this volume.

create paradisiacal conditions?[2] Or should his statements be understood symbolically,[3] in the sense that God is somehow the Creator but that He uses and oversees a process such as evolution?[4] If the latter scenario was on his mind, it could mean that, over time, life on earth would continue to improve to such an extent that conditions might be reached that would resemble those described in Revelation 21 and 22[5]—or perhaps life on earth would deteriorate more and more, such that cynicism and despair would be humanity's only reasonable response.[6]

This study will explore how the creation theme is used in Revelation, how it relates to the Genesis creation account, and how it contributes to the theology of the Apocalypse today.

REVELATION'S REFERENCES AND ALLUSIONS TO CREATION

In the Apocalypse, John refers to creation repeatedly and uses respective language. In addition, various allusions dominate the book.[7]

---

2. E.g., Jan Fekkes, *Isaiah and Prophetic Traditions in the Book of Revelation: Visionary Antecedents and Their Development*, JSNTSup 93 (Sheffield: JSOT Press 1994), 229, states, "The casual reader of 20.11–21.5 would certainly be left with the impression that a universal destruction and re-creation is in view. A closer look at the language and context does nothing to dispel this opinion."

3. E.g., John Sweet, *Revelation*, New Testament Commentaries (Philadelphia: Trinity Press, 1990), 297, asks, "How can the new heaven and earth beyond space and time contain all the material and measurable elements of Rev 21:10ff.? Surely these belong to the millennial kingdom on earth and have been transposed."

4. Gale Z. Heide, "What Is New about the New Heaven and the New Earth? A Theology of Creation from Revelation 21 and 2 Peter 3," *JETS* (March 1997): 39, notes, "Some have interpreted the vision as physically representative of the planet earth and the sky above it. Others see it as a vision of political and spiritual import, with reference to physical realities being secondary of it all." John Court, *Revelation*, NTG (Sheffield: JSOT Press, 1994), 74, commenting on Revelation 21 and 22, comes to the conclusion that "the vision of hope that is set before them could be understood in terms of spiritual development and blessing for the individual believer. But it also clearly relates to an eschatological fulfillment and vindication that will be closely linked to the earthly facts of daily life in the churches." Carol J. Dempsey, "Revelation 21:1–8," *Int* (October 2011): 402, suggests "that the transformation is already occurring even though it is part of a vision."

5. Postmillennialism especially, and amillennialism to some degree, suggest such a scenario. Eric Claude Webster, "The Millennium," in *HSDAT*, 935–42, provides a short description of amillennialism, premillennialism, and postmillennianlism and shows how throughout history the concept of the millennium was understood. On postmillennialism, see Millard J. Erickson, *Christian Theology*, 2nd ed. (Grand Rapids, Mich.: Baker, 1998), 1213–15. Still, millennial views do not necessarily deny Christ's second coming.

6. See John E. Stanley, "The New Creation as a People and City in Revelation 21:1–22:5: An Alternative to Despair," *AsTJ* 60, no. 2 (2005): 25–38. On page 32 he talks about "fatalism."

7. Jon Paulien, *Allusions, Exegetical Methods, and the Interpretation of Revelation 8:7–12*, AUSDDS 11 (Berrien Springs, Mich.: Andrews University Press, 1987), 175–94, deals

We will begin with the clear references to creation before moving on to allusions and echoes.

EXPLICIT REFERENCES TO CREATION

Explicit references to creation in Revelation appear in the first half of the book, at the center of the book, and in chapters 21–22.

Creation in Revelation 3:14

The first creation reference in Revelation is in 3:14: "To the angel of the church in Laodicea write: The Amen, the faithful and true Witness, the Beginning of the creation of God . . . ."[8]

Allusions to creation are found throughout the messages to the seven churches, but here the noun "creation" (*ktisis*) is used directly.[9] *Ktisis* means "creation" but also describes everything that has been created—every creature.

Jesus calls Himself "the Beginning [*archē*] of the creation of God." The designation *archē* has multiple meanings—for instance, "beginning" (Luke 1:2), "beginner," "origin," "first cause" (Rev. 21:6), and "ruler," "authority" (Luke 12:11).[10] In order to determine the correct meaning in a given case, the context must be consulted. The most important shades of meaning are "beginning" and "ruler."[11] In the Johannine literature, the term appears twenty-one times and—apart from Revelation 3:14—always has the meaning "beginning." However, "beginning" can be understood actively or passively: "beginner" or "beginning."

---

with echoes and allusions. He distinguishes between allusions and echoes on the basis that the former are intentional pointers by the author to previous material, while echoes "do not depend on the author's conscious intention" (172). He has provided three criteria for allusions: "verbal parallels" (179–81), "thematic parallels" (182–84), and "structural parallels" (184–85) and classified allusions into five categories from certain allusions to possible allusions to "nonallusions" (193).

8. Unless otherwise indicated, Scripture quotations in this chapter are from the New American Standard Bible®, Copyright © 1960, 1971, 1977, 1995 by The Lockman Foundation. All rights reserved.

9. *Ktisis* is not used in the Septuagint (LXX) but occurs nineteen times in the New Testament. Three times it is found in the Gospel of Mark and each time spoken by Jesus. Twice Jesus speaks about the time "from the beginning of creation" (Mark 10:6; 13:19) and once about the proclamation of the gospel to all creation, which means every creature (Mark 16:15). Mark 16:15 may not have been part of the original text of the Gospel of Mark. The earliest manuscripts omit 16:9–20. In Revelation 3:14 Jesus uses "the Beginning of the creation of God" as a self-designation.

10. The word *archē* is found fifty-five times in the New Testament.

11. Dan Lioy, *The Book of Revelation in Christological Focus*, StBibLit 58 (New York: Peter Lang, 2003), 130, suggests that the two meanings are complementary.

In Revelation 21:6 the term *archē* is applied to God the Father. God is "the beginning and the end." This does not mean God has a beginning but that He is the Originator of all things. The same is true for Jesus, who likewise is called "the beginning [*archē*] and the end" (Rev. 22:13). Revelation 3:14 should be understood in this very sense: Jesus is the Beginner, the Originator of God's creation.[12]

G. K. Beale argues that Revelation 3:14 is a development of Revelation 1:5 and that the Old Testament background of this statement is Isaiah 65, the new creation. Therefore, "Jesus' resurrection is viewed as being the beginning of the *new* creation"[13] and "Jesus as the inaugurator of the new creation is the focus."[14] Craig Koester disagrees: "Revelation uses 'creation' (*ktisis*) and related words (*ktizein, ktisma*) for the present created order (4:11; 5:13; 10:6) rather than for the new creation (cf. 21:1 . . .)."[15]

Only as Creator does Jesus have the authority to deal with the secularized Laodicean church in judgment. That Jesus is the Creator of all things is confirmed by other New Testament texts. As Creator He is God (John 1:1–3; Col. 1:15–16; Heb. 1:2). In Revelation He shares with God the Father divine titles, such as "the Alpha and Omega" and "the beginning and the end" (Rev. 21:6; 22:13) for the very reason that He is God.[16] As God the Father works through Jesus to achieve final salvation and consummation, so He has also brought about creation and salvation here and now through Him.

As mentioned elsewhere, the New Testament's unique contribution to the theology of creation consists of not only affirming that

---

12. Some English translations (e.g., the NIV) prefer "ruler." However, this does not seem to be likely due to John's use of the term. The meaning "ruler" or "powers" is mostly found with Paul: for example, in Rom. 8:38; 1 Cor. 15:24; Eph. 1:21; 3:10; 6:12; Col. 1:16; 2:10, 15; and Titus 3:11. However, it is not found in Hebrews (see, e.g., Heb. 1:10; 2:3; 3:14; 5:12; 7:3). In addition, John seems to distinguish between *archē* and *archōn* ("ruler, authority") in Revelation.

13. G. K. Beale, "The Old Testament Background of Rev 3.14," *NTS* 42, no. 1 (1996): 136.

14. Ibid., 144. Beale does not, however, rule out original creation as a secondary meaning (ibid., 151).

15. Craig R. Koester, *Revelation*, AB 38A (New Haven, Conn.: Yale University Press, 2014), 336.

16. Richard Bauckham, *The Theology of the Book of Revelation*, New Testament Theology (Cambridge: Cambridge University Press, 1993), 56, states, "That a reference to Christ's participation in God's creation of all things is not out of place . . . is clear from 3:14, where the beginning of the message to the church at Laodicea calls him: 'the origin (*archē*) of God's creation'. This does not mean that he was the first created being or that in his resurrection he was the beginning of God's new creation. It must have the same sense as the first part of the title, 'the beginning (*archē*) and the end', as used of both God (21:6) and Christ (22:13). Christ preceded all things as their source."

God the Father is the Creator but also and especially pointing out that Jesus Christ is the Creator.[17] While in the Gospels and the letters of the New Testament the authors tell us plainly that Jesus is the Creator God, Revelation 3:14 contains a direct claim by the risen Lord that He is the Originator of creation. The issue of creation is thus inseparably linked to what we think and believe about Jesus Christ.

Creation in Revelation 4:11 and 5:13

> The twenty-four elders will fall down before Him who sits on the throne, and will worship Him who lives forever and ever, and will cast their crowns before the throne, saying, "Worthy are You, our Lord and our God, to receive glory and honor and power; for You created [*ktizō*] all things, and because of Your will they existed, and were created [*ktizō*]." (Rev. 4:10–11)

> And every created thing [*ktisma*] which is in heaven and on the earth and under the earth and on the sea, and all things in them, I heard saying, "To Him who sits on the throne, and to the Lamb, be blessing and honor and glory and dominion forever and ever." (Rev. 5:13)

These are two of the seven hymns found in the seal vision. Five of them occur in Revelation 4 and 5 and two in Revelation 7.[18] Revelation 4 and 5 make up the introductory scene to the vision of the seven seals, which runs from Revelation 6:1 to Revelation 8:1. At the same time, it is found right in the beginning of the apocalyptic part of Revelation and may therefore also set the tone for Revelation 6:1—22:5.

The main motif (or emphasis) in Revelation 4 is the throne, and thereby God the Father. Although the one who sits on the throne is not directly identified as God, it is obvious that John is talking about God the Father.[19] The throne motif is a major theme in Revelation. Although it is broader than the circumlocution "he who sits on the throne," the circumlocution by itself "is most prominently featured in the heavenly temple scenes, but it also appears

---

17. See Ekkehardt Mueller, "Creation in the New Testament," *JATS* 15, no. 1 (2004): 57–59.

18. Stephen N. Horn, "Hallelujah, the Lord our God, the Almighty Reigns: The Theology of the Hymns of Revelation," in *Essays on Revelation: Appropriating Yesterday's Apocalypse in Today's World*, ed. Gerald L. Stevens (Eugene, Ore.: Pickwick, 2010), 42, explains how hymns can be recognized.

19. No other New Testament book mentions the throne more frequently than Revelation, and no other chapter employs the term as often as does chapter 4. The throne is found there fourteen times and refers to God's throne twelve times.

in contexts elaborating the day of wrath, the cosmic conflict, the millennial judgment and the new creation."[20] This is important to notice: creation and new creation (Rev. 21–22) are associated with the divine throne, and therefore with the person of God.

Revelation 4 focuses on God, His "majesty and sovereignty,"[21] and His activities. The rainbow around the throne (Rev. 4:3)—reminiscent of God's covenant with Noah and all of humanity (Gen. 9:9–17)—points to the "creator's fidelity to his creation."[22] The two hymns toward the end of Revelation 4 are addressed to the one sitting on the throne and should be understood as informing each other.

The first hymn is presented by the four heavenly beings around the throne: "Holy, holy, holy is the Lord God Almighty, who was, and is, and is to come" (Rev. 4:8, NIV). God is praised for who He is. God's holiness is stressed as a foundational divine quality. "The 'holiness' of God here points to his separation from the created order. He is the 'Wholly Other,' standing above this world and soon to judge it."[23] Along with the threefold "Holy" come three different names for God.[24] They stress His covenant faithfulness, His omnipotence, and the fact that in God there is no beginning and end. God is pictured as transcendent,[25] the potentate of the universe. He is almighty and powerful and out of reach of humans unless He chooses to come close and reveal Himself. One can only prostrate before Him and worship Him.[26]

In the second hymn (Rev. 4:11), God is praised for His work of creation. Twice in verse 11 the verb *ktizō* ("to create, to make") is used. This term clearly refers to creation but does not occur in the Septuagint (LXX) of Genesis 1 and 2. There the more general term *poieō* ("to do, to make") is employed. Still *ktizō* is found twice in Genesis 14 (LXX). In verses 19 and 22 God is called "God Most High, who has

---

20. Laszlo Gallusz, *The Throne Motif in the Book of Revelation: Profiles from the History of Interpretation*, LNTS 487 (London: Bloomsbury T&T Clark, 2014), 116.

21. Grant R. Osborne, *Revelation*, BECNT (Grand Rapids, Mich.: Baker, 2002), 236,

22. Jonathan Moo, "The Sea That is No More: Rev 21:1 and the Function of Sea Imagery in the Apocalypse of John," *NovT* 51 (2009): 167.

23. Osborne, *Revelation*, 237.

24. Cf. David E. Aune, *Revelation 1–5*, WBC 52A (Dallas: Word, 1997), 307, who also suggests that in Revelation 4:8 "the threefold repetition of 'holy' is connected, perhaps by design, to three characteristics of God." See also Stephen Smalley, *The Revelation of John: A Commentary on the Greek Text of the Apocalypse* (Downers Grove, Ill.: InterVarsity, 2005), 123.

25. Cf. Horn, "Hallelujah," 44–45.

26. Bauckham, *Theology*, 45, describes false worship—namely, the worship of the beast—as "false precisely because its object is not the transcendent mystery, but only the mystification of something finite."

made heaven and earth."[27] The reference is clearly the creation account of Genesis 1 and 2. This is also the case in Revelation 4:11:

A You created all things,

   B and because of Your will ["for the sake of Your will"] they existed,

A' and were created.

This statement contains a number of important points. First, the "you" is emphatic. An extra personal pronoun—"you"—is used although the Greek verb form already contains the second person singular. This device stresses and highlights God as the Creator and the one who is worthy to be praised.[28]

Second, God created all things. This includes all living beings and all inanimate things. But God is not part of creation. There is a marked difference between Creator and creation, although they relate to each other.[29]

Third, creation by God is expressed twice in this verse: once in the indicative mood—"God created"—and once in the passive—"they were created." The passive is a divine passive. The phrase is formulated in the third person plural, possibly indicating that no being can claim that it does not exist as a result of divine creation.

Fourth, creation is not an accident or mere coincidence. Creation is rooted in the will of God.[30] It is possible to translate this verse "because of your will" or "for the sake of your will." Stephen Smalley suggests that "both meanings appear to be present. Creation came about by the operation of God's will; but the universe came into being through Him precisely so that His holy purposes for humanity could be accomplished. His is the ultimate and gracious power, in creation and salvation."[31]

---

27. The Hebrew text is typically translated as "possessor of heaven and earth."

28. See Gregory Stevenson, "The Theology of Creation in the Book of Revelation," *Leaven* 21, no. 3 (2013): 140. Noel Due, *Created for Worship: From Genesis to Revelation to You* (Tain: Christian Focus, 2005), 220, suggests that "the particular focus in Revelation 4 is on his nature as Creator (4:11)."

29. Paige Patterson, *Revelation*, NAC 39 (Nashville, Tenn.: Broadman and Holman, 2012), 159, writes, "The contemporary religious scene tends to regard God as somehow a part of the created order or perhaps the created order as a part of the 'body or being of God.' Over against this is the stark declaration of Scripture that God has no beginning and that he is to be kept clearly distinguished from his creation, which owes its initiation and continuance totally and completely to his sovereign will." See also Koester, *Revelation*, 371; and Steven Grabiner, *Revelation's Hymns: Commentary on the Cosmic Conflict* (London: Bloomsbury, 2015), 94.

30. Grabiner, *Revelation's Hymns*, 94, talks about "intentionality" and "the universal dimension of creation."

31. Smalley, *Revelation of John*, 125.

Fifth, while the order of the verbs—"created," "existed," "were created"—is strange, having the term "existed" prior to the second mention of "created," it is not a denial of the fact that creation precedes existence. Rather, this arrangement seems to be a literary device. In this case, the stress would be on God sustaining creation.[32] God is "active in the world, which he created. . . . The world is God's world."[33]

At this time, we have to return to the preceding hymn. The two hymns are not independent of each other. They occur in the same immediate context of worship. It is the holy God who sits on the throne, the Lord God Almighty, the one who was and is and is to come, who is the Creator God. In other words, the divine designations in verse 8 must be understood as descriptions of the Creator God. G. R. Beasley-Murray comments on "who was, and is, and is to come" (NIV) in Revelation 4:8 and says, "The Lord of creation is also Lord of the ages."[34] At least from chapter 4 onward, the divine names and titles carry with them the notion that God is to be understood as the Creator. Therefore, the creation motif is more pervasive in Revelation than it appears at first sight.

For instance, the term "Almighty" is a translation of the Greek *pantokratōr*. The one who has created all things (*ta panta*) is the ruler of all (*pantokratōr*), also rendered as "All-Powerful" and "Omnipotent."[35] God's power as the Almighty finds expression in creation. This role as Creator of all gives Him the right to be involved in judgment.

> The one God is defined as the One who brought all things into existence. As Creator, he alone has ultimate power over everything. As

---

32. The strange order of verbs has triggered a number of suggestions, among them that God planned creation in His mind before executing it. See, e.g., Robert H. Mounce, *The Book of Revelation*, rev. ed., NICNT (Grand Rapids, Mich.: Eerdmans, 1998), 127. G. K. Beale, *The Book of Revelation*, NIGTC (Grand Rapids, Mich.: Eerdmans, 1999), 335, proposes that the meaning of lines 2 and 3 is that "they continually exist and have come into being." Aune, *Revelation 1–5*, 312, suggests "an instance of *hysteron-proteron*, i.e., the inversion of events, which sometimes occurs in Revelation." On the other hand, Osborne, *Revelation*, 242, suggests an ABA pattern, a chiastic pattern, in which creation is being restated without implying a chronological order.

33. Smalley, *Revelation of John*, 126.

34. G. R. Beasley-Murray, *Revelation*, NCBC (Grand Rapids, Mich.: Eerdmans, 1983), 118.

35. The title *pantokratōr* occurs nine times in Revelation (Rev. 1:8; 4:8; 11:17; 15:3; 16:7, 14; 19:6, 15; 21:22), and only once more in the New Testament (2 Cor. 6:18). In Revelation it refers only to God the Father. Most frequently it appears in the vision of the seven plagues and in other judgment scenes.

creator, to whom all creatures owe their very being, he alone is to be worshipped. . . . The understanding of God as Creator was not only integral to Jewish and Christian monotheism; it was also essential to the development of Jewish and Christian eschatology.[36]

While Revelation 4 portrays the transcendent God, Revelation 5, the second part of this sanctuary scene, depicts Jesus in His self-condescension and sacrifice as the immanent Lord. The third (Rev. 5:9–10) and fourth (Rev. 5:12) hymns are addressed to Jesus. Both stress His sacrificial death. The hymn of Revelation 5:9–10 talks about salvation for humans, the new status of believers, and the future reign of the saints, pointing to their millennial reign (Rev. 20:4, 6) and their eternal reign in the new creation (Rev. 22:5).[37] Thus, while the second hymn of the five in Revelation 4 and 5 praises God as the Creator (Rev. 4:11), the third, called a new hymn, addresses the work of salvation (Rev. 5:9–10).

The fifth hymn is directed to God the Father and the Lamb. It concludes and summarizes the worship in the entire throne room scene of Revelation 4 and 5. Here direct creation language is used again: "I heard every creature [*ktisma*] in heaven and on earth and under the earth and in the sea, and all that is in them" (Rev. 5:13, ESV). The noun *ktisma* refers to "creatures" and "everything created." It also occurs in Revelation 8:9, the second trumpet, where a third of the sea creatures die. Here, however, God's creatures include "every creature in the universe."[38]

"The added phrase 'and all that is in them' stresses that no living creature failed to join in the great and final hymn of praise (cf. Phil. 2:9–11)."[39] Grant Osborne lists those included: "angels, humans, demons, as well as all birds, animals, and fish."[40] Creation surpasses our world and is not limited to this earth and the solar system. There are created beings in heaven of whom God is the Creator. Consequently, the New Testament teaches that God created not only the earth, its surroundings, and life on this earth but also extraterrestrial life forms, which are not part of the creation we encounter and to which we belong.

---

36. Bauckham, *Theology*, 48.
37. Cf. Osborne, *Revelation*, 260–61; and Smalley, *Revelation of John*, 564–66.
38. See Beasley-Murray, *Revelation*, 128.
39. Mounce, *Revelation*, 138.
40. Osborne, *Revelation*, 264.

The throne scene in Revelation 4 and 5 emphasizes the importance of creation and salvation. For the author of Revelation these two concepts belong together and are inseparable. Within the context of a world of sin, one cannot exist without the other, or else there would arise logical and biblical inconsistencies. Without creation, no salvation! Without salvation, no new creation! "Where faith in God the Creator wanes, so inevitably does hope for resurrection, let alone the new creation of all things. It is the God who is the Alpha who will also be the Omega."[41]

Creation in Revelation 10:6

And swore by Him who lives forever and ever, WHO CREATED HEAVEN AND THE THINGS IN IT, AND THE EARTH AND THE THINGS IN IT, and the sea and the things in it, that there will be delay no longer. (Rev. 10:6)

Revelation 3:14 is part of the messages to the seven churches, and therefore is part of the first septet of Revelation. Revelation 4:11 and 5:13 are part of the second septet, the seven seals. And Revelation 10:6 occurs in the third septet, the seven trumpets. We have already mentioned Revelation 8:9, a text that talks about the death of a third of the creatures of the sea and belongs to the trumpet vision. That means that so far, all major visions of Revelation clearly contain creation language—not to mention allusions.

Revelation 10:6 occurs in the expansion of the sixth trumpet. The sixth trumpet portrays the demonic army of two hundred million beings who are opposed to God's people[42] and kill a third of humankind (Rev. 9:15–16, 18). But the survivors do not repent (Rev. 9:20–21). The seventh trumpet describes the second coming, divine judgment, and the reign of God. The expansion of the sixth trumpet in Revelation 10:1—11:14, placed between the sixth trumpet proper and the seventh trumpet, deals with the time of the last events and the role of God's word and His people during this time.[43]

---

41. Bauckham, *Theology*, 51.

42. In the parallel section of the seal vision, God's "army" is depicted as 144,000 people (Rev. 7:4).

43. Revelation 10 portrays John as eating a scroll that tastes sweet first but later turns out as a bitter experience. The chapter ends with a call to mission. Revelation 11a refers to the measuring of the temple and the experience of the two witnesses. The last part of Revelation 11 contains the seventh trumpet that describes the fact that "the kingdom of the world has become the kingdom of our Lord and of His Christ; and He will reign forever and ever" (Rev. 11:15).

The message is that the divine promises regarding the end of this evil age will be fulfilled.[44]

The strong angel of Revelation 10 is probably Jesus. This angel is clothed in a cloud, a rainbow surrounds His head, His face shines like the sun, and His feet resemble pillars of fire (Rev. 10:1). The last two characteristics remind the audience of Jesus in Revelation 1:9–20. The cloud was mentioned in Revelation 1:7 in connection with Jesus, while the rainbow in Revelation 4:3 is linked to the throne of God. Furthermore, the angel resembles the heavenly being of Daniel 10–12, especially Daniel 12:7.[45] Beale mentions that the angel has divine attributes and therefore is either Christ or the angel of the Lord,[46] who again would be Jesus.[47] Other scholars admit the similarity of this angel to Jesus in Revelation 1:9–20 but avoid identifying the angel with Him.[48]

This angel from heaven first places His right foot on the sea and then His left on the earth (Rev. 10:2), swearing an oath by the one who lives eternally, the Creator God.[49] Here the elements of creation found in verse 6 are already present. Gerald Stevens points out that the order is decisive. According to the next vision (Rev. 11:19—14:20), the first beast of Revelation 13 comes out of the sea, while the second beast comes from the earth.

> The mighty angel's legs like pillars of fire standing on both sea and land is an image that symbolizes God's authority over the major

---

44. Cf. Ranko Stefanovic, *Revelation of Jesus Christ: Commentary on the Book of Revelation*, 2nd ed. (Berrien Springs, Mich.: Andrews University Press, 2009), 333.

45. Cf. Jim Hiner Jr., "Is the Angel of Revelation 10 a Divine Being?" *JATS* 8, nos. 1–2 (1997): 106–19.

46. Beale, *The Book of Revelation*, 522, says, "If he is an angel, he is an extraordinary one, since he is described in a majestic way, unlike any other angel in the Book. He is given attributes that are given only to God in the OT or to God or Christ in Revelation. Therefore this heavenly being is either the divine Christ himself or the divine angel of Yahweh." Beale discusses the angel extensively on pages 522–26. Cf. Jacques B. Doukhan, *Secrets of Revelation: The Apocalypse through Hebrew Eyes* (Hagerstown, Md.: Review and Herald, 2002), 91; and Francis D. Nichol, ed., *Seventh-day Adventist Bible Commentary*, 7 vols. (Hagerstown, Md.: Review and Herald, 1957), 7:797.

47. Cf. Beale, *The Book of Revelation*, 525.

48. So Simon J. Kistemaker, *New Testament Commentary: Exposition of the Book of Revelation* (Grand Rapids, Mich.: Baker, 2001), 308–9; Osborne, *Revelation*, 393; and Mounce, *Revelation*, 201–2, who admits "the phrases by which he is described are elsewhere used of deity" (p. 201).

49. While most commentators understand the oath to be sworn to a person other than the angel Himself (e.g., Patterson, *Revelation*, 232), Nichol, *SDABC*, 7:798, suggests that the angel "swears by himself." This makes sense if the angel is Christ. Even in the Old Testament God would swear by Himself, having no one greater to swear by (Deut. 32:40).

characters to arise in the second half of the Judgment Cycle to come. This authority over sea and land further is affirmed in the oath taken by the mighty angel, who swears by the creator God who made sea and land (10:6a).[50]

The phrase "who created heaven and the things in it, and the earth and the things in it, and the sea and the things in it" reminds Bible students not only of Genesis 14:19, 22 (LXX) but also and even more so of Nehemiah 9:6, Psalm 146:6, Acts 4:24, 14:15, and the Sabbath commandment in Exodus 20:11, emphasizing God's universal creatorship and therefore His universal authority.[51] The threefold repetition of the phrase "and the things in it" heightens the stress on the Creator's power and sovereignty.[52] The Sabbath commandment is of special importance because it not only has a literary connection to creation but is further connected through the element of the seventh day. The Creator and Lord of the Sabbath "precedes all things, and he will bring all things to eschatological fulfillment. He is the origin and goal of all history. He has the first word in creation. He has the last word in the new creation."[53]

The contribution of Revelation 10:6 to Revelation's creation theology is that it links protology to eschatology.[54] It is the Creator God who controls the events on earth and ushers in the end in the form of judgment and new creation.[55]

Creation in Revelation 14:7

"Fear God, and give Him glory, because the hour of His judgment has come; worship Him who made the heaven and the earth and sea and springs of waters." (Rev. 14:7)

---

50. Gerald L. Stevens, *Revelation: The Past and Future of John's Apocalypse* (Eugene, Ore.: Pickwick, 2014), 415.

51. There is also a connection to Revelation 5:13, discussed in the section of this study titled "Creation in Revelation 4:11 and 5:13," 409.

52. Beale, *The Book of Revelation*, 538, states, "This emphasis is intended to connect God's universal sovereignty over the beginning of creation to Christ's absolute rule . . . over creation in the latter days of the church age and of the coming new creation."

53. Larry L. Lichtenwalter, "Creation and Apocalypse," *JATS* 15, no. 1 (2004): 127. Cf. Sweet, *Revelation*, 178, who says "it is God the *Creator*, who made the world according to his will, whose final will is to be done."

54. See Stevens, *Revelation*, 386.

55. Mounce, *Revelation*, 206, points out, "To speak of God as creator underscores his power to accomplish that which he set out to do. For the Seer it means that the One who brought all things into being can carry them through in fulfillment of his redemptive purpose. The end of history, as was the beginning, is under the sovereign control of God."

This text is part of the central vision of Revelation, which, after a short introduction in Revelation 11:19, begins with the birth of the Messiah and His ascension to God (Rev. 12a). It describes the persecution of God's true church (Rev. 12b) and focuses on last events related to the faithful remnant (Rev. 12:17; 13:1–18). While the remnant have to face economic boycott and a death decree (Rev. 13:15–17) and everything looks hopeless, they are presented as the victorious 144,000 who are with Jesus on Mount Zion. This faithful remnant proclaims God's last message for humanity (Rev. 14:6–12) just prior to Christ's second coming (Rev. 14:14–20). The text containing the creation reference is part of the first angel's message, the message to be proclaimed in the last days of earth's history in conjunction with the other two messages.

The two creation texts, Revelation 10:6 and Revelation 14:7, appear in a parallel context, shortly before Christ's second coming. They are quite similar and yet different.

1. While Revelation 10:6 uses the verb *ktizō* ("to create") to describe creation, Revelation 14:6 uses the broader term *poieō*. However, *poieō* is employed in Genesis 1 and 2 (LXX), as previously mentioned.[56] *Poieō* means "to do" or "to make" and does not need to refer to creation. However, here as well as in Genesis 1 and 2, it does. By using *poieō* instead of *ktizō*, the connection of Revelation 14:7 to Genesis 1 and 2 is even more clearly established, even if it is through Exodus 20:11 ("For in six days the Lord made [*poieō*, LXX] the heavens and the earth, the sea and all that is in them").

2. While Revelation 10:6 enumerates three spheres of creation (heaven, earth, and sea) plus "what is in them," Revelation 14:7 contains four elements (heaven, earth, sea, and springs of water). But both contain the first three elements in the same order, and both allude to the Sabbath commandment (Exod. 20:8–11). Yet, even the connection to the Sabbath is clearer in Revelation 14:7[57] because the

---

56. Applied to God's creative acts, *poieō* is found in Genesis 1:1, 7, 16, 21, 25, 26, 27 (3x), 31; 2:2 (2x), 3, 4, 18. According to Genesis 3:21, God made garments for Adam and Eve.

57. See Jon Paulien, "Revisiting the Sabbath in the Book of Revelation," *JATS* 9, no. 1–2 (1998): 179–86.

context also refers to the Decalogue.[58] These ringing words in Revelation 14:7 are thus a call to people who live on earth in the last days to acknowledge the Creator by respecting Him and His will. The Sabbath is clearly linked to this acknowledgement of God's will in the text, and we argue that Revelation 14:7 is a call to restore the Sabbath observance God instituted at creation (Exod. 20:8–11).

3. While contextually both texts deal with final events, Revelation 10:6 describes the action of the strong angel, whereas Revelation 14:7 is an appeal to humanity to make right choices. In Revelation 13–14 the issue of whom to worship reaches its climax. "All the world is encouraged to worship the true creator (4.11) rather than his idolatrous shadow (13.15)."[59] While Revelation 10:6 points out the sovereignty of God, Revelation 14:7 calls people to commit themselves completely to the Creator. In mentioning that judgment has come, Revelation 14:7 also contains an indirect warning about the choices made here and now.

4. The conflict in Revelation 13–14 culminates in true and false worship pitched against each other.

In addition to these similarities and differences, Revelation 14:7 is introduced by verse 6. In this verse the message of verse 7 is designated and confirmed as eternal gospel.[60] In other words, the

---

58. Revelation 11:19 mentions the ark of the covenant, which contained the Ten Commandments (Exod. 25:21; Deut. 10:1–2). Observance of the commandments occurs in Revelation 12:17; 14:12, rejection in Revelation 12:4, 15 and 13:15 (killing); 13:4, 8, 12, 14, 15 and 14:11 (idolatry); 13:6 (blasphemy).

59. Smalley, *Revelation of John*, 363.

60. It has been argued by various scholars that the term "gospel" here has to be understood in a restricted sense, pointing primarily to judgment. See, e.g., Mounce, *Revelation*, 270–71; Smalley, *Revelation of John*, 361; and Kistemaker, *Revelation*, 407. Cf. Aune, *Revelation 6–16*, 825–29. G. B. Caird, *The Revelation of St. John the Divine*, Harper's New Testament Commentaries (Peabody, Mass.: Hendrickson, 1987), 182, disagrees: "For whether it has an article or not, the word *euangelion* can only mean 'good news', and it is improbable that John should have thought of using it in a cynical sense. Moreover, he says nothing about the gospel being good news for Christians; this is a gospel to proclaim to the inhabitants of earth. . . . Nor is it any casual or ephemeral news; it is an eternal gospel, a gospel rooted and grounded in the changeless character and purpose of God. If the angel carried a gospel which was eternal good news to every nation, tribe, tongue, and people, it is hard to see how this could differ from *the* gospel." In the context of Revelation, and especially in view of the prologue (Rev. 1:4–8), *euangelion* should indeed be understood as good news. In other words, the prologue of the Apocalypse contains a

eternal gospel appears here in the context of divine creation. This reminds the audience of the interdependence of creation and salvation in Revelation 4 and 5. Creation, salvation, and judgment (eschatology) are interdependent. One cannot have one without the others. The proclamation of the gospel presupposes and includes creation by the sovereign Lord.[61]

Acts 14:15 is another interesting parallel to Revelation 14:7. Paul and Barnabas appealed to the Gentiles to turn from the vain things to the living God "WHO MADE THE HEAVEN AND THE EARTH AND THE SEA AND ALL THAT IS IN THEM." They confronted Gentiles with the Creator God. Likewise, the eternal gospel is to be preached to "those who live on the earth, and to every nation and tribe and tongue and people" (Rev. 14:6). In both texts proclamation of the Creator God is the mission of true believers and the church. All humanity is called to repent.[62] "The inhabitants of the earth have been amazed by the powers displayed by the beast and his false prophet (13:12–14); they are now reminded that they have to do with one who is mightier than the beast—with him who is the source of all things in heaven and on earth."[63]

Creation in Revelation 21 and 22

The terms *ktizō*, *ktisis*, and *ktisma* ("to create," "creation/creature," "creature"), with their clear reference to creation, appear in Revelation up through chapter 10. Revelation 14:7 unmistakably describes creation using the term *poieō* ("to do, make"). Revelation 21:5 does the same: "And He who sits on the throne said, 'Behold, I am making all things new.' And He said, 'Write, for these words are faithful and true.'" However, even without this statement it would be clear that Revelation 21 and 22a describe the new creation. So far, the readers and hearers of Revelation have encountered the original creation in Genesis 1 and 2. Now they are confronted with a new, yet future creation.

---

clear description of the gospel. Revelation 14:6 must be read with this background. The author knows and understands the gospel, the good news. When he refers to it, he must have in mind the major features of the gospel, including the details that he will mention in the next verses.

61. Alain Coralie, "A Word to Worship Leaders: Reflections on Revelation 14:6, 7," *Ministry*, April 2016, 8, states, "God cannot be Savior and Judge unless He is Creator."

62. See George Eldon Ladd, *A Commentary on the Revelation of John* (Grand Rapids, Mich.: Eerdmans, 1991), 193.

63. Ibid., 194.

Here is an outline of Revelation 21–22b:

Introduction (Rev. 21:1–2)	
A new heaven and a new earth	
The holy city	
Voice from the Throne (Rev. 21:3–4)	
The presence of God with humanity and its results	
God's Speech (Rev. 21:5–8)	
"I am making all things new" (v. 5a)	
"these words are faithful and true" (v. 5b)	
God's self-disclosure and what He does for believers and unbelievers (vv. 6–8)	
The Speech of the Angel (Rev. 21:9)	
"I will show you the bride"	
The Action of the Angel (Rev. 21:10–27 and 22:1–5)	
He "showed me"—the bride as the holy city	• Description of the city (21:10b–14) • Measuring of the city and its wall (21:15–17) • Description of the city continued (21:18–27)
He "showed me"—a river, the tree of life, and the throne	• Water of life and tree of life (22:1–2) • The presence of God (22:3–5)

This outline shows that the last two chapters of Revelation, dealing with the new creation, contain three speeches of heavenly beings that follow the short introduction.

First, there is the unidentified voice from the throne with a short but crucial message. This message explains the presence of God among the redeemed with sanctuary language. God tabernacles with His people as He did in the garden of Eden in Genesis 2.[64] The wonderful result is described with the positive affirmation that in fatherly love God will take care of all the tears of His children. Personally and in tenderness He removes what creates hurt and injury. This is followed by the undoing of four detrimental aspects of present life that were not found in the first creation: death, mourning, crying, and pain. Jonathan Moo notes that with these positive effects, the curse of the Genesis 3 Fall is undone.[65]

---

64. In Jesus God also tabernacled among humans, however, in a more hidden way (John 1:14).

65. Moo, "The Sea That is No More," 165, states, "Of the seven items John lists, the middle five can in biblical tradition be related ultimately to the effects of the curse and the expulsion from Eden described in Gen 3: *death, mourning, crying, pain,* and—echoing

This voice is followed by the voice of God the Father Himself declaring that He makes everything new. Laszlo Gallusz outlines the speech in the following way:

A 21.5a – the promise of the new creation . . .
B 21.5b – the trustworthiness of the divine promise . . .
A' 21.6a – the accomplishment of the new creation . . .
C 21.6b – the guarantee of the new creation . . .
A 21.6c – the new creation as a reward . . .
B 21.7 – the climax of the divine promise . . .
A' 21.8 – the new creation as a punishment . . . [66]

This divine speech is made by the One who sits on the throne, God the Father. While Jesus speaks repeatedly in the book—for example, all the messages to the seven churches come from Him—God the Father utters only two direct speeches: the one found here and the other one in the prologue of the Apocalypse (Rev. 1:8).[67] Both are related to Him being the Creator and contain the divine designation Alpha and Omega. Revelation 1:8 states, "'I am the Alpha and the Omega,' says the Lord God, 'who is and who was and who is to come, the Almighty.'" The context of chapter 1 clearly identifies the speaker as God the Father. Both speeches come from the throne (Rev. 1:4; 21:5), situated in the heavenly sanctuary (Rev. 7:15).[68] Sanctuary and garden of Eden creation imagery are intertwined. The new aspect in the new creation and eschatological sanctuary, however, is the issue of salvation.[69]

The third voice is that of one of the angels with the bowls of Revelation 15 and 16. Only now does the audience get a more detailed picture of what the new creation entails. The message is addressed to John, who is to come and see, and introduces the rest of the new creation as described in Revelation 21b and 22a. The verb *deiknymi* ("to show") links the angelic speech concerning the "bride, the wife of the

---

Zechariah 4:11, but with Gen 3:17 looming in the background—πᾶν κατάθεμα [*pan katathema*] (*everything cursed*)."

66. Gallusz, *Throne Motif*, 131.

67. See Bauckham, *Theology*, 50.

68. See Gallusz, *Throne Motif*, 122.

69. Elias Brasil de Souza, "Sanctuary: Cosmos, Covenant, and Creation," *JATS* 24, no. 1 (2013): 25–41. See page 34 for the reference. He also writes, "In Revelation, interconnections between salvation and creation occur within the framework of sanctuary imagery. As the concluding chapters of Revelation clearly show, the ultimate outcome of salvation is the full restoration of creation when 'the tabernacle of God is with men' (Rev. 21:3)" (p. 37). On the original Eden as sanctuary, see Ángel Manuel Rodríguez, "Genesis 1 and the Building of the Israelite Sanctuary," *Ministry*, February 2002, 9–11; Rodríguez, "Eden and Israelite Sanctuary," *Ministry*, April 2002, 11–13, 30; and de Souza, "Sanctuary," 34–35.

Lamb" (Rev. 21:9) to the subsequent action of the angel. However, what the angel shows John is "the holy city, Jerusalem" (Rev. 21:10), "the river of the water of life . . . from the throne of God [the sanctuary[70]] and of the Lamb" (Rev. 22:1), and the tree of life (Rev. 22:2). So John portrays the new Jerusalem as a bride, as a city, and as a garden.[71] Richard Bauckham describes what is happening here under the headings "The New Jerusalem as Place," "The New Jerusalem as People" (based on Revelation 21:3), and "The New Jerusalem as Divine Presence" (also based on 21:3).[72]

This angel ends his portrayal of the bride of the Lamb in Revelation 21:3–5 by returning to the beginning of Revelation 21 (especially verse 3)—that is, to the presence of God among His people. With the new creation God dwells again with humankind. The intimate fellowship between God and humanity that existed in Eden is restored. Redeemed humanity will see the Creator and Savior face-to-face, will serve Him, and will reign forever (Rev. 22:3–5). Sigve Tonstad describes the situation with the following words: "Revelation pictures God relocating from heaven to earth, distance and separation made unthinkable now that God and humans share the same address."[73] Bauckham adds, "As a result [of God's holy presence] the city itself becomes the temple. As well as features already mentioned, the most striking sign of this is its perfectly cubic shape (21:16). In this it is like no city ever imagined, but it is like the holy of holies in the temple (1 Kings 6:20)."[74]

---

70. Gallusz, *Throne Motif*, 121, reminds his readers that "the divine throne is referred to four times in the context of new creation mentioned in chs. 21–22." The texts are Revelation 21:3, 5 and 22:1, 3.

71. Wes Howard-Brook and Anthony Gwyther, *Unveiling Empire: Reading Revelation Then and Now* (Maryknoll, N.Y.: Orbis, 1990), 189, declare, "While it is the amplified feature of urban architecture that dominate the first part of the description of New Jerusalem, the city is also envisioned as the primeval garden—Paradise or Eden (cf. 2:7)." Michael J. Gorman, *Reading Revelation Responsibly: Uncivil Worship and Witness: Following the Lamb into the New Creation* (Eugene, Ore.: Cascade, 2011), 164, concludes, "Thus this paradise is not just a garden but an urban garden, or even better, a *garden-city*. This tells us that it is not civilization/culture/the city itself that is evil, but the distortion of city/culture/civilization caused by evil people and powers." See also Bruce J. Malina, *The New Jerusalem in the Revelation of John: The City as Symbol of Life with God* (Collegeville, Minn.: Liturgical Press, 2000), who suggests that the city is the new earth, "the equivalent of perfection and harmony" (p. 56) and "heightened holiness" (p. 55).

72. Bauckham, *Theology*, 132–43. On page 132, he concludes, "As a place, the New Jerusalem is at once paradise, holy city and temple."

73. Sigve K. Tonstad, *God of Sense and Traditions of Non-Sense* (Eugene, Ore.: Wipf and Stock, 2016), 386.

74. Bauckham, *Theology*, 136. See also Kistemaker, *Revelation*, 572–73; and Malina, *New Jerusalem*, 54–56.

While Revelation 21 and 22a add new concepts to what is found in Genesis—such as the bride, the holy city, and the end of suffering and pain—there are many parallels and allusions to Genesis 1 and 2, which we will explore later.

Summary

The explicit creation texts and passages in Revelation lead to the following conclusions:

1. The book of Revelation contains a number of clear and explicit texts dealing with creation. These text form a creation theme or network in Revelation that goes beyond individual texts, linking many terms in Revelation under the theme of creation.

2. Creation is assumed as a given in Revelation. Apart from Revelation 21 and 22a, the creation passages in Revelation refer to the original creation mentioned in Genesis 1 and 2 and in other passages of Scripture.

3. Not only is God the Father clearly described as Creator in Revelation, but Jesus Christ is also. This places Jesus on the divine level. The book of Revelation assumes a definite beginning of the world's history through the creative activity of God. But there is no hint that He uses processes such as evolution.

4. Jesus is Creator but also Savior. Creation and salvation appear together in Revelation. The Fall of Genesis 3 makes salvation necessary. The evil effects of sin and the partial undoing of creation must be overcome by a new and permanent creation that needs to be and will be established.

5. God created all things. This includes everything not only in our solar system but also in the universe. But God is not part of creation. There is a marked difference between Creator and creation, although they relate to each other.

6. In some parts of Revelation, creation has an eschatological dimension pointing to the promise of consummation, and therefore to a future new creation. This future creation is described most clearly in Revelation 21 and 22.

7. Creation and Sabbath go together in Genesis 2 and in New Testament passages dealing with creation—for instance, Revelation 14:7.

8. Knowing what creation means and how it closely links humanity to God allows people to find meaning in life.

REVELATION'S ALLUSIONS AND POTENTIAL ALLUSIONS TO CREATION[75]

So far we have dealt with the more explicit creation texts and passages in Revelation. We now turn to allusions to creation, beginning with Revelation 21 and 22a, the longest among the explicit creation texts. Following that, we will list other allusions to creation. There will not be an extensive discussion on these allusions; rather, the aim is to get an impression of the wide range of the creation motif in Revelation.

Allusions to Creation in Revelation 21 and 22a

Commonalities as well as differences are found between the original creation and the new creation. Differences include the new Jerusalem as the Holy City, the bride of the Lamb, the end of death, and the nations that are associated with the New Jerusalem. But there are also striking similarities:

1. *Heaven, earth, and sea.* These are mentioned in Revelation 21:1 and Genesis 1:1, 9 (although in the plural form). In both passages, heaven and earth appear as a pair. The reference to the sea may be different in meaning in Genesis 1:9 and Revelation 21:1.[76]
2. *The presence of God.* God "tabernacles" among His people (Rev. 21:3). His throne is in the garden-city and the redeemed will see Him (Rev. 22:3–4). According to Genesis 3:8, the Lord walked in the garden, where He met Adam and Eve.
3. *The concept of life.* Life is associated with the creation of flora and fauna, and such terminology occurs explicitly in Genesis 1:20, 21, 24 and 2:7, 9, 19. In the new creation, death will be replaced by life (Rev. 21:4). There is the book of life (Rev. 21:27), the spring/river of the water of life

---

75. We do not claim that all allusions have been identified in this study. That may not even be necessary in such a limited treatment of the topic of creation in Revelation. Nevertheless, the picture emerges clearly enough to demonstrate that Revelation is saturated with creation references and concepts.

76. See Moo, "The Sea That is No More," 148–67.

(Gen. 2:10; Rev. 21:6; 22:1), and the tree of life (Gen. 2:9; 3:24; Rev. 22:2).

4. *Precious stones and gold.* They are associated with the new Jerusalem (Rev. 21:11, 18–21). They also appear in Eden (Gen. 2:12).

5. *Sun and moon, as well as light.* The sun and moon are not needed in the new Jerusalem because the glory of God provides light (Rev. 21:23; 22:5). The sun and moon appear in Genesis 1:16 as two great lights. Light is important in the original creation account because it appears on the very first day and may be associated with God Himself (Gen. 1:3–5). On the fourth day, the two great lights, plus the stars, were created to give light to the earth (Gen. 1:14–19).[77]

6. *Day and night.* Days will exist on the new earth, but nights will no longer (Rev. 21:25; 22:5). In Eden, and obviously on the entire planet, the rhythm of days was established with the seven creation days (Gen. 1:5, 8, 13, 19, 23, 31; 2:2–3). Night and day appear in Genesis 1:5 and in Genesis 1:14, 16, 18, where day and night are separated and associated with heavenly bodies. While "day" refers to the light part of a twenty-four-hour period, it also describes the entirety of this very period.

7. *Humans reigning/ruling.* The redeemed "will reign forever and ever" (*basileuō*, Rev. 22:5). Adam and Eve received the mandate to rule (*archō*, Gen. 1:26, 28, LXX).

Other Allusions and Possible Allusions to Creation

1. *The phrase "from the foundation of the world."* This phrase appears in Revelation 13:8. Here we are not interested in the interpretation of the text but rather the understanding of the phrase "from the foundation of the world." For instance, David Aune states that "the crucifixion of Jesus, was an event predetermined from the beginning of creation."[78] The NIV translates the phrase "from the

---

77. See William H. Shea, "Creation," in *HSDAT*, 420.

78. David E. Aune, *Revelation 6–16*, WBC 52B (Dallas: Word, 1998), 747. Mounce, *Revelation*, 252, proposes, "It is better in this case to follow the order of the Greek syntax and read, 'the Lamb that was slain from the creation of the world.' That is, the death of Christ was a redemptive sacrifice decreed in the counsels of eternity."

creation of the world," which seems to be the correct meaning.

2. "*It is done.*" This phrase occurs in two different forms in Revelation 16:17 and 21:6. It is translated "It is done" or "It is finished" (NLT). The Greek consists of one word: *Gegonen* (Rev. 16:17, singular, "it is done") or *Gegonan* (Rev. 21:6, plural, lit. "they are done"),[79] respectively. The difference between the declarations (Revelation 16:17 and 21:6) is that the first is uttered by "a loud voice . . . out of the temple from the throne" that designates the end of judgment, whereas in the Revelation 21:6 it is clearly God's voice that speaks, declaring final salvation in the new creation order.[80] *Gegonan* is derived from the verb *ginomai*, which has various meanings, depending on the context.[81] This term is frequently used in Genesis. It relates especially to God's creative acts in Genesis 1, where it appears no less than twenty-six times.[82] Depending on the verbal form, *egeneto* in its context means "let there be" (Gen. 1:3), "it was" (Gen. 1:5), or, together with the particle *houtōs*, "it was so" (Gen. 1:6). This verb links the Genesis creation account and the completion of creation there with the new creation in Revelation 21 and 22 and its completion.[83] Revelation 21:6 continues to point to God as Alpha and Omega, Beginning and End, thus strengthening the allusion to creation.[84] It also alerts us to the possibility that when it occurs in other places in Revelation, a creation reference may be intended:

---

79. The plural may refer to the "words" and/or "all things" in verse 5.

80. See Brian K. Blount, *Revelation: A Commentary*, NTL (Louisville, Ky.: Westminster John Knox, 2013), 381; and Smalley, *Revelation of John*, 540–41.

81. These meanings include "to be born," "to be produced," "to be made," "to be created," "to come about," "to happen," "to become," and "to be." See *NIDNTT*, 1:569–74.

82. Genesis 1:3 (2x), 5 (2x), 6 (2x), 8 (2x), 9, 11, 13 (2x), 14, 15, 19 (2x), 20, 23 (2x), 24, 30, 31 (2x), 2:4, 5, 7. See the chapter by Jon Paulien, "Creation in the Gospel and Epistles of John," 225, in this volume.

83. Cf. Kistemaker, *Revelation*, 559; Ulrich B. Müller, *Die Offenbarung des Johannes* ÖTK 19 (Gütersloh: Gütersloher Verlagshaus Gerd Mohn, 1984), 352; and Jürgen Roloff, *Revelation*, CC (Minneapolis, Minn.: Fortress, 1993), 237. Beale, *The Book of Revelation*, 1055, also refers to the cross: "There [Rev 16:17] it stressed God's promises to judge the ungodly, but here [Rev 21:6] it designates the accomplishment of the new creation, which was set in motion at the cross when Jesus cried, 'It is finished!'"

84. Ben Witherington III, *Revelation*, The New Cambridge Bible Commentary (Cambridge: Cambridge University Press, 2003), 256, speaks about God as "Creator or Author of Life" being now "the Finisher or Completer of Life" and continues, "And so, we will hear of creation renewed, restored, and re-created in the new heaven and new earth."

the silence under the seventh seal is described with *ginomai* (Rev. 8:1), as is the undoing of creation under the trumpets (Rev. 8:7, 8, 10) and the plagues (Rev. 16:2, 3, 4, 10, 18, 19).

3. *Silence in heaven.* Silence in heaven is mentioned in the seventh seal (Rev. 8:1). The context suggests that the sixth seal ends with the second coming of Jesus, the day of the Lord (Rev. 6:14–17). While the unbelievers ask the rocks and mountains to fall upon them in order to avoid seeing God and the Lamb, the question is raised, "Who is able to stand" (Rev. 6:17)? This question is answered by Revelation 7. Those who are able to endure the second coming are the 144,000, the great multitude. The 144,000 are described as being on earth, while the great multitude finds itself in front of God's throne in the heavenly sanctuary. They are cared for by Jesus. There will no longer be suffering, hunger, thirst, or scorching heat. They are led to the "springs of the water of life; and God will wipe every tear from their eyes" (Rev. 7:17). This is a description not of the new earth but of the condition of the redeemed in heaven. Therefore, Revelation 7b may describe the millennium. The silence follows the millennium. In the Old Testament silence is associated with judgment.[85] If this is also the case here, the seventh seal would be an indirect reference to the executive judgment that takes place in front of the great white throne (Rev. 20:11–15) and the inauguration of the new creation (Rev. 21:1).[86]

4. *The beast that comes out of the earth (13:1).* In Revelation 13, the combination of sea and earth from which two beasts arise may have a creation background, as previously mentioned. The second beast in particular, the one coming out of

---

85. See, e.g., God is silent—Isa. 42:14; humans/the earth are silent when God executes judgment—Exod. 14:14; Pss. 37:7; 76:9; Hab. 2:20; Zeph. 1:7; Zech. 2:13. Cf. Mounce, *Revelation*, 170.

86. See especially Beale, *The Book of Revelation*, 445–53. He declares, "These Jewish reflections on the silence in connection with the exodus confirm our earlier contention that the silence in Rev. 8:1 is directly associated with both judgment and new creation" (p. 50). Blount, *Revelation*, 157–58, comes to the following conclusion: John amplifies the judgment theme with the declaration of silence. Though the seer uses the word *sigē* ("silence") only here, in both Old Testament and Jewish contexts the term conjures images of divine judgment. The relationship between the moment of silence and the breaking of the seventh seal is reminiscent of the silence that preceded God's creation of heaven and earth. In this case, following the cataclysms of the final judgment, God will create a new heaven and a new earth.

the earth, seems to reflect the creation motif. Ángel Rodríguez makes the following suggestion: "The Hebrew term
translated 'animal' in Genesis 1:24 is the equivalent of the
Greek *therion*, 'beast,' used in Revelation 13:11. . . . According to Genesis, bringing a beast into existence from the
ground or earth is a divine act of creation, a manifestation of
divine power. Since this is the only parallel to Revelation
13:11, we would have to conclude that the second beast
comes into existence as a result of a divine act of creation."[87]

This second symbolic beast will later develop into an opponent
of God and His people, but this does not rule out its divine origin.

CREATION THEMES IN REVELATION

Having dealt with explicit references to creation and allusions to
creation, this section will briefly mention some other creation themes
that appear in Revelation. The difference between creation themes
and allusions is mainly their frequency of occurrence.

DIVINE DESIGNATIONS

Early in the Apocalypse God calls Himself "the Alpha and the
Omega" (Rev. 1:8) and later also "the beginning and the end" (Rev.
21:6). In Revelation 22:13 Jesus calls Himself "the Alpha and the
Omega, the first and the last, the beginning and the end." The three
designations overlap in meaning. "The beginning [*archē*] and the end
[*telos*]" seem to have creation overtones since Jesus, as the "the
Beginning of the creation" (Rev. 3:14), is the Originator (*archē*) of
creation, and the End (*telos*) appears in a verbal form with a prefix
in Genesis 2:1 (LXX): "Thus the heavens and the earth were com-
pleted/finished [*synteleō*]." Gregory Stevenson suggests, "The term
end here is therefore not so much the cessation of something, but
the culmination of something. Stating that God is the *arche* and the
telos means that God has put something into motion for a specific
purpose and that something is heading toward a predetermined
goal. That goal, in Revelation, is new creation."[88] Now, whether *telos*

---

87. Ángel Manuel Rodríguez, *Future Glory: The 8 Greatest End-Time Prophecies in the Bible* (Hagerstown, Md.: Review and Herald, 2002), 114.

88. Stevenson, "Theology of Creation," 141, where he also proposes that these divine titles are cosmological titles that describe God as the sovereign ruler of and caregiver to all creation.

refers to the end of the creation process in Genesis 2 or to the new creation in Revelation 21 and 22, it seems clear that the phrase "the beginning and the end" has creation overtones. This would then also be applicable to the parallel phrases "the Alpha and the Omega" and "the First and the Last." Larry Lichtenwalter may be right when he asserts, "God precedes all things, and he will bring all things to eschatological fulfillment. He is the origin and goal of history. He has the first word in creation. He has the last word in the new creation."[89]

The term *pantokratōr* has already been mentioned. It seems also to refer to creation because it is used in the creation context of Revelation 4.

"MAKING" (*POIEŌ*)

As indicated above, the verb *poieō* is used in Genesis 1 and 2 (LXX) to describe the divine activity in creation. In Revelation it is used for believers, evil powers, and God Himself. Five texts are important for our discussion:

1:6	Jesus has made us a kingdom and priests.
3:12	Jesus will make the overcomers pillars in God's temple. They have an important function to fulfill in God's sanctuary.
5:10	Jesus has made believers a kingdom and priests.
14:7	God has made heaven and earth, the sea, and the springs of water.
21:5	God promises to make all things new.

While Revelation 14:7 talks about the original creation, Revelation 3:12 and 21:5 refer to the future new creation. However, Revelation 1:6 and 5:10 describe a kind of spiritual creation in the interim between the Genesis creation and the eschatological new creation. Jesus is active now in changing the lives of people. He alters their status, making them a kingdom and priests for God. From that perspective God has not ceased to be creatively active.

THE UNDOING OF CREATION IN THE TRUMPETS AND BOWLS

The trumpet vision has various Old Testament and New Testament backgrounds that refer to trumpets, series of sevens, or the

---

89. Lichtenwalter, "Creation and Apocalypse," 127.

actual content of some of the trumpets.[90] The seven trumpets come in two groups: a group of four that affects nature and a group of three that affects humanity.[91] The group of three is also called the three woes. However, the trumpet series in Revelation 8–11 refers not only to the Egyptian plagues or the blowing of trumpets in the Old Testament but also to elements of creation that are at least partially destroyed. Hail and fire, mixed with blood, burns a third of the earth, a third of the trees, and the grass (Rev. 8:7). A mountain is cast into the sea, and a large part of the sea becomes blood (Rev. 8:8). A great star falls from heaven with devastating effects (Rev. 8:10). The sun, moon, and stars are partially darkened (Rev. 8:12). The abyss (Rev. 9:1–2, 11) is opened and immense smoke comes out of it, darkening the sun, followed by a locust plague that tortures humans (Rev. 9:4–6).[92] This torture of humanity is intensified under the sixth trumpet. Horse-like beings with serpent-like tails kill a third of the people on earth (Rev. 9:7–11). Part of the trumpets seem to refer not only to the exodus from Egypt and the fall of Babylon[93] but also to an undoing and reversal of creation. J. Ramsey Michaels notes, "The four areas affected—earth, sea, fresh water and sky—made up the whole of the human environment as the ancients perceived it. These four spheres were what Jews and Christians acknowledged as God's creation (compare 14:7)."[94] Simon Kistemaker talks about "an area of God's creation" that is affected with each trumpet that is sounded.[95]

The same is true for the last seven plagues/bowls, only that the plagues are an intensification of the trumpets, a third being replaced by the fullness of the impact of God's wrath.[96] The first plague affects the earth, the second the sea, the third the waters/springs,

---

90. For a discussion of some of these backgrounds, see Gordon J. Wenham et al., eds., *New Bible Commentary*, 4th ed. (Downers Grove, Ill.: InterVarsity, 1994), 1437; Blount, *Revelation*, 160; and Caird, *Revelation*, 108–11.

91. See Kistemaker, *Revelation*, 267.

92. Paulien, *Interpretation of Revelation 8:7–12*, 181, shows the parallel between Revelation 9:2 and Genesis 1:2 (LXX) and comes to the conclusion: "Here the author of Revelation introduces the flavor of the creation account into the plague narrative. This plague is returning God's creation to its pre-creation chaotic state."

93. See Kenneth A. Strand, "The Eight Basic Visions in the Book of Revelation," *AUSS* 25, no. 1 (1987): 107–21; and Witherington, *Revelation*, 148.

94. J. Ramsey Michaels, *Revelation*, The IVP New Testament Commentary Series 20 (Downers Grove, Ill.: InterVarsity, 1997), 121.

95. Kistemaker, *Revelation*, 273.

96. For parallels between trumpets and bowls, see Aune, *Revelation 6–16*, 497–99.

the fourth the sun, the fifth brings intense darkness, and the sixth Armageddon so that humans are directly affected (Rev. 16). U. B. Müller suggests that with the pouring out of the first four bowls, the entire creation of earth, sea, rivers, and heavenly bodies is affected.[97] It seems that the trumpet series describes a partial undoing of creation, while the parallel and yet distinct bowl series describes the complete undoing of creation and, therefore, stands in contrast to the new creation in Revelation 21 and 22a.[98]

THE ABYSS

The abyss appears in Revelation 9:1–2, 11; 11:7; 17:8; 20:1, 3. It is found in Genesis 1:2 (LXX). In this verse, the "surface of the deep," which is connected to the state of planet earth being formless or void, is translated with the term *abyssos*. "'Over the surface of the deep' parallels 'over the waters' in the subsequent clause. . . . On the second and third days these waters are eventually separated from the expanse and land masses when the waters are called 'sea' (vv. 6–10)."[99] After the separation, sea (*thalassa*) and earth (*gē*) became visible. It is precisely from these two areas that the two beasts of Revelation 13 come forward, the sea beast and the beast out of the earth. In Revelation 17:8 another beast emerges from the abyss. Although in the New Testament the abyss receives a slightly different meaning, it can be assumed that John takes his imagery from the creation account in Genesis 1.[100]

SOULS OF HUMANS

The term *psychē* occurs in Genesis 2:7 and seven times in Revelation. The word can be translated "soul," "life," "self," "person," or "creature." According to Genesis 2:7, the body formed by God plus the breath of life from God make this lifeless entity a living soul/being. In other words, the soul in Genesis 2:7 designates the entire human being with all its faculties as created by God. In the Apocalypse, the

97. Müller, *Die Offenbarung des Johannes*, 281.

98. The trumpet series is still rooted in and depicts processes in history, while the bowl series describes eschatological events, in this case the judgment that culminates in Christ's second coming.

99. Kenneth A. Mathews, *Genesis 1–11:26*, NAC 1A (Nashville, Tenn.: Broadman and Holman, 1996), 133.

100. For a more detailed discussion of the abyss, see Ekkehardt Mueller, "The Beast of Revelation 17—A Suggestion (Part 1)," *Journal of Asia Adventist Seminary* 10, no. 1 (2007): 40–50.

first usage of "soul" comes in Revelation 6:9, talking about the souls "slain because of the word of God, and because of the testimony which they had maintained." As in Genesis 2:7,

> these *souls* are not disembodied spirits. They are, after all, visible to John. Nor are they the "lives" or "selves" of slaughtered victims as a kind of abstraction, nor are they typical of what theologians like to call "the intermediate state" (the interval between a believer's physical death and the final resurrection). Rather, at least within the horizons of John's vision, these *souls* are people with voices and real bodies, like the "beheaded" souls of [Rev.] 20:4. They are martyrs, not just in the sense of bearing *testimony* (Greek *martyria*, v. 9), but in the sense of having been "killed" (v. 11) for their testimony. Like Abel, the first martyr, who "still speaks, even though he is dead" (Heb 11:4; compare Gen 4:10), they cry out for justice to be done.[101]

In Revelation 8:9, which is part of the second trumpet, the "souls" are associated with "creatures" (*ktismata*). Therefore, the NASB translates "the creatures which were in the sea and had life [*psychē*]," and the ESV renders the phrase as "living creatures." The parallel text in the second plague states, "Every living thing [*psychē*] in the sea died" (Rev. 16:3).[102] In Revelation 12:4 *psychē* must be understood as self or life, not as part of a human being. In 18:13 "human souls" are sold as merchandise; they seem to be identical with the preceding "bodies"[103] and describe humans as wholistic entities (see Gen. 2:7). In Revelation 18:14 "your soul" (ESV) means "you" (NASB).

---

101. Michaels, *Revelation*, 106. Larry Lichtenwalter, "'Souls under the Altar': The 'Soul' and Related Anthropological Imagery in John's Apocalypse," *JATS* 26, no. 1 (2015): 66, writes, "That Revelation would 1) twice portrays [sic] sea creatures as having (8:9) or being (16:3) souls; 2) equate the human soul with the body (18:13); and 3) place the soul in juxtaposition with death as opposites (12:11; 16:3) reveals how it echoes anthropological realities found in the Genesis narrative. Genesis 2:7 records that "the Lord God formed man of dust from the ground, and breathed into his nostrils the breath of life; and man became a living being" . . .; i.e., a living soul. One does not have a soul; he is a soul—a living being, a living person. The breath of life unites with the inanimate body transforming it into a living being."

102. Typically, the phrase is understood as referring to fish, sea mammals, and other life forms in the oceans. However, Beale suggests that in Revelation 16:3 *psychē* should also be understood as humans. Beale, *The Book of Revelation*, 815, notes, "πᾶσα ψυχὴ ζωῆς ἀπέθανεν [*pasa psychē zōēs apethanen*] can be translated 'every *living soul* died.' . . . This may refer to the death or suffering of people who depend on a maritime economy. The second trumpet judgment involved the death of sea creatures 'having *life*' (ψυχάς [*psychas*]) . . . . The death of humans themselves appears to be the point of 16:3, especially since every other use of ψυχή [*psychē*] in Revelation, except technically in 8:9, refers to people (6:9; 12:11; 18:13, 14; 20:4)."

103. See Mounce, *Revelation*, 334.

In Revelation 20:4 the souls are again human beings in their totality, created and later raised by God from the dead.

THE SEVEN CHURCHES WITH THEIR PROMISES TO THE CONQUERORS

The messages to the seven churches end with promises to the overcomers/conquerors. The first and the last messages to the seven churches have clear references to creation—either the original creation or the new creation—speaking about eating of the "tree of life which is in the Paradise of God" (Rev. 2:7) and about Jesus as the Originator of creation (Rev. 3:14) upon whose throne the overcomers will sit with Him (Rev. 3:21). But the messages to the churches other than Ephesus and Laodicea also have at least indirect creation overtones.[104] These overtones relate to the new creation. The overcomers in the church in Smyrna are promised to be protected against the "second death" (Rev. 2:11; 20:6, 14; 21:8). Those in Pergamum will receive a white stone and a new name, obviously in the future kingdom of Christ (Rev. 2:17). To the overcomers in Thyatira the promise is made that they will have authority over the nations (Rev. 2:26). The nations are mentioned in Revelation 21:24, 26 and 22:2, in the context of the new earth and the new Jerusalem. The overcomers in Sardis will receive white garments and are assured that their names will not be blotted out of the book of life (Rev. 3:5). Those will enter the new Jerusalem "whose names are written in the Lamb's book of life" (Rev. 21:27). The promise to the overcomers in Philadelphia was previously mentioned—namely, being pillars in the temple of God. But in addition they are told that they "will not go out from it anymore" and the name of the new Jerusalem will be written on them, the name of the city "which comes down out of heaven from My God" (Rev. 3:12). Thus, the promises to the overcomers in the seven churches are related to the new creation of Revelation 21–22. The conquerors have the assurance of resurrection to eternal life—a kind of new creation—on the new earth. An additional promise to the overcomers is found in Revelation 21:7. This is in the very context of the new creation and is clearly linked to the creation theme.

---

104. Stanley, "New Creation," 29, proposes that "John links six of these conquering promises with a reward in Revelation 20–22." We would suggest that all the promises to the overcomers of the seven churches contain a creation/new creation reference.

RESURRECTION

The resurrection is mentioned for the first time in Revelation 1:5 and then again in Revelation 1:18. It is associated with life—that is, coming to life. The resurrection of Jesus is the paradigm for all resurrections, whether in the past or the future. The resurrection of the two witnesses is described as "the breath of life from God" coming into them (Rev. 11:11). The "breath of life" appears in Genesis 2:7 in connection with the creation of Adam, although slightly different vocabulary is employed.[105] Revelation 20:4–6 mentions the future first and second resurrections of humans. Those resurrected to life will enjoy the new creation. So resurrection—at least the first resurrection—is linked to the new creation, reminding the audience of what took place in the garden of Eden. To resurrect people who have completely disintegrated is a creative act of the almighty God. Stevenson writes, "Christ's resurrection provides a model for understanding the new creation of Revelation 21–22 . . . John describes the ending of the first heaven and first earth in terms reminiscent of death. In light of the resurrection of Christ, however, death becomes merely an ending that inaugurates a new beginning."[106] This statement could be interpreted differently. People could assume that death is the way to eternal life, but it is Jesus Christ who guarantees the first resurrection to those who believe in Him. Bauckham states,

> Creation is not confined forever to its own immanent possibilities. It is open to the fresh creative possibilities of its Creator. This is how the hope of resurrection was possible. The Jewish hope of resurrection was not based on belief in the inherent capacity of human nature to survive death. . . . It was fundamentally a form of trust in God the Creator, who, as he gave life that ends in death, can also give life back to the dead. More than that, he can give *new* life—eschatologically new life raised forever beyond the threat of death. . . . But Jewish eschatological hope was not just for the resurrection of individuals. It was hope for the future of God's whole creation. It was hope for *new* creation.[107]

---

105. Genesis 2:7 (LXX) has *pnoēn zōēs*, while Revelation 11:11 uses *pneuma zōēs*. There should not be a substantial difference. *Pneuma zōēs* describes the living beings that will die in the flood (Gen. 6:17; 7:15). In Genesis 6:17 they seem to refer to both animals and human beings. In Ezekiel 37:5 God speaks to the dead bones: "Thus says the Lord GOD to these bones, 'Behold, I will cause breath to enter you that you may come to life'" [*pneuma zōēs*]. See also Ezekiel 37:10.

106. Stevenson, "Theology of Creation," 141.

107. Bauckham, *Theology*, 48–49.

SUMMARY

Our study has pointed out a significant number of clear creation references. In these verses and passages creation vocabulary has been used. The Apocalypse affirms God and Jesus Christ as Creator and bases itself squarely on the Genesis creation account and its reverberations in the Old and New Testaments.

However, the creation references do not provide the entire picture of the importance of the topic of creation in the Apocalypse. Many allusions and potential allusions to creation round out the picture. These could be further explored.

Finally, what has been termed "creation themes" are allusions to creation that occur more frequently throughout the book, adding considerably to the overall topic. Taken together, these references, themes, and allusions reveal an impressive and theologically significant network of the creation theme throughout Revelation.

METAPHORIC OR NON-METAPHORIC UNDERSTANDING OF THE CREATION MOTIF IN REVELATION?

Before we explore the theological significance of the creation theme in Revelation, we must address the question of whether creation in the Apocalypse should be understood primarily or exclusively metaphorically and spiritually or it also points to actual creation events as described and implied in Genesis 1 and 2. As pointed out, Revelation refers predominantly to the Genesis creation but occasionally also to a spiritual creation and extensively to the new creation at the end of time. We are here concerned with the creation of a hospitable environment and life on planet earth. Is this creation to be understood symbolically or not? Furthermore, would it be correct and fair to read into biblical texts our present understanding of scientific theories and suggest that these are the intended meaning of Scripture? And if they are not, would we be justified to reinterpret Scripture, accommodating it to our present worldview and the next generations to theirs?

This is certainly a larger hermeneutical issue that cannot be fully discussed here. The answer depends to some extent on one's own presuppositions and decisions on the origin, role, and authority of Scripture. Still, we will attempt to respond to part of the issue.

It is no secret that Revelation should be primarily understood symbolically (Rev. 1:1). While its letter frame (Rev. 1–3; 22:6–21) is more straightforward and not as rich in symbolism, needing to be understood more literally than figuratively, the apocalyptic part (Rev. 4:1—22:5) is full of symbolic descriptions and entities. Theoretically, this might allow for understanding the creation motif metaphorically. However, we need to add some cautionary remarks.

Even the symbolic portions of Revelation are not completely symbolic. There is always a mixture of metaphorical and non-metaphorical language. For instance, the term "God," which appears ninety-six times in Revelation, is not once used figuratively. It always describes the supreme being, the Creator of the universe. A purely symbolic text would hardly be understandable, and it would be extremely difficult to unlock the biblical meaning of its symbols if all terms were used only figuratively. The task of the expositor is to find out which terms should be understood figuratively and which ones should not be interpreted that way. If one really wants to understand the author's intended meaning, this cannot be based on personal preference but must be grounded on sound principles.

Without controls, figurative language can be misused and given a multiplicity of artificial meanings that disregard the message of the document under investigation. Such interpretations may even be contradictory. While we recognize that texts may speak differently to different readers, the authors typically pursue one specific goal rather than remaining completely vague about the meaning of their message.

Therefore, symbolic language must be unlocked. This may occur, for instance, through the study of the context, the use of the respective symbols, and their explanation by the author as well as through intertextual connections between different authors—in this case Old Testament and New Testament authors—who live and work basically within the same framework, worldview, and fabric of thinking.

The creation motif occurs in the apocalyptic part of Revelation as well as in the messages to the seven churches, without major differences. Consider, for example, the creation vocabulary,[108] divine designations related to the creation motif, and allusions such as resurrection

---

108. A good example may be the word family *ktiz-* ("create, creation").

that are not spiritualized in Revelation.[109] This bridging of creation language without shift from the letters to the apocalyptic section of the book suggests that the language of creation remains literal and nonmetaphoric.

Revelation uses clear references and allusions to the Old Testament creation account and Old Testament and New Testament passages based on them. They describe who God is and what He does. These references to creation appear in different literary genres without losing their basic meaning. Creation is intrinsically linked to the nature and being of God and should not be interpreted completely differently in different biblical documents. God is and remains the Creator God. While biblical authors may highlight various aspects of God's creative activity, there is no reason to believe they doubted that God had actually created the universe and life in it, including on planet earth.

Jesus appears in many roles in Revelation, one of them being as Creator. This is in line with New Testament statements such as the ones found in John 1:1–3, Hebrews 1:1–2, and Colossians 1:15–16. "According to Colossians 1, Jesus is not only the "firstborn of all creation" (v. 15) but also the "firstborn from the dead" (*prōtotokos tōn nekrōn*, v. 18). Revelation 1:5 also says Jesus is the "firstborn of the dead" (*prōtotokos ek tōn nekrōn*)—using the same phrase—and, according to Revelation 3:14, He is "the beginning of God's creation" (ESV), "the ruler of God's creation" (NIV), or "the originator of God's creation" (NET), which is the same concept as being the firstborn of creation.[110] In both Colossians 1:15 and Revelation 3:14, *ktisis* ("creation") is used, and the person responsible for it is mentioned. The Old Testament background for Colossians 1:15–18 and Revelation 1:5 and 3:14 is Psalm 89:27, 37 (88:28, 38, LXX). John clearly builds on Old Testament and New Testament creation theology.[111]

---

109. On the resurrection in Revelation, see Ekkehardt Mueller, "Basic Questions About the Millennium, Part 2: The Issue of Dispensational Premillennialism," *Reflections* (July 2016): 2–3.

110. Beasley-Murray, *Revelation*, 104, seeing the parallel to Colossians 1, states that the concept of Jesus as the prime source of God's creation "is the same as 'alpha' in the title 'alpha and omega.'" See also Roloff, *Revelation*, 64.

111. Aune, *Revelation 1–5*, suggests that "in all probability, the writer did not formulate this title, for the title ἀρχή, πρωτότοκος ἐκ τῶν νεκρῶν [*archē, prōtotokos ek tōn nekrōn*], 'the beginning, the firstborn from the dead,' occurs earlier in Col 1:18 (in the context of a hymn incorporated into that letter). Since Colossians was circulated in the Roman province of Asia, including Laodicea (Col 4:16), one of the seven churches to whom Revelation was addressed, the title may have become part of the christological tradition of the region." For a

Therefore, since the same terminology is used, we argue that his understanding of the Creator does not differ from Paul's understanding of creation and the Creator. The Gospels remind us that in addition to being the Originator of creation, Jesus affirmed the creation of Adam and Eve (Matt. 19:4; Mark 10:6) and believed in the historical existence of their son Abel (Matt. 23:35; Luke 11:51).

Obviously the Old Testament audience as well as the first-century audience understood that creation happened as described in Genesis 1 and 2, although precise details of how it occurred are not revealed there. But a consistent picture of creation appears throughout both the Old Testament and New Testament, culminating in the one portrayed by John the Revelator. God and Jesus are Creator in the true sense of the word.

Therefore, a metaphorical reinterpretation of creation in Revelation does not seem to fit the data and does not seem to be justified. If the original creation is to be taken seriously, the future one should likewise be accepted and vice versa. Michael Gorman states, "This eschatological reality is *not a fantasy but a certain hope*, guaranteed by the faithful and true God and by the death, resurrection, and exaltation of the slaughtered Lamb, the faithful and true witness."[112] Jon Paulien argues, "It is equally clear that a real creation is necessary to his [John's] theological use of that creation [the new creation]."[113] And Gale Heide affirms, "We can interpret apocalyptic literature as visionary without denying the reality of the essence of the vision."[114]

THE CONTRIBUTION OF THE CREATION THEME TO THE THEOLOGY OF REVELATION

Stevenson proposes that "creation as a theological concept is a central component of the Book [of Revelation]."[115] The question is what this means. This section will take a brief look at the contribution of the creation theme to Revelation's teaching on God and anthropology and briefly mention how it is related to other important topics.

---

discussion of the passage in Colossians 1:15–20, see Ekkehardt Mueller, "The Firstborn in Colossians 1:15," in *Biblical and Theological Studies on the Trinity*, ed. Paul Petersen and Rob McIver (Adelaide: ATF Theology, 2014): 65–86.

112. Gorman, *Reading Revelation Responsibly*, 166.

113. Paulien, "Creation in the Gospel and Epistles of John," 250, in this volume.

114. Heide, "What Is New," 56.

115. Stevenson, "Theology of Creation," 139.

CREATION AND THE GODHEAD

Creation plays a central role in Revelation's teaching about God, His nature, His intentionality, His relationship to the created order, and His role as Savior.

The Nature of God

Being Creator is not only about what God[116] does—His works—but also about His very identity. Human beings, made in the image of God, are by nature creative—some more and some less. God is by nature the Creator, exhibiting unlimited creativity and yet being distinct from creation. Therefore, it is correct to argue that "creation is a fundamental component of who God is." Further, "God's creation of a new heaven and a new earth (21.1) is a testament that God's creative activity was not a one-time event, but an intrinsic part of his nature."[117] In contrast to humanity's creativity and human "creations," God's creativity is related to life. He is the source of life.[118] God the Father as well as the Holy Spirit gives the water of life without cost to those who are thirsty and come to God (Rev. 21:4; 22:17). Those who are redeemed by Jesus have the right to the tree of life (Rev. 22:14). The "breath [or "Spirit"] of life" came into the two witnesses, and "they stood on their feet" (Rev. 11:11), revived.[119]

God has not only created inanimate things, but He has also created various life forms (e.g., Rev. 16:3). In addition, He has created beings that are not only alive but are also candidates for eternal life (Rev. 21:1–4, 27; 22:1–5). Because He has created all things (John

---

116. In this section "God" is to be understood in the wider sense of "Godhead." While in Revelation God the Father is clearly identified as Creator and Jesus is called the Originator of creation, there is less information about the Holy Spirit. However, the Holy Spirit is found in close relationship with God the Father. In Revelation 4, God is praised as Creator (Rev. 4:11). In this creation context the Holy Spirit occurs. Also, the point cannot be missed when one looks at Revelation 5:6. As the Spirit is linked with the Father in Revelation 4, so He is linked with the Lamb in Revelation 5, who is praised as Redeemer. Revelation 4 and 5 contain, among other topics, the themes of creation and salvation. Creation and salvation belong together, as do the Father, Son, and Holy Spirit. Especially from Revelation 5 one can derive that the Holy Spirit is involved in salvation, but so is He in creation. See Ekkehardt Mueller, "The Holy Spirit in Revelation" (unpublished manuscript), 28. Regarding Jesus, Gorman, *Reading Revelation Responsibly*, 167, holds that "Revelation really does engage in the christological reconfiguration of God, especially prominent in chapters 4–5." This is confirmed at the end of the Apocalypse.

117. Stevenson, "Theology of Creation," 140.

118. Or, as Bauckham, *Theology*, 141, expresses the thought, life has its "eternal source in God."

119. For a discussion on whether or not the breath/Spirit refers to the Holy Spirit, see Mueller, "The Holy Spirit in Revelation," 22–24.

1:3) and has done this through His Word (Heb. 11:3), it can be assumed that He created *ex nihilo*. This creative power surpasses the capacities of all of God's creatures. Therefore, God as Creator is unique. From this uniqueness as Creator derives God's authority over all creation. He is the Lord Almighty, the Alpha and Omega, the Beginning and the End (Rev. 1:8, 4:11; 21:6; 22:13). He is the only one to be omnipotent. He is to be praised and worshiped (Rev. 4:11; 14:7). The angel of Revelation 10:6 bases His oath on the surest foundation, the Creator God.

Although Revelation does not directly attribute to God the ownership of creation as, for example, Psalm 24:1–2 does, this concept, found in various places in Scripture,[120] still seems to be assumed in Revelation. Jesus as the Originator of God's creation (Rev. 3:14) reprimands the church in Laodicea. He has "supreme authority and power to execute the word of which he is the guarantor and the faithful and true witness."[121] "He is the source of creation, and therefore he has a legitimate claim on it."[122] God creates, and He undoes creation—either directly or by allowing it to happen.[123] He has the authority, power, and right to do so, and nobody can hinder Him. He engages in just judgments and brings retribution on those who have mistreated and killed others (Rev. 16:5–7). Obviously these abused ones are His own, and God will intervene for them by raising them from the dead and bringing their enemies to justice. He will allow the planet earth to be empty and void for a thousand years (Rev. 20) and then create a new heaven and earth (Rev. 21–22), not allowing any of His creatures to spoil His long-term plans. In the new Jerusalem sanctuary, God's direct presence—His immanence—will be revealed and an unprecedented closeness and intimacy between the Creator and His creation will be established. "The fact that a divine throne is present in the city expresses the idea that the political structure of the new creation is theocracy, a veritable kingdom of God."[124] So He cares for His creation by sustaining it, re-creating it, governing it, and letting His people participate in His reign (Rev. 22:5).

---

120. See, e.g., Ps. 50:12; 1 Cor. 10:26.

121. Beasley-Murray, *Revelation*, 104.

122. Gerhard A. Krodel, *Revelation*, Augsburg Commentary on the New Testament (Minneapolis, Minn.: Augsburg, 1989), 142.

123. See the seven trumpets (Rev. 8–11) and the seven plagues (Rev. 15–16).

124. Gallusz, *Throne Motif*, 172.

Creation is the foundation for the theocentricity of the book of Revelation.[125] Other concepts of God derive from the fact that He is the Creator. From this perspective being Creator is a foundational and encompassing concept. It allows for an integrated understanding of the nature and divine actions of the Godhead—Father, Son, and Holy Spirit—and avoids major inconsistencies in the way the Trinity would relate to the world and its beings were God not the Creator of all.

God's Intentionality

In creating inanimate things and animate beings, God pursued His plan and purpose. While Revelation does not provide the slightest hint that there was in God an inherent need to have a counterpart in creation and that He therefore was more or less forced to create beings in order to achieve self-realization or to exhibit His love and holiness, God decided to create anyway, in free will. Thus creation was no coincidence, and God was not surprised by the appearance of intelligent beings. By His will creation came into existence and is sustained (Rev. 4:11). As bad as it was, even the Fall was not an unexpected shock for the Godhead, and the question of whether or not to find a way of salvation for humanity did not need to be pondered in a divine emergency meeting (Rev. 13:8). The male child of Revelation 12 was the fulfillment of the proto-gospel in Genesis 3:15. Likewise "the New Creation of Revelation 21–22 is not an afterthought."[126] Indeed, God has a plan and purpose. He created so that humans may "fear" and worship Him (Rev. 14:7). He re-creates so that humanity can live in the most intimate relationship with Him. The new creation even surpasses the old creation, especially with God living permanently among humankind, and this is certainly intentional. Therefore, John Stanley may be talking about perfection when he says, "With the one who brought the cosmos into being, *ex nihilo*, there is also the possibility—for there is the will—to bring it

---

125. In Revelation 1:8 God is introduced as the Alpha and Omega, which also means the Beginning and the End (Rev. 21:6). See discussion above in the section of this study titled "Divine Designations." The apocalyptic part of Revelation begins with chapter 4. This is clearly theocentric, and there God appears as Creator, setting the tone for Revelation 5 with Jesus as Redeemer. Revelation 4–5 may not only introduce the seals but also the entire apocalyptic portion of the book, and thus may be foundational. They prepare for the other creation statements in Revelation.

126. Stevenson, "Theology of Creation," 141.

to its intended perfection."[127] Bauckham claims that "Creation has . . . a moral and a religious goal—its dedication to God fulfilled in God's holy presence—and also an aesthetic goal—its beauty fulfilled in reflecting the divine glory."[128]

God's Relation to Creation and His Creatures

Creation—life—is an undeserved, unmerited gift of God. However, the biblical God is not a deist God, winding up a clock and leaving it to itself. He sustains creation and cares for it (Rev. 4:11). "All of [God's] creation, from beginning to end and everything in between, fall under God's sovereign rule and divine care."[129] Jesus the Creator (Rev. 3:14) addresses His church in Laodicea, attempting to bring it to repentance so that it may not be lost, inviting church members to open the door to Him and dine with Him (Rev. 3:20).

Relationship is strongly expressed in the creation passages of Revelation 7 and 21–22. The Lamb, who is Creator and Savior, becomes Shepherd of His people. He guides them and provides what is needed, especially the water of life (Rev. 7:14, 17). God will personally wipe away the tears of His people (Rev. 7:17; 21:4). "Here God himself is said to wipe the tears from the faces of all his suffering creatures. The love of God, for which Revelation rarely uses the word 'love' (cf. 1:5; 3:9, 19; 20:9), could hardly be more vividly depicted."[130]

Relationship is also expressed through the disappearance of boundaries and distances. Interestingly, it is not only humanity that wants to overcome the barrier separating them from God. It is God Himself who wants to be close to His creatures. In the new creation "the tabernacle of God is among men, and He will dwell among them, and they shall be His people, and God Himself will be among them" (Rev. 21:3). Three times in this one verse the loud voice stresses that the distance between God and humanity will have been permanently overcome. Additionally, not only will something be no more, but something else *will be*: "they will be His people" (Rev. 21:3), He will be their God, they will be His children (Rev. 21:7), and God's name will be on their foreheads (Rev. 22:4). Although the redeemed will serve God (Rev. 22:3), they are still His sons and daughters. The

---

127. Stanley, "New Creation," 32.
128. Bauckham, *Theology*, 141.
129. Stevenson, "Theology of Creation," 141.
130. Bauckham, *Theology*, 141.

closeness of God to His people is also expressed with other images: God and the Lamb as the temple (Rev. 21:22), the new Jerusalem that includes the throne of God and the Lamb (Rev. 22:23), and God and the Lamb illuminating the believers (Rev. 21:23; 22:5). The climax will be reached when His own will see His face (Rev. 22:4), something that was not possible for humans throughout history. No human being was able to see God and live (Exod. 33:20). How important it is for good communication and an intimate relationship to see each other's faces. Humans will see God's face.

This is creation theology at its best. It is creation that establishes the possibility to relate to a being beyond our world, the Creator, and there find meaning in and purpose for life.

God, Creation, and Salvation

But with the new creation theme comes another crucial concept: salvation. When through the Fall creation went wrong, God became the Savior. The powerful connection between the two concepts can be illustrated through three points:

1. Revelation 4 and 5 have already linked creation and salvation through the hymns addressed to the Father and Son and both of them. The two concepts are inseparable. God the Father is here portrayed as Creator, and the Son as Savior-Lamb. Creator and Savior are worshiped together.

2. Among others, salvation in Revelation is expressed through the imagery of the slaughtered Lamb, His shed blood (Rev. 1:5; 5:9; 7:14; 12:11), the Lamb releasing humans from their sins (Rev. 1:5), the Lamb purchasing people for God (Rev. 5:9; 14:3–4), people washing their robes and whitening them in the blood of the Lamb (Rev. 7:14), and the redeemed standing with the Lamb on Mount Zion (Rev. 14:1, 3–4).[131] However, this Lamb is Jesus the Creator, who throughout the Apocalypse is associated with God the Father, also described as Creator.

3. Clearly the concept of salvation and new creation are linked again in Revelation 21 and 22. The new home for believers will only be for those who are saved (Rev. 21:7–8).

---

131. For more details, see Ekkehardt Mueller, "Christological Concepts in the Book of Revelation–Part 3: The Lamb Christology," *JATS* 21, no. 2 (2011): 42–66.

Therefore, the call is issued to make a decision and accept the water of life at no cost (Rev. 22:17).

Creation and salvation go together in Revelation. It is inconsistent to separate these two crucial teachings. To do so would typically mean compromising and damaging both. Reinterpreting creation may lead to a reinterpretation of salvation or to a soteriology that is shallow or unsatisfactory. The Creator God is also the Redeemer God. This is the difference between Gnosticism and biblical religion.[132]

CREATION AND ANTHROPOLOGY

Creation also plays a crucial role in anthropology in the book of Revelation.

The Nature of Human Beings

Creation describes, among other things, what humans are. Humans are not an accident of nature. God willed us. We are part of creation and yet can think beyond creation. Having a body with mental/rational and emotional capacities, we are wholistic entities, called "souls" (Rev. 6:9). As humans, we reflect not only on others and our environment but also on ourselves. We are aware of our finitude. While we cannot understand eternity, neither can we fully comprehend that this life here and now is all that there is. We hope for something else. Humans wrestle with the questions: Where do we come from? Where will we be going to after death? And why are we here? And it is precisely these questions, which have to do with the meaning of life, that Revelation's theology of creation answers: Humans come from the hand of God. Our lives gain meaning through our relationship with God. We are not immortal by nature but through Christ can have eternal life and be kept in the Lamb's book of life (Rev. 3:5; 21:27). That means we will have a future beyond life here and now, if we make the right choices.

Obviously, humans are moral beings with our own will and freedom of choice. We can distinguish between good and evil and can choose what is right. If this were not so, God would hardly call us to fear and worship Him as Creator (Rev. 14:7).

---

132. Kurt Rudolph, "Gnosticism," *ABD* 2:1033.

Humans are also created as relational or social beings. We relate to other humans. Some are members of Christ's church or the remnant (Rev. 2–3; 12:17). Some maintain a relationship with God and follow the Lamb (Rev. 14:4). In the context of creation and salvation, Revelation ascribes to the redeemed the status of priests and a kingdom (Rev. 1:6; 5:10; 20:6), which clearly contains relational aspects and tasks.

Creation affirms a basic equality among humans. Male and female are both made in the image of God. Creation recognizes no caste, no human hierarchy. Such systems are made by humans to differentiate groups and regulate communal life, oftentimes to the detriment of the weaker ones. Lichtenwalter writes,

> Human equality is assumed and is an essential part of human creation. There is no fundamental difference in the essential nature of races (and genders). Every nation, all tribes, peoples, and tongues, the small and the great, rich and poor, free men and slave are equally within the Apocalypse's field of vision for both redemption and moral accountability (7:9; 11:18; 13:16; 14:6; 19:5, 18; 20:12). Slavery and trafficking in human lives is a reason for divine judgment (18:13).[133]

Human Responsibilities

With all our privileges, humans are responsible for not only our own decisions and behavior (Rev. 2:4, 14–15, 20; 3:15; 9:20–21; 10:10) but also for creation[134]—that is, their treatment of fellow humans. Throughout the book of Revelation, one encounters injustice, persecution, and murder of humans by humans (Rev. 2:10; 6:10; 13:15–17; 17:6). Revelation 18 contains an economic critique of Babylon. God intervenes with His righteous judgments (Rev. 16:5–6; 19:2, 11; 20:12–13).

But followers of Christ have a responsibility for fellow believers (Rev. 3:2) and for nonbelievers. We are witnesses (Rev. 12:11) and proclaimers of the three angels' messages (Rev. 14:6–11), reminding humanity of the Creator God and His claims. Personally, we emulate Christ's lifestyle (Rev. 14:4–5), and as overcomers (Rev. 2:7, 11, 17, 26;

---

133. Lichtenwalter, "Creation and Apocalypse," 134.

134. The last phrase of Revelation 11:18 is frequently quoted to point to an ecological interest of the Apocalypse. But this text should rather be seen in connection with Revelation 19:2, identifying the destroyer of the earth with Babylon. The interest of Revelation is more spiritual than ecological. Cf. Kistemaker, *Revelation*, 345; and Patterson, *Revelation*, 256.

3:5, 12, 21; 21:7) inherit the promised blessings of the new creation.[135] In addition, Stanley notes, "John's imaginative vision not only creates hope but it bestows an obligation upon us to work with God in building just cities while we await the final city symbolized as New Creation."[136]

CREATION AND OTHER THEOLOGICAL TOPICS IN THE APOCALYPSE

Creation is also linked to other theological topics in the book of Revelation, eschatology, the Great Controversy motif, worship, the Sabbath, and ethics.

Creation, Eschatology, and the Great Controversy Motif

John's Apocalypse covers at least the time from the first century AD until the second coming of Christ, as chapters 12–14 indicate. However, there are references to an early time of human history, especially the repeated emphasis on the original creation and the reference to the Fall, followed by the divine promise encapsulated in the proto-gospel. But Revelation also contains a strong emphasis on end-time events. The entire second half of the book deals with these last events of human history. The seven plagues describe the final divine judgments on apostate humanity before the parousia of Christ (Rev. 15–16). The last two plagues are elaborated in Revelation 17–19. Chapter 19 is a portrayal of Armageddon, in which Jesus, as the rider on the white horse, brings to an end the present evil age. The millennium, framed by the first resurrection and the second resurrection,[137] follows chronologically in Revelation 20.[138] It will come to an end with the creation of a new heaven and a new earth.

---

135. Stanley, in "New Creation," explains how, in his opinion, the Christian mandate in view of the new creation should work itself out: "New creation as the people of God involves conquest over sin and sinful social systems such as imperialism, materialism and the religious syncretism" (ibid., 30). "Today Revelation's New Creation calls for a counter-cultural people who commit themselves to the Lamb and conquer through a lifestyle that distances themselves, as far as possible, from the military-industrial complex, from nationalism, from consumerism, and from the religious syncretism which pervades modern life . . . . If John were writing to Christians in the United States he would instruct them not to recite the Pledge of Allegiance to the flag of the United States because Christians are citizens of the kingdom of God more than any nation state. Such behavior, which combines church and state, violates the New Creation" (ibid., 33–34).

136. Ibid., 35.

137. Stevenson, "Theology of Creation," 142, states, "As the story of Christ is incomplete without resurrection, so too is the story of creation incomplete without resurrection."

138. On the millennium, see Ekkehardt Mueller, "Microstructural Analysis of Revelation 20," *AUSS* 37, no. 2 (1999), 227–55; Ekkehardt Mueller, "Basic Questions About the

So Revelation places eschatology in the context of creation. It paints the large picture of human history from creation to re-creation, from Eden lost to Eden regained, providing even vistas into the angelic world. This encompasses the Great Controversy motif.[139] Gorman observes correctly that "Genesis and Revelation constitute the Bible's two bookends, comprising the canon's own alpha and omega. The grand narrative that began with creation now ends in new creation, as promised by the prophets long ago."[140]

But if this is so, creation should be understood in the same way in the beginning as well as in the end. It is the same Creator God engaged in the same initiative. Scripture indicates that both the Genesis creation and the new creation are actual and real creation events executed by the same Creator God. The Genesis creation account makes possible the creation of a new heaven and a new earth. "Creation theology is essential to eschatology. The One who creates is the One who consummates. God will achieve creation's goal."[141]

Creation and Worship

Worship in the context of creation is very clearly expressed in Revelation 4:8–11 and 14:7. It is such an important theme that the central vision of the book, Revelation 12–14, focuses almost exclusively on the issue of false worship versus true worship. True worship has its foundation in the divine act of creation. It is theocentric and Trinitarian. It maintains the tension between God's immanence and His transcendence. It extols the character and nature of God but also praises His works. True worship is universal and all-encompassing. The completion of the plan of salvation with a new heaven and a new earth is situated in a worship setting. Worship is not only due to the Creator God but also benefits the worshiper. It provides a new

---

Millennium" [part 1], *Reflections* (April 2016): 1–9; and Mueller, "Basic Questions About the Millennium, Part 2," 1–6.

139. Moo, "The Sea That is No More," 167, does not mention the Great Controversy motif and yet may reflect elements of it when he writes, "John's intent is to assure the churches that they have not therefore been abandoned to a world of sorrow, pain and mourning. Instead, the triumph of the 'Lamb that was slain' means that the creator's fidelity to his creation—hinted at in the rainbow around the throne, sign of the Noahic covenant—is expressed finally through nothing less than the renewal of the cosmos, an event in which the world is brought beyond any threat of future rebellion or sin."

140. Gorman, *Reading Revelation Responsibly*, 161.

141. Stevens, *Revelation*, 386; and Stevenson, "Theology of Creation," 140, observes, "Revelation is more about creation than it is destruction; or, to put it another way, it is about how an ending leads to a new beginning, how the old gives way to the new."

perspective to life on earth. Worship of the Creator will continue unendingly.[142]

Creation, Sabbath, and Ethics

The first part of the twofold creation account in Genesis climaxes in the Sabbath (Gen. 2:1–3). Sabbath and creation are combined again in the fourth commandment (Exod. 20:8–11). If there is such a close connection between Sabbath and creation, and creation is a major theme in Revelation, which has such a strong emphasis on worship, then one would also expect to find a reflection of the Sabbath in Revelation. Although the Sabbath is not mentioned directly and by name in Revelation, it is found indirectly in the references to keeping the commandments and especially in the description of the Creator God "who made the heaven and the earth and sea and springs of waters" (Rev. 14:7).[143]

There is some recognition that "the commandments" (Rev. 12:17; 14:12) may refer or does refer to the Decalogue,[144] which includes the Sabbath commandment. The fourfold description of the extent of creation is understood as consisting of three major elements. The last one, "sea and springs of waters" (Rev. 14:7), is considered to be one sector of the cosmos.[145] However, such a description of creation is found in Exodus 20:11, the Sabbath commandment, and John seems to allude clearly to this commandment.[146] A number of commentaries avoid discussing Revelation 14:7 at all,[147] while a few look for the Old Testament background and acknowledge a reference to the Sabbath commandment. J. M. Ford sees in Revelation 14:7 a

---

142. See Ekkehardt Mueller, "Reflections on Worship in Revelation 4 and 5," *Reflections* (July 2012), 1–6.

143. See, e.g., Larry Lichtenwalter, "The Seventh-Day Sabbath and Sabbath Theology in the Book of Revelation: Creation, Covenant, Sign," *AUSS* 49, no. 2 (2011): 285–320.

144. Smalley, *Revelation of John*, 334, states, "The allusion here to obeying God's commands probably refers primarily to the ethical demands of the Decalogue, and then to the need in the Johannine community for its members to obey the love command." See also, Aune, *Revelation 6–16*, 709–10; Kistemaker, *Revelation*, 413; and Ekkehardt Müller, *Der Erste und der Letzte: Studien zum Buch der Offenbarung*, Series: Adventistica: Forschungen zur Geschichte und Theologie der Siebenten-Tags-Adventisten 11 (Frankfurt: Peter Lang, 2011), 373.

145. See Aune, *Revelation 6–16*, 828.

146. See John T. Baldwin, "Revelation 14:7: An Angel's Worldview," in *Creation, Catastrophe, & Calvary: Why a Global Flood Is Vital to the Doctrine of Atonement*, ed. John Templeton (Hagerstown, Md.: Review and Herald, 2000), 19–39.

147. E.g., Edmondo F. Lupieri, *A Commentary on the Apocalypse of John* (Grand Rapids, Mich.: Eerdmans, 1999), 223.

reference to Exodus 20:4–5, the second commandment of the Decalogue,[148] and Müller points to God's works of creation by listing, among other texts, Exodus 20:11.[149]

While the twenty-fifth edition of *Novum Testamentum Graece* mentions in its margin Exodus 20:11 as Old Testament background of Revelation 14:7,[150] the twenty-seventh edition uses the parallel text Acts 4:24 and there lists Exodus 20:11.[151] The twenty-eighth edition uses the other parallel in Revelation 10:6 and there states as reference Exodus 20:11.[152] The fourth edition of *The Greek New Testament* also lists Exodus 20:11 as a parallel of Revelation 14:7.[153] So there seems to be a clear recognition that Revelation 14:7 at least alludes to the Sabbath commandment. This fact may inform the interpretation of other texts in Revelation dealing with the day of worship.[154]

Creation theology in Revelation includes the seventh-day Sabbath. Salvation has been attained by Jesus Christ and can never be earned by His disciples. It is a gracious gift of God that can only be accepted by faith. Believers keep His commandments and pursue an ethical lifestyle because they love and follow Him. They live a righteous and holy life (Rev. 22:11) and thus are distinguished from those rejecting the will of God for their lives (Rev. 21:7–8; 22:14–15). And yet keeping the commandments, including the Sabbath, is not only a consequence of the experience of the gift of salvation; it is also a gift in itself, praised throughout Scripture.

CONCLUSION

In this study we have examined Revelation's references and allusions to creation. We found an unexpected number of such allusions, with a heavy emphasis on the original creation as portrayed in Genesis 1 and 2. There was also a mention of Jesus's activity here and

---

148. J. Massyngberde Ford, *Revelation*, AB 38 (New York: Doubleday, 1975), 248.

149. U. B. Müller, *Die Offenbarung des Johannes*, 267.

150. Eberhard Nestle, Erwin Nestle, and Kurt Aland, eds., *Novum Testamentum Graece*, Editio Vicesim Quinta (London: United Bible Societies, 1969), 639.

151. Nestle-Aland, eds., *Novum Testamentum Graece*, Editione Vicesima Septima Revisa (Stuttgart: Deutsche Bibelgesellschaft, 1993), 330, 660.

152. Nestle-Aland, eds., *The Greek English New Testament:* Novum Testamentum Graece English Standard Version, 28th ed. (Wheaton, Ill.: Crossway, 2012), 1514, 1532.

153. Barbara Aland et al., *The Greek New Testament*, 4th ed. (Stuttgart: United Bible Societies, 2001), 863.

154. See Ranko Stefanovic, "'The Lord's Day' of Revelation 1:10 in the Current Debate," *AUSS* 49, no. 2 (2011): 261–84.

now in changing lives, which is described in creation language (Rev. 1:6; 5:10). However, this aspect remains a minor focus in Revelation. Yet a strong emphasis was found on the eschatological new creation, which is described in terms of the creation account of Genesis 1 and 2, reflecting but also surpassing it. Gorman notes regarding the final vision of Revelation, "This vision . . . is the *climax of the book of Revelation, the New Testament, the entire Bible, the whole story of God, and also the story of humanity.*"[155]

So the Genesis creation and the eschatological new creation are linked and invite us to consider the two in tandem. In Revelation both need to be understood as real events and should not be interpreted metaphorically. They provide meaning for human beings, inspiring us with hope and confidence.

The theological significance of the creation motif is considerable. The creation motif makes a substantial contribution to the understanding of the nature of God. That God is the Creator is foundational to His nature. It shows His intentionality in bringing about inanimate objects and various life forms. But the Creator God seeks a relationship with His creation, especially humankind, even though He is not dependent on it. Therefore, He supports and sustains creation, and when through the Fall it went wrong, He moved to bring salvation. Revelation maintains that creation and salvation form an inseparable package that cannot and should not be severed.

The creation motif also helps us understand the nature of human beings and our responsibilities. It highlights the Great Controversy theme. It calls human beings to the worship of God Almighty, and it challenges us, as those who have been saved, to live in a close relationship with our God. That involves justice, righteousness, holiness, an ethical lifestyle, and obedience to the one who has made us and loves us (Rev. 1:4–8).

---

155. Gorman, *Reading Revelation Responsibly*, 163 (emphasis original).

CONCLUSION

Kwabena Donkor, PhD

Biblical Research Institute
Silver Spring, Maryland, USA

A THEOLOGICAL PERSPECTIVE ON CREATION IN THE BIBLE

INTRODUCTION

Evolutionary thought is popular in contemporary culture, making creationism a hot theological topic. The debate between these two ideas is multifaceted, sometimes incorporating scientific and philosophical concepts. Nevertheless, considering the increasing popularity and acceptance of evolutionism, it seems important to enunciate ever more clearly the view of those who still affirm the biblical notion of the fiat creation of the world by a personal God.

Colin Gunton's subtle critique of Christian theology regarding the relation between the eternal and the temporal should be well received. He notes that when it comes to saying something about the relation between that which preceded the created world and that which, in whatever sense, caused it, most theologians have allowed science to make the statement. Then, Gunton observes, "when science apparently requires a deterministic or mechanistic view of the relation between the eternal and the temporal, Christian theology at least is hard pressed to maintain its traditional voice which speaks of the free creation of the world by a personal God."[1]

---

1. Colin E. Gunton, ed., *The Doctrine of Creation: Essays in Dogmatics, History, and Philosophy* (Edinburgh: T&T Clark, 1997), 2.

In these two volumes of *The Genesis Creation Account,* authors have explored various perspectives on creation by the biblical writers. The goal of the present chapter is to systematically express the biblical view of creation. This discussion explores the thesis, based on a high view of Scripture,[2] that the entirety of the Bible presents a common, consistent picture of creation by a personal God. We hope to elucidate this position by looking at the subject of creation in the Bible from the perspective of four key themes: (1) the Bible presents the creation by God as the primordial/temporal origination of all reality in the heavens and the earth; (2) the Bible presents the view that all reality had no material cause but came out of nothing (creation *ex nihilo*); (3) the entirety of the Bible understands all of reality to have come about as a result of the power of God's word; and (4) the Bible understands creation to be willed by God and, therefore, purposeful.

CREATION AS PRIMORDIAL/TEMPORAL ORIGINATION OF ALL REALITY

Several ideas come to mind when we think of biblical creation as a statement about the primordial beginning of everything we know and experience. A first key idea of Genesis 1:1 is that as historical time began there were two realities: God and His creation (affirmed in the New Testament by the term *ta panta*, Eph. 3:9; Rev. 14:11). As for the phenomenological situation *before* creation, which the statement does not address, the implication seems clear that there was God and nothing, where "nothing" had no metaphysical reality of its own, but simply indicates "no reality." Here we are introduced to the notion of *ex nihilo* creation. God's creative act brought into being something other than God—something that, though not coterminous with God, acquired its being from God.[3] Hence the phrase "in the beginning God created" in Genesis 1:1, while denoting origination, discourages a notion of origins whose inner structure would be

---

2. This discussion adopts a high view of Scripture, which rejects the view that Darwin's investigations and other scientific developments (including "scientific" biblical criticism) have called into question the historical and scientific accuracy of the biblical witness.

3. Robert W. Jensen, "Aspects of a Doctrine of Creation," in Gunton, *Doctrine of Creation*, 18–23, expresses the notion of creation as the absolute origination of reality with the following theses: (1) There is indeed reality other than God and it is really other. (2) That there is reality other than God depends entirely on His will. (3) All the above holds precisely in the present tense. The world at any moment would not be had God not willed it to be. (4) The reality other than God has an absolute beginning.

an eternally standing relation with the being of God.[4] The upshot of these observations is that Genesis 1:1 requires an understanding of origins as an absolute historic/temporal beginning that denies mythical interpretation, emanationism, or panentheism.[5] Thus, the suggestion that Genesis 1:1 served a polemic purpose at the time of its composition may today have the same theological significance.[6] Contemporary immanentism, expressed as panentheism and ontological dependence, appears to provide a foil similar to ancient Near Eastern creation mythologies.[7] In drawing these conclusions, we disagree with such sentiments as expressed by Thomas C. Oden, who, while subscribing to the classical consensus that "space and time came into being only with creation," still observes that "the creation narratives do not pretend to describe in empirical detail, objectively, descriptively, or unmetaphorically, the way in which the world came into being; rather they declare the awesome primordial fact that the world is radically dependent on the generosity, wisdom, and help of God, the insurmountable good and powerful One."[8]

The biblical support for the absolute temporal origin of all reality is based on a historical-grammatical reading of the Genesis creation

---

4. Unless otherwise indicated, Scripture quotations in this chapter are from the New American Standard Bible®, Copyright © 1960, 1971, 1977, 1995 by The Lockman Foundation. All rights reserved.

5. Emanationist and panentheistic ideas of creation continue to create theological and philosophical challenges for the discourse on creation because of the classical Christian understanding of the nature of God as being timeless. The timeless presupposition creates what is noted as a "freedom-nature" dilemma in the discourse. Thus, Jürgen Moltmann, for example, does not care much about "process" and the Neoplatonic emanationist views of creation that he also finds in Paul Tillich because, on such views, one is hard pressed to make adequate distinctions between "God's creatures and God's eternal creation of himself." Yet, Moltmann's own move forward out of the freedom-nature dilemma, presumably based on the Jewish Kabbalistic *zinsum* doctrine of divine self-limitation, has been criticized as panentheistic. In the present author's view, while Moltmann seeks to create history in God's reality to make room for a historical creation, he seems to grant *ab intio*, the fact of divine timelessness. For a discussion of these issues, see Alan J. Torrance, "Creatio ex Nihilo and the Spatio-Temporal Dimensions, with Special Reference to Jürgen Moltmann and D. C. Williams," in Gunton, *Doctrine of Creation*, 83–103.

6. See Gerhard F. Hasel, "The Polemic Nature of the Genesis Cosmology," *EvQ* 46 (1974): 81–102; and Gerhard F. Hasel and Michael G. Hasel, "The Unique Cosmology of Genesis 1 against Ancient Near Eastern and Egyptian Parallels," in *The Genesis Creation Account and Its Reverberations in the Old Testament*, ed. Gerald A. Klingbeil (Berrien Springs, Mich.: Andrews University Press, 2015), 9–30.

7. Thus, Ian G. Barbour, *Issues in Science and Religion* (New York: Harper and Row, 1966), 458, who subscribes to a view of ontological dependence of creation, suggests that the notion of creation as absolute beginning must be given up for the idea of creation as absolute dependence, where "God's priority in status can be maintained apart from priority in time."

8. Thomas C. Oden, *Systematic Theology*, vol. 1 of 3, *The Living God* (San Francisco, Calif.: HarperSanFrancisco, 1992), 233.

story, which reverberates throughout the Bible, as shown in an earlier volume, *The Genesis Creation Account and Its Reverberations in the Old Testament.*[9] Critical to the biblical affirmation that reality had an absolute, historical/temporal beginning is the meaning of the opening phrase of Genesis 1:1 either as a distinct, independent sentence or a subordinate clause qualifying the second verse. In the Old Testament volume of *The Genesis Creation Account*, Richard Davidson makes a strong case for reading Genesis 1:1 as an independent statement. The evidence he adduces for this view include the grammar of the verse regarding the use of *běrē'šît*; the syntax of verse 2 regarding the use of the verb; the short stylistic structure of Genesis 1, which a dependent clause reading of verse 1 vitiates;[10] the theological thrust of the creation account to accentuate the transcendence of God, which an independent reading supports; and the witness of ancient versions and witnesses that support the independent clause reading.[11]

Robert Duncan Culver suggests two additional reasons to treat Genesis 1:1 as an independent sentence:[12] First, he notes that liberal modern scholarship is opposed to the idea of revelation to divinely accredited messengers, which predisposes these scholars to assume that the author of Genesis 1–3 shared the view of the ancient Near East that chaotic matter was already present "in the beginning." Then he observes, "This explains why—although most of them acknowledge that verse one may properly be an independent sentence—they prefer to regard it as subordinate to verse 2. This supports their views of the evolutionary origin of cultural ideas."[13]

The biblical notion of creation as absolute historical origination of reality is worth clarifying and emphasizing because of its immense theological significance. First and foremost, it brings to view the fact of the contingency of created reality. Creation's contingency is rooted

---

9. G. Klingbeil, *The Genesis Creation Account and Its Reverberations in the Old Testament*.

10. Cf. C. F. Keil, "Biblical Commentary on the Old Testament," in *Commentary on the Old Testament*, ed. C. F. Keil and F. Delitzsch, vol. 1 of 10, *Pentateuch* (Grand Rapids, Mich.: Eerdmans, 1985), 46, who explains that a dependent clause understanding, by uniting verses 1–3 into one complex thought, would oppose "the simplicity of style which pervades the whole chapter, and to which so involved a sentence would be intolerable, apart altogether from the fact that this construction is invented for the simple purpose of getting rid of the doctrine of a *creatio ex nihilo*, which is so repulsive to modern Pantheism."

11. Richard M. Davidson, "The Genesis Account of Origins," in G. Klingbeil, *The Genesis Creation Account and Its Reverberations in the Old Testament*, 66–69.

12. The following items are from Robert D. Culver, *Systematic Theology: Biblical and Historical* (Geanies House, Fearn: Christian Focus, 2005), 149–50.

13. Ibid., 150.

first in its temporal origination from nothing, and subsequently in its ongoing dependence on God's providence. The biblical idea is therefore correctly expressed in the view that "though the universe has a being and integrity of its own, its contingency indicates that the universe is neither self-sufficient nor self-explanatory nor self-subsisting."[14] In the New Testament, the idea of creation's contingency is explicitly expressed with reference to Christ. "All things came into being through Him, and apart from Him nothing came into being that has come into being" (John 1:3). "In Him all things hold together" (Col. 1:17). He "upholds all things by the word of His power" (Heb. 1:3).

The contingency of creation means that creation is not a necessary phenomenon in the sense that it *had* to be. It answers the perennial question about why there should be a world at all by proposing that God willed the world to be. Creation, then, is an intentional act expressing, "among other things, the unhindered freedom, sovereignty, and graciousness of God."[15] And since contingency has to do with how two things relate to and with one another, the theological significance of the absolute temporal origin and, hence, contingency of creation cannot be overemphasized. Here we bring into focus the relationship of creation to the Creator, showing how the created order is connected with, conditioned by, subject to, and dependent upon God. Biblical theology begins and ends here. Without biblical creation Christian doctrines would cease to make sense. Creation and its contingency set the context within which we can properly speak about humanity, redemption, and indeed all Christian doctrines.

The biblical view of creation's contingency and dependence on God, however, needs clarification. In view are the theological concepts of preservation and providence, but these concepts need to be interpreted biblically. To begin, the creation account makes clear that there was not only a distinct temporal origin of the created order but also a definite completion: "Thus the heavens and the earth were completed, and all their hosts. By the seventh day God completed His work which He had done, and He rested on the seventh day from all His work which He had done" (Gen. 2:1–2). At the same time, the Bible speaks about some continuing creative activities of God (Ps.

14. Paul Copan and William L. Craig, *Creation Out of Nothing: A Biblical, Philosophical, and Scientific Exploration* (Grand Rapids, Mich.: Baker Academic, 2004), 16.
15. Ibid.

104:30; Isa. 65:17). Although the word *bārā'* (normally meaning "create") is used along with other verbs in Psalm 104:29–30, it is important to distinguish the nature of these acts from the primordial creative act in the Genesis narrative. Hence *bārā'* is translated here in the psalm as "renew." In these verses, the main words are "give" (vv. 27–28), "open" (v. 28), "hide" (v. 29), "take" (v. 29), "send" (v. 30), and "renew" (v. 30). These key words show that God's creative work is over, but His sustaining work goes on, supplying the creatures with what they need by simply opening His hand.[16]

Creation, preservation, and providence should not be confused on the basis of some presupposed philosophical commitment. Such seems to be the case with Oden, for example, when he writes, "The very idea of creation implies this paradoxical conjunction: as *divine* activity, creation is *eternally occurring*, transcending all specific times and places; as *temporal* effect, creation has a beginning and an end, however remote."[17] It seems that Oden relies on the Greek philosophical category of eternity to make room for his evolutionary view of reality. Hence he subsequently suggests,

> Classical Christian doctrines of creation do not necessarily deny an evolution, or the possibility of a natural evolutionary development of nature and history. Matter is created *ex nihilo* in a primary sense, radically given by God, but, as emergently developing through secondary causes, that is, through the processes of natural causality. It can undergo its own development. . . . Everything is created out of nothing, but once something is created out of nothing, then something else can be in due time created out of the prevailing and developing conditions. God continues to create something out of all kinds of somethings. One can posit a gradual evolutionary process that is not a denial of creation.[18]

---

16. R. Ellsworth, *Opening up Psalms*, Opening Up Commentary (Leominster: Day One, 2006), 138.

17. Oden, *Systematic Theology*, 1:261, emphasis added.

18. Ibid., 265. Cf. Wolfhart Pannenberg, *Systematic Theology*, trans. G. W. Bromiley, 3 vols. (Grand Rapids, Mich.: Eerdmans, 1994), 2:34, who also writes, "A trinitarian exposition of the concept of creation makes it possible, then, to relate what is said about creation to the totality of the world from the viewpoint of its duration in time. It does not concern merely the world's beginning. To limit it [creation] to the beginning, as the Old Testament stories seem to do in accordance with Near Eastern myths of a primal era, is one sided. Yet what the two Genesis accounts are really seeking to describe is the normative and abiding basis of creaturely reality in the form of depiction of the initial event. Thus preservation goes with creation. Nor are we supposed to view preservation simply as an unchanging conservation of the forms of creaturely existence laid down at the first. It is a living occurrence, continued creation, a constantly new creative fashioning that goes beyond what was given existence originally."

Conjoining the ideas of an eternally occurring creation with a creation that has a beginning and an end, as Oden does, is inconsistent. This is especially the case when the Bible seems to teach clearly that before the beginning of creation there was "nothing."

ALL REALITY HAD NO MATERIAL CAUSE BUT CAME OUT OF NOTHING (*CREATIO EX NIHILO*)

The biblical view of an absolute, temporal beginning of all reality implies the concept of *creatio ex nihilo*. Indeed, one may argue that the biblical doctrine of creation is synonymous with the concept of *creatio ex nihilo*. Thus, the previous points about the absolute, temporal origination of all reality and its dependence on God are equally pertinent to the discussion here for the concept of *creatio ex nihilo*. Yet, as two aspects of creation theology, we could draw a technical distinction between the concepts of absolute, temporal origination and *creatio ex nihilo*. In what might sound like a paradoxical suggestion, we could say that on one hand *creatio ex nihilo* represents the "material" cause of creation in the sense that "out of *no thing*" (to be distinguished from the Greek philosophical concept of "nothingness" [*mē ōn*]) was brought into existence *things* that are recognized in their essential natures throughout and beyond biblical history. On the other hand, the sui generis event of reality's temporal, absolute origination would represent the "formal" cause of biblical creation. In other words, from the biblical perspective, only an event or occurrence whose inner structure has the character or form of "coming into being" can be characterized as creation. However, the event of "coming into being" must be such that prior to the event there was absolutely "no reality."

This material cause of biblical creation, expressed and explained here as *creatio ex nihilo*, has not been clearly embraced always and by all Christians. True, a formal affirmation of the concept of *creatio ex nihilo* is fairly readily discernible. The biblical and theological grounds for the concept seem firmly conclusive, as this two-volume series tries to show. The biblical and theological evidence for creation's absolute temporal origin also applies to the concept of *creatio ex nihilo*. But it is worth mentioning a few of the multiple attestations to this truth from scholars representing a wide spectrum on the theological landscape. Gerhard von Rad says, "It is correct to say that the verb *bārā'*, "create," contains the idea both of complete effortlessness and creation *ex nihilo*, since it is never connected with any statement of the material. The hidden pathos of this statement [Gen. 1:1] is that God is the Lord of the world."[19] In his analysis of Genesis 1, Kenneth Matthews concludes, "The idea of *creatio ex nihilo* is a proper theological inference derived from the whole fabric of the chapter."[20] Concerning the thrust of the Old Testament's understanding of creation, Thomas McComiskey observes,

> The limitation of this word to divine activity indicates that the area of meaning delineated by the root [of *bārā'*] falls outside the sphere of human ability. Since the word never occurs with the object of the material, and since the primary emphasis of the word is on the newness of the created object, the word lends itself well to the concept of creation *ex nihilo*, although that concept is not necessarily inherent within the meaning of the word.[21]

The reverberation of the Old Testament idea in Hebrews 11:3 has been captured by C. F. D. Moule, who states that "the reference seems to be to creation *ex nihilo*, the *visible* having come into being out of the *invisible*."[22] Regarding John 1:3, William Lane Craig writes, "John 1:3 unambiguously states that all things—that is, 'the material world,' came into being through the Word. The implication is that all things (which would include preexistent matter, if that were applicable to the creative process) exist through God's agent, who is the originator of everything. This is borne out by the fact that though the Word *was* (*ēn*), the creation *came to be* (*egeneto*)."[23] Of the New Testament as a whole, Werner Foerster remarks, "Creation out of nothing by the Word explicitly or implicitly underlies the NT statements."[24]

Detraction from these sentiments comes both overtly and covertly. Gerhard May's work appears to be standard for those who explicitly

19. Gerhard von Rad, *Genesis: A Commentary*, trans. John H. Marks (Philadelphia: Westminster, 1961), 47.

20. Kenneth A. Mathews, *Genesis 1–11:26*, NAC 1A (Nashville, Tenn.: Broadman and Holman, 1996), 141.

21. Thomas McComiskey, "*bārā'*," *TDOT* 1:127.

22. C. F. D. Moule, *An Idiom Book of New Testament Greek* (Cambridge: Cambridge University Press, 1968), 168.

23. William Lane Craig, "*Creatio ex nihilo*: A Critique of the Mormon Doctrine of Creation," Reasonable Faith with William Lane Craig, http://www.reasonablefaith.org/creatio-ex-nihilo-a-critique-of-the-mormon-doctrine-of-creation#ixzz3nNRmCmda.

24. Werner Foerster, "*ktizō*," *TDNT* 3:1029.

express the view that the doctrine of *creatio ex nihilo* does not derive from a fair reading of the Bible but that it "was a late second century formulation by Christian theologians responding to Middle Platonic and Gnostic ideas."[25] Mormon theology is similarly explicitly anti-*creatio ex nihilo*: "Latter-Day Saints reject the *ex nihilo* theory of creation. Intelligence and the elements have always existed, co-eternal with God. He is tremendously creative and powerful, but he works with materials not of his own making."[26]

On the other hand, covert diminution of the doctrine of *creatio ex nihilo* appears to stem, in principle, from the detemporalizing of creation. In other words, affirmation of the *creatio ex nihilo* doctrine without the corresponding declaration of creation's absolute temporal origination risks stripping creation of the temporal/historical element, which is critical to the integrity of a truly biblical concept of *creatio ex nihilo*. In modern and contemporary theological thought on creation, such stripping occurs when the temporal origination of creation is neglected in favor of, for example, the idea of the universe's ontological dependence on God. So, while Ian Barbour flatly denies "creation out of nothing" to be a biblical concept, he suggests replacing it with an idea of ontological dependence where "God's priority in status can be maintained apart from priority in time."[27]

Colin Gunton discusses issues connected to this same problem from the perspective of personal agency in creation, the integrity of created reality, and God's relationship to the created world.[28] For Gunton, the issue is one's understanding of causality, his point being that "neither the concept of God as cause nor the attribution of

---

25. Gerhard May, *Creatio ex Nihilo: The Doctrine of "Creation Out of Nothing" in Early Christian Thought*, trans. A. S. Worrall (Edinburgh: University of Edinburgh Press, 1994), discussed in Copan and Craig, *Creation out of Nothing*, 11–13.

26. Lowell Bennion, "A Mormon View of Life," *Dialogue* 24, no. 3 (1991): 60. Craig, "*Creatio ex nihilo*," observes, "Traditionally, Mormonism has held that matter is eternal, and God is (roughly speaking) an Artificer or Shaper or Reorganizer of this eternal matter—or perhaps some semi-substantial *Urstoff* which is neither being nor non-being."

27. Barbour, *Issues in Science and Religion*, 458. Copan and Craig, *Creation out of Nothing*, 10, trace ideas such as expressed by Barbour to Friedrich Schleiermacher. They note that "many thinkers still labor under the influence of Friedrich Schleiermacher, the fountainhead of much of modern theology. He contributed to the eclipse of the doctrine of creation by collapsing the ideas of creation and conservation. The doctrine of creation was de-temporalized by referring to creation as the 'sustaining relation of God to the world, not to his origination of its existence."

28. Colin E. Gunton, "The End of Causality? The Reformers and Their Predecessors," in Gunton, *Doctrine of Creation*, 63–82.

creation to his will prevents theology from lapsing into conceptions of impersonal determinism."[29] Gunton observes that the concept of "causality" is a polymorphic concept with meanings that shade into each other. At one extreme is a notion of causality that clearly involves personal agency. At the other extreme is causality as logical implication. In the latter case, "to cause something is to *entail* it logically."[30] Gunton points out that much of medieval theology's notion of creation by the "will" of God involved ideas that detracted from God's agency in creation in personal terms. He illustrates his point with Augustine of Hippo:

> The most relentless exponent (before Ockham, that is) of the notion of creation by the will of God is Augustine of Hippo. His achievement is crucial for the development of the doctrine of creation and, indeed, of modernity. But, like all of Augustine's legacies, it is ambiguous, and its dubious features are well marked by the fact that later generations found it difficult to maintain an adequately personal conception of divine action in and towards the world. The reason is that although will is an essentially personal concept because it is personal agents who will, it is also one that easily collapses into impersonalism. This is because it can encourage the kind of conception of unmediated divine omnicausality that ultimately undermines rather than establishes the being of that which is willed. God can be conceived to will everything in such a way that the reality of the other is in some way or other imperilled [*sic*].[31]

The significance of Gunton's point for the doctrine of *creatio ex nihilo* emerges in his comparison of William of Ockham with Thomas Aquinas, who stands in the tradition of Augustine:

> So far as differences are concerned, Ockham is far more interested than Aquinas in the doctrine of *creation out of nothing and the distinctive conception of contingency it generates*, one very much derived from a stress on the free willing of the Creator.... The outcome is that, in this case, will has come to predominate over cause, so that causality's tendency to suggest logical links between God and the world is replaced by one suggesting *freely* willed personal creation.[32]

---

29. Ibid., 66.
30. Ibid., 64.
31. Ibid., 65.
32. Ibid., 69, emphasis added.

It is time now to draw out the theological and spiritual implications of this discussion on *creatio ex nihilo*. A clear biblical understanding of this doctrine is important for a proper understanding of the nature of the world's contingent relationship with God. As noted earlier on, from "out of nothing" was brought into existence things that are recognized in their essential natures. To affirm the principle of "out of nothing" creates the intellectual space to affirm "the something" of creation, which ought to be recognized in its essential nature.

Without entering into a detailed discussion of the essential nature of created reality, we should be able to affirm at a minimum that the concept ought to embrace the integrity of the "nature" or "proper substantiality" of the creature.[33] That is, God's relationship to what is "created out of nothing" must be understood in the context of the latter's genuine endowment with God-given autonomy and freedom. It is because God endowed the creation with essential natures that creation and preservation should not be confused in a way that undermines or compromises the integrity of the creature. Expressed differently, the proper affirmation of the absolute temporal origination of reality creates a corresponding proper notion of creation out of nothing, which combines to show that God and the world are related contingently and internally in a way that refutes deism and panentheism. Not only will a true concept of creation "out of nothing" prevent us from attributing eternality to matter and thereby risking falling prey to idolatry—namely, engaging in the false worship of the world itself or of particular things in the world (Exod. 20:3–6; Rom. 1:18–23)—but it will create a true atmosphere within which God's grace and a spirit of gratitude may be cultivated and nourished. In the words of Luther, "For here we may see how the Father has given Himself to us, with all that he has created, and how abundantly he has cared for us in this life."[34]

ALL REALITY CAME INTO BEING BY THE POWER OF GOD'S WORD

The preceding section has drawn some attention to the issue of agency in creation. God as personal Creator is clearly attested in the

---

33. Ibid., 68.

34. Martin Luther, *Luther's Works*, vol. 1, *Lectures on Genesis chapters 1–5*, ed. J. Pelikan (St. Louis, Mo.: Concordia, 1958), 98, quoted in Gunton, *Doctrine of Creation*, 72.

Bible. Here is a sampling of the Old Testament's witness: "You alone are the LORD. You have made the heavens, the heaven of heavens with all their host, the earth and all that is on it, the seas and all that is in them. You give life to all of them and the heavenly host bows down before You" (Neh. 9:6). "Thus says the LORD, your Redeemer, and the one who formed you from the womb, 'I, the LORD, am the maker of all things, stretching out the heavens by Myself and spreading out the earth all alone'" (Isa. 44:24). "Ah LORD GOD! Behold, You have made the heavens and the earth by Your great power and by Your outstretched arm! Nothing is too difficult for You" (Jer. 32:17). Several New Testament texts reflect the Old Testament's viewpoint: "You should turn from these vain things to a living God, WHO MADE THE HEAVEN AND THE EARTH AND THE SEA AND ALL THAT IS IN THEM" (Acts 14:15). "YOU, LORD, IN THE BEGINNING LAID THE FOUNDATION OF THE EARTH, AND THE HEAVENS ARE THE WORKS OF YOUR HANDS" (Heb. 1:10). "By faith we understand that the worlds were prepared by the word of God, so that what is seen was not made out of things which are visible" (Heb. 11:3). "Worthy are You, our Lord and our God, to receive glory and honor and power; for You created all things, and because of Your will they existed, and were created" (Rev. 4:11).

Two interrelated questions are worth pursuing as we try to tease out the biblical idea of a personal God as creation's agency: Who is God, and how did He create? The nature and activity of God are inextricably linked. Richard Davidson deals with the question of who the Bible's Creator God is. He resorts to the two divine names given in the Genesis creation account. First, "in Genesis 1:1–2; 4a, He is ʾĕlōhîm, which is the generic name for God, meaning 'All-powerful One' and emphasizing His transcendence as the universal, cosmic, self-existent, almighty, infinite God."[35] Second, "in the supplementary creation account of Genesis 2:4b–25, another name for the deity is introduced along with ʾĕlōhîm. He is here also YHWH, which is God's covenant name; He is the immanent personal God who enters into intimate relationship with His creatures."[36] Thus, altogether, the Bible's

---

35. Richard M. Davidson, "Genesis Account," 105, remarks that the use of the divine name ʾĕlōhîm here, emphasizing God's transcendence, accords with the "universal framework of the first creation account, in which God is before and above creation and creates effortlessly by His divine Word."

36. See Alexej Muran's discussion of "Who is God?" in "The Creation Theme in Selected Psalms," in G. Klingbeil, *The Genesis Creation Account and Its Reverberations in the Old Testament*, 196–97. See also George J. Zemek, "Grandeur and Grace: God's Transcendence and Immanence in Psalm 113," *MSJ* 1, no. 2 (1990): 133, who writes, "Psalm 113 provides a

Creator God is a transcendent and immanent God. As terms relating to God's relationship with the world, "transcendence" and "immanence" must be interpreted carefully, since they can be used in ways that may not be compatible with the biblical portrayal of God. On the one hand, transcendence in traditional Christian theology has taken different forms, depending on the perspective of God in question—ontological, epistemological, moral, etc. From ontological and epistemological perspectives, Christian tradition has interpreted God's transcendence to mean, among other things, that He "does not have spatial dimensions of location and extension";[37] that He is timeless, meaning "for God there is no past, present and future";[38] and that He is incomprehensible. On the other hand, God's immanence has not received as much attention as His transcendence in the history of Christian thought, being vaguely described as "the presence of God in the world."[39] Indeed, with the Christian doctrine of God, the idea of transcendence, which has always received more emphasis throughout the history of Christian thought, became radicalized.

An accurate view of the biblical idea of transcendence—that "God is separate from and independent of nature and humanity"[40]—is a logical implication of our discussion on both the idea of an absolute temporal origination of reality and the concept of *creatio ex nihilo.* From this perspective biblical transcendence would properly include God's sovereignty, greatness, power, glory, and knowledge, as well as His goodness, holiness, and purity (Isa. 6:1–5; Jer. 10:12–16). All these aspects of God's transcendence become evident in the "how" of His creation. Davidson discusses these elements at length in his characterization of creation as (1) by divine *bārā',* (2) by divine fiat, (3) a polemic, (4) dramatic and aesthetic, and (5) accomplished in the span of six days.[41]

The classical Christian doctrine of God's transcendence, however, seems to go beyond the biblical idea of transcendence. The radicalization of the concept in the history of Christian theology, incorporating

---

natural theological entrance into two corollary truths about God, His transcendence and His immanence."

37. Millard J. Erickson, *Christian Theology* (Grand Rapids, Mich.: Baker, 1990), 313–14.

38. Paul Helm, "Eternal Creation: The Doctrine of the Two Standpoints," in Gunton, *Doctrine of Creation,* 29.

39. Gregory R. Peterson, "Immanence," in *Encyclopedia of Science and Religion,* ed. J. Wentzel van Huyssteen, 2 vols. (New York: Thomson, 2003), 1:450.

40. Erickson, *Christian Theology,* 312.

41. Davidson, "Genesis Account," 107–11.

such Greek philosophical concepts as divine "timelessness" and "simplicity," has significant implications for the nature of God's creative activity. Its consistent application to the Christian doctrine of creation leads to, at a minimum, the concept of an "eternal creation." A timeless God cannot participate in an activity that has the structure of past, present, and future. Paul Helm is forthright on this point: "To say that God exists timelessly, and that he has created the entire material universe, means that for God there is no past, present and future, that he has created the universe *cum tempore*. There was no time when the universe was not."[42] Consequently, Helm is willing to defend the thesis that while a timeless eternal creator does not lead to the "necessary" existence of the universe, it follows that the universe exists "eternally."[43]

Colin Gunton contradicts Helm's thesis on the universe's necessary existence. Gunton argues from the viewpoint of causality via creation by or through God's will.[44] On his part, he defends the thesis that "the assertion of divine willing alone is not adequate to escape a tendency to necessitarianism."[45] For Gunton, to conceive of God as the "cause" of creation or to attribute creation to His will does not prevent "theology from lapsing into conceptions of impersonal determinism."[46] In his view, the medieval theologians of the Christian church construed divine causality in abstraction and made God's creation by His will succumb to this abstraction. This move ties the creation so closely to God that the creation seems to be an extension of Him. Gunton also sees these tendencies in Thomas Aquinas. When Aquinas refuses to assign to God a purpose for creating but says only that in the creation God was completing His goodness and when he denies that creation puts a reality in the creature except as a relation, the substantiality of the creature is compromised and makes creation seem a necessary extension of God.[47] This close connection between

---

42. Helm, "Eternal Creation," 29.

43. Ibid., 30.

44. Gunton, "End of Causality?," 65.

45. Ibid., 74. Gunton reflects on Revelation 4:11: "Worthy are You, our Lord and our God, to receive glory and honor and power; for You created all things, and because of Your will they existed, and were created." He considers the "will" of God and suggests that like "cause" in the history of Christian thought, it is also problematic. He shows that in Augustine, "will" easily collapses into impersonalism (ibid., 65).

46. Ibid., 66.

47. Ibid., 67–68. In Aquinas's *Summa Theologiae* 44.4, he suggests that to think of God as having a purpose for the creation would lead to the conclusion that there was a need in God that the creation fulfilled: "Every agent acts for an end: otherwise one thing would not follow

God and the creation, occasioned by the impact of Greek notions on the Christian concept of God and His relation to the world, is what suggests creation's "necessitarianism" in the classical tradition. Such conceptions of God and His creative activity carry an implicit negation of a truly biblical notion of *creatio ex nihilo*.

While for the greater part of Christian history a concept of God's transcendence contrary to the Bible has been held, contemporary Christian theology has gone in the opposite direction of promoting an unbiblical notion of God's immanence.[48] As with God's transcendence, our interest in the subject of immanence is because of its implications for the nature of the Creator God and His creative activity. Immanence as "God's presence and activity within nature, human nature, and history"[49] receives its truest interpretation within the framework of the concepts of temporal absolute origination of creation and *creatio ex nihilo*. Here it may be worth repeating the comment earlier regarding the creation's contingency: that a proper affirmation of the absolute temporal origination of reality creates a corresponding proper notion of creation out of nothing, which combine to show that God and the world are related contingently and internally in a way that negates deism and panentheism. Perhaps the Bible's notion of God's immanence is best expressed by what has been described as metaphors of governance and sustenance.[50] Metaphors of governance include Yahweh as Judge (Ps. 99:4; Isa. 61:8), King (Pss. 29:10; 96:10; Mark 1:15), Warrior (Exod. 15:1–18; Deut. 1:30), and Father (Exod.

---

more than another from the action of the agent, unless it were by chance. Now the end of the agent and of the patient considered as such is the same, but in a different way respectively. For the impression which the agent intends to produce, and which the patient intends to receive, are one and the same. Some things, however, are both agent and patient at the same time: these are imperfect agents, and to these it belongs to intend, even while acting, the acquisition of something. But it does not belong to the First Agent, Who is agent only, to act for the acquisition of some end; He intends only to communicate His perfection, which is His goodness; while every creature intends to acquire its own perfection, which is the likeness of the divine perfection and goodness. Therefore the divine goodness is the end of all things." In 45.3 he says, "Creation places something in the thing created according to *relation only*; because what is created, is not made by movement, or by change. For what is made by movement or by change is made from something pre-existing. And this happens, indeed, in the particular productions of some beings, but cannot happen in the production of all being by the cause of all beings, which is God. Hence God produces things without movement. Now when movement is removed from, *only relation remains*" (emphasis added).

48. Stanley Grenz and Roger Olson, *20th Century Theology: God and the World in a Transitional Age* (Downers Grove, Ill.: InterVarsity, 1992), 15.

49. Erickson, *Christian Theology*, 329.

50. Veli-Matti Karkkainen, *The Doctrine of God: A Global Introduction* (Grand Rapids, Mich.: Baker Academic, 2004), 27–30.

4:22; Hos. 11:1; Rom. 8:15–16; Gal. 4:6). Metaphors of sustenance include Yahweh as Healer (Exod. 15:26; Jer. 30:17), Gardener (Num. 24:6; Isa. 5:7), Mother (Isa. 49:15–16; 66:13), and Shepherd (Ps. 23).[51] It seems quite clear that these biblical metaphors of God's immanence do not confuse God with the creation.

Contemporary theological thought shows a decided inclination toward an immanent view of God that is quite different from the one just depicted. Much of the current state of affairs is a consequence of the European Enlightenment. Stanley Grenz and Roger Olson show quite convincingly that the history of the Christian doctrine of God since the Enlightenment has been a struggle to reconstruct the shattered classical Christian balance of transcendence and immanence.[52] However, these authors correctly detect that "despite the gallant efforts of its gifted thinkers, as the century moved toward its close theology discovered that it had not overcome the Enlightenment. The emphasis on the *new immanence*, so much a part of the human vision since the Renaissance, continued to lie at the foundation of theology's reconstructed house" (emphasis added).[53] This new immanence, which continues to dog theology's reconstructed house, is panentheistic in nature. From Immanuel Kant's grounding of religion in morality, to Friedrich Hegel's speculative rationalism of Spirit and dialectic, to Friedrich Schleiermacher's intuitive approach and the feeling of absolute dependence on the whole of reality, the path has been slipping toward anthropocentrism. After Schleiermacher, who has been called the father of modern theology, the floodgates seemed to have opened toward a panentheistic view of God. According to Stanley Grenz and Roger Olson, Schleiermacher himself "considered the whole notion of the supernatural to be dangerous. To him it conflicted with the proper God-consciousness of Christians. The supernatural implied that God stands over against the world, and that God and creation relate to each other through relative independence. Christian piety, in contrast, senses God as the absolute infinite power upon which everything finite is utterly dependent and which is itself absolutely nondependent."[54] The flowering of these tendencies is seen, for example, in Jürgen Moltmann, who, while influential in

---

51. Ibid.
52. Grenz and Olson, *20th Century Theology*.
53. Ibid., 25.
54. Ibid., 48.

seeking to restore a biblical doctrine of the Trinity, falls prey to a "Trinitarian panentheism" in his doctrine of creation. "Creation is a fruit of God's longing for his Other and for the Other's free response to the divine love. That is why the idea of the world is inherent in the nature of God himself from eternity."[55] Moltmann's view is that given the nature of the being of God, before He could create anything finite outside of Himself, He had to make room by withdrawing from within Himself for the *nihil* ("finitude"), out of which God created. John W. Cooper mentions several contemporary experts in scientific cosmology, including Ian Barbour, Paul Davies, Arthur Peacocke, Philip Clayton, and John Polkinghorne, and adds, "All affirm the contemporary scientific world picture that the universe is an evolving system of increasingly complex systems and modes of existence. They argue that this world picture points to God and panentheism is the most reasonable synthesis of science and theology."[56]

It is significant to note that unbiblical notions of both transcendence and immanence have one thing in common: the tendency toward monism. And when these unbiblical ideas are applied to God's relationship to the created world, they yield results that are difficult to reconcile with biblical characterizations. Transcendent monism fashions God's relationship to the world after the order of Neoplatonism and makes God's relationship to the world unreal by absorbing the world into God. On the other hand, monism that has an immanent viewpoint compromises the reality of the biblical Creator God by absorbing divinity into nature, as in pantheistic ideologies. In this sense, theology's panentheism could be viewed as a form of monism insofar as the basis of all reality, including God, is reduced to the metaphysical category of "actual entity," of which God is "their chief exemplification."[57]

In the context of contemporary monistic tendencies, intimations of the Trinitarian nature of the Creator God in the Genesis creation account stand in rather striking relief. Davidson observes,

---

55. Jürgen Moltmann, *Trinity and the Kingdom of God: The Doctrine of God* (London: SCM, 1981), 138.

56. John W. Cooper, *Panentheism: The Other God of the Philosophers* (Grand Rapids, Mich.: Baker Academic, 2006), 25–26.

57. Karkkainen, *Doctrine of God*, 181. The same may be said of what is characterized as a new, moderate kind of "dual-aspect monism," called for by people such as British scientist-theologian John C. Polkinghorne, *The Faith of a Physicist: Reflections of a Bottom-Up Thinker* (Minneapolis, Minn.: Fortress, 1996), 21, who is not a monist nor a pantheist but rather a panentheist.

There are intimations of the plurality in the Godhead in creation, with mention of the "Spirit of God" (*rûaḥ 'ĕlōhim*) in Genesis 1:2; the creative Word throughout the creation account (ten times in Gen. 1); and the "let us" of Genesis 1:26, most probably is "a plural of fullness," implying "within the divine Being the distinction of personalities, a plurality within the deity, 'a unanimity of intention and plan' . . . ; [the] germinal idea . . . [of] intra-divine deliberation among 'persons' within the divine Being."[58]

The idea of plurality in God, evident in the Genesis creation account, is pertinent to the account of origins not simply as an identity marker of who the Creator God is. The idea is important for a correct understanding of creation and the Creator-creature relationship. In his critique of Aquinas's theology of creation and its tendency to lapse into impersonal determinism, Gunton observes,

> If we begin with Aquinas, we must emphasize that it is not the case that either personal or trinitarianly conceived agency in creation is completely lacking from his thought; he is in the tradition of Augustine in teaching that creation is the outcome of the free, personal willing of the Creator. The problem is that the act of willing is rather monistically conceived. The Trinity plays little or no constitutive part in his treatment of the divine realization of creation.[59]

For Gunton, the crucial issue lacking in medieval theologies of creation was a principle of mediation,[60] and he applauds the Reformers for supplying the doctrine of the Trinity as a needed corrective. Of Luther he notes, "Recognizing the concepts of mediation in the chapter [Gen. 1] Luther reaffirms that which was scarcely of interest to Aquinas, that God created heaven and earth out of nothing. He can do this because he sees it to take place through the work of the Son, who adorns and separates the crude mass which was brought out of nothing; and the Spirit, who makes alive."[61]

---

58. Davidson, "Genesis Account," 106, including at the end a quotation from Gerhard F. Hasel, "The Meaning of 'Let Us' in Gen 1:26," *AUSS* 13 (1975), 65.

59. Gunton, "End of Causality?," 67.

60. It would seem that philosophically, when God is conceived monistically in any form, the necessary result, as far as God's actions and His relations to those actions are concerned, would be at least one of three forms: emanationism, pantheism, and panentheism. This will be the case because monism as such lacks any mediation between the acting "subject" and the object of those acts.

61. Gunton, "End of Causality?," 71.

THE BIBLE TEACHES THE CREATION
BY GOD TO BE PURPOSEFUL

Theological reflection on the purposefulness of creation should begin by taking into account the nature and manner of its origination as well as the agency by which it came to be and continues to subsist. It has been rightly observed that "the beginning determines the end. Etiology determines teleology. . . . What the universe is derived 'out of' determines the purpose that it proceeds 'unto.' The *ek* determines the *eis*. If you know where it comes from, you can know where its [*sic*] going."[62] These issues have already been covered in this discussion, and we will now show how they inform the purposefulness of creation.

It is clear that biblical creation is creation by fiat. A personal God spoke a word of command, and the result was the absolute temporal origination of phenomena that were *really* other than God and not coterminous with Him. These phenomena acquired their being from God but out of nothing. In the constitution of these created things, the divine word repeatedly affirmed alternately, "God said" "and it was good." Here is implied the purposeful act of the Creator. Robert Jensen observes that in the Genesis story "the 'and it was good' belongs to the creative act itself: things are good in that they are judged good by God. *Tov* in Hebrew works just like 'good' in English: it says 'good *for*' something. Things are good in that God judges that they are good for His purposes."[63] The case for the creation's purposiveness and intentionality may be strengthened by considering the creation metaphor of the "potter," as employed in Isaiah 45:9. The idea of this metaphor is that the "clay protests the potter's *intentions*."[64] The point is simply that the Creator has constituted the

62. James A. Fowler, "The Teleology of Creation," Christ in You Ministries, http://www.christinyou.net/pages/creattele.html.

63. Jensen, "Doctrine of Creation," 22. The sense of purposefulness is heightened further with a careful consideration of the Hebrew word *tov*. Jacques Doukhan, "When Death Was Not Yet," in G. Klingbeil, *Genesis Creation Account*, 331–32, demonstrates that the word's meaning goes beyond the idea of function to include aesthetic beauty. He notes furthermore that "the word may also have an ethical connotation (1 Sam. 18:5; 29:6, 9; 2 Sam. 3:36)—a sense that is also attested in our context of the creation story, especially in God's recognition: 'It is not good that man should be alone.' This divine statement clearly implies a relational dimension, including ethics, aesthetics, and even love and emotional happiness." It is difficult to escape the sense of intentionality and purposiveness in a creation that envisions not only the good in a functional sense but also beauty and happiness.

64. John D. W. Watts, *Isaiah 34–66*, WBC 25 (Waco, Tex.: Word, 1987), 157, emphasis added.

creation purposefully, for good and beauty. The phenomena of creation are good and beautiful because they have been configured to be so. "For what occurs in creation is spatio-temporal and material conditions without which there is no finite existence—without which there is nothing rather than something. Furthermore, what occurs is a certain order of spatio-temporality and materiality which allows for certain things to emerge—'these' with their spatio-temporality and materiality rather than 'those.'"[65]

It seems clear that a good and beautiful creation implies intentionality and purposefulness. But what is it good for? For what good did God create? The concepts of the absolute temporal origination of reality and *creatio ex nihilo* rule out any suggestion of necessity in creation or that God created in order to be fulfilled or perfected. Colossians 1:16 may be a helpful reference point for reflection on these questions. Keeping in mind the divinity of Christ, clearly expressed in the book (Col. 2:9), the passage suggests that "it is *through* him, as the *Agent* in creation, and *with a view to* him or *for* him as creation's *Goal* that they owe their settled state. All creatures, without any exception whatsoever, must contribute glory to Him and serve His purpose."[66] But Colossians shows us that God Himself is the purpose of creation. There seems to be no greater objective for God in creation than to manifest Himself. And His all-glorious character expressed through His creation glorifies Him. Ultimately, the goodness and beauty of the creation is for the purpose of glorifying God. This purpose holds true for all creation, but more so for humans. Hence God, through Isaiah, speaks in reference to "everyone . . . whom I have created for My glory" (Isa. 43:7).[67]

---

65. Daniel W. Hardy, "Creation and Eschatology," in Gunton, *Doctrine of Creation*, 116.

66. W. Hendriksen and S. J. Kistemaker, *Exposition of Colossians and Philemon*, Baker New Testament Commentary 6 (Grand Rapids, Mich.: Baker, 2001), 73.

67. Ellen G. White, *Education* (Mountain View, Calif.: Pacific Press, 1952), 15, states, "When Adam came from the Creator's hand, he bore, in his physical, mental, and spiritual nature, a likeness to his Maker. 'God created man in His own image' (Genesis 1:27), and it was His purpose that the longer man lived the more fully he should reveal this image—the more fully reflect the glory of the Creator. All his faculties were capable of development; their capacity and vigor were continually to increase. Vast was the scope offered for their exercise, glorious the field opened to their research. The mysteries of the visible universe—the 'wondrous works of Him which is perfect in knowledge' (Job 37:16)—invited man's study. Face-to-face, heart-to-heart communion with his Maker was his high privilege. Had he remained loyal to God, all this would have been his forever. Throughout eternal ages he would have continued to gain new treasures of knowledge, to discover fresh springs of happiness, and to obtain clearer and yet clearer conceptions of the wisdom, the power, and the

The frequent placement of creation within the context of praise in the Bible bears out the connection between creation and God's glory made above. It has been noted that "the praise of God is the central reason for the creation theme in the book of Psalms" and "some scholars argue that outside Genesis 1 and 2, creation appears in the setting of praise."[68] Psalm 148 is particularly significant in calling all creation, not just humans, to praise. This universal call for all creation to praise is significant because it is consistent with the view that all creation exists for the purpose of glorying God: "The heavens are telling of the glory of God; And their expanse is declaring the work of His hands" (Ps. 19:1). In Revelation 4:11, when the 24 elders join in the song of the four living creatures, "the content of the song was new, a song in praise of God as Creator."[69]

The connection between creation and praise in the Bible places a responsibility on the creation to worship God. Yet, it is important to point out that the glory with which the creatures glorify God is His own glory. "It is not any alleged self-generated actions or 'works' of man that glorify God, but only His action of expressing His own character in the actions of man unto His own glory. 'I am the LORD, that is My Name; I will not give My glory to another' (Isa 42:8). 'My glory I will not give to another' (Isa 48:11). Glorification, the ongoing purpose of creation, requires the ontological presence of God, His being expressing His character."[70]

Nevertheless, the responsibility remains for all creation to worship and glorify the Creator. Thus, Revelation 14:7, besides calling attention to God as Creator, enjoins worshiping Him as Creator. The question is appropriately asked: how else is the creation "to respond to the Trinitarian God in whose giving is their beginning, sustenance and end?"[71] It is significant that Christ enters the creation not only as its Originator but also as its Redeemer. By His incarnate life, death, and resurrection He brings about a spiritual "new creation" (Gal. 6:15) whereby humans become "new creature[s]" (2 Cor. 5:17) through the reception of the Spirit of Christ in faith. Indeed, the new creation through Christ touches the whole creation (Rom. 8:20–22).

---

love of God. More and more fully would he have fulfilled the object of his creation, more and more fully have reflected the Creator's glory."

68. Muran, "Creation Theme," 191.

69. William H. Shea, "Creation," in *HSDAT*, 439.

70. Fowler, "The Teleology of Creation."

71. Hardy, "Creation and Eschatology," 127.

These reflections suggest a close link between creation and eschatology—more specifically, creation and judgment.[72] In his analysis of creation in the book of Amos, Martin Klingbeil writes about the apparent contradiction where "what starts as a hymn of praise for YHWH the Creator becomes a threatening description of YHWH the Judge."[73] The apparent contradiction disappears in view of the theological connection between creation and human responsibility, creation and eschatology, creation and judgment. Humanity, like the rest of creation, is configured and fitted for worship, and neglect precipitates judgment: "Fear God, and give Him glory, because the hour of His judgment has come; worship Him who made the heaven and the earth and sea and springs of waters . . . . If anyone worships the beast and his image, and receives a mark on his forehead or on his hand, he also will drink of the wine of the wrath of God" (Rev. 14:7, 9–10). Worship and creation go hand-in-hand. It is an acknowledgment, in praise, aroused by an appreciation of the profundity of the gift of creation in its goodness, beauty, and glory.[74]

CONCLUSION

In the conflict between creation and evolution, there is sometimes a tendency to limit one's attention to the agency by which reality came into existence. Among some believers the issue becomes as simple as whether human beings are the product of evolution or personal creation by God. The theme of creation in the Bible, however, is much broader than simply answering the question of how the world came into being. We have tried to explore the breadth and depth of the theme of creation in the Bible by reflecting on the theological ramifications of four simple facts of creation in the Bible: creation in the Bible means that (1) all reality had an absolute temporal/historical beginning; (2) before creation only God existed, thus the creation was not dependent on any preexisting thing; (3) all reality came into being by the word/command of a personal God; and (4) created reality is constituted purposefully. Our reflections demonstrate the integrity of the creation in its complex relation to the Creator. The

---

72. See Laszlo Gallusz, "Radically New Beginning, Radically New End: Creation and Eschatology in the New Testament," 135, in this volume.

73. Martin Klingbeil, "Creation in the Prophetic Literature of the Old Testament," in G. Klingbeil, *Genesis Creation Account*, 270–71.

74. Hardy, "Creation and Eschatology," 127.

Creator is both transcendent and immanent, while the creation is at the same time autonomous (God-given freedom) and dependent. Issues that go to the heart of Christian doctrines arise in the context of this intricate relationship. The doctrine of creation is the grounding doctrine of all Christian thought. In particular, we have noted that creation and judgment/eschatology go hand-in-hand because of the responsibility of worship and praise that the giftedness, goodness, and beauty of creation evokes. The relationships noted among creation, worship/praise, and judgment/eschatology show the importance of paying close attention to these issues today.

APPENDIX
SUPPLEMENTAL MATERIAL FOR CHAPTER 3 BY JAN A. SIGVARTSEN

The first two tables below provide a list of references to Genesis 1–3 appearing in Philo, Josephus, the Apocrypha, and the Pseudepigrapha. Table 1 presents the references according to the creation days of the cosmogony narrative (Gen. 1:1—2:4a), while Table 2 follows the major themes of the Eden narrative (Gen. 2:4b—3:24). Although these two tables are comprehensive in nature, the author does not claim they are exhaustive, as the main objective when creating these lists was to identify clear and distinct references and allusions to the Genesis creation accounts used within the context of the creation, and not echoes of creation language in general. Moreover, the primary focus of this study is on the creation narratives and how they were used, understood, and expanded upon during the Second Temple period and the implications this may have had for New Testament scholarship. The eschatological use of the creation language is a part of a much larger study currently being conducted by the author. Table 3 presents parallels to the Genesis creation account in Second Temple literature. Table 4 presents locations of the phrase the "Lord [God] of Hosts" in the Prophets and Writings.

Table 1: The Cosmogony Narrative (Genesis 1:1–2:4a)

Genesis	Philo	Josephus	Apocrypha/Pseudepigrapha
1:1–2 Introduction	*Somn.* 1.13 §76 *Ebr.* 8 §30 *Leg.* 1.21–24, 43 *Opif.* §§7–15a, 129–30, 170–71 *Spec.* 4 §187 *Virt.* §62	*Ant.* 1.1 §27	*Bar.* 3:32—4:4; 4 Ezra 6:1, 4, 38–39; 16:15; Add. Esth. 13:10; 2 *Macc.* 7:28; Sir. 16:24–30; 18:1; 24:9–10; Wis. 7:12; 8:3–4; 9:8–9; 11:17, 24–25; *1 En.* 48:2–3, 6; 62:7; 2 En. 24:2—26:3; 65:1; 3 En. 23:1; 26:9; Sib. Or. 1.5; 2 Bar. 4:3; 48:7–10; T. Mos. 1:12, 14; Jub. 2:1; 12:19; Jos. Asen. 12:1–2; LAB 28:4; Pr. Man. 2; Hel. Syn. Pr. 3:1; 5:1; 12:25; Pr. Jos. A2–3; Aristob. Frag. 5:9–11
1:3–5 Day 1	*Somn.* 1.13 §75 *Her.* 163 *Opif.* §§15b–35, 55 *Praem.* 45–46 *Spec.* 2.59	*Ant.* 1.1 §§27–29	4 Ezra 6:40; Jdt. 16:14; 2 En. 27:1–4; Jub. 2:2–3; Aristob. Frag. 4:3–4; 5:9
1:6–8 Day 2	*Opif.* §§36–37	*Ant.* 1.1 §30	4 Ezra 6:4, 41; 16:59; 1 En. 18:1–2; 2 En. 28:1–5; 29:1–6; 3 En. 42:1; 2 Bar. 14:17; 21:4–8; 3 Bar. 2:1; T. Adam 1:5; Jub. 2:4; Pr. Man. 3; Hel. Syn. Pr. 3:2–4; Odes Sol. 16:10–11
1:9–13 Day 3	*Opif.* §§38–44 *Spec.* 2.151 *QG* 2.47, 66	*Ant.* 1.1 §31a	4 Ezra 4:19; 6:42–44; 2 En. 28:1–2; 30:1–2; Jub. 2:5–7; Hel. Syn. Pr. 3:8–12; 15:3–5

Genesis	Philo	Josephus	Apocrypha/Pseudepigrapha
1:14–19 Day 4	*Opif.* §§45–61 *Plant.* §118	*Ant.* 1.1 §31b	4 Ezra 6:45–46; Sir. 43:1–10; Wis. 13:2–5; 1 En. 18:4; 2 En. 30:2–7; 40:6; 65:3–4; 3 En. 26:4, 6; 3 Bar. 9:6–7; Apoc. Adam 5:10; 7:41; Jub. 2:8–10; Hel. Syn. Pr. 3:5–7; Odes Sol. 16:11, 15–16; Aristob. Frag. 5:12
1:20–23 Day 5	*Opif.* §§62–63	*Ant.* 1.1 §32a	4 Ezra 6:47–52; Pr. Azar. 57–58; Sir. 43:25; Wis. 9:1–3; 2 En. 30:7; Sib. Or. 1.5–47; Frag. 3:7, 9; T. Ash. 7:3; Jub. 2:11–12; Jos. Asen. 12:11; Hel. Syn. Pr. 3:11
1:24–31 Day 6	*Conf.* 168–83 *Det.* 79–90 *Somn.* 1.13 §74 *Fug.* 68–72 *Mos.* 2:65 *Mut.* 30–32 *Opif.* §§64–88, 134 *QG* 1.54; 2.56	*Ant.* 1.1 §32b *Ag. Ap.* 2:192	1 Esd. 4:2; 4 Ezra 3:4; 6:53–59; 7:11; 8:44; Sir. 15:14; 16:26–30; 17:1–11; 23:20; 33:10; 39:16, 33; 49:16; Wis. 1:14; 2:23; 9:1–3; 10:1–2; 2 En. 30:8–12; 31:3; 44:1; 58:3; 65:2; 3 En. 48C:1; 48D:8; Sib. Or. 1.23, 57; 8.265–68, 402; Frag. 3.12; 2 Bar. 14:18; T. Naph. 2:5–10; T. Mos. 1:12; Jub. 2:13–16; 3:8; LAE 4:1–3; 13:2–16:1; Hel. Syn. Pr. 3:19
2:1–3 Day 7	*Leg.* 1 §§1–18 *Opif.* §§89–128 *Post.* 64	*Ant.* 1.1 §33	Sir. 33:9; 2 En.]32:2; Jub. 2:16–22; Pr. Man. 2; Hel. Syn. Pr. 5:1–3; Odes Sol. 16:12; Aristob. Frag. 5
2:4a Conclusion	*Leg.* 1 §19 *Post.* 65	*Ant.* 1.1 §33	Jub. 2:23–33

Table 2: The Eden Narrative (Genesis 2:4b–3:24)

Genesis	Philo	Josephus	Apocrypha/Pseudepigrapha
2:4b–6 Introduction	Leg. 1 §§19–30; Opif. §§129–33; QG 1.1–3; 2.67	Ant. 1.1 §34a	Jub. 3:1a
2:7 Creation of Adam	Det. 80–86; Leg. 1 §§31–42; Opif. §§134–47; Plant. 18–20; QG 1.4–5, 8; 2.56; Spec. 4.123; Virt. §§203–4	Ant. 1.1 §34b	2 Macc. 7:22–23; 4 Ezra 3:4–6; 16:61; Sir. 33:10; Tob. 8:6; Wis. 7:1; 15:11; 2 En. 30:13–14; Apoc. Adam 1:2–3; 2:5; T. Isaac 3:15; Apoc. Mos. 40.6; LAE 13:1–3a; Hel. Syn. Pr. 3:20–21; 12:37–40
2:8–15 Creation of Garden	Leg. 1 §§43–89; Migr. 37; Opif. §§153–55a; Plant. §§32–45; QG 1.6–15	Ant. 1.1 §§37–39	Sir. 24:26–27; 1 En. 25:4; 32:2–3; 70:3; 77:4; 2 En. 8:2; 31:1; 42:3; 3 En. 5:5; 48D:8; Gk. Apoc. Ezra 2:10–11; 5:20–21; 3 Bar. 4:7; T. Ab. (A) 11:1; T. Levi 18:10–11; Jub. 3:9–12, 15–16; 8:16; Apoc. Mos. 15:1–3; 17:3; LAB 13:10; Hel. Syn. Pr. 12:41; 4 Ezra 2:12; 4:7–8; 7:36, 123; 8:52; 1 En. 24:3–4; 25:4–5; 32:3–6; 2 En. 8:1—9:1; 42:3; 65:10; 2 Bar. 4:6; 51:7–11; Apoc. Sedr. 12:2; 16:6; Apoc. Ab. 21:3, 6; Apoc. El. 5:5–6; T. Levi 18:10; T. Dan 5:12; T. Ab. (A) 11:1, 10; Jub. 4:26; Apoc. Mos. 28:4; 29:6; 37:5 [cf. 40:1–2; 41:1–3]; LAE 25:3; 42:4; Pss. Sol. 14:3–4; Odes Sol. 11:18–19]
2:16–17 First Commandment	Leg. 1 §§90–108; QG 1.15–16; Virt. §205	Ant. 1.1 §40	4 Ezra 3:7a; Sir. 15:14; 17:11; 25:24; Wis. 1:13; 2:23–24; 2 En. 30:15–16; Sib. Or. 1.38–39, 45; Apoc. Sedr. 4:4; Apoc. Mos. 7:1; Jub. 4:29–30; LAE 32:1; Hel. Syn. Pr. 12:43–45

Genesis	Philo	Josephus	Apocrypha/Pseudepigrapha
2:18 Creation of Woman: Part 1	Leg. 2 §§1–18 QG 1.17		Sir. 36:29; Tob. 8:6–7; Wis. 10:1
2:19a Creation of Animals	QG 1.18–19	Ant. 1.1 §35a	2 En. 58:1; 3 En. 45:3
2:19b–20 Naming of Animals	Leg. 2 §§14–18 Mut. 63 Opif. §§148–50 QG 1.20–23	Ant. 1.1 §35a	2 En. 58:2–3; Wis. 10:2; Jub. 3:1b–3
2:21–23 Creation of Woman: Part 2	Cher. 60 Her. 257 Leg. 2 §§19–48 Opif. §§151–52 Post. 33 QG 1.24–28	Ant. 1.1 §§35b–36	4 Macc. 18:7; Tob. 8:6; 2 En. 30:17; Sib. Or. 1.28–37; Apoc. Adam 1:4; 2:2; Jub. 3:4–6, 8 [Apoc. Mos. 29:9a–b]; LAE 3:3
2:24 Marriage	Leg. 2 §§49–52 QG 1.29		1 Esd. 4:20, 25; 4 Ezra 4:20–21; Jub. 3:7; LAE 3:3
2:25 Conclusion	Leg. 2 §§53–70 QG 1.30		Sir. 6:29–31; 17:1–6; 40:27; 49:16; Jub. 3:8–16; Apoc. Mos. 20:1–2; 3 Bar. 4:16; Hist. Rech. 12:3

Genesis	Philo	Josephus	Apocrypha/Pseudepigrapha
3:1–5 Temptation	*Agr.* 94–101; *Leg.* 2 §§71–108; *Opif.* §§156a, 157–66; *QG* 1.31–36	*Ant.* 1.1 §§40–43a	Wis. 2:24; 4 Macc. 18:7–8; 1 En. 69:6; 2 En. 29:4; 31:3–6; Sib. Or. 1.39–41; 8.261; Apoc. Ab. 23:1; Gk. Apoc. Ezra 2:16; Apoc. Sedr. 4:5; 5:1; 3 Bar. 4:8, 13; 9:7; Jub. 3:17–19; Apoc. Mos. 16:4; 17:4; LAE 12:1; 13:2–3; 14:1–3; 15:1—19:2
3:6–7 The Fall	*Leg.* 2 §§53, 64; 3 §§1–48; *Opif.* §§152, 156b, 165–66; *QG* 1.37–40, 45; *Virt.* §205	*Ant.* 1.1 §§43b–44	4 Ezra 3:7b, 21–22; 4:30–32; 7:11a, 48, 117–18, 127–28; 4 Macc. 18:8; Sir. 15:14–17; 25:24; Wis. 1:13; 2:23–24; 1 En. 32:6; 69:11; 2 En. 29:3; 30:15–17; 31:6; Sib. Or. 1.40–49; Gk. Apoc. Ezra 2:12–16; 2 Bar. 17:2–3; 23:4; 48:42–43; 54:15–19; 56:6; Apoc. Adam 1:4–12; 2:8; Jub. 3:20–22; Apoc. Mos. 7:2–3; 10:2; 14:2, 4; 19:1—21:6; LAE 3:2; 33:2–3; 37:2; 44:2–5; LAB 13:10; Hel. Syn. Pr. 3:24a; 12:46
3:8–13 Interrogation	*Leg.* 3 §§49–106; *Opif.* §156c; *QG* 1.41–46	*Ant.* 1.1 §§45–48	4 Ezra 7:13; 2 En. 8:3; 3 En. 23:18; Apoc. Adam 2:4; Apoc. Mos. 8:1; 22:1—23:5; LAE 34:1
3:14–19a Sentencing	*Agr.* 107–8; *Leg.* 3 §§107–251; *Opif.* §§167–70a; *QG* 1.47–50; *Virt.* §205	*Ant.* 1.1 §§49–50	4 Ezra 7:11b–14; Wis. 15:19; 2 En. 31:7–8; Sib. Or. 1.58–64; 2 Bar. 56:6; 3 Bar. 4:3, 8–10, 12–13; T. Iss. 5:5; Jub. 3:23–25a; Apoc. Mos. 8:2; 10:1; 24:1—26:4; LAE 34:2; 37:1–3; 44:1–5; Hel. Syn. Pr. 12:47–48 [Reversal: 2 Bar. 73:6—74:3]
3:19b Death	*Leg.* 3 §§252–53; *QG* 1.51		4 Ezra 3:7c; Sir. 16:29–30; 40:11; 41:10; Tob. 3:6; Wis. 15:8; 2 En. 32:1; Sib. Or. 1.58; 8.261–63; Apoc. Adam 2:9–10; Jub. 3:25b; Hel. Syn. Pr. 3:24b–27; 12:49–50

Genesis	Philo	Josephus	Apocrypha/Pseudepigrapha
3:20 Naming of woman	*QG* 1.52		*2 En.* 30:18; *Jub.* 3:33
3:21 Clothing	*QG* 1.53		*4 Ezra* 2:45; *Jub.* 3:26; *Mart. Isa.* 9:9; *Odes Sol.* 25:8 [Reversal: *T. Ab.* (A) 11:8-9; *Apoc. Mos.* 39:1-3]
3:22-24 Expulsion	*Cher.* §§1-2, 10-11, 20-30; *Opif.* §155b; *QG* 1.54-57	*Ant.* 1.1 §51	*1 En.* 25:4; *2 En.* 8:2; 22:10; 30:1; 32:1; 42:4; *3 En.* 5:1; 22:6; 23:18; 48D:9; *Sib. Or.* 1.50-55, 61; *T. Levi* 18:10; *Jub.* 3:27-35; *Apoc. Mos.* 27:1—29:6; *Hel. Syn. Pr.* 12:46
Concluding Remarks	*Opif.* §§170b-172		

Table 3: The Creation Narrative and Second Temple Period Parallel Accounts

Day	Genesis 1:1—2:4a	Jubilee 2	Philo Opif.	Josephus Ant.	4 Ezra 6:38-54	2 Enoch J24:2b—32:2	Tg. Ps.-J.
	•Heaven and earth •Waters covering earth				Garden [3:6; 6:2]	1. he souls [J23:4–5] 2. Intelligible cosmos 3. Foundation of the Earth •Adoil – light •Arkhas – darkness •Light + darkness = water •Seven circles •God's throne 4. Light, day 5. Darkness, night	1. The Law 2. Garden of Eden 3. Gehinnam Heaven and earth
1	1. Light •Day •Night	1. Heaven 2. Earth 3. Waters 4. The angels 5. The abyss 6. Darkness 7. Light	Intelligible cosmos	1. Heaven–earth 2. Light •Day and night •Evening and morning	1. Heaven 2. Earth 3. Light	1. Collection of waters 2. Dry land, earth 3. Chasm, bottomless sea	1. Light •Day •Night

Day	Genesis 1:1—2:4a	Jubilee 2	Philo Opif.	Josephus Ant.	4 Ezra 6:38—54	2 Enoch J24:2b—32:2	Tg. Ps.-J.
2	1. Firmament • Water above (sky) • Water below	Firmament	Sense-perceptible cosmos: Creation of the firmament or heaven	Heaven from "the rest"—encrusted it with ice	Spirit of the firmament to separate the waters [angels; cf. 8:22]	1. Heavens 2. Fire 3. Angels 4. Fall of the archangel Satan and his division	1. Firmament • Water above (Heaven) • Water below (ocean) 2. The angels
3	1. Water collected • Dry land (earth) • Water (sea) 2. Vegetation • Seed-plants • Fruit trees	1. Dry land 2. Bodies of water 3. Flora 4. Eden	1. Creation of the earth • Dry land • (Earth) • Botanical world	1. Dry land (surrounded by sea) 2. Plants and seeds	1. Bodies of water 2. Dry land 3. Fruit 4. Flowers	1. Vegetation • Fruit trees • Seed-plants 2. Paradise as garden, guarded by angels	1. Water collected • Dry land (earth) • Water (sea) 2. Vegetation • Seed-plants • Fruit trees
4	1. Lights in the sky for signs and times • Sun—day • Moon—night • Stars	1. Sun 2. Moon 3. Stars	1. Heavenly bodies as signs for future events and seasons and to indicate time, light, day, and night • Sun • Moon • Stars	1. Sun 2. Moon 3. Other stars	1. Heavenly bodies to serve humans • Sun • Moon • Stars	1. Heavenly bodies for the seven circles • Sun—day • Moon, stars—night 2. Zodiac	1. Lights in the sky for festivals, time, calendar, and light • Sun • Moon • Stars

Day	Genesis 1:1—2:4a	Jubilee 2	Philo Opif.	Josephus Ant.	4 Ezra 6:38-54	2 Enoch J24:2b—32:2	Tg. Ps.-J.
5	1. Living creatures • Water creatures • Winged birds	1. Sea 2. Monsters 3. Fish 4. Birds	1. Animal world • Water creatures • Winged birds	1. Living creatures that swim/fly	1. Living creatures • Birds • Fishes • Behemoth (land) • Leviathan (water)	1. Fish 2. Feathered birds 3. Reptiles 4. Animals	1. Living creatures • Water creatures • Birds • Great sea serpents • Leviathan • His yoke-fellow • Creeping things
6	1. Land creatures • Livestock • Creatures that crawl • Wildlife 2. Humans • Male and female	1. Wild beasts 2. Domestic animals 3. Reptiles 4. Humans • Male and female	1. Animal world • Land-animals 2. Humans	1. Four-footed beasts 2. Humans	1. Earth beings • Cattle • Beasts • Creeping things 2. Adam	1. Creation of Adam 2. Creation of Eve 3. Garden in Eden 4. Eve's fall 5. Expulsion from garden	1. Land creatures • Cattle • Creeping things, reptiles • Creatures of the earth 2. Humans • Male and female

Day	Genesis 1:1—2:4a	Jubilee 2	Philo *Opif.*	Josephus *Ant.*	4 Ezra 6:38–54	2 Enoch J24:2b—32:2	*Tg. Ps.-J.*
7	1. Sabbath rest 2. Blessed, sanctified	1. Sabbath blessed and sanctified (for Israel) • Sign • Keep and observe	Blessed and made the seventh day holy: It is a festival for the entire universe, the birthday of the cosmos, which Moses honored by instituting the Sabbath	Day of rest, Sabbath		1. Blessed the Sabbath 2. Rested from all His doings	1. Sabbath rest 2. Blessed, sanctified
8						Determination of millennia	

Table 4: The "Lᴏʀᴅ [God] of Hosts" in the Prophets and Writings

Category	Reference	#
Early Prophets	1 Sam. 1:3, 11; 4:4; 15:2; 17:45	5
	2 Sam. 5:10; 6:2, 18; 7:8, 26, 27	6
	1 Kings 18:15; 19:10, 14	3
	2 Kings 3:14; 19:31	2
Latter Prophets	Isa. 1:9, 24; 2:12; 3:1, 15; 5:7, 9, 16, 24; 6:3, 5; 8:13, 18; 9:6, 12, 18; 10:16, 23, 24, 26, 33; 13:4, 13; 14:22, 23, 24, 27; 17:3; 18:7; 19:4, 12, 16, 17, 18, 20, 25; 21:10; 22:5, 12, 14, 15, 25; 23:9; 24:23; 25:6; 28:5, 22, 29; 29:6; 31:4, 5; 37:16, 32; 39:5; 44:6; 45:13; 47:4; 51:15	58
	Jer. 2:19; 5:14; 6:6, 9; 7:3, 21; 8:3; 9:6, 14, 16; 10:16; 11:17, 20, 22; 15:16; 16:9; 19:3, 11, 15; 20:12; 23:15, 16, 36; 25:8, 27, 28, 29, 32; 26:18; 27:4, 18, 19, 21; 28:2, 14; 29:4, 8, 17, 21, 25; 30:8; 31:23, 35; 32:14, 15, 18; 33:11, 12; 35:13, 17, 18, 19; 38:17; 39:16; 42:15, 18; 43:10; 44:2, 7, 11, 25; 46:10, 18, 25; 48:1, 15; 49:5, 7, 26, 35; 50:18, 25, 31, 33, 34; 51:5, 14, 19, 33, 57, 58	81
Minor Prophets	Amos 3:13; 5:14, 15, 16; 6:8, 14; 9:5	7
	Mic. 4:14	1
	Nah. 2:14; 3:5	2
	Hab. 2:13	1
	Zeph. 2:9, 10	2
	Hag. 1:2, 5, 7, 9, 14; 2:4, 6, 7, 8, 9 (x2), 11, 23	13
	Zech. 1:3, 4, 6, 12, 14, 16, 17; 2:12, 13, 15; 3:7, 9, 10; 4:6, 9; 5:4; 6:12, 15; 7:3, 4, 9, 12, 13; 8:1, 2, 3, 4, 6, 7, 9, 11, 14, 18, 19, 20, 21, 22, 23; 9:15; 10:3; 12:5; 13:2, 7; 14:16, 17, 21	46
	Mal. 1:4, 6, 8, 9, 10, 11, 13, 14; 2:2, 4, 7, 8, 12, 16; 3:1, 5, 7, 10, 11, 12, 14, 17, 19, 21	24
Writings	Pss. 24:10; 46:8, 12; 48:9; 59:6; 69:7; 80:5, 8, 15, 20; 84:2, 4, 9, 13; 89:9	15
	1 Chron. 11:9; 17:7, 24	3

Note: The textual references follow the MT when there is a discrepancy in the verse numbering between the Hebrew text and the English translation.

ABOUT THE AUTHORS

Dominic Bornand, MA, serves as an assistant pastor in the German Swiss Conference of the Seventh-day Adventist Church. He is a PhD candidate in New Testament at the Seventh-day Adventist Theological Seminary in Berrien Springs, Michigan. He is completing his dissertation in Pauline Studies, working on how the body relates to law.

Félix H. Cortez, PhD, is associate professor of New Testament literature at Andrews University. He earned a Doctor of Philosophy degree in New Testament Studies from Andrews University. He was president of the Adventist Theological Society and chair of the General Epistles and the Pastoral Epistles section of the International Meeting of the Society of Biblical Literature. He is the author of *Within the Veil: The Ascension of the Son in the Letter to the Hebrews* and has contributed numerous articles and book chapters to the *Journal of Biblical Literature,* Wissenschaftliche Untersuchungen zum Neuen Testament (Mohr [Siebeck]), *Islamkundliche Untersuchungen* (Klaus Schwarz Verlag), Andrews University Press, and the Society of Biblical Literature, among others.

Kwabena Donkor, PhD, is associate director of the Biblical Research Institute of the General Conference of Seventh-day Adventists. A graduate of Andrews University, he earned his doctorate in Systematic Theology with a dissertation published as *Tradition, Method, and Contemporary Protestant Theology: An Analysis of Thomas C. Oden's Vincentian Method.* He has written scholarly articles for journals such as *Andrews University Seminary Studies, Ministry Magazine,* and the Biblical Research Institute's Newsletter, *Reflections.* He has contributed to several books including Millard Erickson et al., *Reclaiming the Center: Confronting Evangelical Accommodation in Postmodern Times.*

Laszlo Gallusz, PhD, is a senior lecturer in the New Testament at Newbold College of Higher Education. He earned a PhD in New Testament studies at Károli Gáspár University of the Reformed Church in Hungary. Before coming to Newbold College in 2019, he served as a lecturer and academic dean at Belgrade Theological Seminary and also as a departmental director at the South-East European Union

(TED). He is author and editor of five books and a number of scholarly articles in English, Hungarian, and Serbian, including *The Throne Motif in the Book of Revelation* and *The Seven Prayers of Jesus*. He is also an associate editor of the *Seventh-day Adventist International Biblical-Theological Dictionary*.

Michael G. Hasel, PhD, is professor of Near Eastern studies and archaeology and director of the Institute of Archaeology at Southern Adventist University. He holds a PhD in Near Eastern Studies and Anthropology from the University of Arizona. He has written and edited more than ten books, including *How to Interpret Scripture*; *The Promise: God's Everlasting Covenant; Jerusalem: An Archaeological Guide*; *In the Footsteps of King David*; and *Domination and Resistance: Egyptian Military Activity in the Southern Levant*, and has contributed more than one hundred and fifty articles to major journals, books, reference works, and church periodicals. He is co-director of excavations and surveys at Khirbet Qeiyafa, Socoh, and Lachish in Israel.

Ekkehardt Mueller, DMin, ThD, was associate director of the Biblical Research Institute of the General Conference of Seventh-day Adventists. Both his Doctor of Ministry degree in Evangelism and his Doctor of Theology degree in Biblical Exegesis and Theology are from Andrews University. He has written numerous articles for scholarly books, journals, and magazines as well as several books in English and German, including *Come Boldly to the Throne: Sanctuary Themes in Hebrews; The Letters of John; Die Lehre von Gott: Biblischer Befund und theologische Herausforderungen* ("The Doctrine of God: Biblical Evidence and Theological Challenges"); and *Der Erste und der Letzte: Studien zum Buch der Offenbarung* ("The First and the Last: Studies on the Book of Revelation").

Kim Papaioannou, PhD, is an author, pastor, and adjunct professor of the New Testament. He holds a PhD in Theology from Durham University. His dissertation on hell was published in 2013 under the title *The Geography of Hell in the Teaching of Jesus*. He also takes a special interest in Pauline theology and Biblical cosmology and has published *Israel, Covenant, Law: A Third Perspective on Paul* and co-edited *Earthly Shadows, Heavenly Realities: Temple/Sanctuary Cosmology in Ancient Near Eastern, Biblical, and Early Jewish Literature*.

Wilson Paroschi, PhD, is professor of New Testament studies at Southern Adventist University. A native of Brazil, he earned his PhD in New Testament from the Seventh-day Adventist Theological Seminary at Andrews University. He has authored several books and articles in Portuguese, Spanish, and English for scholarly as well as popular readership and has been a guest lecturer at several Adventist institutions in South and Central America, the United States, and Europe. As an ordained minister, he has also served as a church pastor and as editor at the Brazilian Publishing House. In 2011, he spent a year of postdoctoral research in New Testament textual criticism at the University of Heidelberg, Germany.

Jon Paulien, PhD, is professor of religion, director of the Center for Understanding World Religions, and director of the Doctor of Science in Religion and Health program at Loma Linda University. He has written numerous articles and books, such as *Present Truth in the Real World, What the Bible Says About the End-Time, John the Beloved Gospel, Meet God Again—For the First Time,* The *Deep Things of God, Letters to the Thessalonians,* and fourteen articles in *The Anchor Yale Bible Dictionary.* His best-known television series is called *Revelation: Hope, Meaning, Purpose,* which is featured on the Hope Channel.

Richard A. Sabuin, PhD, is the director of the Education Department for the Northern Asia-Pacific Division. He earned his doctorate in New Testament from the Adventist International Institute of Advanced Studies. He wrote his chapter for this book when he was serving as the dean of the AIIAS Seminary. He has written scholarly articles for various journals and magazines and has contributed to the *Andrews Study Bible Commentary,* writing the commentary on Ephesians.

Thomas R. Shepherd, PhD, DrPH, is senior research professor of New Testament at the Seventh-day Adventist Theological Seminary. He received his PhD in New Testament studies from Andrews University and his DrPH from Loma Linda University. He is the co-chair of the Mark Passion Narrative Seminar of the Society of Biblical Literature and has been in the leadership of Markan studies for more than twenty years, helping to establish various research sessions. His doctoral dissertation, *Markan Sandwich Stories,* was published in the

Andrews University Seminary Doctoral Dissertation Series, and he has presented scholarly papers at the annual meetings of the Society of Biblical Literature and the Adventist Theological Society.

Jan A. Sigvartsen, PhD, is associate professor of Old Testament and the doctoral program coordinator at the Theologische Hochschule Friedensau. He is also the associate director of their Institute for Biblical Studies and Archaeology and is currently associated with the *Balu'a Regional Archaeological Project* in the Hashemite Kingdom of Jordan. He was a visiting research fellow at the Hebrew University of Jerusalem and holds a PhD from Andrews University, specializing in Old Testament, Jewish Studies, and Archaeology. He has an extensive publication record, with his most recent works published by Bloomsbury T&T Clark and Zondervan Academic. He is best known in his field for his landmark studies identifying and describing all of the afterlife and resurrection beliefs in the Apocrypha and Pseudepigrapha.

Cedric E. W. Vine, PhD, is associate professor of New Testament at the Seventh-day Adventist Theological Seminary at Andrews University. He holds a PhD in Biblical Studies from the University of Sheffield. Among his publications is *The Audience of Matthew: An Appraisal of the Local Audience Thesis.*

Kayle B. de Waal, PhD, is associate professor and postgraduate course convenor at Avondale University. He has postgraduate qualifications in theology and business administration and earned his doctorate in theology from the University of Auckland. He has written and edited seven books on eschatology, mission, and discipleship and has more than thirty other publications, including book chapters, executive reports, and journal articles. His work on mission was translated into German as *Mission Umdenken: Das Geheimnes Der Ersten Christen.*

Clinton Wahlen, PhD, is associate director of the Biblical Research Institute at the General Conference of Seventh-day Adventists. He received his PhD in New Testament from Cambridge University and has written and edited several books, including *Jesus and the Impurity of Spirits in the Synoptic Gospels, Women's Ordination: Does It Matter?* (as coauthor), and *"What Are Human Beings That You Remember Them?"*

He is also the author of numerous articles and has contributed entries for dictionaries published by InterVarsity Press. Most recently, he authored the Luke commentary for the *Andrews Bible Commentary*.

AUTHOR INDEX

S

T

V

W

SCRIPTURE INDEX

Exodus

Malachi

Matthew

Mark

Galatians

Ephesians

1 Thessalonians

1 Timothy

SUBJECT INDEX

Note: Transliterated Hebrew words are indexed according to English alphabetization.

the 144,000, 427

A

Abel, 27, 113, 164n5, 246, 432
  Jesus' references to, 18–19, 168, 205–6, 438
Abraham, 166–67, 217, 263, 372
absolute beginning, 93, 454n3, 455–57, 459–63, 465, 467, 471, 472, 474
the abyss, 430, 431
the "active principle," 31–32
Acts, 147, 419
  Exodus quoted in, 219, 220
  Jesus' baptism in, 195n28
  paean of praise in, 218–19
  return to the Creator in, 219–20
Adam, 23, 27, 44, 101–2, 176. *See also* Adam, Paul on
  animals named by, 190n15
  as archetype, 103–4
  created from dust, 102n46, 253, 341
  and Eve, Jesus discussing, 104–5, 176, 181, 188–91, 200, 438
  and Eve, similarity between, 111
  Eve recognized by, 108, 176, 190, 267, 314
  "generations" of, 166, 402–3
  God breathing into, 208, 220, 237, 377, 379, 434

Adam *(continued)*
  God represented by, 121
  God seen by, 131
  humanity's common origin in, 220–21, 222
  Jesus as second, 113, 132, 148n43, 167, 265, 319–20
  Jesus' genealogy traced to, 217–18
  keeping Torah, 84
  lifespan of, 102
  loneliness of, 314
  reflecting God's glory, 472n67
  sin of, 112–13, 132
  as son of God, 103, 206, 218, 221, 222–23
  work of, in Eden, 84n40, 120, 155, 238, 425
Adam, Paul on, 103–5, 252–53, 256, 263n29, 265, 267–69
  as common ancestor, 220–21
  death linked with, 44, 113–14, 256
  humanity in, 128
  new, Christ as, 132
  typological use of, 27, 148n43, 319–20
adoption, 260
adultery, 58, 289n53, 304n22, 312n52
Aeschylus, 336n56
aesthetics, 442, 471n63, 472, 474–75
agency, 281, 394n36, 461–62, 463–64, 470, 471, 474
  vs. passivity, 466n47
aiōn ("universe, eternity"), 336–38, 350n110

breath of life *(continued)*
Adam receiving, 102–3, 208, 220, 237, 432n101, 434
death as absence of, 207–8, 223, 377, 379
the Holy Spirit and, 227, 237–38
resurrection as, 208, 237n73, 273n46, 434
bride of the Lamb, 421–22, 423. *See also* believers; the church

C

Cain, 12, 113, 246
Cana, wedding at, 243–45
Canaan, rest in, 346–47
causality, 461–62
and formal *vs.* material causes, 459
and will of God, 462, 466
Celsus, 62n126, 372
chaos. *See also* decreation
defeat of, 156, 170n38
Demiurge creating out of, 331, 353
preceding creation, 75n14, 229n19, 352, 353, 456
return to, 430–31
water symbolizing, 213
Chaos (deity), 35
cherubim, 77, 78, 82, 83, 84
chiasm
in 2 Peter, 395–96
in Colossians, 257n10, 257n12
in Hebrews, 356–57, 358–59
in Mark, 185
in Revelation, 412n32
in Romans, 263n28
the Christian life

the Christian life *(continued)*
as "already" and "not yet," 123–24, 129, 138, 145–46
in Christ, *vs.* in Adam, 127–28
reconciliation and, 127–29
christology
creation and, 201, 227n9
in Hebrews, 368
in John's Gospel, 227n9, 384n21
of the new creation, 126
the church
as covenant heirs, 382
creation of, 16, 26, 147–52
cultural challenges in, 267–68, 303–20
false teachers in, 391–402
growth of, using creation language, 208–10, 223, 271, 302
and the house church setting, 316n68
Jews and Gentiles united in, 204, 266–67, 274
mission of, 151
in Paul, 266–69, 274, 303–20
in Peter's letters, 382, 391–92
Plato's influence on, 325n11, 353
Stoic influence on, 62n126, 68–69
church fathers
creation narratives in, 55n118
Philo's influence on, 327
Platonic influence on, 49n87, 328n28, 329
Cicero, 66, 282n28, 283n38, 288n51, 288n52
circumcision, 124–25, 126
cities of refuge, 187n8
citizenship, 446n135
city of God. *See* new Jerusalem
"cleave," 177, 305–6
Clouds (Aristophanes), 56

K

Kabbalah, 455n5

kainē ktisis (new creation), 119–20, 124, 127, 148–50, 266n33

kainon anthrōpon ("new person"), 266n33, 267n34

kainos ("new"), 148–49, 150, 153

katabolē (foundation), 19–20, 167, 206n13, 252, 255n7, 347, 370, 383

katērtisthai ("restore, create"), 352, 353–54

derivation of, 353n127

semantic range of, 353n126

Kenan, 206n14

Ketuvim. *See* the Prophets

kingdom of God

consummation of, 123, 138–39, 146, 147, 181, 365, 414n43, 440

vs. earthly governments, 446n135

and kingdom of heaven, 173, 181

the Spirit's work in, 147

knowledge

the gospel as, 270, 278n10

and the law, 284n41

leading to godliness, 281

tree of, 112–13, 215, 223

kosmos ("order, world"), 35n22, 220, 234, 247, 259n16, 278–79, 337

ho ktisas ("The Creator, He who created"), 175–76

ktisis ("creation"), 257–58, 260–61, 266, 301, 370, 386, 407, 437. *See also kainē ktisis* (new creation)

as present created order, 408

ktisis (continued)

word family, 14–16, 251–52, 255n8, 279, 408, 419

ktisma ("created being, creature"), 14–15, 252, 269, 376, 413, 419, 432

ktizō ("create"), 14, 15–16, 149–50, 234, 389n27

ecclesiological dimension, 16

in Paul, 251–52, 255n8, 256, 257, 260, 264, 265–68, 300

in Revelation, 409, 410–12, 419

kyrios ("lord"), 180n98, 180n99, 220

L

Lactantius, 67–68

Laodicea, church in, 407, 408, 433, 437n111, 440

"last days" and "later times," 140, 141, 391n31

the law, 124–26

as inviolable, 171

in James, 381

and the knowledge of God, 284n41

as part of first creation, 235

Paul on, 260, 276n2

"let there be," 75n14, 169, 180

Leviticus, 111, 210n30, 291, 294n81, 312n50

life. *See also* breath of life; the Christian life; resurrection

in Christ, 264

eternal, 114, 242, 433, 439, 444

extraterrestrial, 413

as gift, 208

God as source of, 126–27, 151–52, 207–8, 220, 237–38

V

valley of dry bones, 237n73, 273n46, 434n105

violence

and death, in myth, 33, 35–39, 41, 46–47, 69, 100, 114, 192

freedom from, in new creation, 116

transfer of power through, 36, 38–39

vision of Peter, 210–12, 223

W

walking on water, 179–80

water. *See also* the Flood

chaos symbolized by, 213

creation through, 391, 395, 398, 400

of life, 155, 156, 420, 422, 424–25, 427, 439

in Peter's letters, 394, 400–401

and the Word of God, 400–401

white horse, Jesus riding, 446

wholistic anthropology, 4, 5, 432–33, 444

will of God, creation as, 6, 411, 441–42, 444, 454, 457, 462, 466, 471–72

Wisdom, 78, 80–82, 92, 231n29, 232, 374n2

and Prologue to John, 230–31, 233n49

Torah identified with, 81–82, 92

wisdom literature, 230–31, 374

women. *See also* gender

creation of, in myth, 41–42

creation of, in Plato, 52

women *(continued)*

as the glory of men, 313, 316

head coverings of, 267–68, 310–16

immodest acts of, 175n70, 175n71, 312

and Roman sexual ethics, 304n22

Word of God. *See also* the Logos

authority of, 169n35

and *creatio ex nihilo*, 355, 359, 440, 454, 460, 463–74

dangers of disregarding, 344–45, 348, 361–62

destruction accomplished by, 401

fulfillment of, 168–69

healing through, 170n38, 170n39, 240, 241

as invisible, 356–58

Jesus as, 233–34, 339

living, 348–49

in Peter's letters, 391, 394, 396, 397, 400, 401

preexistence of, 90, 92

in Second Temple texts, 232–33

theology of creation by, 463–70

from the throne, 131, 420–21, 426

water and, 400–401

worship, 99, 308–9, 418, 447–48, 475. *See also* idolatry; presence of God

around the throne, 412–13

call to, 6, 7, 28, 450, 473, 474–75

creation and, 447–48, 473

false, 109–10, 259, 410n26, 418, 447, 463, 474

neglect of, leading to judgment, 474

pagan, 64, 65, 66, 311